AN ILLUSTRATED ENCYCLOPEDIA OF
JEWISH HISTORY AND JUDAISM

AN ILLUSTRATED ENCYCLOPEDIA OF JEWISH HISTORY AND JUDAISM

A history of the Jewish people, their religion and philosophy, traditions and practices

LAWRENCE JOFFE & DAN COHN-SHERBOK

LORENZ BOOKS

CONTENTS

INTRODUCTION	8
Timeline	10

VOLUME ONE: A HISTORY OF THE JEWS 16

Introducing Jewish History	18
Jewish Traditions and Festivals	20
The Shabbat	26
Life Events	28

CHAPTER 1: ORIGINS OF A PEOPLE, BIRTH OF A FAITH 30

Introduction to the Patriarchs	32
Canaan and the Birth of a Civilization	34
The Israelites Move into Egypt	36
Moses	38
Return to Canaan	40
The Age of Judges	42
Settling on a Monarchy	44
The Great Kings	46
The Royal Houses of Israel and Judah	48
The Age of Prophets	50
The Northern Kingdom Falls	52

CHAPTER 2: EXILE, RETURN AND DISPERSAL 54

Judea Alone	56
By the Rivers of Babylon	58
Reform Under Ezra	60
Hellenism	62
The Maccabees and Hasmoneans	64
Pharisees, Sadducees and Messianism	66
Israel and the Roman Empire	68
Herod's Dynasty	70
Rome and Iudaea	71
Jesus	72
The Rise of Christianity	74
Rabbis Ascendant	76
The Fall of the Second Temple	78
The Final Revolt	80

CHAPTER 3: THE DIASPORA AND THE RISE OF CHRISTIANITY 82

Survival in the Diaspora	84
The Talmud	86
Palestine After the Roman Conquest	90
The Jewish–Christian Schism Deepens	92
Babylon – The New Centre of Jewry	94
Jews Under Byzantium	96
Jewish Communities of the Mediterranean	98
Changing Fortunes in Europe	100
Jews of Pre-Islamic Persia and Arabia	102

CHAPTER 4: JUDAISM AND ISLAM 104

The Birth and Rise of Islam	106
Jews Between Rival Caliphates	108
Karaites and Khazars	110
Spain – A Cultural Melting Pot	112
Rashi and the Jews of France	114

CHAPTER 5: FROM THE GOLDEN AGE TO THE INQUISITION 116

The Golden Age of Spain	118
Kabbalah – Jewish Mystical Tradition	120
The First Jews of Eastern Europe	122
The Age of Maimonides	124
To the Four Corners of the World	126
Jews of Norman England	128
The Crusades and Jewish Life	130
Anti-Semitism in 14th-century Europe	132
Muslim Rulers of the Bible Lands	134

Below The Damascus keter, 1260.   *Below* The Dead Sea in Israel.   *Below* Ark of the Covenant, Capernaum.

Above Auschwitz memorial.

Above Orthodox Jews in New York.

Above Synagogue by Frank Lloyd Wright.

The Fall of the Byzantine Empire	135
Spain and the 1492 Expulsion of the Jews	136

CHAPTER 6: THE SHIFT TO ASHKENAZ — 138
- Jews in New Cultures — 140
- Intellectual Stirrings — 142
- Jewish Communities in Germany — 144
- Jews in the Ottoman Empire — 146
- Turks and Jews in the Holy Land — 148
- The Dawn of the Ashkenazi Ascendancy — 150
- Jewish Life in Holland and Baruch Spinoza — 152
- Jews in England – The Return to Albion — 153

CHAPTER 7: A CHANGING FAITH — 154
- A Crisis of Faith — 156
- Hassidism — 158
- Palestine – A Messianic Outpost — 160
- Jews of North Africa and the Middle East — 162
- The Partition of Poland — 164
- Revolutionary Times — 166
- The Russian Pale of Settlement — 168
- 18th-century Modernity — 170
- The Reform Movement — 171
- Jews and Commerce – The Rothschilds — 172

CHAPTER 8: REVOLUTION AND EMANCIPATION — 174
- Emancipation and Revolutionaries — 176
- The Ostjuden and Yiddish Culture — 178
- The Spectre of Anti-Semitism Revived — 180
- The 19th-century Population Boom — 182
- The USA – A New Promised Land — 183
- Diasporas of the Southern Hemisphere — 184
- Jews of the Late Ottoman Empire — 185
- Jews in 19th-century Art and Culture — 186
- Political Zionism — 188

CHAPTER 9: WORLD WARS AND THE HOLOCAUST — 190
- Europe at War — 192
- Jews and the Bolshevik Revolution — 194
- The Interwar Years — 196
- Hitler Takes Power – Nazism Grows — 198
- World War II Begins — 200
- Holocaust – Final Solution — 202
- The Aftermath of Genocide — 204
- Cultural Responses to the Holocaust — 206

CHAPTER 10: ZIONISM, JERUSALEM AND ISRAEL — 208
- Zionism – The Nationalist Divide — 210
- Early Days in Palestine — 212
- Jews in a Changing Middle East — 214
- Palestine During World War II — 216
- The Revival of an Ancient Language — 218
- Oriental Immigration to Israel — 219
- The War of Independence — 220
- Jewish Demography After World War II — 222

CHAPTER 11: JEWISH CULTURE IN MODERN SOCIETY — 224
- Israel in the Modern World — 226
- Diaspora Life – The USA and Canada — 228
- Diaspora Life – Great Britain and France — 232
- Jews in Germany and Eastern Europe — 234
- The Spread of Jewish Communities — 236
- Diversity and Orthodox Revival — 238
- Women in Jewish Society — 240
- Medicine and Science — 242
- Jewish Artists and Themes in Art — 244
- Jewish Writers and Literature — 246
- Hollywood and Beyond — 250
- Music and Musicians — 252
- Jewish Philosophers and Politicians — 254
- Jewish Architecture Around the World — 256

VOLUME TWO: JUDAISM	**258**	Reconstructionist Judaism	318
		Humanistic Judaism	320
Introducing Judaism	260	Jewish Renewal	322
Jews in the Ancient World	266	Messianic Judaism	324
Rabbinic and Medieval Judaism	264		
Jews in the Early Modern Period	266	**CHAPTER 4: UNTRADITIONAL**	
Jews in the Modern World	268	**JUDAISM**	**326**
		Religious Zionism	328
PART I: JEWISH TRADITIONS	**270**	Secular Zionism	330
CHAPTER 1: ANCIENT JUDAISM	**272**	Modern Kabbalism	332
Ancient Hebrews	274	The Jewish Left	334
Temple Judaism	276	Jewish Feminism	336
Prophetic Judaism	278	Gender Issues	338
Hellenistic Judaism	280	Jewish Buddhists	340
Samaritans	282	Jews and the Environment	342
Sadducees	284	Jewish Vegetarianism	344
Pharisees	286		
Essenes	288	**PART II: JEWISH BELIEF**	**346**
		CHAPTER 5: GOD	**348**
CHAPTER 2: RABBINIC JUDAISM	**290**	The God of the Jews	350
Introducing Rabbinic Judaism	292	Unity of God	352
Early Mystical Judaism	294	Transcendence and Immanence	354
Kabbalistic Judaism	296	Eternity	356
Philosophical Judaism	298	Omnipotence	358
Lurianic Kabbalah	300	Omniscience	360
Karaites	302	Creation	362
Shabbateans	304	Goodness	364
Frankists	406		
		CHAPTER 6: GOD AND ISRAEL	**366**
CHAPTER 3: MODERN JUDAISM	**308**	Providence	368
Orthodox Judaism	310	Revelation	370
Hasidism	312	Torah and Commandments	372
Conservative Judaism	314	Chosen People	374
Reform Judaism	316	Love of God	376

Below Birthplace of the prophet Amos. *Below Jerusalem, mosaic, 6th century BCE.* *Below Jewish teacher and pupil, 1395.*

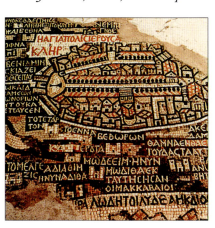

Above The rabbi's visit c.19th-century.

Above Writing a Torah scroll by hand.

Above Girls celebrating bat mitzvah.

Fear of God	378
Promised Land	380
Prayer	382
CHAPTER 7: THE SPIRITUAL PATH	**384**
Bible	386
Mishnah, Midrash and Talmud	388
Ethics	390
Sin and Repentance	392
Compassion	394
Benevolence	396
Justice	398
Holiness	400
CHAPTER 8: MESSIAH AND THE HEREAFTER	**402**
Biblical Messiah	404
Post-biblical Messiah	406
Rabbinic Messiah	408
The Messianic Age and Heaven	410
Hell	412
Jewish Messiahs	414
Anti-messianism	416
Death of the Afterlife	418
PART III JEWISH PRACTICE	**420**
CHAPTER 9: WORSHIP	**422**
Jewish Calendar	424
Places of Worship	426
Worship	428
Sabbath	430
Special Sabbaths	432
Passover	434
Shavuot	436
Sukkot	438

CHAPTER 10: FESTIVALS	**440**
Rosh Hashanah	442
Yom Kippur	444
Fasts	446
Hanukkah	448
Purim	450
Festivals of Joy	452
Holocaust Remembrance Day	454
Tishah B'Av	456
CHAPTER 11: HOME CEREMONIES	**458**
Home	460
Community Life	462
Prayers and Blessings	464
Parents and Children	466
Dietary Laws	468
Conversion	470
Duties of the Heart	472
Ritual Immersion	474
CHAPTER 12: LIFE CYCLE EVENTS	**476**
Birth	478
Rites of Passage	480
Education	482
Higher Education and Courtship	484
Outward Signs	486
Marriage	488
Divorce	490
Death and Mourning	492
Glossary	494
Further Reading	497
Index	498
Acknowledgements	511

Introduction

For nearly 4,000 years the Jewish people have been in existence. Other civilizations – the Sumarian, the Akkadian, the Assyrian, the Egyptian, the Greek, the Roman – have disappeared, yet miraculously the Jewish nation has survived. Today in Israel and the diaspora (outside of Israel), Jewry is as vibrant as ever, and Jewish culture continues to flourish.

This book, containing over 1,000 illustrations, is designed to celebrate the treasures of the Jewish heritage as well as describe the triumphs and tribulations of the Jewish nation through the centuries. Divided into two parts (Volume 1: A History of the Jews; Volume 2: Judaism), the book recounts the epic 4,000-year story of the Jewish people from the ancient Patriarchs and Kings through to the present.

Below The Destruction of Jerusalem by Nebuchadnezzar in 587BCE *by William Brassey Hole.*

The first volume of the book begins in Chapter 1 with a description of the land of Canaan and the lives of the Patriarchs: Abraham, Isaac and Jacob. Their descendants were initially slaves in Egypt, yet under the leadership of Moses they escaped from bondage, conquered the Canaanites, and settled in the Holy Land. Ruled over by a series of judges, they established a monarchy. When the country divided into two kingdoms – Israel in the North and Judah in the South – the prophets emerged, eloquently proclaiming that they must obey God's commands. Eventually the Northern Kingdom (Israel) was conquered in the 8th century BCE by the Babylonians and Jews were driven into exile.

Chapter 2 continues with a description of the Southern Kingdom, the emergence of the Pharisees and the Sadducees, and the Roman conquest of the country in the 1st century CE. This led to the dispersion of the Jewish nation from

Above Menorah Window, Great Synagogue, Jerusalem, Israel.

its homeland. Chapter 3 describes the diaspora, the development of rabbinic Judaism, and the rise of Christianity. Here Babylonian Jewry is depicted in detail as well as the changing fortunes of Jews in Europe, Persia and Arabia. Chapter 4 recounts Judaism under Islam and the eminent Jewish scholars of the medieval period.

From the 8th century BCE and for some 700 years afterwards, Spain displaced Palestine and Babylon as the central focus of Jewish life. Chapter 5 relates the history of this period from the Golden Age to the Inquisition. Chapter 6 then shifts to the Ashkenazi world. This chapter traces the intellectual stirrings during this period in Germany and elsewhere as well as the history of Jews in the Ottoman Empire. The saga progresses in Chapter 7 with the arrival of the false Messiah, Shabbeai Tzvi in the 17th century and the emergence of Hasidism in the next century. The book follows on in Chapter 8 with the history of Jewry in the modern world. With the rise of anti-semitism, Zionism emerged as a central focus of Jewish life. Chapter 9 focuses on the Holocaust

INTRODUCTION

Right A rabbi wraps a tallit (prayer shawl) around the bride and groom during a traditional Jewish wedding ceremony.

and its aftermath. Finally, in Chapter 10, Zionism, Jerusalem and Israel are explored, and the book ends in Chapter 11 with a depiction of Jewish culture in modern society.

Volume Two shifts focus, concentrating on the history of the Jewish religion and philosophy, its traditions and practices until the present day. After a brief outline in Part I of the major Jewish movements of the past in Chapters 1 and 2, Chapter 3 explores the major religious divisions in the modern world. Here Orthodox, Conservative, Reform, Conservative, Reconstructionist and Humanistic Judaism are discussed in detail. This is followed in the next chapter by an account of the various forms of untraditional Judaism including Religious Zionism, Secular Zionism, Kabbalism, Jewish Feminism, Jewish Buddhism and Jewish Vegetarianism.

Part II then proceeds with a description of the major features of Jewish belief. Chapter 5 outlines the central tenets of the Jewish faith: the Unity of God, Transcendence, Eternity, Omnipotence, Omniscience, Creation and Divine Goodness. The next chapter concentrates on various Jewish religious concepts including Providence, Revelation, Torah and the Commandments, the Chosen People, the Love and Fear of God, the Promised Land and Prayer. This is followed in Chapter 7 by a description of the Spiritual Path including sacred literature as well as concepts such as sin and repentance, compassion, benevolence, justice and holiness. Finally, Chapter 8 examines the concept of the Messiah in traditional Judaism.

Part III – Jewish Practice – begins with Jewish religion and concentrates on Jewish worship, the Sabbath, Special Sabbaths, Passover, Shavuot, and Sukkot. Chapter 10 outlines the major Jewish festivals including Rosh Hashanah, Yom Kippur, Fasts, Hanukkah, Purim Festivals of Joy, Holocaust Remembrance Day and Tishah B'Av. Finally, the book concludes with a wide range of ceremonies including prayers and blessings and duties of the heart in Chapter 11 and in Chapter 12 with life cycle events including birth, rites of passage, higher education and courtship, marriage, divorce, and death and mourning. In this two-volume work we have aimed to provide a complete account of the history of the Jewish people from ancient times to the present, and a full description of the Jewish religion and its manifold movements in the present age.

Below Haredim young men during Purim, a Jewish holiday celebrating the salvation of the Jews from genocide in ancient Persia.

Timeline

This is a chronological history of the Jewish people from the time of Abraham and the Patriarchs, through the Exile and the Diaspora, to the modern State of Israel.

Above Expert Assyrian archers like these confronted Israel in 722BCE.

2000–600BCE

c.2000–1700BCE According to tradition, the age of the Patriarchs begins with Abraham. The Bible records how the Israelites leave Canaan for Egypt when famine strikes.
c.1700BCE Joseph is sold into slavery. He later welcomes his family to Egypt.
c.1700–1300BCE Enslavement of the Israelites.
c.1300–1200BCE Moses leads the Israelites from Egypt.
c.1280BCE Torah, including the Ten Commandments, received by Moses at Mount Sinai.
c.1240BCE The Israelites under Joshua conquer Canaan.
c.1200–1000BCE Time of Judges.
1050BCE Philistines vanquish Shiloh and win the Ark of the Covenant. The time of Samuel, prophet and last judge.
1020BCE Saul is first King of the united Kingdom of Israel and Judah; rules until 1007BCE.
c.1004–965BCE King David crowned in Bethlehem. He makes Jerusalem his new capital and installs Ark of the Covenant.
c.965–928BCE Solomon is crowned. The Kingdom expands. First Temple is built.
c.928BCE Kingdom splits into Judah under Rehoboam, and Israel under Jeroboam.
918BCE Shishak of Egypt invades Israel.
c.900–800BCE Time of prophet Elijah.
722BCE Assyrians take over Israel. Ten tribes disperse. Time of prophet Isaiah.
727–698BCE King Hezekiah of Judah introduces major religious reforms.
639–609BCE King Josiah makes religious reforms in Judah. Dies at Battle of Megiddo fighting Egyptian forces and their Assyrian allies.

600–100BCE

586BCE Babylonians conquer Judah and destroy Jerusalem and the Temple. Most Jews are exiled to Babylon (the first Diaspora).
c.580BCE Jews establish a colony on the River Nile island of Elephantine, Egypt.
538–445BCE Persian King Cyrus defeats the Babylonians. Jews return to Israel, led by Zerubabbel and scribes Ezra and Nehemiah. Jerusalem Temple and city walls rebuilt. Canonization of the Torah.
536–142BCE Persian and Hellenistic periods.
c.500–400BCE Canonization of Book of Prophets. Presumed period of Queen Esther and the Purim saga in Persia. Elephantine Temple destroyed in Egypt.
347BCE Time of the Great Assembly, end of kingship.
332BCE Land conquered by Alexander the Great; Hellenistic rule.
285–244BCE 72 Jewish sages in Egypt translate Torah into Greek; called the Septuagint.
219–217BCE Rival Hellenistic dynasties fight for control of Israel. Seleucids finally displace Ptolemaids in 198BCE.
166–160BCE Maccabean (Hasmonean) revolt against Seleucid rule.
42–129BCE Jewish autonomy under Hasmoneans. In Jerusalem the zugot, or pairs of sages, acquire more power.
138BCE Rededication of the Second Temple. Foundation of Dead Sea Jewish sect at Qumran.
129–63BCE Hasmoneans achieve complete independence and expand national borders.

100BCE–300CE

76–67BCE Reign of Queen Salome Alexandra.
63BCE Romans invade Judea. Jerusalem captured by Pompey who names Judea a Roman vassal.
37BCE–4CE Herod the Great rules Judea. Temple in Jerusalem refurbished. Sanhedrin acts as Jewish legislature and judicial council.
c.30BCE–30CE Time of rabbis Hillel and Shammai.
6CE Judea becomes Roman province with capital at Caesarea.
c.20–36CE Ministry of Jesus of Nazareth.
30–100CE The birth of Christianity.
66–73CE The Great Revolt of Jews against Rome.
70CE Jerusalem conquered by Romans who destroy Second Temple.
70–200CE Age of the Tanna'im, sages who organized the Jewish oral law.
115–117CE Abortive Jewish revolt against Rome, the Kitos Wars.
131CE Hadrian renames Jerusalem Aelia Capitolina and forbids Jews to enter.
132–135CE Rebellion of Bar Kochba against Rome. Rome defeats rebels and Emperor Hadrian renames Judea 'Syria Palestina'.
c.210CE Mishnah, standardization of Jewish oral law, compiled by Rabbi Yehuda Ha-Nasi.
212CE Jews accepted as Roman citizens.
244CE Dura-Europos synagogue built in northern Syria.

TIMELINE

300–600CE

220–500CE Period of the Amora'im, the rabbis of the Talmud. The main redaction of Talmud Bavli (Babylonian Talmud) is mostly completed by 475CE.
305CE Council of Elvira forbids Spanish Christians to socialize with Jews.
313–37CE Constantine converts Roman empire to Christianity. Empire is split into two, and Jews come under the rule of the more powerful Eastern, Byzantine empire in 330CE.
313–637CE Byzantine rule.
351CE A Jewish revolt in Galilee directed against Gallus Caesar is soon crushed.
361–3CE The last pagan Roman Emperor, Julian, allows Jews to return to Jerusalem and rebuild the Temple. The project lapses when he dies and his successor Jovian r e-establishes Christianity as the imperial religion.
c.390CE Mishnah commentary, written form of oral traditions, is completed. Hillel II formulates Jewish calendar.
400–50CE Redaction of Talmud Yerushalmi (Talmud of Jerusalem).
425CE Jerusalem's Jewish patriarchate is abolished.
438CE The Empress Eudocia removes the ban on Jews praying at the Temple site.
489CE Theodoric, King of the Ostrogoths, conquers Italy and protects the Jews.
502CE Mar Zutra II establishes a small Jewish state within Babylon.
525–9CE End of Himyar Jewish Kingdom in southern Arabia. Byzantine Emperor Justinian I issues anti-Jewish legislation.
550–700CE Period of the savora'im, sages in Persia who finalized the Talmud.
556CE Jews and Samaritans revolt against Byzantines.
Midrashic literature and liturgical poetry developed.

600–750CE

7th century CE Foundation of the Khazar kingdom in Caucasus, southern Russia.
608–10CE Anti-Jewish pogroms break out from Syria to Asia Minor. Jews riot in Syria against Christians.
613–14CE Persian invasion of Palestine ends Byzantine rule of Syria and Palestine and brings the Byzantine period to an end.
614CE Jews gain autonomy in Jerusalem after a Persian-backed revolt.
622CE Migration of Prophet Mohammed to Medina, marking the start of the Islamic calendar. His new faith, Islam, comes to dominate the Arabian Peninsula. Many Jewish communities there are dispersed, though Jews in Yemen mostly unaffected.
629CE Byzantines retake Palestine and kill many Jews.
632CE Death of Islamic Prophet Mohammed.
637–1099CE Arab rule in Palestine.
637CE Islamic and Arab conquest of Jerusalem. Arabs permit some Jews to return to Jerusalem, including immigrants from Babylon and refugees from Arabia.
640–2CE Arabs conquer Egypt.
691CE Dome of the Rock built on Temple Mount by Caliph Abd el-Malik on the site of the former Temples in Jerusalem.
694–711CE The Visigoths outlaw Judaism in Spain.
700–1250CE Period of the Ga'onim, heads of rabbinical colleges in Sura and Pumbedita, Babylon. New Jewish academies arise in Kairouan, Tunisia, and Fez, Morocco.
711CE Muslim armies invade and within a few years occupy most of Spain.
c.740CE Khazar Khanate royals and many Khazars convert to Judaism.
750–950CE Heyday of the Masoretes in Tiberias, Palestine, who codify Torah annotations and grammar.

Above Isaiah's utopian vision captured in Edward Hicks' painting of c.1840.

750–1050CE

760CE Karaite Jews reject the authority of the oral law and split off from rabbinic Judaism.
763–809CE Reign of Persian-born Harun al Rashid in Baghdad, fifth and most fabled Abbasid Caliph. Jewish diplomat Isaac forges bonds between Harun and Frankish King Charlemagne.
807CE Harun al Rashid forces Jews to wear a yellow badge and Christians to wear a blue badge.
808CE Idris II makes Fez (Morocco) the capital of his Shia dynasty and allows Jews to live in their own quarter (mellah) in return for an annual tax.
809–13CE Civil war in Persia.
900–1090CE The Golden age of Jewish culture in Spain.
912CE Abd-ar-Rahman III becomes Caliph of Spain.
940CE In Iraq, Saadia Gaon compiles his siddur (Jewish prayer book).
953CE Jewish historical narrative, Josippon, written in southern Italy.
960–1028CE Rabbenu Gershom of Germany, first great Ashkenazi sage, bans bigamy.
1013–73 Rabbi Yitzhak Alfassi writes the *Rif*, an important work of Jewish law.
1040–1105 Time of Rashi of France, Rabbi Shlomo Yitzhaki, who writes commentaries on the Hebrew Bible and Talmud.

TIMELINE

1050–1250

1066 Jews enter England in the wake of the Norman invasion.
1090 Muslim Berber Almoravides conquer Granada, ending the period of tolerance. Jews flee to Toledo.
1095–1291 Christian Crusades begin, sparking war with Islam in Palestine. Thousands of Jews are killed in Europe and Middle East.
1099 Crusaders temporarily capture Jerusalem.
1100–1275 Time of the tosafot, medieval Talmudic commentators on the Torah carrying on Rashi's work.
1107 Moroccan Almoravid ruler Yusuf Ibn Tashfin expels Jews who do not convert to Islam.
1135–1204 Rabbi Moses ben Maimon, aka Maimonides, is the leading rabbi of Sephardic Jewry. He writes the *Mishneh Torah* and the *Guide for the Perplexed*.
1141 Death of Yehuda Halevi, who calls on Jews to emigrate to Palestine.
1144 First blood libel, in Norwich, England. The trend spreads to Europe.
1179 Third Lateran Council in Vatican establishes Jewish-Christian relations.
1187 Arab leader Saladin (c.1138–1193) takes Jerusalem and most of Palestine; many Jews arrive.
1200–1300 Zenith of the German Jewish Hasidei Ashkenaz pietist movement.
1240 Paris Disputation. Monks publicly burn the Talmud.
1244–1500 Successive conquest of Palestine by Mongols and Egyptian Muslims. Many Jews die or leave.
1249 Pope Innocent IV in Italy forbids Christians to make false blood libels against Jews.

1250–1480

1250–1300 The time of Moses de Leon of Spain, reputed author of the *Zohar*. Modern form of Kabbalah (esoteric Jewish mysticism) begins.
1250–1517 Mamluk rule.
1250–1550 Period of the Rishonim, the rabbinic sages who wrote commentaries on the Torah and Talmud and law codes.
1263 The Disputation of Barcelona, where Nahmanides (Ramban) defends the Talmud against Christian accusations.
1267 Nahmanides settles in Jerusalem and builds the Ramban Synagogue.
1269–1343 Rabbi Jacob ben Asher of Spain writes the *Arba'ah Turim* (Four Rows of Jewish Law).
1290 Jews are expelled from England by Edward I.
1290–1301 Mamluk rulers allow attacks on churches and synagogues, and segregate Jews and Christians from Muslims.
1300 Time of Rabbi Levi ben Gershom (1288–1344), aka Gersonides, a French philosopher.
1306–94 Jews are repeatedly expelled from France and readmitted. Last expulsion lasts 150 years.
1343 Persecuted in west Europe, Jews are invited to Poland by Casimir the Great.
1348–50 The Plague kills 30 to 60 per cent of Europe's people, and some blame Jews.
1391 Massacres in Spain; Jewish refugees find sanctuary in Algeria.
1415 Pope Benedict XII orders censorship of the Talmud.
1453 Jews welcome Ottoman Turks, who conquer Byzantine Constantinople.
c.1469 *Responsa* by the sage called Rashba published in Hebrew.
1478 The Spanish Inquisition begins.

1480–1550

1486 First Jewish prayer book published in Italy.
1487 Portugal's first printed book is a Pentateuch in Hebrew.
1488–1575 Life of Joseph Caro, born in Spain, who writes the *Shulkhan Arukh*, the codification of halakhic law and Talmudic rulings.
1492 The Alhambra Decree – 200,000 Jews are expelled from Spain. Ottoman Sultan Bayezid II sends ships to bring Jews to safety in his empire. Many Jews survive as conversos (converts) or flee. Columbus reaches America.
1493 Jews are expelled from Sicily.
1495 Jews are expelled from Lithuania.
1497 Jews are forced to convert or leave Portugal.
1501 King Alexander of Poland readmits Jews to the Grand Duchy of Lithuania.
1516 Ghetto of Venice established
1517 Martin Luther starts the Protestant Reformation.
1517–1917 Ottoman rule in Palestine.
1525–72 Rabbi Moses Isserles (The Rama) of Krakow writes a gloss to the *Shulkhan Arukh* for Ashkenazi Jews.
1525–1609 Life of Rabbi Judah Loew ben Betzalel, called the Maharal of Prague.
1534 First printed Yiddish book published in Poland.
1547 First Hebrew Jewish printing house in Lublin, Poland.

Below Maimonides, the greatest Jewish genius of medieval Spain.

TIMELINE

1550–1720

1534–70 Isaac Luria founds the new school of Kabbalists.
1550 Moses ben Jacob Cordovero founds a Kabbalah academy in Safed.
1564 First printed version of Joseph Caro's Code of Jewish Law published.
1567 First Jewish university yeshiva founded in Poland.
1577 Hebrew printing press in Safed, the first of any kind in Asia.
1580–1764 Span of sessions of the Council of Four Lands (Va'ad Arba' Aratzot) in Lublin, Poland. Seventy delegates from local Jewish kehillot meet to discuss issues important to the Jewish community.
1626–76 Life of false messiah Shabbetai Tzvi of Smyrna, Turkey.
1632-77 Life of Baruch Benedict Spinoza, Dutch Jewish philosopher.
1648–55 Ukrainian Cossack Bogdan Chmielnicki leads a massacre of Polish gentry and Jewry that leaves an estimated 130,000 dead. The total decrease in the number of Jews is estimated at 100,000.
1654 The first Jews go to North America.
1655 Oliver Cromwell urges readmission of Jews to England.
1674 The world's first Jewish newspaper is printed in Amsterdam.
1700 Rabbi Yehuda He-Hasid immigrates to Palestine with hundreds of followers.
1700–60 Israel ben Eliezer, known as the Ba'al Shem Tov, founds Hasidic Judaism in eastern Poland.
1701 Foundation of Bevis Marks Synagogue, London, the oldest British synagogue still in use.
1720 Unpaid Arab creditors burn the unfinished synagogue built by immigrant followers of Rabbi Yehuda and expel all Ashkenazi Jews from Jerusalem.
1720–97 Time of Rabbi Elijah of Vilna, the Vilna Gaon.

1720–1800s

1729–86 Moses Mendelssohn and the Haskalah (Enlightenment) movement.
1740 Ottomans invite Rabbi Haim Abulafia (1660–1744) to rebuild Tiberias.
1740–50 Mass immigration to Palestine under Messianic predictions.
1747 Rabbi Abraham Gershon of Kitov is the first immigrant of the Hasidic Aliyah, migration to Palestine.
1755 Jacob Frank tells followers in Podolia, he is the reincarnation of Shabbetai Tzvi and King David.
1765–1783 American Revolution, which resulted in guarantees of religious freedom.
1772–95 Partitions of Poland between Russia, Kingdom of Prussia and Austria where most Jews live. Old Jewish privileges are renounced.
1789 The French Revolution leads France in 1791 to grant citizen rights to Jews, under certain conditions.
1790 In the USA, George Washington writes to the Jews of Rhode Island that he wants a country 'which gives bigotry no sanction ... persecution no assistance'.
1791 Emancipation of Jews begins in Europe. Russia creates the Pale of Settlement.
1799 Failed attempt by the French to seize Acre in Palestine.
1800–1900 The Golden Age of Yiddish literature, the revival of Hebrew as a spoken language and in literature. First major Yiddish theatre founded in Romania in 1876.
1810 Reform Movement in Germany opens first temple (synagogue) in Seesen.
1820–60 Orthodox Judaism emerges in response to Reform Judaism and Enlightenment movements, characterized by strict adherence to Jewish religious law.

Above Touro Synagogue RI, built 1763, is the USA's oldest still operating today.

1800s–1870

1809 Nathan Mayer Rothschild begins dealing in gold bullion in London.
1810 Birth of Rabbi Israel Salanter, founder of the Musar Movement.
1832 First Jewish wedding celebrated in Australia.
1845 David Levy Yulee of Florida is the first Jew elected to Congress. The *Jewish Chronicle* is printed in the UK.
1850s Positive-Historical Judaism begins in Germany. Later known as Conservative Judaism, it advocates a middle path between Reform and Orthodoxy.
1851 Norway allows Jews entry. They are fully emancipated in 1891.
1858 Jews emancipated in England.
1860 Alliance Israélite Universelle is founded in Paris to protect Jewish rights as citizens. The first Haskalah Russian journal, *Razsvet*, is founded.
1860–1945 Time of Henrietta Szold, founder of Hadassah.
1861 The Zion Society is formed in Frankfurt am Main, Germany.
1862 Jews gain equal rights in Congress Kingdom of Poland. Moses Hess writes *Rome and Jerusalem*.
1867 Jews emancipated in Hungary. Karl Marx publishes first volume of *Das Kapital*.
1868 Converted Jew Benjamin Disraeli becomes UK Prime Minister.
1880–90 Russian Zionist groups Hovevei Zion (Lovers of Zion) and Bilu set up Jewish settlements in Palestine, aided by Baron Edmond James de Rothschild. Eliezer Ben-Yehuda revives Hebrew as a spoken modern language.

TIMELINE

1870–1900

1871 Esther Levy publishes America's first Jewish cookbook.
1875 Reform Judaism's Hebrew Union College is founded in Cincinnati.
1877 New Hampshire becomes the last US state to give Jews equal rights.
1881–84, 1903–6, 1918–20 Three waves of pogroms kill thousands of Jews in Russia and Ukraine.
1882–1903 First Aliyah (large-scale immigration) to Palestine, mainly from Russia.
1886 Jews fleeing pogroms in Lithuania swell South African Jewish community.
1887 Conservative Jewish movement founded in America. Birth of Marc Chagall, leading 20th-century artist.
1890 The term 'Zionism' is coined by Nathan Birnbaum.
1891 Jewish Colonisation Organisation founded, prompts Jewish agricultural colonies in Argentina.
1892 Israel Zangwill publishes *Children of the Ghetto* in England.
1894 Alfred Dreyfus, French army captain and a Jew, is falsely convicted of treason.
1896 Theodor Herzl writes *Der Judenstaat* (The Jewish State).
1897 The Bund (General Jewish Labor Union) is formed in Russia. Zionist Congress meets in Switzerland and founds a Zionist Organization.

Below 'Work sets you free' – the cynical motto that greeted Jews at Auschwitz.

1900–1922

1902 The Jewish Theological Seminary becomes the flagship of Conservative Judaism. Herzl publishes utopian Zionist novel *Altneuland*.
1903 The Kishinev Pogrom is caused by accusations that Jews practise cannibalism.
1904–14 The Second Aliyah, mainly from Russia and Poland.
1905 Russian Revolution, accompanied by pogroms.
1909 The first kibbutz and Tel Aviv are founded.
1914 American Jewish Joint Distribution Committee founded.
1915 Yeshiva College and Rabbinical Seminary is established in New York.
1917 British troops drive Ottoman Turks from Palestine. Balfour Declaration gives official British support for 'a national home for the Jewish people'. Russia's October Revolution abolishes the Pale of Settlement and grants Jews equal rights. Russian civil war leads to more than 2,000 pogroms.
1918–48 British Rule of Palestine.
1919–23 Third Aliyah, mainly from Russia.
1920 Histadrut (Jewish labour federation) and Haganah (Jewish defence organization) founded in Palestine. Jewish community (yishuv) sets up National Council. Britain receives the League of Nations' British Mandate of Palestine.
1921 Civil administration of Palestine closes land east of the Jordan River to Jewish settlement. Polish-Soviet peace treaty in Riga. First moshav (cooperative village) founded in Palestine. Albert Einstein wins Nobel Prize.
1922 Transjordan set up on three-quarters of Palestine. Jewish Agency is established. Birth of Reconstructionist movement in USA.

1922–60

1923 Britain cedes Golan Heights to French Mandate Territory of Syria.
1924–32 Fourth Aliyah, mainly from Poland.
1929 Major Arab riots in Palestine.
1931 Etzel (Irgun) right-wing, 'revisionist' Jewish underground organization founded.
1933 Hitler takes over Germany and begins imposing race laws against Jews.
1933–9 Fifth Aliyah, mainly from Germany.
1936 World Jewish Congress founded.
1938 9-10 November: Kristallnacht (Night of Glass) – Nazi violence against Jews.
1939 Britain strictly limits Jewish immigration to Palestine.
1939–45 World War II. Holocaust and the murder of six million Jews.
1946–8 Haganah, Irgun and Lehi militants resume struggle for a Jewish state in Palestine.
1947 Discovery of Dead Sea Scrolls.
1947 29 November: The United Nations approves creation of a Jewish State and an Arab State in Palestine. Violence erupts between Jews and Arabs.
1948 14 May: The State of Israel declares independence.
1948 15 May: Arab–Israeli War erupts. Israel survives Arab attacks, expands borders. Jerusalem divided, influx of Holocaust survivors, flight of Palestinian Arab refugees.
1949 Armistice agreements with Arab states.
1949-50 'Operation Magic Carpet' brings Yemenite Jews to Israel.
1949–54 Mass immigration to Israel of Jews from Arab states.
1952 Prague trials revive anti-Semitic fears in Communist eastern bloc.
1953 Establishment of Yad Vashem Holocaust Memorial in Israel.
1955 David Marshall, son of Baghdadi Jews, becomes Singapore's first Chief Minister.
1956 The Suez War.

TIMELINE

1960–80

1962–5 Jewish–Christian relations improve with Vatican II.
1964 Palestine Liberation Organization (PLO) founded
1966 Shmuel Yosef Agnon (1888–1970) becomes the first Hebrew writer to win the Nobel Prize in literature; jointly with German Jewish author Nelly Sachs.
1967 5–11 June: Six Day War fought between Israel versus Egypt, Syria and Jordan. Israel gains control of East Jerusalem, West Bank, Sinai Peninsula and Golan Heights.
1967 1 September: Arab leader in Khartoum reject recognition of Israel. UN 242 offers 'land for peace' formula and underpins future peace plans.
1968–70 Egypt's War of Attrition against Israel. Jewish settlers occupy houses in Hebron, amid more than 100,000 Palestinians.
1972 Soviets clamp down on 'refusenik' Jews wishing to leave the USSR. Palestinian terrorists kill Israeli athletes at Munich Olympics.
1973 6–24 October: Yom Kippur War. Israel surprised by Egyptian–Syrian attack, retains 1967 territories.
1974 Foundation of Gush Emunim, religious settlers movement. Golda Meir, Middle East's first woman leader, resigns.
1975 USA ties Soviet trade benefits to freedom of emigration for Jews. United Nations resolution equates Zionism with racism. Rescinded in 1991. Israel becomes an associate member of the European Common Market.
1977 Rightist Likud party wins Israeli elections, ousting Labour for the first time since independence.
1978 18 September: Israel and Egypt sign comprehensive peace accords at Camp David. Leftist Israelis found Peace Now.
1978 December: Prime Minister Menachem Begin and President Anwar Sadat are awarded Nobel Peace Prize.
1979 Israel–Egypt Peace Treaty signed.

1980–2000

1982 Israel's withdrawal from Sinai completed. Operation Peace for Galilee removes PLO fighters from southern Lebanon.
1982 June–December: The Lebanon War. Anger in Israel and abroad over Sabra and Chatilla massacre.
1983 American Reform Jews formally accept patrilineal descent. Menachem Begin resigns as prime minister, replaced by Yitzhak Shamir.
1984–5 Operations Moses and Joshua: Rescue of Ethiopian Jewry by Israel. Inconclusive elections result in Labour–Likud coalition.
1987 Beginning of the First Intifada Palestinian uprising against Israeli occupation.
1989 Fall of the Berlin Wall. Leonard Bernstein conducts a celebration concert in a free East Berlin.
1990 The Soviet Union relaxes emigration laws. Thousands leave for Israel.
1990–1 Iraq invades Kuwait, triggering a war between Iraq and allied United Nations forces.
1991 Operation Solomon rescues most remaining Ethiopian Jews. The Madrid Peace Conference starts first bilateral talks between Israeli and Jordanian, Syrian and Palestinian delegations since 1949.
1992 New government headed by Yitzhak Rabin of the Labour party.
1993 13 September: Israel and the PLO sign the Oslo Accords.
1994 26 October: Israel and Jordan sign peace treaty.
1994 10 December: Arafat, Rabin and Peres share Nobel Peace Prize. Palestinian self-government in Gaza Strip and Jericho area.
1995 Broadened Palestinian self-government is implemented in West Bank and Gaza Strip.
1995 4 November: Israeli Prime Minister Yitzhak Rabin is assassinated.
1996 Netanyahu elected, replaced by Ehud Barak in 1999.

Above Itzhak Perlman, one of the best-loved violinists of the modern era.

2000–

2000 24 May: Israel withdraws its forces from southern Lebanon.
2000 Camp David II peace talks between Israel, PLO and America end in failure.
2000 29 September: Start of the second Palestinian uprising, al-Aqsa Intifada.
2001 First Holocaust Memorial Day in Britain. Ariel Sharon elected Israeli Prime Minister.
2002 Spate of suicide attacks on Israeli towns. Israeli military reoccupation of Palestinian urban centres.
2003 US President George W Bush proposes Israeli–Palestinian roadmap to peace. Arab League re-airs Saudi Plan for peace.
2005 31 March: Mahmoud Abbas elected Palestinian president.
2005 August: The Government of Israel withdraws military and Jewish settlers from the Gaza Strip.
2006 Ehud Olmert replaces Ariel Sharon as prime minister after latter falls into coma (he died in 2014), and then wins March election. Islamist Hamas wins Palestinian elections. New war with Hizbollah in Lebanon.
2009 US President Barack Obama hosts first Passover ceremony in the White House. Likud leader Netanyahu returned to power.
2017 December: US President Donald Trump formally recognizes Jerusalem as capital of Israel.
2019 Deadlock in Israel after three indecisive elections.

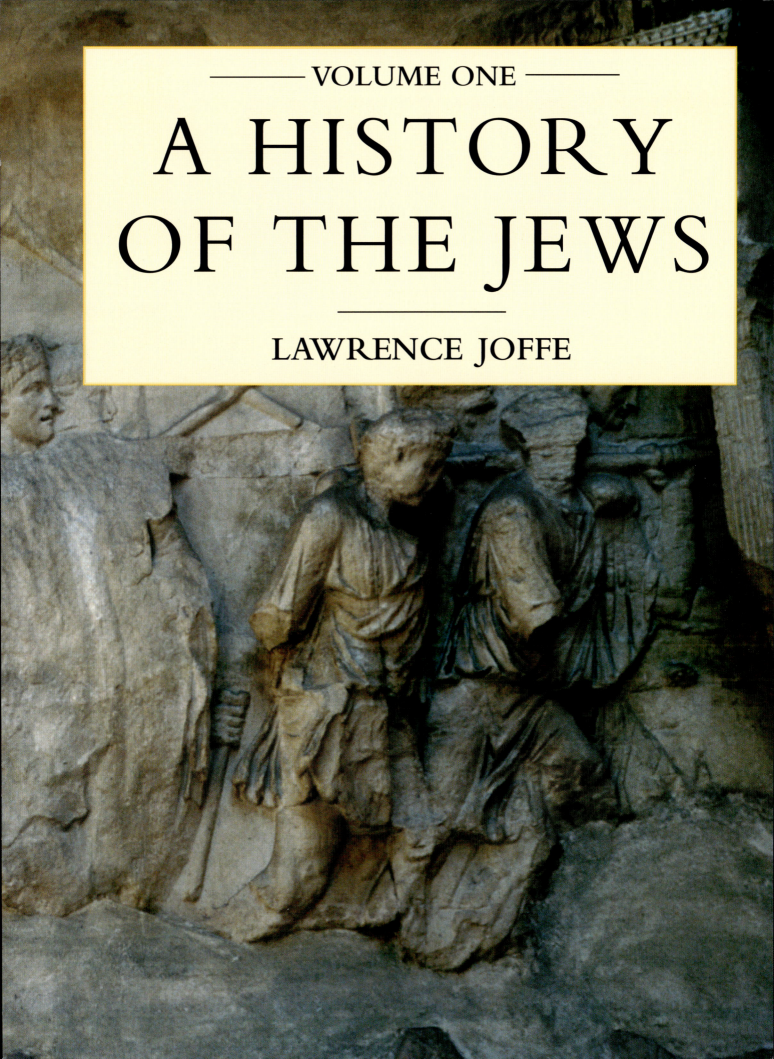

VOLUME ONE

A HISTORY OF THE JEWS

LAWRENCE JOFFE

Introducing Jewish History

OVER A PERIOD OF 4,000 YEARS, JEWISH CULTURE HAS SOMEHOW FLOURISHED, DESPITE ENDLESS ATTACKS AND PERSECUTION. THE JEWISH STORY IS PERHAPS THE MOST INTRICATE STRAND IN HUMAN HISTORY.

The tale of Jewish survival is full of extraordinary drama – triumphs followed by setbacks, and miraculous rebirths coming after periods of near extinction. Such changes in fortune have persisted to modern times, with the devastation of the Holocaust during World War II followed three years later by the founding of the first Jewish State in 2,000 years.

Intrinsic to Jewish history is the theme of returning to the 'promised land', Israel, from the Diaspora, life outside Israel. As Jews have established communities throughout the world, other cultures have enriched the Jewish story and identity. In return, individual Jews have made a profound impact on civilization, from Moses and Jesus Christ to Maimonides and Albert Einstein.

Below *Possible remnants of the fabled Hanging Gardens of Babylon.*

MIDDLE EASTERN ROOTS

In a sense the Jewish story has recently returned to where it began, the Middle East, and in particular a small, pivotal area along the eastern Mediterranean, known as the Land of Israel to Jews and historical Palestine to others.

Jewish history traditionally begins with Abraham, who lived perhaps 4,000 years ago. The Hebrew Bible – what Christians call the Old Testament – encompasses the origins and moral codes of the people. Jews did not leave behind great palaces or artworks, as did the contemporaneous empires of Egypt or Mesopotamia. All that remains is the Bible itself, arguably the greatest Jewish gift to civilization. The Bible's vivid characters have stimulated and informed world literature and art for centuries. Consisting of 24 books in all, the first five, the Books of Moses, are central to Jewish faith.

Above *Ezekiel prophesized the fall of the Temple in Jerusalem, and is seen here in a fresco of 1510 by Michelangelo.*

BIRTH AND SURVIVAL

This book outlines the origin, religion, traditions, culture and artistic, literary, social and scientific contributions of the Jews, both as individuals and as a distinct group in history. It begins with the biblical account of how the descendants of the Patriarchs, Abraham, Isaac and Jacob, became wandering Hebrews, who evolved into 12 Israelite tribes with a belief in one God (monotheism).

Liberation from slavery in Egypt (whether mythical or not) is the pinnacle of this saga, after which charismatic rulers known as the Judges ruled a more settled population back in historic Israel. The Jews then created a briefly united Kingdom of Israel, and forged a national ethos honed by a tradition of Prophets. These men, and sometimes women, acted as a buffer against the excesses and misjudgements of the monarchy. But having disastrously lost ten of their twelve tribes to the Kingdom of Assyria around 722BCE, and the remaining Kingdom of Judah to Babylon two centuries later, their story seemed to be at an end.

LIFE BEYOND ISRAEL

In fact, the destruction of the first Jerusalem Temple in 586BCE and the second in 70CE actually took Judaism and the Jewish people to new places, to explore new directions. The exiles that followed disasters at home invariably sent Jews into the world to form new communities. Throughout Jewish history there is a fascinating tension between its core identity and an ethos that grew through exposure to and opposition to the cultures that Jews found themselves living in: Persian influence, Hellenistic philosophy and Roman rule being only the earliest. Running parallel to this history is the story of anti-Semitism, a virulent and ever-evolving hatred of Jews and their beliefs.

Gradually, the centre of Jewry shifted to Babylon and Persia, and then to western Europe (Ashkenazi), North Africa and Spain (Sephardi). While Jews were everywhere a minority, they formed networks that linked vast areas and thus contributed immensely to the advancement of host societies.

Below Jews who resisted Nazis in the Warsaw Ghetto Uprising are rounded up by the SS, 1943.

Right Anti-Semitic or pro-Jewish? Arguments still rage over Shakespeare's fictional Shylock, seen with his daughter Jessica in Sir James Dromgole's artwork.

CONFLICTING FAITHS

This book explains how Christianity sprang from Judaism, and how this new faith, and later Islam, came to challenge Judaism for dominance. The faith survived, partly thanks to new institutions, not least the compendium of writing called the Talmud, which helped unite Jews in their particular faith and traditions.

It was in the 'Golden Age' of Spain that interfaith cooperation triumphed, producing an era of unprecedented creativity and cultural progress. Sadly, the Golden Age ended when Jews were perceived as a threat by Christian leaders and expelled in 1492. Similar patterns were repeated elsewhere in Europe.

NEW DISASTERS

Some Sephardi Jews fleeing Spain in 1492 were welcomed by eastern Europe, which became the new hub of Jewish life. During the Emancipation and Enlightenment periods, Jews emerged from the physical and notional ghettos that had cordoned

them off from the rest of society. Now, many experienced a crisis of faith, which sharpened an existing divide between traditional and Reform versions of Judaism, or led many to abandon Jewish life altogether.

An explosion of creativity in the late 19th century coincided with extraordinary mass immigration from Europe to America and a proliferation of new ideologies, including Zionism – a movement to reclaim the 'promised land'. However, the catastrophe of the Nazis' World War II Holocaust seemed set to end all such dreams. Miraculously, the Jewish people survived to see the birth of Israel in 1948 and its development, if troubled, as a new axis of Jewish identity.

The Jewish story that emerges is one of survival despite adversity, dreadful miscalculations and remarkable innovations; of a people as tenacious as they are talented; and of individuals who have shone as beacons of hope and inspiration. Timelines and a guide to Jewish festivals introduce readers to the culture, then evocative photography and instructive text bring the narrative to life, telling one of history's most exciting, and devastating stories of human survival.

Jewish Traditions and Festivals

Inseparable from their faith and history, the traditions of feasting, fasting and prayer on special days help to define what it means to live as a Jewish person today.

Above Adam and Eve are tempted by the serpent, an immortal biblical scene from the Golden Haggadah, 14th-century Spain.

The Jewish year follows the 354/5-day lunar calendar, as opposed to the more usual 365/6-day solar year, so while each Jewish festival falls on precisely the same date in each year of the Jewish calendar, the dates will differ on the Gregorian calendar. For synchronicity, and also to keep the months in their appropriate season, a 13th month is added to the Jewish calendar every two or three years. In the northern hemisphere, Rosh Hashanah will always be celebrated between summer and autumn, while Hanukkah always heralds winter and Pesach ushers in the spring, regardless of how different the actual dates will be on Christian calendars.

Jewish holidays always begin at sundown on the day before. The year of celebrations starts around September, with Rosh Hashanah, the Jewish New Year, and progresses through Yom Kippur, the Day of Atonement, which is marked nine days later. Sukkot, the harvest festival of thanksgiving, follows, ending with Simchat Torah, the festival of the Torah. Around December comes Hanukkah, the festival of lights, when gifts are traditionally exchanged. Tu b'Shevat, the Holiday of the Trees, falls around February, and this is followed by Purim, a festival that involves dressing up in colourful costumes, and is considered a kind of Jewish Mardi Gras.

Pesach commemorates Israel's deliverance from Egypt. During this

Below This 18th-century Mizrah scroll, hung on the west wall of the house to indicate the direction of Jerusalem, also illustrates major Jewish festivals.

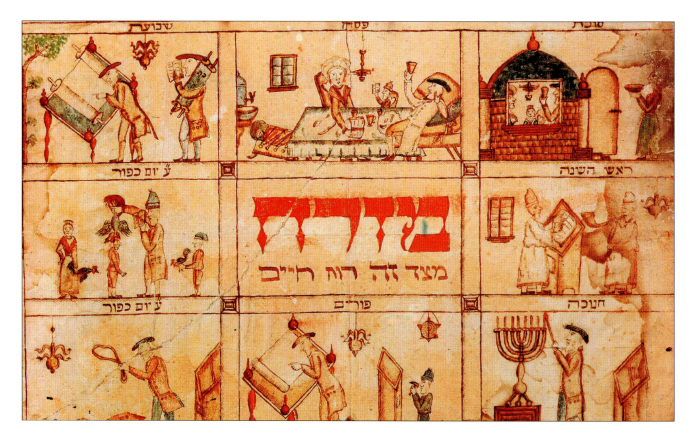

eight-day festival, Jews consume particular foods and drinks, eschewing those that contain leaven. Shavuot celebrates the Giving of the Torah, while Tisha B'Av is a day of fasting, when the Destruction of the Temple is mourned.

Many communities also observe Yom Hatsma'ut, Israeli Independence Day, which is celebrated on 14 May with various festivities. Yom Ha Shoah, the Holocaust Remembrance Day, is observed shortly after Pesach.

ROSH HASHANAH
The Jewish year begins in September or October with Rosh Hashanah, which means the head of the year. This is the start of the Ten Days of Penitence, also called the Days of Awe, which end with Yom Kippur. Jews are encouraged to spend these days in retrospection, considering their behaviour and how to make amends, improving their own lives and the lives of those around them.

The holidays of Rosh Hashanah and Yom Kippur are often referred to as the High Holy Days, and many Jews consider them so important that even if they observe no other festivals in the year, at this time they will go to synagogue, partake of a festive meal, and recite the prayers and blessings.

> ### BLESSINGS FOR ROSH HASHANAH
> Several blessings and benedictions attend this festival, which marks the beginning of the Jewish year. In addition to the blessings printed below, parents give thanks for their children, the challah is blessed as for Shabbat, and a slightly longer Kiddush (sanctifying blessing) is recited over the wine before it is drunk.
>
> **Candle Lighting**
> If Rosh Hashanah falls on the same day as Shabbat, then the blessing is modified and added to accordingly.
>
> *Baruch Ata Adonai Elohaynu Melech Ha'olam, asher Kid'shaynu b'mitzvotav, v'tzivanu l'hadleek neir shel Yom Tov.*
> Blessed are You, Lord God, Eternal One, who enables us to welcome Rosh Hashanah, by kindling these lights.
>
> **Benediction**
> This prayer – Shehecheyanu (the Hebrew for 'Who has given us life') – is recited on Rosh Hashanah and other important occasions.
>
> *Baruch atah, Adonai Eloheinu, Melech haolam, shehecheyanu, v'kiy'manu, v'higiyanu laz'man hazeh.*
> Blessed are You, Adonai our God, Sovereign of all, who has kept us alive, sustained us, and brought us to this season.
>
> **Honeyed Apples**
> Apples and honey represent a sweet new year. Apple slices are dipped in honey, and this blessing is recited.
>
> *Baruch Ata Adonai Elohaynu Melech Ha'olam, boray p'ree ha aytz.*
> Blessed are You, Lord God, Eternal One, who creates the fruit from the tree.

The Ram's Horn
A ceremonial shofar (ram's horn) is blown on Rosh Hashanah, as it is on Yom Kippur. The sound reminds Jews of their history and the covenant between the people of Israel and God.

One tradition (tashlich) calls for penitents to throw all their sins of the previous year into a body of running water. The gesture symbolizes a fresh start for the new year.

Rosh Hashanah begins, as usual, at sundown on the evening before. Candles are lit, the bread is blessed, and the Kiddush is recited over the wine. A festive meal is prepared.

Different Customs
Various ethnic groups have different customs for the holiday. Sephardim eat a fish with the head left intact,

Left The ceremonial shofar (ram's horn) is blown at Rosh Hashanah to welcome in the New Year.

expressing their hopes for a year rich with wisdom, with Israel as the head of the nations rather than the tail.

No sour or bitter foods are eaten at Rosh Hashanah, as no sharp flavours may interfere with the sweetness of the festival. All the new season's fruits are enjoyed.

YOM KIPPUR
The 10th of Tishri, the first month in the Jewish calendar, is Yom Kippur – the Day of Atonement. It also marks God's forgiveness of early Israelites after they worshipped the golden calf while Moses received the tablets of the law on Mount Sinai.

It is a day devoted to spiritual life, when the physical is set aside. Sex is forbidden, as is wearing leather shoes, brushing the teeth, spending money, using perfumes or soap and wearing make-up. Everyone, other than children, pregnant women, and the ill or infirm, is expected to fast.

Making Amends at Yom Kippur

Jews are urged to take stock of their sins, to make amends for any wrongs, and to repent. The ancient Kapparot (expiations) ceremony is still observed in some circles. A live chicken is passed over the head of an individual, so that his or her sins may be transferred to the bird. Many prefer to use a coin instead. The coin symbolizes giving to charity.

On the day of Yom Kippur, Jews go to synagogue, greeting each other with 'Have an easy fast'. Much time is then spent in quiet retrospection as individuals examine their consciences with honesty, aiming to make amends for past misdeeds, and promising to do much better in the year ahead. The Yom Kippur devotions include chanting the Kol Nidre, and the Yizkor, the memorial service at which the dead are remembered and respected. Kaddish, the prayer for the dead, is recited for deceased family members and friends of participants, and for the Jewish martyrs. Candles are also lit for the deceased.

All foods eaten before the fast must be light and simple and not too salty or spicy as it is terribly difficult to fast with a raging thirst. It is intended that penitents should feel a few hunger pangs while they are fasting, but nothing more serious.

A Day of Purity

At Yom Kippur the synagogue is decorated in white, the Torah is draped in white and the rabbi wears a kitl (a white robe), as a symbol of purity. Observant Jews also wear white in the synagogue, and shoes made from cloth rather than leather.

Unlike at other festivals, the candles are lit after rather than before the meal – before the start of Yom Kippur and the festival observances. A pure white tablecloth is draped on the dinner table, and a Bible, prayer book and other sacred religious texts are placed on the table until the observance has been completed.

Families and friends gather together for celebrations to break the fast after Yom Kippur. It is a happy occasion after the solemnity of the day's observance. Sephardim serve eggs, the symbol of life.

SUKKOT

This festival is observed by building a sukkah, which is a little three-sided hut or booth. The Mishnah (the first code of Jewish Law) lays down how this must be done. There must only be three sides, and the roof must be covered with schach, or branches of trimmed greens or palm leaves, with enough open space to permit those inside to see the stars. A sukkah must be a temporary building. Sometimes a few families get together to share the task of building, starting at one house and then moving to the next until all the structures are complete.

If the weather permits, meals during the seven-day festival are eaten in the sukkah. The mood of Sukkot is festive. Friends and family drop by, and if the weather is mild enough, families sleep in the sukkah, too. It is wonderful to catch sight of these sukkahs in big cities where you can see their greenery perched on terraces and in courtyards and gardens.

Right Children spin the dreidel as part of the Hanukkah celebrations.

Left Myrtle and willow branches are placed in the sukkah along with the etrog (citron) and lulav (palm branch).

Celebrating Sukkot

The proper greeting for Sukkot is 'Chag Sameach', which translates as happy holiday. Celebrants give thanks for the previous year, and express hopes for the year to come. At the end of the festival, prayers are offered for rain and the Hebrew dance Mayim may be performed.

Four plants – Arba Minim – decorate the sukkah, and are held in the hands during the blessings each evening. They are: the etrog (a lemon-like citron); the lulav (palm branch); the arava (willow branch); and the myrtle. Each of these has a deep significance. The etrog is shaped like a heart and symbolizes the hope of divine forgiveness for the desires of our heart; this should be held in the left hand. The right hand holds the lulav, which symbolizes Israel's loyalty to God, while the myrtle is shaped like an eye, and represents the hope that greed and envy will be forgiven. Finally, the arava, considered to be shaped like a mouth, symbolizes forgiveness for idle talk and lies. Bright cut-outs are pinned up and fresh and dried fruits are hung from the roof.

HANUKKAH

Throughout the world, beginning on the eve of the 25th of Kislev (which falls in November or December), Jews celebrate Hanukkah, the festival of lights, by lighting an oil lamp or menorah filled with candles. They light one every night for eight nights until all are lit. A shamash (helper candle), is used to light each candle.

The festival commemorates the Maccabean victory over Antiochus IV, who was known as Epiphanes of Greece, in the year 165BCE.

At Hanukkah, Jews eat foods cooked in oil, to remind them of the sacred lamp in the synagogue that burned miraculously without oil for the Maccabees. On the first night, the Shehehayanu (the benediction of thanks) is recited. Each evening a blessing is said over the candles.

Customs and Traditions

Jewish children often make ceramic or papier-mâché menorahs (candelabras) or dreidels (spinning tops) with which to celebrate the holiday. Jews will gather together socially throughout the festival of Hanukkah, greeting each other with 'Chag Sameach', meaning happy holiday, drinking spirits, exchanging gifts or giving money (Hanukkah gelt), and singing songs such as 'Ma-oz Tzur' (Rock of Ages) or the Dreidel Song. This last will often accompany a game of dreidel, when small coins or nuts are gambled away on the outcome of the spinning of the four-sided top. Hebrew initial letters marked on the top signify 'A Great Miracle Happened There', or, if one lives in Israel, 'A Great Miracle Happened Here'.

Hanukkah is a joyous celebration. Indeed, the *Shulkhan Arukh* – the code of law – forbids mourning and fasting during this time, and instead encourages merry-making and feasting.

PURIM

This festival is one of joy, feasting and drinking. It falls on the 14th Adar, around February or March, and reminds Jews of the triumph of freedom and goodness over evil.

The story that Purim celebrates took place in Shushan (now Iran). The main characters are Queen Esther, her cousin Mordecai and the evil First Minister of King Ahasuerus, Haman. The tale relates how Haman, irate that the Jew Mordecai did not show him proper respect, plotted to kill the Jews. Esther went to her husband pleading for the lives of her people. And so, at a banquet designed to honour Haman, the tables were turned. The king hanged Haman on the gallows intended for Mordecai, and the Jews were saved.

Celebrating the Story of Esther

During Purim, children come to the synagogue dressed in costume, often as Haman, Mordecai or Esther. The Megillah, the Scroll of Esther, is read

Left Scrolls of Esther, like this beautifully decorated example from Italy, 1781, are read aloud on Purim.

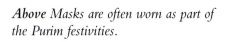

Above Masks are often worn as part of the Purim festivities.

aloud, and when Haman's name is uttered, all make as much noise as they can, by twirling the grogger (noise-maker) or banging things together.

Wine is a sign of happiness and inaugurates many Jewish religious ceremonies, but at Purim it is essential. Indeed, the Talmud exhorts Jews to 'drink so much that you can't tell the difference between Mordecai and Haman'. This is because Esther served huge quantities of wine at the banquet she gave at the palace, when Haman was exposed as a villain.

Special foods are eaten for Purim. In Ashkenazi cultures, triangular pastries filled with nuts, seeds or dried fruit are served. This commemorates Esther, who ate only fruits and nuts in the palace, as the kitchen was not kosher. North African Sephardim eat pastries drenched in honey called oznei Haman (the ears of Haman).

Gifts to Share at Purim

The giving of sweet pastries and fruit, known as shaloch manot, is a Purim observance. Charitable donations are given to at least two individuals or causes. Some Jews observe the fast of Esther, in honour of the queen's fast before she pleaded with the king.

PESACH

The Passover festival, Pesach, is one of the biggest in the Jewish year. Pesach falls sometime around March or April, following the Jewish calendar. It commemorates the story of the exodus of the Hebrew slaves from bondage in Egypt, a flight that turned a tribe of slaves into a cohesive people. It celebrates the fight for freedom of all humanity – the freedom of spirit as well as personal, religious and physical freedom.

'Why is tonight different from all other nights?' asks a small child, quoting from the Haggadah, the narrative read at the Pesach feast. And so the story unfolds.

The word 'pesach' means passing over, and represents the passing over of the houses whose doorways the Israelites had splashed with lamb's blood, so that those inside remained unharmed when the angel of death ravaged Egypt, slaying the first-born sons. This was Egypt's final agony, which convinced Pharaoh to, in the much-quoted words of Moses, 'Let my people go!' And go they did, into the desert to wander for an entire generation until Moses led them to the Promised Land. The festival of Pesach takes Jews on that journey via the Haggadah; the story is relived as the ritual meal is eaten.

For eight days special foods are eaten, and foods that are customarily eaten at other times of the year are taboo. No leavened foods are permitted, which rules out any food allowed to rise or ferment, such as dough containing yeast and flour.

In the weeks prior to the Pesach feast, the entire house is cleaned from top to bottom, especially the kitchen. The day before the Seder or Pesach feast, the head of the household searches for anything that might contain leaven – usually there are napkins filled with crumbs left here and there for the purposes of symbolic removal. Then he or she recites a blessing on the hametz (leavening) that has been gathered which is then burned. In addition to bread, all flour or leavened products are forbidden, as are beer and other alcoholic drinks made with yeast. Observant Jews are very careful about the dairy products that they eat during Pesach. Milk should come from animals that have only eaten grass, not grain, and there must be no risk of contamination with leaven.

Sephardim eat all vegetables and some eat rice, though Ashkenazim eschew many vegetables on the grounds that they could be considered grains or ingredients to make breads or cakes. The list includes corn, green beans, peas, lentils, chickpeas, and other dried beans.

Left Two 18th-century Pesach cups from Germany and an embellished Haggadah from Hamburg, 1760s.

Above A ritual Seder plate.

The Seder

On the first night of the festival (and the second night too, unless the participants are Reform or living in Israel) a ritual meal called the Seder is served. The word seder means order, referring to the fact that the meal has a specific order of events. The meal revolves around the reading of the Haggadah, the story of the exodus from Egypt and slavery. The foods eaten often have symbolic significance and represent elements of the story.

The Seder Plate

Maror (bitter herbs) are placed on the Seder plate to remind Jews of the bitterness of slavery. Horseradish is usually used as maror, but any bitter herb can be eaten. Haroset comes next. Also known as charosses, harosses and halek, this is a blend of sweet fruit and nuts. Mixed with wine to become a sludge, it symbolizes the mortar used by the Hebrews.

The cycle of life is represented by a roasted egg. It is also a symbol of the sacrifices brought to the ancient Temple and a symbol of mourning for the destroyed Temple. A bowl of boiled eggs is usually served with salt water as the first course. Salt water represents the Hebrews' tears.

Also to be dipped in the salt water are spring greens such as parsley or lettuce, which recall the oppression of the Israelites and the renewal of spring.

A roasted shank bone of lamb is placed on the plate as a reminder of the paschal sacrifice at the Temple. Some individuals refuse to eat lamb at the Seder until the Temple is rebuilt. There are no specific rules about what must be on the Seder menu, apart from the restrictions of Pesach itself. Each community has developed its own traditions. A Persian custom commemorating the beating of the slaves, involves hitting each other with spring onions (scallions). Four cups of wine must be poured during the Seder. A fifth is left for the prophet Elijah, the harbinger of the Messiah, who is said to visit every Jewish house on the night of the Seder, drinking from every cup.

SEFIRAH
Between Pesach and the next major festival, Shavuot, is a period called Sefirah. It is a solemn time of observance rather than a festival. Beginning at the end of Pesach, it commemorates the day when a sheaf of young barley – the Omer – was traditionally brought into the Temple in Jerusalem. Observing this period is called Counting the Omer. The solemnity of this period is thought to stem from an ancient superstition. Partial mourning was observed in the hope it would ensure a good harvest of grain.

During this time, the observant do not celebrate weddings, have other celebrations or even cut their hair.

Right Prayers for Shavuot include reading from the Book of Ruth.

LAG B'OMER
This happy day falls on the 33rd day of counting in the month of Lyar and is the one break in the solemn time of Sefirah. It is a day made for celebrating out of doors and picnicking. For observant Jews, Lag b'Omer is the day in spring when you could schedule a wedding or have a haircut.

TU B'SHEVAT
This festival is known as the Holiday of the Trees. It is one of the four holidays that celebrate nature, as mentioned in the Mishnah (part of the Talmud). Tu b'Shevat occurs in early February, when the sap begins to rise in the fruit trees of Israel. Tu b'Shevat is often celebrated by planting trees and collecting funds for reforestation. An old custom of holding Tu b'Shevat Seders has recently been revived. The meal progresses from fruits and nuts, through various juices, all symbolizing the awakening of nature after its slumber during winter.

The Tu b'Shevat Seder contains three different categories of fruits and nuts: hard, medium and soft, which are said to represent the different characteristics of the Jews. Certain fruits also have specific meanings. For example, apples represent the splendour of God, pomegranates represent fertility, , almonds represent divine retribution (because the almond tree blossoms before other trees) and carob represents humility and penitence.

Enjoying a meal made up entirely of fruits and nuts, or simply adding fruits and nuts to a braided loaf of challah are all traditional ways of celebrating the festival of Tu b'Shevat.

Left When the Omer (a sheaf of young barley) was brought into the Temple in Jerusalem the day after Pesach ended, the period of Sefirah began.

SHAVUOT
The word 'shavuot' means weeks in Hebrew, as this festival comes seven weeks after Pesach. In English it is known as Pentecost, from the Greek for 50 days.

It is also sometimes referred to as the Festival of the Torah, because it tells the story of the Israelites wandering through the desert and commemorates the giving of the Jewish scriptures, the Torah, and the Ten Commandments to Moses on Mount Sinai. And it is the Feast of the First Fruits, when the first fruits and grains of the season were brought to Jerusalem as offerings.

Shavuot is celebrated for one day among Israeli and Reform (Progressive) Jews and for two days in other Jewish cultures throughout the world. As with Shabbat, the holiday begins at sundown the night before. The table is set with a fine, festive cloth, wine and challah, as well as fresh spring flowers.

Shavuot is also a time to enjoy meals based on dairy products, although there are no rules that say this must be done. The Book of Ruth is read on Shavuot and provides a dramatic story of a woman devoted to her adopted faith, choosing it over her own family upon the death of her husband.

Shavuot is one of the four times of the year that Yizkor, the memorial prayers in which the dead are respected, are recited.

The Shabbat

The Sabbath or Shabbat is a weekly day of rest for Jews, honouring God's day of rest after Creation. Shabbat is observed from before sunset on Friday until nightfall on Saturday.

The Jewish calendar is punctuated by holidays, festivals and observances, which are shared by the entire community. Personal milestones in the lives of individuals such as bar or bat mitzvahs, weddings and celebrations attending the birth of a baby are also celebrated. Each festival has a special significance, and is accompanied by its own songs, stories, admonitions, activities, food and prayers.

The most important festival and observance of them all is the Sabbath or Shabbat. This is celebrated every week, and forms a model for all the other holidays.

SHABBAT

This is the sabbath, the day of rest. It is arguably the pre-eminent Jewish holiday, and it comes not once a year, but once a week. It is the weekly island of peace amid the sea of hectic life. Shabbat is a day for refraining from work, escaping the chaos of the ordinary working week, focusing on the spiritual, appreciating nature and enjoying family life. Even those who are not observant in other ways will often enjoy keeping Shabbat. The word 'shabbat' means cessation of labour and it is treasured time to relax with the family.

The origins of Shabbat are related in Genesis, the first book of the Bible, which describes how God created the world in six days and rested on the seventh. In the fourth of the Ten Commandments, it is decreed that Shabbat is a day that must be kept holy (Exodus 31:17).

A set of rules has been laid down, encompassing what it means to keep Shabbat. Observant Jews do not do any work, handle money, carry loads, light fires, tear paper, watch television or listen to the radio. They also may not cook.

Above Shabbat begins with the blessings being said over a loaf of challah and a cup of wine.

The Festive Meal

On the eve of Shabbat a festive meal is served. It begins with the lighting and blessing of the candles before sundown. Further blessings are then said over the challah (braided bread), and the Kiddush (sanctifying blessing) is said over the wine.

The lighting of the candles marks the dividing line between the rest of the week and the start of Shabbat. When the candles are lit, traditionally by the woman of the household, she passes her hands lightly over the flame in a movement that seems to gather up the light, then she covers her eyes.

The greeting on Shabbat is 'Shabbat Shalom', often accompanied with a kiss on the cheek, as participants wish each other a Shabbat filled with peace.

Different families have different customs or rituals regarding the blessing of the challah loaf. It is traditional in a number of households for everyone to gather around the table, with their hands on the challah during the blessings, after which they

Left A Californian family praying before the Sabbath meal.

pull it apart, making sure that each person has a bite of the blessed bread.

A welcoming song might be sung, for example 'Shalom Aleichem', and/or 'Shabbat Shalom', a light and evocative melody that welcomes the holiday and puts everyone in a mellow mood.

The meal on Friday night often includes chicken soup. Guests will often be invited, and the table set with white linen, flowers and the finest china and cutlery. Meanwhile, the next day's meal will be simmered slowly in a low oven, as no cooking is allowed on the Shabbat itself. This is usually a dish of beans and meat taken from the Sephardi or Ashkenazi tradition.

MORNING SERVICES

Services of prayer and worship are held on Saturday mornings in the synagogue; this is also a popular time for bar and bat mitzvahs, for boys and girls respectively. If one of these ceremonies is taking place, then a light celebration meal will often be served at the synagogue for the whole congregation.

Shabbat is over when the first three stars are visible in the night sky. At this time Havdalah will be observed. The Havdalah ceremony comes from the word 'hevdal', which means different, to signify the difference or separation between Shabbat and the other days.

The ceremony consists of the blessing over the wine (the Kiddush), inhaling the fragrance of sweet spices and lighting a braided candle, which is then extinguished by a few drops of wine – and so the new week begins.

SHABBAT BLESSINGS

Candle Lighting
This signifies the start of Shabbat and a blessing is recited:

Baruch Ata Adonai Elohaynu Melech Ha'olam, asher Kid'shanu b'mitzvotav, v'tzivanu l'hadleek neir shel Shabbat.
Blessed are You, Lord our God, Eternal One, who lets us welcome Shabbat by kindling these lights.

If children are present, a blessing is said over them. The head of the household places his or her hands on the children and asks that they strive to carry on the traditions of the Jewish people and faith.

A plea is always offered for God's blessing, safety, warmth and protection, and peace.

Friday Night Kiddush
Kiddush means 'sanctification'. The blessing that follows is said over the goblet of Kiddush wine.

Baruch Ata Adonai Elohaynu Melech Ha'olam, boray p'ree hagafen.
Blessed are You, Lord God, Eternal One, who creates the fruit of the vine.

Baruch Ata Adonai Elohaynu Melech Ha'olam, asher Kid'shanu b'mitzvotav, v'rahzah banu, v'Shabbat Kodsho b'ahavah oov'rahzon heen'heelanu, zeekahron l'maasay b'raysheet. Kee hoo yom t'heela l'meekrah-ay kodesh, zaycher l'tzeeat meetzraheem. Kee vanu vacharta ohtanu keedashta meekol ha'ahmeem v'Shabbat kodshecha b'ahavah oov'ratzon heenaltanu. Baruch Ata Adonai M'kadesh HaShabbat. Amen.
Blessed are You, Lord God, Eternal One, who sanctifies us with holy acts and gives us special times and seasons to rejoice. Shabbat reminds us of the times for celebration, recalls the days of Creation of the world and how God rested from that work. Shabbat commemorates the Exodus from Egyptian slavery. God has distinguished us from all people and given us the Shabbat full of joy and love. Blessed are You, Lord God, Eternal One, who sanctifies the Shabbat.

Saturday Midday Kiddush
This blessing is said over the wine to begin the Shabbat meal.

Al ken bayrah Adonai et Yom Hashabbat v'kodsho. Baruch Ata Adonai Elohaynu Melech Ha'olam, boray p'ree hagafen.
Behold, the Eternal blessed the seventh day and called it a holy time. Blessed are You, Lord God, Eternal One, who created fruit from the vine.

Blessing over the Challah
This blessing is said over bread: challah, rye bread, matzo etc.

Baruch Ata Adonai Elohaynu Melech Ha'olam, hamotzi lechem meen ha'aretz.
Blessed are You, Lord God, Eternal One, who creates bread from the earth.

The Birkat Hamazon is the grace said after a meal in which bread or matzo has been eaten.

Life Events

CIRCUMCISION, COMING-OF-AGE CEREMONIES KNOWN AS BAR OR BAT MITZVAHS, AND FUNERALS ARE AN INTEGRAL PART OF JEWISH LIFE FROM THE CRADLE TO THE GRAVE.

From birth to death, Judaism offers ceremonies and observances to mark the rites of passage and key events in the lives of individuals, many of which take place in the synagogue. Each event is always accompanied by abundant festive food and drink.

BRIT MILAH

Male children are ritually circumcised on the eighth day after birth unless they have are at birth, ill or premature; if any of these occur, the circumcision will be delayed until the child is healthy and has achieved a specific weight so as not to endanger his health.

The ritual circumcision is called brit milah in Hebrew, bris in Yiddish. It is usually performed in the home by a community specialist called a mohel, although some Reform Jews have the baby circumcised in hospital by a doctor. In a traditional ceremony, the baby is given no more than a few drops of wine as painkiller and the operation is swift. The baby scarcely gives more than a little cry, but the adults often need a bit more wine or something stronger to fortify themselves after the baby's ordeal.

After the ceremony, which includes blessings and prayers, there is a party, because this is a very happy occasion, when the newborn baby becomes part of the world's Jewish community. At the brit milah, the male child is given a Hebrew name. He is often named after a favourite relative; in Sephardic tradition it is a favourite living relative, in Ashkenazic tradition it is a revered deceased relative.

A girl child will usually be given her Hebrew name at the synagogue, at the age of about a month. In observant families, there is a

Above Circumcision, from a 15th-century Jewish manuscript.

ceremony for the first-born child – Pidyon ha Ben for a boy and Pidyon ha Bat for a girl. This means redemption of the first born and marks the start of the new family.

BAR OR BAT MITZVAH

The next milestone in the lifecycle is a child's bar or bat mitzvah. This coming-of-age ceremony marks the time when the child takes on the religious obligations of an adult.

Bar mitzvah – the ceremony for a boy – means the son of the commandment; bat mitzvah, the equivalent ceremony for girls, means daughter of the commandment. After bar or bat mitzvah the child may be counted as part of a minyan (quorum of ten people required to hold a religious service). In Orthodox communities, ten men are still required to make up a minyan, while in others, such as Reform (Progressive), it is simply ten people – either male or female.

A bar mitzvah ceremony takes place any time after the boy's 13th birthday, while a bat mitzvah takes place after the girl's 12th birthday.

MARRIAGE

Weddings have a special role in Jewish life. They are grand, festive and full of

Below A 19th-century painting shows a rabbi tying the phylacteries to a boy's arm.

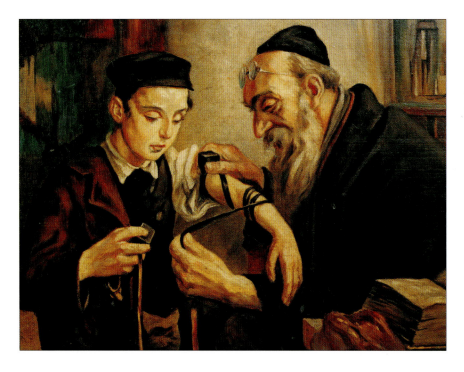

hope. The chatan (groom) and kallah (bride) fast from dawn until after the ceremony. The chatan wears the traditional white robe that is also worn on Yom Kippur. They greet their guests separately, and in Ashkenazi families the mothers of the bride and groom smash a plate, to show that no broken relationship can ever be fully mended. The ceremony takes place under a huppah, a canopy with open sides, symbolically open to friends and family. The marriage is official once the chatan has given an object of value, traditionally a ring) to the kallah. After the reading and signing of the contract, and recital of seven blessings, a glass is broken to remind the couple of their sadness, even on a day of joy, at the destruction of the Second Temple in Jerusalem. There follows a feast and party with foods such as smoked salmon, chopped liver, herring and rye breads, and lots of dancing of the hora.

BEREAVEMENT

Even at the end of life, food plays an important role for Jews. The period of mourning is known as Shiva. Each night during the period of mourning there is a gathering for the purpose of prayer, a minyan. Members of the community bring prepared foods with them when they come to offer support and comfort. Usually these will be traditional, homely foods that warm the soul and are easily digested, for grief is hard on the body. Food, and the act of giving food, sustains the mourners through their ordeal, for even when there is no strength for the task it is still necessary to eat to survive. The preparing, bringing and eating of food is all about survival.

The dead may not be cremated, as this speeds the natural disposal of the body, or embalmed, as this pre-

Right: A Jewish couple marry under the huppah (canopy with open sides) at a wedding in Israel.

FEATURES OF SYNAGOGUE LAYOUT

The synagogue's basic structure is quite simple: a rectangular room, an ark to contain the Torah scrolls (*aron ha-kodesh* or *heikhal*) and a platform from where the Torah is read, called *bimah* by Ashkenazim, *almemar* (after the Arabic *al-minbar*) by central European Jews, and *teba* by Sephardim. Customarily, synagogues allow worshippers to pray in the direction of Jerusalem. Orthodox synagogues segregate male and female worshippers, either by a *me chitza*, or 'low barrier', or a women's gallery overlooking the men.

Reform temples and 19th-century Orthodox United Synagogue buildings in Britain copied Protestant custom by placing pulpits at the front of the congregation to impose decorum. Stained-glass windows are another Christian trait. They illustrate months, zodiac signs or the 12 tribes of Israel, the most dazzling examples being Marc Chagall's windows at the Abell Synagogue in Jerusalem.

Some synagogues in Morocco and Italy deliberately introduce errors, either by misspelling a word in a Hebrew inscription or inserting a false beam, thus acknowledging that only God is perfect.

Today the world's largest synagogues belong to the Ger and Belz Hassidim in Jerusalem, seating 8,500 and 6,000 respectively. Their lavish arks and crystal chandeliers testify to renewed Orthodox vigour. However, the essence of Judaism resides in people meeting, praying and debating, as they have done for 4,000 years. Most Hassidim prefer to pray in humble *shtieblach*, or 'backrooms' given over to daily services.

---

serves it artificially. They must be buried in a simple wooden casket, and all Jews should be buried wearing a simple white shroud, as a symbol their earthly wealth is unimportant and all are equal in death. Flowers are seen as a Christian tradition and not encouraged. At the funeral, seven relatives over the age of 13 each tear an outer garment to symbolize their loss.

CHAPTER 1

ORIGINS OF A PEOPLE, BIRTH OF A FAITH

Are the Jews a people, a race, a nation or a religion? Their early story is encapsulated in the Hebrew Bible, arguably the Jews' greatest gift to civilization. Biblical ideas spawned three faiths, Judaism, Christianity and Islam. In the biblical account, miraculous rebirths followed near extinctions, a cycle that has typified Jewish history to the present day.

Jews trace their origins to ancient Hebrews who emerged in the Middle East some 4,000 years ago. Traditionally, they were descended from Abraham, who followed God's command to leave his native Iraq and settle in Canaan. For four centuries they lived as slaves in Egypt until Moses led the Jews to the 'promised land'. After rule by judges, the Jewish tribes united under kings Saul, David and Solomon, but soon divided into the rival kingdoms of Israel and Judah. Eventually the Assyrians broke Israel around 722BCE.

Opposite Moses leads the Children of Israel across the Red Sea. From the manuscript of a Jewish prayer book from Hamburg, 1427.

Above Abraham Sacrifices Isaac, Persian School, 18th century. The Torah tells how Abraham proved his faith by his willingness to sacrifice his son, and how God showed mercy in return.

Introduction to the Patriarchs

JUDAISM, CHRISTIANITY AND ISLAM ARE THE SISTER FAITHS OF 'ETHICAL MONOTHEISM' (BELIEF IN ONE GOD), WHOSE FOUNDING FATHER, ABRAHAM, MAY HAVE LIVED AROUND 2000-1700BCE.

Our earliest history of the Jewish people comes from the Torah, or Hebrew Bible or Old Testament (essentially the same), and begins with the tale of Abraham's family. They became a clan, which grew into a tribe and then set down roots to become a nation. Over time this nation spawned world religions and sacred texts that together make up the most widely read tome in history. The Torah (Old Testament) inspires 14 million Jews, 2 billion Christians and, through the retelling of its tales in the Koran, has reached 1.5 billion Muslims.

ABRAHAM'S VISION

As the Jews were the first to speak of Abraham, he has a special significance for them. In Hebrew he will always be *Avraham Avinu*, 'Our father Abraham'. Abram, relates the Torah, was a descendant of Noah's son Shem. According to Genesis, Abram and his father left Ur, a town near the Persian Gulf in present-day Iraq, for Harran, 1,600km (1,000 miles) to the east. There Abram had a vision of God, who demanded that Abram and his clan should worship Him alone.

Abram and his wife Sarai took new names – Abraham, 'father of many', and Sarah, 'princess'. In return, God was to lead them to a 'promised land' in Canaan. In the Torah, this was *Eretz Yisrael*, 'the Land of Israel'. The Hebrews (later called Israelites, then Jews) deemed themselves specially chosen to spread the word of God's unity to the world as a 'light unto the nations'. If the Jewish people disobeyed their faith, God would see them punished by disaster or enemy–nation attacks.

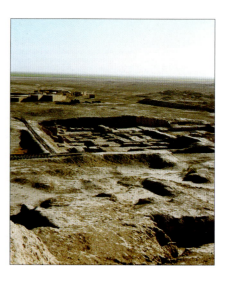

Above View of the ruins of Ur in southern Mesopotamia, where Abraham lived before his family departed for Harran.

TO THE PROMISED LAND

Departing from Harran (in today's south-east Turkey), Abraham and his band travelled south across the Euphrates River. This may explain the name 'Hebrew', meaning 'from the other side'. They then passed through the ancient cities of Damascus in Syria and Hazor in Canaan (a land also later historically known as Palestine). At Shechem Abraham built a small altar and he eventually bought land in Hebron. It was a burial plot, signalling that this was to be his resting place and the heritage of his descendants.

Neither Abraham nor, later, his son Isaac came close to conquering Canaan. Many other nations already lived there. Apart from Canaanites, there were Hittites and Phoenicians to the north, Moabites to the west (in today's Jordan), Midianites in the south (Negev and Sinai) and smaller groups in the central plain. Canaan also hosted wanderers, including the Semitic Amurru (Amorites or 'westerners'). Occasionally erupting into

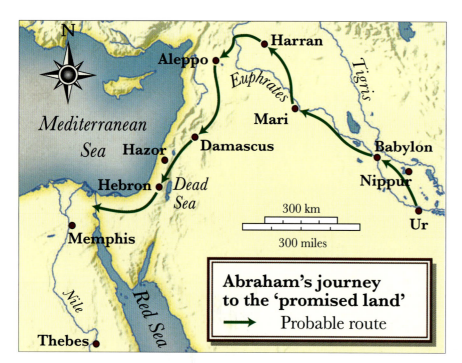

Left The wanderings of Abraham from the ancient city of Ur through Harran and Damascus to Hebron.

Above 6th-century mosaic of the Sacrifice of Isaac from the Beit Alfa synagogue, Heftziba, Israel.

Palestine were the two major powers of the ancient Middle East: Egypt and Mesopotamia. Ultimately, says the Torah, the Jewish people were to forge their identity in exile in Egypt, and it took another 400 years before Moses led them back to Canaan.

THE SONS OF ABRAHAM
Abraham had two sons: first Ishmael, by Sarah's handmaid, Hagar, and then Isaac, by Sarah. Sarah made Abraham banish Ishmael and Hagar to the desert, but God protected Ishmael, who eventually founded a major branch of the Arab nation. Isaac, meanwhile, continued the Jewish line. Some trace the rivalry between Jews and Arabs to these figures.

In Genesis, the ancestors of the Jews emerge as semi-nomadic rural wanderers. Abraham's existence cannot be verified outside tΔ38he Torah, and some regard him as legendary. Even so, he appears a credible 'type' of the age – a tribal patriarch and charismatic trader and diplomat who galvanized his followers into a distinct people.

While Abraham's band was weak compared to the powers of Egypt or Mesopotamia, he was probably not a poor wastrel. In the book of Genesis, for example, he musters a fighting force of more than 300. He was evidently a born leader, who commanded great respect. Primarily, Abraham is portrayed as a man of faith, who uniquely rejected the worship of idols. He had to make hard decisions: travelling into unknown country, circumcising himself and his sons as a sign of the 'covenant' (promise of obligation between his people and God), and finally obeying God's demand to sacrifice his son Isaac. The binding of Isaac on Mt Horeb forms one of the Torah's abiding motifs. Abraham passes the test of faith by showing his willingness to obey God, while God shows mercy by placing a goat in a thicket as a substitute sacrifice.

JACOB'S SONS OF ISRAEL
'Hebrews' came to form a people with a single language, culture, religion, and sense of historical mission. Yet 'Israel' is the name early Jews preferred. It is bound up with Jacob, the third patriarch. Abraham's son Isaac married Rebecca, and they had twin boys, Jacob and Esau. Jacob duped Esau into surrendering his birthright. Thus Jewish lineage passed through Jacob, while the furious Esau went on to found the Edomites. Poetic or Divine justice was at work, however: for seven years Jacob worked for his uncle without pay, only to be married to the wrong sister – Leah instead of Rachel.

In a dream, Jacob wrestled with an angel, who turned out to be a personification of God and gave Jacob the new name Israel, translated as 'He who contends with God'. Jacob had 12 sons and one daughter by his wives and concubines. His descendants adopted the name *Bnei Yisrael*, 'Sons of Israel', or Israelites.

Below Jacob and Esau *by a follower of Caravaggio, c.1625. Esau sells his birthright for a dish of lentils.*

Canaan and the Birth of a Civilization

Canaan lay at the crossroads of civilizations, connecting three continents. If mankind originated in Africa, as is now believed, the ancestors of all Asians and Europeans must have crossed this land.

Precious goods travelled north and south along the King's Highway: from Egypt across the Sinai, through Jordan into Syria and ending at the Euphrates River, the southern border of Mesopotamia. Another route moved east to west, from Arabia to Petra in Jordan, or from India by ship through the Red Sea to the Gulf of Aqaba. Traders then moved on to Beersheva, today in southern Israel, eventually arriving at Gaza, from where they shipped their silks and spices across the Mediterranean Sea.

Canaan was thus a crucial thoroughfare. Its location drew the attention of great empires. Some of the fiercest battles of ancient history took place on or near its soil – including the clash between Egypt's Ramses II (1304–1237BCE) and the Hittites of Anatolia, fought in Kadesh, southern Syria, in 1274BCE.

Naturally this interest made Canaan as much a curse as a blessing to the smaller peoples who lived there! Among those peoples were the ancestors of the Jews.

MYSTERIES OF JEWISH ORIGIN

Material evidence of the first Israelites is scant. The first extra-biblical reference to 'Israel' comes in the Victory Stele obelisk inscribed in the name of the Egyptian king Merneptah (ruled *c.*1204BCE). Mostly we know of the Israelites through the Bible/Torah, which as a historical reference is potentially flawed.

The existence of the Canaanites of Palestine can be verified, as can the Moabites, Amorites and Edomites to their east, and a kingdom of Aram to the north, of which the Bible/Torah speaks. As early as 2350BCE, inscribed tablets from Ebla in northern Syria refer to Canaanites. The Babylonian Mari letters (18th century BCE) and Egyptian Amarna letters (14th century BCE) both refer to wanderers called *Habiru* or *Apiru*, quite possibly the same as 'Hebrew'.

Below A limestone statue of the Ur goddess Narundi, made *c.*2100BCE – perhaps one of the gods that Jewish legend says young Abraham destroyed in his father's idol-selling shop.

Above A 4th-century BCE bronze plaque shows the Phoenician alphabet, from which early Hebrew was derived.

Archaeological evidence shows that indigenous Canaanites had a basic yet sturdy material culture, and the Victory Stele speaks of the Canaanite city-states Gezer, Ashkelon and Yanoam. Yet it only refers to Israel as a people, not a place, which may confirm the biblical version of the patriarchs as being essentially semi-nomadic.

One theory says that the Israelites were a blend of Canaanites and Habiru, or Shasu Bedouin marauders, who later claimed descent from Ur (Abraham's place of origin). Over time it seems they acquired the trappings of civilization, including a sophisticated native tongue. Hebrew belonged to the same Semitic linguistic family as Canaanite, Phoenician and Punic, yet only Hebrew survives. Canaanites also developed the world's first conson-antal alphabet in the 18th and 17th centuries BCE. Spread by the Phoenicians through trade, this alphabet formed the template for the

Hebrew lettering system, and later for Greek, Latin and Arabic as well.

All strata of Israelite society seem to have been literate, which may explain their remarkable endurance. For while Israelites left few impressive edifices, their literacy encouraged story-telling and debate, trade and communication, and an intricate system of law, taboos and ethical codes, which are characteristic of Jewish civilization to this day.

EARLY SUPERPOWERS

Abraham, Isaac and Jacob were small players politically, who variously fought against or allied themselves with nearby tribes. Their neighbours were in turn dwarfed by stronger forces. For most of the 2nd millennium BCE, Canaan was a province of one or other of the great powers of the day: Egypt to the south, or Babylon and Mesopotamia to the north. Both were phenomenally well-organized river-fed civilizations that towered over potential rivals. They boasted advanced systems of governance, employed the latest military technology, traded far and wide and controlled vassal states beyond their borders. No one could escape their influence, either materially, in terms of art and architecture, or spiritually.

Mesopotamian legends and social norms clearly coloured early Jewish customs. For example, the Great Flood story appears in many traditions and probably recalls an actual event. Also, the Jews' covenantal relationship with God resembles in structure Mesopotamian legal contracts, such as Ur-Nammu's constitution or the code of Hammurabi (c.1792–1750BCE), except the Torah says that man was created in God's image, so human life has special value.

SMASHING IDOLS

While the people of Ur worshipped images of as many as 3,000 deities, the Hebrew patriarchs rejected the idolatry that had formerly been part of their culture. Abraham's father, Terah, sold idols for a living, states the Bible. One Jewish fable, repeated in the Koran, tells how Abraham precociously destroyed his father's wares. Child sacrifice was another typically Canaanite custom that the Torah expressly forbids. The scriptures state: 'I give before you life and death: therefore choose life'. Certainly the patriarch's beliefs were revolutionary in their day.

In Canaan the patriarchs built altars in harsh central hill country, such as Bethel and Shechem, situated on a backbone of mountains running from north to south. To their west was the more fertile coastal area, dominated by Canaanites, later by Philistines; to their east, the Jordan River valley, and beyond, desert. Yet before a genuine new faith and nation could be established, the Israelites had to move once more – this time from Canaan to the well-watered pastures of Egypt.

Above A terracotta carving depicting the idol goddess Astarte or Ishtar from Ur, 2100BCE.

Below The Middle East, c.1500BCE, showing the extent of the empire of Hammurabi, the sixth Babylonian king.

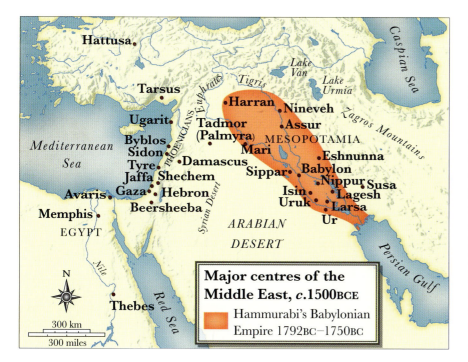

The Israelites Move into Egypt

The River Nile's banks trace a green strip of fertile land that 7,000 years ago helped create the longest-lasting and at times most powerful civilization outside Asia – Egypt.

Pharaoh Djoser (c.2650–2575BCE) built the first pyramid, a step-like structure at Saqqara, as long ago as 2650BCE. He launched the so-called Old Kingdom, centred on Memphis, which succumbed to anarchy around 2180BCE. For nearly 200 years Egypt was split into two kingdoms – Upper and Lower, or southern and northern – until it was reunited as the Middle Kingdom around 2000 BCE and ruled from Thebes.

Reinvigorated, successive dynasties of pharaohs spread their influence northwards to the still embryonic civilizations of the Greek lands and through the Sinai to Palestine, or Canaan, and Syria. Egyptians never settled in these lands in large numbers. Yet their officials built palaces and outposts at places including Beit She'an and Megiddo in ancient Palestine. Egypt was determined to keep trade routes open and hold sway politically. Often this proved a daunting task, given the patchwork nature of Canaan's ethnic divisions, and threats from encroaching northerners.

After 1800BCE, an economic boom in Egypt drew in thousands of foreign sojourners, including Palestinians. They paid taxes and enjoyed certain privileges, but they were never naturalized. Many formed their own distinct communities and had their own kings. Increasingly, as recently discovered papyri show, Egyptian governors must have been drawn from these communities, as they bore foreign and often Semitic names (Semites were the descendants of Shem, the eldest son of Noah).

Above Hebrew slaves building cities for the Egyptian Pharaoh, from the 14th-century Barcelona Haggadah.

HEBREWS IN EGYPT

During the years 1700–1550BCE, one group, known as the Shepherd Kings, or Hyksos, appears to have ousted the indigenous rulers altogether. Exactly who the Shepherd Kings were remains a mystery; some say Semites, others say Indo-Europeans from Anatolia (modern Turkey). Many historians, going back to the Egyptian

Below A 19th-dynasty Egyptian sculpture of Pharaoh Ramses II between god Amun and goddess Mut.

WHAT IS IN A NAME?

When Orthodox Jews want to thank God they say *Baruch Hashem*, 'blessed is the name'. But what is the name of God? Until Moses appears in the Book of Exodus, the Bible uses a plethora of names to denote the One God. Mostly we find the name *El*, which was originally a deity worshipped in Canaan, and which finds later resonance in the Arabic word for God, Allah. Often El is qualified: like '*El-Elyon*', God on High; or '*Elohim*', literally 'gods' (possibly an afterglow of polytheism). Another name used in early passages is '*Shaddai*', God of the Hills, or, in another interpretation, the suckling breasts. There is also '*Melekh ha-Olam*', king of the world; '*Ha-Rachamim*', the merciful one; and a female name for God: '*Shekhina*', denoting the indwelling spirit of the creator. Torah redactors apparently reconfigured names of pagan gods other than El: for instance Adonis, or Adon, from Lebanon, becomes '*Adonai*', Lord. The one name that cannot be said aloud – the true name of God as revealed to Moses – is approximated by the letters YHWH, and rendered in English as Jahweh or Jehovah. Jews pray daily for the world to recognize 'God as one, and his name as one.'

historian Manetho (2nd century BCE), deduce that they must have been Hebrews. According to the account in the bible, Joseph's envious brothers sold him into Egyptian slavery, but he exploited his gift as a dream-interpreter to become a vizier in the pharaoh's court. Joseph eventually got his revenge on his siblings by terrifying them in his guise as an Egyptian potentate; but then relented and granted them and their father, Jacob, a new home in Egypt.

Egypt was the nearest metropolis to Canaan, so assuming that drought did strike – as happens in the water-starved Middle East – the story makes eminent sense. But could it be, ask scholars, that Joseph symbolizes a historical process: the temporary usurpation of Egyptian government by foreigners? Likewise the later enslavement of the Hebrews and their subsequent departure under Moses has been read as mirroring the toppling of the Hyksos monarchs by a resurgent New Kingdom. Under pharaohs such as Tutenkhamen and

Below Prisoners of Ramses III, 1187–1156BCE, who used slaves to rebuild Karnak and Luxor.

Thutmose III, the Egyptian empire expanded south into Nubia and fought the Hittites in Syria.

Egyptian records never refer to Hebrews along the Nile. Even the Bible falls silent about the 400 years between Joseph and Moses. Yet that does not disprove their presence. The proto-Israelites may have been one of the many foreign communities living in Egypt around this time, even if the bulk of the Israelites (as some scholars believe) never left Canaan. Furthermore, Egyptian culture had an impact on the Israelites: for instance, some see ties between the Instructions of Amenemopet of 1200BCE Egypt and the later biblical work the Book of Proverbs.

It is known that the Egyptian king Seti I (1290–79BCE) moved his capital to Avaris at the north of the Nile Delta, where he built huge garrisons. Naturally, building a new capital required significant labour. So while there is no specific mention of Jewish slaves in Egyptian texts, Seti may well have enslaved Hyksos and Jewish and other Semites and forced them to build barricades against any

Above Joseph interpreted Pharaoh's dreams and became a vizier in his court. From a painting by Raphael, c.1515.

attack from the East. Later, Ramses III (r.1186–1155BCE) used slaves to rebuild Karnak and Luxor, and experienced the first recorded labour strike in history.

EGYPTIAN INFLUENCE
Some scholars believe a theological revolution in Egypt influenced the Jewish faith. Amenhotep IV (1353–1336BCE) suddenly outlawed polytheism and insisted on praying to a single deity, Akhen. He even renamed himself Akhenaton. Might this ruler have re-inspired the monotheism of his Hebrew subjects? It remains a theory. What is undeniable is that after Akhenaton's death, Egyptians reverted to worshipping Ra, Isis, Osiris, Ptah, Bes, Toth and other nature- or animal-based gods. And the Egyptians continued to deify their pharaohs, one of whom, says the Bible, so feared the growth of the Hebrew people that he tried to eliminate them entirely.

Moses

Until Moses' day, a few simple beliefs and practices defined the nomadic Hebrew clans. But after Moses received the holy law at Mount Sinai, Judaism embarked on its path to become a world faith.

According to the biblical account, Moses was formidable: a national leader, sage, social engineer and dreamer, a practical teacher, a compassionate man of principle, a radical and sometimes a despot. He led the Israelites' Exodus from Egypt, which experience, at once political and religious, became the prototype for all future redemption. Moses was also the first Hebrew to make an impact on the ancient world. Greeks conflated him with their own gods and heroes.

MOSES IN THE TORAH

The only first-hand source we have for Moses' life is the Torah (the first five books of the Old Testament to Christians). There is no explicit mention of the Exodus in Egyptian texts, yet Moses' centrality to Judaism is undeniable. Strictly speaking, the Torah denotes the Five Books of Moses, or the Pentateuch. Four of them – Exodus, Leviticus, Numbers and Deuteronomy – concern Moses and the Israelites' 40 years in the Sinai desert. The Hebrew for Exodus is *Bamidbar*, 'in the Desert', where Jewish lore says God fed the Israelites manna from heaven.

Moses apparently enjoyed a rapport with God, and he presided over numerous miracles, yet he was never deified, nor were his flaws hidden: his humanity, including his fiery temper, are well-recorded.

ORIGINS IN EGYPT

The name Moses may be Egyptian in origin. To summarize the biblical account, Moses was born the son of Amram, a Levite, and his wife Jochebed. Hebrews had lived for nearly 400 years in relative harmony with Egyptians in the Land of Goshen, in the eastern part of the Nile Delta. When a new Pharaoh came to power, and ordered all newborn Hebrew boys killed, Moses' sister Miriam hid the baby in bulrushes, until Pharaoh's daughter, Thermuthis, discovered him there. The princess named the baby and took him back to the royal court. There he was raised as a prince, and nursed by his real mother, Jochebed, at the entreaty of Miriam. Meanwhile, Pharaoh forced the Hebrews into slavery. The ruler is unnamed in the Bible, but he may be Ramses II (r. 1279–1213 BCE), who launched huge building projects.

Above Moses heard the voice of God in a burning bush, as in this painting by William Blake (1757–1827).

Below This 6th-century CE mosaic of the crossing of the Red Sea is at Dura-Europos synagogue, Syria.

Above Freud believed Michelangelo's Moses *showed him about to break the tablets of the Ten Commandments.*

One day Moses killed a taskmaster who was beating a Hebrew slave. Fearing punishment, he fled to Ethiopia, where he became a military leader. Later he moved to the Jordanian desert and worked as a shepherd for Jethro, high priest of the Midianites. In time Moses married Jethro's daughter, Zipporah, and they had a son, Gershom.

MOSES AS A LEADER

Forty years later, relates Exodus, Moses encountered a bizarre sight while tending his flocks near Mount Horeb. He saw a bush that burned yet was not consumed, and from the bush came a divine voice: 'I appeared to Abraham, to Isaac and to Jacob as El Shaddai (God Almighty) but by my name YHWH I did not make myself known to them.' (Exodus 6:3). The use of this previously unutterable name – Yahweh or Jehovah – signals a new stage in the maturation of Judaism.

Chosen to redeem the 'lost sheep of Israel', says Exodus, Moses returned to Egypt and instigated a slave revolt, possibly the first in history. Pharaoh was punished by ten plagues and eventually allowed the Hebrews to leave. They numbered some 600,000 and they crossed the Reed Sea (incorrectly known as the Red Sea) for the Sinai Peninsula, led by miraculous pillars of fire and smoke. Exodus calls the liberated flock an *erev rav*, mixed multitude, so perhaps slaves of other nationalities joined the Hebrew revolt and left Egypt with them.

THE TEN COMMANDMENTS

Just weeks later, dissatisfied Hebrews began demanding to return to the 'fleshpots of Egypt'. Worse followed when they began worshipping a golden calf idol. Moses brought the Hebrews to Mt Sinai, where he received the Ten Commandments and the oral law from God, says the Bible. This covenant reaffirmed the earlier vows that God had made with Abraham and Jacob. All the myriad laws that govern Orthodox Jewish life stem from the laws derived from the Torah.

Later rabbis identified 613 '*mitzvot*', or commandments: 248 positive ones, and 365 prohibitions, covering almost all human actions, from eating and drinking to hygiene, belief, sex, trade, ethics and keeping the Sabbath holy.

THE SPIES

After less than a year in the desert the Israelites approached the perimeter of the 'land of milk and honey'. Moses sent 12 spies into the territory, one from each tribe. Most reported back that Canaan's cities were heavily fortified and its countryside populated by giants and ghouls. Only Joshua of Ephraim and Caleb of Judah said it was safe to invade. The Israelites were obliged to wander in the desert for 40 years until a new generation was ready to attack Canaan.

FROM MOSES TO JOSHUA

According to Deuteronomy, Moses sent diplomats to the kings of Moab and Edom, south and east of the Dead Sea, who allowed him free passage through their territory. The Pentateuch closes with the poignant image of Moses surveying Israel from Mount Nevo, but denied entry for his failings. So he passed on the mantle to Joshua, son of Nun, his former camp guard. More than a military leader, Joshua now had prophetic powers because of Moses' blessing – but could he hold the tribes together?

Below The Sinai Desert in Egypt, home to Mount Sinai, the site where Moses received the commandments.

RETURN TO CANAAN

THE DRAMATIC FALL OF JERICHO, THE OLDEST WALLED CITY IN HISTORY, REPRESENTED THE ISRAELITES' FIRST BREACH INTO CANAAN, BUT THE FULL CONQUEST MAY HAVE TAKEN YEARS, EVEN DECADES, TO ACHIEVE.

The Book of Joshua tells how the invaders, led by Joshua and Caleb, crossed the River Jordan, encircled the fortified town, blew their trumpets and brought the walls tumbling down on the seventh day.

ISRAELITE INVASION – TRUTH OR FICTION?

So goes the biblical story, but did the siege really happen this way? Archaeological evidence suggests that Jericho's walls had fallen long before the Israelites arrived. Some scholars question whether a military conquest took place at all, and believe that Israelites infiltrated Canaan over two centuries. Biblical accounts of the conquest, from the books of Numbers, Joshua and Judges, show discrepancies.

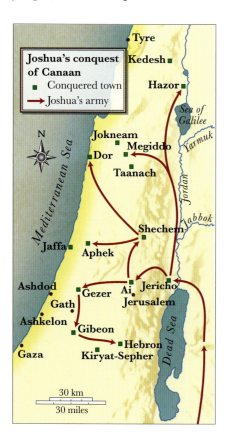

Yet the biblical portrait might have some merit. Excavations show that the Canaanite cities of Lachish, Kiryat-Sepher and Eglon in the south, Bethel in the centre and Hazor, a town of 50,000 citizens in the far north, were all destroyed in the late 13th century BCE. Other evidence confirms that occupation of the hill country took place from east to west, which tallies with the biblical version.

The shrine of Shechem, where Abraham was promised Canaan a millennium earlier, showed no sign of destruction. The Book of Joshua confirms that Israelites were not hindered there. Piecing together evidence from archaeology, biblical sources and the geopolitics of the time, the following reconstruction of events seems possible.

Israelites emerged from the Sinai into Transjordan and prepared to enter Canaan from the east. They were lightly armed and weary after their 40 years in the desert. An assault on Canaan's well-defended cities seemed set to fail. Moreover, the Canaanites had field armies, so conventional battle-field engagements were best avoided.

However, the Israelites used stealth. They took Bethel, Ai and Gibeah by means of feigned retreats and posted spies in Jericho before the siege. Often the Israelites used diplomacy to exploit divisions among Canaan's diverse peoples. For instance, they formed a treaty with the Hivites of Gibeon and neighbouring cities, and helped defend them when four Canaanite city-states attacked.

Left Map of Joshua's conquest of Canaan, showing the route taken by his army as they moved north.

Above Dante's Vision of Rachel and Leah, Rossetti 1855. The Italian poet saw the sisters as symbolizing contemplation and action respectively.

WAVES OF ATTACK

The Israelites advanced in two broad waves. The first consisted of the Rachel tribes (Rachel was Jacob's chief wife), headed by Ephraim and Manasseh of the house of Joseph. They advanced through the Transjordanian kingdoms of Moab and Edom. After fording the River Jordan and taking Jericho, they climbed the mountain range and, once over Mt Ephraim, they fanned out in different directions.

Perhaps a generation later came the second wave; the Leah (Jacob's second wife) tribes led by Judah. After defeating the Amorites, they entered Canaan north of Jericho and moved towards the Judean Hills and the Shefelah Plain nearer the coast. Meanwhile, non-Israelite clans related to Judah, the Calebites, Kenites and Kenizzites, helped them seize Hebron and the Negev Desert.

The Book of Joshua says that the Israelites destroyed 12 fortress towns, but admits that subjugation was far from total. After the initial victories the Israelites suffered reverses, and were forced out of the coastal plains and on to barren hill country.

Right *A 14th-century French illumination by Guiart Desmoulins, showing the 12 tribes of Israel.*

MULTI-ETHNIC CANAAN

The Israelites lived cheek by jowl with other peoples in Canaan. On the northern borders were Phoenicians; to the east, Arabs and other Semitic nomads, such as the Ammonites. Around 1175BCE a new group arrived to upset Canaan's already fragile ethnic balance. These were the Philistines, an advanced race who settled along the southern coast of Canaan.

TRIBAL DEMARCATIONS

Temporarily weakened by internal strife, and disturbed by a spate of earthquakes, Egypt began withdrawing from Canaan around 1150BCE. Each Israelite tribe was allocated an area to settle. Reuben, Gad and Manasseh chose to remain east of the River Jordan. In Canaan proper, four tribes were located north of Shechem: Asher by the coast, Naphtali stretching towards Mt Lebanon, Issachar between Mt Tabor and Mt Gilboa, and Zebulon just east of Mt Carmel. The five remaining tribes all settled south of Shechem. These were Ephraim in the centre, Dan nearer the coast, Benjamin near the northern shore of the Dead Sea, Judah in an arc around Hebron, and Simeon to the south west of the Dead Sea. Members of the priestly Levite caste were not allocated any territory of their own, and instead lived amid all the tribes.

LIFE IN THE PROMISED LAND

The books of Joshua and Judges vividly describe a poor, agrarian, clan-based and egalitarian society, which Late Bronze Age archaeological findings confirm. The Israelites settled on a loosely republican system of government, called the *edah*, congregation or assembly. Its basis was theocracy – politics governed by a religion. Tribal borders shifted over time, depending on battles against or agreements with neighbours. Internal frontier disputes were rare, but the Book of Joshua hints at a growing cultural schism between north and south.

Left This section of a 5th-century CE mosaic map from Madaba, Jordan, shows the city of Jericho and the River Jordan near the Dead Sea.

The Age of Judges

BETWEEN THE RE-ENTRY OF ISRAELITES INTO CANAAN AND THE START OF MONARCHY SOME 200 YEARS LATER, A NEW TYPE OF RULER EMERGED, CALLED THE *SHOFTIM*, OR JUDGES — CHARISMATIC LEADERS FOR PERILOUS TIMES.

Sometimes the Book of Judges hints at a truly national leader. Mostly, though, *shoftim* were local figures, imbued with great charisma. Some came with a pedigree, such as Othniel. As the nephew of Joshua's chief spy, Caleb, he represented continuity from one era to the next. The majority, however, had lowly, even semi-criminal backgrounds.

The Israelites were a Bronze Age people adapting to the new Iron Age, bound together by common ethnicity and beliefs, yet overall remarkably decentralized. The Ark of the Covenant was based at Shiloh in central Palestine, and Israelites held occasional pan-tribal assemblies there, but it was not their capital.

Perhaps one reason for the looseness of the tribal confederation is that Canaan, or historic Palestine, is an amazingly varied locale. The very nature of their environment exacerbated tribal divisions. No one tribe dominated, and even the smallest contributed leaders.

ETHNIC DIVERSITY

Unlike the Book of Joshua, which says all foes were vanquished, Judges presents a more confusing, though probably more realistic, picture. Canaan appears as a multi-ethnic patchwork quilt in which Israelites are one people among many. The Book of Judges 3:5 states: 'The children of Israel dwelt among the Canaanites, the Hittites, the Amorites, the Perrizites, the Hivites, and the Jebusites.'

The stories in Judges share a familiar pattern: every time a judge died the people backslid into bad ways, shirking the one God and worshipping alien deities, especially the Canaanite Baal and his female consort Asherah.

DEBORAH

The only female judge was Deborah, a prophetess who led the Israelites during one of their darkest hours. For 20 years Canaanites under King Javin of Hazor had oppressed her people. Their commander, Sisera, mustered 900 chariots and stood poised to crush the Israelites. Just when all seemed lost, says the Bible, Deborah received a visitation from God promising victory. On hearing the news, the Israelite general, Barak, of the tribe of Naphtali, insisted that she accompany him into battle. The laws of warfare forbade women from participating in war, so Barak's decision showed how exceptional Deborah's personality was.

Spying the Canaanites near the Kishon River, Barak's small force attacked from Mount Tabor, 17 kilometres west of the Sea of Galilee. They then destroyed the enemy by taking advantage of a rainstorm, which caused Sisera's chariots to sink in the mud.

Deborah's song of praises to the Lord is in the Book of Judges, chapter five, and is thought to be one of the most ancient passages in the Bible.

Above The Israelite judge Deborah (1209–1169BCE) invokes her people to battle in this painting by Salomon de Bray, 1635.

Left The Plain of Jezreel was the site of many battles, including those of Deborah and Gideon. Saul and his sons died here fighting the Philistines.

THE AGE OF JUDGES

Above A bronze and gold statuette of a Canaanite god, probably Baal, dated 1400–1200 BCE.

Right Samson, probably the most famous and flawed of the judges, fighting a lion, in this image from a Hebrew Bible and prayer book.

GIDEON AND SAMSON

Deborah was succeeded by the particularly martial Gideon, who 'threshed wheat by the winepress' yet grew into a 'mighty man of valour'. Aided by a cohort of just 300 men, he defended the Israelites from two fearsome besieging groups: camel-borne Midianites from the southern Jordanian desert, allies in Moses' day, turned bitter foes; and Amalekites, distant relatives of the Israelites. When Gideon beat them, the Israelites implored him to be their king. He refused, insisting that 'only the Lord will rule over you'. This was just as well, as his son and would-be successor, Abimelech, turned into a monster who butchered 70 of his brothers and half-brothers.

Most famous of the judges, and probably the most flawed, was Samson. He was a member of the Nazirite sect, puritans who avoided drink and frivolities, and who probably influenced later Jewish strains, like the Essenes, Zealots and Rechabites. Much about the Samson story is mythical, like his superhuman strength derived from his long hair. His tale evokes the romance of a hero, a sinner put to service for good. When he brought down the Temple of Dagon in Gaza, he instilled pride in fellow Israelites. But he was never a conventional ruler, nor did he eradicate the Philistine threat.

THE PHILISTINES

The Israelites and Canaanites had just worked out spheres of influence and fashioned a tense truce, when the Philistines arrived to threaten them both. Today 'philistine' has become a byword for anything boorish, yet the real Philistines were artistically gifted. In fact, they may have been an offshoot of the Mycenean and Minoan civilizations of Crete, Cyprus and the Aegean Islands, or present-day Turkey. Almost certainly they were Indo-European 'Sea People' and not Semitic – a thesis that tallies with the biblical account of the family of nations.

The Philistines were also wise in the arts of war. They used the latest iron swords and 'helmets of brass', as the Book of Samuel reports of the feared warrior Goliath. Evidently the Philistines jealously guarded their

Right This chapter title page from Maimonides's Mishneh Torah gives the title of the Book of Judges – Shoftim.

technology and prevented ironsmiths from working in enemy territory. But in an early instance of industrial espionage, Israelites captured enemy arms in battle and copied them.

SEARCHING FOR A KING

From their coastal locations of Gaza, Gath, Ashkelon, Ekron and Ashdod, the Philistines began encroaching on Canaan's hinterland. Frustrated at being the butt of attack, undermined by myriad schisms and rivalries between the tribes, the Israelites began longing for a national leader who could unite them. So they turned to Samuel, the last of the judges, and asked him to break with tradition and find them a king.

Settling on a Monarchy

JEWISH TRADITION REGARDS SAMUEL AS THE LAST OF THE JUDGES AND FIRST OF THE PROPHETS. HE WAS A CRUCIAL TRANSITIONAL LEADER AS ISRAEL MOVED FROM TRIBAL CONFEDERACY TO MONARCHY.

Samuel arose at a time of crisis when the Israelites, especially the southern tribe of Benjamin, were facing constant attack from the Philistines (c.1180–1150BCE). Samuel's mother, Hannah, was a religious woman of advanced years who came from the remote town of Ramah, and longed for a child. Eventually, Samuel was born in answer to her prayers. So grateful was Hannah, that she entrusted her boy to Eli, high priest at the sanctuary of Shiloh.

When Samuel was 12, the Philistines defeated Israelites at Eben-Ezer and stole the holy Ark of the Covenant. To Samuel this was a seminal moment, after 20 years of Philistine oppression, he summoned an army at Mitzpah and repelled the foe. Now a true national figure, Samuel toured the country dispensing advice. He set up a guild of ecstatic prophets and eventually passed leadership to his sons. But when they proved corrupt, the Israelites begged him to give them a king.

Samuel insisted that choosing a king represented blasphemy against the rule of God. Furthermore, there were many dilemmas: Which tribe should the king come from? Should the monarch be hereditary or popularly chosen? Could a queen be a monarch? And should the king rule on religious matters?

SAMUEL ANOINTS SAUL

In the end Samuel relented, and chose for the Israelites Saul, a farmer from the tribe of Benjamin. Saul seemed modest and principled and, as a Benjaminite, a people who suffered the most from Philistine attack, he knew better than most what it was like to be oppressed.

At first Saul did not want the job and hid when Samuel came looking for him. He was called *nagid* (military commander), and not *melekh* (king), perhaps indicating his unwillingness to fully embrace the monarchic idea. However, Saul proved his mettle when he saved the Benjaminite city of Jabesh Gilead from Ammonite attack. Anointed with oil and crowned king at Gilgal, on the Jordan, he built his capital at his birthplace, Gibeah, from where he ruled for 38 years. Shiloh is believed to have been his alternative capital.

Above King David enthroned. From a Spanish Hebrew manuscript of the Book of Kings, Kennicott Bible, 1476.

Saul, says the biblical Book of Samuel, successfully fought 'enemies on every side', including Philistines, Edomites and Ammonites, urbanized Gibeonites and nomadic Moabites. He and his chief general, Abner, created Israel's first standing army, comprising units based on tribe and territory. He granted land to those close to him, a common practice in the ancient Levant, but until then unknown among Jews.

A tragic figure, Saul grew to be wracked by insecurity and obsessive envy. Increasingly he made arbitrary confiscations and violent arrests. Samuel withdrew his favour when the king disobeyed his orders, thought to come from God, and when Saul lapsed into despotism.

Left Hannah presents her son Samuel to the High Priest Eli. A painting by 17th-century artist Lambert Doormer.

Left Saul resented the harp-playing youth, and this 1646 painting by Guercino shows Saul attacking David.

RISE OF DAVID, FALL OF SAUL

To soothe his melancholia, Saul employed a talented troubadour from the tribe of Judah, David, who befriended Saul's son and chief lieutenant, Jonathan.

David was born in Bethlehem, the son of Jesse and grandson of Ruth, a Moabite convert to Judaism. In time he married Saul's daughter, Michal. According to the familiar story, he killed the Philistine giant Goliath armed only with a slingshot. David's distinctive six-pointed star later became the Jewish national symbol, and the most beautiful psalms are attributed to him.

However, David's triumphs aroused Saul's murderous envy. When David fled, Saul executed Ahimelech and 85 other priests of Nob who gave the young courtier refuge. Often the biblical account hints at social rifts within a still-maturing tribal society. At times it speaks of Jonathan leading Hebrews, as distinct from Israelites. Likewise it says David accepted a fiefdom from the enemy Philistines when he was hiding from Saul.

Another recurrent theme is mercy versus duty. Jonathan, for instance, felt torn between loyalty to his father and love for David. The prophet Samuel rebuked King Saul for not slaying Agag, the defeated Amalekite king. And twice David had Saul in his sights on the battlefield, but chose not to kill him.

Determined to exploit Israelite divisions, the Philistines launched a westward invasion, slaying Jonathan in the opening skirmishes. Saul ultimately took his own life after Philistines defeated his army at Gilboa. When his body was draped on the walls of Beth She'an, the men of Jabesh remembered his earlier service and buried him in their town.

ISH-BOSHET AND DAVID

Saul's captain, Abner, proclaimed Ish-Boshet, Saul's son, king *c.*1007BCE. His two-year reign was undistinguished. David, meanwhile, was crowned rebel king of Judah. Even Abner deserted Ish-Boshet for David's side, and in 1005BCE David's partisans defeated the formal king's forces. Ultimately Ish-Boshet was murdered by two of his own captains, after which David was anointed, allegedly by Samuel, as king of Judah and the northern tribes of Israel.

David immediately executed Ish-Boshet's treacherous killers. Disloyalty was not to be tolerated as he began his major task, the consolidation of a truly united Kingdom of Israel. And Jewish history was to enter a new phase under his reign, the crowning glory of which would be the taking of Jerusalem.

Below Samuel anoints David. A 2nd-century fresco from Dura-Europos, Syria, one of the world's oldest synagogues.

THE GREAT KINGS

DAVID AND SOLOMON TRANSFORMED TRIBES INTO A NATION. THEY MADE JERUSALEM THE CAPITAL OF A UNITED ISRAEL, ESTABLISHED PEACE AND BUILT THE TEMPLE AS JUDAISM'S SPIRITUAL FOCAL POINT.

The biblical account of King David's life is probably unique in early Near Eastern literature. Few sagas contain so much personal detail, psychological insight or information about contemporary society. David almost certainly existed: in 1993 archaeologists working in Tel Dan, northern Israel, uncovered an ancient basalt artefact bearing the words 'House of David' and 'King of Israel'. The books of Samuel and Chronicles describe how after fleeing Saul's court, David recruited a roving army of general malcontents who terrified the tribal elders of Judah. David convinced Judah's elders that only he could protect them.

JERUSALEM IS CAPITAL

In his eighth year David attacked and overwhelmed Jerusalem, making it his new capital. The original Jebusite inhabitants were not massacred or expelled, but continued to live in the city. David even purchased land from Jerusalem's former ruler, Melchizedek, to house the Ark, repository for the commandments.

King David was to rule Jerusalem for the 33 remaining years of his 40-year monarchy. He completed the process begun by Saul in pacifying Canaanite enclaves, and then established Israelite control over Moab, Edom, Ammon and Aram–Damascus in the north-east. Yet he ended his reign with a sense of incompletion, because he never built his desired temple for the Ark.

DAVID'S SONS

Absalom was David's favourite son, and just as David proved a thorn in the side of his mentor, Saul, so Absalom grew to defy his father. He harnessed the ten northern tribes against Judah, but he lost the battle and was stabbed to death by Joab. David chose as his heir his surviving

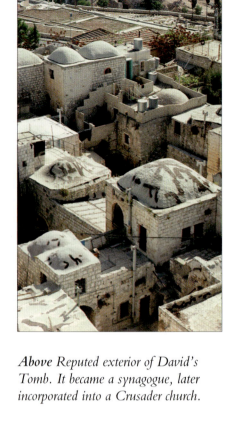

Above Reputed exterior of David's Tomb. It became a synagogue, later incorporated into a Crusader church.

son, Solomon, a scholar-judge, whom he instructed on his deathbed to 'walk in God's ways'. Other Israelite leaders had fought and won battles, but none had so thoroughly stymied Israel's foes as David. The Philistines could not dent Judah's borders for hundreds of years, and Solomon (whose name means 'his peace') enjoyed the luxury of governing for decades without ever having to fight a war.

Solomon was no great military general, but he proved that he could be ruthless. On taking power he replaced all his father's ministers (murdering some) and stopped recruiting conscripts from the northern tribes of Israel, whom he never really trusted. Next, Solomon divided Israel into 12 tax districts, and expanded trade by marrying daughters of all the neighbouring princes. His best-known dalliance was with

Left An illumination from a Jewish manuscript of 1728–9 showing the Temple of Jerusalem.

Above A Muslim miniature from Persia showing Solomon surrounded by courtiers, angels, demons and wives, c.1570.

the beautiful Queen of Sheba, from Yemen or Ethiopia. One result was Israelite control over trade in the valuable myrrh, frankincense and spices from Arabia.

TEMPLE AND EMPIRE

The honour of building the Temple passed from David to Solomon in 973BCE. He chose the highest point in the city, what Jews call '*Har ha-Bayyit*', the Temple Mount, and Muslims call the Noble Sanctuary. The biblical account is remarkably explicit about the Temple's dimensions. It also details how King Hiram of Tyre, south Lebanon (969–936BCE) helped to fund and build the structure.

Solomon probably won more acreage by negotiation and diplomacy than his predecessors had done by warfare. His imperial borders stretched from the Nile to the Euphrates and encompassed former enemies, including Philistines. Proof of the kingdom's extent was found in 1902 with the discovery of the remains of Ir Ovot, a plateau fortress in the Negev Desert. Now in southern Israel, the site dates back to the 10th century BCE.

ECONOMIC GENIUS

Trade was the essence of Solomon's economic success, especially trade by sea. From his Mediterranean ports of Akko (Acre) and Jaffa he shipped goods to and from Tarshish in Spain and Chittim in Cyprus. He built a vast merchant fleet at his southernmost port, Etzion-Geber, near present-day Eilat on the Gulf of Aqaba. Solomon also became an arms dealer, and traded Cilician horses for Egyptian chariots.

However, power corrupted Solomon in his later years. He built chariot cities and royal depots, a sumptuous palace and three new royal fortress cities, at Hazor, Gezer and Megiddo (Armageddon), but these were expensive to fund. So he raised taxes and instituted a corveé on Canaanite and northern Israelite subjects, who laboured for no pay. Northerners resented his Temple cult, as did religious purists, who saw Jerusalem as absolutist and dictatorial, veering towards idolatry. He was also intolerant of local shrines at Bethel and Shechem. So when Solomon died, in 925BCE, northern Israelites insisted that his son Jeroboam be crowned in their area, Shechem.

PSALMS AND PROVERBS

The scriptures include numerous passages ascribed to David and Solomon, the most famous being the psalms, where David's poetic genius and religious passion come across powerfully. Rabbis believe the Book of Proverbs is Solomon's handicraft, and perhaps the famously erotic and spiritual 'Song of Songs', too.

David and Solomon also greatly influenced Judaism's sister faiths. The Book of Matthew, for instance, traces the lineage of Jesus back to David to prove Christ's messianic claim. In Islam *Tawrat* refers to the Torah, but a separate name, *Zabur*, denotes the Psalms of David. Likewise Solomon (as Suleiman) is popular in Persian Muslim art, and the king features in numerous fables. David and Solomon have been immortalized in the three monotheistic faiths but, in historical terms, their deaths created a void that swiftly led to the splitting apart of their united kingdom.

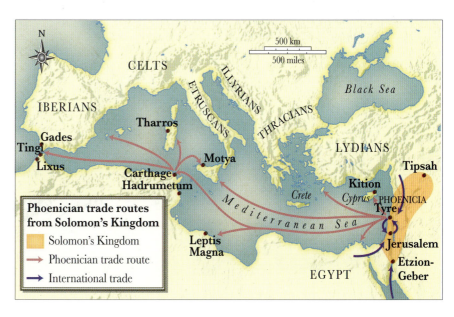

Right Map showing Phoenician trade routes from Solomon's kingdom to Europe and northern Africa.

The Royal Houses of Israel and Judah

After King Solomon died in 927BCE the united Kingdom of Israel split into Israel in the north and Judah in the south. At times they even fought each other, and both suffered religious backsliding.

For decades the ten tribes in the north had felt uneasy about accepting the family of David as their overlords. Only the wisdom and guile of Solomon had managed to hold the squabbling tribes together.

CAUSES OF STRIFE
The immediate cause of the rift was a clash between Rehoboam, Solomon's son and heir, and Jeroboam, an Ephraimite rebel from Solomon's court. Jeroboam fled to Egypt and became a protégé of Pharaoh Shoshenq I (945–924BCE). When Solomon died, Rehoboam took advice from younger counsellors to increase taxes, and thereby stamp his authority over all Israelites. The northern tribes revolted and Jeroboam agreed to lead them. He rebuilt Shechem (near modern-day Nablus) as his capital. But while the smaller southern kingdom consisted only of the tribes of Judah and Benjamin, it had three winning assets: the city of Jerusalem; its Temple; and a healthy economy.

Jews from the north enjoyed travelling to Jerusalem three times a year, for Passover (*Pesach*), Tabernacles (*Sukkoth*) and Weeks (*Shavuot*). Jealous of Jerusalem, Jeroboam fired his Levite priests, replaced them with his own priesthood and built golden calves to be worshipped at Dan in the north and Bethel in the south.

Jeroboam's plans backfired: Judah thwarted the northern Israelites and many died. Ahijah, formerly Jeroboam's prophetic mentor, foretold that his entire dynasty would be exterminated. Jeroboam died soon

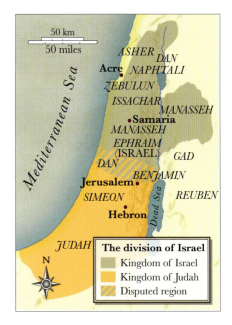

Above Map showing the division of the kingdom between Israel in the north and Judah in the south.

afterwards, leaving the throne to his son Nadab. Two years later the prophet Ahijah's prophecy came true when a soldier called Baasha murdered Nadab and made himself king.

JUDAH'S GOOD KING ASA
Meanwhile, conditions were far from perfect in Judah. Asa inherited a backlog of inefficiency when he took Judah's throne around 908BCE. Asa's stable rule contrasted dramatically with the chaos of northern Israel, and thousands immigrated southwards to Judah, especially from the tribes of Ephraim and Manasseh.

During the years of peace, Asa strengthened Judah's fortifications. His wisdom was proven when a massive force of Egyptian-backed Ethiopians attacked. Asa's army defeated them, thus safeguarding Judah from Egyptian interference for nearly 300 years.

In Asa's 36th year King Baasha of Israel attacked his kingdom. A desperate Asa took gold and silver from the Temple to pay off Ben-Hadad I (died c. 841BCE), King of Damascus and Israel's ally. The ploy worked, as Ben-Hadad began to attack cities

Below Jeroboam's Idolatry, 1752, by J. H. Fragonard. To distinguish his reign from Judah, Jeroboam set up a rival temple cult worshipping golden calves.

belonging to the northern tribes of Dan and Naphtali. Diverted by this Syrian assault, Baasha had to call off his invasion of Judah.

BAASHA TO THE OMRIDS

A military dictator who sealed his borders to prevent immigration to Judah, Baasha built vast fortifications at Ramah from which to raid his enemies. Born into the tribe of Issachar, he ruled for 23 years.

Baasha's descendants fell into vicious infighting until in c.882BCE the military commander Omri took over and launched a new dynasty. Israel's new king immediately moved his capital from Shechem to Samaria (Shomron). Though condemned in the Bible for heresy, Omri was a statesman of some talent. He ruled for 12 years and his son, Ahab, for 20. Economic prosperity returned as the Omrid dynasty nurtured peace with Judah and the Sidonites of Lebanon.

AHAB AND JEZEBEL

Often the Omrids sealed diplomatic pacts with dynastic marriages, the most famous being the union of Ahab and Queen Jezebel (died c.843BCE), daughter of Sidon's King Ethbaal.

Right Athaliah killed all the royal children, except her grandson Joash, in revenge for her son Ahaziah's murder.

The prophets railed against Jezebel for introducing the worship of the pagan god Melkart. She in turn had many of them killed.

Under Omri and Ahab, Israel increased its territory and created new cities. Judah, under King Jehoshaphat (c.873–849BCE), reconquered Edom. Together, the Jewish kingdoms knew prosperity.

ALLIANCE AND REVOLT

Jehoshaphat fought against the Baal cult and sent Levites to instruct common folk in the law. A pragmatist who reigned for 25 years, he allied himself with successive Israelite kings – Ahab, Ahaziah and Joram – though with mixed military results.

The only queen of Judah was Athaliah, who succeeded her husband, Jehoram, and their son, Ahaziah, on the latter's death. She revived Baal worship after Jehu killed her extended family in Israel. Athaliah also killed all but one of the House of David. That survivor was her one-year-old grandson, Joash, who was hidden and raised secretly by the priest Jehoiada.

Six years later Joash was placed on the throne and Athaliah was slain before she could quell the revolt. Joash ruled for 35 years, although Jehoiada acted as his regent in the early years. When Jehoiada died, though, Joash turned to pagan habits. Judah faced constant threat from the Aram Syrians, and hopes of reform receded.

THE KINGS OF ISRAEL AND JUDAH

A UNITED KINGDOM
Saul c.1047–1007BCE
Ish-Boshet c.1007–1005BCE
David c.1005–967BCE
Solomon c.971–928BCE

DIVIDED KINGDOMS

ISRAEL	JUDAH
Jeroboam I 928–906BCE	Rehoboam 928–911BCE
Nadab 907–905BCE	Abijam 911–908BCE
Baasha 906–882BCE	Asa 908–867BCE
Elah 883–881BCE	
Zimri 881BCE	
Tibni 881–876BCE	
Omri 882–870BCE	
Ahab 871–851BCE	Jehoshaphat 870–845BCE
Ahaziah 851–850BCE	Jehoram 851–840BCE
Joram 850–839BCE	Ahaziah 840BCE
Jehu 839–811BCE	Queen Athaliah 839–833BCE
Jehoahaz 812–795BCE	Joash 833–794BCE
Joash 797–781BCE	Amaziah 795–764BCE
Jeroboam II 792–751BCE	Uzziah 797–735BCE
Zechariah 750–749BCE	Jotham 794–733BCE
Shallum 749BCE	
Menahem 749–739BCE	
Pekahiah 738–736BCE	
Pekah 736–730BCE	Ahaz 732–716BCE
Hoshea 731–722BCE	
Fall of Samaria 722–721BCE	
Fall of Israel 718BCE	Hezekiah 715–686BCE

The Age of Prophets

The words and deeds of prophets run like a golden thread through Jewish lore. They also acted as a counterbalance to corrupt rulers and reflected the conscience of the people.

One third of the Old Testament/Tanakh is devoted to the Prophets' writings. Taken literally, *nevi'im*, the Hebrew word for prophets, means proclaimers, probably a reference to visionaries who roamed the countryside shouting predictions and praise for God. Apart from being mystics and channellers of divine messages, prophets often played political roles, as royal advisers, promoters of national feeling or moral compasses.

MAJOR AND MINOR PROPHETS

Some regard all the patriarchs, judges and other early figures, such as Job, Joshua, Samuel and Moses, as prophets. In Islam even Adam is called a prophet. However, the Jewish consensus is that the term 'professional prophet' refers to three major prophets, each with a book in the biblical division Nevi'im/Prophets, and 12 minor prophets, whose writings constitute one book. The major figures are Isaiah, Jeremiah and Ezekiel. The minor ones, so called only because their writings are shorter, are Hosea, Joel, Amos, Obadiah, Jonah, Micah, Nahum, Habbakuk, Zephaniah, Haggai, Zechariah and Malachi. Other prophets, like Neriah, Baruch and Huldah, are just quoted among other biblical writings.

One of the most human stories in the Bible concerns the northern Israelite prophet Jonah. He was born near Nazareth and lived around the years 780–740BCE. Jonah's short book is read on Yom Kippur, the Jewish Day of Atonement. It describes what seemed like an impossible mission, when he was told to persuade the evil-doing people of Nineveh, capital of the Assyrian empire, to mend their ways. After surviving a storm at sea and being swallowed by a whale, Jonah finally did convince the citizens of Nineveh to repent; only to lambast God for so easily forgiving these former sinners while making his own life so difficult!

ADVOCATES OF JUSTICE

Time and again prophets would chide the monarch of the day for neglecting the poor and the weak. In the words of Jeremiah: 'Thus says the Lord, "Do justice and righteousness, and deliver the one who has been robbed from the power of his oppressor. Also do not mistreat or do

Left A late 16th-century Islamic Ottoman miniature shows the story of Jonah and the whale.

Above The Vision of the Prophet Ezekiel by Raphael, 1510. Ezekiel lived in Babylonian exile c.500BCE.

violence to the stranger, the orphan, or the widow; and do not shed innocent blood in this place."'

Prophets wielded huge influence and acted as a counterbalance to an often overbearing monarchy. Put another way, the prophet represented God's conscience, and advocated the welfare of the common people. It would be too much to liken the prophet to an 'official opposition' in the parliamentary sense. However, if anyone could remind the king that he was not above the law, it was the prophet. The priests of Judah were not immune from prophetic criticism either. One of the last prophets, Malachi (c.420–400BCE), explicitly condemned Jerusalem's priests for failing in their duties. Elijah went as far as leading an insurrection against the false priests of Mount Carmel, when he inspired a mob to kill dozens of them at the Kishon River. Born into poverty, a member of the fundamentalist Rechabite sect, the revolutionary Elijah none the less wrote that God's true spirit was 'not in the earthquake, nor in the fire, but in the still, small voice' (1

THE AGE OF PROPHETS

Kings 19:12). His disciple, Elisha, continued his mission to even greater effect against Ahab's heir, Joram.

The Bible speaks of prophets having special powers. Some, like Elisha, could revive the dead; many anointed kings; and most were adept at predicting the future, as well as describing the messianic age to come. Certain prophets seem to argue directly with God, like Habbakuk; others, such as Obadiah, specialize in attacking the enemies of 'God's people'; and social prophets, like Micah and Amos, target the avarice of the rich.

ISAIAH

The most prolific and oft-quoted prophet, Isaiah, lived during a particularly difficult era in Jewish history, the 8th century BCE. From Judah, he witnessed Assyria's destruction of the northern kingdom of Israel, a tragedy that is reflected in his poignant verses. Isaiah prophesied during the reigns of four kings of Judah – Uzziah, Jotham, Ahaz and Hezekiah. Owing to the long time-span of this period, some imagine that there must have been two Isaiahs. Of aristocratic birth, yet deeply concerned for the downtrodden, Isaiah advised King Ahaz to trust in the Lord and not seek help from Assyria. Ahaz ignored him, though Hezekiah wisely heeded his warning in 711BCE to stay out of a conflict between Assyria and Egypt.

Isaiah strongly condemned idolatry, yet he went further than other prophets in asserting that God rejected even Jewish rituals if the practitioners were cruel and unjust.

Above The coming of Elijah at Passover, from the Washington Haggadah, created in north Italy by Joel ben Simeon, 1478.

When Israel forgets her mission, he wrote, she is like a wife deserting her husband, God. At the same time he saw God as king of the world, not only of Israelites. To Christians, Isaiah's repeated phrase 'the holy one of Israel' is a prediction of Jesus. Perhaps his most powerful words concern making God's kingdom on earth, when peace reigns and 'swords are beaten into plough shares'. The United Nations has adopted this as its unofficial motto.

Prophetic writings abound in dazzling poetry and stirring polemics that have inspired thinkers well beyond their immediate Jewish audience. The prophets had varying approaches, but all saw a divine purpose underlying history. They spoke to the individual, helping him or her make sense of life. In short, the prophets broadened Judaism from tribal concerns and rituals. In Babylonian captivity they were to embrace the idea of a universal God who heeds human suffering.

Left The Peaceable Kingdom *by Edward Hicks depicts the messianic age, when, as the prophet Isaiah predicted, the lion would lie down with the lamb and men would learn war no more.*

The Northern Kingdom Falls

FOLLOWING THE DEVASTATION OF THE NORTHERN KINGDOM OF ISRAEL BY THE ASSYRIANS IN 722BCE, TEN OF THE TWELVE ISRAELITE TRIBES WERE ASSIMILATED OR BANISHED, AND LOST TO HISTORY.

Seen in context, the northern kingdom's destruction was a subtext of a larger story of two empires, Assyria and Babylonia, battling for control of Mesopotamia. Paradoxically, the sacking of northern Israel resolved an ongoing battle between the ten tribes in the north and the two tribes of the south. If the Assyrians had not triumphed, suggest some scholars, Jews may never have refined their faith, written the Bible or survived as we know them today.

ASSYRIAN EXPANSIONISM

The story begins with Ashurnasirpal II (884–859BCE), who developed the Assyrian war machine by using heavy chariots, the latest iron weaponry and fearsome discipline. Shalmaneser III (859–824BCE) continued Assyria's westward thrust but faced a formidable pact headed by Damascus and Hamath (present-day Hama). One key member of this alliance was Ahab the Israelite, who, according to the historian of the document known as the Kurkh Monolith had 2,000 chariots and 10,000 men. In 853BCE the two sides fought the largest battle in history to date at Qarqar. The clash proved indecisive, but apparently disabled the alliance, which spelt trouble for Israel.

ISRAEL'S YEARS OF DECLINE

After King Ahab's death, his son Joram (r. 850–839BCE) took over Israel's crown and began a string of disastrous military campaigns. He lost control of Edom (today, southern Jerusalem) and was defeated by the Arameans from Syria at Ramoth-Gilead. Eager to restore order, the prophet Elisha backed a popular Israelite military revolt in 842BCE led by Jehu ben Nimshi (r. c.842–815BCE). Jehu soon killed off the entire Ahab/Joram dynasty and eliminated all worship of Baal. The prophets praised Jehu's purge for its spiritual purity, but in political terms it weakened Israel dreadfully. Judah soon broke its alliance with Israel and when Assyria turned its attention to northern ventures, Aram's leaders Hazael and Ben-Hadad III turned Jehu's son and heir, Jehoahaz (735–720BCE) into little more than a vassal.

Some relief came in the form of a decisive Assyrian blow against Damascus in 796BCE. Israel's new king, Joash, recovered lost cities from a weakened Aram and acknowledged Assyria as Israel's protector. Joash went on to capture Jerusalem, plunder the Temple, and briefly imprison King Amaziah of Judah.

ISRAEL REVIVES

Israel enjoyed its greatest period just before the fatal Assyrian blow. By the time Jeroboam II (792–751BCE) succeeded Joash, as King of Israel, Aram was losing its grip over Syria–Palestine. Jeroboam took advantage of Assyria's Armenian campaigns in the far north to attack and take Damascus and Hamath.

Military success paid economic dividends. Israel controlled the trade routes connecting Anatolia and Mesopotamia to Egypt, and, when it conquered Bashan and Hauran,

Above Assyrian archers. Assyria was a world power and Israelites were just one of the many peoples they deported.

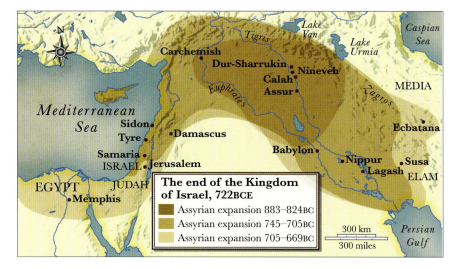

Below Map of Assyrian conquests at the time of the defeat of the northern kingdom of Israel, c.722BCE.

it recovered access to 'the wheat granary of Israel'. Jeroboam opened up new territories to Israelite settlement. Chronicles speaks of Reubenite tribesmen grazing their flocks as far north as the River Euphrates.

JUDAH'S NEW PROSPERITY
Jeroboam's counterpart in Judah, Uzziah, son of Amaziah, became ruler and later king 784–733BCE. Judah conquered the southern port of Eloth, near modern-day Eilat on the Red Sea, which allowed Uzziah to control the two great trade routes of historic Palestine. International commerce boosted Judah's economy to an extent not seen since the united kingdom days. Where Uzziah fatally erred was in attempting to participate directly in Temple services, for which sin, says tradition, he contracted leprosy and died. Even so, his son Jotham continued his father's expansive policies, this time into transjordan.

Below This obelisk marks the triumphs of Shalmaneser III (859–824BCE) and his defeat of Israel's king Jehu.

LOST TRIBES

What happened to the ten 'lost tribes' of Israel remains a mystery. Most exiles were settled near Gozan on the Khabur River, today near the Syrian border with Turkey. Others served as Assyrian garrison troops in Medea. A few maintained Jewish practices but most were assimilated with surrounding Arameans within Greater Assyria.

Above A Beta Yisrael synagogue in Ethiopia, whose people claim descent from the tribe of Dan.

Jewish folklore speaks of lost Jews who await the Messiah's arrival, but remain marooned across the mythical Sambatyon River, which stops flowing every Sabbath. Less fancifully, many refugees from Israel fled south to Judah. Others probably mixed with gentiles in Samaria and became Samaritans or blended into the gene-pool of today's Kurds.

Supposed descendants of the ten appear in all places: David Reuveni, a false messiah, swore he was from the tribe of Reuben. The Ethiopian Jews (Beta Yisrael or Falasha) claim descent from the tribe of Dan, as do some Yemenite Jews. Evidence suggests the priestly sect of the Lemba of southern Africa has a gene marker typical of Cohens. A group from India called Shimlung say they are the offspring of Manasseh.

Even among non-Jews, people claim Lost Tribe ancestry: the Yousefzai clan of Pathans in Afghanistan, for instance, wear side-locks and ritual tassels, like Orthodox Jews. Others who claim such descent include the Celtic Irish and Cornish, the Japanese Makuya sect, a distinctive Ghanaian community, Muslim Kashmiris, certain Native American tribes, and the Ibo of Nigeria.

ASSYRIA ATTACKS SOUTHERN RIVALS

King Jeroboam II's death in 751BCE marked the beginning of Israel's ultimate decline. A power-hungry usurper named Menahem massacred an entire village and crowned himself king of Israel in 747BCE. Two years later, in 745BCE, Tiglath-Pileser III (r. 745–727BCE), one of the most effective military commanders in history, took over the Assyrian kingdom. In 739BCE, Tiglath defeated Judah's King Uzziah in battle. Six years on, he conquered the Philistine-ruled Mediterranean coastline, then turned inland, defeating Damascus, occupying Israel and annexing Galilee.

ISRAEL'S ENDGAME

Israel's new ruler, Hoshea, was king in name only: he controlled little more than Samaria (the ancient capital of Israel). All seemed lost when in 729BCE Tiglath crushed Assyria's greatest foe, Babylon, and assumed control over all of Mesopotamia. After Tiglath's death in 727BCE, King Hoshea chose to revolt by ceasing payment of tributes to Assyria, and turned to Assyria's old enemy, Egypt, for help. But it was too late: Tiglath's successor, Shalmaneser V (726–721BCE), devastated Samaria, took Hoshea captive and deported him to Assyria.

In 721BCE Sargon II seized power in Assyria, crushing a series of regional revolts, and defeating an Egyptian army. He rebuilt Samaria as capital of the Assyrian province of Samerina. He deported 27,290 Samarian Israelites, and resettled the land with colonists from other parts of his empire. Some scattered Israelites remained, but the Kingdom of Israel was no more.

CHAPTER 2

EXILE, RETURN AND DISPERSAL

The year 721BCE seemed to mark Judaism's demise. Ten of Israel's twelve tribes were driven out and lost forever, and the kingdom of Assyria stood poised to destroy Jerusalem. Somehow the little kingdom of Judea survived. But 136 years later its rulers were marched off into Babylonian captivity. Curiously this apparent nadir marked a rebirth of sorts. In exile, Jews developed new scribal and proto-rabbinical traditions. Once Persia allowed them to return after 539BCE, sages rebuilt the Jerusalem Temple and compiled the final version of the Hebrew Bible. Dual rule by king and prophet gave way to more democratic if theological bodies. Two centuries later, Hellenism challenged Jews politically and culturally, until Hasmonean 'kings' reasserted Judean autonomy. Direct Roman control after 37BCE spawned new sects, of which the Jesus followers were one. Finally an ill-fated revolt led to the Second Temple's destruction in 70CE and in time the collapse of Judea as the centre of Jewish life.

Opposite Ezra in Prayer by Gustave Doré, 1865. Born in Babylonian exile, Ezra's return to Judah with the blessing of Persia marked a crucial turning point in ancient Jewish history.

Above Exotic animals swirl around the word melekh, 'king' in Hebrew, taken from a Hebrew prayer book, late 13th-century Germany.

EXILE, RETURN AND DISPERSAL

JUDEA ALONE

WITH NORTHERN ISRAEL SHATTERED, JUDAH WAS LEFT VULNERABLE TO ASSYRIAN ATTACK. THE LITTLE KINGDOM SURVIVED FOR 136 YEARS, UNTIL POLITICAL AND MORAL BLUNDERS INVITED NEW DISASTERS.

The dispersal and loss of the ten tribes of northern Israel in 722BC represented a devastating blow to the Jewish people. Arguably, however, Assyria's destruction of northern Israel rescued Judaism. For with the Israelite capital Samaria vanquished, Jerusalem regained its status as the centre of Jewish devotion and the House of David regained its status.

The very name *yehudim*, or Jews, derives from the tribe of Judah (Yehuda). Benjamin, Judah and remnants of Simeon and the priestly tribe of Levi were the only Israelites to survive the Assyrian conquest of 721BCE intact. Today, most Jews trace their lineage from the southern tribes of Judah and Benjamin. The name 'Israel' lingered on in religious passages and medieval poetry, but only regained political expression with the creation of the State of Israel in 1948.

Below Attacking through the Judean desert, Assyrians laid waste to northern Israel and nearly took Jerusalem too.

SURVIVING DEVASTATION

Hezekiah (*c*.715–686BCE), son of King Ahaz, was the 13th king of an independent Judea when Assyria took the Israelites into captivity. He felt that the Israelites' annihilation had been divinely ordained because they had strayed from the true path. Unwilling to see Judea suffer a similar fate, he set about reforming his small kingdom. Hezekiah railed against unethical behaviour, banned idolatry and foreign gods, and even threw Moses' 'brazen serpent' from the Temple, as people had begun praying to it. Another challenge was how to cope with the influx of Israelite refugees who had escaped the Assyrian dragnet. Some say as many as 70 per cent fled south to Judea where they were absorbed into the surviving southern kingdom. But how could Hezekiah accommodate these newcomers in a crowded Jerusalem whose population was set to increase fivefold over the next century? Adopting a pragmatic approach, the king expanded city boundaries to the west, and made engineers build a canal to deliver water from the spring of Siloam to the city. This venture also provided work and housing for Israelite migrants.

Above Hezekiah's Tunnel, built c.701BCE, linked the Gihon Spring to the Pool of Siloam and saved besieged Jerusalemites from dying of thirst.

HOLDING ASSYRIA AT BAY

The Assyrian tyrant Sennacherib (*d*. 681BCE) grew angry when Hezekiah allied himself with rebellious Ekronites, Egyptians and Arabs. He besieged Jerusalem in 701BCE. Hezekiah stood fast, reports the biblical Book of Kings, and prayed to the Lord, who the next morning 'smote 185,000 in the Assyrian camp'. Assyrian records state that Hezekiah paid off the invaders with a tribute purloined from his temple. The Greek historian Herodotus suggests, conversely, that a horde of mice spread plague in the Assyrian camp and thus halted their assault on Jerusalem. Yet another view says that black African Kushite soldiers, fighting under the Egyptian banner, stormed through the Sinai and devastated the Assyrians.

56

On the hexagonal Taylor prism, dated 689BC, Sennacherib, 'perfect hero, mighty man, first among princes', boasts of levelling with battering rams 46 walled Judean cities. After 'diminishing the land of Hezekiah', he shut up the king 'like a caged bird in Jerusalem, the royal city'. Eventually, though, Sennacherib abandoned his Judean vendetta and sent his troops home to counter more pressing rebellions by Elam and Babylon.

JUDEA UNDER KING JOSIAH

Assyria's departure was a welcome respite for Hezekiah, who continued building, consolidating and reforming Judea. Unfortunately his son and successor, Manasseh (687-642BCE), undid much of his hard work, and it was left to Manasseh's grandson, Josiah, to restore order to Judea. In his 18th year in power he cast out idols to Baal and Ashterah, restored the long-neglected Temple, and seems to have rediscovered the lost scroll of Deuteronomy (the last of the Five Books of Moses).

Praised by the prophetess Huldah and the prophet Jeremiah, Josiah also extended Judean control over most of what had been northern Israel. Unfortunately for him, a new power was rising in the north – Chaldea, which adopted the ancient name 'Babylon'. King Necho II of Egypt set off northward with a mighty army, determined to nip this rival in the bud. Judea lay in the way.

If Babylon opposed the old enemy Assyria, reasoned Josiah, then he must ally with Babylon. Josiah tried to curry favour with Babylon by blocking Necho at the battle of Megiddo (later Armageddon). But he died on the battlefield in 603BCE. Necho marched on Jerusalem, and he replaced Josiah's successor, the popularly elected Jehoahaz, with his elder half-brother, Jehoiakim.

BABYLONIAN CONQUEST

King Necho II then concentrated on his feud with Assyria and left Jehoiakim to his own devices. King Nebuchadnezzar II (*c*.630–*c*.561BCE) of Babylon, who saw Judea as a crucial staging post in his fight with Egypt, promptly invaded Jerusalem. Jehoiakim was taken captive, along with the prophet Daniel, and later returned to the Judean throne as a mere vassal. An inept ruler, Jehoiakim famously tore up parchments bearing the prophet Jeremiah's criticisms and then rebelled against Babylon. Nebuchadnezzar's response was swift: Chaldean, Amorite, Moabite and Ammonite troops attacked and pillaged the whole of Judea.

In short, mediocre Judean rule frittered away the advantages won by Hezekiah and Josiah, and prepared the way for the fall of Judea and Jewish exile in Babylon. It looked as if Judah's 200-year interregnum had been a mere prelude to national annihilation. In fact, banishment to Babylon was to prove a catalyst in the maturation and survival of both the Jewish people and their faith.

Below A sight that Judeans dreaded: two Assyrians riding a chariot, 8th-century BCE stone relief.

Above Found in Nineveh and dated to 689BCE, the Taylor prism luridly describes Sennacherib's destruction of Judean cities and siege of Jerusalem.

By the Rivers of Babylon

EXILE PROFOUNDLY ALTERED JEWISH LIFE. ONCE OVER THE SHOCK OF EXPULSION, JEWS LEARNT HOW TO PRESERVE THEIR IDENTITY AND SURVIVE, WHILE SYNAGOGUES MADE FOR A MORE EGALITARIAN FAITH.

For centuries the Assyrians dominated the northern Middle East. They boasted fine libraries, intricate legal structures, advanced cities and lavish royal courts. But all great empires attract rivals, and over a period of 150 years the Chaldeans, or neo-Babylonians, contested Assyrian supremacy.

After King Ashurbanipal died in 627BCE, the Babylonians and Medeans (probably ancestors of today's Kurds) wrested Nineveh from Assyria in 612BCE. Seven years later Babylon defeated superpower Egypt at the battle of Carchemish. Babylonian King Nebuchadnezzar II added the former Assyrian provinces of Phoenicia and Syria to the rump of his empire in Mesopotamia.

In 597BCE, when Judah's King Jehoiakim rebelled, the Babylonians plundered Jerusalem. They killed the king, banished his son Jehoiachin to Babylon, and placed his brother, Zedekiah, on Judah's throne.

THE TEMPLE DESTROYED

The Bible relates that Zedekiah, too, ignored prophetic warnings and joined a new insurrection led by Egypt. An enraged Nebuchadnezzar destroyed the Temple after an 18-month siege and annexed Judah in 587BCE. So began a second mass deportation of Judah's social elite to Babylon. Others fled east to Moab, Ammon and Edom in modern Jordan.

A Jewish governor, Gedalia, persuaded many refugees to return. But chaos followed when a Judean royal murdered him, and thousands of Jews now sought asylum in Egypt. A third and final expulsion to Babylon in 581BCE sealed the fate of the once-independent Kingdom of Judah. For the first time since Joshua's days, Jews lost political control over even the smallest part of historic Palestine.

It seemed as if a new Jewish state within a state might develop by the rivers of the Tigris and Euphrates –

Above A 5th-century CE terracotta tile from Tunisia, North Africa, showing Daniel in the lions' den.

ironically not far from ancient Ur, birthplace of the patriarch Abraham. Egypt formed another pole in what became known as the Diaspora, Greek for 'dispersal'.

After 50 years of exile, a few Jews began to return to Judah. However, their stay in Babylon profoundly altered their religion and identity. And large numbers chose to remain, thus giving birth to the 2,500-year-old Jewish communities of Iraq and Iran.

IN THE LIONS' DEN

Some of the Bible's most moving verses describe the shock and the dislocation of exile. 'By the rivers of Babylon, there I wept when I remembered Zion. For how can we sing the Lord's song in a strange land?' runs Psalm 137. The Lamentations of the prophet Jeremiah, include a powerful depiction of Jerusalem's desolation. And centuries later talmudic authors used the term 'Babylon' to denote the condition of Diaspora and Exile.

By contrast, the Book of Daniel expresses hope. It enriched the English language with some compelling

Left A detail from Belshazzar's Feast *by Rembrandt. At the banquet, Daniel predicted Babylon's fall.*

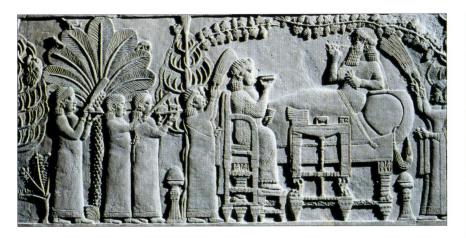

Above A 693BCE Assyrian relief shows Ashurbanipal and his queen feasting in the gardens of Babylon.

phrases. An exile himself, Daniel survived a night in the lions' den. According to Daniel, his fellow Jews, Shadrach, Meshach and Abednego, emerged unscathed from the tyrant's furnace. At Belshazzar's feast God places strange 'writing on the wall'. Daniel tells the arrogant rulers the words mean: 'You have been weighed in the balance and found wanting'. These mystical signs suggested that Jews would survive exile, return home and outlast their enemies. As Daniel's interpretation of Nebuchad-nezzar's dream explains, even great emperors have 'feet of clay'.

LESSONS FROM BABYLON

Jews saw their exile as divine punishment, but life in Babylon was not as harsh as slavery in Egypt. Many Jews became merchants, bankers, artisans and land owners. Former King Jehoiachin of Judah had a seat at the table of Merodach, son of Nebuchadnezzar; and Daniel rose to high rank in the imperial court.

Jews learnt a great deal from the Babylonians. New theological elements filtered into Judaism – migration of souls, celestial angels, and the first notions of a messianic age to come. Jews also absorbed Gnostic ideas of the clash of good and evil, and they adopted a new square script based on local forms. Called *ashuri*, or 'Assyrian', it is still used for writing Hebrew today.

Babylonian Jews were allowed to practise their faith freely, so scribes began writing down the holy texts. In time the scribes displaced the prophets in importance, and the first rabbis and synagogues appeared.

Exile encouraged social change: old tribal divisions that made sense in Israel now dissolved and created, arguably for the first time, a unified sense of 'Jewishness'. In addition, Jews learnt it was possible to live as Jews in exile. If they were treated civilly, advised the prophet Jeremiah, they should offer

Left Ezra flies over Jerusalem's destroyed Temple. From a 1583 Muslim Ottoman work, the Fine Flower of Histories.

Above From a French Christian Bible, 1364, a depiction of the prophet Daniel in the lions' den.

their gentile rulers their loyalty. As he told fellow Jews: 'Seek the peace of the city whither I have caused you to be carried away captive, and pray unto the Lord for it'.

RISE OF CYRUS THE GREAT

Babylon, like Assyria before it, seemed impregnable. Nebuchadnezzar II created in Babylon, his capital, the most astonishing urban civilization of the day. His hanging gardens were considered a wonder of the world.

But soon a new Indo-Iranian contender arose from the East to challenge Babylonia's primacy. In 539BCE Cyrus the Great of Persia won over disgruntled Medes, then conquered Babylon and absorbed its territories.

While the exact reason for Babylon's collapse remains a mystery, for Jews the Persian victory was a godsend. Wishing to demonstrate his tolerance for his neighbours, Cyrus ordered captive populations to return to their ancestral lands. However, Cyrus' generosity carried a political price: from now on Judah was to be Persia's subject-province. Also, returning Jews found Samaritans, whose Jewish claims they rejected, occupying swathes of their former land.

REFORM UNDER EZRA

THANKS TO PERSIAN LIBERALITY, JEWS RETURNED TO JERUSALEM AND REBUILT THEIR TEMPLE. OLD TRIBAL DIVISIONS MATTERED LESS NOW THAN SETTING UP A LEGISLATURE AND CODIFYING THE BIBLE.

The prophet Isaiah described Persia's King Cyrus as the 'shepherd of God' and 'the anointed one' because of his role in delivering Jews from exile. Restoration of a temple in Jerusalem was central to his imperial policy, and in 538BCE, the same year that he proclaimed liberty for his non-Persian subjects, a party of 42,360 Jews returned to Judah. However, the newcomers faced many troubles, and Judah only truly stabilized when Ezra and Nehemiah arrived several generations later. These charismatic figures reformed the Jewish faith, organized a proper system of government and law, and determined the final shape of the Bible – an 'institution' more crucial than the Temple itself.

A NEW TEMPLE

In 536BCE Judah's governor, Zerubabel, laid a foundation stone for the second Temple in Jerusalem. The actual building of the new shrine was to prove more problematic than they first imagined.

Those Jews who had never gone into exile, the humbler, indigenous Jews, resented the privileges that Persia bestowed on the aristocratic newcomers. Together with neighbouring Arabs and Edomites, they interrupted building work in protest. Zerubabel offended the Samaritans when he rebuffed their offer to help construct the Temple. Persia froze funding when rebellions broke out in the empire, and work stopped after Cyrus the Great died in 529BCE. The Temple was only finished at the instigation of the prophet Haggai in 516BCE. It was smaller and lacked the ark of the covenant of the first. But it had the required two courts, twin towers, altars and inner sanctum for the high priest.

EZRA ESTABLISHES ORDER

The arrival of Ezra in 458BCE shook up Judah's Jewish community. Renowned among Babylonian Jews and Gentiles alike, he brought with him a party of 1,500 Levites, priests, singers and other Temple functionaries. A teacher, scribe and ally of Persia's ruler Xerxes, Ezra was sent to Judah in part to guard against an anti-Persian revolt in neighbouring Egypt turning into a region-wide conflagration.

Likened to a 'second Moses', he addressed himself to the 'people of exile', and largely ignored the humbler indigenous Jews. He asked that Jewish nobles and priests separate from their non-Jewish wives. He also began the custom of determining Jewishness through one's mother.

Left The Pool of Bethesda in Jerusalem, a reservoir dating to the Second Temple period.

Above God appearing to Ezra, from a French Christian Bible, 1526.

Ezra summoned a *Knesset ha-Gedolah*, or 'Great Assembly', which effectively became Judah's legislature and the high court of Jewish people everywhere. This body ruled until the 2nd century BCE, in lieu of a monarch. Jews did not wish to run the risk of questioning Persian royal authority. Nonetheless, they hoped that one day a new king would arise from the House of David. The Assembly's 120 members canonized the Hebrew Tanakh (Bible), which Christians call the Old Testament. Several members wrote biblical texts, such as Ezra and his ally Nehemiah, and the last prophet, Malachi.

NEHEMIAH'S REFORMS

In 445BCE, 13 years after Ezra arrived in Judah, Nehemiah, formerly cup-bearer to King Ataxerxes of Persia, became governor of Jerusalem. A skilled statesman as well as a social radical, Nehemiah persuaded Persia to allow Jews to rebuild Jerusalem's city walls. He enlarged the capital's population by insisting that 10 per cent of the populace of Judah lived there. He also provided for regular payment of a Temple tithe and ensured that its benefits spread to the poorer Levites. Judah paid substantial taxes to the Persian court, yet also enjoyed fiscal autonomy and had a small army.

Ezra and Nehemiah were contrasting figures, one conservative and pious, the other radical and worldly wise. They cooperated, however, in galvanizing society in Judah and purging it of 'impurities'. Significantly, they read out the entire Torah in one public sitting, effectively proclaiming it as the constitution of the Jewish people. They established the essential structure of Jewish life that has arguably lasted to the present day.

Ezra was not unique in having ties to both Jerusalem and Babylon: many rabbis crossed between the two up to the late medieval period. However, centuries of separation also moulded distinct identities and encouraged a sense of rivalry between the two great Jewish centres.

Jews in the Persian province of Trans-Euphrates are thought to have enjoyed a decentralized leadership based around the first synagogues. They worked in agriculture, fishing and minor government service, though little extra detail is known,

Below Illuminated heading from a book of Hebrew prayers for the Day of Atonement, Germany, c.1320–5.

except for what can be gleaned from Book of Esther in the Bible. This book has themes that would reappear in Jewish history, namely assimilation, acceptance, dissimulation, survival and political influence.

STRUCTURE OF THE BIBLE
The Jewish biblical canon is called Tanakh, an acronym for Torah (Law), Nevi'im (Prophets) and Ketuvim (Writings). Sometimes the whole is referred to as Torah, and the first section – the Five Books of Moses – is called Humash (The Five) in Hebrew, or Pentateuch, in Greek.

The most sacred parts of the bible are the Books of Moses. These are, in order: Genesis, Exodus, Leviticus, Numbers and Deuteronomy. Orthodox Jews believe that the Hand of God wrote all but the last.

The Book of Prophets is divided into Early and Later Prophets. The first contains four books: Joshua, Judges, Samuel I and II, and Kings I and II. Later Prophets has Isaiah, Jeremiah, Ezekiel, and a book devoted to the 12 Minor Prophets.

Writings comprise the three Books of Truth – Psalms, Proverbs and Job; five Megillot (Canticles): Song of Songs, Ruth, Lamentations, Ecclesiastes, Esther; and three 'other

Above The feast of Purim celebrates the lives of the Persian Jew Mordechai and his niece, Queen Esther; here painted by Aert de Gelder, 1685.

writings': Daniel, Ezra-Nehemiah, and Chronicles I and II (also by Ezra).

According to a model established by Ezra 2,500 years ago, the Torah is read in synagogues in yearly cycles, on Mondays, Thursdays and Saturdays (Sabbaths). Alongside the Torah portion, Jews also recite a *haftarah* (excerpts from the other books, Prophets and Writings). These readings were chosen to tally with the Torah portion, and often give the rabbi material upon which to base his sermon.

On festivals there are also readings from other parts of the Bible. For instance, Lamentations is read on the Fast of Tisha B'Av and Jonah on Yom Kippur (Day of Atonement). Quotations from the Psalms, Prophets, Proverbs and later from medieval poetry, outside the Bible, appear in the three Jewish daily services, *shacharit*, or 'morning', *mincha*, or 'afternoon', and *ma'ariv*, or 'evening'. One work that was not accepted into the Tanakh, *The Wisdom of Ben Sira*, became the basis of the most important daily Jewish prayer, the Amidah.

HELLENISM

GREECE POSED A FORMIDABLE INTELLECTUAL CHALLENGE TO JEWS EVEN BEFORE ALEXANDER CONQUERED THE LEVANT. NOW JEWS WERE TORN BETWEEN DYNASTIES, AND SUBJECT TO CULTURAL TENSIONS.

Until the 4th century BCE the main axis of Middle Eastern power politics ran north to south – essentially, a struggle for influence between the poles of Egypt and whoever controlled Mesopotamia. That pattern was shattered by the arrival of a potent new force from the West: Greece, or more precisely, Greek-derived Hellenism.

BEFORE ALEXANDER

Greek culture had seeped into the Middle East through trade and culture long before Alexander the Great (336-323 BCE). Greeks brought an entirely new way of looking at the world, one that challenged all Levantine peoples, including the Jews. Politically, there was the innovation of democracy, introduced in Athens under Pericles in the 5th century BCE. Greek playwrights first posited the idea of moral choices facing the individual. Philosophers echoed the call that 'man was the measure of all things'. Successive schools, from the Stoics and followers of Socrates, Plato and Aristotle, down to the Cynics and Skeptics, applied rational techniques to the most profound ethical, political and metaphysical questions.

Greece did not conquer the Middle East until the Hellenic period. One reason might be that Greece lacked a single central authority, much like the pre-monarchy Israelites. Greek *polis*, or 'city-states', cherished their autonomy. They would unite in bodies like the Achaean or Hellenic Leagues when fighting a common enemy (invariably Persia), only to dissolve into divisive turf battles, most famously between Sparta and Athens.

Above Roman mosaic of Alexander, who spread Hellenism across the Middle East. Jews hailed him as a liberator.

Even when Persia was outmanoeuvred, successive kings, such as Darius the Great (522–486BCE) and Xerxes (485–465BCE) blocked the Greeks from encroaching into the Middle East. Meanwhile, Greeks established cities along the coastal rim of Anatolia (present-day Turkey).

Xerxes spent much of his reign battling the Greeks. A century after he died, Greek civilization in the guise of Macedonia overwhelmed Xerxes' heirs. This titanic clash between East and West was to have profound ramifications for Jewish history, thought and culture.

IMPACT ON JUDAISM

Many aspects of Greek culture alarmed Jews: tolerance of public nakedness and homosexuality; the proliferation of 'graven images'; a rational spirit which doubted claims of divine revelation; and democracy, which questioned the priestly right to govern. There were certainly Jews who resisted the Hellenic embrace, fearing the authentic core of Judaism was being lost. Assimilation, they argued, would eradicate the Jews as a distinct people. Other Jews, however, welcomed Hellenic sophistication.

Below Ptolemy II of Egypt, shown in a painting by Vincenzo Camaccini, 1813, asked Jewish sages to translate the Hebrew Bible into Greek.

Above Proof positive of Hellenic influence: a Greek stele, c.50CE, from the Jerusalem Temple exterior wall.

In time, Jews adopted Greek names, and Greek rationalism informed Jewish thinkers. Under Ptolemy II (285–246BCE), 70 Jewish sages in Alexandria translated the Hebrew Bible into Greek. This Septuagint, meaning 'seventy' in Greek, became the main scriptural source for Greek-speaking Jews. The Septuagint also opened Hebrew wisdom to gentiles: many became 'God-fearers', while several thousands converted to Judaism outright. Traditionalist Jews protested that only *ha-lashon kodesh*, or the 'holy language', Hebrew, was valid. However, paradoxically, the 'alien' Greek tongue was now spreading the ancient faith to new adherents, and bolstering the beliefs of Jewish communities in the Diaspora (from the Greek for dispersal, literally 'scattering of seeds').

ALEXANDER THE GREAT

The chief disseminator of Hellenic culture was Alexander. He was not Greek, but was the son of Philip, King of Macedon, a Greek subject province in the Balkans. Philip conquered Greece in 338BCE and was assassinated two years later.

Alexander, aged 22 and a student of the Greek philosopher, Aristotle, vowed to fulfil his father's dream of eastward expansion. In four years he defeated the entire Persian empire. By 332BCE Hellenic Macedonians controlled all of Asia Minor (Anatolia), Mesopotamia, Persia, Egypt, Syria and Palestine. Next, Alexander led his troops through Afghanistan, up to the Indus River in northern India, and north into south Russia and Uzbekistan. Within ten years he had created the largest empire ever seen.

CONTENTIOUS PALESTINE

Alexander died in Babylon in 323BCE – of fever, poison or heavy drinking – before he could designate an heir. Immediately his *diadochi*, or 'generals', started fighting over the spoils. By 315BCE the empire had been split into four zones. Generals Ptolemy Soter and Seleucus won control of Egypt and Syria respectively. Each founded a dynasty.

Palestine became a bone of contention between the two dynasties. Jerusalem changed hands seven times during 319–302BCE. The Ptolemies prevailed until in 200BCE Palestine fell to the Seleucids. By then, Hellenic governors had populated much of the land with military and later civilian Greek settlers, in cities such as Akko (renamed Ptolemais) and Beit She'an (Scythopolis). Canaanite nobles generally adopted Greek ways, though Jews initially kept their distance.

NEW LIFE IN EGYPT

Generally the first three Ptolemies were good to their Jewish subjects. They allowed the high priest and his council of elders to run affairs in Palestine, as long as they paid an annual tribute. The Ptolemies also encouraged Jews to settle in Egypt, where they largely prospered, built synagogues, and increasingly began speaking Greek. From Alexandria in the north to the Nile island of

Right Alexander, or Iskander, with seven sages, from the Quintet or Khamsa *by Nizami. Persian, 1494.*

Above Aristotle teaching Alexander, a detail from the French manuscript Romance of Alexander.

Elephantine in the south, Egypt became the second great centre of the Jewish Diaspora after Babylon.

Jews fared considerably less well under the fourth Ptolemy, Philopater (221–203BCE), who persecuted them mercilessly and tried to storm the Temple's holy of holies and defile it. In 198BCE a dynamic Seleucid ruler, Antiochus III (223–187BCE), defeated Epiphanes, successor to Philopater, at Panion in the Jordan Valley and won control of all of Palestine.

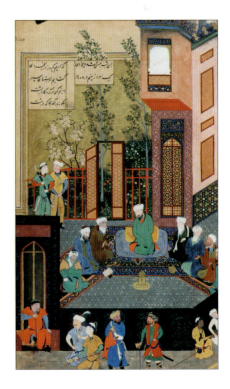

The Maccabees and Hasmoneans

THE SELEUCID RULER ANTIOCHUS III TOOK PAINS NOT TO UPSET THE JEWISH PRIESTS OF JERUSALEM. HOWEVER, HIS ILL-CONSIDERED FOREIGN ADVENTURES ULTIMATELY LED TO REVOLUTION IN PALESTINE.

Goaded on by Hannibal, the defeated Carthaginian ruler, Antiochus III decided to invade Greece itself – a foolhardy move, as the rising power of Rome was Greece's ally. In 190BCE a Roman force inflicted a humiliating defeat on Antiochus and took his son hostage. The Seleucids had to pay reparations, and Antiochus' successor, Seleucus IV (187–175BCE), taxed his subjects to meet the bill.

Onias, the high priest in Jerusalem, condemned such payment as sinful. By contrast his brother, Jason, wanted to pay, hoping that the Seleucids would then grant him the priesthood. When Antiochus' son Epiphanes returned from exile in Rome, he took over the dynasty after Seleucus IV was murdered in 175BCE. He called himself Antiochus Epiphanes, 'the illustrious one'. He immediately removed Onias from office and installed Jason in his stead. Jason built Greek *gymnasia*, or 'schools', in a city that he renamed Antioch-in-Jerusalem. Three years later Epiphanes replaced him with Menelaus.

Above King Antiochus receiving the Judean leaders, from the Book of Maccabees, 11th-century Latin Bible.

Below A Roman bronze sculpture of Antiochus IV, whose insensitivity sparked a revolt by pious Jews.

REVOLT OF THE PIOUS

The *hassidim*, or Jewish 'pious ones', were disgusted that Antiochus Epiphanes nurtured a priesthood open to the highest bidder. Not averse to punning in Greek, they renamed Antiochus IV *Epimanes*, or 'the madman'. Soon farce turned to tragedy. On hearing Antiochus had died, Jason overthrew Menelaus but the rumours proved false, and Antiochus sacked Jason and reinstated Menelaus. This prompted a civil war between partisans for Jason and those for Menelaus, who were backed by the Tobiads, fabulously wealthy Hellenized Jewish tax collectors.

Worse followed when Rome thwarted Antiochus' attack on Ptolemaic Egypt in 168BCE. In revenge Antiochus tore down Jerusalem's city walls, massacred thousands, ordered the Jewish scriptures destroyed, brought prostitutes to the Temple, and executed anyone caught practising circumcision. The final outrage came in December, when Antiochus entered the Temple and sacrificed a pig in honour of the Greek god Zeus.

THE MACCABEE BROTHERS

What followed was probably the first successful guerrilla war in history. In Modi'in, outside Jerusalem, a priest named Mattathias the Hasmonean killed a Jew who was about to sacrifice to a Greek idol. Mattathias and his five sons then fled to the hills of Judea, and became folk heroes. One son, Judah ha-Maccabee, or 'the hammer', led their makeshift dissident army after Mattathias died and harried Seleucid forces up and down the country. By 165BCE the Maccabee brothers took Jerusalem itself. General Lysias, preoccupied

Above A 13th-century Spanish Hebrew Bible shows implements and vessels of the Temple.

Above From the same Spanish Bible, the menorah, which the Maccabees relit after cleansing the defiled Temple.

with strife in the Seleucid capital, Antioch, granted the Jews religious freedom. The Maccabees then cleansed the Temple, reinstituted Jewish worship, and named Judah's brother Jonathan as high priest. According to legend, there was only enough oil to light the Temple lanterns for a day, but it lasted for eight. This small miracle symbolized the greater miracle of national redemption and is still commemorated in the joyous eight-day-long wintertime festival of Hannukah.

THE HASMONEAN DYNASTY

No sooner had victory been achieved than divisions emerged. Judah was imbued with holy fervour and continued fighting. Others wanted to consolidate their gains and sign pragmatic treaties with neighbouring powers.

Judah died in battle in 160BCE, and his successor, Jonathan, was recognized as civil governor in 150BCE. With his brother Simon, Jonathan conquered Jaffa in 147BCE, thus winning Judea a desperately needed outlet to the sea. The biblical book 1 Maccabees praises Jonathan for making peace in the land: 'Israel rejoiced with great joy, for every man sat under his vine or his fig tee, with none to disturb him.'

When Jonathan died in 142BCE, Simon Maccabee, Mattathias' last surviving son, became both high priest and army commander. That same year Syria's King Demetrius II granted Judea political independence. The Roman Senate confirmed this status a few years later. From then until 37BCE, a Hasmonean dynasty governed the first truly autonomous Jewish state since the Babylonian conquest 500 years before.

A HOUSE DIVIDED

Simon Maccabee's son and successor, John Hyrcanus (134–104BCE) proved energetic and able. Calling himself nasi, or 'president', not king, he fended off an attack by Antiochus VII of Syria who besieged Jerusalem in 130BCE. John also forcibly converted the Edomites/Idumeans to Judaism, crushed the Samaritans and expanded the kingdom's borders. Hasmonean rulers failed to live up to expectations, however. They adopted Hellenistic customs and Greek names and usurped the post of high priest, hitherto reserved for the tribe of Levi. Also, they quarrelled among themselves, some supporting the Ptolemies, others the Seleucids.

After John died, his son, the high priest Aristobolus, imprisoned his mother and brothers and titled himself king. After his death his widow, Salome Alexandra (d. 67BCE), freed the prisoners. One of these, Alexander Yannai, reigned from 103 to 76BCE. He further extended national borders, repelled invaders, introduced new coinage and formed a pact with Egypt's Queen Cleopatra (51–30BCE). He persecuted the Pharisee sect and during 94–86BCE he fought a civil war against them that claimed some 50,000 lives.

Internal divisions made Judah vulnerable to the ever-growing regional power of the Roman empire, which had initially favoured the Jews as an ally against their mutual enemies. Now Rome feared that Judah's aggressive policies of conversion and land acquisition east of the Jordan might impede their own imperial growth.

Left Judah ha-Maccabee gives money for sacrifices, from the Hours of Constable Anne de Montmorency, France, 1549.

Pharisees, Sadducees and Messianism

MASS POLITICAL PARTIES DID NOT EXIST IN THE ANCIENT WORLD. INSTEAD, RIVAL FACTIONS CONTENDED FOR CONTROL OVER UNDEMOCRATIC LEADERS. IN JUDEA, REFORMERS CLASHED AGAINST ALOOF PRIESTS.

In the 2nd century BCE Judea was more a theocracy than a monarchy. Its chief factions – Pharisees and Sadducees – grew out of differing theological trends. Both groups belonged to the Great Sanhedrin (assembly), a religious as well as a legislative body.

Over time the Pharisees and Sadducees clashed over how they regarded the outside world. Generally, Sadducees favoured accommodating Persia, Ptolemaic Egypt, Seleucid Syria and later Rome. This remained true even when Judea gained independence after 142 BCE. The Pharisees, by contrast, despised all Hellenistic influences and preferred to assert Jewish autonomy, even at the risk of causing war with neighbouring gentile powers.

SADDUCEES, GUARDIANS OF THE TEMPLE CULT

Exactly when the Sadducees and Pharisees emerged as identifiable groups remains uncertain. Probably named after Zadok, King Solomon's high priest, the Sadducees claimed lineal descent from Aaron and officiated over the Temple cult.

Gradually the Sadducees grew into a hereditary aristocratic caste with a conservative outlook. In religious terms they sought to preserve

Above Horsemen of the apocalypse, a Christian vision of the messianic age from a Mexican church, 1562.

their divinely ordained privileges. They read the Torah literally, distrusted innovation, denied the legal force of oral traditions and stressed ritual aspects of faith. Politically the Sadducees favoured a centralized state where priests, administrators and generals all gathered in Jerusalem. Sadducees also became pivotal to Judea's economy. Yet while they regarded their wealth as a sign of blessedness, their enemies called them corrupt and venal.

Sadducees accepted foreign rulers as long as they tolerated priestly customs. Excessive nationalism was dangerous, they reasoned, as past rebellions against Assyria and Babylon had proven. While Judah ha-Maccabee had been willing to risk a holy war, his surviving younger brother, the high priest Simon, preferred accommodating Judea's stronger neighbours. By the 2nd century BCE Sadducees began associating with the Hasmonean dynasty and also with Hellenism, some out of pragmatic calculation, some out of genuine admiration.

MESSIANISM

From the 2nd century BCE onwards a new theme emerged in Judaism. Called messianism, it drew on the prophetic writings of Isaiah, Elijah and Ezekiel, and gained political impetus as a backlash against Hellenism. Messianism articulated the dream of better days ahead. Its central figure was a moshiach, 'one anointed in oil', a saviour drawn from the Royal House of David. According to the belief, he will restore divine sovereignty to Israel and usher in a golden age of universal peace when God rules the earth. The notion gradually developed of two messiahs – one to redeem the Jews, followed by another to save all mankind. Messianism also promised the revival of the dead at the 'end of days', when an apocalyptic battle between good and evil was followed by a final judgement. The belief revolutionized Jewish thought and comforted Jews wary of the flawed secular world. A potentially dangerous ideology, it spawned many false messiahs during the 2,000 years of exile. It also influenced Kabbalah mysticism. Christians see Jesus as the promised messiah; to Jews, the messiah has yet to come. Though he will come, insisted the medieval sage Maimonides – 'even though he tarries'.

Above The anointing of David, from the Macclesfield Psalter, c.1330.

Right Jewish Maccabees fight the Greek followers of Bacchus. 15th-century illustration by Jean Fouquet.

PHARISEES, INTERPRETERS OF A LIVING FAITH

Literally meaning 'the separated ones' (from the Hebrew *perushim*), the Pharisees were initially a small group of religiously learned laymen. Sincere worship and social justice mattered more to them than Temple rites. Spiritually they harked back to the prophet Isaiah, who wrote: 'To what purpose is the multitude of your sacrifices unto Me? saith the Lord. Bring no more vain oblations; it is an offering of abomination unto Me. Cease to do evil; learn to do well; seek justice, relieve the oppressed, judge the fatherless, plead for the widow'.

Pharisees owed much to the scribal tradition of Ezra, yet politically they grew out of the anti-Seleucid *hasidic* movement. At first the Pharisees supported the Hasmoneans, until they felt the revolution was being betrayed. On the religious plane, Pharisees interpreted an oral law which they said was delivered to Moses at Mt Sinai, alongside the written Torah. Unlike Sadducees, they believed in human free will and divine retribution, as well as resurrection and the afterlife, and a conviction that a messiah would come. Pharisees believed that God was everywhere, not just in the Temple. Their preferred institution was the synagogue, decentralized and open to participation by all. Hence many consider them to be precursors of the rabbis.

BATTLE FOR POWER

Ultimately Rome's destruction of the Second Temple in 70CE removed the Sadducees' raison d'être. Even without a Temple, Jews today maintain a Sadducee ritual when Cohens or Levis recite the priestly benedictions – daily in Orthodox Israeli and Sephardi communities, only on high holy days for Ashkenazi Jews in the Diaspora. But the Pharisees provided the model for Judaism's development, and were the true precursors of today's rabbis.

Left Roman destruction of the Second Temple as imagined by the 19th-century Italian artist Francesco Hayez.

ISRAEL AND THE ROMAN EMPIRE

FROM A BACKWARD PROVINCIAL ITALIAN KINGDOM, REPUTEDLY FOUNDED BY TWIN BROTHERS IN 753BCE, ROME GREW INTO THE MIGHTIEST POWER THE WORLD HAD SEEN. AND IT SOON SET ITS SIGHTS ON JUDEA.

Rumours of Rome's prowess swept the Middle East when, in 202BCE, Scipio vanquished the Semitic Carthaginians of Tunisia. So when the Roman Republic signed a treaty with Judea in 161BCE, Jews thought they had a powerful ally in their battle against the Seleucids.

MASTER OF THE MEDITERRANEAN

Rome clearly wanted to own the Mediterranean region. It quelled Macedonia and imposed crippling terms on the Seleucid Antiochus III (223–187BCE) with the Treaty of Apamia (188BCE) after beating him in battles at land and sea.

By 168BCE Roman consuls were ensconced in Egypt; in 100BCE Rome crushed Jugurtha of Numidia (Algeria). Rome's eastern commander, Pompey, defeated Tigranes II of Armenia in 66BCE. The next year Rome overwhelmed its most dogged foe, King Mithridates VI of Pontus, northern Anatolia, and Pompey cleared the eastern Mediterranean of pirates.

The gateway now lay open to the Middle East. Civil strife and attacks by Persian Parthians had severely weakened the Seleucid realm. Finally Pompey deposed Antiochus XIII and turned Syria into a Roman province in 64BCE.

POMPEY ENTERS JERUSALEM

Most Jews regarded Rome's triumph over Syria as divine comeuppance. They also hoped that Rome might help a benighted Judea. For ever since the Hasmonean queen Alexandra Salome died in 67BCE, her two sons, Hyrcanus II and Aristobolus II (reg. 66–63BCE), had waged a ruinous battle for succession. The latter was triumphant in battle and took the crown.

The grievances took an ideological turn when the Pharisees supported Hyrcanus, and the Sadducees, Aristobolus. During Passover of 63BCE, Hyrcanus and his ally the Arab sheikh Ametas of Petra trapped the Sadducees in the Jerusalem Temple. Somehow, Aristobolus smuggled out a message to Pompey's consul in Syria, Marcus Aemilius Scaurus, promising him 6,000kg in silver if he could help. Aemilius duly ordered Ametas of Petra to lift the siege. When Pompey himself arrived in Jerusalem in 62BCE, Aristobolus gave him 800kg in gold. But when Aristobolus rashly accused the consul Aemilius of theft, Pompey switched sides and backed Hyrcanus. Roman forces then joined Pharisees in attacking the Sadducees. Following a three-month siege, they breached the Temple sanctuary with battering rams and catapults.

Now it was Pompey's turn to miscalculate: he entered the Holy of Holies and allowed his soldiers to

Right Pompey the Great (106–48BCE), the general who made Judea a client of Rome.

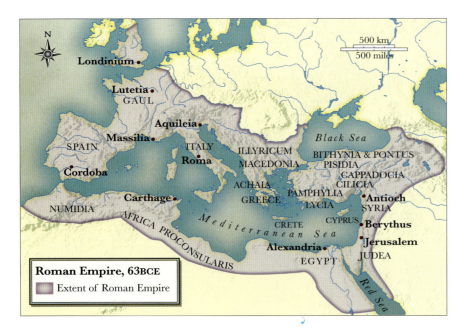

Left The Romans called the Mediterranean 'our sea'... their writ ran from Morocco in the west to Palestine and Egypt in the east.

Right Romulus and Remus, the twin brothers who legend says founded Rome. Sculpture dated c.500–480BCE.

make a sacrifice to their standards. Jews saw this as blasphemy, and the incident cast a pall over future relations with Rome.

Having turned Judea into a client kingdom, Pompey left to pursue his duties as joint ruler of Rome. Hyrcanus was enthroned as Judea's high priest and *ethnarch*, or 'national leader'. Aristobolus was banished and Roman forces annexed some 30 Judean cities that were exclusively populated by ethnic Greeks.

CAESAR AND ANTIPATER

Initial Jewish optimism for Roman rule turned sour in 57–55BCE, when Syria's governor, Aulus Gabinius, retrenched Hyrcanus' powers and favoured Judea's Greeks over Jews. One beneficiary of Roman rule was Antipater, an Idumean of Arab stock

Below A focal point of Rome's 2,200-year-old Jewish community, the Great Synagogue blends classical Italian and neo-Babylonian styles.

and a Jewish convert. Decades earlier Alexander Yannai had appointed him general of all Judea. Antipater later became chief aide to Hyrcanus, advisor to Pompey and governor of Idumaea. He then helped Gabinius thwart Aristobolus' last attempt to regain power in 55BCE, and steadily encroached on Hyrcanus' authority. Antipater then ingratiated himself with Julius Caesar after he defeated Pompey's armies. He persuaded Egyptian Jews to back Caesar and recruited Jewish and Nabatean soldiers to the fight. In 47BCE Caesar made Judea a direct subject of Rome. Having crushed revolts by two Hasmonean aspirants, Antipater became Judea's regent, procurator (chief minister) and tax collector.

Caesar restored Jewish confidence by granting Jews greater political autonomy. He reduced their taxes, exempted them from army service, guaranteed freedom of worship and returned some land to Judea. The shock of his assassination in 44BCE threw the future into doubt. Antipater now switched allegiance to the equally canny Cassius, administrator of Syria, against Rome's new emperor Mark Antony. A Syrian–Judean alliance seemed imminent, until Antipater was poisoned by a rival and died in 43BC.

Wisely, Antipater had guaranteed his legacy by ensuring that his sons, Herod and Phasael, were governors of Galilee and Jerusalem. Herod was to found a dynasty that supplanted the Hasmoneans and changed the course of Jewish history.

SONS OF ROME

There is a curious twist to this story. Pompey had taken thousands of Judean prisoners to Rome in 62BCE. After they were freed they settled beyond the River Tiber. There they formed the hub of a unique Diaspora Jewish society called Benei Roma (Sons of Rome), or Italkim. They were led by *archontes*, or 'rulers', and *gerousiarchoi*, or 'synagogue presidents'. Despite thriving in Rome, resentment simmered under the surface. In 55BCE the orator Cicero called Judaism barbaric, and defended a proconsul of Asia accused of seizing Temple gold donated by Jews. A fraud case saw Jews temporarily expelled from Italy in 19CE. But the community was enhanced when a new influx of Jewish prisoners came to Rome after the destruction of Jerusalem's Temple in 70CE. The community still exists, and its liturgy and cantorial techniques may preserve the closest approximation of original Judean tradition today.

HEROD'S DYNASTY

HEROD DISPLACED JUDEA'S HASMONEAN DYNASTY WITH ROME'S APPROVAL. HIS NOTORIOUS CRUELTY BLIGHTED HIS REPUTATION AS A MASTER BUILDER AND REGIONAL POTENTATE.

Pax Romana, or the 'peace of Rome', took an unexpected blow in Judea when Parthians overran Asia Minor, Syria and Judea in 40BCE. Working in cahoots with renegade Roman commander Labienus, the Parthians deposed Judea's Hyrcanus II, cut off his ears, and replaced him with his nephew Antigonus who was fated to be Judea's last Hasmonean ruler. In Rome, Mark Antony met Herod, recently deposed as governor of Galilee, and crowned him 'king of the Jews'. Herod then headed a Roman army that recovered Jerusalem after a five-month siege in 37BCE. Antigonus was overthrown and beheaded.

HEROD THE GREAT

The controversial new king became known as Herod I the Great (37–4BCE). The Christian Gospels tell of his 'massacre of the innocents' in his quest to kill the newborn 'king of the Jews', Jesus Christ. Jews recalled how he had also slain religious rebels in Galilee while governor. During Herod's reign he killed 47 members of Judea's Sanhedrin soon after his enthronement. He married Mariamne, daughter of the Hasmonean queen, Alexandra, but put her to death, as well as her mother and brother, and even his two sons, as his paranoia took grip.

Herod saw himself as monarch of all Jews and not just those in Judea. He appointed Hananel, a descendant of Zadok, as high priest, and funded synagogues, libraries, baths and charities for burgeoning Jewish communities in Antioch, Babylon, Alexandria and Rome itself. Generally he favoured Pharisees over Sadducees, and fellow Hellenized (Greek-influenced) Jews over traditionalists.

A MASTER BUILDER

A financial genius, Herod monopolized the extraction of asphalt from the Dead Sea and relieved drought in Judea by importing grain from Egypt. Herod was fanatically loyal to Rome and cleverly heeded non-Jewish concerns beyond Judea's borders. He single-handedly revived the Olympic Games, refurbished Antioch and Byblos, built a forum in Tyre and theatres in Sidon and Damascus.

Certainly the greatest Jewish builder since King Solomon, Herod sought to modernize what he saw as a backward Judea. He recast Samaria as 'Sebastia' and he created a mountain villa-fortress overlooking the Dead Sea at Masada, and another, Herodium, just south of Jerusalem. He also built the sumptuous port of Caesarea, complete with a vast artificial harbour.

Below A genius of construction, Herod built Herodium as his hilltop palace and fortress south-east of Bethlehem.

Above Herod captures Jerusalem with his Roman allies, 38BCE. From Jean Fouquet's 15th-century French manuscript, Antiquites Judaïques.

In Jerusalem Herod built an amphitheatre and the imposing Antonia fortress, and vastly expanded and ornamented the second Temple, drawing millions of visitors, Jewish and gentile alike. He encouraged lavish Temple sacrifices and the three pilgrimage festivals, yet confined the Sanhedrin to purely religious matters.

A ROYAL DYNASTY

Herod established a hereditary dynasty, but his successors were weak. Herod Archelaus (b. 22BCE–d. c.18CE), his son and heir by the Samaritan queen, Malthace, proved so unpopular and incompetent that in 6CE Rome deposed him as national leader of Judea. Rome now chose to rule through procurators in Caesarea, answerable to the Roman legate in Antioch. Herod the Great's grandson, Herod Agrippa, raised in elite circles in Rome, proved more able and governed Judea from 37CE until his death in 44CE. (His brother, Herod III, ruled southern Lebanon over the same period.) Agrippa was allegedly assassinated by Romans who feared his growing power. Rome then re-imposed direct rule, sowing the seeds for Jewish revolt.

ROME AND IUDAEA

INEPT RULE BY HEROD'S SUCCESSOR INVITED ROMAN INTERVENTION AND THE CREATION OF IUDAEA. HERE, JEWS REJECTED TAX, BATTLED THE GREEKS AND ADOPTED MILITANCY AGAINST THE OCCUPIERS.

Long dormant troubles surfaced after Herod the Great died in 4BCE. Rioting broke out and only ceased when Roman authorities crucified 2,000 rebels. Eventually opposition to Rome combined with religious and class schisms and led to nationwide uprisings, the Temple's destruction and the end of Jewish statehood. Amidst the turmoil a new religion was born – Christianity.

DIRECT RULE AND TAXES

In 6CE Emperor Augustus heeded calls from Jews and Samaritans and ousted the inept Herod Archelaus. What followed was less welcome: Rome fused Judea into a directly governed province called Iudaea, which included Idumea (Edom) and Samaria but excluded Galilee, the Golan Heights and Perea. So Galilean Jews were cut off from their kinsfolk in a policy of 'divide and rule'.

Below The ruins of Masada, last outpost of the 66-73CE Jewish Revolt. Here some 960 Jewish Zealots and their families took their own lives, it is said, rather than surrender to Roman forces.

Publius Sulpicius Quirinius became governor of Syria, and Coponius ruled Iudaea as its first prefect (based in Caesarea). Judas of Galilee, driven as much by cultural and theological motives as by economic ones, led a violent revolt when Quirinius ordered a regional census for the purposes of taxation. Of all Rome's subject peoples, Jews especially refused to accept Roman culture as superior.

ZEALOTS

Jerusalem's high priest Joazar condemned the tax revolt, which Rome anyway soon crushed. Nonetheless, wrote the contemporary Jewish historian Flavius Josephus, Judea now had a fourth sect after the Pharisees, Sadducees and Essenes. These 'Zealots' drew on messianic rhetoric and sent vigilantes, the Sicarites, to kill Romans, Greek colonists and suspected Jewish collaborators with their sicus, or 'short sword'. Zealots saw Rome as a kingdom of arrogance, the antithesis of what God had promised his 'chosen people'.

Above Pontius Pilate, Roman procurator at the time of Jesus, by an unknown Italian painter, 1510.

Roman procurators, or prefects, governed Iudaea until 41CE, the most infamous being Pontius Pilate (26–38CE). King Herod Agrippa I, a favourite of emperors Caligula and Claudius, reigned over Iudaea from 41 to 44CE and managed to placate Romans and Jews to some extent. Direct Roman rule returned after Agrippa's assassination. Immediately two sons of Judas of Galilee, Jacob and Simon, led another abortive Zealot revolt.

ONE IN TEN ROMANS...

Some seven million Jews lived in the Roman empire by 44CE; another million were located outside the imperial borders, mostly in Babylonia. Thus the vast majority of the world's Jews came under the Roman ambit. They constituted fully 10 per cent of the empire's population.

Of that number, fewer than 2.5 million Jews dwelt in Judea itself. Thus when Herod the Great claimed to speak for all Jews, not just Judeans, he gained influence out of proportion with the size of his kingdom.

Jesus

OUT OF 1ST-CENTURY JUDEA A PREACHER EMERGED WHO WAS TO MAKE A MASSIVE IMPACT ON CIVILIZATION. JESUS WAS BORN, RAISED AND ARGUABLY DIED A JEW, BUT HIS STORY SPAWNED CHRISTIANITY.

Jesus of Nazareth is the most famous man in history. He is the inspiration of the world's largest religion, Christianity. To Christians he is the messiah promised in the Book of Isaiah, and the Son of God. No other figure has been so celebrated in art, and his teachings have been translated into virtually every known language. Jesus profoundly affected the development of Western civilization. Christians, moreover, see Jesus as the saviour of humanity.

Jesus' story – as told in the four Gospels, Matthew, Mark, Luke and John – is deeply rooted in the Jewish narrative. 'Jesus', an anglicized form of the Greek Iesous, is Greek for Joshua (*Yehoshua* in Hebrew, which means 'YHWH is salvation'). 'Christ', from the Greek *Christos*, or 'anointed one', is equivalent to the Hebrew messiah. He was born to a Jewish family in Bethlehem, David's royal city. He studied under rabbis, preached almost exclusively to fellow Jews and often quoted Jewish scriptures. Apart from one trip to Egypt, his life and mission was located within historic Palestine. His followers sought to prove that his arrival fulfilled Old Testament prophecies. Matthew traces his descent from David, as a Jewish readership would expect such lineage before they could consider him as messiah.

JESUS THE MAN

Despite some discrepancies in the gospels and folklore that attached to later accounts, the historic Jesus is fairly well documented, although precise dates are not certain. He was probably born in 4BCE, shortly before Herod the Great died. His parents were Joseph and Mary (Miriam); Matthew and Luke affirm a virgin birth. The family came from Nazareth but went to Bethlehem for Herod's census.

When Jesus was eight his family fled to Egypt to escape persecution by Herod Archelaus. In 7CE, say the Gospels, the 12-year-old Jesus amazed the Jerusalem Temple priests with his knowledge. After this he returned to Nazareth to help his carpenter father. There then follow several missing years. Jesus' ministry began in around 26CE, after John the Baptist anointed him messiah in the River Jordan. Around that time Pontius Pilate became prefect of Judea, and Caiaphas was appointed high priest in Jerusalem.

JESUS' GOSPEL

In autumn 26CE Jesus cleared the money changers out of the Temple in Jerusalem, and in summer 27CE four Galilean fishermen became his first followers. By winter 28CE he had 12 disciples; in the spring he preached his 'sermon on the mount', as found in Matthew 5–7, in which he laid down the foundations of the new teaching ethic founded on the law of love in contrast to the old law of retribution. He also began conducting miracles. Soon the disciples were also spreading Jesus' gospel and performing healing.

Above The Tree of Jesse, from a 13th-century psalter, demonstrates Christ's lineage from Jesse, father of David, and hence his claim to messianic inheritance.

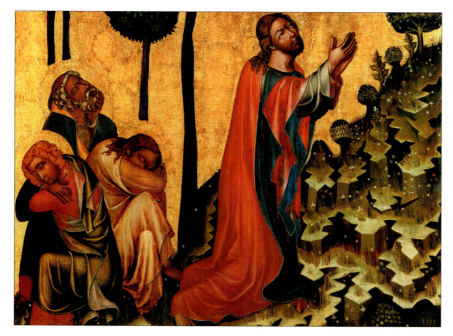

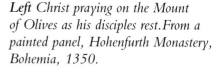

Left Christ praying on the Mount of Olives as his disciples rest. From a painted panel, Hohenfurth Monastery, Bohemia, 1350.

Jesus predicted his own death in 29CE. The next year he entered Jerusalem. Betrayed by his disciple Judas Iscariot during the Passover festival, Jesus was arrested in the Garden of Gethsemane, tried by the Sanhedrin, or Temple officials, for blasphemy, and sentenced by Pilate, seemingly for insurrection. He was then crucified at Golgotha.

ORIGINS AND INFLUENCES

The Gospels famously condemn both Pharisees and Sadducees as hypocrites. On closer inspection, suggest some scholars, Jesus himself

Above An early Christian painting of Christ and the Samaritan woman at the well, Roman catacombs, c.320BCE.

might have been a Pharisee, albeit a radical one. Certainly he was no Sadducee: he damned excessive wealth and corrupt Sadducean practices. Jesus apparently resembled one Pharisaic strain, the *hakhamim*, or 'itinerant wise men'. Like them he was a populist rabbi, or teacher; he delivered lessons through parables, akin to rabbinic *midrashim*. Jesus never refuted the Torah's law and commandments in the Gospels. He did, though, stress that faith, love, hope and charity are in God's eyes superior to the legalism ascribed to by Pharisees.

Some scholars define Jesus as an Essene (see box), but he rejected their ascetic tendencies. His use of messianic imagery recalls the Zealots. But his message – 'turn the other cheek' – clashes with their militancy. Jesus chided disciples who wanted to attack Rome; he paid the

THE ESSENES

The Essenes emerged in the 2nd century BCE when anti-Hellenist Jews, furious that Maccabeans had usurped the high priesthood, left Jerusalem and lived monastically in the wilderness, seeing themselves as the 'True Israel'. Essenes lacerated the Pharisees in stronger terms than Jesus. The Dead Sea Scrolls contain one Essene psalm that promises salvation to 'the humble, oppressed in spirit and those who mourn', echoing Jesus' word. But while Essenes were reclusive and refused female company, Jesus preached to all.

Temple tax and said 'render unto Caesar what is Caesar's'. Whether he can be subsumed into a sect or not, Jesus certainly drew on his Jewish heritage. After his death a new religion emerged, one that both spread Judaic principles and clashed with the parent faith.

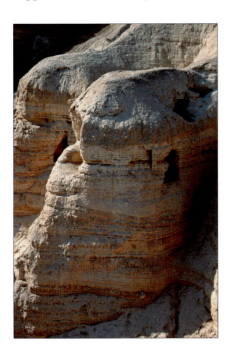

Left Scrolls from this cave at Qumran have intrigued scholars ever since they were found in 1947.

Right Similar jars from Qumran held the Dead Sea Scrolls, whose Essene writings call to mind Jesus' teachings.

THE RISE OF CHRISTIANITY

PAUL HELPED FORM CHRISTIANITY INTO A DISTINCT RELIGION. 'JEWISH CHRISTIANS' WITHERED AWAY AS GENTILES ACCEPTED THE NEW FAITH AND JEWS BAULKED AT GOSPEL ACCOUNTS OF CHRIST'S DIVINITY.

At first the 'Jesus movement' was basically another Jewish sect. Gradually, though, the two separate religions emerged and by 150CE Judaism and Christianity were competing faiths, heading in different directions.

SISTER FAITHS DIVIDED

Three factors may explain this schism. First, St Paul's mission of spreading Christ's words to gentiles (non-Jews) accelerated the process of absorbing 'alien' Hellenistic customs into the faith. Core Christian texts were written in Greek and Latin, which further divorced the religion from its Hebrew, Aramaic and Jewish roots. Second, the notion of a resurrected Jesus and the developing doctrine of God's incarnation in human form tested Christianity's ties with Judaism to breaking point. Third, Jews considered that the Christian New Testament depicted Jews as enemies of God's will. Christian dogma spoke about their followers replacing Jews as the 'true elect of Israel'. And when the Roman empire adopted Christianity in the 4th century CE, the faith became a religion of power. This seems ironic, given Christ's stress on humility, modesty and the meek. By contrast, after the destruction of the Temple, Judaism seemed like a credo of the dispersed and dispossessed.

CRACKS APPEAR

Initially, Jesus' mission seemed over when he died on the cross in 30CE. The Gospels, however, related that Jesus then reappeared to his disciples before being recalled to heaven. He had died in a bodily sense but was reborn to eternal life. Most Jews understood that a messiah should herald an age of universal peace, or at least expel the Romans from Judea. Christians replied that Christ planned a second coming and ultimate redemption.

The Gospels were completed around 90CE, long after Christ's death. Their passages speak of how the Temple shuddered when Christ was crucified. Christians interpreted this as predicting that the Temple would fall because of Jewish complicity in the Lord's death. However, because the texts were finalized after Jerusalem's destruction, some scholars suppose that these 'predictions' may have been added to 'prove' the superiority of Christianity.

Below St Stephen's stoning to death in Jerusalem c.34CE typified the Jesus sect's tribulations. Painting by Francesco Bissolo, 1505.

Above St Peter holding the keys to the Kingdom of Heaven. Austrian altarpiece panel by Friedrich Pacher, c.1508.

JERUSALEM CHURCH

Members of the early Jerusalem Church considered themselves fully Jewish. Led by James (Jacob) – the first Christian bishop and reputedly the brother of Jesus – they prayed in the Temple, observed the Jewish Sabbath and obeyed Torah commandments. Certainly they differed from fellow Jews in seeing Jesus as the Messiah. Yet most stopped short of calling him the Son of God and questioned the doctrine of virgin birth.

While open to proselytes, the Jerusalem Church wanted gentiles to convert to Judaism before they could become Christian. Gradually, distinctive elements entered their practice. Initiates were baptized, as Christ was by John. The church became a community that shared possessions, heard reports from the apostles and stressed the virtues of love, repentance and charity. It also spread tidings of 'Christ's Way' and his return. Allied congregations in Galilee survived after a Sadducean priest killed James in 62CE. Yet the Roman sacking of Jerusalem in 70CE decimated the sect.

CHRISTIANITY'S FOUNDERS

Some scholars regard Paul, not Jesus, as the real founder of Christianity. He was born Saul, a Pharisee from Tarsus in Cilicia, southern Turkey; a rabbi and tent-maker by trade, yet also a Roman citizen. Paul was about to persecute dissident Christ-believers in Damascus in 34CE when, he wrote, he was struck blind and saw Jesus in a revelation.

Paul preached Christian doctrines during 45–57CE, initially to Diaspora Jews in Antioch, Ephesus, Sardis, Iconium and Philadelphia (all in modern Turkey) as well as in Jerusalem, Corinth, Rome and Alexandria.

He went a step further by promoting Christianity among gentiles. Hitherto, gentile males wishing to convert to Judaism would have to undergo circumcision. Paul argued that Christ's 'new covenant' – a term originally used by the prophet Jeremiah – entirely replaced the old Mosaic code. Christians no longer needed to obey Judaism's laws of kashrut, or 'kosher food', or observe Jewish festivals, or circumcise their male children. Gentiles would thus find conversion more attractive. Further, Paul said, one could only enter the Kingdom of Heaven through personal faith in Jesus as the messiah. Such views were anathema to normative Jews.

Born at Bethsaida on the Sea of Galilee, Peter was one of the original 12 disciples. He changed his name from Simon to Peter, Greek for rock, as Jesus told him: 'Upon this rock I will build my church'. In time, Peter was hailed as the first bishop of Rome. The Jewish sage Gamaliel the Elder persuaded fellow Sanhedrin members to spare Peter's life when they threatened to execute him. Peter and Paul were partners in propagating the new faith, although Paul accused Peter of 'Judaizing' the religion. Some say Paul resented Peter for knowing Jesus.

MARTYRS AND *MINIM*

Both Roman and Jewish authorities sporadically persecuted Christians. Many apostles were martyred, beginning with Stephen, stoned to death by a Jerusalem mob around 34CE at the behest of a pre-Paul Saul. Christian tradition relates that Emperor Nero blamed Christians for the great fire of Rome in 64CE and consequently had Peter crucified and Paul beheaded.

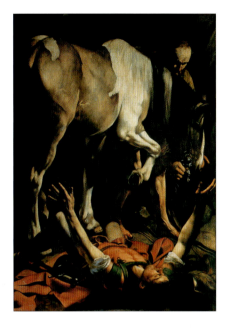

Above Caravaggio's dramatic depiction of St Paul's conversion on the road to Damascus, 1601.

Jewish Christian sects called Ebionites, or the 'poor ones', and Nazirites survived for a while in Judea. In the mid-2nd century CE, however, Gamaliel II, son of Gamaliel, ruled that Christians of any ilk were *minim*, or 'dissidents' who could no longer pray with other Jews.

It is known that Ebionites largely fled Judea for Pella, across the Jordan, when Judea revolted in 66CE. So some ascribe a political element to Gamaliel's charge. Put simply, Jewish Christians voluntarily dissociated themselves from the Jewish people. As Pauline Christians saw them as heretics, too, they quickly disappeared from history.

Left Jesus with James the Less, from a 12th-century column capital, Cathedral of St Lazare, Autun, France.

RABBIS ASCENDANT

JUDAISM MAY NEVER HAVE SURVIVED AS WE KNOW IT HAD A RABBINICAL TRADITION NOT BEEN ESTABLISHED. BUT WHO EXACTLY WERE THE FIRST RABBIS, AND WHAT DOES THE TERM MEAN?

'Rabbi' derives from the Hebrew for 'great teacher'. As a professional title it was first applied to Judah the Prince (Yehuda Ha-Nasi), in the Mishnah, the summary of oral law. Judah compiled the Mishnah around 200CE and based it on nearly 350 years of scholarship and debate by people we would call rabbis.

According to Jewish tradition, custodianship of the Torah passed down an ancient chain of wisdom, from patriarchs to the elders, then to the prophets, the Great Assembly, the Pharisees, and finally to the sages or rabbis. The Great Assembly's creed became the rabbis' motto: 'Be patient in judgement, raise up many students and build a fence around the Torah'. This aphorism is one of many encapsulated in the Mishnah's *Pirkei Avot*, or 'Ethics of the Fathers'.

THE SANHEDRIN

The bedrock of the rabbinic tradition were the *zugot*, or 'pairs of rabbis, who presided over each generation, starting in 142BCE when the Maccabeans re-established Judean independence. Convention decreed that one of the *zugot* was the *nasi*, or 'president of the Great Sanhedrin', while his partner was the *av beit din*, or 'chief justice and vice-president'.

Above A simple yet stark image of the Temple menorah, from a 2nd–3rd-century CE synagogue near Tiberias.

The Great Sanhedrin combined the functions of supreme court and legal assembly. Its 71 members debated in the Temple's Hall of Hewn Stones.

Each city could have its own Lesser Sanhedrin of 23 members. Hence power was devolved and local customs respected. Lower courts encouraged independence from the Temple cult, yet only the Great Sanhedrin could put the king on trial, extend the borders of Jerusalem or act as final arbiter in any controversy. While hardly democratic in the modern sense, the Sanhedrin enjoyed considerable powers of scrutiny. Shemaya and Abtalion, Pharisees who presided during the rule of Hyrcanus II, even summoned Herod, then governor of Galilee, to answer charges of murdering the rebel leader Hezekiah. Shemaya is quoted in *Pirkei Avot*: 'Love work, hate authority and don't get friendly with the government'.

HILLEL AND SHAMMAI

Under the *zugot* system, each issue tended to generate two viewpoints. The Mishnah recorded which was accepted yet preserved the minority decision for future scholars to ponder. *Zugot* often represented different approaches, too. The most

Left A rabbi teaches Hillel's golden rule. Depicted by Samuel Halevi in the Coburg Pentateuch, Bavaria, 1395.

famous duo was Hillel the Elder and Shammai, active in King Herod the Great's reign. Hillel was universalistic and innovative; his lenient rulings stressed the spirit of the law and tried to make compliance easier. Shammai, a builder by trade, was stricter, conservative and more concerned about detail.

Hillel's views usually prevailed over Shammai's. Once, goes the legend, a sceptic challenged Hillel to explain the whole Torah while he stood on one leg. 'Whatever is hateful to you, do not do to your fellow', replied the sage. 'The rest is commentary. Now go and study'. Hillel was born in Babylonia and left for Jerusalem to learn under Shemaya and Abtalion. The story is that he could not afford to pay the academy's entrance fee, so he perched on the roof and listened in. One cold Sabbath the determined student had to be rescued from under a layer of snow. Eventually he became the *nasi*, and is thought to have taught Jesus.

Many Hillel parables and sayings appear in *Pirkei Avot*, including his three rhetorical questions: 'If I am not for myself, who will be for me?' 'If I am only for myself, what am I?' And 'If not now, when?'

THE SANHEDRIN'S POWER

Over time the Great Sanhedrin became in effect a political counterweight to the *cohen ha-gadol*, or the Temple High Priest, an office that was increasingly dominated by wealthy Hellenized appointees.

In Roman times charismatic rabbis advised and sometimes criticized secular Jewish rulers. Often they ruled on sensitive political matters. For example, Gamaliel I (the elder) of the House of Hillel persuaded the Sanhedrin to accept Christians within the Jewish fold. The new sect's messianic claims, he suggested, had yet to be proven or disproven. Johanan Ben Zakkai was probably the most politically effective rabbi; he rescued the Sanhedrin from Jerusalem as the Temple was about to fall and negotiated with Rome to re-establish the institution in Jabneh.

Above Rabbi Yehuda Ha-Nasi led Judea's Jews during late 2nd century CE Roman rule. Entrance to his burial catacomb, Beit She'arim, Israel.

TEMPLE TO SYNAGOGUE

Alongside the rabbis, one other institution allowed Judaism to survive beyond the Temple that was soon to be destroyed. This was the synagogue, a Greek word that means the same as the Hebrew *beit ha-knesset*, or 'house of assembly'. The first probably arose in Babylonian exile, but it truly developed in Second Temple Palestine, at Caesarea, Capernaum, Dor and Tiberias. Unlike temples, synagogues require no expensive priestly rites. Religious services could be held as long as the Torah and a *minyan*, or 'quorum', of ten adult men were present. Jews throughout the Diaspora copied the model, with the synagogue in Alexandria being the most lavish. Only one Diaspora community – a military colony of Jews on the Nile island of Zeb, or Elephantine, near Aswan in Egypt – built an alternative temple. But it withered when the 29th Egyptian dynasty replaced Persian rule in 399BCE.

PHILO OF ALEXANDRIA

Philo was a contemporary of Hillel and the first major Jewish contributor to Western philosophy. Born into a respected Egyptian Jewish family *c.* 20BCE, he still excites controversy in orthodox Jewish circles. Philo's synthesis of Judaism and Hellenism built on foundations laid by Aristobolus of Paneas. He left behind a vast literary output: philosophical works, a legal explanation of the Pentateuch, a biography of Moses, a book on the Creation, 18 treatises of allegorical interpretations, an investigation into biblical dreams, and rhetorical analyses of several Jewish texts.

Philo aimed to show that Judaism formed a coherent ethical system. He blended universalism with a conviction that Jews should be 'priests of humanity'. In his view the Jewish deity was identical to Plato's form of the good. Philo greatly influenced Hellenized Jews. His concept of God interceding in the world via the *logos* (word or idea) also coloured Christianity: John's Gospel opens with 'In the beginning was the word'. Philo anticipated later Jewish thinkers who engaged with the secular world, like Spinoza, Marx and Freud. Unlike them, he believed in the intrinsic truth of the Torah.

Above Known as the Jewish Plato, Philo pioneered the blending of Greek and Judaic learning.

The Fall of the Second Temple

THE JUDEAN REVOLT OF 66–73CE WAS A DISASTER FOR THE JEWISH PEOPLE, YET IT MARKED A NEW BEGINNING. JEWS CHANGED THEIR SELF-DEFINITION AND ESTABLISHED THE STATUS OF THE DIASPORA.

Anger at colonial rule certainly contributed to the Judean revolt. Tiberius, who became Caesar in 14CE, had upset Jews by stealing Temple treasures to pay for an aqueduct. After he died in 37CE his successor, Caligula, provoked rioting when he tried to place a statue of himself as Jupiter in the Temple.

Another factor was the dashing of expectations raised during the reign of Herod Agrippa I, an independent Jewish king whose reign coincided with the first years of Emperor Claudius. Agrippa ruled Galilee after 38CE and also Judea, Samaria and the Golan after 41CE. A friend to Caesars and fluent in Roman ways, he championed Jewish interests while generously funding Hellenized towns. When he died in 44CE – possibly murdered – Rome re-imposed direct rule, and replaced military prefects with harsher civilian procurators.

ROMAN PREJUDICE

More broadly, Roman rulers resented Jews' refusal to bow to imperial superiority, and feared an empire-wide conflagration as pagans, Jewish proselytes and new Christians locked horns in theological battle. Apion, Tacitus, Lysimachus and other Greek and Roman writers derided Jewish practices as bizarre and outdated. Some chastized Jews as enemies of mankind, and Emperor Claudius warned Alexandrian Jews against 'spreading a general plague throughout the world'.

In Judea, Greek settlers dominated the province's civil service, merchant class and Roman cohorts, while ordinary Jewish farmers suffered from taxation and banditry. Ethnically mixed cities such as Caesarea, Sephoris and Joppa (Yaffo) represented islands of wealth in a sea of growing poverty, and were also focal points for clashes between rival Greek and Jewish communities. The previously marginal Zealots benefited from these tensions, and their messianic fervour began attracting a formerly cautious and moderate Jewish middle class.

Opportunism also played its part in the timing of the revolt. Rome was battling Persian Parthia on its eastern flank, so Jews saw a chance to strike when the empire seemed weak. They expected Parthia to rally to their side, and recalled how in 166BCE the Greco-Syrians had crumbled before the Maccabeans. Finally, the uprising sprang from long-simmering divisions within Jewish society. In 50CE, Herod Agrippa II became a Roman vassal-king. In 63CE he completed Temple restorations; but Judeans knew that true power resided with the procurators who colluded with wealthy priestly families of Diaspora origin.

THE SPARK

Eventually in 64CE, the notoriously megalomaniac Caesar, Nero, replaced procurator Albinus with the even more bigoted Gesius Florus. Having encouraged anti-Jewish riots by Greeks in Caesarea, in May 66CE Florus marched into Jerusalem, a city already choking with Jewish refugees from the countryside. It proved a fatal miscalculation. Roman troops massacred Jews in the market, prompting a ferocious counterattack by street-fighting rebels. After a stunned Florus withdrew his men, rebels toppled the hapless Agrippa, and by June Jerusalem had an independent aristocratic government.

Above The iconic image of Jewish defeat: soldiers carry away Temple vessels. From Rome's Arch of Titus.

Below This map of revolts against Rome 66–74CE shows Judean rebels wrested power from Rome, but eventually imperial forces crushed all resistance.

DIVIDED REVOLUTION

The loss of first the city of Jerusalem and then Joppa alarmed Rome, as other subject nations might well rise up if the revolt were not crushed soon. So, in October 66CE, the Syrian legate, Cestius Gallus, invaded Palestine. After initial success he was repulsed at Jerusalem and defeated at Beit-Horon.

Agrippa's supporters attacked Eleazar ben Simon, the Jewish victor over Cestius. Galilean Zealots then captured Jerusalem's Antonia fortress before a former high priest, Anan ben Anan, declared a second aristocratic government in November 66CE. Soon Jews were fighting each other: northern guerrillas under John of Giscala battled 40,000 troops loyal to Simon bar Giora, a radical of Edomite origin.

JOSEPHUS

The leader of Galilee's rebels, Joseph ben Matthias, proved particularly mercurial. Galilee was a crucial buffer province as 60,000 Roman and allied troops and cavalry advanced from Syria. But Joseph neglected war preparations, whether out of incompetence or deliberate treachery. General Vespasian's men massacred thousands of Jews at the fort of Yodfat (Jotapata) in July 67CE; all remaining defenders killed themselves, except Joseph and one other.

Joseph then passed on military intelligence to Vespasian and his son Titus, both future Roman emperors. Today Joseph is better known as Flavius Josephus, author of *The Jewish War, Jewish Antiquities and Against Apion*. Notwithstanding his tendency to self-promotion, he was a brilliant stylist in Greek, later translated into Latin, a fascinating example of a Jew straddling two cultures, and one of the greatest historians of his age.

THE TEMPLE FALLS

After 67CE three Roman legions retook Tiberias, Gamla, Mount Tabor, Giscala, Azotus, Jamnia, Jericho and Qumran. Neither Parthia nor the Jewish Diaspora supported what seemed like a lost cause, especially given Judea's political instability. Jerusalem changed hands in 68CE when John of Giscala overthrew the aristocrats, and again in April 69CE when Simon bar Giora ousted him in turn.

Below Nero, Vespasian and Titus are shown battling Jews in a 15th-century Histoire des Juifs *by Flavius Josephus.*

Above End of an era – Titus Destroys the Temple in Jerusalem *by Nicolas Pouisson (1594–1665).*

Vespasian left Judea in 69CE, and between April and September 70CE his successor Titus besieged Jerusalem. At first rebels burnt the Roman assault ramps, but the legionaries blockaded the city and starved its inhabitants. Eventually they captured the fortress, torched the Temple, hunted down fugitives and sacked the rest of Jerusalem.

To celebrate his victory Titus toured the east and later constructed the Arch of Titus in Rome. It shows soldiers carrying the menorah and other Temple artefacts, and stands next to the Coliseum, a building probably funded by Judean loot and built by Jewish slave labour.

The Judean revolt finally ended in 73CE with the mass suicide of Zealots holed up in besieged Masada, an imposing Herodian-built fortress overlooking the Dead Sea. Agrippa II reassumed Judea's throne for another 17 years, and Rome re-established respectful relations with surviving Jews, but genuine Jewish statehood was no more.

THE FINAL REVOLT

THE YEARS FOLLOWING THE FALL OF THE TEMPLE SAW ROME BARRING JEWS FROM JERUSALEM, AND JEWISH RISINGS AGAINST ROMAN RULE, CULMINATING IN THE BAR KOCHBA REVOLT OF 132–5CE.

The fall of Jerusalem was not quite the end of the Jewish revolt. Ringleader Simon bar Giora was executed in spring 71CE, but Roman 'mopping up' operations dragged on for at least two more years. Finally, the cities of Herodian, Machereus and Masada fell, the last after a fearsome attack and the supposed mass suicide of its inhabitants: Sicarite fighters as well as women and children. Certain Israeli army combat units still use Masada as a site for swearing in graduates, because of its emotional symbolism.

SANHEDRIN SAVED

While some contemporary Jews hail Masada's commander, Eleazar ben Ya'ir, as a hero, others see him as a dangerously misguided extremist. By contrast, they regard Yohanan ben Zakkai as the only figure to emerge from the revolt debacle with any dignity. Yohanan was a revered rabbi in Jerusalem who, though initially affiliated with the Zealots, soon realized that the revolt was a hopeless cause. According to Talmudic legend, Yohanan had himself smuggled out of the besieged city of Jerusalem in a coffin. He then struck a deal with the Romans allowing him to reconstitute the Sanhedrin, formerly located in the Temple precinct, in Jamnia (Yavneh) on the southern Palestinian coast. So when Jerusalem fell in 70CE, the central authority for Jewish law survived. In 80CE, Gamaliel II replaced Yohanan and further bolstered the strength of the institution.

ROMAN PRAGMATISM

Rome barred Jews from Jerusalem after its destruction but otherwise adopted a moderate policy towards them, if only for pragmatic reasons. It was imperative to keep open the trading routes that carried grain from Egypt, through Palestine, to Rome. Likewise, Rome was determined to prevent its main enemies, the Parthians, from exploiting unrest in Palestine. If Parthia was to capture Palestine, as it had briefly managed to do earlier, this could drive a wedge through the Roman empire.

Around the year 95CE the Emperor Diocletian agreed to recognize a Jewish patriarch in Galilee as spokesman for Jews throughout the empire. This office, invariably held by a Pharisee, lasted until 425CE. In addition, Jews were granted exemption from the customary Roman demand that all subject peoples participate in the official imperial cult of emperor-worship.

Above The façade of the Temple in Jerusalem on a bronze coin that dates from the Bar Kochba revolt, 132–5CE.

DIASPORA UNREST

Despite these concessions, the Temple's destruction had nonetheless shocked Jews in the Diaspora to the core. Between 115 and 117CE, Jews revolted against both Roman rule and antagonistic Greek neighbours in several major centres: Alexandria, Cyprus, Mesopotamia and northern Africa. All were quelled, and extremely brutally in the case of Alexandria, where Trajan's forces destroyed the city's synagogue.

Below Aerial view of Betar in the Judean hills, Bar Kochba's headquarters and last stronghold to fall in 135CE.

Below Ruins of the Jewish camp at Masada where Jewish Zealots succumbed to Rome in 73CE.

THE FINAL REVOLT

Above This Second Revolt era coin shows a palm frond that Jews brought to the Temple on the festival of Sukkot.

Collectively the uprisings are known as the Kitos Wars after a Moorish general in Roman service, Lucius Quietus. Having crushed Jewish rebels in Mesopotamia, Quietus became procurator in Judea, where he razed several towns, encouraged idol worship on the Temple Mount and killed troublesome Jewish leaders.

With hindsight these upheavals were a prelude to the final revolt, but Jews initially welcomed Hadrian when he replaced Trajan as emperor in 117CE. Hadrian recalled Quietus to Rome and had him executed. He promised Roman subjects throughout the empire that he would respect their cultures and rehabilitate their cities. In 130CE Hadrian toured the ruins of Jerusalem and Jews understood – or rather, misunderstood – that he would allow them to rebuild the Temple. Their mood soon changed when he outlawed circumcision as a bodily mutilation. Then in 131CE Hadrian mandated Judea's governor to start work on Aelia Capitolina, a new pagan city to be built on the ruins of Jewish Jerusalem.

THE BAR KOCHBA REVOLT

The sage Rabbi Akiva persuaded the Sanhedrin in Yavneh that Simon ben Kosba was the messiah who would finally rid Judea of the Roman scourge. Simon changed his name to Bar Kochba, 'son of a star' in Aramaic, thus fulfilling a prophecy in the Book of Numbers. He then launched a full-scale revolt from Modi'in.

Bar Kochba proved to be a military genius. He trapped a Roman garrison in Jerusalem and soon conquered the entire country. This time, unlike in 66CE, the Jewish forces were united. Jewish volunteers from the Diaspora helped overrun coastal towns. Rome's desperate Emperor Hadrian summoned troops from Britain and the Danube. Eventually ten legions arrived in Palestine, a third of the entire imperial forces, and considerably more than Titus had commanded. One whole Roman legion was exterminated, and Jewish naval forces even engaged the mighty Roman fleet.

Simon Bar Kochba was crowned Nasi (Prince) of a sovereign Jewish state, while a Sanhedrin headed by Rabbi Akiva revived sacrifices. Proudly, the Nasi minted coins with a Temple image and star on one side, and on the other the inscription 'Year one of Israel's redemption'. However, to follow was one of the most vicious wars in antiquity. Roman forces gradually subdued Galilee, expelled rebels from Jerusalem, and cornered them in the fortress of Beitar. So furious was this last siege, relates the Jerusalem Talmud, that the Romans 'went on killing until their horses were submerged in blood to their nostrils'. The Romans suffered huge losses, while according to the Roman historian Cassius Dio, 580,000 Jews (probably overstated) were killed, and 50 fortified towns and 985 villages were razed. As for Bar Kochba, legend says he held out with rebels in desert caves.

The Romans put Rabbi Akiva to death, drove Jewish survivors into slavery, ploughed Jerusalem under and renamed the land 'Syria Palestina' after the virtually extinct Philistines. In this way they deliberately effaced the name of Judea. Somehow Jewish life continued in Galilee, but the south was a wasteland. Jewish fugitives crammed every Mediterranean port, and thousands of Jews were sold into slavery across the empire. Later generations wondered whether Bar Kochba had been a false messiah.

In the Diaspora, Jewish communities quickly learnt that cooler heads than Bar Kochba's should prevail if the Jewish people and faith were to survive.

Below The Ecce Homo Arch, once part of Aelia Capitolina, the Roman city built on the ruins of Jerusalem, 136CE.

CHAPTER 3

THE DIASPORA AND THE RISE OF CHRISTIANITY

The Jewish Diaspora began to dominate Jewish life after the revolts of 68–73 and 130CE decimated Judea. Bereft of the Temple, rabbis transcribed the Talmud, which became a portable constitution for Jews in exile. The Talmud fostered debate and study, and remains a unique repository of Jewish folklore, ethics, law, history and literature. Gradually, Babylon replaced Galilee as Jews' cultural and religious epicentre.

Meanwhile, the related faiths of Judaism and Christianity went their separate ways. Acrimony grew when the Roman empire adopted the new religion around 314CE, and after Visigoths overran Rome in 476CE, the surviving Eastern Roman empire, called Byzantium, increased persecution of non-Christians. Still, Jewish communities displayed remarkable resilience in Libya, Greece, Turkey, Syria, Yemen and newly Christianized Europe.

Opposite *Rock relief of the triumph of Shapur I over the Roman emperors Valerian and Philip the Arab. Shapur had good relations with the Jewish community.*

Above The Flight of the Prisoners *by James Tissot focuses on the exile of the Jews from Canaan to Babylon.*

Survival in the Diaspora

AFTER TWO FAILED REVOLTS, THE LOSS OF JERUSALEM AND DREAMS OF STATEHOOD DASHED, JEWS NONETHELESS SURVIVED AND AT TIMES EVEN THRIVED IN THE LANDS TO WHICH THEY FLED.

Initially, the failure of the Bar Kochba revolt against the Romans seemed like the end of the world to most Jews. An estimated million lost their lives during Judea's two uprisings; tens of thousands were taken into slavery. With their focus of worship, the Second Temple, destroyed, and most of Judea devastated, Jews wondered if they could survive.

However, Jewish life continued in the burgeoning Diaspora, which had been largely shielded from the worst effects of the Judean upheavals. Even in Palestine, once the initial trauma abated, there were signs of survival and rebirth.

THE DEMISE OF SECTS
In religious terms, the Sadducees were all but decimated as a caste when they could no longer perform their Temple rites. Evidently some assimilated into the Roman aristocracy; others, hereditary Cohens and Levis, rejoined the general Jewish population; yet others left Judaism altogether. Similarly, little more is heard of the Essenes. Perhaps their tendency to monasticism, celibacy and separation of the genders simply reduced them to unsustainable numbers.

Revolutionary Zealots also suffered. Although a few Zealots fled to the Diaspora, where they helped revive moribund communities, as a distinct political movement they were finished. After 135CE the number of Jewish Christians also fell. They found themselves doubly ostracized: conventional Jews accused them of lack of patriotism and 'heresy' regarding the Torah, while Pauline Christians (followers of St Paul) shunned them for rejecting the divinity of Jesus.

By contrast with Sadducees, Zealots, Jewish Christians and Essenes, the Pharisees enjoyed a new lease of life as rabbis. They dominated the Sanhedrin, which was re-established at Yavneh. Under Gamaliel II they moved up to Galilee. Having learnt

Above Josephus, 1st-century CE Romano-Jewish historian, whose books have invaluable information about Jewish sects.

the bitter lessons of two failed revolts in 66–73CE and 132–5CE, Jews concentrated on quiet self-government according to religious law. By the early 3rd century the Sanhedrin head, Judah the Prince ('Hanasi'), had established cordial relations with Palestine's Roman administrators.

NEW SOCIAL STRUCTURES
The absence of meaningful Jewish sovereignty over Palestine deprived the old landed aristocracy of communal respect and access to wealth. Merchants, traders and artisans could more easily emigrate and start life anew in the established Diaspora.

Most Jews, though, belonged to the group that sages called *am ha'aretz* (people of the land). They proved remarkably adaptable. Some returned to Palestine or gravitated to other Jewish outposts. And while Judea itself remained largely a war-ravaged wasteland, many *am ha'aretz* reconstituted their life in Galilee.

JEWS IN A ROMAN WORLD
Once the threat of Judean nationalism had been crushed, the Roman empire tolerated and even welcomed Jewish minorities. Jewish commerce and industry benefited the ports and cities; their literacy and multi-

Below The remains of a 5th–6th century CE synagogue in the Golan Heights.

lingualism were useful assets. Roman law absolved them from military service and usually granted them religious freedom and a measure of civic autonomy.

In 212CE Jews shared the new citizenship rights that Emperor Caracalla (198–211CE) bestowed on all non-slave subjects of the Roman empire. What was once the privilege of a few, and hence the cause of envy and strife, was now widely available. Citizenship improved access to travel, trade, education and professional advancement. Paradoxically, Jews only began suffering serious reverses with the rise of their sister faith, Christianity.

The long-established Jews of Alexandria in Egypt were probably the wealthiest, best educated and most politically independent of Diaspora communities. Successive Ptolemies had assigned them two of the five city districts to safeguard their customs from pagan influence. Mostly relations with the Hellenistic Ptolemies were amicable; Jewish scholars tutored the kings, and Jews excelled as perfumers, jewellers, silversmiths and fine weavers.

Alexandrian Jews paid dearly, however, when they rioted against Roman governors, first in 66CE, in sympathy with the great Judean revolt, and next in 115–17CE. In putting down the second uprising, wrote the great historian Josephus, Roman forces under Trajan killed up to 50,000 Egyptian Jews. The community then atrophied when some members became Christians.

After a long decline, Jewish life in Egypt revived in the 4th century CE. They rebuilt synagogues, forged ties with Palestinian Jews, and increasingly spoke and wrote in Hebrew, not Greek. They still enjoyed secular pastimes, however, especially theatre, and their writings and artefacts suggest a continued blend of Jewish, Hellenic and local Egyptian features.

ASIA MINOR AND BABYLON

On the north side of the Mediterranean, significant Jewish communities were already well established in Asia Minor, modern-day Turkey; and in Delos, Athens and Corinth on the Greek mainland. Both Jews and Samaritans built synagogues in Ptolemais (Akko, on the Palestinian coast) and the three Greek sites. Asia Minor and the Aegean peninsula were under Roman rule, although they remained Hellenistic in culture. The ever-shifting border in eastern Turkey represented a crossing from the Roman empire into Persian-ruled territory. The Persian realm included the ancient cradle of civilization, Babylon, which grew in status as a Jewish centre after Jewish institutions in Palestine began to wither after 400CE. Babylon became a haven for Jews fleeing economic hardship and political turmoil elsewhere in the Roman empire.

Bar Kochba's debacle had seen many Jews literally sold into slavery, and as Rome settled a depleted Judea with foreigners, the centre of Palestine's Jewish population moved to Galilee. For a while Emperor

Above Trajan's Column, commemorating the Roman emperor who crushed a Jewish revolt in Egypt after 114CE.

Hadrian prohibited the practice of Judaism itself. Almost everywhere else Jews formed a minority. While they survived as a religion and ethnicity, they no longer constituted a single political entity. The breach with Christianity, too, became final.

All these factors would shape Jewish history for nearly two thousand years. Yet Jews proved impressively resilient and disciplined. They drew sustenance from their tradition and veneration for scholarship, even when they replaced Hebrew with Greek as their everyday language. Their population shifted dramatically, westward towards Spain, Gaul and the Rhineland, and eastward towards Babylon. Jewish communities bargained for and won a measure of internal independence; and fugitives who fled Judea actually strengthened Judaism in the Diaspora. For in Babylon, in tandem with the work of the Jabneh sages, the Talmud emerged as a pinion of Jewish culture and identity.

THE TALMUD

THE PALESTINIAN AND BABYLONIAN TALMUDS ARE INTRINSICALLY RELIGIOUS BUT ALSO EMBODY A PORTABLE CONSTITUTION THAT HELPED JEWS SURVIVE FOR NEARLY 2,000 YEARS IN THE DIASPORA.

The Talmud can be understood in two senses. More narrowly, it refers to two specific books each called the Talmud: the shorter and earlier Jerusalem or Palestinian Talmud, written around 400CE, and the longer and much more detailed Babylonian Talmud, dated 500CE.

Literally, Talmud means 'learning'. Yet it is so much more than that. To many the Talmud represents the religious and civil constitution of the Jewish people, a portable constitution that helped them survive for nearly two millennia in the Diaspora. Others consider it the summation and repository of all traditional Jewish knowledge.

More broadly, 'talmud' stands for a centuries-long process, a way of life for its scholars and a guide to living for all observant Jews. It encapsulates strict law, ethical debates, sayings of the sages, history and philosophizing, questions and responses, commentaries on hidden meanings in the Bible, even folktales and aphorisms. Within this immense *oeuvre*, which continues to the present and by definition will never end, the actual books named Talmud form only one, albeit pivotal, part.

WRITING THE ORAL LAW

The Palestinian and Babylonian Talmuds, narrowly defined, are themselves explications of the Oral Law. Jewish tradition says Oral Law accompanied the Written Law, or Torah/Hebrew Bible, at Mt Sinai and was then conveyed orally by prophets, elders, Pharisees and rabbis to their pupils down the generations.

The bedrock of all Jewish legal rulings are the 613 *mitzvot*, or 'commandments', that appear in the biblical books of Deuteronomy and Leviticus. They acquire additional meaning when allied with the Oral Law. So, for instance, where the Torah simply says 'thou shall not cook the calf in its mother's milk', the Oral Law builds on this edict a whole edifice of legislation determining how and why one should not cook milk and meat products together.

Above Ha'ari synagogue, Safed, Israel. Ha'ari means lion and was the nickname of the great Talmudic scholar Joseph Caro of Safed.

The first summary of Oral Law to be written down is called the Mishnah. Rabbi Yehuda Ha-Nasi, head of the Sanhedrin, edited this compilation *c.* 200CE. Essentially the Mishnah summarizes the debates of past centuries and from these it defines the obligations of Jews in all spheres of life. Rabbi Akiva (50–135CE) is credited with devising the process of linking each traditional practice to a basis in biblical text. This process is called exegesis in Greek. Akiva also helped systematize the vast amounts of material that went into the Mishnah.

But why did Rabbi Yehuda decide to write down the Oral Law in the first place? Some say that because so many scholars died during the two Judean revolts, including Akiva, the old system of a rabbi instructing his pupils would no longer suffice.

MISHNAH

In structure the Mishnah consists of six 'orders' or 'divisions'. Another name for the book is Shas, an acronym of

Left Yemenite rabbis studying the Talmud, 1906. The shortage of books meant the book was read from all sides.

the Hebrew expression *shisha sidrei mishnah*, the six orders of the Mishnah: *Zera'im*, or 'seeds', *Mo'ed*, or 'festivals', *Nezikin*, or 'damages', *Nashim*, or 'women', *Kodashim*, or 'holy things', and *Taharot*, or 'purifications'.

Each order contains numerous tractates (63 in all) some of which veer from the subject matter of the order's title. For instance, under *Zera'im*, which is meant to explain the agricultural rules of ancient Palestine, the most famous tractate is *Brakhot*, or 'blessings'. Orthodox Jews believe the whole world is a sacred gift from God. Hence they feel obliged to bless apparently mundane actions, like eating, drinking, going to sleep or waking up. (Jesus' blessing of the bread and wine shows the prevalence of the custom.)

FESTIVALS AND MARRIAGE

The order called *Mo'ed*, or 'festivals', specifies in its 12 tractates the oral laws for *Pesach* (Passover), *Purim* (the festival of lots), *Rosh Hashana* (New Year), *Yom Kippur* (Day of Atonement), and *Sukkot* (Feast of Tabernacles). Its longest tractate is called *Shabbat*, and consists of 24 chapters, detailing 39 types of 'work' that are forbidden on the Sabbath. Many of the smaller tractates have odd titles: *Beitza* (egg) deals with general practices on festive days; *Megillah* (scroll) refers to the Scroll of Esther, which contains the story of Purim; *Shekkelim* (coins) considers Temple tithes.

The ten tractates of *Nezikin* (damages) essentially summarize Jewish civil and criminal law. *Nashim* (women) covers issues between the sexes, including laws of marriage, *kiddushin*, and divorce, *gittin*. *Kodashim* outlines the laws of ritual slaughter and sacrifices, which ceased when the Temple was destroyed, but have been studied since, along with other tractates and orders, by students in *yeshivas* (rabbinical academies).

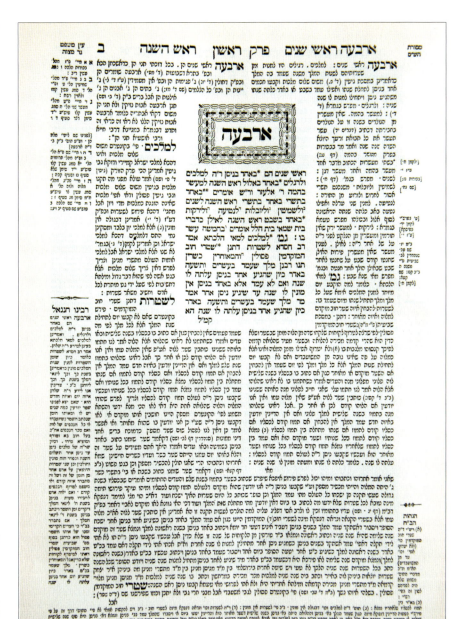

Above A page of the Talmud, showing the typical pattern of text conveying an ongoing dialogue. In the middle, a short Mishnah section with Gemara below. Surrounding this, Rashi, Tosafists and other commentators in each margin.

Left An early copy of Maimonides' *Mishnah Torah*, dated 1351, which summarized the subject divisions and conclusions of the earlier-written Talmud.

THE DIASPORA AND THE RISE OF CHRISTIANITY

Above The Semag, a 14th-century book of Halakha, *showing God creating his world.*

Finally comes the order *Taharot*, which details the laws of purity and impurity. It encompasses decisions as to which food is *kosher* (clean), or *tereif* (unclean). Eminently practical in purpose, its tractates include Hebrew titles that translate as vessels, tents, cow (concerning the rare red heifer required for Temple sacrifices), ritual baths and seminal emissions.

MORAL GUIDANCE

At first glance most of the Mishnah can appear dry, legalistic, even pedantic and didactic. However, Rabbi Yehuda wisely added minority viewpoints as an aid to future debate. He also included some extraordinary statements of universal ethics.

One tractate in particular – *Pirkei Avot*, or 'Ethics of the Fathers' – is entirely devoid of law, and comprises instead much-loved aphorisms attributed to the earliest rabbis. It focuses on character development and universally applicable moral principles.

GEMARA AND TALMUD

The Mishnah marked the end of one process and the start of another. It set in written form what had previously been conveyed orally. It also stimulated intense discussion among rabbis, and these debates were later compiled as a detailed commentary on the Mishnah, called *Gemara*, derived from the Aramaic word for 'study'. Whereas Mishnah is in Hebrew, the Gemara is overwhelmingly written in Aramaic, which was the secular lingua franca of the region.

The Talmuds that emerged, the Palestinian and Babylonian, are essentially a repetition of Mishnah tractates followed by passages of Gemara. Both books cover similar ground, although the longer, clear and detailed Babylonian version is considered the essential Talmud.

Scholars date the Palestinian version to the years 350–400CE; it emerged from the school of Johanan ben Napaha in Tiberias, and was annotated by Rav Muna and Rav Yossi. Its Gemara component consists of discussions between rabbis mainly from Tiberias and Caesarea.

The Babylonian Talmud is four times the size of the Palestinian, runs to 5,894 folio pages and is usually printed in 12 volumes. The leading debaters quoted are Abbaye and Rava; two other Babylonian sages, Ravina and Rav Ashi, are credited with completing the work around 550CE. It probably took centuries to finish entirely. Although it covers only 36 of the 63 Mishnaic tractates, most subject matter is addressed in the Gemara to other tractates.

The rabbis cited in the Mishnah are called *Tanna'im*, Aramaic for 'teachers'; those quoted in the Gemara are known as *Amora'im*, 'interpreters'. If there is a dispute on an issue commented on by both Tanna'im and Amora'im, Jews regard the former as authoritative. This is based on the principle that they were closer in time to Moses.

Right A Jewish family reads sacred texts at Passover. From Agada Pacatis, *a 15th-century Hebrew manuscript.*

WALKING AND TALKING

Within the Talmud there are essentially two types of subject matter. *Halakha* – derived from a Hebrew root for 'walking', as in, on a path – refers to legal rulings and associated discussions. This material makes up nearly 90 per cent of the Talmud. Whatever does not count as Halakha – whether ethics, business and medical advice, history or folklore, even mystical poetry – is collectively called *Aggada*. The name comes from the Hebrew for 'narrative', and relates to the word Haggadah, the traditional telling of the Exodus story around the Passover table.

Closely linked to Aggada is Midrash – the custom of adding to familiar biblical stories, or retelling them in allegorical guise. Some *midrashim* appear separately, others in the Talmud itself.

STUDY

One notable feature of Talmud study is its method. There is a fourfold way of analysing a text, especially when applied to Midrash and Aggada. This method is often summarized in the word *pardes*, which means 'orchard' or 'paradise' (the name entered Hebrew from Persian). Pardes forms an acronym for four components: *pashut*,

Above The tomb of Rabbi Meir, Baal ha-Nes, the miracle-maker, at Tiberias on the coast of the inland Sea of Galilee.

or 'the basic meaning'; *remez*, or 'the hint of something deeper'; *darash*, or 'discussion and interpretation', where the passage's words are compared with similar usages elsewhere; and finally, *sodi*, or 'the secret, hidden or mystical element of a passage'. Some say that the redactors of the Midrash concentrate on *remez* and *darash*, leaving the *sodi* approach to the mystical writers of the Kabbalah.

TALMUDIC PERSONALITIES

The Talmud abounds with engaging personalities. One was Bruriah, a much-quoted sage and the sharp-witted wife of Rabbi Meir. According to a midrash on Psalm 118, she once chided her husband for praying for the destruction of the wicked, rather than for their repentance. If that story were true, Rabbi Meir was probably acting out of character. He was famously generous towards the destitute, even though he was poor himself. Meir, reputedly the grandson of Emperor Nero, insisted that people should bless God for good things and bad. Even the holiest people, he warned, had to guard against the *netzer ha-rah*, or 'evil impulse'.

Meir's real name was Nehora'i and he was also called 'master of miracles'. For example, when his sister-in-law was falsely imprisoned, he reputedly sprang her from jail by mollifying guard dogs when he invoked God's name. Roman authorities launched a huge manhunt to catch him after the ill-fated Bar Kochba rebellion, which he supported. Meir left Palestine, died in Asia and was buried in Tiberias, today in Israel, where pilgrims still visit his tomb.

In Babylon there was friendly rivalry between two great sages. Abba Arika, best known simply as 'Rav', was the first Babylonian *Amora*, or 'interpreter'. He led the yeshiva at Sura, and enjoyed genuine respect in the Persian royal court. Rav's counterpart was Samuel, who re-established the famous Nehardea yeshiva in Pumbedita, after the former was overrun when Palmyrene Arabs fought Parthian Persians. Samuel was an astronomer and doctor. He established that *Dina d'malchuta dina* – essentially, 'the law of wherever you live (your kingdom or government) should be your law'. This enlightened principle enabled Jews to live securely in non-Jewish countries. It served as a retort to Jews who refused to obey secular authorities on spurious nationalistic or religious grounds. Samuel's ruling probably curbed messianic excesses and tailored Jewish political expectations to the reality of Diaspora life.

CONTINUITY AND CONTROVERSY

Between 550 and 700CE Babylonian rabbis called *Savora'im* (explainers) put the Talmud in its final form. Oppressive Byzantine rule in Palestine hampered their counterparts from similarly rationalizing the Jerusalem Talmud. Between 700 and 1250CE, after the Arab conquest of Babylon and Persia, Jews throughout the world consulted the *Ga'onim* (heads of the yeshivas) at Sura and Pumbedita about legal and theological matters. Their *responsa* informed further glosses in the Talmud.

For the last thousand years the Talmud has faced heavy criticism. Christian medieval clerics feared the Talmud as a demonic work and either censored it heavily – especially after the invention of printing – or publicly burned the books. Among Jewish sects, Karaites rejected the Talmud as a deviation from the Torah. Centuries later, Reform Jews questioned the relevance of studying the minutiae of Temple sacrifices, which have had no practical application for 2,000 years. Others say the Talmudic method encourages *pilpul*, or quibbling.

Certainly the Talmud has enormously influenced Jewish life, providing liturgy used in synagogues and subject material for rabbinical sermons. Talmudic exegesis inspired Christian and Muslim theologians in both form and content. For Orthodox Jews the Talmud approximates a living constitution. Secular Jews feel less positively, yet welcome the *dina malchuta* ruling that limits the Talmud's remit over civil society.

Below Students at the Beit Shmuel (House of Samuel) Yeshiva in Israel studying and discussing the Talmud.

PALESTINE AFTER THE ROMAN CONQUEST

AFTER THE ROMAN CONQUEST OF PALESTINE, JEWS GAINED LIMITED AUTONOMY. GREAT CHANGE OF THE EMPIRE BEGAN UNDER EMPEROR DIOCLETIAN, WHICH WERE TO AFFECT JEWISH CULTURE IN PALESTINE.

Palestine's Jewish population fell sharply after the Bar Kochba revolt of 132–5CE. Many thousands had died; many more emigrated. Rome, meanwhile, encouraged Greek and Roman colonists to repopulate the country. Southern Judea remained largely a wasteland, and Jews were barred on pain of death from visiting Jerusalem, except on *Tisha B'Av*, the 9th of the month Av. That date marks the fall of both Temples, and it is still observed as a festival of mourning.

CLINGING TO POWER

Jews tentatively renewed communal life and re-established the Sanhedrin assembly. By the late 2nd century it had branches in Tiberias on the Sea of Galilee, Sephoris, the old Galilean capital, and Lydda in northern Judea.

Below *The synagogue of Dura-Europos, a Hellenistic, Roman and Parthian border city above the Euphrates River.*

The Sanhedrin sage Judah instituted the office of *nasi* (prince). In effect he became Judea's executive administrator, if not ruler. Roman authorities turned a blind eye to the fact that his supposedly civil courts judged and sentenced criminal cases.

The Roman empire reached its zenith under Trajan (reg. 98–,117CE). Rival peoples – Goths, Gauls, Parthians – beset the realm from every quarter. So it made sense to allow the Jews limited autonomy, if only to ward off another unwelcome Judean rebellion. And while Palestine raised little revenue, it remained valuable as a trade thoroughfare and bulwark of imperial defence.

Militarily weak though the Jews were, they could still wield political leverage. In the late 2nd century CE war broke out between two Roman generals, Lucius Septimius Severus and the cruel governor of Syria and Egypt, Niger Pescennius. Jews sided with the half-Berber half-Phoenician

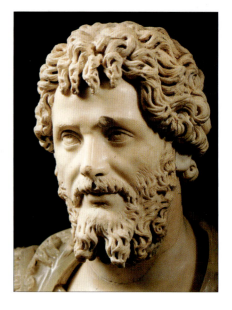

Above *Septimius Severus, Roman emperor 193–211CE, who enjoyed his Jewish subjects' support.*

Severus, who won the contest and was crowned Caesar in 193CE. He remembered his Jewish supporters and set up a dynasty that established good relations with the community. Severus banned conversion to Judaism or Christianity but allowed Jews to acquire whatever office they merited. One successor, Alexander Severus (222–35CE), was particularly praised in the Talmud for allowing Jews to visit Jerusalem. A number settled there with informal Roman approval. Lydda and western Judea experienced something of an urban boom. And the oldest synagogue complex in western Europe, at Ostia, Rome's port, was renamed in Alexander's honour.

DIVIDED PALESTINE

Outside Palestine the Severan tendency towards military autocracy fostered political and economic instability. Determined to rectify this situation and facilitate easier management, Diocletian (284–305CE) divided the empire into two zones, east and west. He applied a similar model of reorganization to Palestine, by attaching to it to the southern part of the Roman province of Arabia.

Diocletian's process culminated around 400CE, when Palestine was split into three distinct zones. Palestina Prima, with its capital at Caesarea, covered Judea, Samaria, Idumea, Perea and the coastal plain. Palestina Secunda consisted of Galilee, Golan, and the Decapolis – ten largely autonomous Hellenistic cities, including a rebuilt Damascus, in southern Syria and today's Kingdom of Jordan. Palestina Tertia incorporated the Negev Desert and took the ancient Nabatean city of Petra, hewn out of red rock, as its capital.

CONSTANTINE AND THE JEWS

Life grew harder for Jews when the Roman empire under Constantine legalized Christianity in the Edict of Milan of 313CE. Christianity became the state religion. Pagan Romans had tolerated other religions; Christians, however, wanted all to convert. They had particularly strong feelings about Palestine, where their saviour Jesus had lived and died.

In 324CE Constantine took control of both halves of a divided empire and marched into Aelia (Jerusalem) to open the city to Christian pilgrimage. Two years later he built the Church of the Holy Sepulchre in Jerusalem. Palestine's Jews felt ambivalent about such developments. Christian pilgrimage benefited all locals, and a massive influx of capital transformed the area. But Christian appropriation of ancient sacred sites troubled Jews, many of whom moved to the Upper Galilee and Golan Heights to secure a realm separate from the emerging Christian Terra Sancta (Holy Land).

In Sephoris and Horazin, Jews revolted unsuccessfully against the harsh governor, Gallus, after he was made 'Caesar of the East' in 351CE.

A brief reprieve arrived when Julian the Apostate ruled as Rome's last pagan emperor in 360–3CE. In 362CE he declared that all religions were equal before the law. In 363 he ordered the Jewish Temple rebuilt, which Alypius of Antioch set about doing. What happened next is unclear: some say an earthquake destroyed the foundations, others, that Christian arsonists sabotaged the project. Julian died in battle against the Sassanid Persians in 363CE and his successors broadly returned to Constantine's Christian path, leaving the Jewish Temple unbuilt.

MOVING FROM PALESTINE

In 395CE Palestine was absorbed within the ambit of the Byzantine or Eastern Roman empire. Limited Jewish autonomy continued until 415CE, when Rabban Gamaliel VI, the *nasi*, was condemned to death by emperors Honorius and Theodosius II for building a synagogue without authorization, and defending Jews against Christians. After Gamaliel died in 426, imperial officials decreed that moneys once owed to the nasi would go to the Roman treasury.

By the 6th century CE, 43 Jewish communities remained in Palestine: 12 on the coast, in the Negev and east of the Jordan, and 31 in Galilee and the Jordan valley. Jewish life in Palestine was ebbing away. The Jewish centre of gravity was moving to other centres, such as Asia Minor, Babylon and the Mediterranean rim.

Above Hellenistic and Jewish culture combine in this zodiac mosaic in Sephoris, once Galilee's largest city.

Below Palestine, c.400CE, showing the district capitals of Scythopolis, Caesarea and Petra.

The Jewish–Christian Schism Deepens

ROME'S UNEXPECTED ADOPTION OF CHRISTIANITY AS ITS IMPERIAL RELIGION MARKED A HISTORICAL WATERSHED – AND INSECURITY FOR JEWS AT THE HANDS OF A NEWLY EMPOWERED RIVAL FAITH.

The closeness of Christianity and Judaism provoked problems from the outset. Christians venerated the Hebrew Bible as their Old Testament, yet they interpreted the text as prefiguring Jesus. Increasingly they called themselves the 'New Israel', which antagonized Jews. Eusebius, bishop of Caesarea (c. 264–340CE), said he loved the ancient Hebrews yet hated the present-day Jews who rejected Christ. During this period most Jews and Christians lived in a slowly crumbling Roman empire. They competed for converts among Rome's pagan majority, and Christians won over poorer artisans and slaves with the simplicity of their beliefs – compared with Judaism – and the promise of eternal salvation in the afterlife.

Below A 1530 fresco shows Christians persecuted by the imperial authorities, as they often were before Rome adopted Christianity as a state religion.

CHRISTIANS PERSECUTED

Until Emperor Constantine's conversion to Christianity in 312CE, Christians had actually been more victimized than Jews. Rome accepted Judaism as a *religio licita* (a legitimate religion), whereas they considered Christianity a bizarre cult. They blamed Christians for the plague, fed believers to the lions, and threatened to kill them for not sacrificing to Roman gods.

Many Christians hid in subterranean catacombs, and most of the early saints were martyred. Roman viciousness reached its zenith under Emperor Diocletian (ruled 284–305CE) and his successor Galerius. Churches and scriptures were destroyed and Christians subjected to punishments such as blinding, mutilation and castration. Outside the empire, pagan Gothic rulers also persecuted Christians, whom they saw as a threat.

Above The Emperor Constantine and his mother, Helena, in a 7th-century fresco from Elmali Kilise, Turkey.

ROME TURNS TO CHRIST

Thousands of Jews had been enslaved after the failed Judean revolts of 68–74CE and 132–5CE. Some were forced to build Rome's Coliseum, itself funded by riches looted from Jerusalem's Temple. After Rome regained political superiority, however, most slaves were freed and Jews were tolerated, even prized, as contributors to the imperial economy and cosmopolitan culture.

Their circumstances began to change when Constantine legalized Christianity with the Edict of Milan of 313CE. The hitherto despised faith gained power and new followers as Christian bishops targeted non-believers. In 315CE Constantine denounced Jews as 'Christ killers', thus shifting blame for the crucifixion from his own imperial predecessors. In 323CE Christianity replaced paganism as Rome's favoured religion. And in 337CE Constantius outlawed Jewish proselytizing, forbade Jews to own non-Jewish slaves, banned intermarriage with Christians, and stopped rabbis meeting.

The pagan emperor Julian (360–3CE) interrupted this trend when he promised to rebuild the Jerusalem

Temple; and his Arian Christian successor, Valens (364–78CE), strengthened the Jewish patriarch. However, Theodosius I (379–95CE) confirmed mainstream Christianity as Rome's sole state religion in 380CE, and imposed a deluge of statutes on non-conformists.

While most emperors still upheld the religious rights of Jews, Christian clerics sought to curb their influence. When in 388CE a mob burned down a synagogue along the Euphrates River, Theodosius ordered it rebuilt at Christian expense, only to rescind his order under church pressure.

THEOLOGICAL RIVALRY
According to St Augustine (354–430CE), Jewish survival was part of God's design, as their travails bore witness to the truth of the new religion. Christians felt that God had spurned the former 'chosen people' and wanted Palestine transformed into a Christian Terra Sancta, or Holy Land.

Not all contact between Jews and Christians was negative. Origen, the 2nd-century Egyptian Christian theologian had spent long hours

Below St Jerome translating the Bible from Hebrew into Latin. A 15th-century Netherlandish painting on panel.

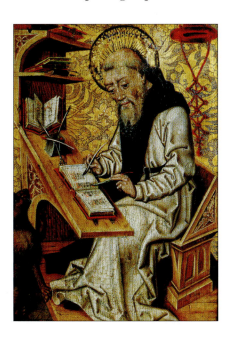

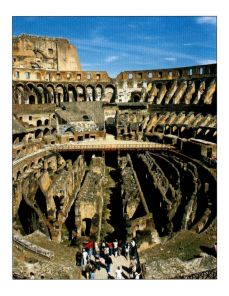

debating with rabbis. St Jerome (347–420CE) translated the Old Testament from Hebrew into Latin, and his scriptural commentaries show the influence of Philo and the Alexandria Jewish school.

Conversely, a 4th-century archbishop of Constantinople, John Chrysostom, is credited with pion-eering a specifically Christian brand of anti-Semitism, called synagogues the dens of scoundrels and warned against 'Judaizing' Christians who observed Jewish fasts and feasts. It seems his views bore political fruit in 418 when Jews were barred from Roman public office.

During 419–422CE Syrian monks raided Palestine, burned synagogues and destroyed Jewish villages. Less violent missionaries sought to 'save Jewish souls' through conversion, a venture that only partly succeeded. Churchmen especially resented the Palestinian office of the nasi, or Jewish patriarch. His status as 'remnant of the house of David' undermined their idea of Jesus as David's rightful heir. Some Jews countered with polemic of their own, including veiled references in the Mishnah to Jesus as an impostor, a magician, or even the ill-egitimate son of a Roman centurion.

In 429CE Byzantium abolished the 350-year-old patriarchate, and, with Palestinian Jewry duly weakened,

Left Rome's Colosseum, 70–82CE, was probably built by Jews, taken as slaves after the Palestine revolt.

Samaritans offered the only real armed resistance to the spread of Christianity in Palestine.

Although the Western Roman empire ended in 476CE, Christianity survived in the Eastern Byzantine empire. By now it had taken root among Rome's barbarian conquerors too. There were moments of reprieve in Christian–Jewish relations. But harsher laws were to follow; and outside Christendom, the Jews of Babylon enjoyed better conditions.

SAMARITAN FORTUNES

Christ's 'Good Samaritan' parable in the New Testament hints at the traditional enmity between Jews and Samaritans in Palestine. Although religiously and ethnically related to Jews, many Samaritans helped Rome crush the Jewish Bar Kochba uprising of 135CE.

Samaritans were later punished by Rome when they refused to worship Roman gods, and the triumph of Christianity merely sharpened the conflict.

In the 4th century CE, Baba Rabbah revived the Samaritan sect and repeatedly defeated Roman invaders with his armies. In 483CE, Samaritans massacred Christians and burned churches after Theodosius II extended anti-Jewish statutes to their community.

In 529CE, Emperor Justinian I crushed an uprising to establish a Samaritan state, after which many converted to Christianity. Thousands fled when Muslims conquered Palestine in 634CE.

The Samaritans once numbered millions; today some 600 remain, divided between Nablus in Palestine and Holon in Israel.

Babylon – The New Centre of Jewry

FROM THE TIME WHEN PERSIANS CONQUERED BABYLON, JEWS REMAINED IN THE ANCIENT REGION. GENERALLY THEY FLOURISHED, AND THEIR RELIGIOUS CENTRES RIVALLED THOSE IN PALESTINE.

After the fall of Jerusalem, the central focus of Jewish life gradually shifted from Palestine to Babylon, a region under Persian rule since the 6th century BCE. The core of Babylon's Jewish community was formed by exiles from the Kingdom of Judah. Over time, immigrants replenished their population, including Jews fleeing turmoil within the Roman empire and Jewish farmers from Palestine, who suffered from heavy taxes, currency devaluation and military requisitions to billet Roman soldiers.

BABYLONIAN JEWS

In the 1st century CE the Jewish historian Josephus wrote: 'The Jews beyond the Euphrates are an immense multitude and not estimated by numbers.' Their rulers were Parthians, a north-east Persian clan which in 129BCE had conquered Babylon and the rest of Mesopotamia, including most of present-day Iran and Iraq.

Babylon's Jews were furious when Romans desecrated Jerusalem in 70CE. So when the Parthians fought Rome, the community lent its protectors full support. The Parthians reciprocated by funding anti-Roman zealots in Judea, and raising the status of local Jewish communal leaders in Babylon.

Jewry received a boost when Queen Helen of the satrapy of Adiabene and her son Izates converted to Judaism in the mid-1st century CE. Helen contributed greatly to the second Temple in Jerusalem, and the royal family supported a notable yeshiva in Arbela (modern Irbil, in Iraqi Kurdistan). The Parthians already prized their Jewish subjects as revenue collectors and in 140CE they permitted them an exilarch or *resh galuta*, Head of the Exile. He interceded with the royal court on his community's behalf, and often directly influenced Persian foreign policy. Even so, he still had to contend with the authority of the yeshivas, especially in Sura, Nehardea, and later Pumbedita. The yeshivas benefited immensely from an influx of Palestinian Pharisees, such as the students of Rabbi Ishmael, a great sage of Yavneh.

THE RISE OF THE SASSANIDS

In 224CE Ardashir, an ambitious Persian provincial governor, overthrew the Parthians and crowned himself Shahanshah, 'king of kings'. His Sassanid dynasty promoted Zoroastrianism and gave their empire a more centralized structure. Ardashir and his successor, Shapur, conquered Roman lands in Asia Minor, such as Antioch, though not Palestine.

Rome's nadir came when the Sassanids captured Emperor Valerian in 260CE. That same year Sassanid armies killed some 12,000 Hellenized Jews defending Mazaca-Caesarea in Cappadocia. Babylon's own Jews feared that the Sassanids might end their political autonomy and religious freedom. However, Talmudic Jewish scholars Abba Arika and Samuel won security for Jews living under the new regime.

RIVALRY WITH PALESTINE

In earlier days Babylonian Jews regularly paid their Temple tax to Jerusalem; after the destruction they continued to fund the rabbinate in Palestine. Rivalry between the two centres grew, for while Palestinian rabbis were influenced by Roman and Greek culture; the Babylonians were oriented more to Eastern traditions. New influences emerged in the 4th century, however, when Persia's neighbour Armenia adopted Christianity, and Jews arrived from a crumbling Roman empire.

Above Relatives of Sanatruces I, 1st century BCE king of Parthia, whose descendants gave Jews honoured status.

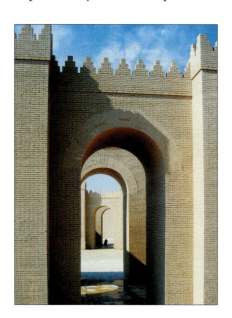

Left Modern rebuilding of Babylon, where Jews flourished under Persian rule until persecution returned c.400CE.

Above The remains of Queen Helen of Adiabene's residence. She converted to Judaism and lived in Jerusalem.

> ### DURA–EUROPOS
> In 1935 a remarkable synagogue was discovered in Dura–Europos in northern Syria. The city was founded by Seleucids in 303BC. Its synagogue is dated to 245CE, and is the earliest preserved example to survive. It features walls of mosaics that charmingly depict the Torah's best-known characters and stories. Dura–Europos was originally Hellenistic, yet as a border town it changed hands several times. The city came under Parthian control in the 2nd century BCE, was captured by Romans in 165CE, and fell to the Sassanid Persians in 257.
>
> It is tempting to extrapolate a sense of Persian or Babylonian Jewish culture from Dura–Europos, whose synagogue remains are now in Damascus. Strictly speaking, the city lay outside the Babylonian orbit and its mosaics defy the biblical stricture on graven images. Even if atypical of the period and region, it shows previously unimagined artistic creativity and bolsters the view that the earliest churches were modelled on Jewish houses of worship.

The Palestinian school claimed precedence, partly because they remained in the Holy Land and partly through such personalities as Johanan, Akiva and Yehuda Ha-Nasi, who determined the sacred calendar. Babylonian rabbis claimed a purer Davidic lineage than the Palestinians. They argued that their interpretations were less sullied by outside influence. And Jews from Palestine and beyond sought guidance from the Babylonian exilarch after the Palestinian Jewish patriarchate fell in 429CE.

Around 500 Babylonian sages produced the *Talmud Bavli*. Unlike the Palestinian Talmud, it concentrated less on rites connected to the Land of Israel and became the paramount version in all Jewish yeshivas, whether of European Ashkenazim, Spanish-origin Sephardim or Middle Eastern *mizrakhim*.

The Babylonian Talmud vividly records the real life of Jews in Babylon. It tells that the second Sassanid king, Shapur I (241–72CE), reinstated religious tolerance and befriended such sages as Samuel and his disciple, Judah. Shapur II, whose mother was Jewish, rescinded earlier oppressive legislation. Yazdegerd I (399–421CE) married a Jewish noblewoman, Shushandukht, and habitually hosted Talmudic sages in his royal court.

Jews flourished as date cultivators, fishermen, artisans and river navigators. And for two months each year – when fieldwork ceased – ordinary farmers would pour into the academies to study Torah.

MIXED FORTUNES

Unfortunately this halcyon period did not last: fanatic Zoroastrian priests, threatened by Byzantine inroads from the west, forced King Yazdegerd III to persecute Jews, Christians and Manicheans. In 455CE Persia's rulers passed an edict banning the Sabbath. Eventually this prompted a full-scale Jewish rebellion in 511 when the Jewish exilarch Mar Zutra usurped power from Kavadh I (ruled 488–531CE) for seven years.

Kavadh's successor, Khosrau I (531–79CE), restored Persia to its former glory, repelled Byzantium and improved conditions for his Jewish subjects, which may explain why Jews so enthusiastically backed Persia's invasion of Byzantine-ruled Palestine in the early 7th century CE.

Below 3rd-century CE relief of Shapur I of Persia, whom the Talmud praises as a friend to Jews and patron of scholars.

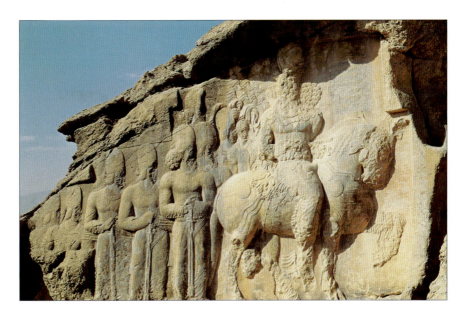

JEWS UNDER BYZANTIUM

JEWS EXPERIENCED A CHEQUERED EXISTENCE UNDER BYZANTINE RULE – PRECARIOUS IN PALESTINE AND PROSPEROUS IN THE CITIES. BUT, AS THE EMPIRE FALTERED, JEWS WERE INCREASINGLY OPPRESSED.

'Byzantine' has become a byword for anything unnecessarily complex. The notion probably originated when rough-hewn Crusaders encountered the sophisticates of Byzantium. Modern medievalists now argue that Western European prejudice obscured the truth – the Byzantines outlasted the Roman empire by a thousand years.

BYZANTIUM GROWS

Greek colonists founded Byzantium at the Anatolian gateway to the Black Sea in the 7th century BCE. It grew in stature after Emperor Diocletian reconfigured the Roman empire as a tetrarchy (led by four people) in 292CE. In 330CE his successor, Constantine, built a 'second Rome' on its site, which seven years later became Constantinople, capital of the Eastern Roman empire. The east–west split became permanent after the death of Theodosius I in 395CE, the last emperor to rule both zones simultaneously.

Rome and Byzantium shared a faith, but political, cultural and religious schisms grew as Byzantium became the seat of Greek Orthodoxy, while Rome championed Latinate Catholicism. The final rift came when Byzantium rejected the authority of the pope in 1054.

Byzantium came to dominate much of the Middle East and all of Asia Minor, and influenced the Jews who lived in those regions. In 330CE – the same year that Byzantium became Nova Roma – Constantine made Jerusalem part of his realm. Christian pilgrims began flocking to Jerusalem, and successive emperors built churches in the city, including on the former Temple Mount. Other great ancient cities of the region – like Antioch, Damascus and Alexandria – became Christian archbishoprics under the Byzantine aegis. Meanwhile, Byzantium and Sassanid Persia fought over border territories.

Above A Byzantine mosaic from 1210 showing the construction of the Tower of Babel, as told in the Hebrew Bible.

FROM PRIVILEGE TO PERSECUTION

The Byzantine age was certainly chequered for its Jewish subjects. Palestine's Jewish patriarchate was abolished less than a century after Jerusalem became Byzantine. While Palestinian Jews suffered, those Jews already living under Byzantine rule in Asia Minor and Egypt appeared to fare better, at least at first. They were granted leave from having to join civic associations; and the Emperor Arcadius reinforced privileges for their patriarchs and communal elders. But rioting by Jews in Palestine fuelled anti-Jewish feeling in Constantinople, and things worsened under Emperor Theodosius II (408–50CE), who bowed to clerical pressure and enforced anti-Jewish laws.

Despite legal restrictions, Jews maintained important positions in Byzantine society. They controlled half the shipping fleet in Alexandria, and evidently dominated the dyeing industry from the 6th to the 15th

Below By the 3rd century CE, Jewish communities had spread throughout southern Europe and northern Africa.

Right Today a mosque, the imposing Hagia Sophia in Constantinople, present-day Istanbul, was the world's largest cathedral for a thousand years and the spiritual epicentre of Byzantine Orthodox Christianity.

centuries. Culturally, Jewish life influenced Byzantine Christianity: Hebrew poetry (*paytanim*) blossomed in Palestine, and one monk, Romanos, an apostate from Judaism, introduced Jewish poetic modes into Byzantine liturgy.

The Byzantine appointee Bishop Cyril of Alexandria (c.375–444CE) demanded the expulsion of the city's Jews. Ten years later, in 425CE, Theodosius II issued his Code of Law, which limited where Jews could live and what they could wear and subjected them to extraordinary taxation. Jews could no longer build synagogues or own slaves, which ruined Jewish farmers. Intermarriage with Christians was punishable by death. In 439CE, Theodosius prohibited Jews from holding public office or positions involving control of money; he also re-enacted a defunct law outlawing the building of new synagogues.

JUSTINIAN, PHOCAS AND HERACLIUS

Justinian I (527–65CE) also deprived Jews of civil and religious privileges. In 535CE he outlawed Judaism in the re-conquered lands of North Africa; in 553CE he banned the recitation of Hebrew in synagogues, and forbade the use of the Mishnah to help congregants understand the Torah. As the empire weakened under the blows of enemies within and without, successive emperors used Jews as scapegoats. Eventually, in 608CE, when Emperor Phocas (602–41CE) initiated a new wave of forced conversions, the Jews of Antioch revolted and killed the city's bishop.

Desperate to revive Byzantine fortunes, Emperor Heraclius (610–41CE) promised to protect the Jews in Palestine as he launched a counter-attack against Persia. When Heraclius took Jerusalem in 629CE, he went back on his word. He barred Jews from living within a three-mile radius of the holy city, and allegedly allowed Byzantine troops to kill any Jew they could find.

BYZANTIUM FALTERS

Within the Byzantine realm, indi-genous Christians of minority sects (Nestorians, Assyrians, Monophysites, Copts and others) resented the arrogance of Greek Orthodox clerics. Seemingly endless battles eventually exhausted all parties, effectively leaving the door open for the Muslim Arab conquests of the early 7th century CE. Byzantium's loss of swathes of land to Muslim Arabs then spelt the end of Christian patrimony over the Middle East.

Jews faced repeated attempts at conversion to Christianity by the emperors Basil I (in 873CE) and Romanus I Lecapenus (in 943CE). In 1204 Latin Crusaders sacked Constantinople and burned down the Pera district, today Beyoglu in Istanbul, south of the Golden Horn and home to Genoan, Venetian and Jewish merchants and silk weavers. Byzantium eventually fell to Muslim Turks when the Ottoman Sultan Muhammad II took Constantinople on 24 April 1453.

Below Tiberias, major port on the Sea of Galilee, where Jews launched their final revolt against Byzantine rule in 614CE.

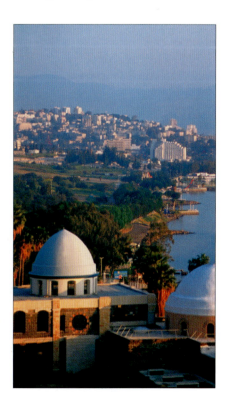

Jewish Communities of the Mediterranean

Undisturbed by the rise and fall of empires, Jews from Libya, Syria, Greece and Turkey formed a network that traded in goods, services and ideas across the Mediterranean.

Outside Egypt and the Middle East, Jewish communities played a huge role in the life of the Mediterranean basin, a position they maintained after the Roman empire collapsed in the late 5th century CE. These included outposts in Morocco and Tunisia – especially the cities of Kairouan, seat of a noted yeshiva; and the island of Djerba. Other sites included Spain, Greece, Anatolia, southern France and Cyrenaica, in what is now Libya, west of Egypt.

CYRENAICA

The region of Cyrenaica consisted of five main Hellenistic cities – Cyrene, Berenice, Appolonia, Teucheria and Ptolemais – known collectively as a pentapolis. In *The Antiquities of the Jews*, Josephus writes that Jews first came to Cyrenaica from Egypt, under Ptolemy I (323–285BCE). Originally, it seems, they were regarded as the fourth 'class', after citizens, peasants and metics (later settlers). Rome acquired the territory from the Ptolemies in 96BCE, and, after an interim of civil strife, turned it into a Roman province in 74BCE. One Cyrenaican Jew was Jason of Cyrene, whose five volumes in Greek on the Maccabean revolt were summarized in II Maccabees. Jason later helped instigate the failed Egyptian Jewish rebellion against Trajan in 115CE.

DAMASCUS

A Jewish community has probably existed in Damascus for millennia, and it lays claim to being the oldest continually inhabited city on earth. Egyptian Mari documents of the 18th century BCE call it the Land of Apum, ruled by Western Semites, and the name Damascus occurs often in the biblical books of Chronicles and Kings and in the Dead Sea Scrolls. Given Syria's geographical proximity, the city formed a natural place of refuge for Jews fleeing trouble in Palestine or the Land of Israel. (One known 'refugee' was King Herod, who hid in Damascus when the Sanhedrin accused him of treating Galilean Jewish rebels brutally.)

The Talmud speaks of Damascus as 'the gateway of the Garden of Eden', such was its economic renown. And we know of Damascus' importance from the books of Paul, who as a rabbi was sent to punish the recalcitrant 'heretical' Christ-believers among the Jews who dwelt in Damascus'

Left A shiviti, *a contemplative artwork traditionally placed on the eastern wall of a room or synagogue, facing Jerusalem, which reminds Jews of God's presence.*

Above A bust of Jason of Cyrene, a Jew who wrote a history of the Maccabees up to the victory against Greco–Syrians.

Straight Street. Scholars believe that Damascene Jews farmed and traded, but they were not noted as religious sages, unlike Jews in Aleppo, north Syria.

Both indigenous Christians and Jews suffered under Byzantine rule. There also seems to have been rivalry between the two communities. When Damascene Jews helped Persia oust local Byzantine rulers in the early 7th century CE, they suppressed the Christians of Tyre (now in Lebanon), the main port outlet for landlocked Damascus.

GREECE

Documentary evidence shows that Jews lived on the Greek mainland from 300BCE; some possibly arrived as early as the Babylonian exile. Over time they formed a community called Romaniotes which was distinct from both Sephardi and Ashkenazi Jews. They had their own *minhag*, or 'local customs', and a unique language called Yevanic, a Greek dialect written in Hebrew characters. The early medieval Jewish traveller Benjamin of Tudela wrote that the largest Romaniotes community was in Thebes, where Jews

Above A ruined synagogue at Sardis, ancient capital of the Lydian kingdom and known for its fabulous wealth.

were respected as cloth-dyers and makers of silk garments. They also lived on the islands of Corfu and Aegina, and in Corinth, Athens and Thessaloniki, which became the largest Greek Jewish city when Sephardi Jews arrived from Spain after 1492. Later the fortified *kastro* section of Ioannina, a town in northwest Greece, south of Albania, became the Romaniote centre.

ASIA MINOR

Vast in size and opulent in its decoration, the marble-floored, two-tiered synagogue of Sardis was truly a wonder of ancient Anatolia. Its rediscovery in the 1960s overturned previous theories about Jewish life in Asia Minor and indicated that Jews had formed a prosperous and confident minority long after Christianity had supposedly eclipsed all other faiths.

Formerly capital of the Lydian kingdom, Sardis was known for its fabulous wealth, as captured in the expression 'as rich as Croesus', its 6th-century BCE king. Jews had lived in Lydia since the 4th century BCE, and traded extensively along routes that passed through Sardis to Persia and beyond. Their great synagogue was built in 3rd-century CE Sardis, the metropolis of the Roman province of Lydia, the city having been previously ruled by Athenians, Persians and Macedonians. Located on a street full of elegant shops, many of them Jewish-run, the synagogue was attached to a magnificent bath-gymnasium and contained 80 Greek and seven Hebrew inscriptions. All these facts indicate Jews were thoroughly integrated into the life of a mainly pagan and later Christian city.

Jewish mercenaries in the Greco-Syrian army of Seleucus were among the first inhabitants of Antioch, an Anatolian port created in the 3rd century BCE. From then on Jews wielded enormous influence, whether as wealthy merchants in the suburb of Daphne, rice-growing farmers to the north east, or bakers, metal workers and weavers within the city itself. Rome conquered Antioch in 64BC, and 100 years later Titus, returning in triumph after crushing the Judean revolt, imposed on its Jewish population a special tax called a *ficus Judaicus*. In effect that meant that Antioch's Jews had to pay two denarii to Rome instead of to Jerusalem as before. However, the city's Jews still enjoyed high status after the empire became Christian. In 391CE they helped fund a new synagogue in Apamea, 50 miles away. Fourth-century sources reveal that Jews, pagans and Christians lived and worked harmoniously together, while the Jews still worshipped separately and maintained strong links with their Palestinian brethren.

Right Paul preaching to the Jews in the synagogue at Damascus, 12th-century Byzantine mosaic.

Changing Fortunes in Europe

JEWS TRADED ACROSS GERMANY, FRANCE, SPAIN AND ITALY AFTER THE ROMAN EMPIRE COLLAPSED. SOME BEFRIENDED EMPERORS AND POPES, BUT OTHERS WERE PERSECUTED BY NEWLY CHRISTIANIZED PAGANS.

Jews fleeing Palestine naturally gravitated to colonies of fellow Jews who already lived in the Diaspora. Although the actual Jewish population of the world appears to have dropped markedly, from eight million around 50CE to 1.5 million around the year 1000, Jews managed to carve out new roles for themselves on the back of Roman colonization. Equally remarkably, they survived and even expanded after the Western Roman empire itself collapsed, despite being vulnerable to the whims of the rulers of the day, and certain zealous priests.

MOVING INLAND

Jews had followed the Roman empire's military encampments into inland Europe. It is known that Jews established trading posts in Germanic frontier towns, such as Bonn, Triers and Cologne, as testified by an imperial decree of 321. Here they first encountered the 'barbarians' who were encroaching on Rome. Conceivably these Jews were the first Ashkenazim, who make up some 90 per cent of Jews today. The name Ashkenaz derives from an obscure biblical location. It was used during medieval times to denote the lands of Germany and northern France which earlier Jewish sources called Allemania.

For the most part, Jews were welcomed in German towns as international traders to the East. New communities emerged in southern central Germany in the 11th century. There then followed a period of persecution during the 12th to 14th centuries, when Jews moved north and east, and began practising money-lending.

Above Pope Gregory I (reg. 590–604CE) called Jews blind to Christ's truth, yet he also allowed them freedom to worship.

JEWS IN ITALY AND SPAIN

Increasingly, pagan rulers and their peoples converted to Christianity, which often led to persecution of Jews – but not always so, as in the case of Theodoric the Great. In 500CE Theodoric safeguarded the right of the Jews of Italy to determine civil disputes and worship freely. In 519, Christians in Ravenna burned the local synagogues, and he ordered the town to rebuild them at their own expense.

By contrast, the Visigoth King Recared of Spain (586–601CE) renounced Arianism in favour of Catholicism in 587CE and with the Third Council of Toledo in 589CE proceeded to persecute Jews. He banned intermarriage, forbade Jews to own slaves or hold positions of authority and ordered that children of mixed marriages be raised as Christians. Defenders of Recared's record say he rejected bribes from wealthy Spanish Jews and that he rescinded the death penalty for Jews who proselytized.

EARLY POPES AND THE JEWS

Several of the first popes were martyred, sometimes with their congregations, and it was only really

Below A 15th-century woodcut from Munich of the Judensau or Jewish pig, which anti-semites said suckled Jews.

Above In this 14th-century manuscript, Entree d'Espagne, *Charlemagne (742–824) gives audience to his subjects.*

with the Edict of Milan in 313CE that the papal institution began to acquire its later power. Essentially the pope is the bishop of Rome, bishop meaning 'overseer' in Greek. Rome was one of four central cities for Christians, the others being Antioch, Jerusalem and Constantinople.

Popes often proved more tolerant than local bishops, presumably because they had to consider the economic and political well-being of the empire and not just populist concerns. The most influential early pope, Gregory the Great, formulated official church policy towards Jews in 590CE. He banned forced conversions and granted Jews the right to worship freely. Gregory thus set a standard for successors to follow – not that they always did – and Jews felt they could appeal to the pope when threatened by local bigotry.

Formally, the schism between Roman Catholics and Greek Orthodox occurred in 1054, but the two churches had been moving in different directions for centuries. By and large, the 'barbarians' who now ruled different parts of the former Western Roman empire adopted Christianity; they followed the pope in Rome as their spiritual guide, rather than the patriarch in the still-surviving Eastern Roman or Byzantine empire.

CHARLEMAGNE AND JEWISH LIFE IN FRANCE

One barbarian convert was Charlemagne, King of the Franks, who was crowned emperor of the west in 800CE. Credited with being the first true 'European', he expanded his realm from northern France to include all of Germany, northern Italy, Holland, Austria and the zone between France and Muslim Spain. While he forced other barbarians to adopt Christianity, he showed a rare respect for Jews and Judaism, borne as much by appreciation of their economic utility as by ethical considerations. Militant priests chafed at the privileges he gave Jewish traders – especially the Radhanites from Persia – but he resisted clerical attempts to curtail Jews' rights.

Generally, anti-Jewish rhetoric from the pulpit found little traction among ordinary Christian Franks, and Charlemagne was happy to keep it that way. As the borders of the 'Holy Roman empire' expanded, it encompassed such Mediterranean locales as Massalia, the first Greek outpost in western Europe. Later called Marseilles, it began attracting Jews soon after it was founded c.600BCE. (Today it houses the third-largest urban community of Jews in Europe.) Another French port with a significant Jewish presence was Narbonne, whose loyalty to the Frankish monarch won them the right to be ruled by their own Jewish 'king' of his community and effective city treasurer.

The security that was enjoyed by Charlemagne's Jews might have been exceptional. Recared's successor in Spain, Sesbut, prohibited Judaism in 610CE. Although exiled Jews returned to Byzantine Spain under his successor, Swintilla, a new law 18 years later decreed that only Catholics could live there – an edict that many Jews clearly ignored. Christianity had largely united post-Roman Europe, yet it was to prove extremely problematic for Jews who had long lived there.

Below A German woodcut showing the alleged ritual child murder of Simon by Jews in 1475 in Trent, Italy.

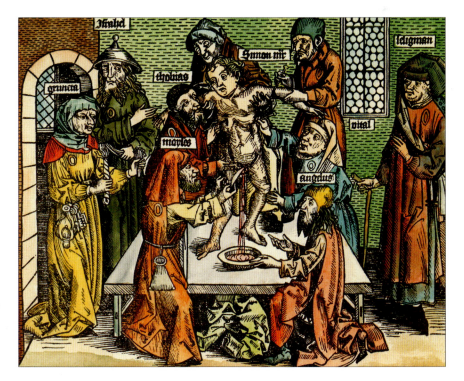

Jews of Pre-Islamic Persia and Arabia

OVER TIME, JEWS FLEEING PALESTINE CAME TO LIVE AND WORK ALONGSIDE THEIR ETHNIC COUSINS, THE ARABS, AND THE YEMENITE KINGDOM OF HIMYAR EVEN BRIEFLY ADOPTED THEIR FAITH.

In 614CE the Persians conquered Jerusalem and ruled it until 629CE. The two former centres of Jewish life, Palestine and Babylon, were briefly reunited. However, both the Persians and their rivals, the Byzantines, were about to face a potent new threat from Arabia.

Mobilized by the monotheistic faith of Islam, Arabs conquered large parts of Sassanid Persia in 634CE. Damascus fell in 635CE, Jerusalem in 637CE, and by 650CE all of Persia and Iraq was in Arab hands.

COUSINS DIVIDED?

A broad definition of the word 'Arab' denotes any speaker of Arabic, which today covers most of the population of the Middle East and North Africa. A narrower usage applies only to the so-called 'pure' Arabs of the Arabian desert and Persian Gulf area, often referred to as Bedouin (literally, 'those who dwell outside'). However, both definitions are fraught with complexities. After the Arab and Muslim conquests of the 7th century, Syrians, Egyptians, Amorites, Berbers and Greek settlers, among others, adopted the new language. Some kept their original faith, invariably Christianity, yet still proudly called themselves Arab.

The Bible only occasionally uses the term Arab. Usually Arabs are referred to as Ishmaelites, the descendants of Abraham's first-born son by Hagar, Ishmael. The

Above An 18th-century Persian painting of the Sacrifice of Abraham, showing the angel with the ram.

Bible and the Koran agree that the Jewish line runs through Ishmael's younger half-brother, Isaac, so that would make Jews and Arabs first cousins. Certainly the Bible refers to both Arabs and Jews, or their Israelite ancestors, as the progeny of Noah's son, Shem – hence the word Semites. Linguistic and genetic research appears to confirm this commonly accepted tradition.

One minority view even states that the words Hebrew (*Ivri* in the Hebrew language) and Arab (*Aravi*), stem from the same Semitic root, and may once have been interchangeable. *Ivri* broadly means 'those who dwell across [the river]'; *aravi* suggests either 'of the desert' or 'those who mingle', like the blending of daylight and darkness at dusk. In all cases, there is a suggestion of the nomadic ways of the earliest biblical patriarchs and the Bedouin Arab sheikhs.

JERUSALEM UNDER PERSIA

After Jerusalem's fall in 70CE, many Jews migrated to Perea and Arabia Felix, Roman provinces east of Judea. Proto-Arabs such as the Idumeans (Edomites) had already been converted to Judaism, and to a limited extent this happened further east.

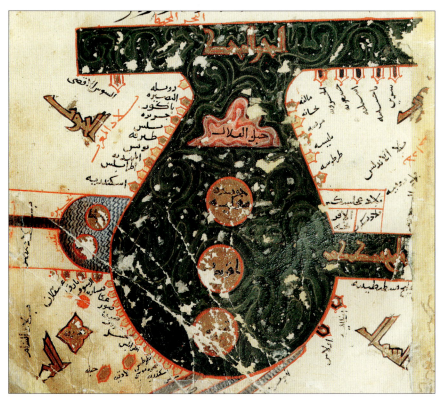

Left A 10th-century Arabic geography, Book of Routes and Provinces, showing the Mediterranean.

Right Islamic Palestine in the 7th century CE, showing the Persian conquest, the Byzantine reconquest and the Arab invasion.

Mostly, though, Arabic-speaking Jews of the vast Hijaz area dwelt alongside pagan Arabs, but separately, and they were respected as traders.

THE INDEPENDENT KINGDOM OF HIMYAR

Jews evidently reached southern Arabia, around Yemen, in the 1st century BCE, and Herod the Great sent a Jewish brigade to the region in 25BCE. The Arabic Kingdom of Himyar, founded in 115BCE, was centred around Yemen and the southern Najd area (of today's Saudi Arabia). It controlled most of southern Arabia by the 4th century CE. Successive Himyarite kings, Ab Karib As'ad in the 5th century CE and Dhu Nawas in the 6th, adopted Judaism. Jewish affiliation intensified among the populace when Christian Abbysinians (Ethiopians) and Byzantines threatened to capture the economically strategic region. Ultimately, declining trade

Below A modern Yemenite Jewish girl in traditional ceremonial dress. Goldsmiths are among the craftworkers who emigrated to Israel from Yemen.

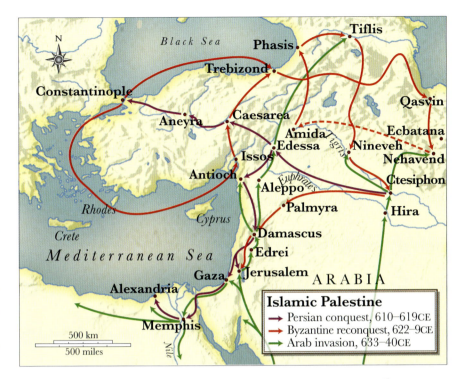

destroyed Himyarite power and the Jews lost an ally.

JEWS OF PERSIA AFTER THE 5TH CENTURY CE

Between 614 and 629CE, Jerusalem and all of Palestine came under Persian rule. Most Jews at the time were suffering under the yoke of the Byzantines and thus welcomed the new invaders. The Jews of Damascus had already helped the Persians to attack and occupy that formerly Byzantine-ruled city in 613CE. In Jerusalem, the Persian conquerors destroyed many Christian churches, and later reneged on promises to re-establish Jewish sovereignty. Jews – who numbered 150,000 in all of Palestine – were barred from the holy city to a radius of three miles. Within decades, however, Arabs had control of Jerusalem and the entire Levant, which opened up new challenges and opportunities.

THE RADHANITES

Long before Marco Polo 'discovered' China, Jewish traders from Persia used the Silk Road to the East. Up to 1,000 merchants, the Radhanites, dominated trade in China and Europe, between Muslim and Christian worlds.

Some say their name refers to a Babylonian province; others think it is from the Persian for 'those who know the way'. Others believe that it points to the River Rhône, where the major routes to the East began.

Radhanites travelled by boat down Russia's Volga River, across the Mediterranean, or by sea from the Persian Gulf to India. They also carried goods by camel-back to Egypt, or from Khazaria across deserts to China. They traded beaver skins, slaves, eunuchs, brocade and swords from the West and from the East came musk, camphor, cinnamon, silk, oils and jewellery. The Radhanites spoke Persian, Greek, Arabic, Spanish, Frankish and Slavonic. Some say they introduced Chinese papermaking to the West, and that their use of credit notes inspired early banking systems.

CHAPTER 4

JUDAISM AND ISLAM

Early in the 7th century CE, Islam was born. Islam was the third of the three great monotheistic religions that were to arise in the Middle East, this time from Arabia. Much of the Islamic Koran, a text considered by its adherents to be the verbatim word of God, revisited the Hebrew Bible, and Jews and Muslims share remarkably similar beliefs and practices. Islam's rapid rise profoundly affected Jewish history. A rift during Mohammed's lifetime led Muslims to expel Jews from Arabia, but generally Jews were to find relations with Muslims easier than their encounters with Christians.

The encounter of the three faiths in Spain after 712CE, known as the Golden Age of Spain, spawned a period of religious tolerance when arts, sciences and trade flourished. Meanwhile, dramatic events included the Khazar Kingdom's conversion to Judaism; a Jewish rebellion against the rabbis, which resulted in the new Karaite sect; and the first stirrings of a distinctively European Ashkenazi culture of Judaism in France.

Opposite A painting of Noah's Ark, from The Fine Flower of Histories, *a work of political and religious world history by Ottoman historiographer Seyyid Loqman Ashuri, 1583.*

Above The Dome of the Rock was built on the Temple Mount of Jerusalem, on the presumed site of the Second Temple, thus making the area sacred for both Muslims and Jews.

The Birth and Rise of Islam

LITERALLY MEANING SUBMISSION TO GOD'S WILL, AND DERIVED FROM THE ROOT WORD FOR PEACE, ISLAM CLAIMS TO COMPLETE THE DIVINE MESSAGE RECEIVED BY JEWS AND CHRISTIANS.

According to Muslims, the Angel Gabriel relayed the Koran, Islam's holiest text, to Mohammed. Today there are more than 1.6 billion adherents of Islam, making it the world's second largest faith.

The rise of Islam and defeat of Persia in the 7th century CE ended polytheism in most of the known world. Judaism now faced two competing monotheistic faiths. Arab victories in the Middle East and North Africa also re-united formerly split poles of Jewish life, and by 732CE Islam ruled Spain and reached Tours in France. Now 90 per cent of the world's Jews lived within the Islamic ambit, a factor that profoundly influenced Jewish history.

THE LIFE OF THE PROPHET

Born in the southern Arabian town of Mecca in 570CE and orphaned at five, Mohammed was raised by his uncle and worked as a shepherd. Legend says that when he was 12 he visited Syria, where his first encounters with Jews and Christians gave him respect for these *ahl al-kitab*, or 'People of the Book'. Illiterate yet canny, in 594CE he acted as a caravan agent for a wealthy, older tradeswoman, Khadija, whom he married.

Mohammed reported his first revelation, of being visited by the Angel Gabriel, in 610CE and began preaching in 613CE. His beliefs won him some converts, but the powerful Quraysh tribal confederation felt

Above The Ka'bah is a granite building that, according to Islamic tradition, dates back to the time of Abraham. Muslims all over the world turn towards it in prayer.

threatened. Mohammed had damned the Quraysh as oppressors, even though he belonged to the Banu Hashim, a minor clan in the tribe. They dominated Mecca's lucrative trade routes and also controlled the Ka'bah, a cube-shaped shrine and object of pagan pilgrimage.

As a trader Mohammed often travelled to the desert oasis of Yathrib – later called Medina – where he encountered Jewish tribes, possibly descendants of refugees from Palestine in Roman times. In 622 Mohammed settled in Medina with his *muhajiroun*, or 'migrants', after Meccan authorities threatened to kill him. He converted the Aws and Khazraj, local majority pagan tribes; founded the first Muslim community; and skilfully arbitrated between rival factions. The Muslim calendar actually begins at 622CE, the year of the *hijra*, or 'immigration';

Left A 16th-century Turkish painting shows the Archangel Gabriel inspiring Mohammed. Traditional Muslim strictures on showing the face of the prophet means his face is flooded with white light.

later Muslim scholars defined the pre-*hijra* period as *jahaliya*, or 'the age of ignorance'. From a Jewish viewpoint, Medina's new constitution allowed them to maintain their religion and guaranteed their financial autonomy. It also decreed that Jews and 'believers' (Muslims) were part of a single community and pledged mutual support if either were attacked. Only Mohammed, though, could authorize war.

Mohammed expected to win over Medina's Jews to his cause. He urged Muslims to pray in the direction of Jerusalem and to assemble on Friday afternoons as Jews prepared for the Sabbath. The *Koran*, or 'reading', affirms strict belief in one God, Allah in Arabic, and is full of ethical precepts partly derived from the Ten Commandments. Islam and Judaism had and still have much in common in terms of practices such as regular prayer, fasting, circumcision and shunning certain foods.

Most of the tales in the Koran are familiar to readers of the Hebrew Bible and Midrash. It was probably first compiled in 650CE during the early caliphate, 18 years after Mohammed died. The Koran is divided into 70 *suras*, or 'chapters', one of which is called Bani Israil (Children of Israel). Moses, or Musa in Arabic, is mentioned in 176 verses, and according to Muslim belief Abraham (Ibrahim) was the first Muslim – literally, 'one who submitted to Allah'. The Koran often repeats that God first revealed Himself to the sons of Israel. All but one of the Koran's chapters opens with 'In the Name of Allah, most merciful and most compassionate'. To believing Muslims, the Koran is perfect and free from contradictions.

RIFT WITH JEWS OF MEDINA
The Jews of Medina initially sided with Mohammed, but then some reputedly mocked him for his imperfect grasp of Jewish texts. Ultimately they rejected his claim to be the last prophet and preferred to keep their original faith. Mohammed changed the direction of prayer, or *qibla*, to Mecca, although Jerusalem was to become the third holiest site in Islam after Mecca and Medina. Mohammed had a number of disputes with Jewish tribes, including the Banu Qunayqa (who he expelled from Medina), the Banu Nadir and the Banu Qurayza. After conquering the oasis of Khaybar, he married Saffiya bint Huyay bin Akhtab, daughter of the executed Jewish sheikh of the Banu Nadir.

Mohammed also overcame many non-Jewish tribes. In 630CE he attacked Mecca and stripped the Quraysh of power. The Koran reports several alliances between Jews and early Muslims. One Hadith, or 'saying of the prophet', praised a brave Jewish general who fought for Mohammed. In another Hadith, the prophet upbraided Muslims who mocked Jewish converts over their origins. Later Muslims often invoked Khaybar, whenever tension rose with Jewish subjects. Jews were largely expelled from central Arabia after the Khaybar battle yet remained untouched in other areas where Arabs adopted Islam, especially in Yemen.

Mohammed died suddenly in 632CE, without an obvious successor in place. Widespread tribal rebellion erupted, although it was stemmed when Abu Bakr was chosen as caliph (*khalif*, or 'God's deputy') and re-imposed Islamic government over Arabia. Omar ibn al-Khatib succeeded Abu Bakr in 634, and over ten years subjugated Syria, Palestine, Egypt, Mesopotamia and Persia. Vastly more Jews than had ever lived in Arabia now found themselves under Arab rule.

The pace of the Arab conquest was astonishing. Desert nomads forced the Byzantine empire back into

Above Mohammed, the founder of Islam, with his father-in-law Abu Bakr, who became caliph when Mohammed died.

its Anatolian heartland, while Persia dissolved entirely as an independent political unit. Most of all, Islam galvanized the Arab people and gave them a sense of unity, pride and identity that they never had before.

Some Jews and Christians converted, but most kept their original faiths. Formally, Muslims tolerated them as 'people of the book' and held them in higher esteem than pagans and idolaters. Moreover, the Koran stated that there should be 'no compulsion in religion', though certain overzealous Arab commanders ignored this stricture.

In practice, Arab leaders probably considered Jews less threatening than Christians, who they feared harboured loyalties to the Byzantine foe. Generally the Arabians were pragmatic; instead of antagonizing local populations, they employed them as builders, administrators, teachers and traders. They sought to consolidate their expanded borders and came to respect the more settled and refined cultures of the Levant. Overall, Jews fared better under early Islam than they did in the Europe of the day.

Jews Between Rival Caliphates

THE DRAMATIC ARAB CONQUEST OF PALESTINE, PERSIA AND NORTH AFRICA UNITED MOST OF WORLD JEWRY UNDER MUSLIM RULE. GENERALLY, JEWS WERE PROTECTED, PROVIDED THEY PAID TAXES.

Above A 7th-century CE mosaic from a shrine in the courtyard of the Umayyad Mosque in Damascus. The date palm may represent the tree of life in the garden of Paradise.

From the outset, Muslims were uncertain how to treat Jews and Christians. 'To you be your religion, and to me my religion', runs one Koranic verse. On the other hand, certain Koran verses suggest that Muslims should fight non-believers, including Jews and Christians. The Koran also chides Jews for spurning the prophets.

MILITARY TRIUMPH

The question of other monotheist religions sharpened when Muslims came to rule over millions of Christians and Jews after Mohammed's death in 632CE. In fact, the second Caliph, Omar, acquired more territory more quickly than anyone before in history. His camel-borne fighters struck north and conquered large parts of Sassanid Persia in 634CE. He then swung south and took Damascus in 635CE and Jerusalem in 637CE. Egypt fell in 640CE and by 650CE all of Persia and Iraq were in Arab hands. Within decades warriors from the Arabian hinterland controlled the entire Middle East and North Africa, and by 717CE had added northern India and most of Spain to their realm.

Jews in Palestine and Babylonia were glad to be rid of Byzantine domination and Persian caprices, yet they also recalled how severely Mohammed had treated Arabian Jews in Khaybar. Most, though, welcomed Arabs as fellow Semites and followers of a monotheistic faith.

DIVISIONS IN ISLAM

The size of the Arab victory dissuaded defeated peoples from rebelling. Meanwhile, the Muslim *umma*, or 'community of believers', was divided over how to choose a successor to Mohammed. They settled on having a caliph, literally God's 'deputy', as a combined spiritual and political leader.

Sunni Muslims, Islam's majority trend, called the first four caliphs – Abu Bakr, Omar, Othman and Ali ibn Abi Talib – the righteously guided ones. However, the latter's followers claimed that the Sunni were impostors, and spawned a dissident Shia party after Ali was murdered in 661CE and his son in 680CE, both in Iraq. This clash began the Sunni–Shia schism that persists today.

Another division was cultural and geographic in nature. After Ali died, Mu'awiya, governor of Damascus, established the Umayyad Caliphate and moved Islam's centre from the Arabian Peninsula to Damascus. He employed Christian officials and set up *diwans*, 'Byzantine-modelled bureaucracies', to run a realm from Egypt to Iran. He also introduced hereditary leadership, which earlier Muslims had rejected.

PACT OF OMAR

The 622CE constitution of Medina protected Jews but did not cover rule by Muslims of non-Muslim majorities adequately. One of the first caliphs, Omar, conquered

Left Map of the Umayyad Caliphate showing how the centre of Islam moved from Arabia to the old 'fertile crescent', traversing the edge of the Mediterranean.

Above A 15th-century Syrian artwork of the Umayyad mosque, Damascus, built by Caliph al Walid I, 706–15CE.

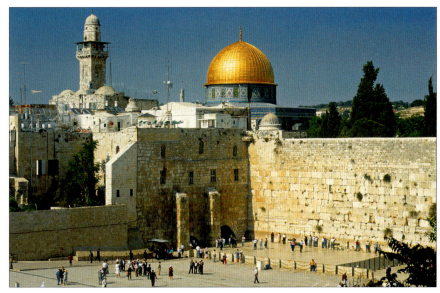

Above The Dome of the Rock, built on the Temple Mount, rises behind the Western Wall in Jerusalem.

Jerusalem, then humbly entered the city on foot and in 637CE signed a treaty with Patriarch Sophronius guaranteeing Christian freedom of worship. The caliph overturned Christian restrictions by allowing 70 Jewish families to move to the city. Omar's successors built the magnificent Dome of the Rock in 692CE and completed the nearby Al Aqsa mosque in 715CE.

The Umayyad Caliph Omar II in 717CE issued a second 'Pact of Omar', which formalized the concept of the tolerated *dhimmi*, or 'protected ones', essentially Jews, Christians and Zoroastrians. *Dhimmi* gained military protection in return for paying a *jizya* (poll tax).

POLITICS AND ECONOMICS

Islamic jurists began dividing the world conceptually into *Dar al-Harb*, or the non-Muslim 'house of war', and *Dar al-Salam*, or Muslim-ruled 'house of peace'. As conditions changed, so did the law. Intermediate categories emerged, like *Dar al-Ahd*, or 'abode of agreement'; and *Dar al-Dhimmi*, or 'zone of tolerance'. These formulations allowed Muslims to live in peace within Christian majority societies, and also permitted Muslim rulers to forge pacts with non-Muslim regimes.

Under the Umayyad Caliphate, which began in 661CE, the ruler became a more political and less spiritual figure. Practically speaking, Umayyads worried that tax revenue from the *jizya* would fall if too many *mawali*, or 'non-Arabs', converted. The land tax forced most Jews to abandon farming and flock to cities, where they were continuing to prosper as officials and craftsmen.

ABBASID RULE

Eventually the Umayyad Caliphate was overturned in 750CE by the Abbasids, a coalition of religious revivalists and *mawali* non-Arabs, who in 754CE made Baghdad their capital instead of Damascus. Abbasid rule coincided with the Jewish geonic period (690–11th century), named after the Geonim, the heads of the rabbinic academies in Babylonia. Gaon meant 'pride of the community'. It is likely that talmudic practices affected the way Muslims developed their own law, the *sharia*. Under Caliph Harun al-Rashid (786–809CE) the Jewish exilarch's office grew in pomp and stature to unimagined levels. However, Jewish life in Jerusalem declined when Damascus lost ground to Baghdad in distinct Mesopotamia.

SAADIA GAON

The greatest figure of the geonic age, Saadia Gaon was born in Fayum, Egypt, in 882CE. Saadia wrote a fearsome polemic against Karaite Jews, who rejected the Talmud and rabbinate. He translated the Bible into Arabic, opening it up to Arabic-speaking Jews; and he wrote one of the most comprehensive Jewish prayer books. Most famously he authored *Beliefs and Opinions*, regarded as the first systematic Jewish theology. Like contemporary Arab thinkers, Saadia argued that there were two ways to truth – reason and revelation (in his view, via the Torah). Saadia synthesised Jewish tradition, Greek rationalism and Muslim Mu'tazili speculative theology. He also helped 'cleanse' Judaism of superstitions, and his work still influences Jewish thought.

Karaites and Khazars

KARAITES REJECTED RABBINICAL POWER AFTER 760CE; TRIBES IN RUSSIA CALLED KHAZARS ADOPTED JUDAISM 80 YEARS LATER. LARGELY VANISHED TODAY, BOTH GROUPS REVOLUTIONIZED JEWISH HISTORY.

The talmudic dictum of 'building a fence around the Torah' helped rabbis maintain their role as arbiters of Jewish life. Yeshivas gained specific regions of control; their *gaon* (head) could appoint judges and impose or suspend a *herem* (religious ban) on transgressors. However, in the late 8th century a new movement from within the body of Jewish believers arose to challenge their authority.

BIRTH OF KARAISM

Anan ben David, a Babylonian Jew of Davidic descent, in effect declared war on Rabbanites (rabbis and their followers), allegedly after he failed to become the exilarch in *c*.760CE. Anan galvanized dormant dissident groups such as the Essenes and Sadducees, as well as schismatics led by Abu 'Isa and Yudghan in Babylonia, and Serene in Syria.

Below Karaite Jews in Odessa, from Anatole Demidoff's Voyage dans la Russie méridionale, *1854.*

Karaites argued that the Talmud had taken Jews down a false path; the only true source of Judaism, they said, was the Torah. Adherents followed its literal reading, insisting that Jews celebrate the Sabbath in the dark and not drink wine after the Temple's demise. They bowed in prayer as Muslims and biblical figures did, kept a different calendar and allowed the eating of milk and meat together.

Anan ben David's *Book of Precepts*, written *c*.770CE, considered astronomy to be witchcraft, recommended long fasts and rejected doctors and medicines because Anan reasoned that God was the only healer. Later Karaite leaders overturned his wilder views, some calling Anan 'chief of the fools'. But all Karaites maintained his core rejection of rabbinic authority.

KARAITE SEPARATISM

The Karaites gained converts when their clerics argued with the rabbis, and exploited resentment against the political clout and elitism of the yeshivas, or 'Talmudic academies'. They called themselves 'roses' compared to the rabbinical 'thorns'. Karaite authors such as Sahl al-Masliah, Yefet ben Ali, Moses Dar'i and the 15th-century poet Abraham ha-Rofe transformed Jewish literature. They adopted advanced Arab models, and replaced Aramaic with Arabic as the default secular language to holy Hebrew. But when they determined practices according to a code called the *sevel ha-yerushah* (yoke of tradition), Rabbanites mocked them for rejecting the 'man-made' Talmud, only to recreate their own tendentious oral laws.

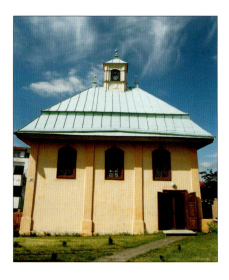

Above Karaite synagogue, Trakai, Lithuania. In the 1500s a group of Karaite Jews were invited to settle in Trakai by Grand Duke Vytautas.

The Karaites saw Diaspora existence as tragic and called for a return to the Land of Israel. Between the 9th and 11th centuries they probably outnumbered Rabbanites in Jerusalem, where they followed ritual purification rites and prayed for redemption at the city gates. Karaism spread to Fez and the Draa Valley

THE KUZARI

Judah Halevi (1086–1145) wrote a book that immortalized Khazaria. *The Kuzari* was an imagined dialogue between King Bulan and a rabbi in which the pagan monarch chose Judaism over Christianity, Islam and Greek philosophy.

Originally published in Arabic and later translated into Hebrew, the book was really a polemic in favour of Jewish beliefs and a lament for Jews in the Diaspora. Halevi depicted the condition of exile as a double bind. Many Jews suffered during the Crusades that raged in his lifetime. As he wrote: 'Seir and Kedar [i.e. Christendom and Islam] may fight their wars but we are the ones who fall'.

in Morocco, Spain, eastern Persia, Byzantine Asia Minor, and later to the Balkans, Russia and Poland. Invariably, Karaites lived among other Jews, but separate from them. Their spiritual leaders were *hakhamim*, or 'wise men', and their house of worship was the *kenesa*.

OUTPOSTS OF KARAITES

One of the most unusual and resilient Karaite communities lived on the Crimea. The Karaim were probably Turkic or Tatar tribesmen who converted to Karaism.

In 1392 Grand Duke Vytautas of Lithuania transplanted large numbers of Karaim to Vilnius and Trakai. There some grew wealthy from trade, and others became renowned scholars. Encouraged by their eccentric 19th-century leader, Abraham Fircovitch, the Karaim called themselves 'gentiles of Mosaic persuasion', thus absolving themselves from Tsarist charges against Jews for killing Jesus.

Small Karaite communities still exist in New York, Lithuania, Israel and, until recently, Cairo. However, polemics against them by Saadia Gaon and their own lack of cohesion, due to reverence for individualist interpretations and responsibilities, explain why they never overcame the Rabbanites. Their number dwindled from an alleged 40 per cent of all Jews to a few dozen thousand today. In 2007, however, Karaites in San Francisco celebrated their sect's first conversion ceremony since 1465, raising talk of a revival as other Jews sought alternatives to rabbinic authority.

KHAZARS CHOOSE JUDAISM

Not far from Crimea, on the estuary of the River Volga to the Caspian Sea, existed a Turkic people called the Khazars. What began as a small khanate in 652CE grew into an empire to rival the Caliphate to the south and the Rus (proto-Russians) to the north. Their royal court converted to

Judaism around 838, and their population apparently became Jewish too. Khazars rejected St Cyril's attempt to turn them to Christianity, and by the 10th century many Khazar documents were written in Hebrew.

During its heyday Khazaria formed a buffer between Christian Byzantium and Muslim powers. The empire derived wealth from its location along the silk road, and enjoyed a reputation for religious tolerance at home, while forcing tributes from neighbouring tribes, the Huns, Bulgars, Slavs and Magyars. The Khazar empire crumbled quickly towards the latter part of the 10th century, assailed by eastern Slavs and

Above Karaite synagogue, Yevpatoria, Ukraine. After Russia annexed the Crimea in 1783, Yevpatoria became a residence of the Hakham, spiritual ruler of the Karaites.

the Rus from Kiev (ironically, a city they may have founded). Khazars were probably dispersed and some suppose that this ethnically non-Semitic people formed the bedrock of the Ashkenazim, who today constitute 85 per cent of world Jewry. Recent evidence has cast doubt on such views, but Khazars undeniably shaped Jewish life in Eurasia.

Below Map of the once-Jewish empire of Khazaria, 10th century CE.

Spain – A Cultural Melting Pot

Over the centuries, Jews played a leading part in the cultural, social and economic life of Spain. They were influential in the Roman, Islamic and Christian periods.

When the Romans invaded the Iberian Peninsula in 218BCE and started settling from 171BCE, they encountered a mixed population including Celts, Phoenicians, Carthaginians and Jewish families who claimed to descend from refugees of the first Temple period.

BEFORE THE ISLAMIC ERA

The Visigoths took over Spain in 551CE, after the fall of Rome, and in 587CE their king Recared (586–601CE) converted to Roman Catholicism, as did his subjects two years later. Christian rulers gave Jews the choice between conversion and expulsion in 613CE, before enslaving those who remained in 694CE. Jewish children were regularly abducted and raised in Christian homes. By the early 8th century CE, however,

Below A cantor in a Spanish Sephardi synagogue reading the Haggadah to illiterate members of the community, 14th century.

Right A street sign labelled 'Judios' commemorates the fact that Cordoba was the centre of Jewish intellectual life in the Golden Age of Spain.

Spain had split into warring fiefdoms, creating a power vacuum that Arab invaders eagerly exploited.

A NEW STATUS FOR SPANISH JEWS

It is said that one Visigoth ruler, Julian, invited Tariq ibn Ziyad to land at Gibraltar in 711CE. The name Gibraltar derives from the Arabic for 'Tariq's mountain'. Leading 7,000 converted Berbers and Arabs from North Africa, Tariq routed the Visigoth armies in the name of the Umayyad Caliph of Damascus, Al-Walid I.

Arabs, or more broadly, 'Moors', conquered Toledo and Cordoba in 711CE, Seville in 712CE and Portuguese Lisbon in 716CE. By 718CE they controlled most of the Iberian Peninsula, which they renamed Al-Andalus (land of the Vandals) with Cordoba as its capital. Moorish forces then crossed the Pyrenees into France, taking Narbonne in 720CE and Autun in 725CE, until the Frankish King Charles Martel stemmed their advance at Tours in 732CE.

Wherever they were victorious the Moors freed Jews from bondage at the hands of Visigoth rulers, and allowed them to reconstitute their communities. North African Jews began following largely Berber armies on to Spanish soil. Meanwhile, indigenous Spanish Jews became translators, advisors and diplomats to Muslim principalities, sometimes interceding with Jewish counterparts in Christian-held territories. They were valued for their facility with languages, long residence in Spain, trading experience and their perceived neutrality, being neither Christian nor Muslim.

RENAISSANCE IN CORDOBA AND TOLEDO

Tariq's men were merely the advance guard for a much larger influx of North African Muslims. They imported irrigation techniques and crops such as rice and oranges from the Middle East, so that Cordoba flourished economically and grew into a city of 100,000 inhabitants, the largest in Europe. Spanish Muslims subdued Christian strongholds in the north and turned them into feudal holdings.

Events in distant Syria were soon to influence Spain. When the Abbasids overthrew the ailing Umayyads there in 750CE, one dynastic survivor, Abd al-Rahman I, fled to Cordoba, displaced the local ruling al-Fihri family, and proclaimed himself Emir (prince) in 756CE. Umayyads reigned in Spain until 1031, and reconfigured the social mosaic by importing cohorts from Jordan, Palestine and Damascus, and implanting them in distinct *junds*, or 'military colonies', in Iberia.

Increasingly, Spain became the cultural centre of the Muslim world and Jews contributed significantly to secular society. Their scholars translated Arabic texts into Spanish, Provençal and French, and rendered Hebrew and Greek works into Arabic. Hebrew literature also blossomed, while Latin scholarship declined, even among clerics. The Jews of Toledo contributed to mathematics, medicine, geography, poetry, botany and philosophy. The introduction of Arabic numerals and the Indian concept of zero encouraged not only the invention of algebra, but also an increasingly sophisticated commercial and banking system.

HISDAI IBN SHAPRUT

Scholars dispute when the 'golden age' truly began, but for Jews it seemed well under way in 929 when Hisdai ibn Shaprut was appointed physician to Caliph Abd al-Rahman III (891–961CE). He soon became director of customs and chief diplomat. Using his mastery of Greek and Latin, he negotiated with Abbot Johannes, emissary of Otto I, the Holy Roman Emperor, and persuaded the Christian kings of Leon and Navarre in northern Spain to sign peace treaties with the caliph.

Within his own community, ibn Shaprut was regarded as a *nagid*, or 'religious leader'. He created a centre for Jewish spiritual studies and a yeshiva, or 'academy', headed by Moses ben Hanokh of southern Italy. These institutions attracted immigrants from the East, loosened Spanish Jewry's bonds with Iraq, and supported poets and scholars such as the linguist Dunash ibn Labrat and the lexicographer Menahem ibn Seruq.

Abd al-Rahman III transformed his Emirate into a Caliphate, and ibn Shaprut served his successor, al-Hakim II (985–1021CE), as foreign affairs advisor. In 970CE al-Hakim founded a magnificent library in Cordoba called 'the jewel of the world'. He also expanded mosques, public baths, orchards, courtyards and aqueducts that served half a million people. Ibn Shaprut could, however, be despotic, as was his successor as *nasi*, or 'communal leader', Jacob ibn Jau, a wealthy silk manufacturer. Both owed their status to royal approval, and were generous benefactors to the poor.

THE SEPHARDIM

Spanish Jews came to call themselves Sephardim, after Sepharad, the name of a biblical site, which they designated as Spain. They spoke an Arabic dialect in Muslim areas and a Judeo-Spanish language called Judezmo or Ladino in Christian areas; they wrote both in Hebrew characters.

Logically, the collapse of the Hispanic Umayyad dynasty in 1031 should have marked the end of cultural advances. Anarchy prevailed as the *ta'ifa*, or smaller Muslim 'party kings', fought vicious turf wars. Jewish insecurity was highlighted when on 30 December 1066 an irate Muslim mob stormed Granada's royal palace and killed the unpopular Jewish vizier along with 1,500 Jewish families.

Above The Jewish quarter of Girona in Spain is criss-crossed with winding streets and narrow flights of stone stairs.

Yet such massacres were aberrations. Arguably the division of power between petty fiefdoms encouraged more diverse patronage of the arts and sciences. And this trend favoured talented citizens, no matter their ethnicity or faith.

Below Spain in the 10th century under the Umayyad dynasty, showing the kingdoms of Leon and the Franks.

Rashi and the Jews of France

RABBI SHLOMO YITZHAKI, OR SOLOMON BEN ISAAC, BETTER KNOWN BY HIS HEBREW ACRONYM 'RASHI', IS REGARDED AS THE GREATEST EXEMPLAR OF EARLY ASHKENAZI JUDAISM, AND HIS WORDS HAVE GUIDED GENERATIONS.

Born in Troyes, the capital of Champagne province, in 1040, Rashi lived during a period of new-found confidence for European Jews who no longer depended solely on edicts from Babylonia to run their lives.

RASHI'S WORK

Rashi returned from studying in Mainz and Worms to found his own yeshiva (academy) in Troyes in 1067. His commentary on the Torah is still unparalleled for its clarity, thoroughness and accessibility for ordinary readers. He synthesized earlier sages' arguments when writing on the Talmud, imbuing his words with a passionate moral spirit that draws on consoling passages from the *aggadah*, or 'sayings'. Rashi also drew on knowledge gleaned during his travels, and his interest in buildings, food, politics and economics. Some say he arrested a trend towards clerical elitism in Judaism and thus helped to 'democratize' the faith. He was also one of the first European Jews whose works were studied by the Sephardim of Muslim Spain.

Rashi built on foundations laid by predecessors, such as Rabbenu Gershom ben Judah of Mayence (960–1028CE) – the 'Light of the Exile'. He reinforced Gershom's ruling to outlaw polygamy, a practice that Sephardi and Babylonian Jews allowed, though seldom carried out. Such rulings marked a distinction between the three branches of Jewry.

Ashkenazi Jewry was still in its infancy and heavily influenced by rites from southern Italy. Their practices were intermingled with superstitions and coloured by popular tracts such as the 10th-century CE Josippon Chronicle, a history from Adam to the age of Titus. *Minhag*, or 'local custom', differed, but generally Ashkenazi, Sephardi and Babylonian rabbis ensured that *halakha*, or 'essential religious law', stayed in harmony. An unusual feature of early medieval Jewry was the extent to which rabbis would travel to meet and debate with their colleagues, despite the fierce wars that were often fought between their home nations.

Since Charlemagne's day, urbanized Jews had established themselves as local financiers and international merchants. They generally got on well with local Christians and often formed the vanguard of new colonies. Yet while the Frankish king Louis the Pious (814–40CE) particularly favoured Jews and their mercantile skills, Archbishop Agobard of Lyons (769/79–840CE) wished to end their role in slave trading – a practice still common in Europe, and not condemned by any of the three sister faiths at the time.

PRAGMATIC SOLUTIONS

Rashi's *responsa*, or 'replies to legal questions', paint a colourful, informative picture of Jewish occupations in 11th-century northern France and the Rhine River Valley. His replies con-

Above The Rashi synagogue in Worms. He was the outstanding figure of early medieval Western Jewry.

Below Savants at the Table of Maimonides. *From left: Joseph Caro, Isaac Alfasi, Maimonides, Jacob ben Asher and Rashi. From a Passover Haggadah.*

cerned particular cases but established principles on sensitive issues. He was known for his devotion to *peshut*, or 'the plain meaning of biblical texts and Talmudic edict', and warned against needless arguments and mystical excesses.

Certainly Rashi was a pragmatic community leader; for instance, he strove to find means by which Jews could lend on interest to one another, which Jewish law until then had forbidden. Often his responsa recommended making transactions through a gentile intermediary. Innovative and flexible, Rashi championed the independence of Jewish communities from each other. Most daringly, he permitted community councils to cancel or ignore 'decisions made by the ancients (i.e. prophets and sages) according to the needs of the time'.

DESCENDANTS OF RASHI

Rashi was so influential that to this day he has a separate column on every Talmud page devoted to his commentaries. The column is written in a distinctive semi-cursive hand, called 'Rashi script', although Rashi probably never used it.

Rashi's three learned daughters, Yocheved, Miriam and Rachel, helped him collate his copious writings and engaged him in constant debate. He insisted that his girls read and study, and thus set an example to more patriarchal or chauvinist households. Yocheved's and Miriam's husbands and sons became known as the Tosafists (addition-makers), the most famous of whom was Jacob ben Meir, the Rabbenu Tam. They, too, have a small column appended to the Talmud; their methods resemble those of Christian scholastics, who were just beginning to develop at the earliest European universities.

ERUPTION OF VIOLENCE

Networks of mutual aid seem to have shielded Jews from external problems, for while western Europe was wracked by famine for much of the 10th and 11th centuries, there is little hint that the Jews of the region suffered more than other groups.

Left An illustrated copy of the first page of Rashi's commentary on the Pentateuch, produced in Italy, 1396.

Above Pope Urban II declares the first Crusade at the Clermont Synod, 1095. German woodcut, c.1480.

Conditions deteriorated during Rashi's lifetime, when, after 1095, Christian Crusaders sent out by the Pope to capture the Holy Land killed Jews along the way, often aided by angry mobs. Jews were offered the choice of conversion or death. How should they react? On the one hand life was sacred and Jewish law regarded suicide as a desecration of God's name; on the other, martyrdom would strike a stand. In one hymn Rashi demanded that the Torah assert itself: 'If there be no Israel [Jewish people] to sing, thou art indeed silenced in every mouth and throat'. He prayed to see the Crusaders expelled from the Holy Land 'in blazing wrath'. At the same time, Rashi respected Christian zeal, and urged Jews to treat kindly those who had chosen conversion over death.

CHAPTER 5

FROM THE GOLDEN AGE TO THE INQUISITION

From the 8th century CE and for some 700 years thereafter, Spain displaced Palestine and Babylon as the central focus of Jewish life. The key that unlocked Jewish creativity was the invasion of Iberia by Arab and Berber soldiers, marching under the banner of Islam. Muslim rulers brought intellectual curiosity, economic vigour and aesthetic sensibilities that strongly influenced Christians and Jews. The 'Golden Age' of Sephardi Jewry produced great sages, linguists, scientists, physicians, diplomats, mapmakers, astronomers and mystics.

Christians reconquered the Spanish Peninsula, and in 1095 the Vatican ordered the Crusades, which soon reached Jerusalem. Jews suffered in the conflicts between Islam and Christendom, and anti-Semitic feeling reached a pinnacle when Jews were expelled from Spain in 1492. However, intrepid communities had planted seeds for survival all over the world in Norman England, Ottoman Turkey, a newly established Poland and even China and Ethiopia.

Opposite Alhambra Palace, Granada. Isabella and Ferdinand flew flags there in 1492, marking the defeat of Muslim Spain and heralding the eclipse of Jewish life on the peninsula.

Above A beautiful illuminated page from the Barcelona Haggadah of 1350, showing a synagogue service in medieval Spain.

THE GOLDEN AGE OF SPAIN

A UNIQUE CONFLUENCE OF CULTURES IN MUSLIM-RULED SPAIN INSPIRED AN EXTRAORDINARY PERIOD OF JEWISH CREATIVITY. SPANISH JEWS BECAME A BEACON FOR ALL OTHER JEWISH COMMUNITIES.

The phrase 'Renaissance man' could have been invented for Samuel HaNagid, but for the fact that he lived in Muslim Spain 500 years before the Renaissance of Catholic Italy.

SAMUEL HANAGID
Born into a Levite family in 993CE, Samuel was steeped in Jewish theology, yet also studied the Muslim Koran and spoke and wrote Arabic and Latin. In time he was elected *nagid* (prince) of Granada's Jewish community and served two successive Caliphs as *vizier* (chief minister).

Samuel was an accomplished poet, philologist, trader, rabbi, diplomat and benefactor. He was a brilliant battlefield commander, winning victories for his Muslim patrons, and becoming the first true Jewish military hero in centuries. Known as Ibn Naghrela in Arabic, Samuel distinguished himself as a fine poet. His remit spread far beyond the boundaries of Spain, to Ifriqiya (Tunisia), Egypt and Iraq.

SUCCESSFUL SUBJECTS
Along with thousands of Jews, Samuel fled Cordoba in 1013 when Berbers attacked and provoked a civil war. In 1025 he became vizier to the king and later to the king's son, Badis. Samuel was an acute political observer. He wrote of the mature state in lines that anticipated the 14th-century Arab founder of sociology, Ibn Khaldun: 'When it grows full and handsome and ripe, from the tree it will certainly fall.'

Samuel had a considerable religious impact: he published an everyman's guide to the Talmud, and he commissioned dozens of scribes to produce copies of *halakhic* works which he disseminated across the Mediterranean. Samuel supported indigent Jews and struggling students. The best ruler, he wrote in one poem, was 'he who forgives his people's misdeeds and toils for the good of the poor'. Berbers, Arabs and Jews all mourned Samuel when he died in 1056.

Yet was Samuel HaNagid an exception to the rule? Outside the royal courts, Muslim subjects often envied Jews for flaunting the restrictions on *dhimmis* (non-Muslim subjects of a state governed by Sharia law) and 'favouring their own'. At times Jews suffered collectively because of such anger: in late 1066 a mob assassinated HaNagid's son Joseph, the new vizier at Granada's Alhambra palace, and killed as many as 4,000 Jews.

Below The 'Carpet page', 1260, from the Damascus keter, one of the earliest manuscripts of the Hebrew Bible that survives from Spain.

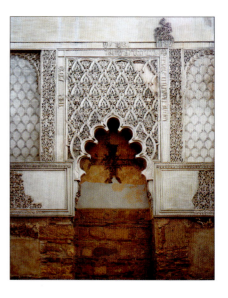

Above The Cordoba synagogue shows the fusion of Jewish, Arab and Iberian cultures that symbolized the Golden Age.

THE INFLUENCE OF ARABIC
Spanish Jews were by no means unique in their exposure to the Arabic language or tenets of Muslim faith. The archbishop of Seville, for instance, had the Christian Bible translated into Arabic because so few of his flock knew Latin. Christian scholars from France, Germany and England reportedly learnt Arabic and travelled to Seville and Toledo to study the classics and Arab algebra, geometry and trigonometry, often from Jewish tutors.

Religious Jews beyond Spain also drew on flourishing secular traditions. The writings of Ibn Sina (980–1037CE), a Persian philosopher known in the West as Avicenna, profoundly influenced both Jews and Muslims. The playful Arabic literary style *adab* helped mould Hebrew poetry and even the structure of the Hebrew language.

MUSLIM SPAIN FALTERS
After the Umayyad Caliphate collapsed in 1031 Muslim Spain split into a number of smaller kingdoms. Christian kingdoms to the north exploited Muslim divisions and re-conquered formerly Christian towns, notably Toledo in 1085. The next year Morocco's powerful and religiously

austere Almorabid Berbers came to the aid of Andalucians. Jewish and Muslim Spaniards were now caught between southern Berbers and northern Christians.

The Almorabids were displaced by the Almohads, and these were defeated by the Christians in 1212, effectively ending their rule over Spain. Cordoba fell in 1236 and Seville in 1248, leaving Granada as the last Muslim outpost on the peninsula.

SOLOMON IBN GABIROL

One of the greatest scholars of the period was Solomon Ibn Gabirol. Born in Malaga in about 1022, he introduced Neo-platonic ideas to Europe, where he had more influence over Christian scholastics than on his fellow Jews in Spain. His masterpiece *Mekor Hayyim*, or 'Fountain of Life', explained the universe as consisting of three elements: God, the material world, and the omnipresent will as the bridge between the two. Ibn Gabirol also wrote in Arabic two powerful yet accessible guides to ethics, *Kitab islah al-akhlaq* (Improving the Qualities of the Soul) and *Mukhtar al-jawahir* (Choice of Pearls).

The Golden Age was also stimulated by scholarly cross-pollination with Ashkenazi Jews. Jacob ben Asher (1270–1343) was born in Germany

Above Solomon Ibn Gabirol, outstanding 11th-century Andalucian Jewish poet, philosopher and moralist.

around 1270 and moved to Spain in 1303. He wrote the *Arba'ah Turim*, or 'Four Rows', a synthesis of the views of Alfassi, Maimonides and earlier Talmud writers.

Abraham Ibn Ezra (1093–1167) typified the spirit of the age. A Spanish-born rabbi, poet, astronomer, astrologer, doctor and thinker, he believed the 'angel that mediates between man and his God is intelligence'. He left Granada when the illiberal Alhomads came to power, and then wandered through France, Italy and England, where he is thought to have died. A crater of the moon is named after him. Ibn Ezra questioned the meaning of exile. He was not the only Jew to dream of an eventual return to Zion. In 1141 Judah Halevi lamented: 'My heart is in the east, but my body stays in the west'; late in life he went to Palestine.

The Catalan rabbi and sage, Moshe ben Nahman Geronti, or Nahmanides (1194–1270) settled in Jerusalem in 1267, where he built the Ramban synagogue, so named after his familiar acronym. Almost single-handedly he re-established Jewish communal life in the holy city, which has continued since.

JEWS IN CHRISTIAN SPAIN

Nahmanides argued that Arab and Greek philosophy should be equal. He also respected Ashkenazi scholarship. In his book *Torat Ha-Adam*, the Law of Adam, the Ramban chastized other rabbis for denying the everyday experiences of pleasure and pain. He argued that humans have a special divine soul that places them above animals. He denied the truth of secular philosophy, and sought mystical meanings in biblical text, as well as professing to believe in miracles and in God's providential plans.

The Ramban lived under Christian rule, mostly at peace, until in 1263 he was summoned to defend Judaism in a 'disputation' in Barcelona. He was questioned by priests anxious to use the Talmud to prove the truth of Christianity. The Ramban debated freely and won the king's admiration – which was certainly not the case in trials in France and Germany around that time. But with hindsight, the Spanish tolerance disguised mounting prejudices against Jews and Muslims, which ultimately led to the 1492 expulsion of the Jews.

Left A synagogue in Fez, Morocco, a city which gave refuge to many Jews fleeing Spain in 1492.

Kabbalah–Jewish Mystical Tradition

KABBALAH IS A MOVEMENT THAT DEVELOPED IN THE GOLDEN AGE OF SPAIN. NOWADAYS THE BEST-KNOWN JEWISH MYSTICAL PATH, THE KABBALAH (MEANING 'TRADITION' OR 'RECEPTION') IS AN ESOTERIC MYSTICISM.

Most forms of mysticism aim to form a perfect union with God and break the bonds of the material world. The same is true of Kabbalah. Two elements, though, set it apart from other belief systems. One is the idea that humans can help God repair a fractured world, a process called *tikkun olam*. The second idea is that the deepest mystical truths are embedded in the Bible and Talmud. Only one who knows these texts can hope to master Kabbalah. Practitioners seek to restore serenity to the individual soul by communing with God. The Kabbalah is also invoked when Jews address ethical issues, such as 'repairing the world' through everyday acts of *hesed*, or 'loving kindness'.

REACTION TO TURMOIL
Some note that Jewish mysticism typically flourishes two or three generations after a catastrophe. Kabbalah was often associated with periods of messianic fervour, and political or social insecurity, with adherents scouring its texts for hints of when the final judgement day will come.

EARLY GROWTH
Abraham Abulafia (1240–91) was a particularly compelling Kabbalist. Born in Spain, he travelled to Greece, Malta and Sicily and died in Italy, where he is credited with pioneering 'ecstatic Kabbalah'. His works include *Book of the Righteous*, *Life of the World to Come*, *Light of the Intellect* and *Words of Beauty*. He tried to spread Kabbalistic doctrines to Christians and Muslims. Other, quieter Kabbalists preached a 'practical Kabbalah'. One such trend that came to dominate in the 16th century, with the school of Isaac Luria, which evolved in Palestine during the 16th to the 18th centuries.

Jewish mysticism developed over five periods: the ancient mystics during the writing of the Talmud; the medieval Hasidei Ashkenaz tradition of the Rhineland; the Kabbalah as it developed in 13th–15th century Spain; Isaac Luria's system; and the European Hassidim who were to open up Kabbalah to the masses.

Mystical elements of Kabbalah come from the writings of the prophets and the 2nd-century CE Mishnah. One inspiration behind Kabbalistic thought is the merkavah, or divine chariot, as envisaged by the prophet Ezekiel. Kabbalists have also used Genesis or its midrashic glosses as an inspiration.

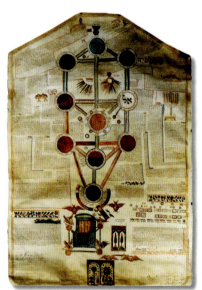

Left A Kabbalistic roll created in Paris, 1604, shows Temple implements and the ten sephirot, *or divine emanations, linked by 32 paths of wisdom.*

Above Ezekiel's vision, which the prophet said he saw in Babylon. The vivid image of a fiery merkavah, *or chariot, inspired later Kabbalists.*

NON-JEWISH INFLUENCE
Secular-minded scholars of Kabbalah detect influences from other traditions, including Gnosticism (with the eternal battle between good and evil); and its Persian religious manifestations, Zoroastrianism and Mazdaism. The Jewish idea of divine emanations in the material world appears to have affinities with the 99 names of God as explained by the Muslim mystical philosopher Al-Ghazali. Hindu and Buddhist models tally with the Jewish tree of life motif, while the Indian Jain religion's diagram of concentric circles of heaven and earth mirrors the Kabbalistic concept of seven worlds.

Kabbalah has in turn influenced Judaism's sister faiths. The Christian mystic and mathematician John Dee of England studied Kabbalah and used its ideas to devise spells, calculate the end-times or dabble in alchemy. Renaissance Christian scholars of Kabbalah included Johannes Reuchlin, Pico della Mirandola and Athanasias Kircher. Kabbalists often explain obscure texts by calculating the numerical value of letters, as do many Muslim Sufis.

KABBALAH – JEWISH MYSTICAL TRADITION

Above The Tree of Life came to epitomize the Kabbalistic world view. From an illuminated Jewish book, northern France, 1290.

THE ZOHAR

By far the best-known mystical text is the Zohar, or 'Radiance'. Part-midrash (midrash means 'searching the scriptures'), part epic poem, the book addresses issues such as good and evil, interceding angels, man's role as master of virtue in bettering creation, the nature of God (part-male and part-female), and how man can ascend by steps to the ultimate 'cause of causes'.

Kabbalists attribute the Zohar to Simeon bar Zakkai of 2nd-century CE Palestine, though it was probably written by Moses de Leon of Spain (1250–1305). Within 50 years of its publication it had spread throughout the Diaspora. It was accepted as 'sacred text'. Zohar verses appear in prayer books, and most leading rabbis, including those deemed rationalist in outlook, have commented on it. Christian scholars saw in certain Zohar passages hints of the holy trinity. According to some traditions no one unmarried, under 40 or female may read the book.

The Zohar was by no means the final mystical text. Later writings include *The Book of the Reed*, *The Wonder* and Moses Cordovero's *Palm Tree of Deborah*. Kabbalistic lore spread from Spain to Provence in the 13th century and received a further boost when, after 1492, Spanish and Portuguese Kabbalists dispersed to Amsterdam, Constantinople and, eventually, Tiberias and Safed.

THE TEN EMANATIONS

Before the Zohar came other works: *Sefer ha-Bahir*, the 'Book of Brightness', which includes mystical divinations with numbers and was published in 12th-century southern France; and *Sefer Yetzira*, the 'Book of Creation', written between the 3rd and 6th centuries CE. The latter addresses the ten *sefirot* or emanations of God's essence, ten being the number of divine perfection. Sometimes these elements are compounded into allied concepts. These are: crown (primordial consciousness), wisdom, love and understanding, mercy and vision, judgement and strength, compassion and symmetry, contemplation, surrender, foundation and memory, and the lower crown or kingdom of accomplishment.

Above Blue, the pacifying colour of the spirit, adorns the tomb in Safed, northern Israel, of 16th-century Kabbalah pioneer Isaac Luria.

TREE OF LIFE

In time Kabbalists devised a diagram called the *Etz Hayyim*, or the 'Tree of Life', on which are draped representations of *sephirot*. They wrote about how the sephirot flowed from one heavenly chamber to another, so as to restore the natural state of harmony. Echoing the Creation is the concept of *tzimtzum*, the expanding power that cracks the shells of the sephirot and releases divine energy.

Right Typifying Kabbalah's current resurgence, worshippers in Tel Aviv perform the tashlich ritual of throwing bread into the sea to cast away past sins.

The First Jews of Eastern Europe

JEWS WELCOMED INVITATIONS TO EASTERN EUROPE FROM SLAVIC RULERS WHO WANTED TO CATCH UP WITH GERMAN NEIGHBOURS AND SAW ENTREPRENEURIAL IMMIGRANTS AS THE ANSWER.

In the summer of 966CE Ibrahim ibn Yacoub, an intrepid Jewish trader and diplomat from Toledo in Spain, set off on a journey into the unknown. Travelling through the furthermost eastern lands of the Holy Roman empire, he arrived in countries we now call Poland and the Czech Republic. This region was in flux. Celts, Huns, Scythians and Goths jostled for control, towns were just being born, and the notion of swapping commodities for money, rather than bartering, was still new.

SETTLEMENT IN POLAND

Ibrahim wrote the first extensive account of Poland. That same year, 966CE, the leader of the newly arrived Polanie tribe, Duke Mieszko I, was baptized into Christianity, an event Poles regard as the birth of their nation. From the start, Jews played a vital part in the Polish story, even if their initial presence was somewhat transient. Jewish traders – Radhanites (medieval Jewish merchants) from Iraq or, like ibn Yacoub, from Spain – used Poland as a thoroughfare along the route linking China and the Orient to Western Europe.

Jews in Poland and Prague, which Ibrahim also visited, were known to sell slaves (hence 'Slavs') to Arabs and Byzantines. They developed a facility for commerce, too, and by 1170 they were running the mint in Warsaw. Jews even made Polish coins with Hebrew inscriptions.

In years to come Poland would grow into the world's largest centre of Jewish life. Some 3.5 million Jews lived in former Polish provinces in 1880 out of a global Jewish population of 7.7 million, yet very little is known about the early settlement.

One theory suggests that Polish Jews descended from Khazar Jews who fled there after the collapse of that Eastern realm. Some think Jewish communities located around Roman camps remained in 'Middle Europe' when the Roman empire collapsed. More likely, Jews poured in from the west. A number fled as persecutions mounted around the year 1000, when Frankish and Germanic Christians enthusiastically expected a second coming of Jesus a millennium after his birth. Anti-Jewish sentiment rose further in the wake of the First Crusade a hundred years later, culminating in the first great expulsion from France in 1182.

PROTECTED STATUS

As to why Jews chose remote Poland, some might have been attracted by its name: *Polin*, Yiddish for Poland, is a pun on the Hebrew expression for 'here you will live'. Poland's early rulers were also notably tolerant to newcomers. In 1203, for instance, they issued a decree allowing Jews to own land in Galicia province, just two years before Pope Innocent III declared that Jews were doomed

Above An old house in Kazimierz, Krakow. Its Star of David testifies to a Jewish presence that began in 1335.

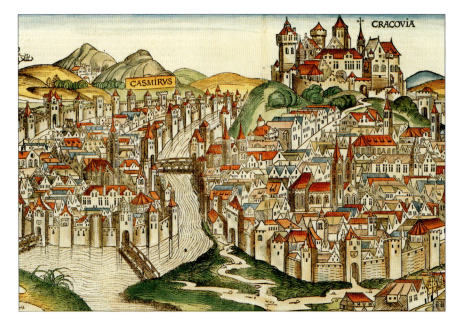

Left The Polish city of Krakow and surrounding hills, from Hartman Schedel's Nuremberg Chronicle, *1493.*

to perpetual servitude owing to the crucifixion of Christ. Polish authorities apparently welcomed literate and industrious Jews as 'agents of modernity' who might drag the Poles out of the dark ages, and allow them to compete with their Germanic neighbours.

Boleslav V the Pious produced a charter to protect Jews in 1264; and Casimir III 'The Great' (1333–70) guaranteed these privileges in 1334. The next year he created a new city for his Jews on an island in the River Vistula, near the capital, Krakow, called Kazimierz. In 1356 Casimir granted Jews autonomy in communal affairs; he extended these rights to the Jews of Lesser Poland and Ukraine in 1367. Privileges were extended by his successor, Grand Duke Vytautas (Vitovt; 1350–1430).

Official persecution began in Poland under King Wladislaus II (1386–1434) after 1399, and Jews found themselves the target of rioters in Krakow in 1407. Kazimierz may well have become Europe's first ghetto in 1494. This *oppidum judaeorum*, or 'Jewish city', was established 22 years before Venetians corralled Jews into a restricted area near iron foundries (*campo gheto*), from which came the term ghetto.

The onset of the Black Death fuelled anti-Jewish sentiment when comparatively few Jews perished, probably because they lived by more hygienic food practices. Economic envy from Christian traders and artisans grew, as did resentment by Catholic clergymen who felt Polish kings showed excessive tolerance to 'non-believers'. Casimir IV the Jagiellonian (1447–92) stemmed attacks on Jews; yet even he felt compelled to issue the Statute of Nieszawa (1454), which abolished ancient Jewish privileges as 'contrary to divine right and the law of the land'.

THE POLISH ASHKENAZ

It is thought that many of the Sephardi Jews expelled from Spain in 1492 eventually went to Poland, where they were probably absorbed into the Ashkenazi community. By the early 16th century, Polish Ashkenazim formed the largest Jewish community in the world. They outnumbered their cousins in the Germano-Frankish Rhineland area, the original 'Ashkenaz'.

Ashkenazim traded with gentiles but kept very much to themselves. They frequented the synagogue, studied the Torah and Talmud, and spoke Yiddish, a vernacular based

Above During the 1348 plague, pogroms in Germany drove many Jews to commit suicide, as depicted in this stylized 1880 woodcut.

on old German with Hebrew additions. After lagging behind Rashi's heirs, Polish scholars, such as Moses Isserles (*c.*1530–72), began rising to the fore.

OUTSIDE POLAND

In other parts of Eastern Europe, Jewish life could be precarious. A church synod in Breslau, chief city of Silesia, ordered Jews to wear special caps in 1267. Dozens were murdered there in 1349, more were expelled in 1360, and 41 Jewish martyrs were burnt at the stake in 1453. In 1421 Jews were imprisoned and forced to leave Austria; that same year a medieval synagogue in Vienna was burnt down together with its congregants. Jews were driven out of Eger in Bohemia in 1430, only months after co-religionists were expelled from Speyer in Germany. Despite setbacks, the seeds were planted for communities that in time became the hub of Jewry around the world.

Left Built in 1270, the Old-New Synagogue of Prague exemplifies a long Jewish presence in Czech lands.

The Age of Maimonides

The greatest of Sephardi polymaths, Moses Maimonides was born in Cordoba. He went on to revive the Egyptian Jewish community and wrote books that still inspire today.

Widely regarded as the greatest Jewish thinker since biblical times, Moses Maimonides (Moshe ben Maimon in Hebrew, and Abu Imran Musa ibn Maimun in Arabic) is also possibly the most enduring medieval philosopher of any faith. He is still studied at Jewish yeshivas, both Ashkenazi and Sephardi; his works are on the core syllabus at Al Azhar in Cairo, the supreme Sunni Muslim college; and he profoundly influenced St Thomas Aquinas, the leading Christian theologian of the Middle Ages.

EARLY LIFE
The story of Maimonides covers several zones – Spain, Morocco, Egypt, Palestine and Yemen – and must also include Christian Europe, which he never visited, but where his books received equal shares of admiration and opposition. An eclectic genius who wrote forward-thinking tracts on all aspects of medicine, he was also a rabbi and talmudic scholar, community leader and judge, philosopher and ethicist, and royal advisor to Caliphs.

Maimonides, often called the Rambam, was born in Cordoba in 1135, the son of a rabbi. At 13 he was forced to flee when Almohads conquered the city. The new rulers decreed that Jews unwilling to convert to Islam would be killed or exiled. For nearly a decade his family wandered from town to town, before settling in Fez, Morocco.

LOGIC AND FAITH
Despite these upheavals and his father's complaints that he was lazy, the 16-year-old Maimonides wrote a brilliant treatise on logic. In later life he called Aristotle his 'first teacher', and the Muslim philosopher Al-Farabi his second. Ibn Sina (Avicenna) was another influence, as was his fellow Cordoban and contemporary, Muslim Ibn Rushd (Averroes) (1126–98).

Yet Maimonides was also a fully committed Jew, who believed Judaism was the highest form of monotheism. His first great work was a commentary on and digest of the 2nd-century CE Mishnah. Next came his 14-volume *Mishneh Torah*, said to be the clearest exposition of the basic tenets of Jewish faith ever written. Composed between 1170 and 1180 in his new home of Egypt, it was a comprehensive and logically organized code of Jewish law written in clear and precise Hebrew. All his other books appeared first in Judeo-Arabic.

GUIDE TO THE PERPLEXED
Even more famous than the *Mishneh Torah* is Maimonides' 'Guide to the Perplexed', first written in Arabic as *Dalalat al-Ha'irin* and translated by Yehuda Ibn Tibbon as *Moreh ha-Nevukhim*. The book is specifically aimed at educated Jews troubled by the disagreements between philosophical learning and the Torah's teachings, but it contains moral insights for all.

Above A contemporary bronze statue of the Rambam, Moses Maimonides, in Cordoba's Jewish Quarter.

Below Arguably the greatest Jewish mind of his time, Maimonides lived in this house in Fez, Morocco, after leaving Spain in 1160.

THE AGE OF MAIMONIDES

Above 'The Guide to the Perplexed', the Rambam's most famous work. Hebrew manuscript title page, Spain, 1356.

Maimonides wrote the first statement of Jewish faith to match those of Christians (the credo) and Muslims (the shahada). These he summarized in 13 core beliefs. Within the Jewish tradition he followed the rationalist path of Philo and Saadia Gaon, and emulated the clarity of Rashi, even if he disagreed with all of them.

THE POWER OF REASON

To Maimonides all prophets had to be philosophers, and prophecy was not confined to Jews. He laboured to show that revelation and all Jewish laws had their foundation in reason. For Maimonides, only a God who transcends the universe could have created it. Later rationalists castigated this approach as contrived, while many rabbis felt it was blasphemous to demand proofs of the divine. Even the supposedly non-philosophical *Mishneh Torah* drew the ire of traditionalists, because it quoted laws without listing the rabbinical arguments that led to them. Rabbis feared

Right Al Hakim Mosque in Fustat, near Cairo, Egypt, where Maimonides lived in the latter part of his life.

that unqualified readers would claim to be experts. Maimonides countered that he had made the Talmud accessible to all and said to his critics: 'I forgive everyone who speaks ill of me through stupidity.'

MEDICAL BREAKTHROUGHS

Maimonides was prone to melancholia and suffered badly for a year, aged 30, when his beloved brother, David, died at sea. He drew on this experience to write a brilliant analysis of depression that is still studied today. His other medical writings are on diet, nutrition, gastroenterology, sexual diseases and fevers. Like his immediate Arab predecessor, Abu Bakr al-Razi (called Rhazes in the West), Maimonides observed patients and their symptoms first hand. Among those in his care was the vizier to the caliph.

HEAD OF EGYPT'S JEWS

Maimonides' Egyptian phase coincided with a political transition in the country. He arrived in Fustat in 1166, having spent several months in Akko (Acre), Tiberias and Jerusalem. In 1171 a Kurdish-origin Muslim, Salah al-Din al-Ayubi (Saladin), overthrew the Shia Fatimid dynasty and restored Egypt to Sunni rule. One of his first acts was to appoint Maimonides as *ra'is al-yahud*, or 'head of the Jews'.

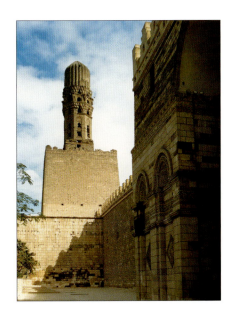

Above Yehuda Ibn Tibbon translated Maimonides' Arabic books into Hebrew. Statue in Granada, erected 1988.

According to legend Saladin's great adversary, King Richard of England, wanted to use Maimonides as his doctor, but the rabbi refused.

LEGACY OF MAIMONIDES

After Maimonides died, in 1204, some rabbis in France began to condemn his works as heretical. In 1232 they persuaded the church authorities of Montpellier to burn copies of his *Guide* and the *Book of Knowledge*. The debate about Maimonides' beliefs simmered in one form or another for decades, even centuries.

In some senses, Maimonides was ahead of his time. However, he never wavered in his faith in God, even if he introduced a strong seam of rational analysis to Judaism. He believed that pursuing truth and seeking God were essentially the same task, and prescribed how to build better societies on earth. In writing about *tzedakah* (charity or justice), Maimonides defined eight stages of giving, with the highest being a donor who employs a poor person or helps him set up his own business, freeing him of the need for aid. This theory is now widely applied.

TO THE FOUR CORNERS OF THE WORLD

AS EARLY AS THE 8TH CENTURY BCE, ISAIAH WROTE OF JEWS IN CUSH, OR ETHIOPIA. SINCE ISAIAH'S TIME DIASPORAS HAVE SPREAD THROUGH CHINA, INDIA AND THE DEEPEST CAUCASUS.

One particularly engaging character of the Jewish Middle Ages was Rabbi Benjamin of Tudela in Spain, who went on pilgrimage to the Holy Land in 1165. He returned home in 1173 having visited 300 cities in Europe, the Middle East and North Africa. His famous book, the *Itinerary*, records Jewish life far and wide. He did not visit every outpost of Jewry, but his accounts bear testimony to the widespread nature of the Diaspora.

ETHIOPIAN JEWS

The Jews of Ethiopia today number more than 127,000. Since the great 'exoduses' of Operation Moses (1984) and Operation Solomon (1991), most now live in Israel. They call themselves Beta Israel (House of Israel) a term they prefer to the familiar but pejorative *Falasha*, or 'stranger'.

Below A 19th-century Ethiopian painting of Solomon receiving gold, ivory and a lion from the Queen of Sheba.

Ethiopia's strong ties with ancient Israel followed a local tradition that said Emperor Haile Selassie was the direct descendant of Menelik, a son born to King Solomon and the Queen of Sheba: thus making Ethiopian royalty the last surviving monarchy from the House of David. Although most Amharic-speaking Ethiopians are Christian, and have been since the earliest days of the faith, one theory suggests many were Jews who converted, hence the similarities between Jewish and Ethiopian Orthodox Christian rites.

The Beta Israel claim to be offspring of Moses, separated during the Exodus, or of the tribe of Dan, which fled southwards through Arabia and across the Red Sea to Africa after the united kingdom divided in the 10th century BCE. Unusually amongst Diaspora Jews, the Beta Israel, who mainly dwelt in the Gondar uplands, used the Ethiopic Ge'ez tongue as their liturgical language, not Hebrew.

Above The intrepid rabbi Benjamin of Tudela riding across the Sahara in a 19th-century engraving by Dumouza.

Despite that, their holy book, the Orit, is essentially identical to earlier sections of the Torah. Also unusually, they knew nothing of the Talmud or later Jewish festivals, like Purim or Hannukah – proof, some say, of their authentic antiquity.

JEWS OF SOUTHERN INDIA

The great Moorish traveller Ibn Battuta (1304–c.1368) wrote of an autonomous hilltop settlement in Malabar, five days' journey from Calicut. Some believe this may refer to one of several known communities dotted around southern India, of which the Jews of Cochin in Kerala state are the most famous. The Cochin Jews, who maintain a now much-visited synagogue, divided themselves into 'white' and 'black' communities. Known for their industriousness, hospitality and cuisine, they have apparently lived alongside Hindus, Christians and, latterly, Muslims for millennia.

JEWS OF KAIFENG

Ibn Battuta also reported entering the Chinese port of Hangzhou through a 'Jews' Gate', and encountering a vibrant Jewish community there. Even earlier, Marco Polo wrote of meeting

Right This village synagogue in Ethiopia's Gondar region once served the Beta Israel Jewish community.

Chinese Jews in Beijing around 1286. It is known that Jews habitually traded up and down the silk road to China. Some must have settled down and they presumably married into local Chinese communities, because for centuries there was a strong Jewish outpost in Kaifeng, Henan province.

The records of the Jesuit missionary and cartographer Matteo Ricci tell how he met Ai Tian, a Jewish mandarin from Kaifeng, in 1605. Westerners had never encountered Jews in the area, and Ricci assumed Ai was Christian. Hearing Jesuit Ricci was a monotheist but not a Muslim, Ai assumed he was Jewish. Ricci later corresponded with the Kaifeng rabbi and produced drawings of his pagoda-like synagogue.

Some Chinese Jews claimed descent from 6th-century BCE Babylonian exiles, and one stone monument dated 231BCE suggests a presence at the time. Certainly Jews and Phoenicians imported Far Eastern goods to Rome and Italy. Later, Jews from Yemen, Persia and Bukhara in Central Asia settled on the south banks of the Yellow River.

Proof of the antiquity of a Jewish presence comes in the form of a business letter written on Chinese paper in Judeo-Persian, dated 718CE. Kaifeng historical records speak of a synagogue, called *libai si*, established in 1163. More details of Jewish history, genealogy and practices appear in stelae, or stone tablets, dated 1489, 1512 and 1663. The middle stele proudly boasts that Jewish soldiers were 'boundlessly loyal' to the Song dynasty emperor of the day.

Below India's oldest synagogue operates in the southern port of Cochin, Kerala, and reflects local architectural influences.

MOUNTAIN JEWS
With a population of 101,000 as of 2004, the so-called Mountain Jews of the Caucasus constitute another rare subset of international Jewry. They call themselves Juhuro, speak a language called Judeo-Tat, differ in many traditions from other Ashkenazi and Sephardi Jews, and for most of their history they lived in Azerbaijan and Dagestan, mainly Muslim areas of the former Soviet Union.

Most Juhuro immigrated to Israel during 1970–90, though some settled in Moscow and the USA. As to their origins, they may descend from hardy Jewish military colonists posted to mountainous regions by Persia's Parthian and Sassanid rulers, or they may be local Tats converted to Judaism. One radical theory states that all Tats were once Jewish, but that most adopted Islam in the Middle Ages. Traditionally farmers and gardeners, the Juhuro were famed for their vineyards, handicrafts and skills as tanners.

JEWS IN MOROCCO
The Berber Jews of North Africa probably descended from local tribes who converted or intermarried with Jews accompanying Roman armies. During the 5th century CE a Jewish community thrived in Mauretania, south of Morocco. Two centuries later Jews escaping persecution in Spain joined them. Legend tells of a Jewish Berber warrior-queen named Kahina who repulsed Muslim Arabs around 680CE.

Many Berbers retained their Judaism after Islam triumphed. The movement caused by the Muslim conquest of Spain linked Iberian Jews to their southern brethren, and the Moroccan-born rabbi Yitzhak Alfassi (1013–73) won renown on both continents for his Torah and Talmud commentary, the Rif.

Morocco again became a haven for refugees after Spanish Christians sacked Seville's Jewish district in 1391. Within 50 years Jews had a special district, or *mellah*, in Fez.

Jews of Norman England

IN 1066, WILLIAM THE CONQUEROR DEFEATED THE SAXONS AT HASTINGS AND IMPOSED NORMAN RULE ON BRITAIN. THIS ALSO INAUGURATED 224 YEARS OF JEWISH SETTLEMENT IN ENGLAND, WHICH ENDED IN TRAGEDY.

The vibrant Jewish community of Normandy, France, had long traded with southern England. So when King William (1027–87) invited the Jewish courtesans of Rouen, the Norman capital, to cross the Channel, many accepted gladly. Jews settled in Oxford, Lincoln, Bath, Norwich and especially London, where Old Jewry road in the City testifies to their medieval presence. Some settled in Ireland, too, and by 1232 Dublin had an established community, while Norwich became home to a small but vibrant Rhineland community.

AN OPTIMISTIC START

Norman England became the best-administered territory in western Europe. As feudal law prevented Jews from owning land or practising any profession besides medicine, they often worked as financiers, bankers and moneylenders – jobs barred to Christians, because Old Testament law forbade lending on interest to fellow believers.

Some Jews grew immensely wealthy and were therefore unpopular when times were hard. For protection they built sturdy stone dwellings. Two in Lincoln are among the earliest English homes to survive, and one may have doubled as a synagogue. Unusually for medieval society, Jewish women often worked in their own right; 10 per cent of Jewish taxpayers were female. Examples include Mildegod of Oxford, a successful innkeeper; and Licoricia, the 13th-century widow of Isaac of York, who lent to King Henry III and helped fund the building of Winchester Cathedral.

ROYAL PROTECTION

William protected his Jewish subjects, and his son and heir, William Rufus (r. 1088–1100), allowed Jews who had converted to return to their faith, against the wishes of Christian clerics. English Jews were generally spared the pogroms that bedevilled their Continental cousins after the Crusades began in 1096. Later King Henry I (r. 1100–35) allowed Jews to live in 26 cities, whereas before they were restricted to just six.

Above Excavated in 2001 in the City of London, this medieval Jewish ritual bath, or mikveh, takes pride of place in London's Jewish Museum.

Below Jewish homes were pillaged by mobs during the reign of England's Richard I. From a painting by Charles Landseer, c.1839.

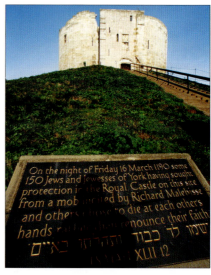

Below Clifford's Tower in York, built by William the Conqueror. Here, Jews tragically met their death in a fire after fleeing a murderous mob in 1190.

Right This anti-Semitic drawing from a 1233 land tax roll shows the Jews of Norwich consorting with demons.

English Jews were unusually creative, even though they probably never numbered more than 16,000. They exported to Europe an Anglo-Norman romance about Sir Bevis of Hampton, which was reincarnated in 1507 as the *Bovo-Bukh*, arguably the first great work of Yiddish secular literature. Whimsical Anglo-Jewish illustrations of the biblical Moses, drawn in the 13th century and now held by the British Library, reveal a society that was pious, cultivated and self-assured. Rabbis Yom Tov of Joigny in York and Jacob of Orleans in London were respected as teachers, community leaders and Talmudic masters.

FROM PROSPERITY TO LIBEL
Jews also prospered under Henry II (reg. 1154–84); for example, when Aaron of Lincoln died in 1186, his 430 debtors owed him a sum equal to three-quarters of the annual revenue of the English exchequer. But conditions worsened as church authorities grew bolder, and prejudice fuelled by Crusader fervour proved more powerful than the law.

A murderous witch-hunt in Norwich in 1144 was the first of many European 'blood libels' that accused Jews of ritually killing Christian children. Another occurred at Bury St Edmunds in 1181 after a debt dispute between Jewish lenders and the local abbey. Similar outrages took place in Gloucester (1168), Bristol (1183), Winchester (1191), London (1244) and Lincoln (1255).

Crusader passions bred more violence, as in 1189, when Jews carrying gifts to Richard I's coronation were denied entry and beaten.

Right Reputedly the oldest domestic building in Britain, Jews House in Lincoln dates from 1158.

The fiasco sparked riots in which many London Jews died, including Rabbi Jacob of Orleans. Richard the Lionheart executed three ringleaders, but new atrocities occurred when he left to fight the Third Crusade. The worst took place in March 1190 when mobs sacked Jewish houses in York and forced nearly the entire community to take refuge in Clifford's Tower. For several days some 500 Jews defended themselves valiantly, until they finally killed themselves, emulating their ancestors in Masada, Judea, a thousand years earlier.

Even Jews who accepted baptism were killed in case they might testify against defaulters. The looters deliberately destroyed records of debts stored in York castle. To prevent future recurrences, Richard's successor, John (r. 1199–1216), guaranteed Jews security, and in April 1233 Henry III formalized the system of *archae* – coffers controlled by two Jews and two Christians, which held copies of each debt owed to a Jew. This system meant that kings no longer lost money if pillagers targeted Jews, nor could murdering a Jew absolve a debtor of what he was obliged to pay.

By the late 13th century, crippling taxes had reduced Jews to penury. The 'Saladin tithe' funded war in the Holy Land, and demanded fully 25 per cent of a Jew's wealth. The Church that had once forced Jews to practise usury now outlawed the profession and retrospectively accused Jews of blasphemy. Christian bankers from Lombardy filled the vacuum and Jews found themselves dispensable.

In 1290 Edward I used the pretext of a dozen alleged counterfeiters to expel all of England's remaining 2,500 Jews. Most returned to Normandy, but after 16 years they were evicted from there, too, along with all other Jews in France. Only in 1656 were Jews formally readmitted to Britain.

The Crusades and Jewish Life

IN THE FACE OF MUSLIM EXPANSION, THE LOSS OF THE HOLY LAND AND THREATS TO CHRISTIAN PILGRIM ROUTES, POPE URBAN II (1088–99) CALLED FOR CHRISTIAN MILITARY EXPEDITIONS KNOWN AS THE CRUSADES.

The Crusades were an unprecedented rallying point, a moment of European self-definition. Some Christians believed fighting would absolve them of earthly sins and prompt Christ's return. Others were motivated by baser motives: knights dreamt of ruling oriental kingdoms, while serfs welcomed the chance to escape the drudgery of feudal servitude.

CALL TO ARMS

Pope Urban II explicitly called for 'holy war' before hundreds of clerics and laity in Clermont, France, on 27 November 1095. Soon Crusader armies set off from Boulogne, Toulouse, Otranto and Flanders, accompanied by peasant militias.

European Jews were cast as the enemy within. 'Why should Christians travel to the ends of the world to fight the Saracens', asked the Abbot of Cluny, 'when we permit among us other infidels a thousand times more guilty toward Christ than the Mohammedans?'

Crusaders looted Jewish property along the Rhineland and forced Jews to convert or be put to death. Some churchmen, including John of Speyer and the Bishop of Cologne, tried to stop townsfolk from joining the melee, but invariably to little effect. Some 800 Jews perished at Worms; another thousand died in Mainz (Mayence); more were killed at Triers, Eller and Speyer. In all, about 5,000 Franco-German Jews died.

MARTYRDOM

Many Jewish mothers took their lives and their children's, wrote Soloman bar Samson, a contemporary eyewitness, rather than submitting to forced conversion or rape and murder. Jewish liturgic poetry memorialized martyrs as exemplars of kiddush hashem, or 'sanctification of God's name'.

More died when the Crusaders advanced along the Danube during 1096, though resistance was now stiffer. Five hundred Jews and 1,000 ducal soldiers repelled Crusaders at

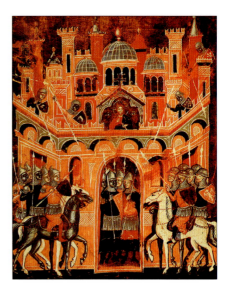

Above Crusaders at Jerusalem's gates, from a 13th-century manuscript by Buchardus Teutonicus.

Vishehrad, near Prague in Bohemia. Henry IV of Germany (1056–1106) rejected papal calls to join the Crusade and allowed forced converts to return to Judaism. Hungary's King Coloman defended Jewish subjects from Frankish marauders.

Still, with entire communities wiped out, Jewish leaders questioned the value of royal charters of protection and began separating themselves from gentile neighbours. The Crusades also caused a huge demographic shift eastwards. By the 13th century, Rothenburg on the Tauber River had replaced Mainz, former seat of Gershom ben Judah (c.960–1040CE), as the leading Ashkenazi study centre. Other Jews settled in Slav-populated areas, especially Poland.

JERUSALEM FALLS

In 1099, Crusaders led by Godfrey of Bouillon reached Jerusalem and mounted a siege. After the Crusaders achieved victory on 15 July 1099, reported Monk Fulcher of Chartres, they had massacred so many Muslims

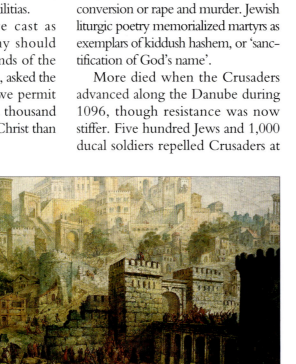

Left: Jews in Metz, France, were among the first Crusader victims in 1096. 19th-century painting by Auguste Migette.

Right Peasants burning down the tower of Verdun-sur-Garonne, Languedoc, where 500 Jews were hiding during the Peasants' Crusade, 1320.

and Jews that the city's streets ran ankle-deep in blood. Jews were corralled into a synagogue and burnt alive. At least 20,000 Jews were killed or captured and sold as slaves in Italy.

Baldwin I was crowned King of Jerusalem, and his successors ruled its environs in relative peace for nearly a century. His was the largest of four main Crusader 'Outremer' (overseas) principalities, the others being Edessa, Antioch and Tripoli.

FURTHER CRUSADES

French and German kings launched a Second Crusade in 1145 after a Turkish warlord, Zengi, conquered Edessa in 1144. By now, however, popular support was lacking. Crusader commanders led an unsuccessful attack on Damascus, until then a Muslim ally against Egypt, which brought Nur ad-Din to power in 1154. In 1171 his successor, Saladin, became Sultan of a united Egypt and Syria that enveloped the Jerusalem kingdom.

Saladin demolished a European army at Hattin in Galilee in July 1187. He then took Ashkelon, Gaza, Acre, Nablus, Sidon and Beirut in September, and captured Jerusalem on 2 October 1187. One of his first acts was to invite Jews to return, which some hailed as the advent of a messianic age.

THE LAST CRUSADES

Richard I of England vowed to return Jerusalem to Christendom. In 1189 he launched a Third Crusade together with the Holy Roman Emperor Frederick Barbarossa and Philip II of France. Despite initial successes, the Crusade floundered and Richard and Saladin agreed a treaty in 1192.

A Fourth Crusade launched in 1202 failed to reach Jerusalem. A Fifth Crusade that began in 1217 ended in failure in 1221.

Eight years later, Crusaders under Frederick II retook Jerusalem with Saladin's consent. However, Muslims still controlled the Temple Mount

Left Saladin (1138–93), who reconquered Jerusalem for Islam. Painting by Cristofano Altissimo, 16th century.

and the city lay in ruins. Eventually, in 1244 Turks ousted the occupiers. By now enthusiasm for holy war was waning in Europe. The Pope refused to sanction a Crusade by Louis IX of France in 1270. In 1291 some 1,600 Christian pilgrims arrived in Acre on a papal mission and began killing local Muslims and Jews, but Mamluk forces soundly beat them, recaptured Acre, and thus ended Christian rule in the Holy Land.

Between 1290 and 1294, a concerted church campaign virtually destroyed Jewish communities in the kingdom of Naples. The original cradle of Ashkenazi Jewry was no more, and Jews who faced extermination converted en masse. Yet Ashkenazi seeds had travelled north of the Alps. There, despite further persecutions, they would later blossom into new settlements. And, in papal Rome, the pope's direct protection of Jews overrode the proselytizing wishes of his more zealous monks.

Anti-Semitism in 14th-century Europe

This was a dreadful period for Europe's Jews as persecution and plague followed repeated expulsions. Despite invitations to return, increasingly Jews left voluntarily for the safer Slavic east.

In France, already saddled with debts from past Crusades, King Philip IV (1268–1314) desperately needed cash for his war against England. When punitive taxes between 1292 and 1303 failed to raise enough revenue, on 22 July 1306 he arrested 100,000 Jews, confiscated their goods, auctioned their properties and pocketed the proceeds. Then he drove them out of France with just the clothes on their backs and 12 sous (pennies) each in a purse.

There was a rash of expulsions from France in 1306, followed by invitations to return when kings found that they needed funds or, as in the case of Louis X of France in 1315, when he discovered that the Italian bankers who had replaced the Jews charged higher interest.

Below A plague scene from a 14th-century manuscript. Simple people sought scapegoats and often blamed Jews or other outsiders for their troubles.

Unlike England, France was neither an island nor a unitary state. Refugees decamped to areas beyond royal control: Burgundy, Lorraine, Savoy, Roussilon, Dauphiné and the southern papal lands of Avignon.

CHRISTIAN PERSECUTION

The French expulsions coincided with the eradication of the southern Italian Jewish community (1290–4) and the eviction of Jews from Norman England (1290). Church politics was clearly one factor behind this pattern of persecution. For centuries the Catholic Church had battled for authority against Europe's monarchs. To succeed it first had to weed out heretics. Having exterminated the Cathar Christian sect, the French clergy next targeted Jews as Europe's last 'Christ-deniers'. In 1240 a Christianized Jew, Nicholas Donin, put the Talmud on trial in what was cynically called a disputation. Defending the scriptures, Rabbi Yehiel of Paris proclaimed: 'Our bodies are indeed in your hands, but not our souls'. In 1242 the Pope ordered monks to burn all copies of the book.

Above 15th-century Jews wearing distinctive round badges, or 'wheels', on their clothing. Contemporary engraving.

Even in places where Jews fared best, such as Rome and Provence, religious prejudice mixed with popular superstition to generate more anti-Semitism. As Crusaders fought the 'infidel' in the east, locals looked askance at the ethnic 'alien' in their midst, the Jew. Rebellious peasants targeted the Jewish moneylender or middleman who peddled goods between town and countryside. Cathedral art showed the synagogue as a blindfolded woman carrying a broken staff, alongside a youthful woman representing Christ's triumphant church. Other symbols for Jews included a brooding owl and the *Judensau*, a pig that they were said to worship.

BLOOD LIBELS

Church propaganda fanned anti-Jewish 'blood libels' across Europe after the first ritual murder accusation hit England in 1144. So potent was the myth that Geoffrey Chaucer described Jews murdering Christian children in his 1387 *Canterbury Tales*, 100 years after Jews left England.

Pope Innocent III drafted a protective 'constitution for the Jews', yet later called them 'a snake around the loins' and urged Christians to combat 'Jewish usury'. In 1298, Jews in Roettingen, Bavaria, were said to have stolen and desecrated the host (wafer) used in Catholic mass. This allegation inspired massacres in Germany and resurfaced in Lorraine and Franconia in 1338–9, when bands of *Armleder*, or 'armband-wearers', and *Judenschläger*, or Jew-beaters, murdered and pillaged at will.

Jews suffered during the Anglo-French Hundred Years War (1328–1453), and were suspected of helping the Tartars who threatened Europe. Anti-Semites targeted Jewish advisors when their royal patrons fell from grace, and in 1320 would-be 'shepherd crusaders' robbed Jews in 120 French communities. These peasants dreamt of fighting Spanish Muslims, and killed Jews who refused baptism, until the pope allowed soldiers in Carcasonne and Aragon to wipe out the zealots.

THE BLACK DEATH

The worst spur to violence was not war, politics, law or witchcraft, but disease. Two out of five Europeans died from the Black Death, a plague that struck Europe in 1348. Superstitious people quickly blamed Templars, heretics, witches, foreign merchants, the poor, the rich and, above all, the Jews.

Pope Clement VI ruled that it was 'absolutely unthinkable that … Jews performed so terrible a deed'. Despite his words, in 1348–9 pogroms engulfed 300 Jewish communities in France, Germany, Austria, Switzerland and even relatively tolerant Krakow in Poland. Thousands of Jews died, many converted under torture, and horrors returned in 1370 when all the Jews of Brussels were wiped out.

German cities soon re-admitted Jews to fulfil essential financial functions. Now, though, they were 'serfs of the city', no longer protected by kings and subject to short-term domiciles that could be cancelled in a trice. Many returnees were widows and orphans, forced to live outside the city gates as lepers and prostitutes. Turbulent times undermined the old Jewish bourgeoisie, and *Shtadlanim* (court intercessors for Jews) fell by the wayside. Instead, communal leadership passed to more mystical or legalistic elements.

Above French Jews put to the flame during the 1316–22 reign of Philip V. Illuminated manuscript, c. 1410.

Below A victorious Church tramples a blindfolded Synagogue underfoot. 13th-century French Christian prayer book.

MEDIEVAL SCIENCE

Levi ben Gershon (1288–1354), also known as Gersonides, was a true polyglot whose work anticipated the Renaissance. Born in France in 1288, he was a rabbi, philosopher, astronomer and mathematician. He is credited with inventing the sailor's quadrant known as Jacob's staff, which for three centuries was used to determine latitude and the local hour.

Most medieval Jewish scientists were Spanish, Portuguese or North African. In Barcelona, the astronomer, mathematician and philosopher Abraham Bar Hiyya (1070–1136) wrote the first book to introduce Islamic algebra to Europe. Isaac ibn Sid, a cantor in Toledo and amateur stargazer, updated astronomical tables.

Another intellectual trailblazer was Isaac Israeli ben Solomon, who died in Kairouan, Tunisia, in 932. A profound philosopher, skilful oculist and court physician to a Fatimid Caliph, he wrote six Arabic books on medicine, which Muslim doctors praised as 'more valuable than gems'.

Muslim Rulers of the Bible Lands

MUSLIMS RULED ALL OF PALESTINE FROM 644CE UNTIL 1099, WHEN THE CRUSADERS TOOK JERUSALEM. IN 1291 THE LAST EUROPEANS WERE OUSTED AND PALESTINE REMAINED UNDER MUSLIM CONTROL UNTIL 1917.

The Crusader reign over Palestine was a 150-year-long Christian interlude in a largely Muslim story. Palestine's Jewish population waxed and waned in size during the 873 years from the Arab victory to the Ottoman takeover in 1516.

EARLY MUSLIM RULE
Arabs conquered Palestine fully in 644CE, having allowed Jews to return to Jerusalem in 638CE. In time, Arab rulers permitted Jews to rebuild a yeshiva in the holy city. Muslims became the majority population, and Arabic the dominant language.

Muslims revered Jerusalem as their third holiest city, and in 691CE Caliph Abd el-Malik built the Dome of the Rock on the presumed site of the destroyed Jewish Temples. The nearby Al Aqsa Mosque was completed in 705CE. Jerusalem was a spiritual outpost, but in 715CE Arabs built Ramle as Palestine's administrative capital. All of what Jews called the Land of Israel was absorbed into Syria, itself governed from Baghdad after 762CE.

Successive Egyptian dynasties then ruled, culminating in the Fatimids, Shia Muslims who took Ramle in 970CE. They tolerated minorities until the advent of Caliph Hakim I (996–1021CE), who in 1009 burned Jerusalem's Church of the Holy Sepulchre and later destroyed its synagogues.

Muslims held supreme political power in pre-Crusader Palestine. Under the surface, though, Jewish life showed surprising vibrancy. From the 7th to the 11th centuries, scholars known as the Masoretes formalized how to read, write, pronounce and sing sacred Hebrew texts. They also organized the Bible into chapter and verse.

CRUSADERS' RISE AND FALL
In 1099, after Crusaders captured Jerusalem, Franks, Normans, Italians and Hungarians settled in Palestine, forming a thin Christian mantle over a mainly Muslim society. The Jewish population dropped to 1,000 families.

In time, Saladin reclaimed Palestine for Islam in 1187 in a victory welcomed by Jerusalem's impoverished Jews. Ultimately the Mamluks, an Egyptian military dynasty, gained Palestine in 1260, and in 1291 evicted Crusaders from their last Palestinian enclave, in Acre.

MAMLUKS AND TURKS
Palestine was now subdivided into three sanjaks, or districts, with capitals in Jerusalem, Gaza and Safed.

Left Saladin conquered Egypt, drove the Crusaders from Jerusalem, and ruled Islam's other holy cities, Mecca and Medina.

Above A 15th-century Arabian illumination shows Mamluk soldiers on horseback.

The Mamluk triumph encouraged some Diaspora Jews to return to the Holy Land, such as the Spanish sage Nahmanides in 1267. Synagogues and yeshivas were built and the Mamluks also improved Jerusalem.

Rabbi Obadiah ben Abraham restored welfare and scholastic institutions after 1488. More Jews arrived following the Spanish expulsions of 1492, bolstering the community.

In 1516 Ottoman Turks conquered Palestine. Suleiman built Jerusalem's city walls in 1538, and the Turks were to rule for 500 years.

Below King Baldwin IV, King of Jerusalem 1174–85, drawn as a boy showing fight wounds to the Archbishop of Tyre.

THE FALL OF THE BYZANTINE EMPIRE

BY THE 11TH CENTURY, BYZANTIUM HAD BEGUN TO RESEMBLE 3RD-CENTURY CE ROME: WEALTHY AND CULTURED, YET POLITICALLY DIVIDED. IT WAS ALSO SUBJECT TO PRESSURES ON ITS BORDERS.

Life was often extremely harsh for the Greek-speaking 'Romaniote' Jews who populated the medieval Byzantine empire. Successive Emperors Heraclius, Leo III and Romanos I demanded their baptism and conversion in 640, 721 and 930CE. Basil I formally tried to ban Jewish religious practices in 873CE, and an enforced 'disputation' between rabbis and monks resulted in further expulsions in 880CE.

Resurgent Byzantine forces repelled Muslims in the 10th century, sparking an economic boom that attracted both Rabbanite and Karaite Jews. Greek became the Karaites' language and Hebrew replaced Arabic in their literature.

In the 11th century, however, Byzantium was attacked from all sides. The empire lost colonies in Sicily and southern Italy. Crusader invasions further unsettled a restive Byzantium after 1096.

INTELLECTUAL DECLINE, COMMERCIAL SURVIVAL

Earlier centuries had seen a literary flowering among Byzantine Jews. For example, many of the 200 liturgical poems by the 7th-century CE master Eleazar Kallir found their way into the Ashkenazi Jewish prayer book.

By the 11th century the Sephardi scholars of Spain had taken over as the academic vanguard of the Jewish world. Constantinople's Jews, as seen by the 12th-century Benjamin of Tudela, were barred from political and administrative office – by contrast with Jews in Muslim lands – and Greeks would beat them in the capital's streets. They 'bore their lot with cheerfulness', wrote Benjamin, but were forced to leave after 'Latins' sacked the city in 1204.

Jewish fortunes improved when Michael VIII restored the empire in 1259. Assisted by his Mongol allies, he recovered Constantinople in 1261,

Above A historical watershed: Ottoman Turks wrest Constantinople from the last Byzantine emperor on 29 May, 1453. From a 16th-century fresco.

welcomed Jews back to the capital and revoked discriminatory laws in exchange for their support. No longer did Jews fear forced conversion, nor was their property stolen by greedy nobles. Indeed, by the 14th century, resident Venetian Jews enjoyed more privileges than the empire's Greek majority, due to favourable terms that Venice had negotiated with Byzantium.

FALL OF CONSTANTINOPLE

Jews felt safer under the Ottoman Turks, successors to the Seljuks, who by the 15th century occupied most of Anatolia. In 1453 the Ottomans won Constantinople after a seven-week siege, ending some 1,150 years of distinctive Byzantine civilization.

In 1472 Grand Duke Ivan III of Moscow married a Byzantine royal, and called his capital the 'Third Rome'. Russia became the new centre of Orthodox Christianity, a successor to Byzantine glory, and another potentate whose actions would profoundly shape Jewish destiny in centuries to come.

Left Rome itself might have collapsed, but Byzantium, the 'Rome of the East', survived its imperial sister's demise for another thousand years.

FROM THE GOLDEN AGE TO THE SPANISH INQUISITION

Spain and the 1492 Expulsion of the Jews

From the 11th century, slowly but surely, Christian principalities recaptured Spain in a process known as the Reconquista. By the mid-1200s Granada was Spain's sole remaining Muslim kingdom.

The Christian mountain enclave of Asturias became the Kingdom of Leon in 913CE, and joined its neighbour and occasional ally, Castile, in driving the Reconquista. Umayyad Andalus dissolved into 23 disparate Muslim 'party kingdoms' in 1030. In quick succession the Muslims lost Toledo in 1085, Valencia in 1092 and Zaragoza in 1118. After decades of stalemate, Christians united to defeat the Muslims at Tolosa in 1211. Cordoba fell in 1236 and Seville in 1248. Spanish Jews now found themselves mostly living under Christian rule. In time, Christian authorities started forcing Jews to convert, imposing pseudo-theological 'disputations' and officially sanctioning massacres.

JEWISH SUCCESS
Jews from France and North Africa had settled in Aragon during the reign of King James I (1213–76), encouraged by property grants and tax

Right Passover customs come alive in the Golden Haggadah, Spain, c.1320.

exemptions. Jews had also benefited from a belated intellectual flowering in Christian Spain. Toledo established a university that taught Greek, Arabic and Hebrew after 1130, and a rabbinical university was set up in Barcelona in 1267. More Jews settled in both cities after the French expulsions of 1306.

RISING ANTI-SEMITISM
However, Spanish Jewry was not immune to developments elsewhere in Europe. In 1215 the Vatican's Fourth Lateran Council instituted the 'Badge of Shame' to distinguish Jews, who were also banned from appearing in public on Good Friday.

Toledo's king and archbishop cherished their city's reputation for co-existence of Jews, Muslims and Christians, called *La Convivencia*. They persuaded the Pope to suspend the badge law in Spain. But Aragon's King James I forbade law courts from accepting a Jew's oath in 1228; and Zaragoza saw the first Spanish 'blood libel' in 1250.

NEW LAWS AND POGROMS
Over time, petty discomforts grew into debilitating legal codes, officially approved mob violence, and finally outright religious persecution. Castile's Siete Partidas, or Seven-Part Code of 1265, allowed Jews to run synagogues and guaranteed freedom from interference on the Sabbath. While this code recommended converting Jews by 'kind words', it also claimed that Jews crucified Christian children over Easter. The Partidas banned sexual intercourse between Jews and Christians, and threatened to burn any Jew who wounded a Jewish convert to Christianity. Thus it provided later rulers with an arsenal of discriminatory powers, and sanctioned torture.

Increasingly, Jews in Spain were blamed for the plague of 1348. Henry of Trastamara unleashed his forces on Toledo's Jewish Alcana quarter in 1355, where they killed more than a thousand. Terrible pogroms in

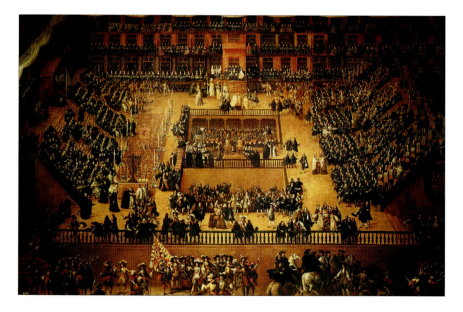

Left Auto-da-fé on the Plaza in Madrid on 30 June 1680 by Francisco Rizi, 1683.

136

Above Interrogation of the Jew, Spanish altarpiece painting, 1485. Seven years later Jews were expelled from the kingdom.

Valencia, Seville and Barcelona in 1391 persuaded many to convert to Christianity. Some *conversos* practised Judaism in secret, so Spaniards called them *marranos* (pigs). Others became militant Christians, like Don Pablo de Santa Maria, bishop of Burgos. By now Spanish Jews faced an awful double bind. Those who kept their faith faced increasing strictures, while Jews who adopted Christianity were accused of doing so for venal motives.

THE SPANISH INQUISITION
During 1413–14 a former Jew named Jose Lorqui led 63 sessions of a disputation in Tortosa whose outcome was predetermined, unlike the earlier 1263 Barcelona disputation. Spanish Jewry's end came with the dreaded Inquisition in 1481. Spain had long resisted this method, which was designed to weed out heretics. It pried into people's lives, robbed local bishops of their authority and confiscated the property of the 'guilty' to the Vatican, not to rulers.

Nonetheless, Queen Isabella of Castile called in the inquisitors when in 1480 she heard that leading 'New Christians' had been caught secretly celebrating the Jewish Passover. Soon the institution reached Valencia, Catalonia and Aragon. Thousands were forced to confess their 'crimes' under torture. Many more were burnt alive in public displays called auto-da-fé (acts of faith). Those who confessed had the dubious privilege of being strangled before the pyre was lit. The Inquisition continued until the late 18th century.

FALL OF GRANADA
In 1469, powerful Jews encouraged the marriage between Castile's Isabella and Aragon's Fernando, hoping that this dynastic union might end persecution. One such advocate was Lisbon-born Isaac Abrabanel (1453–1508), philosopher, financier and advisor to Isabella. The royal couple did not wish to lose the services of their Jewish allies, but they eventually bowed to clerical pressure and expelled all Jews from Andalucia in 1483.

Now the only area where Jews could live safely was Granada. Jews had proven their loyalty in 1453 by fighting for Muslim Granada against Castile. Jews enjoyed the kingdom's hospitable and cultivated environment; Granada's sultans hosted intellectuals, built the fabulous Alhambra Palace and traded with Europe and North Africa. But its political capital was spent, and on January 2, 1492, Isabella and Fernando's armies defeated this last outpost of Muslim rule in Spain.

DISASTER AND NEW HOPE
Of the 200,000 Jews who left Spain, at least 50,000 went to North Africa or Ottoman Turkey, and another 100,000 crossed into Portugal, only to be expelled four years later. In Spanish Malta, Jews had to pay 'compensation'

Right Respectful debate or thinly veiled show trial? Disputations between rabbis and monks increasingly heralded persecution. Illustration to Heinrich Heine's Disputation, 1851.

Above Damned by the Inquisition by Eugenio Lucas Velázquez, 1850.

for the effect of their departure on the economy.

Another event of 1492 was Christopher Columbus' expedition to the New World. On board was Luis de Torres, the expedition's official Arabic translator, a *converso* (a Jew who had been forced to convert to Christi-anity). By some accounts Columbus himself was half-*converso*. Whether true or not, he almost certainly used the maps of the Spanish Jew Abraham Crescas and the navigational tools of another Jewish scientist, Gersonides.

CHAPTER 6

THE SHIFT TO ASHKENAZ

For Jews everywhere the Spanish expulsions of 1492 seemed to snuff out a light that would never be relit. In fact, the calamity coincided with several new opportunities. That same year Columbus sailed to the 'New World', opening up previously unimagined prospects for traders. Printing technology disseminated knowledge more easily than ever before. And the Ottomans allowed Spanish exiles to settle across their empire, including Palestine.

Within two centuries, Dutch Sephardim became the first Jews to return to England, and Amsterdam produced Baruch Spinoza, arguably the greatest of early Jewish freethinkers. Yet Italy invented the ghetto, and a German reformist Christian movement known as Protestantism turned from sympathizing with Jews to deriding them. Overall, the period from 1492 saw a gradual passing of the torch from Sephardi to Ashkenazi culture, as Poland grew in stature as a Jewish centre, Yiddish flourished as a language and Rabbi Loew spearheaded a Jewish Renaissance in Prague.

Opposite The Dutch master Rembrandt (1609–69) often painted Jewish subjects, such as this striking portrait of a rabbi. Amsterdam became home to Jews, both Ashkenazi and Sephardi.

Above Bridge to the Jewish ghetto in Venice. A sudden influx of Spanish Jewish refugees led to the founding of the first established ghetto in the world in March 1516.

THE SHIFT TO ASHKENAZ

JEWS IN NEW CULTURES

THE LATE 15TH CENTURY SAW JEWS EVICTED FROM SPAIN AND PORTUGAL, NAPLES AND NUREMBERG. YET FRESH COMMUNITIES SPROUTED IN POLAND, THE NETHERLANDS, PERSIA, AND EVEN THE AMERICAS.

Jews survived despite the expulsions and persecution of the turbulent 16th century. They created new institutions, harnessed new technology and kept alive old traditions of scholarship. Jews thrived by creating intricate trading networks that linked their new places of refuge – Ottoman Turkey, North Africa, the Netherlands, Poland and Lithuania.

NEW HAVENS
Paradoxically, the expulsions put Sephardi and Ashkenazi Jews in contact with each other to their mutual advantage. This was especially true of the Netherlands and, later, north-west Germany, areas that came under Protestant rule and accepted 'New Christians' (converted Jews) from Spain and Portugal. As a result of this, Jews repopulated the shores of the Atlantic after years of absence, just as the Atlantic began to take over from the Mediterranean as the prime focus of European trade.

Iberian (Sephardi) Jews also flocked to the Ottoman empire, while most German Ashkenazim moved *en masse* to Poland. Thus Sephardi–Ashkenazi co-operation grew as Poland became the chief transit for expanding overland trade between the Ottomans and central and western Europe.

THE GHETTOS
In March 1516, panicked by a sudden influx of Spanish Jewish refugees, Venice set up the world's first ghetto, so called because the area was an old iron foundry (*ghetto* in Italian). Most of the original inhabitants were of German origin; Jews from the Levant got their own ghetto in 1541. Other Italian cities set up ghettos: Rome in 1556, Florence in 1571, Verona in 1605, Mantua in 1612 and Ferrara in 1624.

The word ghetto has come to signify an area of urban depravity, but there were positive aspects: during nightly curfews Jews were protected from bigots outside the walls; during daylight hours they still traded in the city. They alone were allowed to pursue loan-banking, a trade which, although it never yielded vast fortunes, spread prosperity throughout some 300 Italian communities during the period 1300–1500. Isolated from gentile society, these Jews nurtured a distinctive culture within the ghetto.

FALSE HOPE IN PORTUGAL
By the 13th century Portugal's Jews numbered 200,000, a fifth of the total population; and King João II valued his Jewish financiers and gun-makers for most of his 1481–94 reign. After some 150,000 refugees poured across the border from Spain in 1492, however, João declared non-domiciled Jews to be slaves, and ordered that Jewish children should be separated from their parents. João's successor, Manuel, reversed these decrees, only to order all Jews to leave Portugal in October 1497. Three thousand Iberian crypto-Jews died in a pogrom in Lisbon in 1506.

Above A beautiful ketubah, *Jewish marriage contract, from Modena, Italy, 1723, with a view of Jerusalem.*

Below Established in 1516, the Venice Ghetto set a pattern for similar enclaves for Jews across Europe.

In 1531 Pope Clement VII (1478–1534) began a Portuguese Inquisition aimed at 'secretly Jewish' Maranos: several thousand were imprisoned and many more fled.

SICILY, MALTA AND ITALY

The Spanish expulsions and the period leading up to them affected Jews well beyond the Spanish mainland. In 1391 some 300 were murdered by mobs in Majorca. After 1492, Jews were forced out of Spanish-ruled Sicily and southern Italy. Most constructed new secure lives in Ottoman territory.

Pope Alexander VI (1431–1503) allowed Jews from Sicily, Sardinia and Spain to settle in his Italian states. Many fled to papal Naples, but after it fell to Spain, Jews were evicted in 1510 and 'new Christians' (converted Jews) in 1515. As late as 1587, the duchy of Milan banished 900 Jews when it, too, came under Spanish rule. Nor were all popes so benign: in 1556 Paul IV (1478–1559) sent 24 Portuguese Maranos to burn at the stake in Ancona.

THE NEW WORLD

In 1502, on his final visit to the New World, Christopher Columbus left behind 52 Jewish-origin families in Costa Rica.

The Spanish and Portuguese began to hunt down insincere converts in their New World colonies. As early as 1515 the authorities deported one 'secret Jew' from Hispaniola (now Cuba) to face the Inquisition in Spain. Maranos were offered the choice of death or 'true conversion' at autos-da-fé in Lima, Peru (1570), Mexico City (1574), Cartagena, Colombia (1610) and Havana.

By 1640, Jews and Maranos were living safely along the Brazilian coast under Dutch rule. One town, Bahia, was even nicknamed 'The Rock of Israel'. After Portugal reconquered Brazil in 1654, resident Jews fled to nearby Surinam and Cayenne and to the Caribbean. Twenty-three Brazilian Sephardim arrived in Dutch-ruled New Amsterdam (later called New York), where they established She'arit Israel, the first Hebrew congregation in North America.

PERSIA

Meanwhile, Jews thousands of miles to the east suffered too. In 1511 the usually downtrodden Shia sect took over Persia and established its first empire since the Fatimids ruled Egypt. Their clerics forced Persia's new Safavid rulers to discriminate against Jews and Christians.

Above Lorenzo de Medici (1449–92), ruler of Florence, who protected his Jewish subjects from expulsions.

Respite came when the urbane Abbas I (1588–1629) invited Jews to settle in his new capital, Isfahan, in 1592. They welcomed his peace treaty with the rival Ottoman Caliphate and his expansion of seafaring trade with Europe, in which they played a pivotal role.

Next, Shah Abbas II of Persia (r. 1642–66) drove Jews from Isfahan in 1652 on grounds of 'ritual impurity', and forced 100,000 Jews to adopt Islam. Confronted by a Jewish delegation in 1661, Abbas relented and allowed Jews to revert to their old faith, as long as they wore a distinctive patch.

Life improved for Jews in 1736 when invasions by Sunni Muslim Afghans destroyed the Safavid dynasty. Many became physicians, pharmacists and international merchants. However, they never reached the intellectual heights of their co-religionists in a Europe where the Renaissance promised new hope.

Left *The current building for Congregation She'arit Israel, New York City, for a community established in 1654.*

Intellectual Stirrings

During the Renaissance and the Reformation, Jews remained the only religious minority within Christendom. The advent of printing led to increasing interest in Hebrew texts.

Europe of the 15th, 16th and 17th centuries was a ferment of change. The Italian Renaissance encouraged artistic individualism, rational inquiry and renewed interest in long-neglected classics. Protestants in Germany and France challenged the 1,200-year-long dominance of the Roman Catholic Church and were soon to split the continent apart. Other truth-seekers rejected Christianity altogether.

Meanwhile, scientific breakthroughs allowed for voyages of discovery and helped create Europe's first overseas empires. In time the new mercantile class began seeking greater domestic freedoms. Europeans often oppressed the peoples of Africa, Asia and the Americas, however, and colonial rivalries led to bloody wars abroad and at home. In addition, developing colonies demanded slaves, which led to a trade in human cargo that shamed their liberal and Christian values.

EUROPE'S SOLE MINORITY

Throughout this period Jews remained the only religious minority within Christendom. The changes around them had decidedly mixed effects on their community, for while attacks on Church authority created space for free expression, challenges to religion threatened their faith as well. Anti-Semitism refused to disappear despite the spirit of liberalism.

Jews who initially welcomed Protestantism, for instance, were shocked when Martin Luther took to Jew-baiting. Even the great Dutch humanist Desiderius Erasmus of Rotterdam wrote: 'If it is the part of a good Christian to detest the Jews, then we are all good Christians'.

Above The first book printed in Lisbon, the *Book of Abraham*, *published in Hebrew by Eliezer Toledano, 1489.*

PRINTING REVOLUTION

One escape from isolation came via printing, which democratized knowledge and defied borders. After Johann Gutenberg made the world's first Bible with movable type in 1445, Jews produced at least 180 Hebrew printed titles between 1472 and 1500. Most were religious works.

The first printing press of any language in the Orient was a Jewish firm, which printed Hebrew books in Constantinople in 1493. Italy became the centre for Hebrew printing, although many master printers were German Jews. The Jewish Soncino family, for instance, originally hailed from Bavaria and settled near Milan. They also printed in Brescia, Rimini, Pesaro, Constantinople and Salonika.

Perhaps the most accomplished craftsman of all was Daniel Bomberg, a Christian from Belgium, primarily active in Venice between 1516 and 1549. He printed the entire multi-volume Talmud between 1520 and 1523 in Venice and set the pagination standards for Talmuds for all time. The technical advance of printing spread Jewish knowledge like wildfire.

Below Solomon and the Queen of Sheba, *c.1555, by Tintoretto, an Italian Renaissance artist fascinated by Jewish and biblical themes.*

INTELLECTUAL STIRRINGS

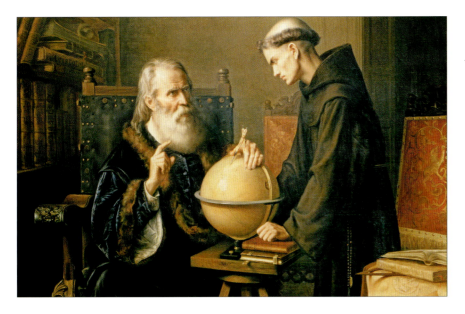

Left Galileo explaining his daring scientific insights at Padua University; from a painting of 1873, Mexico.

OFFICIAL CENSORSHIP

Catholic governors were worried about dissident literature being spread, so they introduced tight censorship and ordered Talmuds and other Jewish books burned in 1554. Production resumed 11 years later, but only once copies were vetted to rid them of negative references to Jesus or gentiles.

Censorship was not unknown to Jews. Conservative French rabbis persuaded Dominicans to burn copies of Maimonides' 'Guide' in Montpellier, France, in 1233. Nine years later they watched as thousands of Talmuds were set ablaze in Paris by papal order, aware that they had precipitated this self-inflicted tragedy.

THE RENAISSANCE

A 15th-century revival of interest in Greek and Latin classics soon spawned curiosity in texts in Hebrew, which Italian and later German scholars came to regard as the third of the great 'classical literatures'. For Jews, literature, music and the sciences presented better chances for creative expression. One Jewish pioneer was the court composer Salomone di Rossi, who wrote European-style melodies for the ancient synagogue liturgy.

FREE THINKERS

The Renaissance encouraged Italian Jews to broach taboos and to discuss ideas with gentile interlocutors. Azaria di Rossi, for instance, revisited contentious issues of belief first raised by the 1st-century Egyptian Jewish philosopher Philo. Leone Modena taught Christians about Jewish practices and did much to demystify Jews in the public eye.

One of the most daring Jewish thinkers was Solomon Ibn Verga (c.1450–c.1525). He wrote *The Rod of Judah*, sometimes called the first secularist Jewish history since Josephus. A dedicated rationalist, Ibn Verga criticized the Talmud and mocked Maimonides, chided Jews for being 'twice naked' by neglecting political and military science, and blamed anti-Semitism on Jews who 'show themselves lords and masters, therefore the masses envy them'.

The Renaissance spirit also took hold in Holland under Calvinist Protestant rule, where the established *ma'amad*, or 'executive body of the Sephardi community', had no truck for dissent. Uriel da Costa set an example to other Jewish freethinkers. Born in 1585 in Oporto, Portugal, and raised as a Jesuit, he reconverted to Judaism and fled from persecution to Holland. He questioned the Oral Law and wrote scathingly about the ritualistic 'Pharisees of Amsterdam', who excommunicated him. Da Costa rejoined the community in 1640, but killed himself after being forced to receive 39 lashes in the synagogue by way of 'recantation'.

Below An anti-Semitic pamphlet from Frankfurt, 1601, shows a ritual murder and Jews suckling a pig.

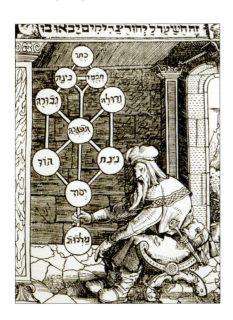

Below: Jewish Kabbalist holding a 'tree of life' diagram of divine attributes; from a book of magic, *Portae Lucis*, 1516.

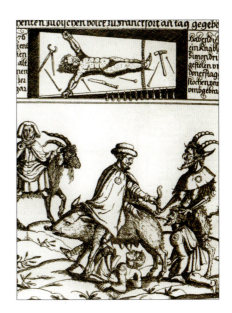

Jewish Communities in Germany

BY THE 16TH CENTURY, THE HOLY ROMAN EMPIRE SEEMED LIKE A THROWBACK TO MEDIEVAL TIMES, WHEN RELIGION AND MONARCHICAL DYNASTIES, NOT NATIONALITY, DEFINED EUROPE.

Germany was not a distinct state until the mid-19th century. Before that, the Holy Roman empire encompassed most of what is today Germany, as well as Switzerland, Austria, Slovenia, Belgium, Luxembourg, the Czech Republic and Holland, plus parts of France, Poland and northern Italy. Far from being a truly united entity, the empire comprised hundreds of smaller kingdoms, principalities, counties and free imperial cities.

EASTERN EXTREMITIES

From a Jewish perspective, greater Germany was particularly uninviting in the 15th century: Jews were expelled from Vienna, Linz, Cologne,

Below Built in 1175, this synagogue in Worms, sometimes called Rashi's Chapel, is the oldest in Germany.

Right Martin Luther, the dynamo behind the Protestant Revolution, at first inspired hope in Jews. Danish altarpiece, 1561.

Augsburg, Bavaria and Styria, southern Austria, in 1496. Increasingly Jews moved eastwards, through the empire's extremities to Moravia, Bohemia and on to Poland.

Jewish fortunes revived by the late 16th century: the Emperor Maximilian II (r. 1557–76) allowed Jews to return to towns in Bohemia, and in 1577 his son, Rudolph II, gave them a charter of privileges. Poland, meanwhile, emerged as the new Ashkenazi heartland; some Jews made fortunes there and further east, effectively running vast Ukrainian and Lithuanian estates that provided grain to expanding western Europe.

THE PFEFFERKORN AFFAIR

Jews discovered friends in unexpected places, such as Johannes Reuchlin, a German Christian humanist and Hebrew scholar inspired by the winds of change emanating from Italy. In 1509 Johannes Pfefferkorn, a Jewish-born Dominican monk in Cologne, declared: 'Whoever afflicts the Jews is doing the will of God'. He sought to kidnap Jewish children and raise them as Catholics. He also won imperial approval to confiscate all Jewish books, especially the Talmud. Soon Jewish tomes were set alight in Frankfurt; while 38 Jews were burned in Berlin on trumped-up charges of child murder. Reuchlin argued for the Jews, forcing the emperor to rescind his edict in 1510. The controversy raged for years.

THE REFORMATION

For more than a millennium, Roman Catholicism reigned in most of Europe. As the Byzantine empire drew to a close in 1453, Greek or Christian Orthodox pockets in western Europe, such as Ravenna in Adriatic Italy, died out. The Church of Rome isolated and eliminated competing trends, like Gnosticism and Arianism in the 3rd century, the Cathars in the 14th and Hussites in the 15th. All were called heresies, and several movements were ostracized precisely because they seemed to be too close to Judaism.

With the pope at its head the Catholic Church seemed impregnable. However, a string of corrupt popes weakened it, and resentments came to the boil in the 16th century. Disgusted by the offering of bogus 'indulgences', the rebel monk Martin Luther nailed his 95-point thesis to the door of the Wittenberg Palace All Saints' Church in late October 1517. So began the Protestant Reformation, which was to revolutionize Europe. At first Jews welcomed the new religious trend: they were no longer the only non-conformists in Europe, and some imagined that Protestants would be their natural allies. Luther published a pamphlet stressing the links between Jews and Christians, called

JEWISH COMMUNITIES IN GERMANY

Right A historical turning point? When thugs looted Frankfurt's Jewish ghetto in 1614, Habsburg Emperor Matthias hanged the instigators and restored Jewish property.

Christ was Born a Jew. And while his aim was always to convert Jews, he insisted that this should be done with gentleness.

THE PROTESTANTS TURN

Jews soon learnt Protestants could be just as anti-Semitic as Catholics. When Jews rejected Luther's advances he issued a virulent attack on them in 1543, recommending a programme of arson, expropriation, hard physical labour and ultimately, 'if we are afraid that they may harm us', driving them 'out of the country for all time'.

After reforms in 1356, German emperors had given local princes or imperial 'electors' the right to tax Jews. Once Jews could appeal directly to the emperor; now they had to contend with the whims of local fiefs. Eventually, in 1614, Emperor Matthias (r. 1612–19) stood up against anti-Semites and hanged the ringleaders of a pogrom in Frankfurt. He then ceremonially restored the Jews to their homes.

Below The vast and sprawling Holy Roman empire was generally inhospitable terrain for Jews.

Generally, Jews fared better in the northern German states of the Hanseatic League. Semi-autonomous from the empire, the League afforded opportunities for trade with Scandinavia and the Baltic states. By the 16th century Jews from Spain and Portugal migrated to the region. They soon forged lucrative links with fellow Sephardim in Holland and Ashkenazim in Germany.

THE RISE OF COURT JEWS

Jews also benefited from the Thirty Years War, which erupted in 1618 between the Holy Roman empire and an array of foes, both Catholic and Protestant. Almost single-handedly one Jew, Jacob Bassevi of Prague, saved the imperial Habsburg army from bankruptcy with loans and a food-supply network in eastern Europe. Some Jews profited from supplying the opposition; other Jews became contractors to Swedish forces. In sum, the war brought about two changes. First, Jewish communities who used to suffer from any conflict were now treated better than others. Second, there were 'court Jews' who funded capital projects in peacetime as in war, who advised rulers, and who capitalized on these factors to safeguard the interests of poorer Jews.

Below This painting by Flemish artist Sebastien Vrancx depicts the Thirty Years War, 1618–48, during which some Jews shrewdly gained influence.

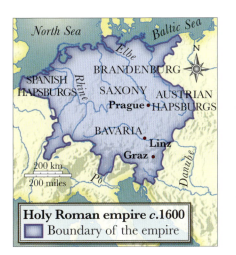

Jews in the Ottoman Empire

AFTER MUSLIM TURKEY THREW SPANISH JEWS A LIFELINE IN 1492, SEPHARDIM REVIVED JEWISH COMMUNITIES ACROSS THE OTTOMAN-RULED BALKANS, EASTERN MEDITERRANEAN AND NORTH AFRICA.

To the beleaguered Jews in 15th-century Spain, the sight of offshore sailing masts belonging to the Ottoman fleet was particularly reassuring. Between 1490 and 1492 the naval commander Kemal Reis sent ships to hug the Iberian coastline, picking up load after load of refugees and transporting them to Turkey and the Ottoman provinces. Even after Granada fell to Christian Spaniards, Reis bombarded the ports of Almería and Málaga on behalf of fellow Muslims suffering in Spain, and in 1506 he rescued the last consignment of Jews and Arabs who wished to escape the Spanish Inquisition.

BAYEZID'S INVITATION

Whereas Christian nations accepted Jews begrudgingly, Sultan Bayezid II (r. 1481–1512) made it Ottoman policy to welcome them. He was keen to engage worldly-wise entrepreneurs in building up his nascent empire. Adroitly calculating that Christianity's loss could be Islam's gain, he openly invited the Jews to immigrate, and he said of Spain's king, Ferdinand: 'Can you call such a king wise or intelligent? He is impoverishing his country and enriching my kingdom'.

Turkey's existing 50,000 Jews generously helped their brethren, performing 'unlimited great deeds of charity, giving money as if it were stones', reported the chronicler Rabbi Elijah Capsali. About 150,000 arrived, of whom 40,000 settled directly in Constantinople. Jews also came to Salonika in Greece, whose Jewish population rose to 20,000 by 1553; to Izmir (formerly Smyrna); and to Adrianople, now Edirne in European Turkey, site of an earlier influx of Ashkenazim from France and Germany. Adrianople's rabbi,

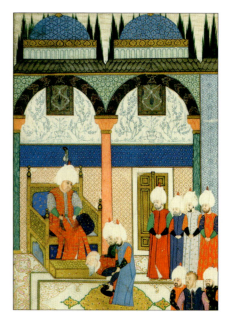

Above Ambassadors paying homage to the Ottoman Sultan Suleiman the Magnificent; from a 16th-century manuscript about his campaigns.

Isaac Sarfati, even posted letters to communities in Hungary, Moravia and the Rhineland praising the liberality of the Sultanate.

Once ensconced as citizens of the empire, Sephardi Jews did well, establishing the first Gutenberg press in Constantinople in 1493, and working as skilled craftsmen, iron-casters and makers of gunpowder.

OTTOMAN RULE

During the reign of Suleiman the Magnificent (1520–66) the Ottoman empire controlled Asia Minor, Egypt, North Africa, the eastern Mediterranean and all of the Middle East apart from Persia. In fact the dynasty originated as a small *beylik* (principality) abutting Byzantine territory. After Mongols vanquished Anatolia's powerful Seljuk Turks, the Ottomans began their inexorable rise, led after 1281 by Osman (known as Ottoman to Europeans).

Left The Etz Hayyim ('tree of life') synagogue in Chania, Crete, a Greek island long under Ottoman control.

JEWS IN THE OTTOMAN EMPIRE

Above Once a haven for Jews under Turkish rule, Safed houses this synagogue named after a famous rabbinical resident, Joseph Caro.

The first Jewish community under their control was Bursa in north-west Anatolia, taken in 1326. Osman's son, Orhan, allowed Jews to build the Etz Hayyim (Tree of Life) synagogue, and Jews immigrated from as far as Arabia. In swift succession the Ottomans took over parts of Romania and Bulgaria, Serbia, Albania, Macedonia and Greece, most of which had small Jewish populations.

Having captured Byzantium in 1453, Sultan Mehmet II (1432–81) confirmed Moses Kapsali as chief rabbi. The Greek-born Kapsali was known for both his impartiality as a civil magistrate and tax supervisor, and also for his friendship with Mehmet and Bayezid II. Scrupulous in matters of religion, he defended normative Judaism against Karaite attack and youthful rebels. Mehmet encouraged Jews from Crete and the provinces to live in Constantinople. In 1556 he

Right Sephardi Jews breathed new life into the Ottoman empire, which by the 1500s included Jerusalem and Mecca.

sent a Jewish regiment called 'Sons of Moses' to fight rebel Christian forces in Belgrade. Leading the enemy army was the monk John Capistrano, a notorious persecutor of Jews in Italy, Sicily, Bavaria, Silesia, Austria and Poland.

SEPHARDIM DOMINATION

Supremely confident that they originated from the most refined culture in Europe, Sephardi Jews set up their own synagogues. Soon a familiar pattern was repeated, but with a difference: in the past there had been rivalry between Babylonian rite synagogues and Palestinian; now it was Spanish versus indigenous. Ottoman authorities asked synagogues to collect taxes, so they became fiscal bodies as well as spiritual and communal centres and schools.

In places where each community had its own synagogue (Italian, Sephardi, Ashkenazi, Romaniote), an umbrella *kehillah*, or 'Hebrew community', came to represent them all. Moreover, ad hoc Jewish general assemblies administered internal affairs, while Ottoman Jewish law courts enjoyed more autonomy than their equivalents in Christian Europe. Ottoman prestige rose among European Jews, too, when Palestine fell to Turkish hands in 1516.

JOSEPH CARO

The Ottoman subject who made the greatest impact on Jews was rabbi and mysticist Joseph Caro (1488–1575). He was born in Spain, moved as a child to Portugal and lived in Adrianople, Salonika, Constantinople, Safed and Jerusalem. Probably even more than Moses Maimonides, Caro determined the authoritative code of law and practice for generations of Orthodox Jews. His magnum opus, *Beth Yosef* (House of Joseph) was an overview of 32 authorities on Talmudic rulings. Caro intended to rationalize the rapidly diverging Sephardi and Ashkenazi approaches to law.

His much shorter abridgement of *Beth Yosef*, entitled *Shulkhan Arukh* (Prepared Table), achieved immortality. Published in Venice in 1574, it was to be 'carried in one's bosom and referred to at any time and any place'. Critics found it didactic; Caro himself suggested it was mainly for simpletons or beginners. However, aided by the printing revolution, the 'Table' gained popularity in both Ashkenazi and Sephardi households.

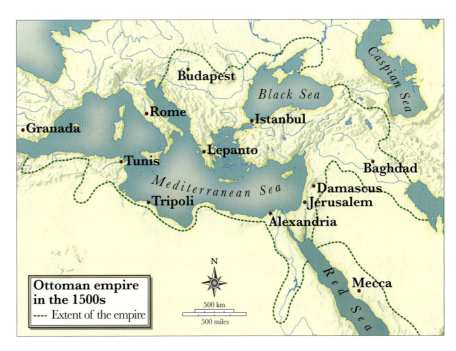

Turks and Jews in the Holy Land

THE OTTOMANS ELEVATED THE OFFICE OF CHIEF RABBI AFTER TAKING PALESTINE IN 1516, AND ALLOWED JEWS SUCH AS DONA GRACIA HITHERTO UNPARALLELED INFLUENCE IN IMPERIAL AFFAIRS.

Unlike his predecessors who were obsessed with European campaigns, Selim I the Grim (r. 1512–20) turned east after taking the Ottoman throne in 1512. He defeated Shah Ismail of Shia Persia in 1514, took Palestine and Syria in 1516, occupied Egypt in 1517 and gained possession of Arabian territories from the Mamluks.

At a stroke Selim became steward of Islam's three holiest cities – Mecca, Medina and Jerusalem – and declared himself Caliph over all Muslims. Ottoman rule reunited Jewish communities in the Balkans, North Africa and the Middle East. Significantly, from a Jewish perspective, Turks ruled the Land of Israel and Jerusalem, and would do so for another 400 years.

Below Jewish doctors often served the Ottoman court; drawing by the French geographer Nicolas de Nicolay, 1568.

CHIEF RABBI OF THE LEVANT

In 1452 the Ottomans had established the office of chief rabbi, and after 1517 the officeholder became in effect Exilarch of the Levantine Diaspora. Formally this included Palestinian Jews, too. The incumbent rabbi was Elijah Mizrahi, a Romaniote Jew. He was proficient in Arabic, Hebrew, Italian and Greek, wrote a famous commentary on Rashi's Torah, accepted Karaites as students and as a mathematician reputedly discovered how to extract the cube root.

The Ottomans set up the *kakhya*, or 'office for secular administration', headed by Shealtiel, a Turkish-speaking Jew. Jews were recognized as a separate ethno-religious community, alongside Greek Orthodox, Armenian Christians and others. However, Muslims outnumbered the minorities, Jews and Christians had to pay protection and head tax, and the Chief Mufti held a cabinet post, unlike the spiritual leaders of the Christian and Jewish communities.

Generally 16th-century sultans favoured Jews over Christians, and several rose to positions of power, such as Mehmet II's minister of finance, Hekim Yakup Pasha, and Murad II's physician, Ishak Pasha. Selim followed the trend by appointing Abraham Castro master of the mint and *nagid*, or Jewish community leader, in Egypt. Closer ties came during the 1520–66 reign of Suleiman the Magnificent, who rebuilt Jerusalem's city walls. He won popularity when his troops captured Rhodes in 1522, freeing and gaining fighters from 4,000 Jews whom the ruling Knights Hospitaller had been using as slave labourers.

Above Sultan Selim the Grim, who took Palestine and Syria in 1516, thus uniting Eastern Jews under one rule.

FAMILY RELATIONS

The Jewish pair who wielded the most power was Don Joseph Nasi, born as the Portuguese Marano João Micas around 1524, and Dona Gracia, his aunt and mother-in-law. They turned a precious-stones enterprise into a banking empire. Cultured and charming, Gracia left Portugal via England for Antwerp, mingled with European nobles and arrived in Venice in 1545. Turkish diplomats intervened when she was denounced as a Judaizer. She arrived in Constantinople in 1553 and was reunited with her nephew, having arranged escape passages for other Portuguese Maranos.

In Constantinople Don Joseph regularly met foreign ambassadors and counselled sultans on matters of policy, especially concerning the Middle East. He became a *muterferik*, or 'gentleman of the royal retinue', and Duke of the island of Naxos. In 1560, he and Gracia were allowed to develop a Jewish colony at Tiberias, near the Sea of Galilee, to the betterment of all its inhabitants.

Joseph, now Lord of Tiberias, encouraged Suleiman to attack Cyprus, a Venetian possession. At the subsequent naval battle off Lepanto in 1571,

Above Born in Portugal, Dona Gracia became in her day the most influential woman in the Ottoman empire.

however, a combined fleet of Spanish, Venetian and papal ships humiliated the Ottoman navy. Turkey secured Cyprus in 1573 and Tunis the next year, but Joseph, blamed for his Lepanto miscalculation, was never named king of Cyprus.

JEWISH DIPLOMATS
Turkey used Jews to negotiate with European political figures. Joseph's rival, Solomon Ashkenazi, represented Turkey in peace talks with Catholic Venice, despite Venetian reluctance to meet a Jew. He later got Venice to cancel a threat to expel its Jews. Don Joseph called for an embargo of the Adriatic port of Ancona, after the Inquisition began targeting the Portuguese Maranos living there. The embargo was opposed by Italian Jews who feared papal retribution and ultimately failed. Yet it signalled an early use of economic power as a political weapon.

SAFED VERSUS JERUSALEM
Palestinian Jews benefited economically after the Ottoman conquests of 1516–17. Contacts grew with Jews in Syria and Egypt, and soon 1,500 Jewish families were living in Jerusalem. By the late 16th century some 15,000 Jews were drawn to Safed, both by its holiness and its trade with nearby Damascus. Their prosperity, though, stoked resentment in a poorer Jerusalem.

One wealthy Safed spice dealer, Rabbi Jacob Berab, also harboured millennial ambitions. He wanted to revive the Great Sanhedrin, and persuaded Joseph Caro and others in Safed to reinstate the Temple custom of *smicha*, or 'priestly ordination by the laying on of hands'. But Jerusalem rabbis declared that such practices were forbidden until the Temple was restored.

DECLINE AFTER SULEIMAN
After Suleiman died in 1566, Muslims in Tiberias protested against Jewish plans to build city walls, and local governors imposed burdens on residents, especially Jews. Meanwhile, the Ottoman conquest of Hungary in 1526 had brought thousands of Ashkenazi Jews into the Turkish fold. Most felt comfortable, yet Christians perceived a Muslim threat to their security, and often cast their suspicion at the Ashkenazi population of eastern Europe.

Left A 1517 etching of the Ottoman capture of Erzerum, which opened the gateway to the Middle East.

> ### LADINO: THE SEPHARDI LINGUA FRANCA
> As Yiddish is to Ashkenazim, so is Ladino to the Sephardi Jews – a much-loved hybrid language filled with pathos, wit and charm. Again, like Yiddish, the number of its speakers has sadly dwindled; only about 80,000 Jews in Israel and a few thousand others outside still understand Ladino. The sole surviving Ladino newspaper is printed in Istanbul (formerly Constantinople).
>
> Also known as Judeo-Spanish, Judezmo, Spanyol, or Haquitiya in Spanish Morocco, the word Ladino derives from 'Latin'. The language is based on medieval Castilian with lashings of Hebrew, Aramaic and a little Turkish, Arabic, French and Italian. Until recently Ladino was written in Hebrew characters, using a cursive 'rabbinic' typeface. Its heyday came after the 1492 expulsion, and the first Ladino Bible translation appeared in the 1700s in Constantinople. The most famous Ladino work was *Me'am Lo'ez* (1730), a retelling of Bible stories. There was a strong oral rather than written culture until the 19th century. Ladino is being revived as a literary language in academic circles and, in a curious reversal of normal practice, it might as a result be catching on again as a spoken language. This is partly driven by a revival in Ladino music.

The Dawn of the Ashkenazi Ascendancy

ASHKENAZI COMMUNITIES GREW IN SIZE AND SELF-CONFIDENCE AS THEIR MEMBERS FOUND NEW ROLES IN 16TH-CENTURY PRAGUE, KRAKOW AND PREVIOUSLY OBSCURE LANDS EAST OF GERMANY.

Precisely when Ashkenazi Jews separated from Sephardi Jews is hard to say. Some attribute the break to 1000CE, when Ashkenazim outlawed polygamy while Sephardim still allowed it. Others believe the rift dates from the adoption of the Ladino language by Sephardim and Yiddish by Ashkenazim, possibly around the same period.

In 1571 Rabbi Moses Isserles of Krakow appended notes to Joseph Caro's definitive legal summary, the *Shulkhan Arukh*. His glosses were called *Mappah*, a 'table-cloth' to dress the Sephardi Caro's 'prepared table'. They defined Ashkenazi customs such as avoiding rice over Passover. Since then, the Ashkenazi *Shulkhan Arukh* has come with the *Mappah* attached. It denotes a connection to the world of Sepharad yet also a declaration of independence from it.

*Below Torah binders (*Mappah *in Hebrew) indicate vibrant cultural creativity among Ashkenazi Jews.*

A JEWISH RENAISSANCE

By the 16th century, Mediterranean Jews were beginning to be outnumbered by their fellow Ashkenazim, with most living in Poland and eastern Europe, rather than their original heartland of Germany. Many reasons explain Poland's attraction: though Jews were temporarily expelled from Krakow in 1494, Poland's Jagiellon monarchs usually favoured Jews as economic entrepreneurs who could develop their empire's hinterland.

In 1501 King Alexander of Poland readmitted Jews to the Grand Duchy of Lithuania, and he appointed Jacob Polak as Poland's first chief rabbi in 1503. After 1551 Jews got to elect their own chief rabbi. The royal court and rabbis granted Jewish councils the power to tax their flock. This benefited the crown, which kept 70 per cent of takings, leaving 30 per cent for communal welfare and official salaries.

Rabbis approved easy access to credit finance, which allowed Jews to join forces with Polish landowners and develop wheat-growing areas in the east. Jews leased estates, ran tolls, distilleries and mills, imported wine, cloth, soap and furs, and created entire townships anew, known as *shtetls* in Yiddish. Jews also came to dominate river traffic to Baltic ports and exported grain by sea to western Europe.

In 1534 King Sigismund I (1467–1548) abolished the law that forced Jews to wear special clothes. In this freer atmosphere, Jews felt encouraged to start the first Hebrew printing house – in Lublin, 1547. Twenty years later they founded the first Jewish university/seminary in Poland.

Above An etching of Prague's Jewish Town Hall, c.1898, symbolizing the autonomy Jews enjoyed in Bohemia.

16TH-CENTURY PRAGUE

Rabbi Polak was credited with inventing *pilpul*, the Talmudic system of study that involves what some call needlessly hair-splitting argumentation. Other Ashkenazi centres preferred a less insular approach to learning, one that was more relevant to the outside world and the scientific changes spawned by the Renaissance.

One such place was Prague, whose Jewish roots began in the 10th century, and where 3,000 Jews lived at the end of the 16th century. The community included some especially creative figures, such as Judah Loew ben Betzalel (1525–1609), rabbi, Talmudic sage and community leader. The Maharal, as he was known, was both a mystic and a devotee of rational science and philosophy. He was associated with the Golem, a mythical creature of mud who protected Jews after being brought to life by uttering the word *emet*, or 'truth'.

Isaiah Horowitz (c.1565–1630) became rabbi of Frankfurt and Prague, leaving for Palestine in 1620. A phil-anthropist, he survived a kidnapping in Jerusalem when ransomed by the Turkish pasha. His *Shnei Luhot Ha-Berit*, 'Two Tablets of the Covenant', is a classic compendium of ethics and mysticism that promotes joy in every action, and converts evil into good.

A different sort of Prague figure was Marcus Meisel, who provided the Holy Roman (German) Emperor Rudolph with art and scientific equipment. Meisel also financed Rudolph's war against Turkey. An archetypal court Jew, he protected his community, paved roads, built synagogues and cemeteries, provided charity for the poor, and won the right to bar police from entering the Jewish quarter.

COUNCIL OF FOUR LANDS

The growth of the Jewish population of Poland was dramatic: under 30,000 in 1500, about 150,000 by 1575, and as many as 450,000, or 4.5 per cent of Poland's population, in 1650. By then Polish Jews constituted about half of the world's Jews.

In 1580 Polish monarchs granted Jews a measure of political autonomy unprecedented in Europe until then. The resultant Council of Four Lands was an autonomous assembly which lasted for nearly 200 years. It consisted of 70 delegates drawn from the *kehillot*, or 'Jewish communities', of Greater Poland, Little Poland, Ruthenia and Volhynia. The Council met half-yearly, and at times also included Podolia, now a region of Ukraine.

Above Jews displaced from Germany, Hungary and elsewhere found havens in Poland and its environs.

Ukraine remained open to the Jews even after Ivan the Terrible, Tsar of Russia (1530–84), barred them from his territory. By 1648 there were 115 Ukrainian Jewish settlements which farmed taxes, advised magnates and governments, and ran entire colonies. However, Christian Ukrainian peasants despised the Catholic Poles, and even more so the Jews who served as their middlemen. From 1648 to 1654 Ukrainian pogroms killed perhaps 100,000 Jews. This disaster devastated the Council of Four Lands, which ceased operating in the first partition of Poland in 1764. Thereafter, most Polish Jews came under the authority of Moscow.

GLÜCKEL OF HAMELN

In faraway Hamburg, near the former epicentre of Ashkenaz, the first named Jewish female author of modern times, Glückel of Hameln (1646–1724), wrote in her memoirs of other crises – the false messiah Shabbetai Tzvi and the expulsion of Jews during the Polish–Swedish war. Glückel's stoical account written in Yiddish suggests the indomitable spirit that allowed Jews to survive.

YIDDISH: THE LANGUAGE OF THE ASHKENAZIM

'Glitch', 'chutzpah', 'shlep', 'nosh' and many other colloquial words derive from Yiddish. The language fuses German dialects with Hebrew, Slav and Romance languages. It probably began when Jews left France and Italy for the Rhineland in the 10th century. There they met Jews who still used Aramaic and French Jews who spoke Laaz, a Latin-based argot. Yiddish was probably first written down *c.*1270, and rendered in Hebrew characters.

Above Performance in Berlin by the Moscow Art Theatre, 1935, of a play by Yiddish writer Peretz Hirschbein.

During 1250–1500, Yiddish acquired words and grammar from Polish and Russian. Eastern Yiddish displaced Knaanic, a Slavic Jewish dialect. In France and Germany, Old or Western Yiddish faded in the 1600s as urban Jews began using national languages, and 18th-century intellectuals preferred Hebrew as the 'authentic' Jewish language. Detractors saw Yiddish as a crude patois, but supporters hailed it as the essence of Ashkenazi folk culture. The 19th century saw a boom in Yiddish literature; until assimilation, the Holocaust, Soviet oppression and the promotion of Hebrew in Israel nearly suppressed it. Yiddish today is enjoying a revival, mainly spoken by ultra-Orthodox Jews.

Jewish Life in Holland and Baruch Spinoza

JEWISH TRADERS PROBABLY ACCOMPANIED ROMAN SOLDIERS IN ANCIENT TIMES, AND A FEW ASHKENAZIM LIVED IN THE NETHERLANDS AFTER THE 12TH CENTURY, BUT THE 1580S SAW THE GREAT EXPANSION OF JEWISH LIFE.

Modern Dutch Jewry began when 20,000 vendors and scholars, including Maranos, left Antwerp for Holland in 1585. More Jews came after Dutch cities offered charters for settlement in 1604, including Don Samuel Palache, representative of the Sultan of Morocco.

Holland gained its first Sephardi rabbi just as Amsterdam was becoming the centre of world trade. Jewish merchants refined sugar, sold tobacco and silk and came to dominate the diamond-polishing industry. They accompanied Dutch expeditions to the Americas and held shares in the East India Company. Families such as the Machado, Pereira, de Medina and Suasso provisioned Holland's army and benefited when Holland spearheaded European opposition to France after 1672. Dutch Jews were also celebrated as book printers at a time when Holland was attracting foreign philosophers such as John Locke and René Descartes.

DUTCH FREEDOM?
Many Jews discovered the Dutch republic's reputation for freedom was not entirely deserved: guilds still barred Jews from key trades and the city of Utrecht refused to admit them. Nor was the Jewish community liberal: the Sephardi freethinker Uriel da Costa took his life in 1640 after a public recantation at the Portuguese synagogue in Amsterdam.

BARUCH SPINOZA
Unlike da Costa, who was brought up as a Jesuit in Portugal, Benedict (Baruch) Spinoza was raised in a Jewish environment. Born in 1632 to Maranos (crypto-Jews) from Portugal, he studied the Torah and Talmud under Menasseh Ben Israel, who persuaded England to welcome back Jews. He also studied Kabbalah and the Jewish philosophers, Maimonides, Gersonides and Crescas.

Far from being an atheist, as he was accused of being, Spinoza devoted his life to the 'intellectual love of God', a view expressed in his posthumous *Ethics* (1677). His *Theologico-Political Treatise* (1670) was controversial since it was a systematic critique of Judaism and organized religion. He saw God as part of nature and thought the idea of a God who hears prayers or has a divine universal plan was absurd.

Turning to Judaism specifically, Spinoza wrote that Torah laws 'have no relationship with happiness'. They were obsolete after the

Left The Jewish Bride, *also known as* Isaac and Rebecca, *by the Dutch master Rembrandt van Rijn, 1667.*

Above The pioneering Dutch-born philosopher Baruch Spinoza left his Jewish faith and helped lay the foundations for the Enlightenment.

Temple's destruction and constituted 'statutes that were not good and by which none could live'. Religion should guide us towards an ethical life, he believed; but rabbis were more concerned about self-preservation, and Christian persecution merely hardened their stubbornness.

HERETIC OR NOT?
In July 1656, Sephardi community elders issued a *herem*, or 'act of excommunication', against Spinoza, in terms that still chill: 'Cursed be he when he lies down and cursed be he when he rises up... the anger and wrath of the Lord will rage against this man'. Only much later did some suggest that Spinoza pre-empted the Hassidic belief that 'all is in God' – called pantheism.

Baruch Spinoza headed a circle of rationalists while supporting himself as a lens-polisher. He died in 1677, still shunned by the Jewish community. Even detractors, however, respect his intellect. In one Hassidic tale a pupil tells his rabbi about Spinoza's belief that there is no basic difference between humans and animals. 'In that case', replies the rabbi, 'why have no animals produced a Spinoza?'

Jews in England – The Return to Albion

Officially, the 1290 expulsion order was never rescinded and England remained 'Jew-free' for 366 years. However, a strange sequence of events subsequently led to their readmission.

England had not been officially open to Jews since 1290, but after 1492 several Maranos from Spain and Portugal made their homes in London. Rodrigo Lopez, royal physician to Queen Elizabeth I, was a prized member of this community before he was accused of plotting to poison the monarch and was executed in 1594. (Two years later William Shakespeare wrote *The Merchant of Venice*, reputedly basing his depiction of Shylock on Lopez.)

ROYAL SPIES AND TRADERS

In 1635, the Portuguese merchant Antonio Fernandes Carvajal (c.1590–1659) settled in London and revived a Marano community that had dwindled after the Lopez scandal. He won a contract to supply corn to the English army, ran ships to the Caribbean, Brazil, India and the Canaries, and annually imported £100,000 in silver.

England was engaged in a fierce trading war with colonial rivals, so Carvajal and his fellow Maranos used their contacts to spy on Spanish ambitions in the New World. Grateful British authorities agreed to waive the usual strictures on foreigners and make Carvajal a denizen in 1655. They turned a blind eye to the fact that he and other nominally Catholic Portuguese worshipped at a secret synagogue in London's Creechurch Lane.

CROMWELL'S SUPPORT

In 1649 King Charles I was executed following the Second English Civil War, and Oliver Cromwell became Lord Protector in 1653. Cromwell listened favourably when Menasseh Ben Israel travelled from Holland in 1650 and presented him with his tract, 'Hope for Israel'. In it the Madeira-born rabbi and printer argued – somewhat fancifully – that Native Americans were the lost Hebrew tribes, and England was the only place on earth without Jews. Readmitting them would hasten the coming of the Messiah, and also prove a financial and strategic asset.

Although readmission was never formally agreed, it became accepted. By 1690 about 400 Jews, mainly Sephardim from Holland, had settled in England. Their first synagogue was the now officially consecrated house in Creechurch Lane. In 1702 a new synagogue in Bevis Marks, City of London, opened.

IN THE CITY

The City accepted Jews as bankers and brokers, even though anti-Semitic sentiment lingered. When Dutch prince William of Orange invaded England in 1688 he became King William III of England, and many Jewish financiers left The Hague to help create London's new stock market.

Parliament passed a Jewish Naturalization Act in 1753 after Tory MPs raised an outcry about 'abandonment of Christianity'. A number of Sephardim chose to baptize their children to gain fair chances.

LIFE OUTSIDE LONDON

While Sephardim entered parliament as Christians – in time they saw Benjamin Disraeli elected as Prime Minister in 1874 – Ashkenazi newcomers from Germany and the Hanseatic League began settling in England. Most were small traders who lived in coastal towns such as Plymouth and Bristol. Slowly, new congregations emerged in Leeds, Manchester and Edinburgh. And mass migration of poorer immigrants from Russia, Poland and Romania followed, although full emancipation only came in 1858.

Right Menasseh Ben Israel, the Dutch Sephardi rabbi who convinced Cromwell to readmit Jews to England.

Below Built in London in 1702, the Bevis Marks Sephardi Synagogue is a miniature of the Esnoga in Amsterdam.

CHAPTER 7

A CHANGING FAITH

Disasters have typically inspired messianic hopes of redemption among Jews. This was certainly true after Ukrainian pogroms and Polish wars engulfed mid-17th-century Europe. From Cairo to Amsterdam, Jews flocked to the cause of a charismatic rabbi from Turkey named Shabbetai Tzvi, who drew from the mystical Kabbalah tradition of Safed, Palestine.

When Shabbetai proved to be a fraud, new trends emerged to fill the void. One was Hassidism, a return to Orthodox faith infused with spiritual joy that rejected elitism and intellectualism. Another was the Haskalah, a Jewish variant of the European Enlightenment, which defined Jews as a nationality worthy of full civil rights. The Haskalah in turn inspired the modernizing Reform Judaism movement, while revolutions in 18th-century America and France seemed to promise an age of equality. The historian Leopold Zunz said Jews made a dramatic transition from a prolonged Middle Ages straight into the modern era. But when Tsarist Russia corralled Jews from a dismembered Poland into a vast Pale of Settlement, such dreams of tolerance and progress became delusions.

Opposite A 17th-century Turkish folk art depiction of a rabbi holding a Torah aloft, chanting the traditional words: 'This is the Torah Moses set before the Children of Israel'.

Above The First Great Sanhedrin, supreme court of the Jewish people, which Napoleon granted to Jews in France, symbolizing his scheme to be patron of a Jewish national revival.

A Crisis of Faith

BATTERED BY WARS AND POGROMS IN UKRAINE AND POLAND, EUROPEAN JEWS EAGERLY LOOKED TO TURKISH RABBI SHABBETAI TZVI, ONLY TO DISCOVER HE WAS A FALSE MESSIAH.

From his vantage point in late 16th-century Prague, Rabbi Judah Loew was relieved that the expulsions of the Middle Ages had come to an end. But his optimism was to prove misplaced: at least 100,000 Jews were slaughtered in the Ukraine during 1648–54 in the so-called Chmielnicki massacres. The upheaval also generated impossible messianic expectations, which, once dashed, set Jews back for decades if not centuries.

JEWS BETWEEN TWO FAITHS

Mid-17th-century Europe felt threatened by Muslim Ottomans. The Ottomans had besieged Vienna in 1529 and taken most of Hungary and Transylvania by 1546. They fought Poland to stalemate after a 15-year-long war that ended in 1606, and launched a campaign against Venice in 1645. Many Christians suspected their Jewish neighbours were acting as a Turkish fifth column.

However, the great Ukrainian pogroms arose not out of any Muslim–Christian clash, but from a vicious fight within Christendom. In 1569 the newly created Polish–Lithuanian Commonwealth took over large parts of Ukraine where Catholic Polish landlords encouraged Jews to run their estates. By now some 75 per cent of the world's Jews may have lived in Greater Poland.

But Ukraine's peasants were Orthodox Christian, not Catholic, and felt closer to Russians than to Poles. In addition, the Cossacks of central Ukraine, a militant caste, yearned for independence. Most Ukrainians therefore despised the Polish nobles and hated their Jewish administrators with even greater venom. In 1648 the Cossack commander Bogdan Chmielnicki (c. 1595–1657) rebelled against the Polish yoke, telling peasants that the Catholics had sold them 'into the hands of the accursed Jews'. He quickly repulsed Commonwealth forces and declared himself 'sole autocrat of the Rus' in 1649.

Churches were burnt, priests and nobles slaughtered and estates pillaged. Nearly a million are thought to have died. Proportionately, Jews suffered worst, with 300 population centres destroyed and more than 100,000 killed. Though contemporary estimates of up to 500,000 are probably exaggerated, the killings surpassed in brutality the pogroms of the Crusades and of the Black Death, and dispelled illusions that eastern and central Europe had adopted Enlightenment values.

Tsarist Russia absorbed a weakened Ukraine in 1654 and then attacked Poland. Russian troops killed 100,000 Jews mercilessly during the resultant Russo-Polish war (1654–67). Finally 'The Deluge', or series of 'misfortunes' following the Swedish invasion and occupation of the Polish Commonwealth (1655–60), created yet more havoc.

FLIGHT NORTH AND WEST

The gruesome four-way war between Ukraine, Russia, Poland and Sweden drove thousands of Jews westward, reversing a trend of eastward migration that had prevailed for two centuries. Many Ashkenazi refugees settled in Amsterdam alongside the existing Sephardi community. Others fled to Lithuania in the north, where local communities raised ransoms to redeem fellow Jews kidnapped by Tartars, the temporary allies of the Cossacks.

Above Hero to some, villain to many – statue completed in 1888 of Bogdan Chmielnicki, in Kiev, Ukraine.

Below: Chief Rabbi Jacob Loew's grave in Prague's Old Jewish Cemetery, Czech Republic, where his nephew Rabbi Judah Loew, the Maharal of Prague, is also buried.

MESSIANIC STIRRING

Increasingly, Jews turned to mysticism for solace. Could these torments, they wondered, be the apocalypse that preceded the coming of the Messiah? Rumours began to pour in about a Kabbalistic 'system' that explained the mysteries of the world. The creators of this system were Rabbi Isaac Luria (1534–72), a friend of Joseph Caro, and his disciple Haim Vital (1543–1620). Both lived in Safed, in Galilee, the highest city in Ottoman-ruled Palestine and spiritually almost on a par with Jerusalem.

Luria likened the state of exile to *tzimtzum*, or God's 'withdrawal' or 'contraction' from the world at the tumultuous act of creation. Each human soul, he said, contained a *nitzotz*, or 'spark' of the divine. To move from exile to redemption, everyone, and especially Jews, should practise *tikkun olam*, or 'repairing the world', by gathering the sparks that escaped on the first day, according to Genesis. Humanity could thus achieve global harmony, explained Luria, by appeasing God through good acts, or *mitzvot*.

Jews outside Safed began reading into Luria's beliefs a radical explanation and a possible cure for historical disasters. While 'purer' Kabbalists warned against the vulgar mixing of Lurianic mysticism with ideas of a coming saviour, many felt the genie was out of the bottle.

THE FALSE MESSIAH

The man who most dramatically and disastrously inspired public passion was Shabbetai Tzvi, a Sephardi Jew born in Smyrna (Izmir), Turkey, in 1626. The son of a trading agent for Dutch and English firms, Tzvi oscillated between ecstasy and gloom, which would suggest symptoms of extreme manic depression.

Expelled from Smyrna, Salonika and Constantinople, Tzvi fled to Palestine where he visited a Lurianic Kabbalist called Nathan of Gaza (c. 1643–80) in the hope of a cure. Instead Nathan, an Ashkenazi, persuaded Tzvi that he was the foretold messianic descendant of David. Together they 'revealed' themselves on 31 May 1665: Tzvi rode around Gaza on horseback, appointing ambassadors to summon the lost tribes of Israel, while Nathan became his prophet and 'holy lamp'.

Jews in Poland, Holland, Germany, Syria, Greece, Egypt and even England were swept up in the year-long, intense craze and spread Tzvi's message. Tzvi returned to Smyrna, broke into the main synagogue and announced the date of redemption – 18 June 1666 – when he would depose the Sultan and divide the world into new kingdoms.

SHABBETAI'S APOSTASY

Nathan announced that the Lurianic system was now overthrown and that Israelite armies were gathering in the Sahara to greet the messiah. Many Jews sold all their goods and did penance in preparation for their 'return

Left Shabbetai Tzvi, the false messiah, blessing Jews in Smyrna, Turkey, from a contemporary woodcut, c. 1665.

Above Nathan of Gaza, Shabbetai's chief ally, is blamed for dashing the hopes of a generation of Jews.

to Zion'. Others deliberately contravened the holiest Jewish laws and indulged in sexual lewdness.

Understandably perturbed, Ottoman officials arrested Tzvi when his ship entered Turkish waters, and jailed him in Constantinople. In September 1666 a Polish Kabbalist denounced him as an impostor. Faced with the choice of conversion or death, Shabbetai Tzvi became a Muslim, renamed himself Aziz Mehmed Effendi and was appointed the Sultan's official gatekeeper.

A shocked Jewish world fell suddenly silent, and the Sultan exiled Tzvi to Albania for his safety, where he died in 1676. Shabbateanism survived in pockets thanks to Nathan the master publicist, who explained that Tzvi's apostasy merely disguised his descent into evil to restore the last lost sparks. But most Jews felt badly deceived.

As to why mass obsession took root, it seems that crisis and upheaval so troubled a vulnerable 17th-century group that they readily believed a delusional mystic's utopian promises.

Hassidism

IN THE 18TH CENTURY, THE BA'AL SHEM TOV FOUNDED HASSIDISM, A RELIGIOUS AND SOCIAL MOVEMENT THAT FLOURISHES TODAY. HE TAUGHT THAT A PURE HEART IS MORE IMPORTANT THAN MUCH STUDY.

Rabbis seemed powerless to protect their flocks after the calamities of the 17th century, including the Ukrainian Chmielnicki massacres, the Russian and Swedish invasions of Poland, and the Shabbatean crisis. A century later, another 'false messiah', Jacob Frank, led followers into apostasy when he converted to Catholicism in 1759. Furthermore, the Polish Diet (parliament) ended the Jewish Council of Four Lands in 1764, and many Jews died in Ukraine's 1768 Koliyivshchyna rebellion. In 1772 Austria, Prussia and Russia were planning the dismemberment of Poland itself.

But this time another movement offered comfort to Jews seeking guidance and leadership. Also centred around Podolia, where Frank was born, Hassidism reinvigorated Jewish life with its passion. Its name derived from the Hebrew root, *hassid*, meaning 'piety' or 'loving kindness'. Hassidism addressed the same concerns as the Shabbateans and Frankists, but, unlike them, it never attacked the basic tenets of Jewish faith.

THE BESHT
Israel ben Eliezer (1698–1760), the founder of the Hassidic movement, is better known by his nickname, the Ba'al Shem Tov, or 'Master of the Good Name', or by the acronym Besht. Born in Okopy (now in Ukraine), he settled in the Podolian town of Mezhbizh in 1740. He was orphaned young and not formally educated. He worked as a clay digger and innkeeper, and wandered alone in the Carpathian Mountains.

Known as a healer, soothsayer and holy man, the Besht appealed to ordinary Jews who lived in villages and resented the didactic pronouncements of the *yeshivot*, or 'seminaries', of northern Europe. Many of those attracted to Kabbalah found the door to its wisdom barred by 'specialist' practitioners. Meanwhile, Jews who returned to Ukraine after the restoration of Polish rule in the 1690s were open to new ideas.

The Besht preached sincere love of God and fellowship among men. To the lay person he conveyed his ideas through his earthy personality and beguilingly simple parables; to the more learned, such as his disciple Meir ben Tzvi Hirsch Margolioth, he provided deeper spiritual insights.

The Besht wrote nothing himself, but his disciples transmitted his ideas orally and later set them down as an integrated system of beliefs. Soon dynastic Hassidic 'courts' spread across Ukraine, Belarus, Galicia and central Poland, and *magids*, or 'wandering teachers', inspired devotees by their force of personality.

Left The Ba'al Shem Tov – untutored, charismatic founder of Hassidism, who challenged the rabbinical establishment.

Above The Besht's tomb in Mezhbizh, Ukraine, now a place of pilgrimage for Hassidic devotees.

RABBI DOV BER
After the Besht died, his mantle passed to Rabbi Dov Ber of Mezhirech (1710–72), an extreme ascetic whom the Besht persuaded to participate in society. Enemies of Hassidism accused Dov Ber of neglecting Torah study and introducing forbidden new rituals. In fact, Hassidism drew on Isaac Luria's Kabbalastic idea that God is to be found in all aspects of life and thus can be served in performing even mundane activities.

The Hassidim stressed *devekut*, or the attempt to bridge the gap between God and man. That this could be achieved with the help of song, dance and even tobacco and alcohol infuriated more mainstream rabbis. They also practised *kavanna*, or 'concentration in prayer', and valued *tikun olam*, or 'repairing the world'; through acts of help and kindness. In that way, they said, people could gather the shards of goodness in a fractured niverse.

WONDER RABBIS
Rabbi Dov Ber, in his turn, inspired Elimelech of Lizhensk, Levi Yitzhak of Berdichev, Menachem Nahum of Chernobyl, and the Besht's grandson, Rabbi Boruch of Mezhbizh. After Dov Ber's death, his four disciples subdivided Europe into distinct territories. In time, this led to the creation of Hassidic courts and even

Above Not the usual Hassidic headgear! – Orthodox Jews celebrate Purim in Jerusalem, 2005.

'dynasties'. They spread the message with tales of *wunder-rebbes*, 'wonder rabbis', who explained their essential beliefs in a charming and accessible way. Within half a century Hassidism claimed the adherence of up to half of all Jews in eastern Europe, despite the fierce opposition of established rabbis, particularly in Lithuania, where Elijah Zalman tried to get Hassidim banned as heretics.

THE SCHOOL OF CHABAD

An acronym from Chochma, Binha and Da'at, Chabad stands for Wisdom, Understanding and Knowledge. By the 19th century the Chabad movement had its own courts and dynasties, the largest of which was based around Lubavich in Russia. Today, Lubavich Hassidim, headquartered in New York, are the most influential Hassidic sect in the world. They actively seek out wayward Jews, whom they bring back to Judaism as *hozrei b'teshuva*, or 'returnees to faith'.

INTO THE BALKANS

Hassidism also spread south across the Carpathian mountains and into Ruthenia, Romania and Hungary. The Teitelbaum family spawned many sects, including the famous Satmar Hassidim. Hassidic beliefs generally did not suit educated German Jews and faced resistance from Orthodox and Reform Jews.

> ### THE VILNA GAON, 'DEFENDER OF ORTHODOXY'
> Elijah Ben Shlomo Zalman (1720–93), usually called the Vilna Gaon, signed two orders of *herem*, or 'excommunication', against the earliest Hassidim, in 1772 and 1781. However, his true role in Judaism was more positive. Known in adulthood as the *gadol ha-dor*, or 'giant of his generation', he began as a child prodigy who mastered even the more obscure branches of rabbinical literature. The Vilna Gaon regarded secular study as necessary, though only in so far as it aided understanding of Jewish sources. He opposed the casual study of Kabbalah (mysticism) yet was himself an adept Kabbalist who believed in the power of spells and charms. Though not a rabbi by appointment, the Gaon was the acknowledged spiritual leader of Lithuanian Jewry, which under his steerage became the acme of religious scholarship.
>
> His main disciple was Haim of Volozhin (1749–1821), who in his book *Nefesh ha-Haim* (Spirit of Life) accused Hassidim of idolatry for venerating their rabbi-leaders. Haim also took issue with established practice in yeshivas, by outlawing *pilpul*. At Volozhin he established a rota so that someone would be studying the Torah and Talmud at all hours. His life's motto was 'Man must participate in the sufferings of others and help them'.

Similarly the trend made few inroads among Sephardi Jews, despite the proximity of the southern Hassidic heartland to Turkey and the Black Sea, and the fact the earliest hassidim adopted a Sephardi *nusach*, or 'prayer rite'. Only with the creation of the State of Israel have some *Mizrachi*, or 'oriental', and Sephardi Jews joined Hassidic sects. Even so, many social historians believe that Hassidism rescued Orthodox Judaism.

HASSIDIC CUSTOM

In their distinctive gabardines and Homburg hats, fur *shtreimels*, or 'large caps', Hassidic men are familiar sights in London, New York, Jerusalem and Bnei Brak near Tel Aviv in Israel. Women dress modestly, though children put on colourful costumes for the festival of Purim. Many theories abound about the origin of the costume. Some say Hassidim imitated Polish nobles of the day; others say this was typical east European Jewish dress, only most non-Hassidim have since abandoned the custom. Yet others suggest an oriental influence, and compare the long black satin robe called the *bekishe* to Shia imams' garb in Iran. Other aspects – the *pe'ot* 'sidelocks', and *tzitzit*, or 'side-tassels' – are normative Orthodox requirements, shared with other *haredim*, or 'ultra-Orthodox Jews'. Small differences in clothing (sock length, buttons, ties or no ties) distinguish one sect from another. That they exist in such large numbers is almost miraculous, given the devastation suffered in World War II.

Right A rabbi in traditional Hassidic dress stands beside the door of Yosef Caro's synagogue in Safed, Galilee.

Palestine – A Messianic Outpost

KABBALAH MYSTICISM DREW JEWS TO 16TH-CENTURY SAFED, YET THEY FORMED A MINORITY OF PALESTINE'S TOTAL POPULATION. WITHIN 300 YEARS, OTTOMAN NEGLECT LED TO ARAB REVOLT.

Perched on a hill overlooking the Sea of Galilee, Safed is one of the four holy cities to Jews, alongside Jerusalem, Hebron and Tiberias. Under Ottoman rule in the 16th century, it rapidly grew into the largest and most developed town in Palestine with the second-largest Jewish population in Asia. It also acted as a magnet for some of the greatest scholars in Jewish history. Here the Kabbalah, the main Jewish mystical tradition, truly developed – a phenomenon that gave comfort and guidance to millions, but also, in the wrong hands, spawned the false messiah movements that imperilled the Jewish faith everywhere.

Below Ceiling of the Abuhav Synagogue, Safed, built in the 16th century and full of mystical Kabbalistic imagery.

Right Mohammed Ali, Pasha of Egypt, whose actions sparked revolt in Palestine after 1834.

RABBI ISAAC LURIA – THE LION

More than any other, Rabbi Isaac Luria (1534–72) revolutionized Jewish thought with his new system of the Kabbalah. Known as the Ha-Ari, or 'The Lion', he was born in Jerusalem in 1534 to an Ashkenazi father and Sephardi mother. He studied Torah in Egypt, made a living as a spice merchant, and arrived in Safed in 1569 where he studied directly under the great Kabbalist, Moses Cordevero (1522–70). Yet while this teacher was a master of close textual analysis of the Zohar, the prime book of Jewish mysticism, his pupil went in another direction.

EXILE TO REDEMPTION

Rabbi Luria described how in the imperfect world after Creation, the *shekhina*, or 'divine presence', known as the indwelling spirit or the feminine aspect of God, is itself in exile. Redemption would come when exile ended. For many Jewish listeners, such ideas had relevance in the real world and excited messianic expectations. On a national level they suggested there would be a Jewish return to Palestine, or the Land of Israel.

Gentle-natured and intuitive, Luria wanted his doctrines kept secret, in case they were misinterpreted. Luria wrote little himself, but his protégé Haim Vital recorded his thoughts and fashioned Lurianic Kabbalah into an intricate system of moral and spiritual empowerment. After Luria died during an epidemic in 1572, aged 38, his disciples disseminated his works via the printing presses of Safed, Vilna, Constantinople and Livorno.

RISE AND DEMISE OF SAFED

Beyond the mystical, Safed became a thriving industrial centre based on manufactured cloth, which in the still-new Ottoman empire was a novelty. Wool was imported from Macedonia in the Balkans and

then shipped to the town of Safed by way of Sidon and Tripoli. In Safed, master weavers turned the wool into cloth that after dyeing was ready for export. Safed families also traded in food and spices with Lebanon and Syria, where there were active Jewish communities. Within Safed, Jews ran a close-knit welfare and administration system that tried to conform to Torah and Talmud precepts.

After the initial boom, problems began to emerge: Safed, like Jerusalem, Tiberias and Hebron, lacked an agricultural hinterland, thus limiting chances of expansion. New sultans neglected provincial towns, and some Turkish or Arab governors of Safed distrusted the town's Jews. Security deteriorated and robbers stalked the highways. In the mid-17th century an influx of zealous Shabbatean devotees, who had given away their worldly belongings, further strained Palestine's battered economy.

Below A 16th-century Torah scroll and traditional casket associated with Rabbi Isaac Luria, in Safed.

ASHKENAZIM IN PALESTINE

Poor Jews in Jerusalem badly needed aid, so *shlichim*, or 'emissaries', were sent from the Holy Land to wealthier Diaspora communities in Alexandria, Constantinople, Izmir and Ashkenazi centres. Diaspora Jews regarded *hallukah*, or 'donating charity', as an honour. Some, such as the esteemed Rabbi Isaiah Horowitz, personally immigrated; he settled in Jerusalem in 1620.

In 1740 the Muslim ruler of northern Palestine invited Haim Abulafia (1660–1744), Rabbi of Izmir, to rebuild the city of Tiberias. That same year the Ottoman Sultan Mahmud I allowed Christians to worship in Jerusalem, and come under the jurisdiction of their European homelands. Perhaps it was this ruling that encouraged more pious Ashkenazim to settle in 'Eretz Israel': first Hasidim from Belarus, Ukraine and Poland, and then, after 1780, Perushim, the 'separated ones' or disciples of the anti-Hassidic Vilna Gaon of Lithuania. By now Jerusalem had eclipsed Safed in importance.

SEEDLINGS OF JEWISH AND ARAB NATIONALISM

As of 1609 Palestine was subsumed within the province of Greater Syria; though Jerusalem was treated as a

Above Johann Gutenberg at work – his printing revolution of 1447 profoundly altered Jewish society too.

separate *sanjak*, or a district under a military governor. Most inhabitants of Palestine were neither Turkish nor Jewish, but Sunni Muslim Arabs. Like their Jewish co-residents, Palestinian Arabs loathed the Ottoman tax collectors; unlike them they often protested vigorously.

Their largest revolt came after the Egyptian ruler Mohammed Ali, a former Ottoman vassal, wrested Syria and Palestine from a weakened Turkey in 1831–41. In May 1834 Arab sheikhs from Nablus, Jerusalem and Hebron refused to offer Ali conscripts; they briefly took Jerusalem, Safed, Tiberias and Haifa. Ali and his son, the Egyptian army commander Ibrahim Pasha, eventually crushed the uprising. Arab historians call it the 'Syrian Peasant Revolt', although others detect the first strains of a specifically Palestinian Arab nationalism.

For their part, Jews also harboured nationalist dreams but they felt that return from exile should come from a divine agency. They generally favoured Ottoman rule of law, which helped bind one Diaspora community to another.

JEWS OF NORTH AFRICA AND THE MIDDLE EAST

FROM TIMBUKTU IN AFRICA TO BUKHARA IN CENTRAL ASIA, JEWS WERE DYNAMIC TRADERS, WHILE SEPHARDI IMMIGRANTS REVITALIZED ANCIENT LEVANTINE COMMUNITIES.

The Sephardi Jews who were exiled from the Iberian Peninsula at the end of the 15th century generally felt safe under Ottoman rule. They no longer needed to fear persecution, or hide their identity in public. However, later sultans and governors proved less accommodating than earlier ones, economic slowdown hampered scholastic development, and wars between Europe and Turkey interfered with ties between Jews in both zones. The first challenge facing Sephardim in the 16th century was how to co-exist with the old Jewish communities of North Africa and the Middle East.

Jewish merchants of the Ottoman empire from the 16th to the 19th centuries, transported merchandise to the great cities of Salonika and Constantinople, just as they had done under the Romans 1,500 years earlier. Jews were invaluable to commerce with Europe because many could speak German, French, Italian and Spanish.

Old Jewish firms in Muslim ports like Basra and Alexandria imported foreign products and exported raw materials. New Jewish-run industries, especially weaving, boomed in Salonika, Safed, Izmir and Algiers.

CAIRO

The Ottomans took Cairo in 1517, a year after occupying Jerusalem. There they encountered a mixed Jewish community, which included Sephardi descendants of the 12th-century Spanish scholar Maimonides. Spanish rabbis came to dominate synagogues, with only limited local *mughrabi* opposition. Sultan Selim I (1512–20) appointed Abraham Castro head of the Egyptian mint.

Sephardim settled in Alexandria, Cairo and Rosetta, as well as Damascus and Aleppo in Syria. They founded new yeshivas (rabbinical seminaries); poetry and rabbinic scholarship flourished to the benefit of Egypt and Palestine. Trade was revitalized in the 16th century

Above A 19th-century African Mizrah showing the direction of Jerusalem and blending Islamic art and Jewish symbols.

as peace returned to the eastern Mediterranean and Maghreb (North Africa). Some immigrant Sephardi Jews benefited from the capitulation agreements that Sultan Suleyman (1520–66) signed with Venice and France to protect foreign citizens.

TUNISIA

Talmudic sages had arrived in Tunisia in the 2nd century and Jews built an esteemed yeshiva in Kairouan soon after Muslim Arabs established it as their fourth holiest city in 670. Spanish raids in the 16th century drove Jews inland and to the mountains, where they took refuge with Berber tribes. Only in the 17th century did Tunisia return to Ottoman control, and even then Tunisian *beys* (governors) enjoyed autonomy.

In the 17th and 18th centuries Italian Jews from Leghorn (Livorno), known colloquially as Grana, joined indigenous Judaeo-Arabic Jews and earlier refugees from Spain in the 'Berber states' of Tunisia, Algeria and Tripolitana (part of today's Libya).

Left Lighting the candles in the ancient El-Ghriba synagogue on the Tunisian island of Djerba.

Right Jewish Wedding in Morocco, *Eugène Delacroix, 1841.*

They were very European in their dress, attire, speech and habits. In Tunisia they enjoyed the company of the forcibly converted Spanish Muslims who were expelled from Spain in 1609, and who, like the Grana, spoke Spanish.

By contrast, the Jews of the island of Djerba claim descent from Israelites who fled Babylonian persecution. They held to customs that probably originated in First Temple times. Their El-Ghriba Synagogue, the oldest in Africa, is still active and attracts Jews and other pilgrims.

JOURNEY TO TIMBUKTU

Evidently, a thriving Jewish community once existed in the vital trading entrepôt of Timbuktu, Mali. Southern Moroccan Jews imported gold and salt from inner Africa through the city, and many settled there, including Sephardi refugees from Spain. Most later converted to Islam, though pockets remain who proudly recall their Jewish roots and are reviving Judaic traditions in the 21st century.

Below Jewish children in Hara Sghira, Tunisia, learn the Hebrew alphabet.

YEMEN

Jews were already established in Yemen in the 5th century, and in medieval times regularly sought rulings from Maimonides when he lived in Fustat in Cairo. Jews in Sana'a, the capital, kept close contact with the academies in Iraq. The port of Aden also became a vital transit point for lucrative Jewish trade with India.

The Turks conquered Yemen in 1546, but soon lost control of Sana'a to local sheikhs and Zaydi Shia imams who accused the Jews of helping the foreigners. During this period of incessant revolts and forced conversions, the great Yemenite Jewish poet Shalom Shabazi wrote his finest works, such as *Im Nin 'Alu* and *As'alk*.

PERSIAN JEWRY

Shia Persia lay outside the Ottoman realm, and resisted the Constantinople Caliphate's presumption to represent all Muslims. Many Persian Jews had generally suffered under the Shia regimes of the Safavid dynasty, so they welcomed the new Sunni dynast, Nadir Shah (1736–47). He settled numerous Jews in Mashad, a city where the community thrived as rug merchants. They bolstered state coffers by trading in silk and gems with other Jews in Mirv, Khiva, Samarkand and Bukhara in Central Asia, and Herat in Afghanistan. Many thousands migrated to these imperial outposts as well as to Kurdistan, Egypt and India. Politically, Persian Jews served as negotiators between Sunni Turkestanis and Shia Iranians and had their own representatives in local government.

The fragility of Persian Jewish life was shown when the Qajar dynasty, which ruled Iran from 1796 until 1921, restored Shia ascendancy. They persecuted minorities and in 1839 – a century after Nadir Shah – forced the Jews of Mashad to convert to Islam. Elsewhere Jews were quarantined in separate neighbourhoods.

Paradoxically, Qajar excesses attracted the attention of Jews in the West who threw lifelines to their brethren in Persia. In 1865 French Jews represented by the educational association Alliance Israelite Universelle, and Sir Moses Montefiore, an influential English Sephardi philanthropist, interceded with ministers in Tehran to better the lot of Persian Jewry. This pattern was repeated in Ottoman territories.

Despite a promising start at the beginning of the 16th century, therefore, the Sephardim had to call on all their resources of ingenuity to survive in often unstable conditions in North Africa and the Middle East over two centuries.

THE PARTITION OF POLAND

IN 1700 THE POLISH COMMONWEALTH DOMINATED CENTRAL EUROPE. BY 1800 POLAND HAD DISAPPEARED, AND JEWS WHO LIVED THERE FOUND THEMSELVES DIVIDED BETWEEN AUSTRIA, PRUSSIA AND RUSSIA.

A tiny band of Western Jews had played a key role, albeit unintentionally, in events leading to Poland's demise. These 'court Jews' of Germany and Austria were urban cosmopolitans who became closely connected to Europe's new breed of absolutist monarchs.

Absolutism arose out of the centralization of the state that began in the France of Cardinal Richelieu and Mazarin in the early 18th century. The new rulers attacked crafts guilds and church privileges that stood between the sovereign and the individual. They also mistrusted Jews, who seemed doubly alien in their language and religion. The absolutist strain showed itself even in liberal guise, during the French Revolution. Many Jews hoped to be considered equally Jewish and French, yet the state granted Jews everything as individuals, and nothing as a 'nation'. Court Jews realized, however, that there was space within this secular ideology for advancement. Guilds that barred Jews were now powerless, as religious denomination was no longer a hindrance to entry. An individual's worth depended on his or her contribution to the state's well-being, not upon birth, faith or origin.

CONTROLLED SOCIETIES

Instead of excluding Jews from society, as in medieval times, absolutists wanted to make them 'useful' to the state treasury. A 1750 Prussian regulation ensured that Jews had to register their homes and businesses, and that their weddings were supervised. If they obeyed, they were 'protected'; if not, they could be demoted to 'useless' citizens and deported. In practice the new dispensation made privileged Jews richer and other Jews poorer. The latter were forced to work as old-style moneylenders, pedlars or pawnbrokers.

The Edict of Toleration issued in January 1782 by the Holy Roman Emperor of Austria, Joseph II (1765–90) best illustrated absolutism at work. On the one hand, his law decreed that Jews no longer had to wear demeaning badges of ethnic identification or pay the onerous *leibzoll* (body tax) when they entered an area that customarily banned them. On the other, they had to adopt German-style forenames and surnames and were liable for state military service. In addition, Jews

Left German, Polish and East European spice boxes to mark the end of Sabbath, 18th–19th centuries.

Above Catherine the Great, Empress of Russia, 1762–96, under whose reign a million Polish Jews became Russian subjects when borders changed.

were barred from using Hebrew or Yiddish in commercial and communal records, and rabbis lost their juridical autonomy.

Although discriminatory, the law marked an advance. All Jews had been evicted from Vienna in 1670 (though most soon returned) and they had faced severe persecution under Maria Teresa in Bohemia and Moravia in 1745. Emperor Joseph had argued that toleration would serve the 'betterment of Jews' and would make them 'less harmful' to general European society. Other Enlightenment figures followed the ideas of the English social theorist John Toland, whose book *Reasons for Naturalising the Jews in Great Britain* (1714) argued that Jewish culture is intrinsically positive and productive. Toland believed that the Jewish masses, not only the rich, could benefit from the general community.

COURT JEWS

The new Court Jews applied themselves systematically to their tasks and were openly rewarded as a result. Samson Wertheimer (1658–1724), chief rabbi of Hungary and Moravia, and financier to Austrian Emperor Leopold I (1658–1705), for example, made large loans to government during the war with Turkey and purchased numerous palaces and gardens. He also built hospitals, distributed charity in Europe and Palestine, and helped establish 40 Jewish congregations in Hungary.

LOOMING CRISES FOR POLES AND JEWS

The heyday of the Polish empire was long past; in fact, Poland never completely recovered from the Chmielnicki uprising of 1648–54, or the invasions of Russia and Sweden that followed. Powerful nobles, moreover, refused to cede power either to King Stanislaus II (1764–95) or to Commonwealth citizens. They blocked attempts at reform and created a crisis of administration. By the mid-18th century Poland was threatened by neighbours on three sides: Prussia in the north, Austria in the south, and Russia in the east.

THREE PARTITIONS

The three partitions of Poland effectively severed connections between Jewish communities in both towns and regions. The first, of 1772, awarded much of White Russia (Belorussia), to Russia, while Austria gained Galicia, and Prussia received Pomerania. Parliament duly passed a progressive Polish constitution in 1791 and some nobles and intellectuals began calling for Jews to receive civil equality. However, Empress Catherine of Russia sabotaged the venture by sending in troops to reinforce the old order. This prompted the second partition, of July 1793, whereby Russia gained half of Volhynia, all of Podolia and the remaining part of Ukraine. Prussia, meanwhile, seized Greater Poland (Poznan).

The Kosciusko Uprising erupted in 1794 when Poles tried to defend their rights against their new Russian imperial masters. One Jewish merchant from Lithuania, Berek Joselewicz, formed a Jewish Brigade. Their 500-man unit was an entirely new concept for the age, and a sign that some Jews, at least, were willing to take up arms for the cause of society as a whole. The unit was wiped out just east of Warsaw, but their bravery and commitment, both as Poles and as Jews, impressed many gentiles.

Left Interior of the Remuh Synagogue, first built in 1554, one of the oldest Jewish structures in Krakow, Poland.

Above Fiddler on the Roof, *by Carl Spitzweg, 1880 – often taken as symbolizing the precarious nature of Jewish life in eastern Europe.*

Although the uprising collapsed, Joselewicz survived to fight in the Napoleonic Wars, leading to the third Polish partition of 1795. Now Prussia gained the remainder of Poland, including Warsaw; Austria took Galicia and Krakow; and all of Lithuania and its 250,000 Jews passed over to Russia.

RUSSIAN RULE

At a stroke, nearly a million Jews came under Russian rule. At first Empress Catherine defined Jews as part of the town population and even granted them the municipal vote. However, the Russian statute of 1804 reiterated that Jews needed to be 'improved' before they deserved political rights, and ordered Jews to leave all villages within four years, lest they corrupt the peasants by selling them alcohol. It seemed as if history had again played a cruel trick, for just as western Europe was embracing the Enlightenment, eastern Jews found themselves ruled by despotic Tsars. Some nobles and intellectuals began calling for Jews to receive civil equality.

Revolutionary Times

DESPITE THEIR SMALL NUMBERS AND ALMOST ACCIDENTAL ORIGINS, JEWS FOUGHT IN AMERICA'S 1776 WAR OF INDEPENDENCE. SOON AFTERWARDS, THE FRENCH REVOLUTION ENCOURAGED HOPE IN THE OLD WORLD, TOO.

Today the United States of America houses seven million Jews, the largest single Jewish community in the world. By contrast there were barely 2,000 Jews in North America when English settlers declared their independence from Britain in 1776.

NEW WORLD STIRRINGS

A desire for liberty inspired the earliest Jewish migrants to North America. Jews were admitted as burghers (town citizens) and in 1654 they set up their first congregation, She'arit Israel, or 'Remnant of Israel', in New Amsterdam. The city was renamed New York in 1665, and ceded to the English in 1674.

Meanwhile, Rhode Island, founded as an outpost of religious freedom in 1643, attracted 15 Sephardi families from the West Indies to its leading town, Newport,

Below Touro Synagogue, Rhode Island, built in 1763 and the oldest Jewish house of worship in the USA.

Right John Adams, a founding father of the USA, whose ambiguous views on Jews reflected that of many Americans.

in 1658. Almost immediately they set up Congregation Jeshurat Israel and built the first permanent synagogue in North America in 1763. It was named Touro after its dynamic spiritual leader, Isaac Touro.

OLD TESTAMENT PURITANS

Mid-18th-century North America was a patchwork quilt of mostly coastal European colonies – French, Spanish, English, Swedish and Dutch – dotted among a majority population of Native Americans. Most of the English settlers were devout Nonconformist Protestants called Puritans, and although there were hardly any Jews among them, they felt strongly attached to Jewish mores. They likened their departure from England to the flight of the Israelites from Egypt, with the king cast as pharaoh and America

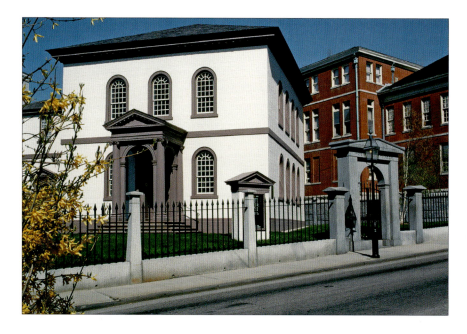

as the Promised Land. Hebrew was widely taught at Yale, Harvard and Princeton universities, and nearly half the 1655 legal code of New Haven quoted from the Hebrew Bible, or Old Testament.

SEEDS OF REVOLUTION

English settlers steadily edged out European rivals, especially after New England colonies united as the Massachusetts Bay Colony in 1691. However, tensions with the mother country culminated in the 1773 tax revolt known as the Boston Tea Party, and finally the Declaration of Independence of 1776. Jews fought on both sides in the resulting war, but overwhelmingly for the rebels. As a community, Jews anticipated more freedom to worship, less interference and better opportunities away from the monarchy.

GUARANTEES OF FREEDOM

Pious and God-fearing though America's founding fathers were, their constitution chose to separate church from state and guaranteed freedom of worship. Legislation did not mention Jews specifically, which was almost an advantage. In Europe, 'enlightened despots' were pushing through supposedly emancipating laws that often forced integration.

Above Decree instituting freedom of worship in France, 1799, showing non-Catholic recipients, including a Jew.

Such rulings reinforced historical prejudices about a dominant culture and religion, which were absent in American law.

American politicians nonetheless felt ambivalent about Jews. John Adams, for instance, wrote that they were 'the most glorious nation that ever inhabited the earth.' Yet he also remarked: 'It is very hard work to love most of them', and he hoped their 'asperities and peculiarities of culture' would be worn away.

LIFE IN THE *ANCIEN REGIME*

In France, life was precarious under the royal system that preceded the 1789 Revolution. Formally France had been closed to Jews since 1394, but for pragmatic reasons successive kings ignored the presence of Jewish communities. Paris did not object, for example, when Maranos fled Spain after the Inquisition and introduced chocolate-making to the south-western town of Bayonne.

Maranos still faced discrimination when they revealed their Jewish identity, and, despite royal proclamations that guaranteed Jews security after 1550, it briefly became illegal to harbour or even speak to them in 1615. The community's make-up changed when anti-Semitic troubles in Provence drove Jews northwards and the Sun King Louis XIV annexed Alsace and Lorraine from Germany. France simultaneously gained a large number of Ashkenazim and a fierce local strain of anti-Semitism. The royal court did, however, abolish the poll-tax on Jews in 1785 and allowed them to settle anywhere in the country.

Intellectuals had nurtured ideas of 'liberty, equality and fraternity' since the early 1700s. After the Revolution of 1789, France's new rulers sought to put the ideas into practice and challenge the monarchies of the day. Many European regimes fell in France's post-revolutionary wars, which, to many Jews, seemed to offer new hope for freedom.

PARTIAL LIBERATION

The Revolution of 1789 had a dramatic effect in France and beyond. That August, the new National Assembly declared that 'no man shall be molested for his beliefs', and in September 1791 it enfranchised all Jews. Revolutionary leaders such as Count Mirabeau and Abbe Gregoire argued strongly for Jewish emancipation. When France's revolutionary army expelled the Pope from Rome in 1798, it broke down the ghetto walls and revoked local laws that restricted Jews.

NAPOLEON'S REFORMS

Throughout this period, reformers were puzzled by two questions: were Jews a religion or a people; and, depending on that answer, should they be accepted or forced to change? Napoleon, who seized power in 1799 and crowned himself emperor in 1804, saw Jews as a distinct nation. Yet he also wanted Jews integrated into France, so he convened an Assembly of Jewish Notables in 1806, dubbed the New Sanhedrin, and in 1807 he classed Judaism as an official religion of France. Two years later, however, he concentrated all Jewish affairs in the hands of a central consistory in Paris. Napoleon's 'Infamous Decree' of 1808 annulled debts owed to Jews, leading to widespread bankruptcy. Thus, what began with emancipation ended with restrictions reminiscent of medieval times.

Below Napoleon reinstates Jewish rights, in an idealized depiction by François Louis Couché, 1806.

A CHANGING FAITH

The Russian Pale of Settlement

DRAMATIC BORDER CHANGES MEANT THAT, OVERNIGHT, JEWS OF POLAND AND LITHUANIA FOUND THEMSELVES UNDER RUSSIAN RULE. GIVEN THE TSARS' FIERCE REPUTATION, THIS PROVOKED MUCH FEAR.

Above The Pale was a place of confinement and state restrictions, yet it also incubated a vibrant Jewish culture.

From a small, landlocked 15th-century Christian principality, cut off from Western civilization, Russia grew into the largest country on earth. Today it covers nearly 6.6 million square miles, stretching from the Baltic in northern Europe to the Sea of Japan in the East. Still larger was the Tsarist empire of which Russia was the rump: it accounted for fully one-sixth of the earth's land surface.

JEWS OF OLD RUSSIA
Small pockets of Jews had existed in what is now Russia, possibly even from First Temple times. Some 4th-century Armenian cities had Jewish populations of up to 30,000; other Jews lived in the Crimea; and the large Khazar khanate adopted Judaism until the Rus (proto-Russians) of Kiev defeated them in 969.

Kiev had a Jewish quarter from the 11th century and there are records of their contacts with fellow Jews in Babylonia. Persian Jewish traders, the Radhanites, traversed Russian territory along the route from Europe to China, and other Jews may have lived in parts of north-eastern Russia during the 12th century. In the 14th century Lithuanians took over parts of western Russia, where they granted privileges to Jews. However, under Ivan IV the Terrible (1533–84) Russia recaptured territory and began treating Jews harshly, forcing some to convert.

The Duchy of Muscovy – the kernel from which Russia grew – shook off its Tartar overlords and laid claim to all ethnic Russian lands in 1480. Soon afterwards it declared its capital, Moscow, an Orthodox Christian 'Third Rome' and barred entrance to any 'enemies of faith' – Jew, Muslim, pagan or even Catholic.

POLISH JEWS IN RUSSIA
When Moscow captured part of Ukraine in 1727 it cleared the area of Jews. For most Polish and Lithuanian Jews the threat of Moscow seemed notional until the first partition of Poland in 1772 gave Russia large swathes of formerly Polish land. The largest transfer of land and people occurred with the second (1793) and third (1795) partitions, when at a stroke Russia 'inherited' nearly a million Jews.

From the start, Russia discriminated against her newly acquired Jewish subjects. By 1791, though, she had learnt that Jews could benefit trade and administration, so she encouraged them to settle in southern territories that Russia had wrested from the Ottomans. When Lithuania passed to Russia in 1795, Tsar Alexander I (1801–25) added it to an area known as the Pale of Settlement.

LIFE IN THE PALE
The Pale was a zone within which Jews could live but not leave. The dimensions of the Pale stabilized around 1812. It included two provinces adjoining the Black Sea: Bessarabia (now Moldova) along the Dnieper in the west, and Taurida in the east. The former included the

Below Founded in 1794, the multi-ethnic southern Russian port of Odessa became a magnet for Jews.

Right Traditional life. Riding to market in Piaski, eastern Poland, 1979, once part of the Jewish Pale of Settlement.

towns of Kishinev and Khotin, and the latter, Sebastopol and Yalta on the Crimean Peninsula. Ultimately the Pale continued in one form or another until the fall of Tsarist Russia in 1917.

FORCED ASSIMILATION

After 1794, Jews in the Pale paid double rates of taxes compared to Christian town dwellers. At times they were banned from certain major towns, including Kiev and Sebastopol. They were also encouraged to live in *shtetls*, or 'small towns', and excluded from running inns or living in the countryside, where as estate managers many had made their living. All these policies increased destitution, and Jewish charities struggled to support the needy.

Conversely, Russia opened public schools to Jews in 1804 in the hope of encouraging them to assimilate, learn Russian and become 'useful' subjects. Many Polish and Lithuanian Jews carried passes allowing them to trade in Russian cities beyond the Pale. Furthermore, other Jews lived semi-secretly in Russian towns, confident that inefficient officials would not enforce the law or might ignore them for a fee.

NICHOLAS I'S CRACKDOWN

When Tsar Nicholas I (1825–55) took power, tolerance gave way to a commitment to destroy Jewish life. In his first year as tsar, Nicholas ordered all Jewish males aged 12 or over to be conscripted into the Russian army where they would spend decades of their life. He had in mind social engineering on a grand scale, whereby Jews would forget their religion and stop speaking Yiddish. He also encouraged Jews to resettle on agricultural land in southern Russia.

Because Jews had not flocked to state schools as intended, in 1844 Moscow decided to create special schools for Jews 'to bring them nearer to Christians and to uproot their harmful beliefs which are influenced by the Talmud'. At the same time the Government disbanded Polish-style Jewish communal structures and replaced them with a state-approved system. Jews could no longer wear traditional clothes or grow *pe'ot*, or 'sidelocks', of Orthodox Jews. Exemptions from the worst restrictions were granted to 'useful' Jews, such as the wealthier merchants.

A RUSSIAN THAW

When Nicholas died he was replaced by the apparently more amenable Alexander II (1855–81). Alexander had abolished serfdom in 1861, but he was less liberal regarding minorities. He forbade Jews from hiring Christian servants, restricted their travel rights and insisted they could own no land. In short, his rule did not bring the hoped-for eman-cipation that Jews west of Russia were, by then, starting to enjoy.

Right Bust of the Vilna Gaon, fulcrum of the 18th-century Jewish community, in present-day Vilnius, Lithuania.

JEWS OF LITHUANIA

Separated from Russia itself, Lithuania was home to a now thriving Jewish community with a distinctive identity. Some, it seems, came originally from Babylon and Palestine around the 8th century, but probably most were descended from German Ashkenazim who fled eastwards after the 12th century. Their population grew rapidly, up to 250,000 in 1792. Living alongside them was a sizeable population of dissident Karaite Jews, mostly transported to Troki in Lithuania from the Crimea.

18th-century Modernity

UNTIL 1800, MOST EUROPEAN JEWS WERE BARRED FROM CLUBS, UNIVERSITIES, POLITICAL OFFICE AND MANY OCCUPATIONS. SLOWLY, AS MONARCHIES BEGAN TO LOSE THEIR GRIP, JEWS STARTED TO LIBERATE THEMSELVES.

A century of European intellectual creativity led acculturated Jews to expect social acceptance. So they were disappointed to learn that several Enlightenment thinkers had deep anti-Jewish prejudices. Voltaire, for example, called Jews 'the greatest scoundrels who ever sullied the face of the globe…our masters and our enemies… the most abominable people in the world.'

On the other hand, the German playwright, freethinker and critic Gotthold Lessing consistently defended Jews against attack. As his model for the learned and humane Jewish sage in his play *Nathan the Wise*, he chose his friend Moses Mendelssohn (1729–86), the leader of what became known as the Haskalah (Jewish Enlightenment).

MOSES MENDELSSOHN
Born a hunchback and the son of a poor rabbi and scribe, Moses Mendelssohn learnt Torah, Talmud and Maimonides as a child, as well as the secular disciplines of Latin and mathematics. He was highly regarded in German circles and his philo-sophical work *Phaedon* earned him the title the German Socrates. However, Jewish critics said that by trying to make Judaism acceptable to Christians, Mendelssohn merely encouraged assimilation. He remained an Orthodox Jew all his life, but all his grandchildren were baptized after his death, including the brilliant composers Felix Mendelssohn and Fanny Mendelssohn-Bartholdy.

THE HASKALAH
Arising from a desire to counter anti-semitism by showing the value of Jewish learning, the Jewish Enlightenment was known as the Haskalah. Jewish *maskilim*, or 'followers of Haskalah', were also aware that there may be faults within Judaism and Jewry. The Haskalah thus pulled in two directions: towards assimilation into general society, and towards defining a Jewish identity to complement and perhaps replace religion as a binding force. Haskalah ideas inspired the birth of Reform Judaism, which sought to modernize worship and allow Jews to adopt the culture wherever they lived.

Mendelssohn felt that gentiles would only embrace Jews as equals if they engaged with current intellectual developments. Born in Dessau, Saxony, he wanted to share Hebrew literary treasures with non-Jews and with Jews who knew no

Left Fanny Mendelssohn-Bartholdy (1805–47), composer, sister of Felix and granddaughter of Moses Mendelssohn.

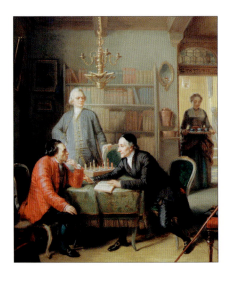

Above Moses Mendelssohn (left) plays chess with dramatist Gotthold Lessing, 1771; painted in 1856.

Hebrew. He tried to revive Hebrew as a spoken language, and translated the Hebrew Bible into the finest German. At the same time he believed Judaism should shed its medieval superstitions and overly ritualistic elements. Like Maimonides before him, he saw no contradiction between religious belief and critical reason, and his works *Jerusalem* and *Morning Hours* explain Judaism as a coherent ethical system.

MENDELSSOHN'S LEGACY
Moses Mendelssohn generously supported *maskilim*, including Solomon Maimon (1754–1800), a Lithuanian-born philosopher whose 1790 work *Transcendental Philosophy* was praised by Emmanuel Kant as the most penetrating of all critiques. In 1784 neo-Hebraists in Germany, Austria and Poland founded an influential periodical called *Ha-Me'assef* (The Collector), while Leopold Zunz (1794–1886) launched a methodical approach to studying Jewish history and literature called *Wissenschaft des Judentums*, or 'The Science of Judaism'. His followers included David Luzzatto in Italy (1800–65) and Salomon Munk in France (1803–67).

THE REFORM MOVEMENT

THE 19TH-CENTURY MOVEMENT CALLED REFORM JUDAISM MARKED THE MOST RADICAL DEPARTURE FROM TRADITIONAL JEWISH BELIEF AND PRACTICE TO DATE, AND SPREAD FROM GERMANY TO ENGLAND AND THE USA.

Reform developed out of Haskalah and aimed to integrate Jews into Europe, bring Judaism up to date with scientific developments and win back those who felt alienated from traditional religion. The idea was to jettison 'obsolete' ritual such as dress codes that attracted suspicion from outsiders, while maintaining and promoting Judaism's ethical core. Reform was thus a natural and perhaps inevitable response to long-brewing cultural developments in Western Jewish society.

NEW METHODS

Reform Jews held services in local vernacular languages. They called their synagogues temples and imitated churches by using choirs and music. Men and women were seated together in prayer, not divided by a *mechitza*, or 'barrier', or segregated into upper and lower floors.

Services were generally shorter and more disciplined affairs than those held in traditional 'shuls' or 'shtiebls'. The centrepiece was a sermon delivered by a rabbi attired in church-like garb. As in a church, the pulpit assumed prominence.

DOCTRINAL REVOLUTION

Reform abandoned what it saw as obsolete laws that only applied in Temple times. Followers questioned that the Torah came from heaven and they rejected the belief in a personal Messiah, resurrection of the dead, return to the Holy Land and the rebuilding of the Temple. They emphasized the prophetic and lyrical (psalm) tradition rather than the legalistic Talmud and Pentateuch.

Reformists also saw Jews as loyal citizens of their states, rather than as a nation in exile.

THE SPREAD OF REFORM

Israel Jacobsohn was the first rabbi to introduce ceremonial reforms in a synagogue established at Seesen, Germany, in 1810. Another pioneer institution was the Hamburg Temple of 1818. Samuel Hirsch gave the movement a philosophical basis, and the great Haskalah scholar Abraham Geiger lent his support. Perhaps the most important Reform journal was *Allgemeine Zeitung des Judenthums*, edited by Ludwig Philippson.

Although mainly an Ashkenazi phenomenon, Reform appealed to those Sephardi Jews detached from traditional practices. The first Reform synagogue in London began as a breakaway from the Sephardi

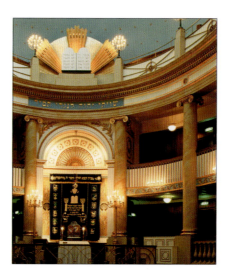

Below Shielded from street view, as then required by Austrian law, and built in 1824–6, Vienna's Stadttempel (city temple) later adopted the Reform liturgy.

Above Abraham Geiger, Reform rabbi pioneer and expert on Judaic influence on Christianity and Islam, 1865.

flagship synagogue, Bevis Marks, in 1841. Other synagogues appeared in Bradford and Manchester, and Reform spawned satellite congregations in Hungary and the USA where it is now the largest US Jewish denomination.

DEBATE AND CRITICISM

At German Rabbinical conferences in the 1840s a split developed between those who wanted profound change and a majority who worried that Reform was becoming estranged from mainstream Jews. One prominent radical was Samuel Holdheim (1806–60), whose Berlin temple transferred the Sabbath from Saturday to Sunday to match Christian practice. Most congregations decided not to go so far. Some traditionalists, now defined as Orthodox, feared that Reform was halfway towards conversion to Christianity or lapsing into atheism.

In between the two poles were responses that adopted certain Reform features – such as a quizzical attitude to divine authorship. Examples include the Neo-Orthodox school of Samson Raphael Hirsch in Frankfurt, the Neologs in Hungary, and, later, the US Conservative and Reconstructionist (synagogue) trends.

Jews and Commerce – The Rothschilds

IN THE 19TH CENTURY THE ROTHSCHILD NAME EXEMPLIFIED WEALTH AND SUCCESS, AND SO IT REMAINS TODAY. THEIR STORY IS ONLY ONE CHAPTER IN THE STORY OF JEWISH FINANCIAL PROWESS.

From modest origins in the back streets of 18th-century Frankfurt am Main the Rothschild family rose to become the byword for financial ingenuity and commercial success worldwide. Apart from their original banking venture the family's interests have embraced such diverse fields as art patronage, politics, diplomacy, textiles, scientific innovation, oil exploration, engineering works, wine-making and philanthropy. And, while the Rothschild saga is exceptional, it throws light on the challenges and achievements of other Jewish enterprises, large and small.

THE FIRST ROTHSCHILD

The story begins with Mayer Amschel Rothschild (1744–1812), a coin and art dealer who was appointed Crown Agent to the Principality of Hesse-Hanau in 1769. In 1785 Mayer's employer, Prince William, inherited the largest private fortune in Europe. In time Mayer used his hard-won post to launch his own career in banking after working at the Oppenheim bank-ing house in Hanover. By 1785 he could afford a large house, which he shared with his wife, Guttele Schnapper, and their five sons.

In the early 1800s Mayer expanded his business and set up interdependent banking branches in five major cities, as a deliberate policy of spreading influence and facilitating pan-European links. One son headed each branch: Frankfurt, Vienna, London, Naples and Paris. The bank adopted a crest showing five arrows shooting out in different directions.

INDEPENDENT FINANCIERS

Initially the Rothschilds followed the example of earlier court Jews, like the Wertheimers and Oppenheimers, except that they spread their interests and acted independently, not so much servants of a prince but masters of their own affairs.

By transcending borders while keeping the business within the family, the Rothschilds arguably founded the first transnational corporation. Thus they insured themselves against the dangers of a change of ruler, as had happened in 1737 when Joseph Oppenheimer's patron, Duke Karl Alexander of Wurttemberg, died and jealous rivals sent Joseph to the gallows the next year.

The Rothschilds' early achievements owe much to a happy twist of fate: the moving of the Anti-Napoleonic League's financial centre to Frankfurt from Amsterdam, which had fallen to France. After the Congress of Vienna (1815), which marked Napoleon's defeat by English and Prussian forces, the Rothschilds extended their business into most European states. They made loans to governments, issued state bonds, liquidated inflated paper currencies, founded floating public debts and funded post-Napoleonic war (1815) reconstruction projects. The Austrian emperor made all five brothers peers by 1822, and from 1815 to 1828 their capital rose from 3.2 million francs to 118.4 million.

ENGLISH BRANCH

Nathan Mayer Rothschild played a pivotal role in his family's banking success, though he was originally sent to Manchester as a textile merchant in 1798, aged 21. He sold English cloth to Europe until Napoleon's blockade threatened English exports. In 1811 he founded the brokering house N.M. Rothschild. The Rothschild family was soon handling most English financial dealings with the Continent. Nathan's branch funded the British war effort against Napoleon and supplied Wellington's troops with gold before the Battle of Waterloo in 1815.

Above Baron Lionel de Rothschild, banker, and first professing Jew elected to Britain's parliament, 1836.

Below Five sons of Mayer Rothschild, each of whom ran a bank branch in a major European financial centre.

Between 1818 and 1835 Nathan Mayer issued 26 British and foreign government loans. In 1824 he floated the Alliance Assurance Company and the following year he helped the Bank of England avoid a liquidity crisis. His own dedication to work was legendary and his marriage to the well-connected Hannah Barent Cohen afforded him a network of business contacts. Like his father he was famously discreet, and used similarly cautious agents to courier funds through Napoleonic France. Above all, he understood the value of accurate and speedy information. His private intelligence service learnt the outcome of the Battle of Waterloo a day before the British Government.

Two of Nathan's descendants were path-breakers in British politics, the first being Lionel de Rothschild, who in 1858 became the first professing Jew to enter parliament. In fact, he was first elected in 1847, 11 years earlier, but he refused to take the Christian oath of entrance and so was barred from the chamber. Only when parliament allowed him to swear on the Hebrew Bible did he take his seat. In 1885 Sir Nathan Mayer

Below The Rothschild Family at Prayer *by the German Jewish painter Moritz Daniel Oppenheim.*

Right Waddesdon Manor, Buckinghamshire, the Rothschild country estate built 1874–89.

Rothschild II entered the House of Lords as the first Jewish peer and established a baronetcy in his family's name.

THE INDUSTRIALISTS
The Rothschilds realized the potential of technological innovation. Salomon Rothschild (1774–1855), head of the Vienna banking branch, built Austria's first railway system. James Mayer de Rothschild (1792–1868), founder of the French branch, played a dominant role in transforming 19th-century France into a major industrial power. He financed mining enterprises and helped found the French railway consortium Chemin de Fer du Nord in 1845. Other Rothschilds backed the newly formed mining conglomerate Rio Tinto Zinc in 1873 and advanced the British Government the money needed to purchase the Suez Canal in 1875.

BEYOND BANKING
Nathan's son Nathaniel (1812–70) moved to Paris, set up a second French branch and acquired a vineyard whose Château Mouton Rothschild wines are among the best in the world.

After the Russian pogroms of the 1880s, Baron Edmond James de Rothschild (1845–1934) set up the Jewish Colonization Association that established 12 settlements in Palestine. Baron Lionel Walter Rothschild was the addressee of the 1917 Balfour Declaration that committed Britain to establishing a 'national home for the Jewish people' in Palestine.

VENTURE CAPITALISTS IN A CHANGING WORLD
Apart from the Rothschilds, Jewish families such as the Warburgs, Mendelssohns and Bleichroeders pioneered merchant banking to meet changing economic needs. Railways were a fruitful source of enterprise: during 1850-70 Samuel Poliakov developed Russia's network, while the Paris-based Maurice de Hirsch (1831–1896) made a fortune in Turkey, Austria and the Balkans. Jews also capitalized American railroads and developed joint stock institutions such as Deutsche Bank, founded in 1870.

Such entrepreneurship built on older traditions of financial innovation. In medieval Baghdad and Cairo Jews had devised *jahbadhiyya*, a system that distributed risk by tying state loans to the savings of the entire Jewish merchant class. Spanish Jews spread to Venice and France other Islamic ideas, such as the cheque (*sakh*) and bill of exchange (*suftaya*). Jewish refugees boosted the prosperity of 16th-century Livorno, Italy, as well as Marseilles, Bordeaux and Rouen in 17th- and 18th-century France. The Henriques family helped found the Bank of England in 1694 and the Ashkenazi Goldsmid banking family joined their Sephardi brethren in the City of London.

In time other Jews realized the potential of a consumer culture. Levi Strauss (1829–1902) invented denim jeans in the US and built a thriving textile business; while in Manchester, England, the Belarus-born Michael Marks (1859–1907) and gentile Thomas Spencer formed in 1894 Marks & Spencers, one of the first major retail chains.

CHAPTER 8

REVOLUTION AND EMANCIPATION

While Jewish civil emancipation proceeded at a snail's pace after the 1815 Congress of Vienna, access to education created a generation of individual Jews whose contributions to art, music, science and politics became considerable. By the late 19th century formal emancipation was achieved, but anti-Semitic factions still survived. Within the community, Orthodox and conservative leaders worried that new liberties might encourage total assimilation, even the disappearance of Judaism itself. Meanwhile in eastern Europe, Jews lacked the opportunities enjoyed in Paris, Berlin or London. Thousands of Russian and Polish Ashkenazi Jews left for America, the 'golden land'. Likewise, Sephardi Jews began deserting an Ottoman empire in decline. Of the Jews who stayed behind, many believed that the betterment of their people was impossible until the whole of society changed. Jews thus flocked to ideologies including Marxism, socialism, and nationalism. Gradually a new strand emerged, Zionism, which sought to 'solve the Jewish problem' by transplanting Diaspora Jews back to the historic Land of Israel, in Palestine.

Opposite An Ashkenazi Rabbi of Jerusalem, *by G.S. Hunter. As the 19th century unfolded, figures of Orthodoxy came under attack from within the Jewish community.*

Above A bustling street scene in New York, 1890s. Jewish immigrants from Russia and Poland flocked to the city that seemed to offer a chance for new beginnings.

EMANCIPATION AND REVOLUTIONARIES

THE FRENCH REVOLUTION RAISED JEWISH HOPES OF ACCEPTANCE INTO CIVIL SOCIETY. BUT THE FIGHT FOR EMANCIPATION WAS LONG AND HARD, WHICH LED SOME JEWS TO ADOPT MORE RADICAL APPROACHES.

The forces unleashed in the French Revolution could not be contained within the country's borders. By August 1792, France declared war on Austria and the republican Girondin party wanted to spread revolution to the whole of Europe. In the spirit of Jacques Rousseau, the Continent would 'be forced to be free'. The major emissary of this new freedom was Napoleon Bonaparte.

Jews throughout Europe greeted Napoleon as a liberator, and many joined French troops and local radicals as they literally tore down the ghetto walls. Some dreamt that the Russian Pale of Settlement – arguably the largest ghetto of all – would fall, too, as French troops marched towards Moscow in 1812.

It was not to be: Napoleon failed in Russia and ultimately lost the Battle of Waterloo in 1815.

THE OLD ORDER RETURNS

Coinciding with Napoleon's last defeat, the Congress of Vienna (1814–15) restored many royals to power. While Jews retained their liberties in Belgium and Holland, in Austria and Italy's papal states, ghettoes were re-established. In Germany – still a loose confederation of 39 states – Jews gained some rights in 1815, though not yet full freedom.

EMANCIPATION IN ENGLAND

English emancipation continued at a gentler pace. As early as 1740, parliament allowed 'foreign Protestants and others' in Britain's American colonies to be naturalized after seven years' residence. In 1753, parliament voted for naturalization in England itself, but backed down after a public outcry. Only in 1826 could Jews become full citizens. Isaac Goldsmid was the first Jew to receive a hereditary title in 1841. A parliamentary act in 1845 allowed Jews to enter municipal office, and in 1855 Sir David Salomons was elected as London's first Jewish Lord Mayor. Fuller political emancipation only arrived in 1858 when Lionel Rothschild was allowed to sit in the House of Commons without taking a Christian oath.

REFORM AND REVOLUTION

Across the Channel, France adopted a constitutional monarchy in July 1830, and soon officially recognized Judaism. Four years on, Jews sat in the French parliament.

Yet not all European Jews welcomed the prospect of emancipation. Traditionalists feared losing the autonomy that preserved religious life. Some supporters of the Haskalah (Jewish Enlightenment) warned that integration might erode Jews' identity.

Many Jews felt that tolerance was not enough, and society needed radical reform. They joined Christian co-citizens in a spate of revolutions that rocked Paris, Berlin, Vienna, Budapest, Rome and Venice in 1848. They demanded equal rights and

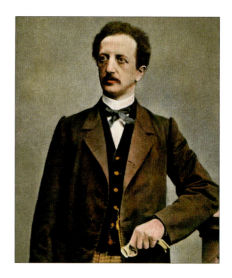

Above Ferdinand Lassalle, a Jewish socialist who advocated general social change above specifically Jewish concerns.

Below The Berlin Revolt of 1848, in which Jews died fighting for their freedom alongside Christian citizens.

written constitutions. It seemed that Enlightenment values had triumphed: Europe's rising middle class came to accept Jews in public office (until then a taboo). Emperor Franz Joseph of Austria (1848–1916) stated in 1849: 'political and civil rights are not based on religion'.

The philosopher Karl Marx came from a Jewish family that had converted to Christianity. His grandfathers were rabbis in Trier and Holland. In 1848 Marx (1818–83) published his *Communist Manifesto* and announced an ideology that would alter the course of history. Marx attacked Jewish traders as a group that 'worshipped money', and later extended his critique to the entire capitalist class. Many Jews defended his apparently anti-Semitic attack as an ironical plea for the economic liberation of Jews.

EMANCIPATION ACHIEVED
Many of the gains of 1848 were temporary: in 1851 Prussia abolished its liberal constitution, which had promised greater democratic

Below Paul Reuter (1816–99), son of a German rabbi, set up Reuters News Agency in London, 1851, spurring on the communications revolution.

HEINRICH HEINE

'Where one burns books, one will, in the end, burn people.' So said Heinrich Heine, the archetypal combination of German patriot and radical Jewish humanist. Born in Düsseldorf in 1797, he yearned for 'the emancipation of the whole world'. He was an early devotee of revolutionary socialism and probably influenced the young Karl Marx.

Paradoxically, he lampooned Jews who chose conversion, 'the entrance ticket to European society', yet he became a Christian himself in 1825. Heine once blamed Judaism for developing 'the fault-finding with human beings'. And he had no respect for Reform Jews who tried to turn 'a little Protestant Christianity into a Jewish company'. Later he rejected Marx as a 'godless self-god', feared the 'dark iconoclasts' of revolution and revisited Judaic themes in essays, stories and his 'Hebrew Melodies' poems. A peerless German stylist, Heine personified European Jewish intellectual creativity, yet also, some say, self-doubt.

Above Heinrich Heine as portrayed by Moritz Daniel Oppenheim. Both painter and subject were Jews who found acceptance in German society.

freedoms for all Germans; in 1853 Austria banned Jews from acquiring real estate or moving to certain areas. True emancipation only arrived with the unification of Italy in 1861 and Germany in 1871.

Legislation for Jewish equality was passed in France first, in 1791, then the Netherlands, Greece, Canada and the Ottoman empire by 1839. Britain, Germany, Austria-Hungary, Italy, Spain, Bulgaria, Serbia, Spain and finally the Russian empire had followed suit by 1917.

JUDAISM MODERNIZED
Liberal views influenced change in European Jewry. Many Orthodox Jews looked to combine social integration with religious observance. Neo-Orthodoxy was a movement inspired by Frankfurt Rabbi Samson Raphael Hirsch (1808–88) and his ethos of *Torah im derech Eretz* ('Torah in the way of the land'), which taught secular alongside religious subjects.

OTHER REVOLUTIONS
Yet more social changes were afoot in the 19th century. New technology and mass production soon led to an economic revolution, and Jewish capitalists were to play a vital role in industrializing Britain, France and America.

From the 1830s, German Jews built up machine, oil and copper enterprises. In Russia, Jewish industrialists developed not only food, textile and tobacco industries, but also river-shipping, metals, mining and urban expansion. Even so, discrimination after the 1870s barred Jews from the Russian bureaucracy, and educational restrictions meant that there were virtually no Russian Jews in the liberal professions.

Beyond Russia, Jews had largely won their civil freedoms. Yet the rise of nationalist parties with explicitly anti-Semitic platforms showed that, while the legal battle had been won, a political struggle was just beginning.

The Ostjuden and Yiddish Culture

Yiddish, the language of Ashkenazic Jewry, became the chief vehicle for spreading information in Jewish eastern Europe. It was the glue that bound a secular sense of 'Jewishness', called *Yiddishkeit*.

In western Europe, Yiddish was increasingly regarded as uncouth; the *maskilim*, or 'enlightened ones', of the Jewish Haskalah, spoke German or French among themselves, and wrote learned books in 'purer' Hebrew. By the 20th century, certain elements in Western Jewry professed disdain for the *Ostjuden*, or 'Eastern Jews', under the Russian yoke.

A minority, though, felt nostalgia and even envy towards their Eastern cousins who seemingly maintained a surer sense of who they were, for all their poverty and political deprivation. Some of the most Jewishly creative places in Europe were precisely those areas where *Ostjuden* and refined Western *maskilim* met, such as the 'borderland' cities of Vienna and Budapest in the Austro-Hungarian empire.

Below Red Guards, Moscow, 1917. At first, many Jews welcomed the Russian Revolution as a chance for change.

MATURATION OF HASSIDISM

Once dismissed as a passing phase, Hassidism (a populist expression of Jewish Orthodoxy) had put down deep roots in eastern Europe by the 19th century. Most sects were usually headed by a *rebbe*, or rabbinic 'master', whose authority often overruled that of the local town rabbi.

Hassidic ways had economic implications, as ordinary followers set up mutual self-help societies and funded *tzadikim*, 'righteous ones' who claimed to mediate between God and the common people. Hassidism entered the USA with the great immigration wave of the 1880s, but the movement found unfertile ground. Many Jewish newcomers welcomed America's freedom from European strictures, whether these were official, anti-Semitic or religious. Only much later did New York become the main destination for Hassidic survivors of the Holocaust.

Above Russia before the Revolution. Jews attacked by Russian thugs, 1903, from a contemporary Italian newspaper.

EASTERN EUROPE

The prevailing ethos east of the Dnieper River was more traditional, but eventually the *haskalah* (Jewish enlightenment), spread from its birthplace in Prussia to Austrian Galicia (culturally Polish Jewish) and on to Tsarist Russia. Eastern Haskalah assumed its own distinct character: rather than attempting to reform Judaism or seek political emancipation – a hopeless cause in Russia – Eastern *maskilim* (Haskalah enthusiasts) concentrated on regenerating their communities on a secular basis.

By the late 19th century some Western Jews, who had felt it their duty to educate the Ostjuden about civilized practices, hired east European *maskilim* to teach their children the rudiments of Judaism. Eastern Haskalah served as a bridge to a West that was losing connection with the wellsprings of Jewish tradition.

THE MAY LAWS

Optimists thought that Russia was becoming more liberal when, in 1862, Jews gained equal rights

Right Klezmer bands were a regular fixture of Ashkenazi life in both eastern Europe and America. This one stands ready at a welcoming party, c.1920.

in Congress Poland, which essentially had been a semi-autonomous puppet state under Tsarist rule since 1815. However, both Poles and Jews suffered when Russia crushed a revolt and incorporated Poland more firmly into the Tsarist realm three years later. Much worse was to follow under Tsar Alexander III (r. 1881–94). Pogroms erupted throughout western Russia and Ukraine and dragged on for three years. Although the authorities did not officially encourage the violence, they did little to stop it.

RADICALIZATION IN RUSSIA

New pogroms, anti-Jewish mass attacks, erupted in 1903–6, coinciding with the abortive 1905 revolution, and yet another wave occurred in 1918–20, during the civil war that followed the Bolshevik Revolution. All told, tens of thousands of Jews died in the period to 1920, during which time two million Jews chose to emigrate, mostly to the USA.

For those who remained in Russia, radicalism set in. Broadly they joined one of four groups: universalist and atheist Marxists; Narodni peasant revolutionaries (who generally did not welcome Jews); the Bund, an all-embracing Russian socialist association specifically for Jewish concerns; or Zionists who laboured for an emancipated Jewish society only in Palestine.

HUNGARY – BETWEEN TWO WORLDS

The distinct worlds of Western Jewry and the Ostjuden touched in Hungary, a land living partly in the shadow of Austria, and blessed with a vast variety of Jewish types: Carpathian mountain Jews, urban German speakers, and Orthodox Jews who preferred speaking Hun-garian to Yiddish. Despite enduring residual prejudices from gentile Magyar nationalists, the Jewish population grew and fostered ties with Jews in neighbouring Serbia and Bosnia.

Hungarian Jews took advantage of the 1783 Edict of Tolerance, the brainchild of Emperor Joseph II (1765–90), and entered universities in search of secular education. Hungary's still-small Jewish population was replenished by the influx of Jews from Poland, Slovakia and Moravia. By the end of the 19th century, some 350 Jews had joined the titled nobility. A quarter of all university students and more than 40 per cent of Hungarian bankers, intelligentsia and artists were Jews, even though they made up just 5 per cent of the general population.

City dwellers favoured Reform practices, imported from Germany; and some Orthodox concocted a Hungarian moderate version of reform called Neolog. By contrast, Hassidic sects separated themselves to safeguard Jewish tradition. They set up dynasties in several towns and introduced a new flavour to Hungarian Jewry.

Meanwhile, in Austro-Hungarian Bohemia, Jews thrived because of the combined effect of the Industrial Revolution and weak local nobility. Families such as the Porges built cotton, calico and linen printing factories and spawned Jewish banking clans in Vienna. In the 1840s the Emperor ennobled the Porges, a sign that economic success could bring social respectability without any need to convert from the Jewish faith.

LITERATURE IN YIDDISH

East European Jews took to literature and theatre with alacrity. They wrote mainly in Yiddish, so their output was for Jewish 'domestic consumption'. Early pioneers included the playwright Solomon Ettinger (1802–56) and folklorist S. Ansky (1863–1920), who built on Ostjuden oral story-telling traditions. Ansky's 1914 Yiddish play *The Dybbuk* has been dubbed an Ashkenazi *Frankenstein* and a metaphor for the nature of Jewish life. He also wrote in Russian, while his contemporary Israel Zangwill (1824–1926) used English. Both men's use of the locally dominant language demonstrated the speed of Jewish acculturation. Yet they preserved a sense of Ostjuden culture.

The Spectre of Anti-Semitism Revived

HOPES FOR JEWISH EMANCIPATION IN RUSSIA WERE SUDDENLY DASHED BY AN OUTBREAK OF VIOLENCE AFTER 1881. EVEN IN THE WEST, MEDIEVAL SUSPICIONS ABOUT JEWS REVIVED.

The 1881 pogroms in Russia altered Jewish history profoundly. They were to lead to the birth of political Zionism – the campaign to create a Jewish national state in Palestine – and the growth of American Jewry. They also led indirectly to the Russian Revolution. However, as an instance of official and popular anti-Semitism, the pogroms were not unique.

ATTACK FROM THE RIGHT

Rightists still feared that Jews were eternal aliens. Even the supposedly enlightened Frederick the Great of Prussia decreed in 1750 that 'extraordinary' Jews (such as Court Jews) could not pass on their privileges to the next generation. 'Ordinary' Jews were barred from professions, and could not allowed to marry or settle in further numbers 'until a careful investigation [had] been made'.

Below The Dreyfus affair of 1894 exposed an underlying cultural anti-Semitism that shocked French liberals.

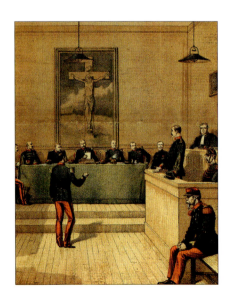

In France, Edouard Drumont published a two-volume racist book, *La France Juive* (1886) whose popularity encouraged him to found the Anti-Semitic League and a daily paper, *La Libre Parole* (1896).

Envy of successful Jewish families such as the Reinachs (who included prize-winning lawyers, politicians, archaeologists and classicists) fuelled French rightist dislike for Jews. A string of malicious conspiracy theories followed the Comptoire d'Escompte banking crisis (1889) and the Panama corruption scandal (1893), which both involved Jews.

ANTI-SEMITISM ON THE LEFT

Diverse groups castigated Jews on economic grounds. In 1891 the Russian Jewish thinker Leon Pinsker noted: 'For property holders, [the Jew is] a beggar; for the poor, an exploiter and a millionaire'.

Some radicals saw Jews as financial protectors of oppressive state structures and nobles. Late 19th-century Russian Narodniks and anarchists jointly attacked nobles and *Zhids* (pejorative Russian for Jews). Often there was a nationalist element at play.

THEOLOGY AND SCIENCE

Theologically, some atheists and secularists blamed Jews, the first monotheists, for all the evils of religion. Enlightenment thinkers of the 18th century set this trend when they criticized Jewish beliefs, in what might have been an attack on Christianity itself. The charges stuck, and a century later fused with a new strand of racial anti-Semitism, to emerge as an offshoot of social Darwinism.

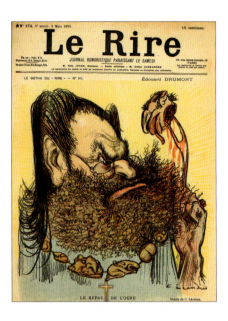

Above Caricature of notorious French anti-Semite Edouard Drumont, from a French satirical journal, 1893.

Ernest Renan, a French philosopher and analyst of religion and nationality, along with like-minded academics, saw Semites in general and Jews in particular as an 'incomplete race' with an 'inferior level of human nature'.

GENTILE FRIENDS

To balance the record of anti-Semitism, Jews also found allies, especially in Britain, such as the parliamentarian and historian Thomas Macaulay, and Walter Scott, whose 1820 novel *Ivanhoe* sympathizes with the plight of Jews in medieval England. Lord Byron's 1815 book of songs, *Hebrew Melodies*, praises Jews' persistence despite exile; and was set to music by a Jewish composer, Isaac Nathan, called the 'father of Australian music'.

Inspired after meeting a learned book cataloguer at the British Library, George Eliot took lessons in Hebrew, visited Palestine in 1869 and often frequented synagogues. Her last novel, *Daniel Deronda* (1878), features an admiring portrayal of a fictitious Jew who rediscovers his identity; his yearning for, and eventual return to, Palestine inspired many Jews to become Zionists. Similar themes appeared in Prime Minister Benjamin Disraeli's novels *Alroy* and *Tancred*.

PROTECTING JEWS' RIGHTS
The murder of a French capuchin friar in Damascus in 1840 (the Damascus Blood Libel) led to the torture and death of three Jews. Two prominent Jews, Sir Moses Montefiore and Adolphe Crémieux, intervened to stop more bloodshed. The affair led to the creation of the Alliance Israélite Universelle in 1860, a coalition dedicated to safeguarding Jewish rights worldwide.

RUSSIAN RESTRICTIONS
Despite the positive movements of Alliance Israélite, the Tsar's May Laws of 1882 re-imposed cruel restrictions on Russian Jews. They were prevented from entering secondary schools, universities and mining institutes, and were dismissed from government services. These laws, whose prime instigator was Konstantin Pobedonostsev, revealed both economic envy and religious prejudice. They stayed on the statute books until 1907 and provided the basis for other acts of discrimination. In 1886, fines were imposed on Jewish families whose sons failed to report for military service; in 1888 Tsar Alexander III (r. 1881–94) rejected recommendations to extend Jewish rights; and in 1891, 20,000 legally resident Jewish artisans were expelled from Moscow.

Considered together, legislation and pogroms encouraged the greatest movement of Jews to date: between 1881 and 1920, two million Jews left Russia. Some went to Palestine, others to Britain, but overwhelmingly they settled in the United States.

Above French poor hitting a Jewish capitalist, probably a response to the Panama affair, 1893.

So, paradoxically, the Russian laws encouraged the still-nascent Zionist movement, and they also quite unintentionally gave birth to the modern American Jewish community, which in the 20th century became by far the largest and most influential in the world. Within Russia they radicalized more secular-minded Jews, and thus contributed to the revolutions of 1905 and 1917.

THE DREYFUS AFFAIR
The Jews of France felt more secure than most as the 19th century drew to a close. However, in 1894 a Jew from Alsace, Col. Alfred Dreyfus, was falsely accused of betraying military secrets to Germany, and convicted of treason. The trial created an uproar, pitting pro-Dreyfus liberals and republicans, notably the campaigning journalist Emile Zola, against anti-Dreyfus clerics and the social and political old guard. It took 12 years before Dreyfus was exonerated and freed from exile on Devil's Island, by which time France had passed pivotal legislation separating church from state, and safeguarding civil rights.

PROTOCOLS OF THE ELDERS OF ZION

'The Protocols of the Elders of Zion' is one of the most potent, influential and longest-lasting of anti-Semitic tracts. It was a forgery concocted by Russian secret police in the late 19th century and based on the wording of a pamphlet directed against Napoleon III, originally written by a French lawyer, Maurice Joly, in 1864. The Protocols pretends to be a master-plan by secret Jewish leaders plotting to undermine all other nations, socially, morally, economically and politically. Though reprinted during the 1905 Russian Revolution, it reached its peak of popularity during World War I and the 1917 Bolshevik Revolution, when rightists persuaded themselves that Communism was entirely a Jewish conspiracy. The document was disseminated in France by clerics who feared Jewish and Masonic influence; and in England where *The Times* launched an investigation into its authenticity in 1920. From the foundation of the independent State of Israel in 1948 it gained a readership in the Arab world, as a putative 'explanation' of Zionism. Indeed, it is probably no coincidence that its original publication coincided with the first Zionist conference in Basel, Switzerland, in 1897. Philip Graves, a reporter for *The Times*, exposed the forgery in 1921.

Above Illustration of Jew with snakes for hair from 1937 Protocol, a forgery that revealed a supposed Jewish plot to control the world.

The 19th-century Population Boom

An extraordinary growth in Jewish population occurred in the 19th century. By 1880 there were around 7.7 million Jews in the world, mostly in Russia, although increasingly in the USA.

Improved health standards, high birth rates, better nutrition and relative peace in central and eastern Europe probably accounted for the unprecedented increase in Jewish numbers during the 19th century. As of 1880, nine-tenths of the world's Jews lived in Europe. Around 3.5 million dwelt in the former Polish provinces under Russian rule. The first Russian empire census of 1897 recorded 5.2 million Jews, of whom all but 300,000 still lived in the Pale of Settlement. Another 1.3 million lived in Poland proper, where they made up 14 per cent of the population.

Ashkenazim thus outnumbered Sephardim and Mizrahim (oriental Jews) by a ratio of 9:1. There was also growth in western European Jewry.

Below: Jewish neighbourhood, Lower East Side, New York, c.1900. Eastern European Jews transplanted their culture to an American urban setting.

WESTERNIZATION

In 1820 some 223,000 Jews lived in Germany, but while that represented a significant rise on previous years, the biggest shift of all began 60 years later, in the USA. There the population rocketed, rapidly turning America into an important new centre in Jewish life. Most of the two million Jews who left Tsarist Russia settled there. In the first 15 years of the 20th century, Jews accounted for 10 per cent of all immigrants to the United States. Jewish Americans numbered 2.5 million in 1914.

By then, a quarter of all Jews in the world lived in 11 cities. By far the largest population lived in New York, with an astonishing 1.35 million Jews. London, another immigrant magnet, had more than 150,000. That left sizeable urban communities in other American and European cities including Chicago, Warsaw and Vienna. Occupational

Above Roman Vishniac's 1930s photograph of a heder, *or religious class typical of those in eastern Europe.*

expectations gradually changed: the grandparents' generation tended to be Torah observant Jews who worked in small trades as salesmen, cobblers or tailors. Parents took advantage of new freedoms and economic expansion to run larger-scale enterprises, often in mass retailing. But genuine social respectability arrived with the third generation, when their children went to university and became lawyers, accountants or doctors.

IMMIGRANT IDENTITIES

Immigrant Jews of the first two generations cherished their membership of institutions called *landsleitsverreine*, or 'fellow countrymen associations'. Jews from certain towns, such as Krakow, would gather together, in their new cities. By the third generation, however, bonds to the old country had weakened, and Yiddish gave way to English in the USA, Canada, Australia and South Africa, or Spanish in Argentina and Mexico. Now Jewish immigrants felt equally American (or Australian or Chilean) and Jewish, but no longer so strongly Litvak (Lithuanian Jewish), say, or Polack (Polish Jewish).

The USA – A New Promised Land

WHEN EARLY 20TH-CENTURY YIDDISH WRITERS SPOKE OF *DI GOLDENE MEDINE*, THE 'GOLDEN LAND', THEY MEANT THE USA. IT WAS A PLACE OF OPPORTUNITY, LARGELY FREE OF 'OLD EUROPE'S' PREJUDICES.

The Anglo-Jewish author Israel Zangwill famously called America a 'melting pot' in which former identities would dissolve and people would emerge as equal citizens. Many Jews thought America signalled the end of 'Diaspora persecution', even if it was not exactly the biblical 'promised land'. Jewish women were important to American social activism, and included such figures as Rebecca Gratz, educator of poor women, and Lillian Wald, a healthcare pioneer.

SETTLING IN THE USA

The first wave of Jews to the USA were Sephardim from Brazil and Holland; the second wave were educated German Jews; and the third and largest were Yiddish-speaking eastern Europeans, originally fleeing the 1881 pogroms in Russia.

Below An American gold prospector wearing Levi's jeans.

Uncomfortable with indigenous religious liberality, some 'third wave' traditional Jews created an Orthodox Congregation Union in 1898. Many others joined the Reform and Conservative movements, which seemed closer to the American ethos, while others clung to Yiddish culture even if they lost their faith.

Between 1800 and 1860 America's Jewish population had leapt to more than 100,000. This growth inspired the creation in 1843 of the *B'nai Brit*, or 'Sons of the Covenant', America's first nationwide Jewish secular organization.

JEWS IN THE WILD WEST AND IN CONGRESS

The great 19th-century move west attracted entrepreneurs such as the Gratz family of Philadelphia, who developed the new terrain with their expertise in banking, insurance and railroads. Likewise, the German-born Levi Strauss (1829–1902) found a ready market for his invention, hardy denim jeans, among the prospectors in the 1848 California Gold Rush.

Meanwhile, in New York, Mordecai Manuel Noah (1785–1851), an eccentric playwright and newspaper editor, led the Democrat Party's political machine. Noah fought to abolish slavery, and also campaigned for a Jewish homeland on an island in the Niagara.

Jews were also represented in the Deep South: as early as the 1670s Sephardim had settled in Charleston, South Carolina. Florida railroad pioneer David Levy Yulee (1810–66) became the first Jew elected to the Senate in 1845. Jewish senator Judah

Above Emma Lazarus was an American Jew born in New York City. Her poem 'Colossus' welcomed immigrants at Ellis Island with: 'Give me your huddled masses yearning to be free.'

Benjamin (1811–84) became war secretary in the southern Confederate cabinet.

REFORM AND CONSERVATIVE JUDAISM

The Bohemian-born rabbi and organizational dynamo Isaac Mayer Wise (1819–1900) effectively founded modern American Reform Judaism in Cincinnati after 1854. Samuel Hirsch (1815–89) from the Rhineland then brought a more philosophical perspective as president of the Conference of American Reform Rabbis in 1869. The flagship Hebrew Union College, created in 1875, soon signalled that American Reform was set on a path distinct from its European roots.

Others balked at Hirsch's radicalism, yet found Orthodoxy too constraining. In 1886 they set up New York's Jewish Theological Seminary to promote their values. Called Conservative Jews and later inspired by the scholastic Rabbi Solomon Schechter, they founded synagogues after 1913 and by the mid-20th century they formed America's largest Jewish denomination.

Diasporas of the Southern Hemisphere

For centuries, Jewish history took place exclusively north of the equator. With 18th- and 19th-century colonial expansion, new communities arose in the Southern Hemisphere.

Many Jews travelled to the Southern Hemisphere after the 1881 Russian Pogroms. Few, if any, Jews lived there already and it was hard to lead a traditional Jewish life. Immigrants exploited economic opportunities in frontier societies that could ill-afford the old prejudices of Europe and soon established new Jewish communities, schools and institutions.

SOUTH AFRICA

There were few practising Jews among the Dutch who settled in South Africa in 1652. More arrived in the 1820s after Britain took over the Cape Colony, and larger numbers followed with the diamond and gold-mining boom in the late 1800s.

Initially, most Jews came from Britain. As travelling salesmen they connected remote farmsteads with larger towns; a bilingual Yiddish–Zulu lexicon helped them trade with Black Africans. A few became the wealthy heads of mining finance houses, like Alfred Beit, Barney Barnato, Lionel Phillips and Solly Joel.

Many more Ashkenazim came from Lithuania and Latvia after 1881, and Jews made up 23 per cent of all immigrants to the Cape 1885–1915. These 'Litvaks' tended to gravitate to Cape Town and Johannesburg where, considerably poorer than the gold magnates, they worked as tailors or small shopkeepers. They encouraged their children to train for the professions, and set up their own Board of Deputies in 1904.

AUSTRALIA

The first Jews in Australia arrived as convicts in 1788. Their descendants bought a burial plot in 1820; in 1832 they formed a congregation under Aaron Levi; and in 1844 built their first synagogue in Sydney. Tasmania was probably the next place of settlement. Gold rushes attracted immigrants to Melbourne in the 1850s, and Perth in the 1890s. One prominent Australian-born Jew of the period was the architect Nahum Barnet, who built synagogues, department stores, factories and theatres.

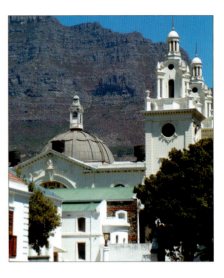

Above Great Synagogue and Jewish Museum in Cape Town, South Africa.

SOUTH AMERICA

Portuguese traders and smugglers in the Rio de la Plata most likely included a few Sephardim, but French Jews established the first true Argentinean community after the country won independence in 1810. A large post-1881 influx of 'Rusos' boosted the Ashkenazi proportion of the population to 80 per cent, while others came from Morocco.

Baron Maurice de Hirsch considered Argentina an alternative Zion and bought farmland in Santa Fe and Entre Rios provinces. Soon Yiddish-speaking gauchos were herding cattle. Over time, their *communas* (small towns) began resembling east European *shtetls*. By 1920, most of Argentina's 150,000 Jews lived in larger cities.

A liberal 1824 constitution and a booming trade in rubber made Brazil the second largest Latin American destination for Jews. Mexican Emperor Maximilian I encouraged German Jews to come to his kingdom, and Sephardi Jews fleeing an ailing Ottoman empire made new homes on the continent.

Left Consecrated in 1877, Mikve Israel Synagogue in Melbourne symbolizes Jewish roots planted in Australia.

Jews of the Late Ottoman Empire

WITHIN A SLOWLY STAGNATING EMPIRE, SALONIKA REMAINED A MAGNET FOR JEWISH IMMIGRATION, A HUB OF SCHOLARSHIP AND INNOVATION, AND A VIBRANT MOSAIC OF CULTURES AND CLASSES.

In 1683 the Turks alarmed Europe when they laid siege to Vienna. Yet two months later they were repelled, after which the Ottoman empire began its gradual decline. Constantinople's reluctance to industrialize hampered its economy, and from the 16th century European trade vessels bypassed the Ottomans, sailing direct to India and the Americas. By the 19th century, Western officials mocked Turkey as 'The Sick Man of Europe'.

DECLINE AND SURVIVAL

Wars deprived Turkey of parts of Greece, Hungary and the Black Sea, and the Congress of Berlin of 1878 further chipped away at the empire. Despite this, belated reforms enhanced civil rights and five Jews sat in the Ottoman parliament by 1887. Some Jews benefited from laws, first introduced in 1536, that privileged foreign traders. Yet the overall effect was negative; Jews in Egypt, for example, felt relieved when the former Ottoman province came under British protection in 1882. The Young Turk revolt of 1908 briefly offered new hope, until in 1914 the empire erred fatally in backing Germany in World War I.

SALONIKA

Ruled by Turks since 1430, Salonika in north-eastern Greece – today, Thessaloniki – became the mainstay of Sephardi Jewry. New immigrants enriched the community: Hungarians after 1376, Bavarian Ashkenazim in 1470, Jews from Venice and Sicily, and most of all Spanish exiles and Maranos, especially after 1492. By 1514 Jews formed more than half the population, and Salonika, an early hub of Hebrew printing, was dubbed the 'Mother of Israel'

Jews were pivotal to the wool and silk trades. After 1515 they provided the Ottoman army with uniforms. Many also worked as miners, jewellers, dockers and fishermen. In 1680 the Jewish communities united to elect one assembly. By 1900 they made up 80,000 of the city's 173,000 inhabitants. Sephardim dominated: local dishes and songs bore an Iberian flavour; gentile Greeks, Armenians and Turks came to speak their Ladino language; and the busy port closed for the Sabbath.

Jewish colleges taught astronomy, medicine and sciences from the 1500s. An Alliance Israélite school in 1874 encouraged liberal attitudes. More Jews became lawyers, doctors and bankers, and Emmanuel Carasso and Marcel Samuel Cohen were prominent Young Turk leaders. During 1880–1910 secular Ladino theatres and newspapers flourished, along with socialist and Zionist clubs. But Orthodox stalwarts often clashed with wealthy families who favoured the French language and Western values.

Jews began leaving Salonika after Greece captured the city in 1912, and fire destroyed homes and businesses in 1917. In 1943 the Nazis deported 95 per cent of those who stayed, up to 56,000 people – almost all perished in Auschwitz.

Today descendants of Ottoman Jews live on in Istanbul, New York, London, Paris and Israel.

Above Jewish porter in the Greek city of Salonika, late Ottoman period.

Left Dolmabahçe Palace, home to the last six Ottoman sultans, in Constantinople (now Istanbul).

Jews in 19th-Century Art and Culture

WHEN UNIVERSITIES OPENED TO JEWS, DOZENS OF NEW CAREER CHOICES WERE UNLOCKED, AND CREATIVITY BLOSSOMED IN THE FIELDS OF MUSIC, OPERA, ART, SCIENCE, POLITICS AND SOCIAL CAMPAIGNING.

The mid-19th century saw an explosion of creativity by Jews in the arts, music, politics and science. According to one theory, analytical skills honed through religious study were concentrated within enclosed Jewish societies. Once the ghetto walls came down, Jews were bound to excel in other fields.

UNIVERSITY LIFE
Jews began to enter university in the 1760s in America, the 1780s in Hungary, and the 1830s in England. They soon flocked to the professions, becoming doctors, lawyers and scientists. In Russia and Romania universities still barred their entry, but Jews from those countries won university places in Vienna, which became an intellectual and scientific magnet. Jews, many of central European origin, won a disproportionate 48 of the 171 Nobel Prizes in physics between 1901 and 2001.

SCIENCE AND INVENTION
Generally, 'culturally neutral' scientific departments welcomed Jews more than arts faculties. Where prejudice lingered, as in medical schools that still prevented them from becoming surgeons, Jews pioneered fields of epidemiology and social medicine. Chemist Fritz Haber (1868–1934) won a Nobel Prize in 1916 for synthesizing ammonia.

The Industrial Revolution further enthused Jews. In Germany, Siegfried Marcus (1831–98) built the world's first petrol-driven vehicle while other Jews were innovative in aeronautics. The social sciences offered fertile ground for Jewish talent, such as the early English economist David Ricardo (1772–1823), the American anthropologist Franz Boas (1858–1942) and the German sociologist Emile Durkheim (1858–1915).

THE CHALLENGE OF ART
Art challenged Jews for two reasons: suspicion of the 'graven image' from within Jewish culture, and resistance to Jews entering the elite salon. Even so, named Jewish artists emerged in the 19th century. A few adopted a cautious approach, such as the Dutch naturalist Josef Israels (1824–1911). Others expressed a radical spirit, such as the Franco-Caribbean impressionist, Camille Pissarro (1830–1903), or the leader of Berlin's avant-garde school, Max Liebermann (1847–1935). Even more daring were the abstract painters and sculptors of Paris

Left Camille Pissarro's Woman Wearing a Green Headscarf, *1893, illustrates his pointillist style.*

Above Marc Chagall's The Red Jew, *painted in 1915 and blending modernity with [Jewish] antiquity.*

on the eve of World War I. Jewish art patrons often acted as adventurous 'taste-makers', like Paul Cassirer (1871–1926), the promoter of Van Gogh and Cézanne.

MUSICAL SUCCESS
Of all the arts, music seemed least alien to Jews because of their long tradition of sacred and secular music. Jews with musical skills could leapfrog social barriers, even in Russia, where by the late 19th century all four violin soloists in the anti-Semitic Tsarist court were of Jewish origin.

Jews revealed a surprising affinity for Western classical musical forms. In Germany, Felix Mendelssohn (1809–47) won fame for his violin concerto and Wedding March theme. His sister, Fanny (1805–47), composed 466 pieces. And the Bohemian–Austrian Gustav Mahler (1860–1911) daringly blurred divisions between symphony, song and concerto. In 1897, Mahler was appointed director of the imperial Vienna Opera.

Nonetheless, there was resistance to Jewish success. In 1850, Richard Wagner wrote an essay translated as 'Jewishness in Music', which lambasted Jews for producing shallow, artificial works that betrayed a lack of

Above Born Jewish and baptised Anglican, Benjamin Disraeli was twice prime minister of Britain.

true 'German spirit'. Perhaps it is no wonder that the Mendelssohns were raised Protestant and Mahler converted to Catholicism.

THEATRE AND OPERA

Unlike Germany, France seemed receptive to artistic expressions of Jewish identity. *La Juive* ('The Jewess') by Jacques Halévy (1799–1862), for instance, became a regular fixture of the French operatic repertory after 1835. Giacomo Meyerbeer (1791–1864) pioneered grand opera, and the German-born French composer Jacques Offenbach (1819–80) helped create the operetta form. Yiddish theatre allowed east European Jews to laugh, to lampoon authority figures, whether the Tsarist commissar or local rabbi, or just to escape reality. While few gentiles knew this tradition, in the West Jews began taking to the mainstream stage. Emancipation now freed the previously suppressed talents of Jewish women, including Rachel (Eliza Felix, 1820–58) and Sarah Bernhardt (1844–1923), both universally celebrated actresses.

Right Henrietta Szold, social campaigner, in Kiryat Anavim, Palestine, c.1935.

MAINSTREAM POLITICIANS

Conversion offered an entry to a political world otherwise barred to 19th-century Jews. The leading example was Benjamin Disraeli (1804–81), the only person of Jewish parentage to become British prime minister. His father, an Italian Jew and historian, baptized his son after a dispute with his synagogue, but the later Conservative statesman never denied his Jewish identity.

In France, Adolphe Crémieux (1796–1880) was twice minister of justice. In 1827 he helped repeal the last pre-revolutionary legislation that disadvantaged Jews. Meanwhile, in Germany Ludwig Borne (1786–1837) became a satirical political writer and campaigner for emancipation, and Gabriel Riesser (1806–63) advocated both Jewish rights and German nationalism while serving in successive Prussian governments. He later became the first Jewish judge in Germany.

SOCIAL ACTIVISTS

Other Jews eschewed conventional politics for social activism. In the USA, Samuel Gompers founded the American Federation of Labour, and Henrietta Szold (1860–1945) taught immigrants English and founded the Hadassah Jewish women's organization in 1912. Later she founded hospitals and social services for Jews and Arabs in Palestine, and helped to rescue Jews from Nazi persecution in Europe in the mid-20th century.

ACADEMICS

Jewish academia flourished across a range of disciplines after universities opened to Jews. Iuliu Barasch (1815–63), born into a Hassidic family in Brody, Galicia, was a pioneer of medical science. Herman Cohen (1842–1918) and Ernst Cassirer (1874–1945) were leading neo-Kantians; the latter founded a 'philosophy of culture'. Henri Bergson (1859–1941) pioneered the philosophy of time and creativity, Other Jews were prominent orientalists, such as the Hungarian Ignaz Goldziher (1850–1921), a founder of modern Islamic studies in Europe.

Knowledge gained in the old world soon crossed the Atlantic: the German-born Franz Boas (1858–1942) was called the father of American anthropology. Nor is it possible to imagine sociology without Emile Durkheim (1858–1915), logic without Edmund Husserl (1859–1938) or psychology without Sigmund Freud (1856–1939).

POLITICAL ZIONISM

ONE OF MANY IDEOLOGIES THAT TRIED TO ANSWER JEWISH YEARNINGS, POLITICAL ZIONISM GRAFTED MODERN NATIONALIST IDEAS ON TO THE ANCIENT CONNECTION OF JEWS TO THE LAND OF ISRAEL.

Above Confident, elegant, romantic yet controversial, Theodor Herzl galvanized the nascent Zionist movement. The text above the picture bears his famous words, 'If you will it, it is no fairytale.'

Coined by the publicist Nathan Birnbaum, the expression 'Zionism' derives from Mount Zion, which adjoins the Old City of Jerusalem. At its simplest, Zionism acknowledges Jewry's attachment to the Land of Israel that broadly covers present-day Israel and the West Bank of the River Jordan. Some draw a distinction between spiritual Zionism, which has underpinned the Jewish religion since the Babylonian Exile, and political Zionism, which crystallized in Europe in the late 19th century.

TOWARDS A JEWISH NATIONALISM

Increasingly, followers of the *Haskalah* (Jewish Enlightenment) defined themselves as a nation, not a religion. And as every nation should have a land, so should the Jews, they concluded. The German Jewish philosopher Moses Hess (1812–75) exemplified this ideology. He wrote in his 1862 book *Rome and Jerusalem* that Jewish national feeling was unquenchable and could only be expressed by physically returning to Palestine. If necessary, Jews should sacrifice emancipation in the Diaspora for this cause.

ODESSA AND THE 1881 POGROMS

Few noticed Hess's book until two men from Odessa, Leon Pinsker (1821–91) and Ahad Ha-Am (1856–1927), revived its ideas. Odessa on the Black Sea was one-third Jewish and housed some 150,000 of the most secular, educated and assimilated Jews in Russia. The pogroms of 1881 shattered dreams of integration and prompted Pinsker to write *Auto-emancipation*, in which he declared: 'For the living, the Jew is a dead man; for the natives, an alien and a vagrant; for the patriot, a man without a country; for all classes, a hated rival'. Jews would only enjoy respect when they liberated themselves, he said.

Pinsker headed *Hovevei Tzion* (Lovers of Zion), which founded Rishon le-Tzion as the first Zionist settlement in Palestine in 1882. Baron Edmond de Rothschild began to help, and Russian Jewish students, called *Bilu*, started the first *aliyah*, or 'ascent', or wave of immigration.

THEODOR HERZL AND THE DIPLOMATIC PATH

Hovevei set up an Odessa Committee in 1890 to plan Jewish farming in Palestine, but lacked political direction. Ultimately it was Theodor Herzl (1860–1904) who filled that need. Earlier he had mused about 'solving the Jewish problem' through mass conversion. While reporting from Paris in 1895, he heard crowds baying for Jewish blood at the court martial

Left 'In Basel I founded the Jewish State', wrote Herzl in 1897. Here he is with delegates at the fifth Zionist conference in the same Swiss city.

of Alfred Dreyfus, a Jewish colonel falsely accused of treason. Now convinced that even cultured France was irredeemably anti-Semitic, he wrote his monograph *Judenstaat*, or 'Jewish State', in 1896, which argued that the Jewish Question was national in essence, not individual; Jews could only enjoy true freedom if they governed themselves, preferably on 'ancestral soil'.

Judenstaat became Zionism's manifesto and Herzl, a man of rare panache and regal bearing, gained messianic status among some east European *Ostjuden*. Most Jews, however, were less enthusiastic. Most Jewish philanthropists rebuffed him as a dangerous dreamer.

THE BASEL CONFERENCE

In 1897 Herzl and his colleague Max Nordau convened the first Zionist conference in Basel, Switzerland. There they created an organization and a 'national fund'. Two trends quickly emerged within Zionism. General or political Zionism followed Herzl's diplomatic path, while Ahad Ha-Am persisted with cultural Zionism. Aaron David Gordon (1856–1922) later led practical Zionists who saw settlement in Palestine as a way to create a 'new Jew' through the dignity of labour.

Herzl wrote in his diary after the conference, 'In Basel I founded the Jewish State… Maybe in five years, certainly in fifty, everyone will realize it'. At the time it seemed an extraordinary prediction; Zionism was only one of dozens of Jewish ideologies.

NEW TRENDS

Gradually a third stream, known as Labour Zionism, became dominant in the early 20th century. It consisted of divergent elements, including a romantic back-to-nature trend called Po'ale Tza'ir (Young Worker) and a more Marxist grouping, Po'ale Zion (Worker of Zion).

Above Jewish men and women pray at the Western Wall, Jerusalem, c.1905.

A fourth stream emerged, Religious Zionism, which opposed both the secularists who dominated the Zionist movement and the anti-Zionists who made up most observant Jews. In 1902 this group held its first conference in Vilna under its leader, Rabbi Yizhak Reines. Finally Nordau and others who came to despair of gradualism advocated what they called Catastrophic Zionism.

THE UGANDA OPTION

Herzl envisaged a Jewish-ruled yet pluralist Palestine, a bourgeois European-style utopian paradise in the Levant, as seen in his 1902 novel *Altneuland* (Old-New Land). Even fellow Zionists mocked its naïve dream of Jerusalem as a capital of world peace, or its belief that Arabs would welcome Jewish settlement.

When Britain's foreign office offered Herzl a tract of land in Uganda/Kenya, he agreed immediately. The seventh congress in 1905, however, rejected the Uganda Option, by which time Herzl had died of exhaustion in July 1904.

Ultimately, Zionism's fate depended on external factors, the collapse of Ottoman rule and Britain's acquisition of Palestine. The challenge was reconciling the national feelings of Jews and the land's indigenous Arab majority. As early as 1891 Ahad Ha-Am warned in *The Truth from Palestine* that it was not, as some imagined, 'a land without people'. The Marxist Zionist, Ber Borochov, dreamt of Jewish and Arab workers uniting; however, Ha-Am noted that if any Arab felt oppressed by Jews, 'rage will stay alive in his heart'.

JERUSALEM – BEYOND THE CITY WALLS

During 1537–42 the Ottoman Sultan Suleiman built Jerusalem's majestic walls and eight gates, which still define the Old City today. Within those walls are Muslim, Christian, Jewish and Armenian quarters. At the centre stands the Temple Mount, or Haram al-Sharif, site of two Muslim mosques and believed by Jews to be the location of the twice-destroyed Temple. Every day religious Jews pray to God for 'remembrance of Jerusalem Your Holy City' and the 'return of the Divine Presence to Zion'.

After 1700 Polish and Moroccan Jews began filling up the Jewish quarter; soon the Old City became overcrowded. In 1860 Sir Moses Montefiore, an English Sephardi benefactor, won approval for Jewish suburbs to be built outside the walls, the first being Mishkenot Sha'ananim. Soon Muslim and Christian Arabs built their own neighbourhoods, though by the 1870s Jews probably constituted the majority of the city's population.

Early Zionists felt ambivalent about the city, because it was a centre for religious Jews who depended on charity and rejected their secular venture. To Zionists, these long-established Jews paradoxically represented the worst aspects of 'non-productive' Diaspora life.

CHAPTER 9

WORLD WARS AND THE HOLOCAUST

More than 20 million people died in World War I between 1914 and 1918, and when fighting ceased, both Jews and Gentiles understandably longed for peace. The interwar years saw individual Jews flower in the arts, sciences and politics as never before. The more radical welcomed Russia's 1917 Communist Revolution, especially when it outlawed anti-Semitism and abolished the pernicious Pale of Settlement.

Yet many ordinary Germans believed that Jews had betrayed the fatherland. Increasingly they backed Adolf Hitler's ultra-nationalist Nazi Party, which vowed to exterminate 'non-Aryans' and, during World War II (1939–45), almost succeeded. In 1942 the Nazis began the industrialized murder of 6 million Jews, including 1.5 million children. Called the Holocaust, or Shoah in Hebrew, this systematic genocide virtually destroyed 1,500 years of European Jewish civilization. Recalled in monuments, museums, novels and films, it remains a benchmark for mankind's capacity for evil.

Opposite Shoes at the former Nazi extermination camp of Auschwitz, Poland. Up to 1.5 million men, women and children, mostly Jews, were murdered there in 1942–4. The Holocaust marked a nadir in human history and nearly wiped out Jewish life in Europe.

Above Prisoners are led through the gates of Theresienstadt concentration camp, c. 1942. Inscribed above the entrance is 'Arbeit macht frei' ('Work will set you free') – a supremely cynical motto.

Europe at War

Some 1.5 million Jews served as soldiers in World War I, the conflict that transformed Europe and indirectly led Britain to promise Jews a 'national home' in Palestine.

Even before World War I broke out, life was turbulent for Jews in eastern Europe. Violence against Jews during Russia's 1905 uprisings led to 154,000 Jews moving to the USA during 1905–6. Smaller numbers went to France and Britain. In 1904–14 40,000 mainly socialist, east European Jews moved to Palestine. This Aliyah, or 'ascent', laid foundations for the Zionist labour movement, the Hebrew press and the *kvutzot*, or 'communal farming settlements'.

THE PATH OF WAR

Austria's Archduke Franz Ferdinand's assassination in Sarajevo, Bosnia, on 28 June 1914 led to the most murderous war to date. By August, a series of alliances had been activated, with the Entente Powers – Britain, France, Serbia and imperial Russia – fighting the Central Powers of Germany and Austria-Hungary, Ottoman Turkey and Bulgaria.

Hopes of swift victory faded as trench warfare came to western Europe. The technology that enabled mass production of electric lighting, telephones, radio, railway networks and cars now drove the world's first truly industrial war. The conflict was fought on land, sea and air and across six separate fronts. Over four years, 65 million troops were mobilized, 8.5 million killed, 21.2 million wounded, and 7.8 million taken prisoner or listed as missing in action. Another 13 million non-combatants probably died through hostilities and disease.

SOLDIERS ON ALL SIDES

All leading German Jewish intellectuals – except Albert Einstein – signed a petition supporting German war aims. Some 100,000 Jews fought for Germany, proportionately more than any other ethnic, religious or political group, and about 12,000 died in battle. Jews from European colonies also enlisted, and Algerian Jewish soldiers were particularly noted for their courage in battle.

Jews in England and America felt uncomfortable joining any alliance with Russia's anti-Jewish Tsar. Despite this, 50,000 Jews served in the British forces, of whom five won the Victoria Cross and 50 the Distinguished Service Order. Many worked in labour corps in Middlesex, Egypt and the French trenches, while a few joined the Zion Mule Corps.

The Russian Imperial Army fielded 400,000–650,000 Jewish troops, more than any other nation; possibly 100,000 Russian Jews died in the conflict. Early in the war, Russian officials expelled Jews from the Pale of Settlement.

After 1915 some 40 per cent of Russian Jews came under German and Austrian military rule. Most welcomed their better treatment yet regretted being cut off from brethren to the east. By 1917, 3.4 million Jews remained under Russian rule, 700,000 of them beyond the Pale.

Above A.J. Balfour, British Foreign Secretary, whose 1917 Declaration pledged a national homeland for Jews.

Left Europe in 1914, showing the disposition of forces before a war that was to claim 21 million lives.

America's entry into the war in April 1917 ultimately tipped the balance and resulted in an Entente victory, but not before a late eastern push by Germany encouraged war-weary Russians to force their Tsar to abdicate in February 1917.

A WAR TO END ALL WARS?
Europe was transformed when the Great War ended with the armistice of 11 November 1918. Gone were the Ottoman and Austro-Hungarian empires and the German Second Reich. New states including Czechoslovakia and Yugoslavia emerged, and Poland was independent for the first time in 100 years.

The war had turned America into a global superpower, and US President Woodrow Wilson promoted a League of Nations to prevent future conflict. Yet the same Versailles Treaty that created the League in 1920 so harshly punished Germany, it virtually guaranteed another war.

BALFOUR'S DECLARATION
Barely noticed amid the clamour of war was a letter that Britain's foreign secretary James Balfour wrote to

Below Jewish soldiers from Austria, Hungary and Poland at prayer, military camp, 1914, first year of World War I. By the Jewish painter O. Ehrenfreund.

> ### THE WAR IN PALESTINE
> Although Zionists and many Jews backed Turkey and Germany over the Allies, dissidents saw an opportunity to plan a future Jewish state by backing the Allied powers. In late 1914, Vladimir Jabotinsky and Joseph Trumpeldor persuaded Britain to create the Zion Mule Corps, a Jewish transportation unit. This disbanded in 1915, but inspired the 1917 establishment of the Jewish Legion.
>
> Palestinian Jewish spies were siphoning information to Britain on Turkish movements, as French troops were mobilizing in Syria and Lebanon. Jews and Arabs, French and British, were all fighting against a Turkish enemy.
>
> Eventually, on 11 December 1917, Britain's General Allenby entered Jerusalem and accepted a Turkish surrender. In 1918 a Jewish Legion battalion led a British crossing of the Jordan River into Palestine. So ended 500 years of Ottoman rule over the Holy Land. Allied and Arab forces took Damascus, Beirut and Aleppo by the end of 1918.
>
> *Above Pte Nathaniel Friedlander, a Jewish barber from London, after signing up to fight with the Army Service Corps, 1915.*

Lord Rothschild on 2 November 1917. In it, Balfour stated that his government 'views with favour the establishment of a Jewish national home in Palestine'. The Balfour Declaration, brief and unspecific though it was, marked the first Great Power approval for a Jewish political entity on 'ancestral soil' in 1,900 years. The letter crowned years of diplomacy by Chaim Weizmann and Nahum Sokolow of the World Zionist Organization. Weizmann's technical assistance to Britain's war effort also helped clinch the agreement. Yet most European Jews remained sceptical about Zionism. And five days after Balfour signed his letter, Russian Bolshevik militants launched a Marxist revolution that raised Jewish hopes for a more promising solution.

Below United in death: German soldiers, one Jewish, one Christian, buried side by side at a French war cemetery.

WORLD WARS AND THE HOLOCAUST

Jews and the Bolshevik Revolution

Russia, home to half the world's Jews, was still a semi-feudalistic state in the early 1900s. The 1917 revolutions marked a dramatic shift, but the Jews were later to suffer under Communist rule too.

By the 1900s, Russia's Jewish socialists were deeply divided. Many belonged to the leading Marxist Social Democratic Party, which was itself split between moderate Mensheviks and radical Bolsheviks. For their part, Socialist Zionists, called Po'ale Zion, or 'Workers of Zion', threw their weight behind the 1917 October revolution.

REVOLUTION, WAR, AND THE END OF THE PALE

The Bund, a Jewish Labour Union, had been founded in 1897 to achieve equality for Jews in the Russian empire. Bundists also led the 1905 revolutionary uprisings, which resulted in limited political reforms.

Below Born to a Jewish family, Leon Trotsky embraced Marxism and helped lead the 1917 Russian Revolution.

However, a backlash led to 500 Odessa Jews being killed in a single day, and Marxists boycotted elections to a Duma (parliament) that was soon dissolved anyway.

Russia entered World War I on 1 August 1914, woefully unprepared and allied with Britain and France against the Central Powers. Fighting largely took place in areas where Russian Jews lived. Tsar Nicholas II took personal command of forces in September 1915, but by 1917 crippling losses caused them to reject rule by the 'Little Father of the People'. In March 1917 Nicholas was forced to abdicate. Russia's new provisional government abolished the Pale of Settlement.

STORMING THE KREMLIN

Exiled Bolsheviks stole back into Russia on board a 'sealed train' from Switzerland in April 1917, led by Vladimir Lenin (1870–1924) and his chief aide, Grigory Zinoviev (born Hirsch Apfelbaum, a Jew by origin, 1883–1936). Defying orthodox Marxist qualms, in October Lenin seized St Petersburg and Moscow and within weeks the centralized empire fell to his Bolshevik cadres.

Their astonishing success would have been impossible without the organizational skills of Leon Trotsky, born in 1878 as Lev Davidovich Bronstein. His father was an illiterate Jewish Ukrainian farmer.

In January 1918 the Bolsheviks banned other parties and declared a Soviet Republic. Mensheviks were tolerated as allies temporarily, but were outlawed in 1921.

Above The future is red – 1924 propaganda poster of Bolshevik revolutionary leader Vladimir Lenin.

RUINOUS CIVIL WAR

In March 1918 Trotsky signed the controversial Brest–Litovsk peace treaty with Germany, which pulled Russia out of the war and ceded Poland and the Baltic States. By now a vicious civil war had erupted between Bolsheviks, or Reds, and Counter-revolutionaries, or Whites, a motley coalition of monarchists, liberals and local nationalists backed by Allied powers. This conflict raged for four years and included rightist pogroms that killed more than 70,000 Jewish civilians. More Jews now backed the Bolsheviks, even though some renegade Red troops had also ransacked *shtetls* (Jewish villages).

JEWS IN NEW RUSSIA

Dozens of Jewish-origin Bolsheviks now wielded power over the largest nation on earth. Lenin was himself part-Jewish, and four of his politburo's seven members had Jewish blood, including Zinoviev, Trotsky and Lev Kamenev. Another Jew, Adolph Joffe, chaired the St Petersburg Military Revolutionary

Committee that overthrew the provisional government. Jews even ran their own Communist party cell, the *Yevsektsiya*.

Soviet rule brought changes for ordinary Jews, initially for the better. In July 1918 the Communists passed a decree 'recognizing the equality of all citizens, irrespective of race or nationality', and Lenin unequivocally proclaimed in 1919: 'Shame on accursed Tsarism which tortured and persecuted the Jews'.

With the Pale gone, Jews could, in theory, live anywhere. Jews formed soviets (workers' councils). The Kremlin decided to transform Jewish pedlars and petty artisans into farmers, to integrate Jews into society and eradicate anti-Semitism. By contrast with trends everywhere else, Jews left cities for the countryside. By 1930 some 230,000 Jews were working on farming communes in Belarus, Crimea and Ukraine.

FREEDOM EXTINGUISHED

Soon Communism revealed a darker side. The authorities penalized small Jewish shopkeepers and artisans as 'bourgeois elements' and closed churches, mosques and synagogues alike after 1921. The Evseksia summarily crushed all other Jewish organizations and ran 'community trials' against 'backward and chauvinistic' Jewish religious practices, before it, too, was disbanded in 1930. As the Russian-born Zionist Chaim Weizmann noted, the revolutionaries 'could not understand why a Russian Jew should want to be anything but a Russian'.

Joseph Stalin gradually monopolized power after Lenin's death in 1924 by sidelining, arresting or expelling rivals, notably including Kamenev, Zinoviev and Trotsky. Agricultural collectivization led to rampant famine, especially in Ukraine, which killed millions. Show trials after 1934 purged most old Bolsheviks, including thousands of Jewish origin, and former tolerance of Yiddish cultural autonomy gave way to enforced assimilation by the late 1930s. But at least the physical survival of Jews was not threatened by communist rule, as it was in Nazi Germany and fascist Europe.

Left Capturing the excitement of a new era, this Bolshevik poster calls on foreign workers to join the Revolution.

Above Soviet Jewish collective farmer Michael Gefen and wife Sheina tend their homestead in Birobidzhan, 1935.

BIROBIDZHAN

The USSR's politburo wanted to assign a homeland to each nationality, including the Jews. Communism opposed Zionism so Palestine was no option. In 1928, the USSR set up the town of Birobidzhan at the end of the Trans-Siberian railway, to be the capital of a Jewish Autonomous Region, Yevreskaya. Yiddish and Russian were its official languages, and Jews were encouraged to farm and work in factories. However conditions were poor, Hebrew and religious instruction were outlawed, and, though the Kremlin boasted 150,000 Jews would live in Birobidzhan by 1937, few actually did. Only 25,000 were there in 1974, and 4,000 in 2008.

Birobidzhan experienced a slight revival after the fall of the Soviet Union, but it never fulfilled its aim of becoming a Marxist 'alternative Zion'.

THE INTERWAR YEARS

AFTER THE DEVASTATION OF WORLD WAR I, THE LEAGUE OF NATIONS WAS ESTABLISHED IN 1919 TO GUARANTEE GLOBAL PEACE. IN FACT THE RESULTANT TREATIES CREATED MORE PROBLEMS THAN THEY SOLVED.

From a Jewish perspective the interwar years presented a portrait of contrasts. On the one hand individual Jews thrived as never before; on the other, hatred against Jews mounted. And after Nazis took over Germany in 1933, both individuals and communities across Europe faced the real threat of annihilation.

JEWISH DELEGATES TO VERSAILES

The Paris peace talks of 1919 aimed to establish a new world order where all peoples had a voice. In this spirit, Jews sent a deputation called the Comité Des Delegations Juives, claiming the support of 12 million people worldwide. Led by US lawyer Louis Marshall and Russian Zionist Leo Motzkin, the Comité demanded protection for Jews as a nationality, albeit a stateless one. In the event Jews were acknowledged as a semi-autonomous minority.

The Versailles Treaty of 1919 recognized a host of new states, including Poland, Lithuania, Czechoslovakia and Yugoslavia. Austria was stripped down to its core area, Hungary won its independence and Germany's Weimar Republic had to cede economically valuable land to neighbours.

Versailles was hardly ideal for Jews. Before 1914 they had lived with other minorities in ramshackle empires but now they felt exposed. Versailles compelled eastern European states to sign minority rights treaties following Comité advice, though Poland, Hungary and Romania subverted this requirement by targeted taxation, or laws to improve trade and sanitation. Furthermore, rifts between pro- and anti-Zionists undermined the Comité and similar bodies such as the Jewish Agency and World Jewish Congress.

THE STAB IN THE BACK

Conspiracy theorists in Germany's ultra-nationalist *Freikorps* group spread the myth that Jews had stabbed Germany in the back by forcing the fatherland to surrender just when it was about to win the war. Meanwhile, rightists in Russia and beyond blamed the Jews for the 1917 revolution and subsequent ruinous civil war; even though most ordinary Jews were apolitical residents of the Pale, remote from events in Moscow and Petrograd.

JEWISH REVOLUTIONARIES IN GERMANY

In November 1918, as Germany sank to military defeat, Jewish socialist Kurt Eisner overthrew the Bavarian monarchy and founded a 'people's republic'. When he was assassinated the next February, other

Left The League of Nations was the brainchild of President Woodrow Wilson, seen here reassuring a nervous USA.

Above Socialist firebrand Rosa Luxemburg, murdered in 1919 after an abortive coup in Berlin.

Jewish revolutionaries, Ernst Toller, Gustav Landauer and Eugene Leviné, established a short-lived Soviet republic there in imitation of the Bolsheviks in Russia.

The best-known Jewish radical of all was the Polish-born Rosa Luxemburg (1871–1919). Formerly the co-founder of the Lithuanian Social-Democratic Party, she moved to Germany in 1898 and soon rejected the parliamentary approach. Her inveterate foe was another Jew, the revisionist Marxist Eduard Bernstein, a Social-Democrat leader and Reichstag member during 1902–18 and 1920–28. Luxemburg took a bolder stance: a fiery critic of imperialism, nationalism and even Bolshevik 'bureaucracy', she co-founded the Spartacist League in 1914, which unlike mainstream socialists opposed the war and supported spontaneous uprising by the masses. Army officers murdered her in January 1919 after a failed Spartacist coup attempt in Berlin. The leftist Jewish historian Isaac Deutscher later called her assassination 'the first triumph of Nazi Germany'.

Neither Rosa Luxemburg nor most Marxists of Jewish origin cared much for Judaism. Nor did most German Jews support their views.

Above The old world meets the new? Erich Lessing's painting shows a Polish Jewish soldier reading a newspaper to his countrymen, 1920.

None the less, the prominence of Jewish revolutionary leaders allowed rightists to tar the whole community with the 'radical' brush.

JEWISH LIFE IN POLAND

Having been missing from the map of Europe since the partition of 1816, Poland was reborn as an independent nation under Marshal Joseph Pilsudski on 11 November 1918. Thousands of Jewish shopkeepers, professionals and petty capitalists voted with their feet and moved there. By 1924, Poland had nearly 3 million Jews, more than 10 per cent of its population. Jews made up about a quarter of all schoolchildren and university students. Polish Jews generally felt well disposed towards Pilsudski, who named himself dictator in May 1926 and implemented the terms of the 1919 Minorities Protection Treaty.

Poland's Jewish urban dwellers increasingly spoke Polish and revelled in a buoyant national culture, whereas poorer rural Jews stuck to Yiddish and cherished traditional ways. Jewish political parties now entered the *Sejm*, or 'Polish parliament', initially as a national council in co-operation with other minorities. After 1928 some Jewish parties joined the government list – a new phenomenon that split Jewish votes and eroded the community's independence.

Leftist and Zionist Jewish groups competed with each other more productively in Poland and Lithuania by building networks of secular schools. Instruction was either in Yiddish or Hebrew and the development marked a breach with previous tradition.

THE MARCH OF FASCISM

All Europe suffered from the Wall Street stock market crash of 1929, and as unemployment and inflation ran rampant, fascism grew in Austria, Hungary and Poland. Fanatics began to follow the model set by Benito Mussolini's Italian Fascists who took power in October 1922. Fascism venerated the state, rejected capitalism and Marxism in equal measure, and marked, in Mussolini's words, the clear, final and categorical antithesis of democracy, plutocracy, freemasonry and the principles of 1789. Every state in Europe was under democratic government in the 1920s; by 1940 only four democracies had survived.

At first fascism was not explicitly anti-Semitic, but it provided an environment within which racism could thrive. Ultimately Nazism, the Germanic variant of fascism, transformed racism into a commanding ideology, dragged the world into a second world war, and all but destroyed the Jews of Europe.

AMERICA – PROGRESS AND PITFALLS

World War I helped establish American centrality in world affairs, and Jews became an integral part of US society. The first Jewish state governor, Moses Alexander of Idaho, was elected in 1915; Louis Brandeis became the first Jew in the US Supreme Court in 1916; and in 1917 Jews made up 5.7% of the US Army, greater than their 3.25% representation in the population.

Above Ku Klux Klan devotees, Long Island, New York State, 1930.

New organizations arose to articulate Jewish interests: the American Jewish Joint Distribution Committee in 1914, and the American Jewish Congress (AJC) in 1918. Reconstituted under Steven Wise in 1924, in 1936 the AJC propelled the creation of a World Jewish Congress. Brandeis, Wise and Felix Frankfurter were powerful advocates for Zionism; and immigrants benefited American science, industry and popular culture.

However, an influx of comparatively unskilled workers strained the economy and led to new quotas. The 1924 Immigration Act capped entrants by area of origin to 2% of any donor country's community present in the USA in 1880, thus targeting Asians and eastern and southern Europeans, including Jews. Latent anti-Semitism came to the fore, with car tycoon Henry Ford disseminating the Protocols of Zion, and others backing the 1924 act on grounds of racial hygiene. Following the 1929 slump, the racist Ku Klux Klan added Jews as another enemy of America, and anti-Semitic organizations, some sponsored by Germany after 1933, lambasted President Roosevelt's New Deal as a Jew Deal. In 1938 the Catholic radio priest Charles Coughlin launched a propaganda campaign against Jews. Despite this, when war erupted in September 1939 most Americans united against Nazi aggression.

Hitler Takes Power – Nazism Grows

For Jews, no country represented civilized aspirations more than Germany. Yet it was here that the most barbaric and devastating anti-Semitic onslaught was devised and realized.

In 1921 the novelist Jakob Wasserman proclaimed, 'I am a German and a Jew in equal measure – one cannot be separated from the other.' That same year the Berlin-born Jewish satirist Kurt Tucholsky wrote: 'Germans have two passions: beer and anti-Semitism. The beer is 28 proof but the anti-Semitism is 100 proof.'

Many Germans believed that Jews had betrayed the nation in war and were steering it to disaster in peace. They blamed Jews for the June 1919 Versailles Treaty, which limited their army to 100,000 soldiers, confiscated territories and colonies and imposed reparations of $32 billion. And they despised the Weimar Republic – instituted on 11 August 1919 – as a Jewish tool, which had wilfully dismantled the monarchy and handed Germany to the socialists.

Below In command – Adolf Hitler addresses a stormtrooper rally, Dortmund, 1933.

NAZISM AND ANTI-SEMITISM

Adolf Hitler's skill lay in turning this minority viewpoint into a mainstream belief and eventually using it to gain absolute power. In 1920 he became *führer*, or 'leader', of the small National Socialist German Workers' Party, better known as the Nazis. From the outset, anti-Semitism was his central motif. 'It is our duty', he said in 1920, 'to whip up and to incite in our people the instinctive repugnance of the Jews'.

Born in Linz, Austria, in 1889, Adolf Hitler fought in World War I and, like millions of ex-soldiers, thought that politicians had 'sold them out' in 1918. Hitler fostered the *Sturmabteilung*, or SA, a cohort of brown-shirted stormtroopers under the fanatic Ernst Röhm, and won the crucial backing of the veteran war hero Erich Ludendorff.

Hitler and Ludendorff instigated a coup in a Munich beer hall in 1923. When it failed, Hitler was charged with treason and jailed for nine

Above An early harbinger of coming genocide – sign designating area for Jews, Berlin Park, c.1935.

months in Landsberg prison, where he began writing *Mein Kampf*, or 'My Struggle'. The book signalled his view that 'Aryans' were the 'master race', and that 'parasitical' Jews caused all Germany's misfortunes and were the enemy of civilization everywhere.

Some Nazis adopted anti-Christian occultism as symbolized in the swastika sign. What made Nazism so potent was its blend of elements, and its exploitation of human psychology. It appealed to Germany's growing petty middle class who envied the wealthy above them, feared the proletariat below and had most to lose from economic recession. Anti-Semitism, once thought uncouth, became more acceptable as political hysteria increased.

HITLER WINS POWER

Most Jews supported the Weimar Republic and welcomed the ascent of Walther Rathenau as foreign minister in 1922. His assassination by right-wing army officers on 24 June 1922 prompted economic panic and the German mark fell from 350 to 4,500 per dollar in four months. The Wall Street Crash and global recession of 1929 hit Germany hard. By 1932 half her factories stood idle and millions were jobless. In 1932,

Above Mein Kampf *('My Struggle')
– Adolf Hitler's manifesto, in which he expresses his hatred against the Jews.*

14 million German voters backed the Nazis, and Hitler was appointed Chancellor on 30 January 1933. In March the Nazis gained 44 per cent support in elections, and Hitler authorized the first concentration camp, at Dachau, for political opponents. Four days later he used a fire at the Reichstag – thought to have been started by Nazis – as the pretext to rule by decree.

LEGISLATING HATRED

Hitler lost little time in putting *Mein Kampf* theories into practice. In April 1933, he ordered a boycott of Jewish lawyers, doctors and shopkeepers and forced a bill through the Reichstag that sacked Jews from the civil service. Paul von Hindenburg wanted to exempt loyal Jewish war veterans from the law but was rebuffed.

Non-Nazi institutions rushed to satisfy Nazi policy with remarkable speed. In May students burned books by Jews, Communists and other 'degenerates', and in July universities began purging Jews from their faculties. By June 1935 Germany's leading medical journal openly compared Jews to the tuberculosis bacilli.

In August 1933 Propaganda Minister Joseph Goebbels began barring Jews from working in broadcasting, cinema, music and the press. Before long, no Jews could attend theatres, film-houses or concert-halls. Having banned rival parties and trade unions, Hitler crushed the SA on the Night of the Long Knives in June 1934 and declared himself *führer* of Germany after von Hindenburg died in July.

NUREMBERG LAWS, 1935

Already, before 1935, Jews could not use hospitals, were barred from higher education, and had to adopt middle names – Sara and Israel. They had identity cards stamped with a J. But anti-Jewish legislation really started with the Nuremberg Laws of 15 September 1935. Their purpose was apparently to cease attacks on Jews by party members, as this harmed the German economy, and to standardize the treatment of Jews, based on a pseudo-scientific racial rationale. Now, Jews were no longer citizens, but 'subjects', stripped of their political rights. The Law for the Protection of German Blood and Honour banned Jews from marrying non-Jews in order to 'preserve the German people'. Jews were categorized as full Jews or first- and second-class mongrels, according to how much Jewish blood they had.

The Nuremberg Treaty established a legal framework for uprooting Jews and reducing them to poverty. Public areas were declared *judenrein*, or 'Jew-free'; individual Jewish 'criminals' were sent to concentration camps in 1937; Jewish businesses were liquidated or 'Aryanized' in 1938; and up to 17,000 Polish Jews were deported to the border in October 1938.

Many German Jews persuaded themselves Nazism was a passing phase, but it became increasingly obvious that trying to ride out the storm would no longer work. About a third of German Jews emigrated. The Confessing Church stood against racism in 1935, as did some Catholic canons. However, most dissidents were exiled, incarcerated or killed. There was no united resistance against the Nazis. Matters worsened as Germany took more European territory in the 1930s.

> ### TALENTED JEWISH REFUGEES
> The Third Reich's race legislation prompted the flight of some of Europe's most talented Jews. The composer Kurt Weill left in 1933, and writer Stefan Zweig in 1934. By the time the Nazis annexed Austria in 1938, flight was far harder. The novelist Herman Broch was rescued by James Joyce and others; and the father of modern psychology, Sigmund Freud, left Vienna for London in June 1938. Philosopher Ludwig Wittgenstein had to pay off officials to get papers to leave for Britain in August 1939. He and Hitler were, paradoxically, classmates at a high school in Linz. Predictions of German weakness due to a Jewish 'brain drain' were overstated, although the flight of 29 Jewish nuclear physicists was to prove a massive blow to Germany when the Allies produced the first atomic bomb. Most famous of all refugee scientists was Albert Einstein, who left Berlin in 1932 and in 1933 helped set up the International Rescue Committee to assist opponents of Hitler.

Right Young Jews prepare to leave Nazi Germany for Palestine in February 1938.

WORLD WAR II BEGINS

THE GERMAN DRIVE FOR *LEBENSRAUM*, OR 'LIVING SPACE', ULTIMATELY SPARKED WORLD WAR II. AS MORE COUNTRIES WERE CONQUERED, SO MILLIONS OF JEWS FELL PREY TO LETHAL NAZI LEGISLATION.

At first, the Nazis only coveted lands lost in 1918. They acquired the port of Danzig after 1933, and overran the coal-rich Saar region in 1935 and German Upper Silesia in 1937. Facing mere rebukes from France, Britain and the League of Nations, Hitler felt emboldened to fuse his native Austria with Germany, although the 1919 Versailles Treaty had expressly forbidden this.

On 12 March 1938, German troops invaded Austria and arrested 70,000 leading Jews, Communists and Social Democrats. Hitler then declared Germany and Austria one, entered Vienna and Linz and applied racial legislation against Austria's 190,000 Jews, about three-quarters of whom lived in Vienna.

Below Internees building Dachau, Germany's first concentration camp, under the watch of an SS guard, 1933.

EVIAN CONFERENCE

By 1938, about 150,000, or nearly one-third, of Germany's 500,000 Jews had emigrated; and more Jews left from occupied Danzig, Saar, Silesia and Sudetenland. In July 1938, US President Franklin Roosevelt convened a nine-day conference to address the refugee issue at Evian-les-Bains, France. All told, some 811,000 Jews managed to find new homes abroad during the period 1933–43: 190,000 went to America, 120,000 to Palestine and 65,000 to England.

NIGHT OF BROKEN GLASS

The true nadir arrived with the cross-continental pogrom against Jews in Germany and Austria on 9–10 November 1938. Dubbed *Kristallnacht*, or 'Night of Broken Glass', this onslaught saw 1,000 synagogues totally destroyed, dozens

Above Kristallnacht, November 1938, when looters ransacked Jewish shops with the connivance of the regime.

of Jews killed, businesses looted, properties resold at forced auctions and wealth stolen by Nazi thugs. Five days later Germany closed all public schools to Jewish children.

Kristallnacht shocked the world and hastened the likelihood of war. Responding to pleas from British Jews, Britain agreed to rescue 10,000 unaccompanied Jewish children in what was called the *Kindertransport*. A similar initiative in America was sadly blocked at Congressional Committee stage.

THE FALL OF POLAND

Adolf Hitler's final gamble was his non-aggression pact with the Soviet Union of 24 August 1939, which effectively neutralized Germany's 'eastern front'. The way was now clear for Hitler to invade Poland on 1 September 1939. Some 20,000 Jews died in the initial incursion, and bombing destroyed up to 95 per cent of Jewish homes in 120 centres. Poland was divided into two zones, German in the west (with 2.1 million Jews) and Russian in the east (with 1.37 million Jews). From

WORLD WAR II BEGINS

Above Lithuanian soldier marching a group of Jews to forced labour in Nazi-occupied eastern Europe.

October 1939 Nazis began corralling Jews into urban ghettos, with the Warsaw Ghetto holding 380,000 and Lodz, 160,000. Conditions were appalling: Jews, nearly a third of Warsaw's population, occupied just 2.4 per cent of the city's area. Thousands died of disease and starvation as Jews were only allocated 253 calories of food per person, compared to 2,613 for Germans. Jews were forbidden to step outside the ghetto and any Pole caught aiding a Jew was killed on the spot.

Within the ghetto Jews ran a *Judenrat*, or 'Jewish Council', and police, schools, libraries and theatres to keep up spirits, until the Nazis forced councillors to choose who should fill quotas for deportation to death-camps. The decision drove many an official to suicide.

WORLD WAR

Hitler's 1939 Polish invasion triggered World War II, which led to Germany invading Norway and Denmark in April 1940, and France, Belgium, Holland and Luxembourg in May. All but Britain fell before the German *blitzkrieg*, or 'lightning war'. Meanwhile, Italy and Japan joined Germany in a Tripartite Axis Pact in September. In July 1939 the Nazis had shut down the *Reichvertretung der Juden in Deutschland*, or 'National Agency for Jews in Germany', a compulsory organization of all Jews in the Reich headed by Rabbi Leo Baeck, and replaced it with a National Association directly run by the Gestapo. Jews in conquered countries were subjected to Nazi race laws, and wartime exigencies meant that emigration was no longer possible.

FRANCE AND ALGERIA

From July 1940 France was divided into a German-occupied zone in the north and the puppet Vichy regime in the south, which collaborated with the Nazis and deported thousands of Jews to German camps.

The Crémieux Decree of 1870 had naturalized Algerian Jews, but that status was revoked when 117,000 Jews felt the weight of the racist Vichy laws in Algeria.

THE RUSSIAN FRONT IN 1941

Having conquered most of mainland Europe, Adolf Hitler turned his attention eastwards. On 22 June 1941, he breached his non-aggression pact with the Soviet Union and launched Operation Barbarossa, which caught millions of Jews in a fatal dragnet. Nazis decapitated Jewish leadership by murdering any Communist commissars they found, and killing all but one or two of Lithuania's 300 communal rabbis.

RESISTANCE FIGHTERS

During April–May 1943, Mordechai Anilewicz (1919–1943) led the first armed Jewish resistance to Nazism in the Warsaw Ghetto uprising. Somehow the residents resisted for five weeks, before succumbing to Nazi soldiers, who razed the site at the cost of 7,000 Jewish lives. The remaining 50,000 were sent to concentration or extermination camps.

Later the Vilna Ghetto rose up and resistance groups formed in Bialystok, Minsk and Kovno ghettos. In Poland, Jews commanded 4 of the 12 partisan units parachuted in in 1944. Despite such bravery, nothing could stop the murder of millions known as the Holocaust.

Below A searing image of infamy: Nazi troops round up Jews after crushing the 1943 Warsaw ghetto uprising.

Holocaust – Final Solution

THE HOLOCAUST IS REGARDED AS THE ARCHETYPAL EXAMPLE OF MAN'S CAPACITY FOR WICKEDNESS. FROM A JEWISH PERSPECTIVE, NAZI RACIAL GENOCIDE PROVED MORE LETHAL THAN ANY ANTI-SEMITISM IN HISTORY.

The Holocaust, or *Shoah* in Hebrew, destroyed Jewish human life on a scale never seen before, eliminated Europe as a leading centre of Jewish civilization, and left an irreparable wound on the Jewish psyche.

Jews were not the only sector of European society to suffer the Holocaust. An estimated 500,000 Roma and Sinti gypsies were also killed, as were homosexuals, mentally and physically disabled people, the 'Rhineland bastards' (offspring of Germans and African soldiers from World War I), and political opponents, including dissident churchmen. Yet Jews were pursued with unparalleled fanaticism and died in far greater numbers.

THE 'FINAL SOLUTION'

SS chief Heinrich Himmler created *Einsatzgruppen*, or 'action forces' before the war to round up and kill Jews, gypsies and Communists. Now their commandos killed Jews on the spot as they ploughed through Ukraine and the Baltic states *en route* to Moscow. Officials sought a more comprehensive approach. On 31 June 1941 Hitler's deputy, Hermann Goering, entrusted the Reich Security overseer, Reinhard Heydrich, with implementing 'a complete solution to the Jewish question', affecting an estimated 11 million Jews throughout the German sphere. Jewish emigration was totally prohibited on 31 October 1941. In January Heydrich convened a conference at Wansee, near Berlin, to co-ordinate the logistics of total extermination. Heydrich was assassinated in May 1942 but the policy lived on.

A NETWORK OF CAMPS

In Germany the prototype concentration camp was Dachau, set up near Munich in 1933. All extermination camps, a 1942 innovation,

Above The view that greeted US soldiers after they liberated Buchenwald concentration camp, April 1945.

were located outside the Reich. The six most infamous were in Poland: Auschwitz, Chelmno, Belzec, Majdanek, Sobibor and Treblinka. Others were located in Croatia (Jasenovac), Ukraine (Janowska) and Belarus (Maly Trostenets).

Prisoners sent to such camps were not expected to last more than 24 hours. Conditions were also atrocious in 'conventional' camps – 70,000 died in Bergen-Belsen and 56,000 in Buchenwald. In 1942 Germany began mass deportations from ghettos at a bewildering pace, as part of Operation Reinhard: 300,000 Jews were shipped over just 52 days from the Warsaw Ghetto to Treblinka, where in total 750,000 Jews were killed.

GAS CHAMBERS

As early as 1933 the Nazis had used carbon monoxide to achieve the 'euthanasia' of physically or mentally handicapped people. But this method was inefficient – hence gas chambers using faster-acting Zyklon B were invented.

Left Jewish women and children marked with the yellow star are forced on to cattle truck trains to the death camps.

The selection process, as to who would die immediately or be forced to work, took the form of a pseudo-medical inspection. Jews selected for death were sent to take 'showers' in rooms that were actually gas chambers, and died within 25 minutes. The Nazis tattooed prisoners with a number on their arm; no one was addressed by name; and badges distinguished groups – yellow star for Jews, pink triangle for homosexuals.

AUSCHWITZ

Based on an old Polish military barracks near the town of Ozwickiem, Auschwitz mutated in 1942 into the largest death camp of all. It became a fully fledged city with street lighting, railway tracks and electrical and plumbing systems. An additional site was added, called Birkenau, plus a factory at Mona. Thirty freight cars of Jews arrived every day.

After victims died, a unit called the Sonderkommando purloined gold teeth, shoes, bones, even human fat which was sent to soap factories, and hair, for stuffing pillows.

Below Prelude to the Holocaust: German soldiers face a synagogue set ablaze by locals after the Nazis occupied Lithuania, 1941.

THE STATISTICS
The following are estimates of the numbers of Jews killed in the Nazi Holocaust and the percentages of each country's pre-war Jewish population who died.

Country	Number	%
Poland	3,000,000	90%
Soviet Union	1,250,000	44%
Hungary	450,000	70%
Romania	300,000	50%
Germany/Austria	210,000	90%
Netherlands	105,000	75%
France	90,000	26%
Czechoslovakia	80,000	89%
Greece	54,000	77%
Belgium	40,000	60%
Yugoslavia	26,000	60%
Bulgaria	14,000	22%
Italy	8,000	20%

All suffered collective punishment if anyone escaped, and many froze to death standing in punishment grounds. Attached to Auschwitz was a unit that experimented on live human beings. Allied airplanes overflew Auschwitz, but were ordered to bomb more militarily valuable targets. Overall, some 1.5 million Jews perished at Auschwitz.

HUNGARY AND GREECE

In April 1944 the Holocaust reached Hungary, on the back of the Nazi invasion. Until then, Hungarian Jews bore burdens but their lives were safe. Immediately Adolf Eichmann, one of the major organizers of the Holocaust, began sending Jews to Auschwitz; 380,000 arrived over six weeks and 300,000 died. Even when the Soviet Army stood at the gates of Budapest, the Germans managed to arrest 40,000 Jews and sent them on a death-march to Auschwitz.

THE FEW WHO HELPED

Certain German-occupied nations distinguished themselves by resisting, such as Finland; Denmark, which

Above Raoul Wallenberg, the Swedish diplomat who risked his life to save thousands of Jews in Hungary.

smuggled most of her Jews to neutral Sweden; Italy, which flouted German deportation edicts; and above all Bulgaria, where resolute government action saved 50,000 Jews. It is also said that King Mohammed of Morocco personally refused to hand over Jews to the Vichy overlords.

A few brave individuals helped Jews at great personal cost. In late 1942 Jules Géraud Saliège, Archbishop of Toulouse, publicly protested against Vichy French deportations. 'All is not permissible against them. They belong to mankind. They are our brethren as are so many others. No Christian can forget that', he wrote.

Another saviour was Raoul Wallenberg, a Swedish diplomat in Hungary who saved perhaps 15,000 Jewish lives by issuing false papers. French Protestants and Catholics in Le-Chambon-sur-Lignon hid Jewish children during 1942–44. And Oskar Schindler, a Sudeten German industrialist, rescued almost 1,200 from certain death by getting them transferred from Auschwitz to work in his factories. Sadly, such cases were the exceptions; most people just averted their gaze.

The Aftermath of Genocide

Whether the Holocaust was the zenith of centuries of anti-Semitism, or a wartime aberration, when standing before the murder of six million Jews, perhaps the most fitting response is silence.

One by one, the death camps were liberated by Allied troops: Auschwitz by the Red Army on 27 January 1945, Buchenwald by the US Army on 11 April, and Bergen-Belsen by the British Army on 15 April.

NUREMBERG TRIALS

From November 1945 to October 1946, an International Military Tribunal put 24 pre-eminent Nazi leaders on trial within the US occupation zone. The location was Nuremberg, doubly fitting because it was the site of the Nazi mass rallies and the Nazis' first systematic racial legislation. Questions were raised about the complicity of ordinary Germans and whether personnel acted on orders from above or on their own initiative.

Below 'Never again' was the pledge made at the Nuremberg International Military Tribunal, where Nazi perpetrators of crimes against humanity were put in the dock, January 1946.

PSYCHOLOGICAL TRAUMA

Jews, too, faced troubling questions: notwithstanding a few uprisings, why had so many been led 'like lambs to the slaughter'? Thousands felt guilty for surviving when relatives had perished, or strove to hide the degradation from their children. Memories of impossible moral choices, like having to decide which child to surrender to the Gestapo, deepened their trauma.

Mostly, Jews felt cheated by Western civilization and the allure of its supposed 'enlightenment'. Survivors who returned to their countries were often shocked by their reception. When in July 1945 200 Jews arrived in Kielce in Poland, local anti-Semites launched a pogrom that killed 42 of them. This massacre convinced Jews that they had no future in Europe. Many tried to escape to America, while thousands joined the *Beriha*, or underground 'flight', of 1944–8 to southern Europe, *en route* to Palestine.

Above A memorial wall in Krakow, constructed of Jewish gravestones that had been destroyed by the Nazis.

An estimated 50,000 reached Palestine during these years, despite a British bar on entrance.

DISPLACED PERSONS CAMPS

Among the eight million people displaced by World War II were some 50,000–100,000 Jewish camp survivors. Another 150,000 Jews soon joined them after fleeing anti-Semitism in Romania, Poland, Russia and Hungary. From October 1945 the newly established United Nations set up a relief administration to run displaced persons (DP) camps in Germany. Meanwhile, the group *Sh'erit Ha-Pletah*, or 'surviving remnant', met in congress at Munich in 1946 and elected representatives for Jews who had nowhere to live

BEHIND THE IRON CURTAIN

The Kremlin ignored the anti-Jewish nature of Nazi actions. If anything, Russian anti-Semitism increased after the war. In August 1952, 13 leading Yiddish poets were executed. Jews were called 'rootless cosmopolitans' and 'American agents' in the official press. Soon hundreds of Russian Jews lost their jobs or were arrested, the zenith being the supposed 'Doctors' Plot' against Stalin. During the Cold

Above Jewish women and children at Belsen concentration camp, Saxony, where British troops found 60,000 barely alive survivors.

War, Soviet authorities banished Jewish activists to the Gulag, and effectively barred ordinary Jews from various professions and universities.

Europe's post-war division into an American-sponsored western bloc and a Russian-backed eastern bloc also had adverse ramifications for Jews. Jews in eastern Europe found themselves subject to the same strictures as those in the USSR. They could not leave since Communist governments barred emigration. Worse, Jews were purged from Communist parties throughout the region, culminating in the arrest and execution of Czech party secretary Rudolf Slansky and 11 other leading Jews in November 1952.

PERPETRATORS, VICTIMS AND BYSTANDERS

During genocide, argued the historian Raul Hilberg, everyone is a perpetrator, victim or bystander. To blame German culture uniquely ignores non-German bystanders. A survey of 1941 shows that even before the Holocaust got under way, various peoples were persecuting Jewish citizens. French police arrested 4,000 Parisian Jews and interned them in urban Drancy, near central Paris. Over three years, 65,000 were deported from there, of whom only 2,000 survived. Likewise, Lithuania's 'Order Police' began exterminating Jews as soon as the Soviets left; and in September 1941 Ukrainian collaborators helped Nazi *Einsatzgruppen*, or deployment groups, shoot 33,771 Jews and dump their corpses at Babi Yar, a ravine near Kiev, in the largest single massacre of the Holocaust.

MEMORIALS

As early as 1945, Zionists met in London to plan a project to commemorate the Shoah (Holocaust in Hebrew). The result was the complex known as Yad Vashem (hand of God), which was built over 200 acres in Jerusalem. An avenue recalls the 'Righteous' gentiles who risked their lives to save Jews from death.

People also recall the Holocaust's acts of quiet courage, such as when prisoners held secret religious services, even when many asked, 'Where was God in Auschwitz?'

Israel has long held an annual Holocaust Day; now the UN and other nations do the same. In America, several museums mark the genocide. Berlin's Jewish Museum, opened in 2001, features a poignantly empty Holocaust Tower. Berlin also inaugurated a sculptural Memorial to the Murdered Jews of Europe in 2005.

BIRTH OF ISRAEL

The United Nations was founded in 1945 to banish genocide and replace war with dialogue. No doubt these factors hastened the decision to set up the State of Israel in the former British Mandate of Palestine in 1948. To many Jews, the fact that only three years elapsed between the Holocaust's end and the birth of the first Jewish state in 1,900 years was a miracle. But even this triumph cannot lessen the worst disaster to befall Jews in their history.

Below Displaced persons encampment, Bamberg, where thousands of survivors spent the immediate post-war years.

Cultural Responses to the Holocaust

Initially stunned by the enormity of the Holocaust, artists gradually began to create works of dignity against evil, and lasting memorials to Europe's obliterated communities.

In 1945 a philosopher of German Jewish origin, Theodor Adorno, responded to the Holocaust with the line: 'To write poetry after Auschwitz is barbaric'. Many shared his views: what use was Western culture, which German Jews had eagerly embraced, when the cattle-wagons started rolling? Adorno soon admitted he might have been mistaken. After the war, cultural expression served as witness to arguably the greatest humanitarian crime in history. In the longer term it helped Jews come to terms with loss and begin their recovery.

POETRY OF ANNIHILATION

In June 1941, Nazis overran Vilna, shot 10,000 Jews and corralled another 20,000 into two ghettos. Witnessing the liquidation of the smaller ghetto on Yom Kippur, the Yiddish poet Avrom Sutzkever wrote from his hiding place: 'I lie in this coffin the way I would lie in a suit made of wood, a bark tossed on treacherous waves, a cradle, an ark.' Sutzkever transplanted the image of baby Moses into this nightmarish world.

CULTURAL RESISTANCE, WORDS OF TESTIMONY

Sutzkever smuggled guns into the ghetto and conducted play readings and arts events throughout this grim era. Likewise, Mordechai Strigler, future editor of the New York Yiddish daily *Forverts*, or 'Forward', taught Jewish children in Maidanek and Buchenwald and organized literary evenings during which prisoners 'whispered poems and bits of history in order to keep their minds from dying.'

IMMORTAL WORKS

Even more than poetry, prose has been the prime vehicle of commemorating the Holocaust. The three outstanding authors are Primo Levi, Eli Wiesel and Anne Frank. All three personally experienced the trauma of the time. Anne Frank was sent to Auschwitz and then died in Bergen-Belsen after being captured from her hiding place in Amsterdam while still a young girl. Her poignant *Diary* survived and has entranced generations in many languages ever since. Eli Wiesel, born in Sighet, Romania, won a Nobel Peace Prize in part for his classic Holocaust memoirs, *Night*, first published in Yiddish in Buenos Aires.

Left Letter by Anne Frank, dated October 1942, when she was 13. She hid in Amsterdam before being sent to Auschwitz. Her diary is still widely read.

Above Nobel Peace Prize laureate and Holocaust survivor Eli Wiesel at Auschwitz, 60 years after liberation.

Levi, scion of an old Piedmontese Jewish family, was a chemist who survived Auschwitz and wrote several engrossing works in Italian, starting with *If This is a Man*. Later titles, all translated, include *Periodic Table* and essays *The Drowned and the Saved*. Throughout his work, he expresses the indomitable human spirit and the lunacy of war.

MUSIC

Since the 1990s concerts have featured recently recovered musical works by Jews murdered in the camps, thus recalling their creativity and defying their exterminators. The Soviet composer Dmitri Shostakovich set his Symphony no. 13 to Yevgeny Yevtushenko's fierce poem *Babi Yar*, commemorating that 1941 massacre. Neither man was Jewish, yet both were criticizing alleged Soviet denial of Jewish suffering in the crime. And in 2007 the Israeli Lior Navok composed the powerful *And the Trains Kept Coming*, an oratorio based on real documents of the Holocaust period.

CINEMA

American and British films just after the war alluded to Hitlerite anti-Semitism, yet few broached the actual calamity of the Holocaust. Exceptions were *The Stranger* (1946) directed by Orson Welles, which featured footage of the camps; and *Ostatni Etap*, or 'Last Stop', directed in 1948 by Wanda Jakubowska. Herself a Polish-Jewish former Auschwitz inmate, she said she only survived because she felt compelled to document what happened there. One of the most powerful Western documentaries was *Night and Fog* (1955) directed by Frenchman Alain Resnais.

Hollywood films tended to focus on particular cases and were arguably all the more powerful for doing so. One example was *The Pawnbroker* (1964), directed by Sidney Lumet, about a traumatised Jewish survivor who suffers flashbacks about his murdered family while running a shop in Harlem. Another was *Sophie's Choice* (1982), based on William Styron's 1979 novel and directed by a Jewish New Yorker, Alan Pakula; the film featured the agonizing dilemma of a mother made to choose which of two children to surrender to the gas chambers.

FILMS AFTER SHOAH

In 1985 *Shoah*, French-Jewish director Claude Lanzmann's compelling 9.5-hour-long documentary, set a benchmark for viewing the Holocaust in a literal and non-declamatory way. Two years later the celebrated veteran French director Louis Malle brought out *Au Revoir, les Enfants*, or 'Farewell, Children', reprising memories from Malle's own childhood when Jewish pupils were smuggled into his Catholic school, until they and their priest teacher were captured and sent to their death in the camps.

Perhaps most famous of all was Steven Spielberg's 1993 film *Schindler's List*, adapted from Thomas Keneally's 1985 Booker Prize-

Right *A still from* The Boy in the Striped Pyjamas, *a 2008 film directed by Jack Scanlon.*

Right *Deported to Auschwitz in 1944, Primo Levi survived the camps and wrote outstanding much-loved books about the Holocaust.*

winning novel, *Schindler's Ark*. Another notable film in 1997 was Roberto Benigni's *Life is Beautiful*, which was awarded three Academy Awards and was one of the highest-grossing non-English language films. In 2003 Roman Polanski, himself a former child camp survivor, produced the acclaimed and unusually restrained Holocaust-based film, *The Pianist*. Other notable films that explored the subject of the Holocaust are *Fateless* (*Sorstalanság* in Hungarian) in 2005 and *The Boy in the Striped Pyjamas* in 2008.

ACADEMIC WORKS

From the 1960s, academic Holocaust literature has multiplied, as new data emerged and the number of firsthand witnesses dwindled. Possibly the most definitive work remains Raul Hilberg's monumental 1961 tome, *The Destruction of European Jewry*.

Inevitably the subject tends to controversy: the French pseudo-historian Roger Garaudy has denied the Holocaust happened, while the English David Irving minimized its extent and downplayed Hitler's role. Today, Holocaust denial is a crime in Austria, Germany and France.

RESPONSES IN ISRAEL

For many Jews the most powerful cultural response to the Holocaust was a strong and confident State of Israel. That said, there was a certain ambivalence in early years: as the author Moshe Shamir suggested, 1950s Israelis were taught that European Jewish culture destroyed by the Nazis deserved its fate.

The trial of Adolf Eichmann in 1962 for crimes against humanity and war crimes, allowed survivors to give voice to a formerly taboo subject. On Yom Ha-Shoah (Holocaust Day) the siren sounds for a full minute, and Israelis of diverse backgrounds express a shared memory, standing still in their usually busy streets, homes and workplaces.

CHAPTER 10

ZIONISM, JERUSALEM AND ISRAEL

Political Zionism was one of several ideologies that gained credence among Jews in the late 19th and early 20th centuries. Nor was it initially the most popular. In 1948, however, just three years after the Holocaust wiped out a third of all Jews, the United Nations acceded to Zionist pressure and promulgated Israel as the first Jewish state in 1,900 years. Since then, Israel has outgrown its austere beginnings, revived Hebrew as a living language, and fulfilled the Biblical prophecy of 'gathering in the exiles', including most Jews from Europe and the Middle East. Triumph came at a cost, however. Israel has endured numerous wars and is blamed for dispossessing Palestine's indigenous Arabs. In addition, its acquisition of territories after 1967 encouraged settlers whose messianic fervour has stoked controversy. None the less Israel is today culturally vibrant and economically powerful. Demographically it has probably overtaken the United States as the major centre of modern Jewry.

Opposite Israeli flags flutter at a religious ceremony held at the Western Wall, Old City of Jerusalem. The men wear tallit and tefillin according to ancient Jewish custom.

Above *David Ben-Gurion, the first Prime Minister of modern Israel. He became premier two days after Israeli independence in May 1948.*

Zionism – The Nationalist Divide

TURKISH MILITARY DEFEAT AND BRITAIN'S BALFOUR DECLARATION ENCOURAGED ZIONISTS TO REVIVE THEIR FADING MOVEMENT. DESPITE RESISTANCE, THEY PRESSED FOR A NATIONAL HOME IN PALESTINE.

Two events in 1917 rescued Zionist fortunes: the Balfour Declaration of 2 November, which expressed British governmental support for establishing a 'national home' for Jews in Palestine, and General Allenby's British military conquest of Jerusalem on 11 December. The prime mover behind the Balfour Declaration was Chaim Weizmann. As head of a Zionist delegation to the Versailles peace talks of 1919, he proclaimed that peaceful Jewish autonomy alongside Arabs in Palestine was both possible and necessary. In April 1920 the San Remo conference awarded Britain with mandates to govern Mesopotamia (Iraq) and Palestine, with the Balfour Declaration incorporated into the latter's charter.

Below *A Labour Zionist poster for May Day, 1945, proclaims in Hebrew: 'Workers of all peoples, unite!'*

Not all Jews were convinced that Zionism answered their most perplexing questions. Was Jewish nationalism really the best option? If so, was Palestine the place to locate it? And if Zionism was the way, which type should prevail out of the many contending strands?

ORTHODOX VERSUS SECULAR VIEWS

Until 1789 Jewish political and religious identity had essentially been one; after the French Revolution, Jews gained civil rights and members of the Haskalah (Jewish Enlightenment), began to redefine themselves in social and national as well as religious terms. Secular Zionism grew out of such views, yet drew heavily on imagery from the Torah, Talmud and daily prayer liturgy – nostalgia for the days of Jewish kings, rediscovering ancient Jewry's agrarian past and the mystical concept of redemption and negating the disharmony of exile.

Most Orthodox Jews prayed daily for a return to Zion, which they believed lay in the Creator's hands alone. They saw political Zionism as blasphemous because it was driven by humans, not by God's hand. They felt that the resultant community would be secular, not religious, so not a truly 'Jewish state'.

RELIGIOUS DISSENTERS

Denial of Zionism on religious grounds inspired the first truly global Orthodox political group, World Agudat Yisrael (Jewish Union), founded in Kattowicz, southern Poland, in 1912. A smaller contin-

Above *Theodor Herzl with Zionist delegation on board* Imperator, *on the way to Palestine, October 1898.*

gent of religious Zionists had already since 1902 organized themselves as Mizrachi – an acronym standing for 'religious centre'. They argued that faith without national spirit was only 'half Judaism'. Mizrachi affiliated with other Zionists, relocated to Palestine in 1920 and set up a youth wing, Bnei Akiva, nine years later.

At the opposite end of the religious spectrum, Reform Jews opposed Zionism for different reasons. They saw Judaism as a system of ethical principles and nothing more; nationality ought to depend on where one lived, not ethnic ties. Nazi oppression made many German Reform Jews reappraise that position.

BRITAIN'S VIEW

There are many theories as to why Britain backed Zionism, such as its desire to guard Middle East routes to India, or to ward off German or French aspirations. The Anglo-Jewish establishment was itself split down the middle on the Zionist issue. The leading Liberal politician Edwin Samuel Montagu considered Zionism a 'mischievous political creed'. The deliberate ambiguity of the Balfour Treaty's phrase 'national home' – not 'state' – is often attributed to Montagu's watering down of the more strongly phrased original promise.

REBELLION

Before Balfour, diplomatic disappointments had deepened rifts within the Zionist movement. Some accused Theodor Herzl (1860–1904), the founder of political Zionism, and his successors of defining Zionism too negatively, as a cure for the disease of anti-Semitism. Frustrated at lack of progress over Palestine, the British Zionist Israel Zangwill had split from the Zionist movement at the 7th Congress of 1905 to lead his breakaway Territorialist group, which sought alternative homelands in Africa, Asia and Australia, but the group withered away in 1925. There were also differences between activists in Palestine versus the bureaucrats in Berlin and London; and between political Zionists, who stressed settlement before all else.

SOCIALIST ZIONISTS

More successful was a socialist party called *Po'alei Zion*, or 'Workers of Zion', and the young Russian-born David Ben-Gurion became its chief activist. To his left were Zionists of a more fiercely Marxist hue, who saw their trend as part of a global class struggle. After 1909 some young socialists began setting up *kibbutzim*, or 'collective farming colonies', and championed what they called 'Hebrew labour'. They co-operated with Arthur Ruppin, who in 1908 had founded the Zionist Organization's Palestine Bureau.

ARAB RESISTANCE

A few Palestinian Arabs welcomed the economic boost brought by Jewish immigration, but when the influx grew their suspicions increased. Arabs disliked the alien nature of Zionist socialism and felt that the 'Hebrew labour' policy discriminated against them in the workplace. Palestinian Arab newspapers such as *Karmil* (founded in 1908) ran campaigns against selling land to Zionists, and *Filastin* (1912) decried increased Jewish immigration. Above all, Arabs feared that Europeans might usurp or outnumber them.

Between 1873 and 1914 the Ottomans replaced the old administrative unit, *Jund Filastin*, or 'Palestine Province', with three separate *vilayets*, or 'governorates'. Most Palestinian Arabs, however, referred to themselves as part of Greater Syria. In

Above David Ben-Gurion signing the State of Israel document, 14 May 1948, marking the end of the British Mandate.

January 1919 their delegates attended a General Syrian Congress in Damascus that rejected Zionism, as well as a French mandate over Syria. They wanted to see Palestine incorporated within a united independent Syria and join the Arab delegation at the Paris Peace Talks.

Also in January, Chaim Weizmann met Emir Faisal, Sharif of Mecca and putative Arab leader. The two signed agreement for mutual cooperation, but this proved void when Britain and France, in Faisal's view, reneged on promises to grant him a kingdom.

A US commission of inquiry led by Henry King and Charles Crane in 1919 interviewed Jews and Arabs and provided a report that opposed major Jewish immigration. It also advised against a Jewish national home in Palestine, which could lead to 'dispossession of non-Jewish inhabitants'. Their views notwithstanding, the perils of anti-Semitism in 1920s Europe and especially the rise of Nazism in the 1930s continued to drive thousands of Jews to Palestine.

Left Some 450 Jewish refugees arrive at Haifa, 1946, onboard the Haviva Reil. *The slogan reads:* 'Keep the gates open, we are not the last.'

Early Days in Palestine

SINCE 1922 AND AFTER SEVERAL WAVES OF JEWISH IMMIGRATION, PALESTINE'S BRITISH GOVERNORS FOUND THEMSELVES CAUGHT BETWEEN TWO ACRIMONIOUS COMMUNITIES, JEWS AND ARABS.

Zionism was always more than an immigration movement or political trend. Its more radical ideologies aimed to transform Jewry. To 'normalize', individual Jews should re-engage in simple handicrafts and farming and leave the world of the cerebral and mercantile. The most extreme Zionists wished to negate the Diaspora experience altogether.

THE ALIYOT

Zionism was from the start a collective enterprise, and as such it spawned distinct waves of immigration (*aliyah* in singular, *aliyot* in plural), each with its own unique characteristics. The First Aliyah (1882–1903) consisted of 25,000 mainly Russian Jews who were set on becoming farmers. They founded the first 28 *moshavot*, or privately owned rural settlements.

The Second Aliyah of the years 1904–14 was better organized and clearer in ideological intent. Its *halutzim*, or 'pioneers', established the collectivist kibbutz, set up Hebrew printing presses and the first Hebrew high school in 1906, formed the Hashomer guards, and in 1909 created the first all-Jewish city, Tel Aviv, as an offshoot of ancient Jaffa.

POST-WAR DEVELOPMENTS

After the interregnum of World War I, revolution in Russia and pogroms in Hungary and Poland, a Third Aliyah of over 40,000 began in 1919, boosting Palestine's Jewish population to 90,000 by 1923. They established a defence group, the Haganah, in June 1920. Five months later they founded the Histadrut, an organization that quickly assumed a pivotal economic role as monopolist employers, trade union congress and even a health and welfare system.

With the Bolsheviks restricting Russian emigration after 1923, and America tightening up immigration after 1924, a Fourth Aliyah (1924–8) brought in a quite different sort of immigrant. Half of these 67,000 newcomers were middle-class Poles, including artisans and shopkeepers; they were less ideologically com-

Above Founders Square in Tel Aviv commemorates the 69 people who founded the city in 1909.

mitted than predecessors, and many found life in the Levant trying. By 1927 twice as many Jews left Palestine as arrived. Yet this fourth wave did create industries that stood Palestine in good stead later on.

PALESTINE MANDATE 1922

In 1921 Britain had excluded from the proposed Palestine mandate all the territory east of the Jordan River; Transjordan henceforth became a separate area. What remained was a land of some 10,000 square miles, about the size of the US state of Maryland. Its population was divided in 1922 between 84,000 Jews, settled mainly along the coastal plain, and Arabs, 71,000 of whom were Christian and 589,000 Muslim, generally in the hinterland. Cities such as Jaffa, Haifa and Jerusalem had mixed populations; otherwise Jews and Arabs tended to live separately.

In 1923, the Jewish Agency took over from the Zionist Commission as the putative government of Jews in Palestine. Chaim Weizmann held the central ground as president of the World Zionist Organization (1920–31 and 1931–46). The rising

Left President Dr Chaim Weizmann addressing the Knesset (Israeli parliament) flanked by David Ben-Gurion (right) and Moshe Sharett (left) the first two prime ministers of Israel, 1949.

Above The first kibbutz was Degania Alef, by the Sea of Galilee, built by Romanian Jews in 1909.

power in the new Yishuv (Jewish residents in Palestine) were the Labour Zionists. David Ben-Gurion led the largest Labour faction called *Mapai* after 1930. Under their guidance the essential features of the 'state to come' took form: kibbutzim, Histadrut, or General Federation of Labour, Jewish National Fund, the Hebrew University (founded in Jerusalem in 1925) and the adoption of the Hebrew language.

1925 also saw a long-simmering dispute come to the boil with the emergence of Vladimir Jabotinsky's Revisionist trend. Revisionists insisted that only an 'iron wall' military policy would convince Arabs that Jews were implacable in their intentions.

ARAB REVOLTS

All British attempts to create a joint Arab and Jewish executive failed. Arabs mistrusted Jewish intentions and saw them as colonial usurpers. Anti-Zionist Arab riots broke out in Jerusalem in 1920 and Jaffa in 1921.

Worse violence followed in 1929 in Jerusalem, Safed and Hebron, where some 67 unarmed religious Jews perished. The 1929 riots transformed the Haganah's status: it grew to encompass nearly all Jewish adults and youths, and its cadres began training programmes, set up arms depots and even made their own weapons.

Most tumultuous of all was the 1936–9 Arab Revolt. It caused 5,000 Arab and a few hundred Jewish deaths, and pitted forces loyal to the Mufti, Hajj Amin al-Husseini, appointed 1921, against the British and rival clans. Jews took advantage of Arab–British clashes to build 50 new 'stockade and watchtower' settlements. In 1931 Revisionists created a militant offshoot of Haganah, called Irgun, which after 1936 stepped up 'retaliatory actions' against Arabs and attacked Mandate forces after 1939.

BRITAIN'S CALCULATIONS

Determined to appease Arabs, the October 1930 British Passfield White Paper recommended limiting Jewish immigration. With violence in Palestine still raging, in 1937–8 the Peel and Woodhead commissions recommended splitting the territory into a small Jewish state and a large Arab one. Finally, a White Paper of 17 May 1939 dropped the partition idea and restricted Jewish rights to purchase land.

Most galling from a Jewish perspective was the paper's decision to limit Jewish immigrants to 75,000 in total. During 1933–9, Nazi persecution in Germany and beyond threatened the lives of all European Jews. With gates shut in Britain and America, Palestine had seemed like the only feasible refuge.

DEMOGRAPHICS IN PALESTINE

Year	Jews	Arabs
1800	6,700	268,000
1880	24,000	525,000
1915	87,500	590,000
1931	174,000	837,000
1947	630,000	1,310,000

In 1933 Zionists created Youth Aliyah to help young threatened Jews. In 1934 the Haganah and the He-Halutz movement began chartering ships to bring refugees over illegally; after 1938 the British Navy began firing on illicit vessels. The number of Jews in Palestine rose during 1936-9 from 250,000 to 475,000 as a consequence of Fifth Aliyah immigrants from eastern Europe and Germany. Most new *olim* were neither Zionist nor Socialist. In time, their entrepreneurial spirit and cultural sophistication would add distinctive elements to the Zionists' 'state to come'. The advent of World War II put the Palestinian question on hold, yet, with hindsight, only postponed an inevitable clash between growing numbers of Jews and Palestine's Arab majority, each of whom dreamt of their own independent state.

Below The establishment of Tel Aviv, 1909, on sand dunes north of Jaffa.

Jews in a Changing Middle East

THE MIDDLE EAST, CRADLE OF CIVILIZATION, IS ALSO THE BIRTHPLACE OF JEWS. ABRAHAM GREW UP IN TODAY'S IRAQ; JACOB'S DESCENDANTS SPENT 400 YEARS IN EGYPT; AND PALESTINE, NOW ISRAEL, LIES AT THE REGION'S FULCRUM.

Some half a million Jews lived in the Arab Middle East (Mashriq) and North Africa (Maghreb) by 1900. Though they represented a generally poorer minority of global Jewry, improved education hinted at a better future. However, within 70 years they had fallen to a few thousand.

ARAB NATIONALISM

Why did a century that began so promisingly end in the depletion of entire communities? Four political developments may explain this phenomenon: the liberation of Arab countries from Ottoman rule after 1918; European interference and mandates; the gradual winning of Arab independence; and, above all, the creation of the State of Israel.

In the late 19th century, some 'emancipated' Mizrahim, often known as 'Arab Jews', adopted leftist stances. Other Mizrahim identified with the mandate powers of the day (especially France in North Africa), but they paid for this as Arab nationalism grew. With the exception of Yemenite Jews, most chose not to go to Palestine until after 1948.

From the early 1920s Arab nationalism regarded Zionism as a threat. Such feelings often fed anti-Jewish sentiment. By making life hard for their Jews, Arab rulers contributed to their migration to Palestine and later Israel. Thus, paradoxically, they reinforced the population of the very state they wished to demolish.

In March 1945 the newly established Arab League pledged to fight Jewish statehood in Palestine and to defend Palestine's Arabs. In November 1947 the UN General Assembly voted for partition. After the 1948 war, fury at the fate of Palestinian Arab refugees often found expression in anger at local Jews. Each successive war – in 1956, 1967 and 1973 – saw an upsurge in anti-Zionism, causing yet further Jewish emigration to Israel from Arab League states.

Above Intricate wooden latticework and high ceilings distinguish the houses of the Bataween district of central Baghdad, once home to Iraqi Jews.

MOROCCO'S HISTORY

More than 265,000 Jews lived in Arab-ruled Morocco by the mid-20th century. Jewish success, however, stoked instances of local envy and occasional wildfire pogroms. In 1438 Jews were confined to a *mellah*, or 'special quarter', in Fez, a pattern repeated elsewhere in the realm. Even before 1492, Sephardim and Maranos had begun arriving from Spain and Portugal, and settled in Tangier, Rabat, Meknes, Safi, Mogador, Marrakech and Mazagan. Sephardim influenced Moroccan musical forms, architectural latticework, and cuisine, including *pastilla*, a pigeon pie that is one of the Moroccan–Jewish signature dishes.

European trading influence grew in the 18th century, and France ruled Morocco as a protectorate after 1912. During World War II Sultan Mohammed V defied the Vichy regime's Nazi-inspired racist laws against Jews and pointedly invited all of Morocco's rabbis to his 1941 coronation.

The first Arab–Israeli war stoked anti-Jewish sentiment with dozens killed in Oujda and Djerada in June

Below Signing of the Arab League charter, 1945, which pledged to defend Arabs of Palestine against Zionists.

1948. Many Jews left for Israel and France in a trend that accelerated after Morocco won independence in 1956. Another 80,000 Jews departed over three years after bars on emigration were lifted in 1961, leaving behind 35,000 Jews by 1971 and less than 17,000 today.

IRAQ – ANCIENT COMMUNITY DEPLETED

Jews of Iraq claimed to be the world's oldest continually existing Jewish community and until 1040 their exilarch (grand communal leader) was respected as head of all Eastern Jewry. The opening of the Suez Canal in 1869 and education at Alliance schools spawned a generation of Jewish lawyers, doctors, entrepreneurs and administrators. In 1922 Great Britain created modern Iraq out of three former Ottoman provinces, the mainly Kurdish Mosul, Sunni Baghdad and Shia Basra. Most of Iraq's estimated 150,000 Jews now lived in Baghdad and called themselves *Yahud ibn Arab*, loosely, 'Jewish Arabs'.

After British troops quelled a revolt by Nazi-backed army officers, Iraq's only pogrom erupted in June 1941 and 180 Jews were killed. This two-day *farhud* shocked the community and made many consider leaving for Palestine. After 1948, Iraq banned emigration, as did most other Arab League members. Despite growing popular prejudice, Baghdad's rulers still valued Jewish economic contributions. But in March 1950 they agreed that Jews could leave if they surrendered their citizenship and sold their property. They were surprised when 85,000 registered to depart. Iraqi and Israeli authorities co-ordinated Operation Ezra and Nehemiah, a massive airlift that carried 120,000 to Israel over 18 months in 1951–2.

Above The Mellah of Fez, Morocco, established as a Jewish quarter in 1438.

SCANT HOPE OF RETURN

Since the ousting of the Baathist regime in Iraq in 2003, most of the remaining Jews in Iraq emigrated, including in 2006 the last rabbi, Emad Levy. Jewish exiles have voted in Iraqi elections from their new places of residence, in Britain, America and even Israel. There was talk of allowing tourists to visit the burial places of the Jewish prophets along the Tigris and Euphrates rivers. However, the post-2003 conflicts have spoiled these plans. Iraqi authorities have also rejected calls by the World Organization of Jews from Arab Countries for compensation of properties lost. Virtually no former Iraqi Jews have chosen to return, and the same applies in most Arab countries, including Egypt and Tunisia.

Few Jews have gone back to live in Morocco – though many visit even on Israeli passports. Today, Mizrachi culture persists in Israel, often in hybrid or modern guise. Mizrahim and Sephardis make up an estimated half of Israel's Jewish population.

JEWS AND ARABS IN BAGHDAD

Jews had lived in Baghdad ever since it was founded as the capital of the Arab Muslim Abbasid dynasty in 762. The yeshivas of Sura and Pumbedita relocated to the city where Jews worked as goldsmiths and shopkeepers. They experienced intellectual creativity and peace with their Arab neighbours.

Baghdad later became the arena of a struggle between Sunni Ottomans and Shia Persians. Local Jews helped the Ottomans oust the Persians on 31 December 1534. The Turks ruled until 1623 and again from 1638 to 1917.

Above The Caliph of Baghdad receiving Jewish leaders, 937CE.

Conditions had declined by the early 19th century, but one English traveller praised Baghdad's rabbis and Jewish philanthropists for creating a virtual Jewish welfare state within a state, thus ensuring no one went poor.

Baghdad's Jews grew in number from 20,000 in 1860 to 50,000 around 1900. They set up printing presses, ran newspapers, hospitals and schools and became prominent musicians on Iraqi radio. As late as 1947, 10 of the 17-strong Baghdad Chamber of Commerce were Jews. Jews also ran 28 educational institutions, 60 synagogues and two hospitals offering free treatment to the poor. However, at times of trouble prominent families left, often for India. After the anti-British revolt of 1941 and the creation of Israel, anti-Zionist feelings were often conflated into anti-Semitism. The final demise of the Baghdadi Jewish community came with the public hanging of 11 Jews as alleged Israeli spies in 1969.

Palestine During World War II

ZIONISTS WERE PULLED IN DIFFERENT DIRECTIONS DURING THE WAR. MANY FOUGHT WITH BRITISH UNITS, OTHERS TERRORIZED BRITISH TARGETS IN, OR SMUGGLED REFUGEES INTO, PALESTINE.

In early 1939, with world war looming, Britain hosted a last ditch attempt to solve the Palestine problem. London hoped to reconcile the competing demands of the Jews who had been promised a homeland in the Balfour Declaration and the Palestinian Arabs who were resident in the region.

Concerned that Arab nations might side with Germany and Italy, on 17 March, London released the McDonald White Paper, which dropped the Peel partition plan of 1938 and vowed to establish an independent and unitary Palestine by 1948. The paper also restricted Jewish immigration to 75,000 over the five-year period, 1940–44. Palestine's Jews did not welcome a unitary state where Arabs would outnumber them by 1.2 million to 550,000. However, Jews feared Germany more than they resented Britain for breaking past promises.

PALESTINE'S JEWS IN WORLD WAR II

In late 1940, 26,000 Jews and 6,000 Arabs joined a British infantry division in Palestine nicknamed the 'Buffs' (the East Kent Regiment). Britain also helped create the Palmach in May 1941, a strike force of the Zionist militia, Haganah, to counter Nazi threats to Syria and Lebanon. Even the militant Irgun, the Revisionist Zionist underground, ceased sniping at Mandate forces and supported Britain's war effort.

BEHIND ENEMY LINES

Palestinian volunteers showed remarkable courage in Europe, despite criticism that they should have acted sooner. In 1943 the Budapest-born Hannah Szenes, a poet and playwright, was one of 33 who parachuted behind enemy lines in Slovakia and the Balkans, teamed up with anti-Nazi resistance fighters and sought out beleaguered Jewish communities. In June 1944 she crossed into her native Hungary, but was captured, tried and executed in November. In September 1944 the British formed the 5,000-strong Jewish Brigade, which fought in Italy and helped Jews in German Displaced Persons (DP) Camps after the war. Their military skills were passed on to Haganah, or the Socialist Zionist underground militia.

Above Three young Jewish survivors of Buchenwald concentration camp, en route to Palestine.

SMUGGLING IN 'ILLEGALS'

Haganah cadres now started smuggling in *ma'apalim* ('illegal Jewish refugees') from war-torn Europe. Over 100,000 tried to enter Palestine on 120 boats in an oper-ation dubbed 'Aliyah B', and 70,000 succeeded. There were setbacks too: the British blockaded the coast and interned 50,000 would-be immigrants in Cyprus, Mauritius and Atlit prison, Palestine.

In November 1940 Haganah seized an illegal vessel, the *Patria*, with 1,800 refugees on board. When the British threatened to divert the refugees to Mauritius, Haganah saboteurs bungled an attempt to disable the ship and it sank off Haifa, killing 267. Survivors stayed in Palestine as 'an act of grace'.

OPTING FOR STATEHOOD

As the attempted annihilation of Europe's Jews entered its final stage, Zionist and non-Zionist Jewish groups agreed on a common strategy. At an emergency meeting in New York's Biltmore Hotel in May 1942, delegates declared the goal of a Jewish state, or 'commonwealth', in all of Palestine, which exceeded the terms of the Balfour Declaration.

Below Erwin Rommel, the 'Desert Fox' who dreamt of leading German forces through North Africa to Palestine.

Above Jewish pilot training school near Rome in November 1948, when the newly formed Israel Air Force was still in combat against Arab foes.

SEASON OF TERROR

In 1940 the Polish-born Revisionist Abraham Stern had formed Lehi, an underground unit also dubbed the Stern Gang. Lehi attacked British forces during the war, unlike fellow Revisionists in Irgun.

With war still raging in Europe, on 1 February 1944 Irgun declared its own 'revolt' against Britain. Its leader was Menachem Begin, who served in the Polish army in 1941. At first, Irgun sabotaged police stations and tax offices in Tel Aviv, Haifa and Jerusalem. Irgun and Lehi soon moved from sabotage to terror, and in August 1944 Lehi tried but failed to assassinate the British High Commissioner for Palestine, Harold McMichael. Two Lehi hit-men shot dead Lord Moyne, British Minister Resident in the Middle East, on 6 November 1944 in Cairo. This was a step too far for the Jewish Agency. They barred Lehi and Irgun members from jobs, and, in what was dubbed the Saison (season), Haganah and Palmach helped the British round up dissidents.

ANGLO-AMERICAN COMMISSION

The appalling images of Nazi death camps after World War II ended in May 1945 had radicalized Jewish feeling. Operation *Beriha* began siphoning 'illegals' from eastern Europe to Palestine via secret land routes. Lehi and Irgun blew up oil pipelines in Palestine, and after July the Haganah suspended the Saison and joined its former foes in a joint Resistance Movement that launched 19 attacks over ten months.

An Anglo-American committee of inquiry spent four months in 1945–6 interviewing Jews in Displaced Persons (DP) camps in Vienna and Arabs in Cairo. Their unanimous report of April 1946 proposed the immediate entry of 100,000 Jews into Palestine; an end to the land purchase restrictions of 1940; and the eventual establishment of a bi-national state under United Nations trusteeship. Britain's premier Clement Attlee said Jews could only enter Palestine when Zionist and Arab militias were disarmed. Even so, 1,500 Jews were let in each month after October 1946, half from detention camps on Cyprus, to the anxiety of Palestine's Arabs.

ANGER AT THE BRITISH

Fury over British policies prompted the worst act of Jewish terrorism, the Irgun's July 1946 bombing of Jerusalem's King David Hotel, site of the Palestine government secretariat and British military headquarters. In total, 91 people died. A curfew was imposed on the Jewish area of Haifa.

One of Britain's last acts during its mandate over Palestine helped push the UN towards making Israel independent. When in July 1947 the chartered ship *Exodus* entered Palestinian waters with 4,500 Holocaust survivors from European Displaced Person (DP) camps on board, British naval vessels trailed and eventually boarded the ship. Encountering aggressive resistance to their taking over the vessel, British soldiers resorted to force. Three passengers were killed and 30 wounded. Would-be illegal immigrants were eventually sent back to DP camps in Germany, and the *Exodus* became a media *cause célèbre*, symbolizing Jewish desperation to reach Palestine.

Below King David Hotel bombing, 1946, when Jewish saboteurs destroyed the British Army HQ, killing 91.

The Revival of an Ancient Language

APART FROM THE CREATION OF THE STATE OF ISRAEL, SOME SAY THAT THE REVIVAL OF HEBREW IS THE GREATEST SINGLE ZIONISTS ACHIEVEMENT. IT IS NOW WIDELY SPOKEN, AND A FOUNT OF VIBRANT SECULAR LITERATURE.

The founder of modern Zionism, Theodor Herzl (1860–1904), envisaged a Palestine where Jews all spoke German. Opposed to Herzl, a growing movement preferred Hebrew as the Jewish people's lingua franca, and their view prevailed. There was a problem, however: few Jews spoke Hebrew as a living language.

BEN-YEHUDA AND HEBREW

The foremost champion of modern Israeli Hebrew was Eliezer Ben-Yehuda (1858–1922). He insisted on speaking only Hebrew to all Jews even before he arrived in Palestine in 1881. When his son Itamar was born the next year, he and his wife Deborah decided to raise him as the first all-Hebrew-speaking child in modern history. This caught on with other families in Jerusalem, and Ben-Yehuda then pioneered educational instruction in Hebrew with the head of Alliance Israelite schools in Jerusalem. From 1884, he edited a newspaper, *Ha-Tzvi*, and he and his family also compiled a dictionary. In 1890 he set up what later became the Hebrew Language Academy.

LINGUISTIC SOCIAL ENGINEERING

In 1905, Zionists founded a language committee to popularize Hebrew as the national tongue of Palestine's Jews. Those who spoke French, German, Arabic, Russian, Yiddish, Ladino and Hungarian were moulded into a single monolingual community. Hebrew became the cultural binding agent of the Zionist ideological project.

Hebrew none the less faced challenges: few were qualified to teach it at first, and Orthodox Jews felt awkward speaking *lashon kodesh* (holy language). Also, there was confusion over pronunciation. In the end, language officials favoured a broadly Sephardi (Spanish Jewish) and Mizrachi (Oriental) system, despite the Ashkenazi origin of most early Zionist settlers. In practice, Hebrew developed organically, with speakers borrowing from French, Aramaic, Arabic and English, and purists faced a struggle to keep Hebrew true to its Semitic roots.

LANDMARKS

During the Second Aliyah period, Hebrew was used in schools and adopted for public meetings, even by the World Zionist Organization in Europe. Haim Nahman Bialik (1873–1934) became the great Hebrew national poet of the era, and Yiddish writers such as Sholem Aleichem and Isaac Leib Peretz also wrote in the tongue. Hebrew's battle to become a language of 'higher culture' climaxed in 1913, when the Yishuv rejected a bid by a German-Jewish association to use only German at a proposed college of engineering. The resultant Haifa Technion chose Hebrew, as did the Hebrew University in Jerusalem, which opened in 1925. By then Hebrew had been recognized alongside Arabic and English as one of Palestine's three official languages.

Throughout the Mandate period and after Israeli independence, Zionists fought a campaign against Yiddish, the natural language of most Ashkenazi immigrants. Under the slogan *Ivri Daber Ivri*, or 'Jewish person, speak Hebrew', a League of Language Defenders disrupted meetings in Yiddish. Learning Hebrew rapidly became a crucial aspect of integration. This sparked tensions among Yiddish-speakers. Gradually, Hebrew displaced other Jewish tongues. The Yiddish–Hebrew battle became an existential and symbolic struggle between two 'authentically Jewish' languages.

Above An Orthodox Jew peruses a Hebrew newspaper in Jerusalem's Me'a She'arim neighbourhood.

Below New immigrants learning Hebrew at an ulpan *class, an indispensable part of the Israeli absorption process.*

Oriental Immigration to Israel

ORIENTAL, EASTERN OR MIZRAHI REFERS TO JEWS OF MIDDLE EASTERN AND NORTH AFRICAN ORIGIN. FROM THE START OF STATEHOOD IN 1948 UNTIL 1967, OVER HALF A MILLION JEWS LEFT ARAB LANDS.

Above Ofra Haza (1957–2000) was born to poor Yemenite parents, and won international fame. She was known as 'the Israeli Madonna'.

The first mass airlift into Israel involved 45,200 Yemenite Jews and was nicknamed Operation Magic Carpet. Jews flocked to the British- ruled port of Aden from remote northern Yemen and Hadramaut. While few had even seen cars before, they appeared unfazed by the British and US planes sent to collect them. They believed these were the divine 'wings of eagles' on which the Lord would gather up the scattered of Israel as predicted in the books of Exodus and Isaiah. The secret operation involved 380 flights between June 1949 and September 1950, and took place with the tacit approval of Yemen's new ruler, Imam Ahmad bin Yahya.

In Israel the newcomers met descendants of Yemenites who had arrived with the First and Second Aliyot (or waves of immigration), during 1882–1914.

Below A transit camp, where many Oriental Jewish immigrants spent their first years on Israel's land.

A DIFFERENT OUTLOOK

The conditions of departure varied considerably. In Iraq, Jews were initially forbidden to leave, while in Egypt they were expelled after 1956. Most Jews from Yemen and Iraq were airlifted out; those from Morocco took sea voyages. Jews of the Levant generally fell victim to the Israeli–Arab conflict, whether or not they were Zionist. Beirut was the only Arab capital city whose Jewish population increased after 1948.

For the most part, Jews of the Middle East were not very receptive to Zionism. It seemed bizarre that in Israel they were expected to relinquish their long-held religious values and customs.

THE SECOND ISRAEL?

At first, newcomers were housed in deserted Arab property. When numbers grew, *ma'aborot* (transit camps) were built, tent cities that later became permanent 'development towns', often in the remote Israeli south. Mizrachim arriving in Israel made little attempt to create their own political parties. They went along with existing structures. Some sensed official cultural prejudice and central government neglect. Riots in Wadi Nisnas, Haifa, in 1959 were a prelude to the formation of the radical leftist Sephardi youth group the Black Panthers in 1971. At that stage only 3 per cent of top posts were held by Sephardim, who represented nearly 60 per cent of Israeli Jews. The rightist opposition Likud party won power for the first time in Israel's 1977 elections, largely on the basis of a wave of Sephardi support. Mizrachim began to fill senior state positions.

In recent years, intermarriage has led to a blurring of the divisions between older inhabitants and the newcomers. Mizrahi musicians and artists are emerging in Israel, reflecting a newfound confidence in and recognition of their cultural heritage. Daoud and Salah were famous throughout the Middle East in the 1930s and 1940's, and Daoud's Israeli granddaughter Dudu Tassa is a contemporary success story, her music reviving his Arab melodies.

The War of Independence

THE UN'S DECISION TO GRANT SEPARATE STATES TO JEWS AND ARABS WAS WELCOMED BY MOST JEWS, BUT REJECTED BY ARABS WHO WANTED ONE STATE. WAR SAW ZIONISTS DEFEND THE FLEDGLING ISRAEL.

On 29 November 1947 a United Nations General Assembly (UNGA) voted by 33 to 13 to split Palestine into two states, one predominantly Jewish, the other Arab. The USA and Soviet Union voted for partition, while Britain abstained. Generally, Zionists accepted UNGA Resolution 181, while most Arabs, both in Palestine and the region, rejected it.

FIRST STAGE OF WAR

Within hours of the UN vote, fighting broke out between communities. By January, Arabs were blockading Jerusalem and an Arab Liberation Army entered Palestine. By March, 1,200 Jews had been killed. On 9 April Irgun and Lehi militants invaded Deir Yassin village near Jerusalem and killed at least 100 civilians. Four days later Arabs attacked a convoy of Jewish doctors and patients and killed 80. Arab flight from Haifa and Jaffa gathered pace, and in early May Safed and Jaffa fell to Zionist forces. Most of west Jerusalem was now in Jewish hands, while the Jewish settlement of Gush Etzion fell to Arabs.

INDEPENDENCE

On 12 April 1948 David Ben-Gurion formed a provisional cabinet. War was now inevitable, and future Israeli prime minister Golda Meir made a secret deal with King Abdullah of Jordan. Zionist forces would only minimally attack areas in the eastern half of Palestine (West Bank), an area officially reserved for a Palestinian state but coveted by Jordan in exchange for control over all of western Palestine.

On 14 May 1948 the Jewish state in Palestine, now called the State of Israel, declared its independence. The declaration proclaimed 'the natural right of the Jewish people to be masters of their own fate, like all other nations' and pledged 'equality of social and political rights to all inhabitants irrespective of religion, race or sex.' Ben-Gurion vetoed any mention of specific borders. In a rare moment of concord, the USA and Soviet Union both recognized Israel.

ARAB ARMIES INVADE

As soon as independence was declared, five countries attacked Israel – Syria, Lebanon, Jordan, Egypt and Iraq. The Israelis made gains, except in Jerusalem, which fell to Jordan, and in the Golan, which fell to Syria.

Below A convoy bringing supplies to Jews in Jerusalem, 1948, during the siege by Jordan's Arab Legion.

Above Jewish youths marching in Jerusalem on 30 November 1948, the day after the United Nations' decision to establish a Jewish State.

Right During the war, Israeli forces rebuffed attacks from Egypt, Jordan and Syria, and gained new territory.

On 31 May, Israel's government announced the official disbanding of all separate pre-state Zionist militias. Their members would be subsumed within a single organization, the Israel Defence Forces (IDF), which had 100,000 troops by the year's end. While the IDF held the Syrians at bay in the north, it could not break the siege of Jerusalem until 10 June, when a secret bypass, 'Burma Road', was opened through the Judean Hills.

TRUCES AND CONFLICTS

The UN effected a truce on 11 June and sent Count Folke Bernadotte, a Swedish diplomat who had rescued 21,000 Jews during World War II, to Palestine. Bernadotte proposed that Palestine be annexed to Jordan, with a Jewish enclave attached to assist Arabs economically. Palestinian Arabs and Jews rejected the idea.

Fighting resumed on 9 July with Egyptian attacks in the south, battles in the north, assaults on kibbutzim and Israeli conquests of Lydda, Ramle and Nazareth. A second truce began on 19 July and, on 16 September, Bernadotte released his second plan. This time he acknowledged Israel as a reality, though he recommended awarding the Negev to Egypt and Jordan. His report called for 360,000 Arab refugees to be allowed to return home. The next day Lehi gunmen shot Bernadotte in Jerusalem. Mufti Hajj Amin Husseini's Government of All Palestine was declared in Egyptian-run Gaza, as was a pro-Jordanian Palestinian Congress in Amman, Jordan. Neither was truly independent. In 1950 Jordan formally annexed the West Bank, a gesture only Britain and Pakistan recognized.

The second truce ended on 15 October, after which the IDF relieved Negev settlements, took Beersheva, wiped out the Arab Liberation Army, and, according to Israel's 'new historians', units killed civilians in several Arab villages. In December, Israel entered the Sinai Desert and in March 1949 it secured the southern Negev, including the crucial port of Eilat.

Armistice talks opened on 12 January 1949, and Israel signed agreements with Egypt, Lebanon, Transjordan and Syria. The new state added 50 per cent to the territory allocated to it under the UN plan and linked up split areas.

Many reasons may explain the course of the war including divergent interests and poor strategic co-ordination between Arab forces and secret aid from Diaspora Jewry. For the first time in almost 2,000 years there was a Jewish state, the fulfilment of long-held dreams and a place of refuge for victims of future persecution.

FIRST ELECTIONS AND THE LAW OF RETURN

Israel held its first Knesset (parliamentary) elections on 25 January 1949. In March, David Ben-Gurion became Israel's first prime minister. His coalition government included his Mapai labour party and smaller factions, including a Sephardi list, Arabs from Nazareth and a United Religious Front. Begin led the opposition and Chaim Weizmann became state president after Albert Einstein declined.

In July 1950 Israel's Law of Return granted all Jews the right to immigrate as a defining principle of the nation.

Having survived possible annihilation, the young state faced the challenge of absorbing immigrants and maintaining security. Yet peace has remained elusive ever since.

> ### THE REFUGEE CRISIS
> The 1948–9 War of Independence was seen as a victory for Jews. To Palestinians, however, it was known as the *nakba*, or 'disaster'. Their leaders had rejected the UN partition plan and lost the war, and some 725,000 Palestinians fled the country. Israel now controlled 77 per cent of historic Palestine and 60 per cent of Palestinian people became refugees.
>
> Areas to which most Palestinian Arabs migrated included the West Bank; Gaza Strip; Lebanon; Syria; Transjordan; Egypt and Iraq.
>
> Many of the 190,000 Arabs who stayed in Israel but left their homes are 'internally displaced'.
>
> Currently it is estimated that 14.6 million of Gaza's Palestinians live as refugees. The refugee question constitutes one of the 'final status issues' still at stake in Israeli–Palestinian peace talks.

Right Socialist Zionists defending Kibbutz Gal-On from Egyptian forces, in the southern Negev Desert, 1948.

Jewish Demography After World War II

Since 1948 over 3 million Jews have settled in Israel. Yet Diaspora communities have survived and even blossomed, adding to the ever-changing mix of Jews the world over.

Jewish life altered dramatically in the 20th century. Before World War II some 8.5 out of 10 million European Jews lived in a generally backward eastern Europe and developing Soviet Union. A further 300,000 Jews lived in Asia, 500,000 in Africa and 400,000 in Latin America. Some two-thirds of Jews resided in chastened conditions. After the war, three-quarters of Diaspora Jews resided in advanced countries, USA, Canada, western Europe and a now developed USSR. Comparative affluence and acceptance led Jews to adopt national languages, spelling the demise of Jewish tongues such as Yiddish, Ladino and Judeo-Arabic.

In a history with extraordinary highs and lows, the Jewish people probably experienced more upheaval in the 20th century than ever before. The decimation of the Holocaust, birth of the State of Israel and unprecedented immigration utterly transformed Jewish demography.

There were about 4.75 million Jews globally in 1850, 8.7 million in 1900, 13.5 million in 1914 and 16.6 million in 1939. Today, Jews worldwide total 13 million, 0.23 per cent of the earth's population compared with 33 per cent who are Christians and 20 per cent who are Muslims.

QUESTIONS OF DEFINITION

The debate over who constitutes a Jew partially explains the statistical ambiguities. Normative Jewish religious law, *halakha*, defines a Jew as someone born of a Jewish mother or someone who converts to the faith.

Reform Judaism in the USA opposed intermarriage in 1909, and again in 1947. In 1950 just 6 per cent of American Jews married non-Jews, but by 2000 that figure had risen to 40–50 per cent. In 1983 Reform acknowledged social changes and accepted patrilineal descent. This made it difficult for Orthodox or Conservative Jews to marry Reform Jews. In the same way, 'patrilineal Jews' wishing to settle in Israel may be accepted for citizenship by state law, but they are still deemed non-Jewish when it comes to marrying other Jews.

IMMIGRATION TO ISRAEL

Within Israel, the Jewish populace has grown at least eightfold from 650,000 in 1948. Some 1.5 million Israeli citizens are Palestinian Arabs; and in the territories occupied after 1967 there live at least 3.5 million Palestinians, Muslim and Christian, including a large proportion of refugees from pre-1948 Palestine.

SOVIET JEWS IN GERMANY

Germany attracted droves of Soviet Jewish immigrants after the unification of East and West Germany in 1990. Germany's Jewish population currently stands at about 200,000, the third largest in Europe after

Above Author Maxim Gorky by Isaac Brodsky, a Russian member of the Jewish Society for the Encouragement of the Arts.

Below In 2012 US President Barack Obama hosted his fourth Passover Seder in the White House, Washington DC.

France and Britain, and the fastest growing on the Continent. Former Soviet citizens now make up most of Germany's Jews, and feel under-represented on the Zentralrat, the Central Council of Jews in Germany. Founded in 1950, it is a bastion of indigenous German-speaking Jews, many of whom are descendants of Holocaust survivors. It favours Orthodox Judaism while Soviet Jews, estranged from their roots after 70 years of Communism, prefer US-style Reform founded in 1997.

MIDDLE EAST
During the 20th century, Jews in the Middle East region underwent a demographic revolution: their numbers rocketed from half a million in 1900 to more than five million in 2000, but the distribution of that population was massively skewed. In 1900 most Middle Eastern and North African Jews lived in Iraq, Yemen and Morocco, with smaller pockets in Egypt, Syria, Algeria, Tunisia and Libya. Sizeable minorities also existed in non-Arab countries, Turkey and Iran. After 1948, virtually all Arab states saw their Jewish populations rapidly diminish and in some cases disappear altogether.

Israel was the chief beneficiary, and by 2000 about 95 per cent of the region's Jews dwelt in that one country. Turkey, Iran and Morocco retain Jewish communities of more than 10,000, but these are exceptions to the rule and even there they are a fraction of their size a century ago.

EUROPE TRANSFORMED
At the end of World War II most surviving Jews on mainland Europe were found among the 250,000 located in displaced persons camps. A large number left for Israel, Britain, South America, Canada or the United States. Because Hitler never managed to invade England, Britain became by default home to the largest Jewish community in Europe, although its size has gradually declined since the 1960s. Since then the French community has grown into Europe's largest as Maghrebi (North African) Jews flocked to Paris, Marseilles and other cities.

But Jewish populations in the Czech Republic, Slovakia, Austria, Poland and Hungary are shadows of their former selves. After the 'Iron Curtain' came down in eastern Europe, migration was banned, Zionist groups were outlawed, and only a few intrepid souls managed to get out.

In short, the Holocaust and Cold War divisions transformed the face of Jewish Europe. Other than France, the only country that saw a marked increase in Jewish population after 1970 was, of all places, Germany.

Jews worldwide worry about renewed anti-Semitism which sometimes goes with anti-Zionism. Yet very few face the threats or legally sanctioned prejudice of the past. Most Jews feel financially secure and professionally fulfilled. That this should be so after the Holocaust is particularly impressive.

ISRAEL AS THE JEWISH HOMELAND

Above Israelis celebrate Independence Day with a picnic in the park.

Owing to immigration, Israel's population nearly doubled in its first five years. Jews leaving displaced person camps in Germany were followed by thousands from the Middle East. Absorption camps became permanent towns with persistent social problems, leading to charges of an Ashkenzi discrimination against Jews from Arab lands.

One of the hallmarks of Israel is the way the state and rabbinate reached a 'status quo' from earliest days. Rabbis accepted national laws on most matters, but retained influence over law concerning marriages, burials and questions of identity. Most Israeli Jews are secular, but civil marriage is not allowed so non-believers still require rabbinical blessing for weddings.

Once the 1970s economic crisis was resolved, Israel adopted a more free enterprise system in imitation of America. Agriculture declined compared to industry and high technology. Unfortunately, the competitive economic atmosphere has resulted in increased disparities between rich and poor.

Most Diaspora communities cherish Israel and regard attacks on the country almost as attacks on them. Yet only a tiny minority of US, British or French Jews have emigrated to Israel. Some liberal Jews are critical of Israeli policies and some wish to distance themselves from Israel altogether.

CHAPTER 11

JEWISH CULTURE IN MODERN SOCIETY

Most of today's estimated 14.6 million Jews live in Israel and the USA. While genocide, turmoil and emigration have depleted eastern European and Russian Jewry, other European countries, such as France and Britain, have varied, creative Jewish populations; and Germany, once the birthplace of Nazism, is Europe's fastest-growing community of all. After centuries of discord, Jewish–Christian relations improved dramatically with the passage of the 1964 papal declaration, Vatican II. Jews today contribute to humanity through medicine, science and psychology; and express themselves via myriad paths, from the kibbutz and women-only prayer services to social activism, Jewish cuisine, an Orthodox revival and a plethora of hybrid identities. Individual Jews have depicted modern life in stimulating, sometimes disturbing, ways in art, philosophy and literature. Others pioneered cinema, television, orchestral music and rock bands, or invigorated traditional klezmer and Ladino musical forms. Similarly, synagogue design provides exciting contemporary casings for an ancient faith and ever-adaptable culture.

Opposite After the travails of World War II, both tragedy and hope seem to inform this striking portrait, Jewish Girl, *painted by the Italian artist Armando Pizzinato in 1945.*

Above Moroccan Jews at a celebration honouring the medieval philosopher Maimonides. Today the UK-based Maimonides Foundation fosters relationships between Jews, Christians and Muslims.

Israel in the Modern World

Buffeted by wars and criticized for its actions, the State of Israel has survived for 60 years, absorbing immigrants and redefining Jewish history.

More than 60 years after its found-ation, the State of Israel is militarily strong, economically robust and culturally vibrant. Israel probably now houses more Jews than any other nation on earth. In the words of a Second Aliyah song, Jews came to the land 'to build and be rebuilt', and in many respects that is what has been fulfilled.

HERZL'S DREAM REALIZED?

Jews from every continent have settled in the 'ancient homeland'. Reports say that Israeli Jews, 76 per cent of the population, grew by 300,000 in 2006–7, while the Jewish Diaspora shrank by 100,000. The very existence of the state has altered Jewish history. For the first time in 2,000 years, Jews can stand in the courts of nations and speak for their own national interests.

Jews outside Israel take pride in her considerable achievements in art, science, medicine and literature, on the battlefield, in trade and agriculture, and in her aid to Third World nations. They see everyday life of a Hebrew-speaking nation as a realization of Theodor Herzl's (1860–1904) dream of normalization. Religious Jews welcome the chance to live with dignity and to practise their faith on ancestral soil.

PERSISTENT TROUBLES

However, in many respects Israel remains a dream unfulfilled. Some 60 per cent of Jews still live in the Diaspora. Social disparities have grown, and inter-Jewish ethnic and religious tension remains an issue. Israel's Arab minority – descendants of those indigenous Palestinians who did not leave in 1948 – feel increasingly estranged, while Israel's conduct in the territories she occupied in 1967 has drawn wide criticism.

Most of all, Jews hoped that Israel would be a safe refuge; yet in view of the five major wars that have taken place since independence, two Palestinian *intifadas*, or uprisings, and recurrent terror attacks on its citizens, Israel has sometimes seemed like the least safe place for Jews.

The Israel/Palestine question remains one of the most vexed political issues in the world. What began as a local dispute has been cast as a clash between East and West, and it has acquired religious overtones. Some Arab analysts call it the root cause of all Middle East troubles, while growing numbers challenge Israel's very right to exist.

FROM 1948 TO 1956

Israel endured years of economic austerity and hardship as it absorbed Jewish immigrants in its first decade – 500,000 between 1948 and 1950 alone. The 1950 Law of Return opened the doors to Jews everywhere. Conversely, in that same year Israel's Absentee Property law foreclosed Arab refugees' hopes of returning, which neighbouring Arab leaders

Above For a nation built on immigration, the Ethiopian Jewish exodus of the 1980–90s reminded many Israelis of their raison d'être.

Left US President-elect Richard Nixon chats with Israeli ambassador Yitzhak Rabin (left) and Israeli Defence Minister Moshe Dayan (right), 1968.

made a precondition for further talks. As a result, hopes receded of turning the armistice agreements that Israel signed in 1949 with Jordan, Egypt, Syria and Lebanon into full peace treaties.

Increasingly, Third World and Soviet bloc nations have portrayed Israel as an alien colonial outpost. Palestinian refugees on Israel's borders stepped up attacks as *fedayeen*, or 'self-sacrificers'. Israel's retaliations were often condemned as disproportionate. Egypt's post-1954 leader, Gamal Abdel Nasser, made 'Palestine' central to his pan-Arabist doctrine.

ROAD TO THE SIX-DAY WAR
All these factors raised tensions and set the scene for the October 1956 Suez War, in which the Israel Defence Forces (IDF) captured the entire Sinai and the Gaza Strip. However, UN and American pressure forced Israel to surrender all gains within a year.

In the 1960s Israel drew closer to Washington, and was alarmed when Egypt sponsored the creation of a Palestine Liberation Organization (PLO) in 1964. When Egypt blockaded the Gulf of Aqaba to Israeli shipping, Prime Minister Levi Eshkol (1895–1969) ordered a pre-emptive attack on Egypt, Syria and Jordan on 5 June 1967. In six days Israel defeated all Arab forces and quadrupled the size of land under its control. Up to 200,000 Palestinians became refugees.

A NEW PARADIGM
AFTER 1967
In Israeli and Jewish eyes, David had defeated Goliath. Israel now held the Gaza Strip and the Golan Heights (Syrian). Most significantly it controlled the formerly Jordanian-run West Bank, what religious Jews call Judea and Samaria, the heart of biblical Eretz Israel. This included East Jerusalem's Old City with its Jewish Quarter, Temple Mount and Western Wall. However, Israel was now cast as an occupier, which in turn bred serious internal schisms.

Liberal Israelis envisaged trading territories for peace with Arabs – essentially the idea behind UN Security Council Resolution 242, which Israel signed in 1970. Others felt that expanding Israel's pre-1967 pencil-thin 'waist' would protect against future attack. Few Israelis, though, proposed annexation, as this would enfranchise Palestinian residents and erode the Jewish nature of the state.

Positions soon polarized: in August 1967 the Arab League rejected talks while the PLO recommitted itself to armed struggle. Within Israel buoyant religious Zionists felt that God had delivered victory, and considered it sinful to return an inch of sacred soil.

YOM KIPPUR WAR
Many Israeli policy-makers believed they were invincible after 1967, although a draining 'war of attrition' with Egypt, between 1967 and

Above The Suez Canal blockaded by sunken ships, a symptom of war, November 1956.

1970, should have warned Jerusalem against complacency. In October 1973 Egypt and Syria launched a pincer attack on Israel on Yom Kippur, the Jewish Day of Atonement, and caught the IDF unawares. Israel withstood the blows and after three weeks repelled the enemy, but more than 2,600 Israelis died in combat and national morale was badly dented.

The war prompted the resignation of Golda Meir, the first female premier in the region. It also gave new impetus to Jewish civilians who planted new settlements in the territories, often defying the prime minister, Yitzhak Rabin (1922–95), and contravening international law. A new movement, *Gush Emunim*, or 'Bloc of the Faithful', used messianic religious motifs to champion the settlers. Opposition crystallized in the Peace Now movement, which wanted to return Israel to its former 1967 'green line'.

Above Six-Day War, 1967. A truck full of captured Egyptian soldiers meets an Israeli troop convoy near El Arish.

After Yasser Arafat, leader of the radical Fatah faction, won control of the PLO, international support for Palestinians grew. He addressed the UN in 1974, and the General Assembly soon passed a resolution equating Zionism with racism. Israel and the USA blamed Arafat for encouraging attacks inside Israel and against Israeli and Jewish targets abroad, including the murder of Israeli athletes at the 1972 Munich Olympics.

PEACE TREATY WITH EGYPT

In the May 1977 elections, Likud defeated Labour for the first time. The head of the new government, Menachem Begin (1913–92), was renowned for supporting 'Greater Israel'. He thus surprised critics by hosting a groundbreaking visit by Egypt's President Anwar Sadat – the first by any major Arab leader – in November 1977. Following talks at Camp David, Maryland, Israel and Egypt signed a peace treaty in 1979. Israel agreed to return all of the Sinai Peninsula to Egypt. The treaty, however, failed to initiate negotiations over Palestinian autonomy.

LEBANON WAR AND PALESTINIAN UPRISING

In June 1982, Israelis became embroiled in the Lebanese civil war. By August they had occupied Beirut, HQ of the PLO since 1971, and forced them to evacuate. The Lebanese conflict temporarily clipped the PLO's wings, but also bred a new enemy in the radical Shiite militia, Hizbollah.

Palestinians revolted against what they called 'an illegal occupation' after December 1987, starting in Gaza and spreading to the West Bank in December 1987. Less than a year into this 'intifada', Arafat hinted that he might negotiate and Jordan relinquished its claim to the West Bank. However, Israel doubted Arafat's sincerity and the intifada continued.

FROM WAR TO PEACE

Impatient with Israel's continual settlement expansion and wary of another war, America pressured Israel and Arab states to meet in Madrid in October 1991. So began the first direct bilateral negotiations between Israelis, Jordanians, Syrians and a Palestinian delegation since 1949.

Madrid seemed to release Israel from its status as a pariah. The UN rescinded its 'Zionism is racism' vote, and Jerusalem created or restored relations with Russia, India, China and 56 other nations. Labour's Yitzhak Rabin won elections in 1992 and pledged action for peace; his foreign minister, Shimon Peres, envisaged a 'New Middle East' based on open borders and economic and cultural co-operation.

Ultimately secret discussions in Oslo led in September 1993 to mutual recognition between Israel and the hitherto shunned PLO. Palestinians gained limited auton-

Below The West Bank settlements are a source of pride to many Zionists, but are considered by others to be illegal and an impediment to peace.

Left Yasser Arafat, Shimon Peres and Yitzhak Rabin at the Nobel Peace Prize ceremony, Stockholm, 1994, a year after signing the Oslo Accords.

omy in Jericho and Gaza, to which PLO leaders returned in 1994. That October, Israel and Jordan's King Hussein signed a peace treaty. Arafat's new Palestine Authority (PA) gained control over Ramallah, Tulkarm, Nablus and Jenin.

SETBACKS AFTER 1994

Distrust remained, particularly over expanding settlements and threats from Palestinian militants. Matters worsened when Hamas, a militant Islamic movement founded in 1988, launched a string of terror attacks in 1994.

Religious Zionists felt betrayed: and after a peace rally on 4 November 1995, Yigal Amir, a right-wing Jewish extremist, shot Yitzhak Rabin dead after a peace rally. Peres succeeded Rabin, but the peace process slowed down when Likud under Benjamin Netanyahu (1949–) narrowly defeated Labour in early 1996. During 1996–9, settlement building increased and relations with Egypt and Jordan deteriorated.

NEW UNREST AFTER TALKS FAIL IN 2000

Ehud Barak (1942–) led Labour back to power in 1999 and after failing to clinch a peace deal with Syria, he withdrew Israeli troops from southern Lebanon in May 2000. Then in July he began talks with Yasser Arafat, hosted by Bill Clinton at Camp David. For the first time Israelis and Palestinians officially addressed the 'core issues' of Jerusalem and final borders.

Israelis said Barak generously offered to give up 95 per cent of captured territories for lasting peace and security. Palestinians felt they were being cajoled into surrendering Jerusalem and refugees' rights in exchange for a non-contiguous 'bantustans', not real statehood.

The talks failed and a new *intifada* began in late September 2000, sparked by a visit by Israeli opposition leader Ariel Sharon to the Temple Mount/ Haram al Sharif. Protest spread through the territories and Palestinian factions led by Hamas began suicide attacks in Israeli civilian centres.

Israel responded by sealing off West Bank and Gaza towns, setting up dozens of roadblocks and conducting 'targeted killings' of enemy leaders, including *Hamas* founder Sheikh Ahmed Yassin in 2004. By January 2008, 1,047 Israelis and 5,103 Palestinians had died in the conflict.

ROADMAP TO PEACE

Israeli public opinion swung against Labour in late 2000s, with rightists blaming the 'Oslo criminals' for arming the Palestinians. Ariel Sharon, who won elections for Likud in 2001 and 2003, confined Arafat to Ramallah. In 2003 Sharon and Arafat accepted US President George Bush's 'roadmap to peace' that would result in Palestinian independence. But the war in Iraq diverted attention and continuing violence thwarted the plan's implementation. Sharon's decision to evacuate settlers from Gaza in 2005 upset the Israeli right, and the next year's war with Lebanon and electoral victory of Hamas in the territories made peace a distant dream.

More recent history has been marked by ongoing tensions, conflicts and ceasefires in the region. Official peace negotiations began again in 2013 but were suspended a year later. The country of Israel celebrated 70 years of independence in 2018, but the conflict with Palestine remains unresolved.

Below Prime minister Benjamin Netanyahu at a press conference, 2018.

Diaspora Life – The USA and Canada

For most of the 20th century, America had the world's largest Jewish population. It remains a pillar of modern Jewry, while Canada has the fourth largest Jewish Diaspora community.

The bedrock for today's American Jewish population were the 2.5 million who arrived during 1880–1920, overwhelmingly from eastern Europe. Life was not always easy in the supposed Golden Land: during the 1890s three-quarters of Jewish breadwinners were manual labourers, but this proletariat status was preferable to the insecurities of being hawkers and middlemen in Europe.

AN EVOLVING COMMUNITY

By the 1930s more Jews took up commerce, fewer worked in industry and nearly 30 per cent were self-employed compared with the under 12 per cent national average. Jews began leaving inner cities for the suburbs and economic opportunities on the west coast. Increasingly they spoke English, not Yiddish, and entered universities and the professions, despite occasional discriminatory admission quotas that persisted until the 1950s.

Jews became 'Americanized' as their ties to their original European city or *shtetl* loosened. Yet they maintained a distinctive identity through such organizations as the long-established Bnai Brith welfare and advocacy network. Synagogue affiliation also leapt from 20 per cent in 1920 to 60 per cent in 1960. Another 100,000 Jews arrived from central Europe in the 1930s. American Jews helped rehabilitate brethren in eastern Europe and Arab countries through the United Jewish Appeal, founded in 1939. Yet they could not stop the Holocaust, which may explain why they backed the State of Israel so passionately after 1948.

CULTURAL INTEGRATION

By the 1950s, individual Jews had become leaders in mainstream literature, art, and jazz, classical and rock music, and above all in cinema and television. Jews also prospered in the professions, most notably in medicine and law. In large part this derived from a veneration for education: the figures are debated but US Jews were estimated to number five to six million in 2020, just over 2 per cent of the population. They account for five per cent of all college enrolments and a quarter of Ivy League students.

REDISCOVERED IDENTITIES

American Jewry's rediscovery of identity has taken many forms. Holocaust education has grown as a subject and about 100 universities now run regular Jewish studies courses. While comparatively few US Jews immigrate to Israel, many more involve themselves in school exchanges, educational visits, or buy a second home in Israel.

Meanwhile, those of a less Zionist bent have revived interest in the Yiddish language and

Above 'Bugsy Siegel', a Jewish-American gangster who helped establish Las Vegas, in 1941.

Left Leonard Bernstein conducting Beethoven in Berlin, 1989, after the fall of the Berlin Wall. He was a hugely successful Jewish-American composer.

klezmer music tradition of the Ashkenazic Jews of eastern Europe. And Jews seeking spirituality, many of whom dallied with Eastern mysticism in the 1960s, have eagerly embraced hybrid forms of worship in the Jewish Renewal and Havurah movements, or sought out fashionable Kabbalah workshops with varying levels of authenticity.

POLITICAL INTERESTS

Jews were enthusiastic unionists in the early 20th century, especially in the garment industry. A large number were anarchists or Communists, associations that came back to haunt them during the McCarthyite era. Since World War II Jews have tended to be Democrats. Despite their comparatively small numbers, Jews' traditionally high voting turnout and concentration in the key 'swing states' – New York, California, New Jersey and Florida – gives them enhanced influence. Hence politicians pay attention to what are seen as 'Jewish concerns'. Jews form a high percentage of the political body, although the number fluctuates.

Below Jewish studies enter the academic mainstream: Center for Jewish Life at Princeton University.

FOOD-FEST ON MAIN STREET

Food is a classic manifestation of Jewish culture, and in few cities is this more obvious than in New York. Delicatessens serve trusted staples of the Jewish table such as chicken and matzo ball soup and bagels with lox (smoked salmon). Not to forget wurst (garlic sausage), pastrami on rye, lokshen (noodle) pudding, and the Sabbath loaves called challah.

Florence Greenbaum published her *International Jewish Cook Book* in New York in 1919, featuring European, Ashkenazi dishes. Since then, Jews from Syria, Turkey, Israel, Bukhara and Morocco have introduced such foods as couscous, hummus and falafel.

Above Bagels and other Jewish specialities in a New York deli.

GROWTH OR DECLINE?

Every December civic squares in suburban America feature Hannukah menorahs alongside Christmas trees. Yet to some, the freedom American Jews enjoy endangers their survival. Freedom means the right to practise one's faith but also to abandon it. Some Jews, it is said, feel such harmony between American and Jewish values that they neglect their culture.

Conversely, the recent 'return to faith' trend has boosted the number of young Orthodox Jews. Likewise, refugees from Iran, Iraq, Syria and Egypt have replenished a declining Jewish community, as have migrants from Russia, Georgia and Bukhara since the 1970s and from Israel after the 1990s. Brighton Beach is a magnet for Russian Jews, Beverley Hills for Iranians and Houston for South Africans.

CANADA

Jews arrived in Canada in 1760 as British Army soldiers, and established Bnai Brith Canada in 1875 as a powerful advocate for human rights and communal defence. Canada's Jewish population rose to 100,000 by 1914, the year in which a new Jewish public library made Montreal a focal point on the Yiddish and Hebrew writing circuit.

Several Jewish organizations joined a Canadian Jewish Congress (CJC) in 1919, and a brief influx after 1924 followed when the US curbed immigration, until Canada, too, blocked entry to European migrants in 1930. Almost all the 50,000 Jews who entered Canada in the interwar years came from the USA or Britain. Only 1 per cent of Jews fleeing Nazism found refuge in Canada; xenophobia simply ran too high.

During World War II about 17,000 Jews fought for Canada. Conditions improved markedly after-wards. Canada's Jewish population grew to 260,000 by 1961, after 40,000 Holocaust survivors entered in the late 1940s, Hungarians arrived in the 1950s and francophone Sephardi Jews from North Africa settled in French-speaking Montreal. Traditionally leftist in their politics, Canadian Jews suffered from suspicion during the Cold War years.

Today, Canada's 380,000 Jews constitute the fourth largest Diaspora community in the world. Most reside in Ontario and Quebec. Some 30,000 left Montreal after French separatists threatened English-speakers, although the crisis has abated since 1985. Despite recent anti-Semitic incidents, Jews feel secure, and have contributed disproportionately to Canadian culture.

Diaspora Life – Great Britain and France

SEPARATED BY THE CHANNEL, BRITAIN AND FRANCE NOW HAVE TWO OF EUROPE'S LARGEST JEWISH COMMUNITIES. IN BOTH IMMIGRANTS HAVE REPLENISHED ONCE-DECLINING COMMUNITIES.

The influx of Romanian, Russian and Polish Jews to Britain was so intense in the late 19th century that reportedly the Jewish Free School in London's East End had 4,000 pupils, more than any other school in the world.

A few wealthy Anglicized Sephardi and Western Ashkenazi families, dubbed the cousinhood, dominated the Board of Deputies of British Jews (established in 1760), the United Synagogue (1870), the Anglo-Jewish Association (1871) and the Maccabeans professional dining club (1891). Recent arrivals gradually acquired more power, but the old elite put up stiff resistance.

FROM ALIENS ACT TO BEATING THE BLACKSHIRTS

Some established Jewish grandees campaigned against immigration and supported the Aliens Act of 1905 that blocked entry to 'undesirable indigents'. The act left the door open to refugees fleeing persecution, and funded improved amenities in crowded urban ghettoes.

After the Great War, Jews increasingly entered the professions and many succeeded in business, such as the Sieffs who developed Marks & Spencer, and the Cohens who founded Tesco. Within a generation the children of Yiddish and German speakers were fully at home in English, and a number joined the erudite Bloomsbury group of writers and artists. In the 1930s, émigrés such as Sigmund Freud, Ludwig Wittgenstein, Isaiah Berlin, George Steiner and Albert Einstein enhanced British academia.

Even celebrated figures faced a residue of xenophobia, and

Above Dubbed 'The Jewish Dickens', Israel Zangwill (1864–1926) also coined the phrase 'the Melting Pot'.

proto-Nazi ideas gained currency after Oswald Mosley founded his Blackshirts movement in 1932. Jews, Irish Catholics and anti-fascists confronted Mosley's bullies in the East End's October 1936 'Battle of Cable Street', which passed into folklore as a time when the fascists were beaten.

NEW ARRIVALS

Small numbers of Jews arrived after 1945 from former colonies or protectorates: South Africa, Rhodesia, Gibraltar, Aden, Iraq and Egypt.

Below A mural marking the 1936 Battle of Cable Street, when east London Jews beat off Mosley's Blackshirts.

DUTCH COURAGE

Communist dockworkers went on strike to protest against Nazi race laws in April 1941, the only such incident in Europe, and the Dutch underground hid up to 30,000 of Holland's 140,000 Jews. About 75 per cent of Jews were deported to the camps and killed, leaving a post-war community which, though safe, wealthy and well integrated, stood at 24,000 in 1954 and about 41,000 today. While most affiliated Jews are Orthodox, progressive trends have made inroads in recent years.

Latterly pockets of Israelis have sprung up in parts of London. The Board of Deputies and weekly *Jewish Chronicle* (established in 1841) represent Jews to the broader community and now champion interfaith harmony.

More recently, judges like former Lord Chief Justice Harry Woolf have profoundly affected the British legal system, while the Chief Rabbis Immanuel Jakobovits (1921–99) and Jonathan Sacks gained wide respect for their ideas on ethics.

Jewish families moved to London's leafier north-west suburbs from the East End, where Bengali and Somali immigrants have replaced them. Provincial communities in the cities of Leeds, Bristol, Glasgow, Birmingham and Bradford declined over time, and only Manchester maintained its critical mass with its distinctive blend of old Sephardi Jews, children of Ashkenazi textile merchants and a growing Orthodox community.

POLITICAL SHIFTS

After 1945 Jews experienced a conflict of loyalties between their British patriotism and their sympathy for fellow Jews fighting Mandate authorities in Palestine.

In the immediate post-war era, British Jews were mostly loyal to Labour. Affluence returned after austerity, and gradually more Jews gravitated to the Conservatives in the Margaret Thatcher era. As a child her family had taken in a teenage refugee from Austria, a possibly formative influence. Notable Jews in her government included Nigel Lawson, Leon Brittain, Shirley Porter, Edwina Currie and Michael Howard. Later many Jews navigated towards the Labour party, especially under Tony Blair, although some retreated due to perceptions of anti-Semitism that developed in the Corbyn era; promises of change were made by the new leader Sir Keir Starmer in early 2020.

Right A 19th-century neo-Moorish extravaganza, this London ark suggests a new sense of arrival for British Jews.

CHANGES IN FRENCH JEWRY

In the 30 years to 1914 some 25,000 Greek, Turkish, Polish, Bulgarian, Russian, Algerian and Romanian Jews arrived in France, reinvigorating an indigenous community of only 60,000 in 1880. Leon Blum of the socialist Popular Front became prime minister in 1936–7 and 1938. He served as premier in 1946–7, having survived Nazi incarceration in Buchenwald and Dachau, where he wrote his famous essay, 'For all mankind'.

Many Jews who fled Germany and Austria for France before 1939 perished in the Holocaust. All told, 76,000 Jews were deported to death camps from occupied France and the Vichy puppet regime in the south. France's first post-war president, Charles de Gaulle, welcomed Jews as full co-nationals, and some camp survivors, like the Romanian-born poet Paul Celan, made France their home.

CRIF, an umbrella group dedicated to preserving Franco-Jewish life, was secretly created in 1943. By the 1950s CRIF absorbed Jews arriving from North Africa, who soon outnumbered indigenous Ashkenazim. They ensured that France had the largest Jewish population in Europe for the first time in a millennium.

France's close ties with Israel, at least until 1967, boosted the status of French Jews. Since then anti-Semitism has risen, but despite right-wing Holocaust denial, left-wing anger at Israeli policies, and degrees of tension between Jews and a few of France's six million post-war Muslims, figures like Bernard-Henri Lévi, Raymond Aron and Simone Veil have profoundly shaped public thinking in modern France.

Below Jews dancing in the Rue des Rosiers, Marais Quarter, Paris, 2010.

Jews in Germany and Eastern Europe

RUSSIA, POLAND AND GERMANY WERE ONCE THE HEARTLANDS OF JEWRY. MASS EMIGRATION AND CALAMITIES IN THE 20TH CENTURY SEEMED IRREVERSIBLE, YET SHOOTS OF REVIVAL HAVE REAPPEARED.

After taking control of Russia in 1917, the Bolsheviks dismantled the despised Pale of Settlement and outlawed anti-Semitism. Jews gained access to education and new professions. Leon Trotsky, Lev Kamenev and Grigori Zinoviev reached the highest echelons of Soviet power.

Liberation came at a price: the authorities banned Torah classes, confiscated religious property and had shut down half the synagogues by 1934. Jews who backed Zionist, Bundist, liberal or social-revolutionary parties faced persecution; even the Communist Party's Jewish division, the Yevsektsiya, was liquidated in 1930.

SHTETL CULTURE

The flight to the cities loosened bonds to the *shtetl*, the semi-rural heartland of Russian Jewry. New political borders divided formerly interconnected communities on the borderlands of Russia, Ukraine and Poland. The *shtetl* structure survived civil war pogroms and Stalinist totalitarianism. Yet what Communism did not extinguish, World War II did.

The Nazi–Soviet Pact of 1939–41 imposed a news blackout. When the Germans invaded in late 1941 it was too late for Jews living between Poland and Russia. Nazi *Einsatzkommandos* and local cohorts began the Holocaust with the mass shooting and gassing of 1.5 million Jews in western Soviet Union.

AFTER WORLD WAR II

Barred from fleeing south or west, many Jews went east, which saved lives but destroyed social cohesion. The Jewish Anti-Fascist Committee encouraged a brief cultural revival after 1943, but five years later Stalin had its leaders killed as traitors. The Kremlin barred publication of the 'Black Book', first-hand reports of Nazi atrocities against Jews, lest it detract from the preferred version of the 'Great Patriotic War'.

Above Jewish Socialist Workers Party supporters celebrate revolutionary times under a Yiddish banner; Russia, 1918.

NEW DISCRIMINATION

Israel's military victory in 1967 intensified anti-Zionism in Russia and officially approved attacks on Judaism itself. University quotas for Jews reduced their presence from 18 per cent of Soviet scientific workers in 1947 to 7 per cent in 1970. Under Brezhnev not one Jew was admitted to Moscow University in 1977–8. Some 250,000 were allowed to emigrate in 1971–4, after which the doors closed and 'refuseniks' (those refused an exit visa) were jailed on bogus security charges.

COLLAPSE OF THE UNION

The collapse of Communism across Europe in 1989 and the break-up of the Soviet Union in 1991 created a ripple effect on Jewish life in the region. Mass migration to the USA and Israel ensued, and some predicted the demise of Jewish life in Russia itself. Today most former Soviet Jews live in Israel, followed by the USA, with the Confederation

Left Austria finally returned Gustav Klimt's portrait of her aunt to Maria Altmann in 2006. In all, Nazis stole six of her family's artworks in 1938.

Above Soviet Jewish refugee families reach Vienna on their journey out of the USSR, 1979.

of Independent States (successor to the USSR) taking third place. It is thought about 300,000 Jews now live in Russia, 122,000 in Ukraine and 25,000 in Belarus.

Predominantly Muslim former Soviet Central Asian states have not discriminated against Jews. However, most Jews have emigrated, leaving behind small, aging populations. Only 3,600 Jews remain in Lithuania, once the centre of Jewish religious life.

EASTERN EUROPE

Throughout eastern Europe the events of World War II reduced once- vibrant Jewish communities to fractions of their former size. Thousands left for Israel and the West. The most dramatic decline was in Poland, whose pre-war population of 3.3 million Jews, accounting for 27.2 per cent of all city dwellers in 1931, had shrunk to 5,000 by the 1980s. Many Jews who had survived the Holocaust fled Hungary after the violent suppression of an anti-Stalinist revolt in late 1956.

Czechoslovakia's Jews played a leading part in the Communist establishment in the early days, and Czech arms helped a nascent Israel survive the 1948 war. Then in 1952 party secretary Rudolf Slansky was accused of being a crypto-Zionist, ousted, and executed along with 11 other Jews. Three years later Czechoslovakia became the chief conduit for Warsaw Pact weapons to Israel's Arab neighbours. This switch in policy fed Israel's sense of entrapment, and in part persuaded her to side with Britain and France in the Suez War of 1956.

Two organizations represent the Jews of a newly united Europe: the European Council of Jewish Communities, first established in 1968, and the European Jewish Congress, founded in 1986. Since 1996, 26 European countries have participated in an annual European Day of Jewish Culture. In an event scarcely imaginable just ten years earlier, Poland, Hungary, Slovakia, the Czech Republic, Slovenia, Latvia, Lithuania and Estonia all joined the European Union in May 2004, and Bulgaria and Romania followed in January 2007. As a result Jewish communities in the West and East began meeting each other again after decades of division.

GERMAN RESETTLEMENT

The country that truly defied expectations was Germany. Jews have settled there in large numbers. Most come from the former Soviet Union and many others are Israeli; by 2000 they outnumbered the German descendants of Holocaust survivors, who in 1950 had set up a *Zentralrat*, Central Council, to rebuild their community. West Germany taught schoolchildren about the Holocaust, and after 1952 paid reparations to Jewish survivors for wartime suffering and property stolen, totalling $25 billion by 1987. Bonn also established firm relations with Israel and offered former refugees German citizenship.

Right Once a symbol of a divided Europe, the Berlin Wall's ruins now stand for future hope of tolerance and lasting peace. Photographed in 1989.

> ### VATICAN II
> Relations between Roman Catholics and Jews took a turn for the better in 1965 with the rulings of a council called Vatican II. The key document, *Nostrae Aetate*, 'In Our Time', proclaimed: 'Jews should not be presented as rejected or accursed by God.' The Church, 'mindful of the patrimony she shares with the Jews', condemned persecution of Jews and for the first time absolved them for killing Jesus.

East Germany was less forthcoming about acknowledging wartime crimes, so Jews were wary at the prospect of reunification after the Berlin Wall came down in 1989. But Jewish life is mostly thriving.

THE AUSTRIAN CONUNDRUM

Austria saw itself as 'Hitler's first victim' and unlike Germany denied guilt for killing its Jews. There was scandal over the alleged SS wartime record of Austria's 1986–92 president, Kurt Waldheim. Vienna's Jewish population fell from 200,000 pre-war to 8,000 by the 1980s, but Jews have since made a positive impact on post-war Austrian life.

The Spread of Jewish Communities

GLOBALIZATION IS NOTHING NEW FOR JEWS WHO LEFT EUROPE AND THE MIDDLE EAST TO MAKE NEW LIVES IN SOUTH AMERICA, SOUTH AFRICA, AUSTRALIA, HONG KONG AND SINGAPORE.

Today four out of every five Jews live in either Israel or the United States. Of the remaining 2.3 million, 550,000 are found south of the US–Mexican border. Paradoxically most of these Spanish- and Portuguese-speaking Jews are not Sephardi but Ashkenazi.

Tighter US influx controls made South America more attractive after 1924, and drew immigrants from far and wide. This created great variety: Venezuela with its 35,000-strong half-Ashkenazi, half-Sephardi community; Uruguay with 40,000 Jews in 1980; Cuba, reduced from 12,000 pre-revolution to 1,000 today, and Guatemala, home to many German Jews. In Mexico, 45,000 European, Damascene and Sephardi Jews have largely moved from commerce to the professions. 'Judaizing' sects of *mestizos* (half-Indians) claim Jewish ties.

Below Daniel Barenboim, born in Argentina in 1942, conducting the Arab-Jewish Divan Orchestra, 2010.

Right Templo Libertad, Buenos Aires, a synagogue that symbolizes Judaism thriving south of the equator.

South American states helped pass the 1947 UN Partition Plan that created Israel, spawning strong intercontinental ties ever since.

JEWS OF ARGENTINA

Argentina accounts for nearly half the continent's Jews. Its Italian and Spanish inhabitants attracted 88,000 Jews in 1901–14, and another 74,000 Russian Jews in 1921–30 joined groups from Morocco and Syria.

Anti-Semitism rose with German encouragement in the 1930s, though 30,000–40,000 refugees from Nazism entered Argentina during 1933–43, many illegally. Post-war Argentina absorbed former Nazis and in 1966 the military junta sacked civil servants who were Jewish. In 1967 nearly half the world's anti-Semitic incidents occurred in Argentina and 1,500 Jews are still counted as 'missing', presumed killed by the state. In 1994, 85 people were killed in a terrorist bombing on the Asociación Mutual Israelita Argentina in Buenos Aires, the centre of the Argentinian Jewish community.

Today, Jews are well integrated and contribute to society, arts and sciences, especially since the end of junta rule.

BRAZILIAN JEWS

Unreliable figures suggest millions of Brazilians have 16th-century Jewish or Marrano (crypto-Jewish) ancestry. Moroccan Sephardim founded a synagogue in Belem in 1824; but today's community of about 150,000 are mainly of Russian, Polish and Hungarian descent. Communal activities started in Porto Alegre in 1910 and soon extended to São Paulo and Rio de Janeiro, where most Jews now live. Jews also farmed on ICA communes along the Rio Grande, though by 1958 most had left for the cities. Each wave of immigrants brought its own flavour. Some 24,000 Jews arrived from west and central Europe in 1931–39 and 12,000 from Arab countries in 1957–60 joined an existing 5,000-strong Egyptian-Jewish community in São Paulo.

SOUTH AFRICA

Although South African Jews number fewer than 71,000, just 0.5 per cent of the population, their impact remains significant. The community is known for its strong Lithuanian origins. The youth groups Habonim, Beitar and Bnei Akiva nurtured Zionist ties, and per capita South African funding of Israel exceeds all other Diaspora communities. Until the recent building of yeshivas (academies), and renewed religiosity in Johannesburg, all chief rabbis were imported from Britain.

Rabbis and community heads were slow to condemn apartheid, but individual Jews helped lead the anti-apartheid struggle, including Ronnie Kasrils, Albie Sachs and Joe Slovo. For 13 years, Helen Suzman was a lone parliamentary voice against official racism.

Some 40,000 Jews had left before black majority rule was attained in 1994. Many pursued careers in Britain, including the former attorney for Nelson Mandela, later to be Law Lord Joel Joffe; and earlier the future Israeli foreign minister Abba Eban, and Lord Solly Zuckerman, chief UK science advisor.

Below Consecrated in 1863, the Old Synagogue, Cape Town, is the oldest in South Africa.

Since 1994 fear of crime and reduced employment opportunities have seen Jews move to Australia. Some 80 per cent of emigrants leave with university degrees, whereas few of their Lithuanian forebears had finished secondary school. By the same token former Zimbabweans and Israelis are replenishing South Africa's otherwise aging community.

AUSTRALIA AND NEW ZEALAND

Today, South African and recent Soviet immigrants make up nearly a quarter of Australian Jews. They joined British Sephardim, who developed businesses, galleries and libraries in the 19th century. Refugees from Germany revived a community that seemed to be losing its identity. Its population grew from 70,000 in 1968 to 120,000 today. Australia has 81 synagogues, numerous day schools, low intermarriage rates and an above-replacement level of Jewish children.

Far smaller in size is the Jewish community of New Zealand, which numbered just 5,000 in the 1990s. Even so, 'Kiwi Jews' included Sir Julius Vogel, twice premier in the 19th century; and the novelist, Benjamin Farjeon, who edited the islands' first newspaper. Since then

Above Twice Prime Minister of New Zealand, Sir Julius Vogel (1835–99) campaigned for women's suffrage.

there have been many prominent Jewish doctors, hoteliers, retailers, university professors and steel industrialists.

ASIA

Americans and Israelis boosted Hong Kong's Jewish population from 200 in 1974 to 4,000 in the 1990s. The first settlers were English- and Arabic-speaking Baghdadi Jewish traders, who also built a tiny, vibrant community in Singapore. One of their descendants, David Marshall, became the first premier of Singapore after independence in 1955.

In India, Baghdadi Jews represent a third wave of arrivals. Other Jews settled in Cochin in the 10th century. The Bene Israel of Bombay, known as 'Sabbath-observing oil pressers', claim descent from 3rd-century shipwreck survivors. India took in refugees from Nazi Germany and Poland, though after independence numbers fell from 45,000 to under 6,000, with many leaving for Israel. General Jack Jacob spearheaded India's victory in the Indo-Pakistan War of 1971. In 2012 he declared, 'I am proud to be a Jew, but am Indian through and through.'

Diversity and Orthodox Revival

PROBABLY NEVER BEFORE HAS THERE BEEN SUCH DIVERSITY IN JEWISH BELIEF AND WORSHIP. WHILE THOUSANDS OF JEWS ABANDON ALL TIES TO JUDAISM EACH YEAR, THOUSANDS MORE HAVE 'RETURNED TO FAITH'.

Today there are rabbis who insist that only commitment to all 613 commandments counts as Judaism, and others who deny the existence of God altogether. Judaism has experienced schism before, between Pharisees and Sadducees, Karaites and rabbis, Sabbateans and mainstream Jews, Hassidim and Mitnagedim. Since the mid-19th century, a formerly divided Orthodox camp closed ranks against new perceived common enemies: first Reform Judaism and the Haskalah, then overt atheism, revolutionary socialism, political Zionism, and latterly Western consumerism.

Today pious non-Hassidic Jews also don the black gabardines considered typical of Hassidim, in areas of New York, Stamford Hill in London, Me'ah She'arim in Jerusalem and Bnei Brak outside Tel Aviv.

Below Circle dancing to celebrate harvest at Kibbutz Tuval, Galilee. Communal activities are a vital part of kibbutz life.

These so-called ultra-Orthodox are collectively dubbed *haredim*, literally 'those who tremble [before God]'. With the exception of the Habad movement Lubavich, they tend to live apart from other Jews.

POST-WAR RECOVERY

The Holocaust destroyed traditional centres of Hassidism, and 70 years of Communist suppression virtually extinguished the trend in western Russia, once part of the Hassidic heartland. After the Soviet Union fell, Hassidism – and particularly the Lubavich – has experienced a revival. Today, Hassidic sects, invariably named after their place of origin, are thriving in America and Israel.

The Satmar group provides a remarkable example of Hassidism's phoenix-like recovery after the Holocaust. Now probably the largest Hassidic sect of all, it derives its name from the Hungarian city of Satu Mare. Under the dynamic leader-

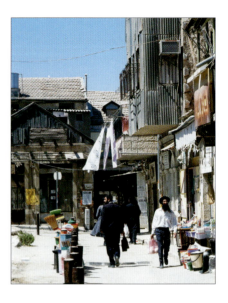

Above Jerusalem's strictly Orthodox Me'ah She'arim quarter – a throwback to 18th-century Europe.

ship of Rabbi Joelish Teitelbaum, who escaped Nazi persecution to Switzerland and briefly Palestine, Satmar reconstituted itself in Williamsburg, New York, and grew enormously by absorbing remnants of other Hungarian, Romanian and Transylvanian Hassidic sects.

RETURN TO FAITH

Ba'alei teshuva, signifying 'returnees to faith', represent perhaps the most remarkable Jewish religious trend of the past 20 years. Many found a home

THE KIBBUTZ

Perhaps the most thorough experiment in community living anywhere, the kibbutz or Israeli communal agricultural collective posited an alternative Jewish society free from religious domination. Money was banned, gender equality stressed and no one could study or travel outside without committee permission. After banking crises in the 1980s, kibbutzim could only survive by joining the economy, and utopian dreams were largely shelved.

in the Habad movement, another name for the Lubavich school of Hassidism. Lubavich has made a point of finding disaffected Jews seeking meaning in their lives.

Many factors account for the *ba'al teshuva* tendency: youthful rebellion during the 1960s, pride in Jewish identity after Israel's victory in the 1967 Six Day War, and disenchantment with Western social values. Some say *Ba'alei* resemble born-again Christians or Muslim *Salafi* revivalists.

SECULARISM AND RELIGION

Israel is not a theocratic Jewish state. The elected Knesset (parliament) determines all major laws, and rabbis rule over limited aspects of personal status. Today some 44 per cent of Israeli Jews call themselves secular, 36 per cent broadly traditionalist, 10 per cent religious and 10 per cent Haredi. Many strictly Orthodox men study full-time in yeshivas, and rely on working wives, charity and state remuneration to support their typically large families.

THE SETTLER MOVEMENT

Situated between the *haredim* and 'secular' Jews, are modern Orthodox Jews, called in Israel *dati leumi* or 'national religious'. Unlike the black-hatted *haredim*, they welcomed the State of Israel as 'the beginning of redemption' and preferred to integrate their faith with involvement in secular society. After 1967 the movement affiliated with the more radical beliefs of the Gush Emunim settler movement, and saw in Israel's conquest of the West Bank (location of ancient Judea and Samaria) a sign of an impending messianic age.

Extreme affiliates opposed attempts to trade land for peace; one zealot killed Prime Minister Rabin in 1995, and ten years later the Government's evacuation of Jewish settlements in Gaza prompted a minor revolt against a state that they felt had abandoned them.

Above Orthodox Jews cast bread into the Hudson, New York, for the tashlikh ceremony during Rosh Hashanah.

A NEW SPIRITUAL THIRST

Young American Jews and Israelis demobbed from the army, caught up in the counterculture mood of the 1960s, felt a craving for spirituality and a new interest in Kabbalah. Out of this arose attempts to reconstruct a hybrid Judaism for the New Age: the *Havurah*, or 'fellowship', movement; Jews in the Woods, an ecological movement nicknamed 'Fruity Jews'; the Jewish Renewal Project; and the New Jewish Catalog, a popular 1970s manual of customs and practices.

ATHEIST JUDAISM?

Standing outside mainstream Judaism are movements called Jews for Jesus and Messianic Jews, both of which see Jesus as fulfilling ancient Judaic promises. Their followers like Hebrew prayers and wish to retain Jewish culture, so they choose this path, not outright conversion to Christianity. Other Jews have organized counter-missionary activity to ward off their attempts to win followers.

20th-century America has produced two innovations for Jews who felt Jewish by identity, yet believed science had disproved the existence of a personal God. Under Mordechai Kaplan (1881–1983), Reconstructionist Judaism posited Judaism as an ever-changing civilization, the result of natural human development. It has 100 synagogues and favours inclusivity for woman. Humanistic Judaism, founded in 1958 by Rabbi Sherwin Wine (1928–2007), with perhaps 40,000 active members, takes pride in Jewish cultural achievements and ethical teachings. It comes closest to overt atheism and raises again the old question, can one be Jewish and not believe in God?

Below Revellers in costume at the Boombamela New Age festival at Nitsanim beach near Ashkelon.

Women in Jewish Society

'Patriarchal' Judaism is often seen as chauvinistic, yet even Orthodox Jews now strive for gender equality. Jewish women have contributed greatly to the arts, sciences and professions.

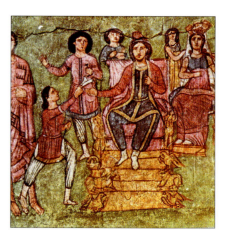

Above Biblical heroine Queen Esther with her uncle Mordechai. Dura-Europos mosaic, 2nd-century Syria.

While outsiders see discrimination against women in the ultra-Orthodox community, the Bible often suggests a different attitude. Women probably sang in Temple services and prayed with men at the Sanctuary in David's time. The matriarchs Sarah, Rebecca, Leah and Rachel are venerated as 'mothers of the Jewish people'. Moses' sister Miriam was called Israel's first prophet; the judge Deborah led in battle; and Queen Esther saved Jews from destruction in Persia. For all that, the abiding impression of the Old Testament is of a man's world.

Similar contradictions apply to Jewish practice. On the Sabbath a husband sings to his wife that she is a woman of worth; and the Talmud calls on a man to love his wife as himself and respect her even more. Yet there is a daily prayer for men to thank God for not making them women, and women in Orthodox synagogues cannot be rabbis, cantors or choristers. Separated from men by a *mechitza*, or 'barrier', they may not handle the Torah nor publicly recite from it, and cannot qualify for a *minyan*, or the quorum of ten men needed for a full service. Religious women hide their hair beneath *sheitls*, or 'wigs' or 'scarves'. Perhaps most controversial today is that Jewish law restricts women's activities during menstruation.

CHECKS AND BALANCES

Defenders of Orthodoxy argue that post-Talmudic checks and balances have guarded against sexist abuse. Formally a man may divorce a woman and not vice versa; yet the medieval Rabbeinu Gershom allowed women to petition a rabbinical council for an annulment and outlawed polygamy.

Women are exempt from many Torah commands because, argue the rabbis, they are innately more spiritual than men. They ruled that running the household equalled religious ritual. Many feminists see such attitudes as anachronistic and patronizing.

HISTORICAL COMPARISONS

In the past, Jewish women were not necessarily more oppressed than Christian and Muslim women. Jewish women were powerful independent merchants in England after 1066 and Judaism insisted that all women be literate. Apart from converts, someone is only Jewish if their mother is; the father's faith is irrelevant.

RELIGIOUS REFORM

Enlightenment values wrought significant change in certain synagogues. Reform thinkers referred back to the gender equality presumed in Genesis: 'God created man in His own image; male and female created He them'. As a result, both men and women lead services, read from the Torah and sing in choirs at American Reform and some Conservative synagogues. In 1922, Reconstructionist Rabbi Mordecai Kaplan had his daughter Judith take the first bat mitzvah, equal to the bar mitzvah for boys. However, only in 1935 was Regina Jonas ordained as the first female Reform rabbi, in Germany.

Unlike strictly observant Haredi and Hassidic Jews, modern Orthodox have gradually tried to make women feel more a part of religious services. They adopted a variant of the bat mitzvah, and since the mid-1970s

---

WOMEN PIONEERS

Increasingly, Jewish women are being recognized for their contributions. Some changed history, such as Dona Gracia who led Portuguese refugees to Turkey and Palestine, and Tannait Asenath Barzani of Mosul, yeshiva head in 17th-century Kurdistan. Women like Rahel Levin in Berlin, Genevieve Straus in Paris and Ada Leverson in London hosted salons, a practice revived by Gertrude Stein and Alice Toklas in 20th-century America. Western feminism is unimaginable without Betty Friedan, Andrea Dworkin, Erica Jong and Naomi Wolf.

Prolific Jewish women writers have included the South African Nobel laureate and enemy of apartheid Nadine Gordimer; Emma Lazarus, Lillian Hellman and Cynthia Ozick in America; Margo Glanz of Mexico and Marjorie Agosin of Chile; and Shulamit Hareven and Shifra Horn in Israel. Prominent women scientists include Rosalind Franklin, who helped unveil the DNA double helix; and Italy's Rita Levi-Montalcini, 1986 Nobel laureate for discovering the protein that makes nerves grow.

Above Hannah Arendt, political theorist and the first female professor at Princeton University, in 1960.

Above Pioneering child psychoanalyst Anna Freud in 1927 with her father, Sigmund Freud, and her niece Eve.

a Tefillah Network has arranged separate women's prayer groups and 'partnership *minyans*' where they read directly from the Torah.

FEMINISM

Jewish women were extremely prominent in the post-1960s feminist movement, but few addressed specifically Jewish concerns. A more pointedly Jewish critique started with Trude Weiss-Rosmarin, an American educationalist whose seminal 1970 article, 'The Unfreedom of Jewish Women', inspired a group to change Jewish laws. Tamar Ross, Rachel Adler, Paula Hyman and the Reform thinker Judith Plaskow (author of *Standing Again at Sinai*) have since amplified her views.

PROMINENT THINKERS

Jewish women often helped define 20th-century trends in society at large. They range from the cult novelist Ayn Rand to the political theorist Hannah Arendt. Susan Sontag wrote radical essays on photography and popular culture, while Yale professor Seyla Benhabib of Turkey addresses issues of globalization and multiculturalism.

AMBIGUITIES IN ISRAEL

In Israel, women serve a mandatory two years in the army. The kibbutz demanded absolute gender equality. In 1969 Golda Meir became Israel's prime minister, the first woman premier in the Middle East. Israel adopted laws of affirmative action for women in 1993. Yet women's rights, championed by politicians such as Yael Dayan and Ada Maimon, usually play second fiddle to issues of war and security.

Today campaigners fight Orthodox strictures on women's right to pray at the Western Wall; others challenge new Hebrew words that betray sexist bias; and the New Israel Fund has shelters for battered women. Women in Black have long marched in solidarity with Palestinians, and Machsom Watch monitors abuses at checkpoints in the territories. In response, rightist settlers set up their own Women in Green.

Female Israeli and Palestinian legislators jointly demanded greater women's involvement in peace brokering in 2005. Sceptics may doubt their chances, yet the record of the Four Mothers lobby, which forced Israel to withdraw from Lebanon in 2000, suggests further surprises in future.

Below Israeli woman soldier, Jerusalem, 1990. Women have been part of Israel's military since 1948.

Below A girl reads from the Torah for her bat mitzvah, initiation into the community equivalent to the bar mitzvah for boys.

MEDICINE AND SCIENCE

THE JEWISH DOCTOR HAS LONG BEEN A RECOGNIZED FIGURE ALL OVER THE WORLD. THE OPENING OF UNIVERSITIES TO JEWS DURING THE 19TH CENTURY LED HUGE NUMBERS INTO THE SCIENCES.

In the Bible, God is called the great healer. Because mankind is seen as completing God's worldly plans, the doctor is regarded as performing divine work; Jews are obliged to value *peku'ah nefesh*, or 'preservation of life'.

Whole sections of the Talmud prescribe remedies and cures, and concern embryology, pathology and intricate examination of medical conditions. Jewish philosophers often practised medicine, such as the 9th-century master of ophthalmology and court physician to the Fatimid Isaac Israeli. Many rabbis combined their duties with medical practice. Maimonides, the most obvious example, wrote ten medical works including *Aphorisms of Moshe* and *Regimen Sanitatis*, written in Judeo-Arabic. His view that a healthy body is essential for a healthy soul influenced doctors for generations.

FROM THE MIDDLE AGES TO THE 18TH CENTURY

During periods of liberality Jews studied medicine in the School of Salerno in 9th–12th century southern Italy, and at Jewish centres in 12th–13th century southern France. Jews served as physicians to Christian kings in Zaragoza, Toledo and Barcelona, and to Muslim sultans in Cairo and Cordoba. The 1492 Iberian expulsions disseminated Jewish medical knowledge to Holland, Germany, Denmark and the Ottoman empire.

MEDICINE IN EUROPE

Jews were still mostly excluded from the best European medical schools until two events dramatically changed matters: the Austrian Edict of Toleration of 1782 and the French Revolution of 1789. Jews poured into the universities and soon achieved remarkable successes. Tsarist edict still barred them from reaching their potential in Russia, and in Germany they were denied access to prestigious fields like surgery. None the less, they were pioneers in ignored areas – notably microscopy, neurology, biochemistry, haematology and psychiatry.

20TH-CENTURY BREAKTHROUGHS

Progress accelerated in the 20th century, although now the stress was on practical application of accumulated knowledge. Paul Ehrlich helped create chemotherapy and invented the first effective drug against syphilis in 1910; shortly after, Casimir Funk showed how vitamin B could counter beri-beri. Partially realizing Ehrlich's dream of a 'magic bullet' to destroy bacteria, the English Nobel Prize-winner Sir Boris Chain isolated penicillin, while other Jews, Harry Eagle and Maxwell Finland, pursued the new field of antibiotics.

In America, Jonas Salk discovered the polio vaccine and in 1963 founded the famous Salk Institute for Biological Studies at La Jolla, California. Albert Sabin, a pioneer in immunology and the relationship of viruses to cancer, invented the oral polio vaccine, which largely eliminated the disease after it was publicly released in 1961.

PHYSICS

As with medicine, Jewish scientists, physicists and chemists flourished with the academic advances of the 19th century. Similarly, the advent of Nazism in the 1930s saw a decided shift in talent from old Europe to America. One early pioneer was the Breslau-born Arthur Korn, who

Above Hans Krebs, German-born British doctor and biochemist who won a Nobel Prize in 1953.

Below Jonas Salk (1914–95), whose invention of a safe and effective polio vaccine in 1952 has nearly eradicated the disease worldwide.

transmitted the first photograph by wire. In the USA innovation and enterprise often went hand in hand, a prime example being Isaac Singer's famous sewing-machine invention, whose export to Britain in the 1860s boosted the still-nascent and Jewish-dominated tailoring trade.

There were few fields where Jews did not leave their mark. Abraham Sztern (1762–1842) pioneered early calculating devices, Siegfried Marcus (1831–98) invented an ignition device in 1864 and the first petrol-driven vehicle in 1870; David Schwartz (1852–97) built the first dirigible airship in 1896 (Count von Zeppelin bought the plans from his widow in 1898). Theodore von Kármán (1881–1963) pioneered supersonic aerodynamics, while Mikhael Gurevich, together with A.I. Mikoyan, built the first supersonic Soviet jet airfighters, the MiGs.

ALBERT EINSTEIN

Apart from creating the greatest upheaval in scientific thinking since Isaac Newton, Albert Einstein (1879–1955) became a prominent figure in Jewish affairs.

Einstein used his platform to criticize politicians and lambasted the abuse of science: 'In the hands of our generation these hard-won achievements are like a razor wielded by a child of three.' Einstein resigned his post at the Royal Prussian Academy of Sciences when Hitler took power in 1933 and never returned to Germany. Instead he travelled to Oxford, England, and eventually settled in Princeton, USA. He protested against the use of nuclear arms, although he was largely responsible for the technology that created the bomb.

A Zionist (if an idealistic and sometimes sceptical one), who agitated for peace between Jews and Arabs, Einstein was offered the presidency of Israel in 1950 but declined. Proud of his Jewish roots, he was an agnostic, although he said that 'The mysterious stands at the cradle of true art and true science'.

Above Two giants of nuclear physics conferring: Albert Einstein and Robert Oppenheimer.

CHEMISTRY

Jewish scientists have found chemistry a particularly fruitful field. In 1916 Fritz Haber won a Nobel Prize for synthesizing ammonia. The Austrian Karl Landsteine discovered the basic blood groups and the Rhesus blood factor. In Israel, Aharon Katzir (Katchalski) gained world fame for his work in polymer chemistry, while his brother, Ephraim, an expert in proteins at the Weizmann Institute, created synthetic fibres for use in internal stitching, and became Israel's fourth state president (1973–8). Aaron Klug, a South African, won a Nobel for his study of the three-dimensional structure of nucleic acids, proteins and viruses.

THE LIFE SCIENCES

Jews in zoology, botany and biology included Julius Sachs, the creator of experimental botany; Lawrence Bogorad, professor of biology at Harvard; and Moses Ezekiel, one of the world's leading economic botanists. Waldemar Mordecai Haffkine developed the first effective vaccine against cholera in 1892. Otto Loewi and Sir Bernard Katz won Nobel Prizes for discovering how nerves work. From 1950 to 1967 Jewish scientists won 11 of the 46 Nobels for biology.

SPLITTING THE ATOM ...

Jewish scientists, who won 48 of the 174 Nobel Prizes in the field of physics from 1901–2004, have played a disproportionate role in atom-splitting studies, the best known of all being Albert Einstein. Another was Max Born, an early master of quantum physics and probability theory.

It was Einstein's letter to President Roosevelt that launched America's top-secret Los Alamos Manhattan Project and created the world's first atomic bomb. The Manhattan team included many great Jewish nuclear physicists, like the American Robert Oppenheimer, and Edward Teller, later credited with inventing the hydrogen bomb.

Left Italian neurologist and 1986 Nobel Medicine prize-winner Rita Levi-Montalcini celebrated her 100th birthday in style.

Jewish Artists and Themes in Art

ART HAS LONG POSED A QUANDARY FOR JEWS: THE TALMUD PRAISES BEAUTIFUL HOLY OBJECTS BUT THE TORAH ITSELF FORBIDS THE 'GRAVEN IMAGE', THUS PRODUCING ART WAS SOMETIMES SEEN AS REJECTING JUDAISM ITSELF.

Although synagogues banned human images, Pharaoh, Moses, Egyptians and Israelites peopled the pages of illustrated Passover *haggadahs*. Calligraphy became a fine art, as did micrography, which formed patterns and pictures from tiny marginal notes in the Torah.

DAWN OF THE NAMED ARTIST
Notions of the named individual artist bypassed Jews, until Moritz Oppenheim (1800–82) began painting elegant portraits of Jewish notables and biblical themes in German Romantic tones. Polish-born Maurycy Gottlieb (1856–79) painted *Shylock and Jessica* and *Jews Praying on Yom Kippur*.

In Holland the contemplative Jozef Israels (1824–1911) was hailed as a reincarnation of Rembrandt. Max Liebermann (1847–1935) shocked German salons with his overtly Jewish painting of *Twelve-year-old Jesus in the Temple*, though he later became the doyen of genteel portraiture and landscapes.

REBELLION AND SUPPRESSION
In eastern Europe the 1881 pogroms bred not only works of despair, but also Lazar Krestin's defiant *Birth of Jewish Resistance* (1905). Not all Jews felt obliged to paint 'Jewish themes'. The work of pioneering Impressionists Camille Pissarro and Isaac Israels reflected little explicit Jewish content.

Paris fostered new trends during 1900–40 such as Fauvism, Cubism, Dadaism and Surrealism, attracting Russian Jews like Marc Chagall and Chaim Soutine and Sephardi Jews like Amadeo Modigliani (Italian) and Jules Pascin (Bulgarian). This 'Jewish School' varied in style from Modigliani's African inspirations to Soutine's anxious Expressionism; only Chagall depicted Jewish imagery. 'Were I not a Jew', he wrote in his 1931 autobiography, 'I would not be an artist at all.'

Stalinism and Nazism stamped out individual expression. In 1933 Nazis sacked Max Liebermann as president of the prestigious Berlin Art Academy.

Above Prolific and ever innovative, the artist Marc Chagall celebrates his 90th birthday in 1977.

Work by Jews was judged 'degenerate' and all non-representative art was considered the handicraft of Jews, even if the artist was 'Aryan'. Paradoxically, this drove creative talents into exile where they spread their radical ideas.

BRITAIN AND THE USA
A remarkable flowering of Jewish artists occurred in Britain at the turn of the 20th century. The movement's godfather was Sir William Rothenstein, an Impressionist painter and principal of London's Royal College of Art (1920–35). His most talented pupil was Mark Gertler (1891–1939), who never forgot his Jewish roots, as seen in *The Rabbi and his Grandchild* (1913).

In 1914 David Bomberg's London Group organized the first exhibition of modern Jewish artists. Two German Jewish painters arrived in Britain in the 1930s: Sigmund Freud's grandson Lucian, a leading Representational portraitist, and the earthy Expressionist Frank Auerbach. England's Cecil Roth was the first true historian of Jewish art.

American art took the lead in daring abstraction, such as the 'colour

Left Jacob Epstein's powerful group sculpture *Social Consciousness*, 1954, stands today in Philadelphia.

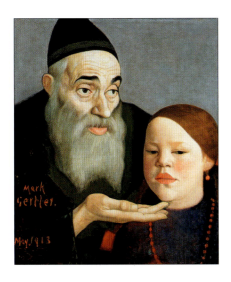

Above The Rabbi and his Grandchild, *a compelling portrait by Anglo-Jewish artist Mark Gertler, 1913.*

> ### ART THAT SERVES FAITH
> Jews have used art from earliest times, often in the service of religion. The *mezuzah*, a doorpost prayer case, can be made of wood, ivory, metal or even sculpted coloured plastic. Ashkenazic coverings for Torah scrolls are made from embroidered cloth, and silver breastplates, and Sephardi *tik* boxes from wood or metal. The Torah is decorated with silver crowns and bells and a *yad*, an ivory pointer shaped like a tiny hand. Jewish craftsmen decorate the Sabbath loaf cloth, twin candlesticks and spice boxes.
>
> Over time calligraphers and miniaturists illustrated flowers and pretty scenes on the *ketubah* or 'traditional marriage document'. Particularly beautiful *ketubot* (pl.) were made in Bohemia, Italy, Egypt, Persia, Jerusalem, Yemen, India and Afghanistan. Other objects treated artistically include kiddush cups, Hannukah lamps, Passover plates and even circumcision tools.

field' innovations of Mark Rothko and Adolph Gottlieb. Pop artist George Segal (1934–) invokes classical Jewish topics, such as Abraham sacrificing Isaac.

THE SCULPTED IMAGE
Even more than painting, sculpture represented a special taboo due to its association with idols. The first Jewish pioneer was Vilna-born Mark Antokolski (1843–1902), whose early Realist sculptures depicted such scenes as 'The Talmudic Debate' and 'Jewish Tailor'. More modern in ethos, the American-born British sculptor Jacob Epstein (1880–1959) continually quoted biblical themes: Adam, the Sacrifice of Isaac, Genesis, and Jacob and the Angel. Even more influential was the Cubist sculptor Lithuanian-born Jacques Lipchitz (1891–1973), who escaped Paris for America as Nazis invaded in 1941.

ART IN ISRAEL
Zionist ideologues wished to create a 'new Hebrew' on Palestinian soil. Biblical scenes inspired Jakob Steinhardt; Yemenite settlers and local Arab farmers caught Reuven Rubin's imagination. Both studied at the Betzalel art and crafts academy, named after Moses' master craftsman and founded in Jerusalem in 1906 by Boris Schatz, a court sculptor in Bulgaria. In 1965 Betzalel's gallery turned into the Israel Museum, now the world's largest repository of Israeli art. Since then, Israelis have moved from 'Jewish imagery' to more universal, individual and abstract concerns.

PHOTOGRAPHY
When US galleries admitted photographs by Alfred Stieglitz, other Jews, such as the French Surrealist Man Ray and Hungarians André Kertész and Laszlo Moholy-Nagy began turning craft into fine art. Several exploited photography's documentary potential, for example German-born Alfred Eisenstaedt and Budapest-born Robert Capa in *LIFE* magazine, or Roman Vishniac, who shot the last days of Europe's *shtetls* and Jewish quarters.

Mary Ellen Mark, Diane Arbus and Lee Friedlander observed contemporary US life, and Judah Passow and David Rubinger have chronicled Israel at war and peace. Examples of creative commercial portraiture and fashion include the baroque style of Irving Penn, the psychological work of Arnold Newman, the experimentalism of Cindy Sherman (USA) and Jeanloup Sieff (France), and Annie Leibovitz's elegant, often ironic studies of celebrities.

> ### LOOTED ART
> During World War II the Nazis took 100,000 art pieces from France alone; some 60,000 were recovered, of which 45,000 were returned to their owners or heirs, invariably Jews. Reparation for lost or 'looted' art is a controversial issue now and has proven a good opportunity to re-inspect some fabulous gems. Ironically Germans seemed passionate for abstract art, or art by Jews, given what Nazi propaganda called it.

Right A chronicler of a lost world, *photographer Roman Vishniac shot this image of a child in Warsaw, 1938.*

Jewish Writers and Literature

IT IS OFTEN QUESTIONED WHETHER ALL WRITING BY JEWS IS BY DEFINITION 'JEWISH LITERATURE'. MANY ARGUE THAT EVEN WHEN JEWS WRITE ABOUT GENERAL TOPICS A JEWISH SENSIBILITY INFORMS THEIR WORDS.

Creative writing by Jews, even when its content is secular, has had a powerful impact on surrounding cultures: imagine German literature without Heinrich Heine or Franz Kafka, American writing without Saul Bellow or Arthur Miller, or Chilean literature without Ariel Dorfman.

THE BIBLICAL WELLSPRING

Before the 19th century, Jews concentrated on religious writing. Many wrote commentaries on what is arguably the most widely read and influential of all literary works, the Hebrew Bible. The Bible contains literary elements: plots, characterization, drama and violence, family sagas and personal rivalries. Though mostly written in prose, the Bible also includes the first instances of Hebrew poetry, in the songs of Deborah and Miriam, and the Song of Songs.

Below A scribe, or sofer, *painstakingly writing out holy verses before the advent of printing. From Rothschild Miscellany, northern Italy, c.1450–80.*

From the Oral Tradition came the Talmud's Aggadah, Midrashic stories loosely based on the Bible, and later mystical works such as the Zohar. These inspired medieval Spanish Hebrew poets including Samuel ibn Nagrela and Solomon Ibn Gabirol, who described intimate personal feelings alongside religious themes. Peaceful times brought cultural cross-fertilization: Judah Halevi and Moses Ibn Ezra incorporated Arabic metre into their poetry, and Joseph ibn Zabara's popular *Book of Delights* showed intimate knowledge of Arab, Greek and Indian folklore.

WRITING IN YIDDISH

Early Yiddish exponents included such women as Glückel of Hameln, or were specifically aimed at women, such as the Bible compendium *Tsena u-Rena*. Abraham Goldfaden was hailed as the 'Yiddish Shakespeare'. In 1876 in Romania he founded the first professional Yiddish language theatre. He wrote 40 plays, before he died in New York. Some have dis-

Above Ludwig Zamenhof, who wrote the first grammar of Yiddish.

missed his works as 'low culture', and his rival the Russian-born American playwright Jacob Gordin responded with adventurous plays like *The Jewish Queen Lear*.

L.L. Zamenhof, who gave respect to Yiddish with its first grammar book, written in 1879, was the same man who invented Esperanto. The trio of Yiddish masters were Mendele Moikher Sforim, social critic and idealist; Sholem Aleichem, much-loved author of Tevye tales (later staged as *Fiddler on the Roof*); and Isaac Leib Peretz, a modernist who believed in self-emancipation.

Since the 1970s a desire to 'return to roots' revived Jewish interest in Yiddish culture. While secular Yiddish remains mainly a studied language, the remarkable growth of Orthodox families guarantees that the argot survives in New York, London and Jerusalem.

Three institutions epitomized the extraordinary outpouring of Yiddish creativity in the 1930s: the Moscow State Jewish Theatre, founded in 1920; the YIVO Jewish Scientific Institute, founded in 1925; and after 1929, 'Young Vilna', a leftist band of artists, writers, polemicists and educators. YIVO and Young Vilna were devastated by the Holocaust, and survivors fled to the Soviet Union or America, where the Singer brothers, Isaac Bashevis and Israel Joshua, had already taken refuge.

POETIC REBIRTH IN PALESTINE AND ISRAEL

Hebrew began replacing Yiddish and Ladino as 'the' Jewish language in 20th-century Palestine, and the greatest Hebrew writers of the 1920s, Haim Nahman Bialik, Ahad Ha-Am and Saul Tchernichowsky, settled in Tel Aviv. By 1940 more books were published for Palestine's 500,000 Jews than for their 5 million American cousins.

Israeli novelists are now widely read and often raise uncomfortable issues, at times questioning Israel's founding myths. S. Yizhar wrote two novellas during the 1948 war, *Khirbet Khizah* and *The Prisoner*, which contrasted Jewish experience of pogroms with their contemporary attitudes to Arabs. Yizhar belonged to the War of Independence generation of writers, as does the nationalist poet Haim Gouri and author and playwright Moshe Shamir. The more sceptical Aharon Appelfeld is the author of *Badenheim 1939*, a darkly satirical work.

Below Topol played the lead in Fiddler on the Roof, *from Sholem Aleichem's stories about Tevye the milkman.*

Internationally recognized stars of the post-1967 generation include Amos Oz, A.B. Yehoshua and David Grossman, who trace the interplay of memory, love, friendship and responses to conflict. Newer voices have expressed fresh views, such as Etgar Keret's cartoon-like pop fables. Additionally Israeli Arabs such as Anton Shammas, Emil Habiby and Sayed Kashua have used dark humour in Hebrew to express the ambiguity of non-Jewish indigenes living in a Jewish state.

HEBREW ON STAGE

Founded in Moscow in 1917, Habimah (The Stage) was probably the first Hebrew theatre company in the world. Tel Aviv's Kameri theatre won acclaim for plays by the popular satirist Hanoch Levin and others. Smaller groups, including Arab and Jewish troupes in Akko and Jaffa, address intercommunal strife and the trauma of regional conflict.

New writers have introduced a distinctive female voice, with Orly Castel-Bloom (1960–) leading the way in her controversial urban satire, *Dolly City*. Others include Savyon Librecht (1948–), Ronit Matalon (1959–), and Dorit Rabinyan (1972–), author of *Persian Brides*. In their different ways, all describe the place of Diaspora memory in contemporary Israeli society.

WRITERS IN THE DIASPORA

Moses Mendelssohn, godfather of the Haskalah, used German and Hebrew in his essays. Later, Heinrich Heine wrote in German, followed by Joseph Roth, Franz Rosenzweig, Franz Kafka and Arnold Zweig. Writers Arthur Schnitzler and Jakob Wasserman urged fellow Jews to fully absorb German culture, until World War II changed their minds. Few Jews still wrote in German after 1945, an exception being the poetess and playwright Nelly Sachs, a 1966 Nobel Prize-winner.

Above A Swedish poet born in Germany, Nelly Sachs shared the Nobel Prize for Literature with Israeli author Shmuel Yosef Agnon in 1966.

JEWISH THEMES

Despite his Jewish origins, Marcel Proust wrote only tangentially on Jewish issues. By contrast, the Swiss-born Jewish essayist Edmond Fleg wrote biographies of Moses, Solomon and Jesus; and Andre Schwartz-Bart's *Last of the Just*, a Jewish historical novel from the Crusades to Auschwitz, is a French classic. George Perec survived the Holocaust to write daringly experimental French literature.

Sholem Aleichem used humour to instruct 'greenhorns' how to acclimatize to American conditions. Generations later, nostalgic books appeared such as *The Apprenticeship of Duddy Kravitz*, by the Canadian Mordechai Richler, or the fictitious Hyman Kaplan, subject of short stories by New York writer Leo Rosten. By now, authors had moved from immigrant literature to the American mainstream. They wrote in English and included two authors fascinated with Zionist settlement, the poet Jessie Sampter, who went to Palestine in 1919, and the intrepid Chicago-born novelist Meyer Levin.

THE JEWISH IMAGE IN LITERATURE

By the late 18th century, Christian writers showed renewed interest in Jewish themes. Gottfried Lessing's German plays *The Jews* and *Nathan the Wise* championed dignified Jews in the face of prevailing bigotry; and romanticism about an ancient, persecuted yet talented people partly countered the anti-Semitic depictions of Jews of 19th-century England.

By contrast, stereotypes of Jewish swindlers persisted, perhaps the most famous being Shakespeare's Shylock in *The Merchant of Venice*. In the 19th century Charles Dickens introduced Fagin in *Oliver Twist*. Shocked when readers saw his depiction as anti-Semitic, Dickens introduced a more sympathetic character in his last completed book, *Our Mutual Friend*, called Mr Riah, 'the gentle Jew in whose race gratitude is deep'.

Above Fagin, Charles Dickens' villain from Oliver Twist, *suggested a negative view of Jews as criminals.*

Literature often treated Jews sympathetically when they were few on the ground, but when their numbers increased the mood changed. In *The American Scene* (1907), Henry James complained of 'a Jewry that had burst all bounds... There is no swarming like that of Israel'. T.S. Eliot and F. Scott Fitzgerald indulged in commonplace anti-Semitism, though by the 1930s backtracked somewhat when such views were associated with Fascism.

One writer who championed the oppressed Jews of Russia was Maxim Gorky (1868–1936). Though not himself Jewish he defended Jewish rights during the 1903 Tsarist pogroms, and after the 1917 October Revolution, which he supported, he wrote his 1918 story *Pogrom*.

AMERICAN WRITERS

Isaac Bashevis Singer was an exception who still wrote in Yiddish. In 1978 Singer became the first Yiddish author to win the Nobel Prize for Literature. Although located in a Jewish setting, Singer's writing discussed issues that affect all society.

Bernard Malamud's Jewish self-awareness shines through in *Dubin's Lives* and *The Jewbird*. 'Everybody is a Jew but they don't know it', he wrote, suggesting Western urbanites now share what used to be a Jewish preserve – displacement and the need to juggle multiple identities.

Canadian-born Saul Bellow, a 1976 Nobel laureate, became perhaps America's top literary stylist who dissected post-war alienation in *Herzog* and *Humboldt's Gift*. Chaim Potok's more populist books threw a spotlight on an Orthodox world long ignored by the US literati, while Joseph Heller, whose *Catch 22* was a cult best-seller, later wrote ribald works like *God Knows* about King David. Even Allen Ginsberg, Beatnik poet and Buddhist convert, drew on his Jewish roots in *Howl* and *Kaddish*.

Norman Mailer's works straddled journalism and fiction, starting with *The Naked and the Dead*, 1948, and essays on Vietnam protest, radicalism and conservatism. Probably most searing in his critique of contemporary Jewry was Philip Roth, with *Goodbye Columbus* and *Portnoy's Complaint*, full of sexual fantasies and jibes at a domineering mother.

ENGLISH AUTHORS

Israel Zangwill (1864–1926), known as the Jewish Dickens, wrote *King of the Schnorrers*, a comedy that shot a few broadsides at the Sephardi elite. His magnum opus *Children of the Ghetto* introduced the vibrant Jewish East End to a wider readership. Later Anglo-Jewish writers have included such bold voices as

Below Isaac Bashevis Singer, first Yiddish novelist to receive a Nobel Prize for Literature, in 1978.

Below South African writer, political activist and winner of the 1991 Nobel Prize for Literature, Nadine Gordimer.

Above Arthur Miller, who received the Pulitzer Prize for Drama in 1949 for Death of a Salesman, *at the United States Jewish Culture Awards in 1995.*

Howard Jacobson, who won the Man Booker Prize in 2010, Clive Sinclair and Linda Grant.

Commonwealth writers include the South African Dan Jacobson, who often depicts the Jewish immigrant experience, and Nobel laureate Nadine Gordimer, an early foe of apartheid (racial segregation), who won the Nobel Prize for Literature in 1991. Smaller numbers of South African Jews wrote in Yiddish, Hebrew and Afrikaans, while in India, Bnei Israel member Nissim Ezekiel was called the leading English-language poet.

RUSSIAN STARS

While in 1897 only 1.3 per cent of the Pale's Jews spoke Russian, the rest Yiddish, 100 years later that ratio was reversed. The trend accelerated after the Revolution and led to passionate writing in Russian from the likes of Isaac Babel, reporter of Jewish Odessa and the vanishing shtetl, and later Boris Pasternak, Vassily Grossman and Nadezhda Mandelstam. Born in Russia and expelled in 1972, Joseph Brodsky, Nobel laureate of 1987, settled in the USA where he stated: 'I am Jewish – a Russian poet and an English essayist'.

THE ITALIAN LEGACY

Italy's small Jewish population has produced an amazing number of authors. Giorgio Bassani in *Garden of the Finzi-Continis* showed wealthier Jews surprised by fascist race laws. Others wrote 'non-Jewish' gems, such as Carlo Levi's paean to peasant life, *Christ Stopped at Eboli*. Primo Levi strove to understand the other Jewish worlds he encountered as a prisoner in Auschwitz. Some call his understated works the most powerful Holocaust literature written. Italian Jewish authors also include Alberto Moravia, Elsa Morante, Cesare Pavese, Natalia Ginzburg and Italo Svevo.

ASHKENAZIM WRITING IN SPANISH

Latin American Jewish writers tend to display spiritual restlessness and a passion for justice. Jacobo Timerman, a Ukrainian-born Argentine and author of *Prisoner Without a Name, Cell Without a Number,* was jailed for his dissident writings. Alicia Partnoy wrote about her experiences as a political prisoner in Argentina in *The Little School*. Cultural anthopologist Ruth Behar writes about her experience as a Cuban Jewish woman.

PLAYWRIGHTS

Loved on both sides of the English-speaking Atlantic, Arthur Miller wrote plays with few overtly Jewish characters, although recognizable Jewish types. Another prolific dramatist who addressed social ills was Lillian Hellman. Her successors have since pricked the nation's conscience on issues from racism and Vietnam to AIDS and infidelity. More recently Yasmina Reza, the French-based daughter of a Persian father and Hungarian mother, both Jewish, won fame in English translation for *Art*, a pastiche of 1990s materialism.

Right British playwright and political activist Harold Pinter was awarded the Nobel Prize for Literature in 2005.

Above Howard Jacobson, celebrated Anglo-Jewish writer and columnist, who won the 2010 Man Booker Prize for Fiction, for The Finkler Question.

In Britain, leading playwrights of Jewish origin include the late Jonathan Miller, Mike Leigh and the Czech-born Tom Stoppard, renowned for witty philosophical dramas. Frantisek Langer was one of Czechoslovakia's leading interwar playwrights. Many musical writers of modern America were Jewish, such as Irving Berlin, Richard Rodgers, Oscar Hammerstein II and Stephen Sondheim, and Jews are well represented as directors and scriptwriters for radio and television drama series. Additionally, Jews have contributed disproportionately to cinema, perhaps the quintessential art form of the 20th century.

Jewish Culture in Modern Society

Hollywood and Beyond

CINEMA DEVELOPED FROM HUMBLE ORIGINS IN THE 1890S TO BECOME PERHAPS THE DEFINING ART FORM OF THE 20TH CENTURY, AND FROM THE START JEWS WERE INTIMATELY INVOLVED IN THE INDUSTRY.

At first promoters and producers, then directors, scriptwriters, actors and composers, by 1912 Jews had set up over a hundred production companies in California, and were pivotal to the creation of the eight super-firms.

RAGS TO RICHES

Almost to a man – and they were all men – the Jewish movie moguls were born into poverty. Carl Laemmle, the 10th of 13 immigrant children, managed a clothes shop before running a string of nickelodeons and in 1912 founding Universal, the first big studio. Louis Mayer joined the junk trade at 8, owned a New York theatre-chain at 22 and produced the epic *Birth of a Nation* in 1915, aged 30. Adolph Zukor, who founded Paramount Pictures in 1917, was born in Hungary, emigrated at 15 and peddled fur garments.

A similar rags-to-riches story applied to the Warner Brothers, sons of a Jewish cobbler from Poland. In 1927 they amazed the filmic world by harnessing new technology to produce the first 'talkie'. Starring Al Jolson, *The Jazz Singer* presented Jewish family dilemmas about tradition and assimilation to a mainstream audience. In the 1930s cinema blossomed. MGM's Irving Thalberg released *Mutiny on the Bounty* in 1936; and David Selznik produced the immortal box-office sensation *Gone with the Wind* in 1939.

FILMS ABOUT JEWISHNESS

Jewish themes became ever more rare, as moguls deliberately played down ethnic traits. The same cannot be said of Yiddish cinema, or of shorter American films that targeted Jewish immigrants. Three basic types prevailed: the ghetto melodrama, the historical pogrom saga and the vaudeville comedy. The Marx Brothers films of the 1930s used humour that was Jewish in origin, and made it universally popular, appealing to anyone who ever had to deal with petty bureaucrats.

Above A Night at the Opera – brothers Groucho, Chico and Harpo Marx hamming it up in 1935.

GERMAN CINEMA

By the 1920s, cinema had spread worldwide, and in Germany, Jewish producer Erich Pommer made *The Cabinet of Dr Caligari*, which set a benchmark for creativity. Fritz Lang directed *Metropolis*, a futuristic critique of industrial society, and *M*, a Kafkaesque murder drama starring a young Peter Lorre. Unlike their Polish cousins, German Jews fostered a cosmopolitan rather than a particularly Jewish sensibility.

Nazism decimated this short-lived flowering, and most Jewish directors, actors, producers and technicians left Germany for London, Paris, Amsterdam or Hollywood. Ernst Lubitsch had already come to America in 1923, and top directors and actors Josef von Sternberg, Billy Wilder, Erich von Stroheim, Fred Zinnemann and the Vienna-born Otto Preminger soon followed. Meanwhile German cinema produced anti-Semitic dramas such as *The Eternal Jew*.

Left Gillo Pontecorvo realized the power of cinema with his searing 1959 debut about the Holocaust, *Kapo*.

Above Woody Allen faces Diane Keaton in his 1977 MGM comedic classic Annie Hall.

ÉMIGRÉS IN BRITAIN

British cinema received a boost from talented central European Jews such as Alexander Korda. He moved to Britain in 1930 and nurtured actors and films tailored to the American market, such as *Rembrandt*, *The Scarlet Pimpernel* and *The Third Man*.

Sir Michael Balcon graduated from Alfred Hitchcock films to Ealing comedies. Canadian-born Harry Saltzman produced the edgy *Look Back in Anger* (1959) and then a string of James Bonds. Karel Reisz, one of 669 Czech Jewish children who Sir Nicholas Winton rescued from the Nazis, defined the social realistic cinema of post-war Britain in *We are the Lambeth Boys*, *This Sporting Life* and *Saturday Night and Sunday Morning*. London-born John Schlesinger picked up the baton with *Billy Liar* and *Midnight Cowboy*. Other Anglo-Jewish directors are Michael Winner and Mike Leigh.

JEWISH THEMES

After World War II many French, Italian, Czech and Polish film directors addressed Jewish themes. In his 1959 directorial debut, *Kapo*, Gillo Pontecorvo broached the awkward subject of Jews who collaborated or adopted false identities to survive the death camps. In France, *Le vieil homme et l'enfant* by Claude Berri focused on Jews who hid in wartime. After his light-hearted *Mazel Tov*, about a Jewish wedding, he won fame in 1986 with *Jean de Florette* and *Manon des Sources*. *Soleil* (1993), by Algerian-born Jewish actor-director David Hanin, began a trend of films about the North African Jewish experience.

The Diary of Anne Frank (1959) was the first Hollywood film to focus on the plight of Jews in the Holocaust; followed by *Judgment at Nuremburg* (1961). There was renewed interest in a pre-American past: *Fiddler on the Roof* revived nostalgia for the *shtetl* while recognizing its imperfections. Jewish women appeared in the 1970s in a non-stereotypical way in *The Way We Were* starring Barbara Streisand, *Hester Street* and *Girlfriends*. New Jewish characters emerged: gamblers, lesbians, cowboys, hit-men and even whorehouse madams.

The comedies of Woody Allen and Mel Brooks turned the comic Jewish *nebbish* (hopeless case) into a representative of late 20th-century angst. *The Frisco Kid* (1979) showed Jewish values and American pragmatism clashing in the US. Steven Spielberg and Roman Polanski viewed the Holocaust anew with *Schindler's List* and *The Pianist*.

Below Film director Steven Spielberg with the cast of Schindler's List, *1993*.

> ### JEWISH HUMOUR
> From the Yiddish writer Sholem Aleichem on paper to the earliest comic films, Jewish humour has been prized as characteristic of its people, even if at times it sails close to the edge of anti-Semitic typecast. What, though, makes it distinctly Jewish? One element is the *nebbish* or hopeless case. Since ghetto days the genre has been reincarnated in Marx Brothers and Woody Allen films.
>
> Mel Brooks and Zero Mostel translated Jewish wit into zany and surreal films, Jerry Seinfeld pushed the boundaries of the television sitcom and the politically incorrect Jackie Mason delighted and shocked audiences. Meanwhile, Sandra Bernhardt, Sarah Silverman, Barbra Streisand and Goldie Hawn have mocked the image of the spoilt JAP (Jewish American Princess) or deliberately subverted the stereotype of the domineering 'Jewish mother'.

> ### ISRAELI CINEMA
> Most Israeli films have focused on a real Israel full of social tensions and ordinary concerns. The real maturation of Israeli cinema came after the 1967 war.
>
> Directors have tackled such former taboos as the treatment of Holocaust orphans (*Summer of Aviyah*), Arabs and Jews in prison (*Beyond the Walls*), homosexuality (*The Bubble*) and the cost of war (*Avanti Popolo, Ricochets, Cup Final* and *Beaufort*).

MUSIC AND MUSICIANS

THE PROPHET ISAIAH PROCLAIMED, 'MAKE SWEET MELODY, SING MANY SONGS, THAT THOU MAYEST BE REMEMBERED'. FORBIDDEN FROM EXPRESSING THEMSELVES THROUGH THE GRAVEN IMAGE, JEWS TOOK TO MUSIC WITH ZEAL.

The songs of Miriam and Deborah are just two examples of early Jewish music. It has thrived, in both sacred and secular formats, while individual Jews have contributed immeasurably to Western classical, jazz, pop and folk.

The Bible and Talmud speak of elaborate musical arrangements associated with Temple rites and sacrifices, and even singing 'duty rosters' for Levite choristers. Performances featured 12 instruments – including pipes, whistles, bells, horns, cymbals, *halil* flutes, the *kinnor* and *nevel* lyres and the *tof* frame-drum.

A great breach occurred when Rome destroyed the Second Temple in Jerusalem in 70CE. After that calamity, Jews shunned the use of instruments for sacred music as a sign of mourning. This ban was soon lifted outside places of worship. Wedding parties stimulated religious melodies and secular festivities wherever Jews settled.

Below *Broadway pioneers George and Ira Gershwin were influenced by Yiddish theatre and popular Jewish music.*

RAM'S HORN
The exception to the ban on synagogue instruments is the *shofar*, the ram's horn, which is blown on Rosh Hashanah, the Jewish New Year. The *shofar* is meant to awaken people from their spiritual slumber and call them to repentance. One name for Rosh Hashanah is Yom Teru'ah, or the 'day of blowing'. The instrument is arguably the oldest known to mankind.

CHANTING AND MELODY
Other than the *shofar* and organs at weddings, all Orthodox synagogue music is sung. One sage called singing 'the fruit of the mouth'. The oldest modes are reserved for chanting weekly portions of the Torah and Prophets, and special markings written above and below the holy words, called *te'amim*, denote their tune.

Early medieval synagogues allowed more tuneful leeway with hymns and *piyuttot*, or liturgical poetry. These were and still are sung to a particular *nusah*, or melody pattern, akin to the Arabic *maqam*, Indian raga, Byzantine hymnody or Roman plainsong. The *nusah* denotes special times, so that someone with a discerning ear can enter a synagogue blindfolded and immediately tell from hearing everyday prayers, like the *amidah*, whether it is the Sabbath, a high holy day, morning service or evening service.

CANTORS AND CHOIRS
Over time the virtuoso *hazzan* (cantor) began to displace the more humdrum *shaliach tzibbur*, or prayer leader, and his role increased as congregants' knowledge of Hebrew diminished. The period between the two world wars is known as the 'golden age of *hazzanut*'.

Above *Frank London and his Klezmatics use jazz to breathe life into old European Jewish klezmer.*

The synagogue choir, originally an *ad hoc* body of harmonic responders, grew in stature and opulence with exposure to Western classical music. In 1882 the Polish-born Jewish composer Louis Lewandowski scored an entire choral service, *Todah ve-Zimrah*, or 'Thanks and Song', for Berlin's Oranienburgerstrasse Temple.

KLEZMER
From the 16th century, eastern European *Klezmorim*, or 'wandering folk musicians', and the *badchen* (jester or compère), were staple fare at weddings. Like their Sephardi counterparts, Ashkenazim absorbed local tunes and techniques into their repertoires. Players employed plaintive or ecstatic ornamentation and also mimicked the synagogue *hazzan* or fervent Hassidic *nigun* (often wordless improvisations). The resultant mixture gives *klezmer* its distinctive 'Jewish feel' to this day.

Since the 1970s klezmer and ladino have revived as Diaspora Jews rediscovered their roots. Some adherents favour hybrids with rock, folk and jazz, such as the American group, Klezmatics. Interestingly, some of the most skilful klezmer practitioners are non-Jewish Germans, like Tickle in the Heart, or Poles, like Kroke.

Above Gustav Mahler, *perhaps the greatest composer of Jewish origin, in the loggia of Vienna Opera House, 1907.*

CLASSICAL COMPOSERS

Medieval Arab theorists inspired Jews to study music as a science, and in time certain Italian and Provençal Jews embraced secular music composition.

The 19th-century enlightenment led to an explosion of Jewish talent in Germany and France, with composers like Felix and Fanny Mendelssohn, Claude Offenbach, Fromental Halévy, Giacomo Meyerbeer and Gustav Mahler. Many became Christians, thus casting doubt on their definition as 'Jewish composers'. Even so, hints of *klezmer* and synagogue melody appear in the majestic orchestrations of the newly Catholic Mahler.

Arnold Schoenberg shocked audiences with atonal experimentations, and inspired numerous imitators after fleeing Austria for America in 1934. More conventional were the American Jewish composers Aaron Copland and Leonard Bernstein. Both evoked a specifically American classical oeuvre, as in Copland's *Appalachian Spring* and Bernstein's *West Side Story*. In more contemplative works such as *Chichester Psalms* and his Third Symphony *Kaddish*, Bernstein set Hebrew texts to modern music.

Jews including Philip Glass and Steve Reich pioneered minimalism and experimentation with electronics in the 1960s. Both addressed Jewish themes – Glass in his *Einstein on the Beach* and Reich in *Tehillim* (Psalms), *Proverb*, *The Cave* (about Abraham and Hebron) and *Different Trains*, which evokes trucks en route to Auschwitz.

Jews have excelled as virtuoso performers, including pianists Arthur Rubinstein and Vladimir Ashkenazy.

JEWS AND JAZZ

From the early 1900s, black American and Jewish musicians practised and performed together in large cities like Chicago and New York. Several Yiddish tunes were reinterpreted as Jazz numbers, including *Burton on the Ritz*, derived from *Bei Mir Bist Du Shein*. Al Jolson moved from traditional Jewish music to become a leading Jazz, blues and ragtime singer.

Others who followed Jolson's Tin Pan Alley path included the songwriter Irving Berlin and Brazilian jazz diva, Flora Purim. George Gershwin bridged the chasm between 'high classical' music and Jazz with such rousing works as *Rhapsody in Blue*. The great swing clarinettist Benny Goodman was born in Chicago to Jewish immigrants and broke down racial segregation in America by working with black musicians.

Below Stan Getz (1927–91), *the American saxophonist who blended Brazilian bossa nova with jazz.*

Above Arthur Rubinstein, *classical pianist, received international acclaim for his interpretation of Chopin.*

ROCK AND ROLL

It is hard to imagine modern rock music without Jewish songwriters Jerry Leiber and Mike Stoller who helped launch the genre. Phil Spector pioneered the 1960s 'wall of sound' technique. In Britain, Brian Epstein managed the Beatles. Notable performers include Gene Simmons of Kiss, Marc Bolan of T Rex, Beastie Boys, Bob Dylan, Leonard Cohen, Ramones, Simon and Garfunkel, Paula Abdul, and converts to Judaism Sammy Davis Jr and Ike Turner.

THE SOUNDS OF ISRAEL

The sensitive songwriter Naomi Shemer drew heavily on the French chanson tradition of the 1960s, before releasing her song *Yerushalayim Shel Zahav* (Jerusalem of Gold) just before the Six Day War. It became in effect a second national anthem.

By the 1980s the singers Ofra Haza, Zehava Ben and the band Ethnix blended East and West to great effect. Hybrid forms and originality now typify Israeli music, examples of which include Yehuda Poliker, of Greek Jewish origin, who shifts from playing bazouki to hard electric rock, and Ahinoam Nini, who mixes jazz, 'indie' folk and Yemenite sounds.

Jewish Philosophers and Politicians

EVEN IN REJECTING ASPECTS OF TRADITIONAL JUDAISM, THINKERS SUCH AS FREUD AND DERRIDA SHOWED SIGNS OF ENGAGING WITH JUDAIC CONCEPTS, THUS REVEALING A SHARED JEWISH IDENTITY.

Perhaps the most revolutionary Jewish thinker of the 20th century was Sigmund Freud (1856–1939), who created psychoanalysis and explored the human unconscious. Convinced that neurosis resulted from repressed impulses and sexual drives, Freud drew on medicine, myth and dreams to explain how the mind works. Freudian terms such as the ego, the pleasure principle, paranoia, guilt feelings, subconscious, peer pressure and regression are repeatedly used and misused in everyday English conversation.

PSYCHOLOGY AND THEORY

Sigmund Freud was not a practising Jew and his books *Totem and Taboo* and *The Future of an Illusion* spoke of religion as the antithesis of reason and experience. None the less he accepted that faith was part of the human psyche. All his psychologist colleagues bar Karl Jung were Jewish. Sigmund's daughter, Anna, became a pioneer in child psychology.

Freud influenced other thinkers, including Jews such as Franz Boas (1858–1942) and Claude Lévi-Strauss (1908–2009) the founder of structural anthropology. While Lévi-Strauss analysed 'primitive' societies, Raymond Aron (1905–83) and Walter Benjamin (1892–1940) cast their gaze at modern civilization. The Parisian-born Aron asked how ordinary people made sense of industrial progress and political competition.

SOCIOLOGISTS

Walter Benjamin killed himself while trying to escape Nazis on the Franco-Spanish border. Even more than Freud, this translator, essayist and philosopher wrestled with his Jewish identity. He individualistically applied the ideas of Goethe, Marx, Brecht and Jewish mysticism to current literature and aesthetics, and his prescient posthumous works *Illuminations* and *Arcades* considered the shopping mall and street life as epitomizing contemporary society. One of his last books, *Theses on the Philosophy of History*, addressed the Jewish quest for a messiah and humanity's clash with nihilism.

Another Jewish-origin pioneer of the link between words and ideas was the Austrian-born Cambridge philosopher and former 'logical positivist', Ludwig Wittgenstein. He and other Jewish thinkers such as Benjamin, Levi-Strauss and Theodor Adorno laid the basis for a post-war school called structuralism. Its most celebrated figure was Jacques Derrida (1930–2007). Derrida pioneered 'deconstruction', a method of minutely interrogating texts for signs of true meaning obscured by written convention, which has been profoundly influential.

Above Hermann Cohen. German neo-Kantian philosophers wrestled with Jewish topics in his many books.

***Below** Hailed as the father of modern anthropology, Franz Boas studied people in their physical environment.*

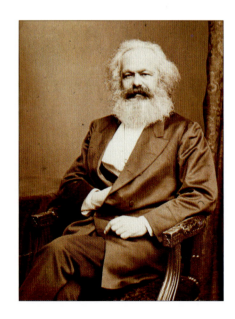

***Below** 'Philosophers have interpreted the world; the point, however, is to change it' – Karl Marx, 1875.*

PIONEERS IN ECONOMICS

New thinking in economics, jokingly called 'the dismal science', also owes much to Jews. Born into an English Sephardi family in 1772, David Ricardo became one of the most influential political economists. Monetarist Milton Friedman inspired Thatcherism in 1970s Britain and President Reagan's supply-side economics in America. Academic development economist Jeffrey Sachs draws on Jewish philosophy, not least Maimonides' theory of facilitating self-help as the highest form of charity. He has advised many Latin American and post-communist states.

Finally, George Soros of Hungary has turned his billions gained in speculation to promoting 'open societies' worldwide. Soros' ideas come from Jewish philosopher Karl Popper, who championed transparency as the ultimate tool against authoritarian systems.

Interestingly, many Jews in the Marxist camp veered from narrower economic analysis to investigating social change.

NEW THINKING IN JUDAISM

Thousands of believing 19th-century Jews sought a middle path, one that married Jewish heritage with modern realities. Exposure to Western academic methods led to radical new outlooks. From the 1950s onwards French philosopher Emmanuel Levinas (1906–95) popularized Talmudic methods to a new generation of secular scholars. More mainstream Orthodox Jews responded to the Haskalah spirit and Hassidic fervour by promoting the Mussar movement of contemplation and ethical introspection started by Rav Israel Salanter (1810–83). Salanter was inspired by the writings of Moshe Chaim Luzzatto (1707–46, an Italian kabbalist and rabbi.

THE NON-JEWISH JEW AND DIASPORA POLITICIANS

And yet the question remains, is there anything specifically Jewish about thinkers on general matters who just happen to be Jewish? To Isaac Deutscher (1907–67), the Polish-born British historian, Marxist activist and biographer of Stalin and Trotsky, it was possible, indeed almost inevitable, to be a 'non-Jewish Jew'. He felt himself a 'Jew by force of my unconditional solidarity with the persecuted.' The

Left Claude Lévi-Strauss, pioneer of structuralism, at the opening of the Musée du Quai Branly, Paris, 2006.

Above Sigmund Freud, the founding father of psychoanalysis.

Israeli historian Shlomo Sand, author of *How I Ceased to be a Jew*, calls himself 'a post-Zionist and non-Zionist because the justification of this land is not historical right'.

Germany's Chancellor from 1909 to 1917 was Theobald von Bethmann Hollweg, a descendant of a prominent Frankfurt Jewish banking family; while in Italy two Jews, Sydney Sonnino and Luigi Luzzatti, became prime ministers in 1909–10 and 1910–11 respectively. France has had five Jewish-origin prime ministers in the last century, most notably Leon Blum before World War II and Pierre Mendes-France after, both from the left. For 12 years Bruno Kreisky was Austria's Chancellor, and Henry Kissinger, who arrived in America in 1938 as a refugee from Nazi Germany, rose to become possibly Washington's most influential Secretary of State during 1973–77. Perhaps most powerful of all was Benjamin Disraeli, the first and only British Prime Minister of Jewish origin in 1868 and 1874–80; he spoke proudly of his people's heritage, though he was converted to Anglicanism aged 13.

Jewish Architecture Around the World

The quintessential Jewish building must surely be the synagogue. Like a barometer of Jewish history, it represents the self-image, tribulations and triumphs of the people.

King Solomon built Jerusalem's first Temple and fortifications in Hazor, Megiddo and Gezer *c.*970-930BC. A millennium later, King Herod transformed the smaller second Temple into an imposing Hellenistic white stone structure. Rome ended large-scale Jewish ceremonial architecture, when it destroyed the Temple ten years after its final refurbishment. Absalom's tomb in Jerusalem's Kidron Valley offers a rare hint of ancient Jewish hybrid style with its Egyptian-like up-ended siphon roof.

The first synagogue was probably built during 6th-century BC Babylonian exile, and became the chief institution of decentralized Jewish worship after the Temple's destruction. More than 400 synagogues existed in the Judea and Galilee of Jesus' day; in function and form they influenced early churches and mosques. Two Toledo synagogues show the Spanish–Moorish Mudéjar imprint most powerfully. One, now the El Transito Church, has amazing floral decorations, Nasrid stucco-work and Hebrew inscriptions; the other, founded in 1180 and now the Church of Santa Maria la Blanca, features Arabesque horseshoe arches, Almohad brickwork and white inner columns.

FALLOW YEARS

Bereft of statehood, Jews generally looked inward and so did their buildings. Small-scale Palestinian gems include 2nd–6th centuries CE catacombs in Beit She'arim, Lower Galilee, with squat Roman columns topped with Levantine-figured capitals, or zodiac signs on mosaic synagogue floors at Hamat and Beit-Alpha. Outside Palestine, Syria's Dura-Europos synagogue unusually displayed frescoes of human images, and the huge 6th-century synagogue complex at Sardis, Turkey, suggested a wealthy, integrated and self-assured community.

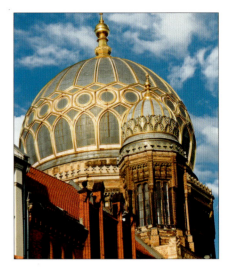

Above The Neue Synagogue, Berlin, 1866, is Moorish in style.

THE CLASSICAL PERIOD

Europe's oldest active synagogue is Prague's Altneuschule ('Old-New Synagogue'), a Gothic twin-nave structure in the Jewish quarter, finished in 1270. The Nazis destroyed many *shuls*; among those that survived are the ones in Hungary, Budapest, Florence, Trani, and, Poland's oldest, the 15th-century Kazimierz in Krakow, renovated after the war.

The Paradesi synagogue of Cochin, India, founded 1568, still operates, as does London's oldest synagogue, the Sephardis' Bevis Marks in the City, completed 1701. Possibly the finest Georgian synagogue is America's oldest, the Touro on Rhode Island.

IMPACT OF REFORM

In the 19th century, Reform Jews rejected ideas of a rebuilt Jerusalem and named their synagogues 'temples'. Men and women sat together, choirs and organs were introduced and new styles adopted: such as the Greek-temple look of Beth Elohim (1840) in Charleston, South Carolina; Byzantine in the West London Synagogue (1870); and a majestic Moorish–Gothic blend in the New Synagogue, Oranienstrasse, Berlin (1886). British Orthodox Jews developed grandiose 'cathedral synagogues', though the

Below National Assembly, Dhaka, Bangladesh, by US architect Louis Kahn.

largest was Reform's 1929 flagship Temple Emanu-El on Fifth Avenue, New York.

TRADITION AND RENEWAL

In the 20th century, the pendulum swung from pomp and ornament towards abstraction and functionalism, and then to post-modernism. Louis Kahn's Temple Beth-El in Chappaqua, New York State, for example, imitates Poland's now lost pagoda-like wooden synagogues. Geometry reappeared in Erich Mendelsohn's 1950 observatory-style Park Synagogue in Cleveland, Ohio; in Max Abramowitz's funnel-like Temple Beth Zion, Buffalo; and in the triangles of Percival Goodman's Temple Beth Emeth, Albany, NY.

Recently, English Reform and Liberal congregations have started housing old arks and *bimahs* rescued from Czechoslovakia in modern synagogues. Equally indicative of renewal is Munich's modern Ohel Jakob synagogue, inaugurated in 2006, 68 years after Nazis destroyed its predecessor. A glass ceiling recalls the portable Tabernacle, a white stone base evokes the Temple in Jerusalem, and large windows are a sign of transparency and trust.

Below Frank Lloyd Wright's Beth Sholom Synagogue, Pennsylvania, 1954.

ISRAELI INNOVATORS

Palestinian Jewish architecture was transformed by the German and Central European influx of the 1930s. Against these Bauhaus stylists were ranged 'orientalists' who tried to incorporate local elements and reflect the people's diverse origins. Zvi Hecker drew on plant design and Arab village terracing for his 1963 Spiral House in Ramat Gan. Moshe Safdie built the Yad Vashem Museum, Jerusalem.

Architects inspired by Le Corbusier pioneered public housing in Beersheva and then developed Jerusalem. Some tried to incorporate 'Jewish emblems' such as Moses' tablets or stars of David. More successfully, the Israel Museum's 1965 Shrine of the Book pays homage to the bedouin urn that contained the Dead Sea Scrolls. Water-ways in Jerusalem's outstanding Supreme Court of Justice, built by the brother and sister team of Ram Karmi and Ada Karmi-Melamed in 1992, echo the psalmist's description of justice on high reflected in law below.

MODERN ARCHITECTS

Frank Gehry and Daniel Libeskind are among the 21st century's leading architects. Canadian Gehry uses fish shapes and curves, as in Seattle's Experience Music Project, Hanover's Gehry Tower, Prague's Dancing House and Bilbao's Guggenheim

Above Tel Aviv Opera House, designed by Ya'akov Rechter, opened in 1994.

Museum. Libeskind's fractal designs and surprising use of symbolism appear in faith-related projects: the zigzag-shaped Berlin Jewish Museum; Bar Ilan University's Wohl convention centre, fashioned like a book; and the Danish Jewish Museum, whose design traces the Hebrew word *mitzvah*, or 'good deed', in tribute to Denmark's wartime rescue of Jews. Whether angular or flowing, the lines of contemporary Jewish architecture may be said to reflect the peaks and troughs of Jewish history.

Below The Shrine of the Book, Jerusalem, houses the Dead Sea Scrolls.

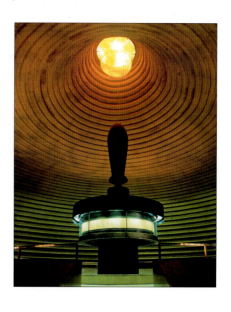

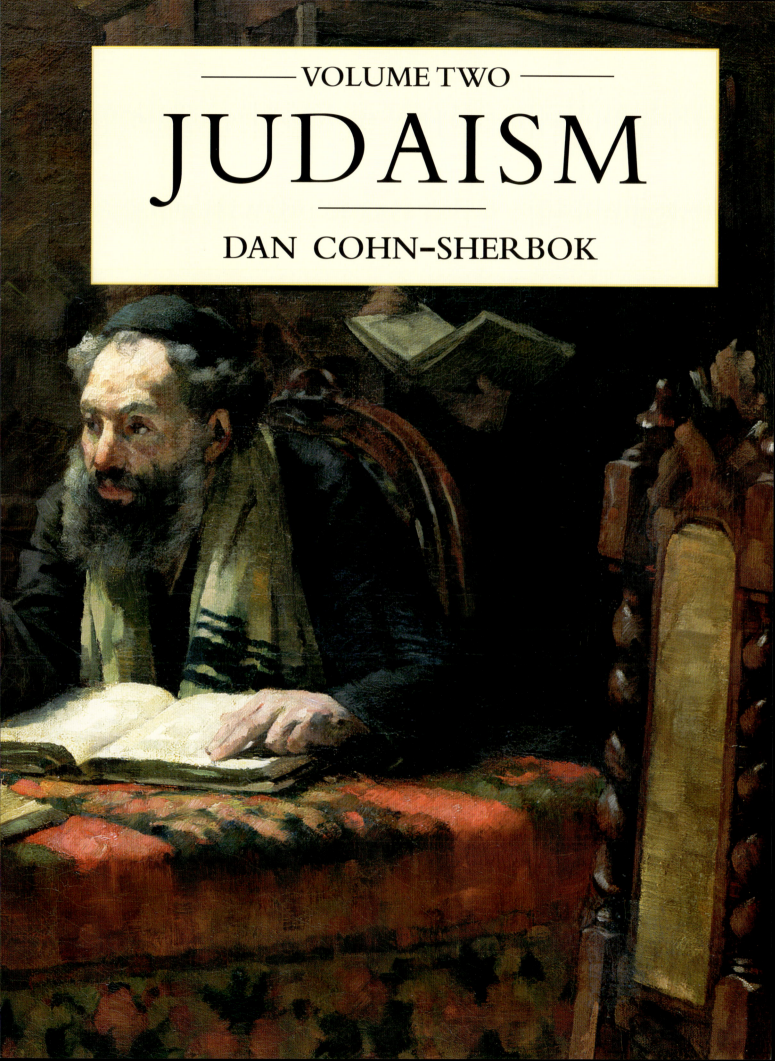

Introducing Judaism

IS JUDAISM A UNIFIED RELIGIOUS TRADITION, OR HAVE A VARIETY OF JUDAISMS EXISTED THROUGH THE CENTURIES? DO ALL JEWS SUBSCRIBE TO THE SAME BELIEFS? DO THEY ALL OBSERVE THE SAME RITUALS?

These are the central questions that this volume seeks to explore. Divided into three major sections – Traditions, Belief and Practice – this work begins with an outline of the variety of forms of Jewish life that emerged in the history of the faith. Throughout it draws heavily on images of the Jew as portrayed in the Western artistic tradition.

JEWISH TRADITIONS
Beginning with ancient Judaism, the book examines a range of Judaisms that flourished from the time of Abraham to the Hellenistic period. Although all these ancient Judaisms embraced a belief in the God of the Hebrews, believers followed distinct spiritual paths in the quest to fulfill the divine will. Similarly, in the rabbinic and medieval periods, new forms of Judaism arose as Jews sought to make sense of their world.

Below *A rabbinical disputation about Jewish law; a 17th-century Dutch painting by Jacob Toorenvliet.*

Rabbinic Judaism, mystical Judaism, and philosophical Judaism were rooted in Scripture, yet these new forms of Judaism provided alternative interpretations of the tradition. The Karaites, Shabbateans and Frankists, however, were intensely critical of the rabbinic establishment and founded movements which were bitterly denounced by traditionalists. The modern world has witnessed the efflorescence of Jewish life and the establishment of a wide range of Judaisms each with its own religious ideology. From Orthodoxy to Humanism, from Zionism to Jewish feminism, modern Jews have strived to integrate Jewish values with contemporary concerns.

JEWISH BELIEF
This presentation of the multifarious nature of Judaism is followed by an extensive outline of Jewish belief, beginning with a discussion of the primary religious doctrines of the faith. Each section highlights biblical

Above *A Jew wearing phylacteries and a prayer shawl, and holding a Torah. By Marc Chagall, c.1930, a pioneer of modernism and leading Jewish artist.*

teaching and traces its development from rabbinic times to the present. Commencing with a survey of Jewish belief about God's unity, the book goes on to examine traditional doctrines about God's nature, including such concepts as divine transcendence, eternal existence, omnipotence, omniscience and divine goodness. Turning to a consideration of God's action in the world, the subsequent sections focus on such subjects as providence, revelation, Torah and

Below *A Sabbath Afternoon by Moritz Daniel Oppenheim, often regarded as the first Jewish artist of the modern era.*

INTRODUCING JUDAISM

Above Jews praying at the Western Wall in Jerusalem. A 19th-century German painting by Gustav Bauernfeind.

mitzvot, and the promised land. There then follows an examination of ideas specifically connected with the Jewish spiritual path. Here such topics as the Bible, Talmud, midrash, sin, repentance, forgiveness, and reward and punishment are examined in detail. This discussion concludes with sections exploring the nature of Jewish eschatology.

JEWISH PRACTICE

The final part on Jewish practice, opens with a depiction of an outline of the Jewish calendar, and Jewish worship embracing such institutions as the sanctuary, Temple and synagogue. This is followed by an outline of the major festivals in the yearly cycle including Sabbath, Pilgrim Festivals, New Year, Day of Atonement, Days of Joy and Fast Days. The next sections discuss home ceremonies and personal piety as well as major life cycle events from birth through circumcision to marriage, divorce, death and mourning. Throughout this illustrated presentation of Jewish life, readers are encouraged to engage with the material and to reflect on the issues that emerge.

A LIVING FAITH

As this volume seeks to illustrate, in the past the Jewish community was united by belief and practice. Yet, all this has changed in the modern world. Prior to the Enlightenment in the 18th century, Jews did not have full citizenship rights of the countries in which they lived. Nevertheless, they were able to regulate their own affairs through an organized structure of self-government. Within such a context, Jewish law served as the basis of communal life, and rabbis were able to exert power and authority in the community.

However, as a result of political emancipation, Jews entered the mainstream of modern life, taking on all the responsibilities of citizenship. The rabbinical establishment thereby lost its status and control, and the Jewish legal system became voluntary. In addition, Jews took advantage of widening social advantages: they were free to choose where to live, whom to marry, and what career to follow. By gaining access to secular educational institutions, the influence of the surrounding culture also pervaded all aspects of Jewish life.

As a consequence of all this, Jewry in modern society has become fragmented and secularized. With the advent of the 21st century, the Jewish community faces new challenges as never before.

For nearly 4,000 years Judaism has been a living faith: if it is to continue, Jews will need to adapt to these changes in Jewish life and chart a new path into the future. What is at stake is no less than the survival of the Jewish heritage.

Below A boy reads the Torah during his bar mitzvah, a major life cycle event, with his rabbi and parents, at the Progressive Jewish community synagogue in Amsterdam.

Jews in the Ancient World

Jewish civilization began in a polytheisitic context in the ancient Near East. According to Scripture, God called Abraham to go from Babylonia to the land of Canaan.

The history of the Jewish people began in Mesopotamia where successive empires of the ancient world flourished and decayed before the Jews emerged as a separate people. The culture of these civilizations had a profound impact on the Jewish religion – ancient Near Eastern myths were refashioned to serve the needs of the Hebrew people. It appears that the Jews emerged in this milieu as a separate nation between the 19th and 16th centuries BCE. According to the Bible, Abraham was the father of the Jewish people. Initially known as Abram, he came from Ur of the Chaldeans. Together with his family he went to Harran and subsequently to Canaan, later settling in the plain near Hebron. Abraham was followed by Isaac and Jacob, whose son Joseph was sold into slavery in Egypt. There he prospered, becoming a vizier in the house of Pharaoh. Eventually the entire Hebrew clan moved to Egypt, where they remained and flourished for centuries before a new Pharaoh decreed that all male Hebrew babies should be put to death.

THE EXODUS

To persuade Pharaoh to let the Jewish people go, God sent a series of plagues upon the Egyptians. After this devastation, Moses, the leader of the Jewish people, led his kinsfolk out of Egypt. After wandering in the desert for 40 years, the Hebrews finally entered into the land that God had promised them. Under Joshua's leadership, the Hebrews conquered the existing inhabitants, the Canaanites. After Joshua's death the people began to form separate groups. At first there were 12 tribes named after the sons of Jacob. During this period the Hebrews were ruled by 12 national heroes who served successively as judges.

Above *Moses receiving the Ten Commandments*, during the 40-year sojourn in the desert. From the 14th-century Spanish Sarajevo Haggadah.

Frequently the covenant between God and his chosen people was proclaimed at gatherings in national shrines such as Shechem. Such an emphasis on covenantal obligation reinforced the belief that the Jews were the recipients of God's loving kindness. Now in a more settled existence, the covenant expanded to include additional legislation, including the provisions needed for an agricultural community. During this period it became increasingly clear to the Jewish nation that the God of the covenant directed human history – the Exodus and the entry into the Promised Land – were viewed as the unfolding of a divine plan.

THE PERIOD OF THE JUDGES

Under the judges, God was conceived as the supreme monarch. When some tribes suggested to Gideon that he deserved a formal position of power, he declared that it was impossible for the nation to be ruled by both God and a human king. None the less, Saul was sub-

Below *The Exodus from Egypt through the Red Sea*, a 17th-century painting by Frans Francken the Younger.

sequently elected as king despite the prophet Samuel's warnings against the dangers of usurping God's rule. Later, the Israelite nation divided into two kingdoms. The northern and southern tribes were united only by their allegiance to King David but when his successor, King Solomon, and his son Rehoboam violated many of the ancient traditions, the northern tribes revolted. The reason they gave for this rebellion was the injustice of the monarchy, but in fact they sought to recapture the simple ways of the generation that had escaped from Egypt. It is against this background that the pre-exilic prophets, including Elijah, Elisha, Amos, Hosea, Micah and Isaiah, endeavoured to bring the nation back to the true worship of God.

DECLINE AND DESTRUCTION

During the 1st millennium BCE the Jews watched their country emerge as a powerful state only to see it sink into spiritual and moral decay. As a punishment for the nation's iniquity, the northern kingdom was devastated by the Assyrians in 722BCE. Two centuries later the southern kingdom fell to the Babylonians. Following the Babylonian conquest in 586BCE the Temple lay in ruins and the people despaired of their fate. Yet, despite defeat and exile, the nation rose from the ashes of the old kingdoms. In the centuries that followed, the Jewish people continued their religious traditions and communal life. Though they had lost their independence, their devotion to God and his law sustained them through suffering and hardship.

RETURN TO JUDAH

In Babylonia the exiles flourished, keeping their religion alive in the synagogues. These institutions were founded so that Jews could meet together for worship and study; no sacrifices were offered since that was the prerogative of the Jerusalem Temple. In 538BCE King Cyrus of Persia permitted the Jews to return to their former home and the nation was transformed. The Temple was rebuilt and religious reforms were enacted. The period following the death of King Herod in 4BCE was a time of intense anti-Roman feeling among the Jewish population in Judea as well as in the Diaspora. Eventually such hostility led to war, only to be followed by defeat and the destruction of the Second Temple. In 70CE thousands of Jews were deported. Such devastation, however, did not quell the Jewish hope of ridding the Holy Land of its Roman oppressors. In the 2nd century CE, a messianic rebellion led by Simon Bar Kochba was crushed by Roman forces. Yet despite this defeat, the Pharisees carried on the Jewish tradition through teaching and study at Jabneh, near Jerusalem.

Above *In 70CE, the Romans under Emperor Titus destroyed the Temple in Jerusalem. 15th-century Flemish picture.*

Below *Babylonian cuneiform tablet from 700–500BCE, with inscription and map of Mesopotamia. In the centre Babylon is surrounded by Assyria and Elam.*

Below *Abraham, father of the Jewish people, preparing to sacrifice his son Isaac, from a 1700s Arabian manuscript.*

Rabbinic and Medieval Judaism

The emergence of rabbinic Judaism has fundamentally changed the nature of Judaism. From the Hellenistic period to today the rabbis have dominated all aspects of Jewish life.

From the 1st century BCE Palestinian rabbinic scholars engaged in the interpretation of Scripture. The most important scholar of the early rabbinic period was Yehuda Ha-Nasi (135–c.220CE), the head of the Sanhedrin (a group of distinguished Pharisaic scholars), whose main achievement was the redaction of the Mishnah, or 'compendium of Jewish law', in the 2nd century CE. This volume consisted of the discussions and rulings of sages whose teachings had been transmitted orally.

According to the rabbis, the law recorded in the Mishnah was given orally to Moses along with the written law. This implies that there was an infallible chain of transmission from Moses to the leaders of the nation and eventually to the Pharisees.

The Sanhedrin, which had been so fundamental in the compilation of the Mishnah, met in several cities in Galilee, but later settled in the Roman district of Tiberias. Other scholars simultaneously established their own schools in other parts of the country where they applied the Mishnah to everyday life, together with old rabbinic teachings, which had not been incorporated in the Mishnah.

During the 3rd century CE the Roman Empire encountered numerous difficulties including inflation, population decline and a lack of technological development to support the army. In addition, rival generals struggled against one another for power, and the government became increasingly inefficient. Throughout this time of upheaval, the Jewish community underwent a similar decline as a result of famine, epidemics and plunder.

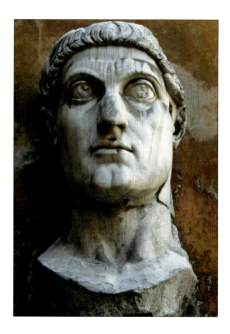

Above *Head of a colossal statue of Constantine the Great, who extended official religious toleration to Christians.*

THE RISE OF CHRISTIANITY

At the end of the 3rd century CE, the emperor Diocletian (ruled 284–305CE) inaugurated reforms that strengthened the Roman empire. In addition, Diocletian introduced measures to repress the spread of Christianity, which had become a serious challenge to the official religion of the empire. However Diocletian's successor, Constantine the Great (ruled 306–37CE), reversed his predecessor's hostile stance and also extended official toleration to Christians in the empire.

By this stage Christianity had succeeded in gaining a substantial number of adherents among the urban population; eventually Constantine became more involved in Church affairs and just before his death he himself was baptized. The Christianization of the empire continued throughout the century and by the early 400s CE Christianity was fully established as the state religion.

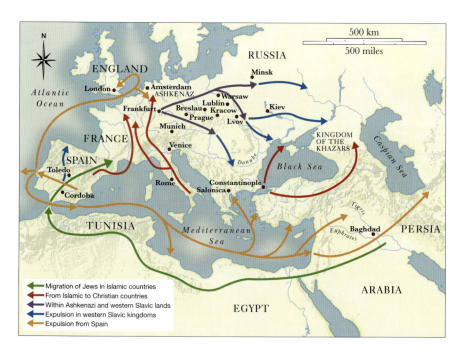

Below *Medieval migration of Jews showing their expulsion from Spain and some Slavic countries and movement to Islamic and other lands.*

IN THE DIASPORA

By the 6th century CE the Jews had become largely a Diaspora people. Despite the loss of a homeland, they were unified by a common heritage: law, liturgy and shared traditions bound together the scattered communities stretching from Spain to Persia and from Poland to Africa. Living among Christians and Muslims, the Jewish community was reduced to a minority group and its marginal status resulted in repeated persecution. Though there were times of tolerance and creative activity, the threats of exile and death were always present in Jewish consciousness during this period.

UNDER ISLAM

Within the Islamic world, Jews along with Christians were recognized as 'Peoples of the Book' and were guaranteed religious toleration, judicial autonomy and exemption from the military. In turn they were required to accept the supremacy of the Islamic state. During the first two centuries of Islamic rule under the Umayyad and Abbasid caliphates, Muslim leaders confirmed the authority of traditional Babylonian institutions. When the Arabs conquered Babylonia, they offi-

Right *A Jewish scholar presents a translation of an Arabic treatise to Philippe d'Anjou, 13th century.*

cially recognized the position of the Jewish exilarch, who for centuries had been the ruler of Babylonian Jewry. By the Abbasid period, the exilarch shared his power with the heads of the rabbinical academies which had for centuries been the major centres of rabbinic learning.

During the 8th century CE messianic movements appeared in the Persian Jewish community, which led to armed uprisings against Muslim authority. Such revolts were quickly crushed, but an even more serious threat to traditional Jewish life was posed later in the century by the emergence of an anti-rabbinic sect, the Karaites. This group was founded in Babylonia in the 760s CE by Anan ben David. The growth of Karaism provoked the rabbis to attack it as a heretical movement since these various groups rejected rabbinic law and formulated their own legislation.

THE DECENTRALIZATION OF RABBINIC JUDAISM

By the 8th century CE the Muslim empire began to undergo a process of disintegration; this process was accompanied by a decentralization of rabbinic Judaism. The academies of Babylonia began to lose their hold on the Jewish scholarly world, and in many places rabbinic schools were established in which rabbinic sources were studied. In the Holy Land, Tiberias was the location of an important rabbinical academy as well as the centre of the masoretic scholars who produced the standard text of the Bible. But it was in Spain that the Jewish community was to attain the greatest level of

Left *A 13th-century South German illumination showing Moses receiving the Ten Commandments, from the Regensburg Pentateuch.*

achievement in literature, philosophy, theology and mysticism.

In their campaigns the Muslims did not manage to conquer all of Europe – many countries remained under Christian rule, as did much of the Byzantine empire. In Christian Europe, Jewish study took place in a number of important towns such as Mainz and Worms in the Rhineland and Troyes and Sens in northern France. In such an environment the study of the Talmud reached great heights; in Germany and northern France scholars known as 'the Tosafists' used new methods of talmudic interpretation. In addition Ashkenazic Jews of this period composed religious poetry modelled on the liturgical compositions of 5th- and 6th-centuries CE Israel.

Yet, despite such an efflorescence of Jewish life, the expulsion of the Jews from the countries in which they lived became a dominant policy of Christian Europe. They were driven out of Rome in 139 BCE, from England in 1290, from Germany in 1348, from Spain in 1492 and from many other states. Repeatedly, Jewish communities throughout Europe suffered violent attack, and Jewish massacre became a frequent occurrence.

Jews in the Early Modern Period

DURING THE EARLY MODERN PERIOD, JEWISH SCHOLARS CONTINUED TO CONTRIBUTE TO JEWISH LIFE. HOWEVER THE LONGING FOR MESSIANIC DELIVERANCE CONTINUED TO ANIMATE JEWISH CONSCIOUSNESS.

By the end of the 14th century political instability in Christian Europe led to the massacre of many Jewish communities in Castile and Aragon. Fearing for their lives, thousands of Jews converted to Christianity at the end of the century. Two decades later Spanish rulers introduced the Castilian laws that segregated Jews from their Christian neighbours. In the following year a public disputation was held in Tortosa about the doctrine of the Messiah; as a result increased pressure was applied to the Jewish population to convert. Those who became Maranos, or apostates, found life much easier, but by the 15th century anti-Jewish sentiment again became a serious problem. In 1480 King Ferdinand and Queen Isabella of Spain established the Inquisition to determine whether former Jews practised Judaism in secret. To escape such persecution many Maranos sought refuge in various parts of the Ottoman empire.

RABBINIC SAGES

Prominent among the rabbinic scholars of this period was Joseph ben Ephraim Caro (1488–1575), who emigrated from Spain to the Balkans. In the 1520s he commenced a study of Jewish law, *The House of Joseph*, based on previous codes of Jewish law. In addition, he composed a shorter work, the *Shulkhan Arukh*, which has become the authoritative code of law in the Jewish world. While working on the *Shulkhan Arukh*, Caro emigrated to Safed in Israel, which had become a major centre of Jewish religious life. Talmudic academies were established and small groups engaged in the study of Kabbalistic (mystical) literature as they piously awaited the coming of the Messiah. In this centre of Kabbalistic activity one of the greatest mystics of Safed, Moses Cordovero (1522–70), col-

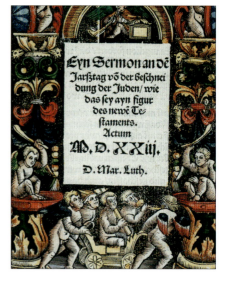

Above *16th-century Jews often found life insecure, as evidenced by this sermon of Martin Luther condemning the Jews. His anti-Semitism had a persistent influence on German attitudes towards Jews.*

lected, organized and interpreted the teachings of earlier mystical authors. Later in the 16th century, Kabbalistic speculation was transformed by the greatest mystic of Safed, Isaac Luria (1534–72).

THE MYSTICAL MESSIAH

By the beginning of the 17th century Lurianic mysticism had made an important impact on Sephardic Jewry, and messianic expectations had also become a central feature of Jewish life. In this milieu the arrival of a self-proclaimed messianic king, Shabbetai Tzvi (1626–76), brought about a transformation of Jewish life and thought. After living in various cities, he travelled to Gaza where he encountered Nathan Benjamin Levi, who believed he was the Messiah. His messiahship was proclaimed in 1665, and Nathan sent letters to Jews in the Diaspora asking them to recognize Shabbetai Tzvi as their redeemer.

Eventually Shabbetai was brought to court and given the choice between conversion and death. In the face of this alternative, he converted to Islam. Such an act of apostasy

Below *Many Jews fled Spain to escape the tortures of the Inquisition, shown here in a 19th-century engraving.*

scandalized most of his followers, but others continued to revere him as the Messiah. In the following century the most important Shabbetean sect was led by Jacob Frank, who believed himself to be the incarnation of Shabbetai.

PERSECUTION

During this period Poland had become a great centre of scholarship. In Polish academies scholars collected together the legal interpretations of previous authorities and composed commentaries on the *Shulkhan Arukh*. However, in the midst of this general prosperity, the Polish Jewish community was subject to a series of massacres carried out by the Cossacks of the Ukraine, Crimean Tartars and Ukrainian peasants. In 1648 Bogdan Chmielnicki (1595–1657), head of the Cossacks, instigated an insurrection against the Polish gentry, and Jews were slaughtered in these revolts.

Elsewhere in Europe this period witnessed Jewish persecution and oppression. Despite the positive contact between Italian humanists and Jews, Christian anti-Semitism frequently led to persecution and suffering. In the 16th century the Counter-Reformation Church attempted to isolate the Jewish community. The Talmud was burned in 1553, and two years later Pope Paul IV reinstated the segregationist edict of the Fourth Lateran Council, forcing Jews to live in ghettos and barring them from most areas of economic life. In Germany the growth of Protestantism frequently led to adverse conditions for the Jewish population. Though Martin Luther was initially well disposed to the Jews, he soon came to realize the Jewish community was intent on remaining true to its faith. As a consequence, he composed a virulent attack on the Jews.

By the mid-17th century, Dutch Jews had attained importance in trade and finance. Maranos and Ashkenazi Jews flourished in Amsterdam. In this milieu Jewish cultural activity grew: Jewish writers published works of drama, theology and mystical lore. Though Jews in Holland were not granted full rights as citizens, they nevertheless enjoyed religious freedom, personal protection and liberty in economic affairs.

Below *A 17th-century engraving of Shabbatai Tzvi, a charismatic from Turkey and self-proclaimed Messiah.*

THE ORIGINS OF HASIDISM (ALSO SPELLED HASSIDISM OR CHASIDISM)

By the middle of the 18th century the Jewish community had suffered numerous waves of persecution and was deeply dispirited by the conversion of Shabbetai Tzvi. In this environment the Hasidic movement sought to revitalize Jewish life. The founder of this new sect was Israel ben Eliezer, known as the Ba'al Shem Tov (1700–60), who was born in southern Poland. Legend relates that he performed various miracles and instructed his disciples in Kabbalistic lore. By the 1740s he had attracted many disciples who passed on his teaching. After his death, Dov Baer became the leader of his sect and Hasidism spread to southern Poland, the Ukraine and Lithuania.

Left *The Ba'al Shem Tov (Israel ben Eliezer), founder of Hasidism.*

Below *The Haari synagogue in Safed, home of rabbinic scholar Joseph Caro and mystic Isaac Luria.*

Jews in the Modern World

JEWISH EMANCIPATION IN THE 18TH CENTURY LED TO A REVOLUTION IN JEWISH LIFE. HOWEVER THE RISE OF ANTI-SEMITICISM IN THE 19TH CENTURY LED TO TERRIBLE CONSEQUENCES IN THE 1930S AND 40S.

During the late 18th century the treatment of Jews in central Europe improved owing to the influence of Christian polemicists.

JEWISH EMANCIPATION

Within this environment Jewish emancipation gathered force. The Jewish philosopher Moses Mendelssohn (1729–86) advocated the modernization of Jewish life. To further this advance he translated the Pentateuch into German so that Jews would be able to speak the language of the country in which they lived. Following his example, a number of followers known as the *maskilim* fostered the Haskalah, or Jewish Enlightenment, which encouraged Jews to abandon medieval forms of life and thought.

REFORM JUDAISM

Paralleling this development, reformers encouraged the modernization of the Jewish liturgy and reform of Jewish education. Although such changes were denounced by the

Below *Proclamation of the Independence of the State of Israel by PM David Ben-Gurion, Tel Aviv, 14 May 1948.*

Orthodox establishment, Reform Judaism spread throughout Europe. In 1844 the first Reform synod took place in Brunswick; followed by a conference in 1845 in Frankfurt. At this gathering one of the more conservative rabbis, Zacharias Frankel (1801–75), expressed dissatisfaction with progressive reforms to Jewish worship. He resigned and established a Jewish theological seminary in Breslau. Eventually this approach to the tradition led to the creation of Conservative Judaism. In 1846 a third synod took place at Breslau, but the revolution and its aftermath brought about the cessation of these activities until 1868, when another synod took place at Cassel.

In the United States, Reform Judaism became an important feature of Jewish life. The most prominent of the early reformers was Isaac Mayer Wise (1819–1900), who came to Albany, New York from Bavaria. Later he went to Cincinnati, Ohio where he published a new Reform prayer book as well as several Jewish newspapers. In 1869 the first Central Conference of American Rabbis was held in Philadelphia; followed in 1873 by the founding of the Union of American Hebrew Congregations. In 1875 the Hebrew Union College was established to train rabbinical students for Reform congregations.

ZIONISM

In eastern Europe conditions were less conducive to emancipation, and a series of pogroms took place in Russia in 1881–2. After these events, many Jews emigrated to the United States as well as Palestine. By the late

Above *Theodor Herzl, founder of political Zionism, on a bridge in Basle during the 5th Zionist Congress.*

1880s the idea of a Jewish homeland had spread throughout Europe. At the first Zionist Congress at Basle in 1897, Theodor Herzl (1860–1904) called for a national home based on international law.

By 1900 a sizeable number of Jews had emigrated to Palestine. After World War I, Jews in Palestine organized a National Assembly and an Executive Council. By 1929 the Jewish community numbered 160,000, and this increased in the next ten years to 500,000. At this time Palestine's population was composed of about one and a half million Arabs consisting of peasants and a number of landowners, plus the Jewish population. In 1929 the Arab community rioted following a dispute about Jewish access to the Western Wall of the ancient Temple. This caused the British to curtail both Jewish immigration and purchase of Arab land.

By the 1920s Labour Zionism had become the dominant force in Palestinian Jewish life; in 1930 various socialist and Labour groups joined together in the Israel Labour Party. Within the Zionist movement a right-wing segment criticized Chaim Weizmann, President of the World Zionist Organization, who was committed to co-operation with the

Above *Scene at St Petersburg railway station in 1891 as many Jews fled from anti-Semitism in Russia.*

British. Vladimir Jabotinsky, leader of the Union of Zionist Revisionists, stressed that the central aim of the Zionist movement was the establishment of an independent state in the whole of Palestine. In 1937 a British Royal Commission proposed that Palestine be partitioned into a Jewish and Arab state with a British zone; this recommendation was accepted by Zionists but rejected by the Arabs.

In 1939, a British Government White Paper rejected the concept of partition, limited Jewish immigration, and decreed Palestine would become independent in ten years.

THE HOLOCAUST

As these events unfolded in the Middle East, Jews in Germany were confronted by increasing hostility. The Nazis gained control of the government and curtailed civil liberties. In November 1938 they organized an onslaught against the Jewish population known as *Kristallnacht*, a prelude to the Holocaust. Hitler invaded Poland in September 1939, and later that year incorporated much of the country into Germany; more than 600,000 Jews were gathered into a

Right *An Arab anti-Zionist demonstration in Palestine under the British mandate, 8 March 1920.*

large area in Poland. This was followed by the invasion of Russia in 1941, and the Nazis used mobile killing battalions, the *Einsatzgruppen*, to destroy Russian Jewry. In time fixed killing centres were created at six death camps where millions of Jews and others were murdered.

During the war and afterwards, the British prevented illegal immigrants entering the Holy Land, and Jews in Palestine campaigned against this policy. By 19 November 1947 the General Assembly of the United Nations endorsed a plan of partition, and the Arabs then attacked Jewish settlements. In May 1948, David Ben-Gurion (1886–1973) read out the Scroll of Independence of the Jewish state. Immediately a government was formed, and the Arabs stepped up their assault. Following the War of Independence, armistice talks were held and agreements signed with Egypt, Lebanon, Transjordan and Syria. Later President Gamal Abdel Nasser refused Israeli ships access to the Gulf of Aqaba in 1956, seized the Suez Canal and formed a pact with Saudi Arabia and various Arab states. In response, Israel launched a strike, conquering Sinai and opening the sea route to Aqaba. These events were followed by the Six Day War in 1967,

Above *Existential philosopher Martin Buber deeply influenced Jewish religious thought with his* I and Thou *(1923).*

the Yom Kippur War in 1973, and in 1982 an Israeli offensive against the PLO in Southern Lebanon.

In the ensuing years, hostility between Jews and Arabs has intensified. The *intifada* coupled with repeated suicide bombing led to the creation of a massive wall of defence in the Occupied Territories. Rocket attacks on Israel from Gaza in 2012 has hardened Israeli opinion and made a two-state solution more difficult. For Jews worldwide, the defence of Israel in the face of Arab opposition has become a major feature of contemporary Jewish life.

PART I

JEWISH TRADITIONS

For nearly 4,000 years the Jewish people have flourished, at times in the most adverse conditions. Throughout their long history, they remained faithful to the traditions of their ancestors. Yet, it would be an error to assume that the Jewish faith is monolithic in character. Rather, from ancient times to the present a wide variety of Judaisms has emerged, each with its own character.

In the ancient world, the simple faith of the patriarchs was replaced by an elaborate cultic system in the Jerusalem Temple. This was followed by the emergence of a number of religious groups including the Samaritans, Sadducees, Pharisees and Essenes. In the post-biblical period, the rabbis dominated Jewish life, creating mystical and philosophical systems. In later centuries, the Karaites were critical of the rabbinic establishment as were the Shabbateans and Frankists.

In modern times, traditional Judaism has been challenged by a range of non-Orthodox movements, each with its own ideology and religious orientation.

Opposite: *The menorah, or seven-branched candlestick, is a classic symbol of Judaism that once stood in the Tabernacle and in the Temple in Jerusalem.*

Above *Lighting of the Hanukkah menorah by Barbara Aiello, who was the first female rabbi in Italy, at a synagogue in Milan, 2004.*

CHAPTER 1

ANCIENT JUDAISM

According to Scripture, Abraham was chosen by God to create a new nation. His descendants were to be as numerous as the stars in heaven. The Book of Genesis describes the faith of the patriarchs – Abraham, Isaac and Jacob – and the subsequent history of the ancient Hebrews.

Faith in one God sustained them in Canaan and their long sojourn in Egypt. They were enslaved by the Egyptian Pharaoh, but rescued by Moses who led them into the desert for 40 years. Under Joshua's leadership, the Jewish people conquered the Canaanites and established a monarchy. With the creation of a Temple in Jerusalem, a new form of Judaism emerged, rooted in cultic observance. The emergence of the prophets brought about a profound change in religious orientation with stress on moral action. Under the influence of Hellenism, the Jewish faith underwent further change. In the Northern Kingdom the Samaritans developed their own interpretation of the faith. As time passed, the Jewish nation divided into three major groups – the Sadducees, Pharisees and Essenes – with different religious orientations.

Opposite *Moses and the Burning Bush. A 2nd-century painting from Dura-Europos, Syria, a synagogue with extraordinarily fine frescoes that was uncovered virtually intact in 1932.*

Above *A 19th-century print of the ancient city of Jerusalem showing the city walls and the magnificent Temple of King Solomon towering above it all.*

ANCIENT HEBREWS

THE RELIGION OF THE ANCIENT HEBREWS WAS BASED ON TRADITIONS SURROUNDING THE PATRIARCHS, THE EXILE IN EGYPT AND GOD'S REDEMPTION OF HIS CHOSEN PEOPLE FROM BONDAGE.

The birth of the Jewish people occurred in ancient Mesopotamia. According to Scripture, God called Abraham to travel from Ur of the Chaldeans to Canaan where he promised to make his descendants as numerous as the stars in heaven.

THE ANCIENT NEAR EAST

The rise of ancient Mesopotamian civilization occurred at the end of the 4th millennium BCE in southern Mesopotamia, where the Sumerians created city states, each with its local god. During the 3rd millennium BCE waves of Semitic peoples settled amid the Sumerians. These Semites, known as Akkadians, identified some of their gods with the Sumerian deities. For these peoples, life was under these gods' control. To obtain happiness, it was essential to keep the gods in good humour through worship and sacrifice.

Below *Jacob dreamt of a ladder to heaven during his flight from his brother Esau. 16th-century painting by Nicolas Dipre.*

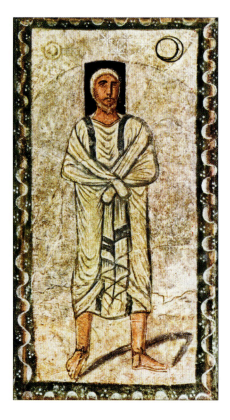

Right *Abraham receives the divine promise that his descendants would be as numerous as the stars. A 2nd-century wall painting from Dura-Europos, Syria.*

THE PATRIARCHS

It was in this polytheistic milieu that the Jews emerged as a separate people in the 19th–16th centuries BCE. According to the biblical narrative in Genesis, Abraham was the father of the Jewish nation. Originally known as Abram, he came from Ur of the Chaldeans – a Sumerian city of Mesopotamia. Together with his father Terah, his wife Sarai, and his nephew Lot, he travelled to Harran, a trading centre in northern Syria. There his father died, and God called upon him to go to Canaan: 'Go from your country and your kindred and your father's house to the land I will show you. And I will make of you a great nation.' (Genesis 12:1–2).

Abraham's belief in one God constituted a radical break from the past. Unlike the Sumerians and Akkadians, who believed in a pantheon of gods, Abraham was committed to the God who had revealed himself to him and ruled over heaven and earth. Scripture records that God made a covenant with Abraham symbolized by an act of circumcision: 'You shall be circumcised in the flesh of your foreskins and it shall be a sign of the covenant between me and you.' (Genesis 17:11). Later, God tested Abraham's dedication by ordering him to sacrifice Isaac, only telling him at the last moment to refrain. Repeatedly in the Book of Genesis God appeared to Abraham, reassuring him of his destiny. Similarly, God revealed himself to Abraham's son, Isaac, and to his grandson, Jacob.

Like Abraham, Jacob was told that his offspring would inherit the land of Canaan and fill the earth. When Jacob travelled to Harran, he had a vision of a ladder rising to heaven: 'And behold, the angels of God were ascending and descending

Below *The Plagues of Egypt. An illumination from a Bohemian Haggadah of 1728.*

THE JOSEPH NARRATIVES

The history of the three patriarchs is followed by a cycle of stories about Jacob's son Joseph. Like his ancestors, Joseph believed in a providential God who guided his destiny. When Joseph was in Shechem helping his brothers tend his family's flocks he angered them by recounting dreams in which they bowed down before him. They reacted by plotting his death. Joseph was eventually taken to Egypt, where he became Pharaoh's chief minister. When his brothers came before him to buy grain because of a famine in Canaan, he revealed his true identity and God's providential care.

The Jewish people were later enslaved in Egypt, an event leading to the Exodus.

Left *This remarkable 19th-century Russian painting has Jacob's eldest son Reuben showing him Joseph's coat.*

on it! And behold, the Lord stood above it and said, "I am the Lord, the God of Abraham your father and the God of Isaac; the land on which you lie I will give to you and to your descendants, and your descendants shall be like the dust of the earth."' (Genesis 28:12–18).

THE EXODUS

The biblical narrative continues with an account of the deliverance of God's chosen people from Egyptian bondage. Here again, Scripture emphasizes that God is active in human history. The Book of Exodus relates that God revealed himself to Moses and commanded that he deliver the ancient Hebrews from bondage: 'I am the God of your father, the God of Abraham, the God of Isaac, and the God of Jacob ... I have seen the affliction of my people who are in Egypt, and have heard their cry because of their taskmasters. I know their sufferings ... Come, I will send you to Pharaoh that you may bring forth my people, the sons of Israel, out of Egypt.' (Exodus 3:6–7, 10)

In order to persuade Pharaoh that he should let the Jewish people go, God sent plagues on the Egyptians, culminating in the slaying of every Egyptian first-born son. After the final plague, Pharaoh released the Israelites, and they fled without even waiting for their bread to rise. However, their perils did not end: Pharaoh changed his mind and sent his forces in pursuit. When the Israelites came to an expanse of water, it seemed that they were trapped. Yet miraculously it was converted to dry land so that they were able to escape. For the ancient Israelites, the belief in a providential God who rescues his people from disaster became a central feature of the faith and is celebrated each year at the Passover festival.

REVELATION ON SINAI

This band of free people then entered the wilderness of Sinai, where God performed miracles to provide them with food and water. After travelling for about 90 days, they encamped before Mount Sinai. God called Moses up to the top of the mountain and told him that if his people would listen to him and keep his covenant they would become God's special people. Moses remained on the mountain for 40 days; at the end of this period, he returned with two tablets of stone on which were inscribed God's laws. These commandments served as the basis for Jewish life as they wandered through the desert for 40 years. Convinced that they were God's chosen people, the ancient Hebrews worshipped the Lord of creation who had chosen them from among all peoples and given them his sacred law so that they could become a priestly nation.

Below *When the people of Israel danced before the Golden Calf, Moses condemned them for setting up an idol. 16th-century fresco by Raphael.*

TEMPLE JUDAISM

THE LIFE OF THE JEWISH NATION WAS ANIMATED BY WORSHIP AND PRAYER. ONCE THEY HAD SETTLED IN THE PROMISED LAND, JEWS OFFERED SACRIFICES IN THE TEMPLE IN JERUSALEM.

During the early history of the nation, the patriarchs prayed to God and offered sacrifices on high places. Later the Jewish people worshipped God in a portable sanctuary. There sacrifices were offered to the Lord of the universe who had delivered his people from slavery. Yet, in time this simple form of worship was replaced by an elaborate cultic system in the Jerusalem Temple. This magnificent structure and its surrounding buildings were constructed by King Solomon in the 10th century BCE.

THE SANCTUARY

For the ancient Hebrews, God was both transcendent and imminent. He had created the universe, yet was intimately involved in the life of his people. Throughout the Genesis narrative, the patriarchs turned to him in prayer. Worship took many forms: petition, confession, praise, thanksgiving, adoration and intercession. In addition, the patriarchs offered sacrifice to God on high places.

Later, Scripture records that Moses made a portable shrine (sanctuary), following God's instructions (Exodus 25–27). This structure travelled with the Israelites in the desert, and it was placed in the centre of the camp in an open courtyard 1,000 cubits (a cubit is the approximate length of a forearm) by 50 cubits (about 1500 x 75 ft/457 x 23m) in size. The fence surrounding it consisted of wooden pillars from which a cloth curtain was suspended. Located in the eastern half of the courtyard, the sanctuary measured 50 cubits by 10 cubits (about 75 x 15 ft/23 x 4.5m). At its end stood the Holy of Holies, which was separated by a veil hanging on five wooden pillars on which were woven images of the cherubim. Inside the Holy of Holies was the Ark of the Covenant, the table on which the shewbread, or 12 loaves representing the 12 tribes of Israel, was placed, the incense altar, and the menorah, or 'candelabrum'. In the courtyard there was also an outer altar on which sacrifices were offered, as well as a brass laver for priests.

THE JERUSALEM TEMPLE

Eventually this structure was superseded by the Temple, which was built by King Solomon on Mount

Above *Two rabbis celebrating Pesach (Passover), from the* Agada Pascatis, *a 15th-century Haggadah manuscript.*

Below *King Solomon overseeing the construction of the Temple in Jerusalem. From an illuminated 16th-century French Bible.*

A NATIONAL CENTRE

Through the centuries the Temple was viewed as a national centre; moreover, since it was the abode of the Ark, it was considered to be the site of the revelation of the Divine Presence and the preferred place for prayer. For this reason individual worshippers directed their supplications towards the Temple even from afar. There the people also gathered in times of distress when the priests would weep between the vestibule and the altar. For the prophets, the Temple Mount (Mount Zion) was the mountain of the Lord, and the Temple was the house of the God of Jacob and the Lord's house. It was the place where God's name was called. In the words of the prophet Jeremiah, it was 'a glorious throne set on high from the beginning.' (Jeremiah 17:12).

Left *A woodcut of Jerusalem and the Temple of Solomon by Melchior Wolgemuth, from the* Nuremberg Chronicle, *1493.*

Right Preparations for the Passover, which in ancient times was observed in the Temple in Jerusalem. Bible illustration, 1470, by Leonardo Bellini.

Moriah in Jerusalem in the 10th century BCE. Acting as the focus of prayer in ancient Israel, the Temple reoriented religious life and took the place of simpler forms of worship. The two principal sources for the plan of the Temple are 1 Kings 6–8 and 2 Chronicles 2–4. Standing within a royal compound, which also consisted of a palace, a Hall of Judgement, the Hall of Cedars, and a house for Solomon's wife, the Temple was 60 cubits long, 20 cubits wide, and 30 cubits high (about 88 x 30 x 46 ft/27 x 9 x 14m).

The main Temple was surrounded by a three-storeyed building divided into chambers with storeys connected by trap doors – these were probably storerooms for the Temple treasures. The main building consisted of an inner room – the Holy of Holies – on the west, and an outer room measuring 20 by 40 cubits (about 30 x 60 ft/9 x 18m) on the east. Around the Temple was a walled-in compound. At the entrance to the Temple stood two massive bronze pillars. Within the Holy of Holies stood the Ark, which contained the Two Tablets of the Covenant with the Ten Commandments.

In the outer room stood an incense altar, the table for the shewbread, and ten lampstands made of gold. In front of the Temple stood a bronze basin supported by 12 bronze cattle. A bronze altar also stood in the courtyard, which was used for various sacrifices.

THE LEVITES

In addition to sacrificial worship, it was customary for the Levites who served in the Temple to sing to the accompaniment of lyres with harps and cymbals. Many psalms in the Bible are ascribed to these Levite singers. Primarily, the Temple was a place of assembly for the entire people for purposes of sacrifice, prayer and thanksgiving. They would come to Jerusalem to bring sin and guilt offerings as well as burnt offerings, peace offerings and meal offerings either in fulfilment of vows or as offerings of thanksgiving. These sacrifices had to be eaten within a day or two of their slaughter, and were apparently brought to the accompaniment of songs and in procession.

FESTIVAL WORSHIP

Special importance was attached to public processions in celebration of festivals. The people travelled to the Temple to worship before the Lord on Sabbaths and New Moons, at appointed seasons, and during the three pilgrim festivals (Pesach, Sukkot and Shavuot). Coming from Judah and beyond, the festal crowd would proceed in a throng with shouts and songs of thanksgiving; the procession was accompanied by the playing of musical instruments. The right to serve in the Temple was assigned to the priests who were descended from Aaron, who were assisted by the Levites. The king enjoyed a status of holiness in the Temple, but in contrast to the priests, he was not permitted either to enter the sanctuary or to burn incense.

Below Coin depicting the kind of lyre that may have been used in the Temple in Jerusalem, dated 134–5CE, the third year of Bar Kochba's war against the Romans.

PROPHETIC JUDAISM

THE PROPHETS OF ANCIENT ISRAEL WERE THE VOICE OF CONSCIENCE. REPEATEDLY THEY WARNED THE PEOPLE TO TURN FROM THEIR EVIL WAYS AND EMBRACE THE COVENANT IN ACCORDANCE WITH GOD'S WILL.

Once the ancient Hebrews settled in the Promised Land, they were ruled over by a series of judges. Eventually, a monarchy was established, at first over the entire country; and later, when there were two kingdoms (Israel in the north and Judah in the south), two royal houses reigned over their respective kingdoms. As time passed, a series of prophets emerged who pronounced against the evils of the nation. Prophetic Judaism championed the rule of justice and God's determination to punish his people for their iniquity unless they turned from their evil ways.

THE NORTHERN KINGDOM

In the 8th century BCE, Israel prospered for 40 years. Towards the end of Jeroboam II's reign, Amos, a shepherd from Tekoa who firmly differentiated himself from the official cultic prophets, proclaimed that Israelite society had become morally corrupt. Many Israelites had become rich, but at the expense of the poor. Israel had sinned, he declared:

> because they sell the righteous
>   for silver
> and the needy for a pair of shoes –
> they that trample the head
>   of the poor
> into the dust of the earth,
> and turn aside the way
>   of the afflicted.
> (Amos 2: 6–7)

Amos's later contemporary, the prophet Hosea, echoed these dire predictions. Israel had gone astray and would be punished. Yet through personal tragedy – the infidelity of his wife, Gomer – Hosea was able to offer words of consolation and hope. Just as Hosea's love for his wife had been rejected, so God's love for Israel had been despised. But despite the coming devastation, God would not cease to love his chosen people.

Just as Hosea could not give up his wife, God could not abandon Israel: 'How can I hand you over, O Israel! My heart recoils within me, my compassion grows warm and tender.' (Hosea 11:8)

THE DESTRUCTION OF ISRAEL

As predicted by these pre-exilic Northern prophets, Amos and Hosea, the nation's fate was sealed. God had threatened destruction unless the people repented.

Left *A stone stele showing two Assyrians driving a chariot, 8th century BCE.*

Above *View of the River Tel and Tekoa, a village in the hills south of Jerusalem. The prophet Amos was born in Tekoa.*

At the beginning of the 8th century BCE the Assyrian King Shalmaneser V (727–722BCE) conquered Israel's capital Samaria after a siege of two years. The annals of Shalmaneser's successor, Sargon II (ruled 721–705BCE), record that 27,290 Israelites were deported as a result of this conquest. This marked the end of the northern kingdom. Following this assault, the kingdom of Judah was under threat.

Below *According to Scripture, the tribes were descended from Jacob's sons, apart from Ephraim and Manasseh, who were sons of Jacob's son Joseph. Benjamin and Judah were in what became the southern kingdom of Judah, and the others in the northern kingdom of Samaria.*

Above *An 18th-century engraving of the Tower of Babel, the Hanging Gardens and the Royal Palace, Babylon.*

THE SOUTHERN KINGDOM

To avoid a similar fate in the south, King Ahaz of Judah (*c.*735–720BCE) continued to pay tribute to Assyria and encouraged the nation to worship Assyrian gods. However, the prophet Isaiah was deeply concerned about such idolatrous practices. He believed the collapse of Israel was God's punishment for sinfulness, and he foresaw a similar fate for Judah. Isaiah warned his country that God was not satisfied with empty ritual in the Temple:

What to me is the multitude of your
    sacrifices? says the Lord.
I have had enough of burnt offerings
    of rams and the fat of fed beasts;
I do not delight in the blood of bulls,
    or of lambs, or of he-goats.
    (Isaiah 1:11)

A contemporary of Isaiah, the prophet Micah, also criticized the people for their iniquity and foretold destruction:

Hear this, you heads of the house of
    Jacob
and rulers of the house of Israel,
who abhor justice and pervert
    all equity ...
because of you Zion shall be
    ploughed as a field;
Jerusalem shall become a heap of
    ruins. (Micah 3:9,12)

Ahaz, however, refused to listen to these words; trusting in his own political alliances, he believed his kingdom was secure.

In the next century, the prophet Jeremiah similarly warned that the southern kingdom would eventually be devastated by foreign powers. The Lord, he declared, had this message for the southern kingdom:

Break up your fallow ground
and sow not among thorns.
Circumcise yourselves to the Lord,
remove the foreskins of your hearts,

O men of Judah and inhabitants
    of Jerusalem;
lest my wrath go forth like fire
and burn with none to quench it,
because of the evil of your doings.

Declare in Judah, and proclaim
    in Jerusalem, and say,
'Blow the trumpet through
    the land';
cry aloud and say,
'Assemble and let us go into the
    fortified cities!'
Raise a standard toward Zion,
flee for safety, stay not,
for I bring evil from the north,
and great destruction.
    (Jeremiah 4:3–6)

DESTRUCTION AND EXILE

In the following century Isaiah, Micah and Jeremiah's predictions were fulfilled: after a siege of 18 months, Jerusalem was conquered in 586BCE; all the main buildings were destroyed, King Zedekiah of Judah (597–86BCE) was blinded and exiled to Babylon.

The anguish of the people facing the tragedy of Babylonian conquest and captivity is reflected in the Book of Lamentations. Here the exiles

Right *Hosea was a compassionate prophet who exhorted the people of Israel to reform. A panel from Sienna Cathedral, 1308.*

bemoaned their fate as predicted by the prophets. The nation had betrayed the covenant and God poured out his wrath as he warned. Reflecting on their holy city, Jerusalem, they declared:

How lonely sits the city that was full
    of people!
How like a widow she has become,
She that was great among
    the nations! ...
The roads to Zion mourn,
for none come
    to the appointed feasts;
all her gates are desolate,
her priests groan;
her maidens have been
    dragged away
and she herself suffers bitterly.
    (Lamentations 1:1,4)

HELLENISTIC JUDAISM

GREEK CIVILIZATION HAD A PROFOUND IMPACT ON JEWRY, AFFECTING ALL ASPECTS OF JEWISH LIFE. YET THESE CHANGES EVOKED A FIERCE RESPONSE FROM PIOUS JEWS LOYAL TO THE TRADITION.

Although it is possible that there was some contact between Greeks and the ancient Hebrews, it was not until the 4th century BCE, during the reign of Alexander the Great (336–323BCE), that Greek civilization had a significant impact on Jewish life. The Hellenistic period was thus marked by the increasing influence of Greek ideas on the Jewish tradition.

THE HELLENISTIC PERIOD

During the centuries after Alexander the Great's reign, Palestine was part of Hellenistic kingdoms, first of Ptolemaic Egypt and then of Seleucid Syria. In the first third of the 2nd century BCE a group of Hellenizing Jews seized power in Jerusalem. Led by wealthy Jewish aristocrats who were attracted to Hellenism, their influence was primarily social rather than cultural and religious. Later, Jason the high priest (175–172BCE) established Jerusalem as a Greek city, Antioch-at-Jerusalem, with Greek educational institutions, such as the gymnasium.

Below *A 2nd-century CE coin of Antiochus IV Epiphanes, the Seleucid king who caused the Maccabean revolt.*

However, Jason was only a moderate Hellenizer compared with his successor as high priest, Menelaus, whose succession provoked a civil war. The Tobiads supported Menelaus, whereas the masses favoured Jason. It was these Hellenizers, including Menelaus and his followers, who influenced the Seleucid King Antiochus IV Epiphanes (175–164BCE) to undertake his persecutions of Jews in order to crush the rebellion of the Hasideans.

GREEK INFLUENCE

Yet, despite such rebellion the influence of Hellenism was widespread in both Palestine and the Diaspora. Greek was substituted for Hebrew and Aramaic; Greek personal names were frequently adopted; Greek educational institutions were created; there was an efflorescence of Jewish Hellenistic literature and philosophy; and syncretism was widespread. The most obvious instance of Greek influence took place in the creation of Jewish literature during the Hellenistic period. The Jewish wisdom writer Ben Sira, for example, includes a number of aphorisms borrowed from Greek sources. The Testament of Joseph and the Book of Judith show Greek influence. Similarly, the Book of Tobit shows Hellenistic influence in the form of its romance. In his paraphrase of the Bible, the Jewish historian made numerous changes. Abraham, for example, is presented as worthy of Greek political and philosophical ideals; Samson is an Aristotelian-like, great-souled man; Saul is a kind of Achilles; and Solomon is like Oedipus.

Above *The battle of the Maccabees during the Hasmonean revolt by Jean Fouquet for Jewish historian Josephus's* Antiquities of the Jews.

HELLENISM IN THE DIASPORA

It seems that there was no systematic pattern of Hellenizing in the Diaspora. Indeed, some Alexandrian Jewish writers argued that the Greeks had borrowed from the Jews. The Jewish Peripatetic philosopher Aristobulus asserted in the 2nd century BCE that Homer, Hesiod, Pythagoras, Socrates and Plato were all acquainted with a translation of the Torah into Greek. The first significant Graeco-Jewish historian, Eupolemus, reported that Moses taught the alphabet to the Jews, who then passed it on to the Phoenicians who transmitted it to the Greeks. The 1st-century BCE Jewish philosopher Philo was profoundly affected by Hellenism: the influence

Below *Painting of the Temple of Solomon from the Hellenistic Dura-Europos synagogue in Syria, 3rd century CE.*

Above Menelaus became high priest after bribing Antiochus IV with tribute money. 13th-century French illustration.

> ### RABBINIC JUDAISM AND HELLENISM
> With regard to the rabbis, a number of tales are told about Hillel, which recall Socratic and Cynic anecdotes. Further, Joshua ben Hananiah's discussions with the Athenian, Alexandrian and Roman philosophers, Meir's disputations with the Cynic Oenomaus of Gadara, and Yehuda Ha-Nasi's discussions with Antoninus illustrate rabbinic interest. Platonism appears to have influenced the rabbis with its theory of ideas. In addition, there are a number of parallels between the Epicureans and the rabbis. The Stoic ideal of the sage as well as the Stoic technique of allegorizing the law appear to have influenced Philo. Possibly the rules for the administration of the Essenes were influenced by Pythagoreanism – Josephus in any case observed that the Essenes followed the Pythagorean way of life.

of Greek thought transcends mere language and affected his entire philosophical system.

ART AND LITERATURE
Beyond literary works, Greek influence is clearly illustrated in Hellenistic Jewish art and architecture. According to Josephus (37/38–100CE), the courts and colonnades of the Temple built by Herod in Jerusalem were in the Greek style. In synagogues in Palestine and the Diaspora, especially at Dura-Europos in Mesopotamia, the artwork was in direct violation of biblical and rabbinic prohibitions. The symbols used represent a kind of allegorization through art, similar to what Philo had attempted through philosophy. There is even evidence that some Jews adopted pagan elements in the charms and amulets they created. It is not surprising therefore that contact with Hellenism produced deviations from the Jewish tradition. Writers and artists who used extreme allegories in their work interpreted ceremonial laws as only a parable. Others relaxed their Jewish observance in order to become citizens of Alexandria. Indeed, the city of Alexandria, where Hellenism was most manifest, was the only place where Christianity seems to have made real inroads in converting Jews.

JEWISH RESISTANCE
The spread of Hellenism gave rise to powerful resistance among the observant. Jewish struggle against Greek and Roman domination was provoked by a reaction to what was seen as spiritual corruption. Jewish monotheism and observance of the covenant were challenged by the influence of foreign ideas. This was most manifest in the Hasmonean revolt. When Antiochus IV conquered Jerusalem in 167BCE, he banned circumcision, Sabbath observance and the reading of the Torah; he also decreed that the Temple should be dedicated to the worship of the Greek god Zeus, that pigs should be sacrificed on the altar, and that all people, including non-Jews, should be allowed to worship there. In championing Hellenism, he underestimated Jewish resistance to such reforms. Many Jews were prepared to die rather than violate their traditions, and in the end the nation triumphed against its oppressors.

Below Seleucid general Nicanor attacked the Palestinian rebel leader Judah Maccabee and the Jews on the Sabbath, during the Hasmonean revolt. Drawing by Gustave Doré, 1865.

Samaritans

IN THE NORTHERN KINGDOM THE SAMARITANS KEPT THEIR OWN TRADITIONS BASED ON SCRIPTURE. AS TIME PASSED, HOSTILITY GREW BETWEEN THE JEWISH AND THE SAMARITAN PEOPLES.

In ancient times the Samaritans constituted a separate people originating from within the Jewish community. This Jewish sect, which occupied Samaria after the conquest of the Northern Kingdom by the Assyrians, developed its own interpretation of the faith. Intermingling with the resident non-Jewish population, its mixed community continued to follow the Jewish way of life while simultaneously adopting pagan practices.

When Cyrus of Persia (590/580–529BCE) conquered Babylon in the 6th century CE, he allowed the Jews to return from Babylonia to their homeland. When the Samaritans offered to help these returning exiles rebuild the Temple, the governor of Judea Zerubbabel, who supervised the repair and restoration of the Temple, refused their offer since he regarded them as of uncertain racial origin and was suspicious of their worship. Recognizing that they would be excluded from the state which these exiles were intent on creating, the Samaritans persuaded the Persian officials responsible for the western empire that the plans for restoration were illegal, thereby delaying work on the Temple for ten years or more. This was the beginning of the enmity between the Jewish and Samaritan peoples, which continued for hundreds of years.

BELIEF AND PRACTICE

Despite their rejection from the Jewish community, the Samaritans remained loyal to traditional belief and practice. In its earliest form, the Samaritan creed consisted of a simple belief in God and the Torah (Pentateuch). For the Samaritans, God is the wholly other – he is manifest in all things, all powerful and beyond comprehension. His purposes for Israel and all peoples were communicated to Moses on Mount Sinai. According to Samaritan tradition, Moses was God's representative who wrote the Torah and authorized Mount Gerizim as the place that God chose for sacrifice. In addition, the Samaritans subscribed to a belief in resurrection and anticipated the arrival of one who would restore all things prior to the final judgement of God.

Given that the Samaritans possessed only the Torah as the sole authoritative source, the Pentateuch served as the basis of their religious practices. Frequently the Samaritans were stricter about the interpretation of biblical law than the rabbis because of their adherence to the letter of the law. In other cases, Samaritan law deviated from rabbinic traditions because of different interpretations of the text.

Regarding the Sabbath, for example, the Samaritans held four prayer services. The first, on the Sabbath eve, lasted for about an hour before the setting of the sun. This was followed on the Sabbath morning by a second service, which began between 3 and 4 a.m. The afternoon service was held only on regular Sabbaths and those that fall during the counting of the Omer; it began at

Above *In the 1920s, arranged marriages among Samaritan children of the West Bank were still common.*

Below *On Passover eve, Samaritans today sacrifice a lamb, which is roasted whole and eaten by the community.*

noon and lasted for about two hours. The fourth prayer service took place at the end of the Sabbath and continued for about half an hour until the sun set.

In addition to Sabbath observance, the Samaritans also celebrated the other festivals recorded in Scripture. For the Samaritan community, the Passover was of central significance. On the eve of the festival, the Samaritans carried out the sacrifice of the paschal lamb on Mount Gerizim. At twilight on the 14th day of the first month, all members of the community gathered at the site of the altar in two groups; the first carried out the sacrifice and the second engaged in prayer. The High Priest then climbed on to a large stool and gave the signal to slaughter the sheep while reading the account of the Exodus from Egypt. Then a number of sheep corresponding to the families present were slaughtered.

Another major festival is Shavuot, when the Samaritans made a pilgrimage to Mount Gerizim. This holiday was celebrated on the 50th day of the counting of the Omer. The per-

Below *A magnificent Samaritan Torah case decorated in gold with images of objects used in the Temple.*

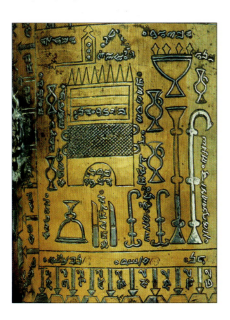

Above *At Shavuot, Samaritans parade at Mount Gerizim, Israel, celebrating the giving of the law on Mount Sinai.*

iod is divided into seven weeks; in each week the Samaritans devoted the Sabbath to one of the places that the children of Israel passed on the Exodus from Egypt before arriving at Mount Sinai. On the first day after the sixth Sabbath, the Samaritans celebrated the day standing on Mount Sinai – there they prayed and read from the Torah (Pentateuch) from the middle of the night until the following evening. The seventh Sabbath is called the celebration of the Ten Commandments. The pilgrimage itself began early in the evening and all places holy to the Samaritans were visited.

LITERATURE

Turning to the literature of the Samaritan community, the earliest work was the Pentateuch, which served as the centre of Samaritan life. The *Defter* constituted the oldest part of the liturgy and was probably written in the 4th century CE. There were also Samaritan chronicles, including the *Asatir*, a midrashic work, and *Al-Tolidah*, which contained various genealogical lists. The Samaritan Book of Joshua recounted the history of the Samaritan people from the initiation of Joshua to the days of Baba Rabbah. The *Annals* by Abu al-Fath were composed in the 14th century and were explained in the 19th to 20th centuries by Jacob ben Harun.

The *New Chronicle* was written in Samaritan Hebrew by Av-Sakhva ben Asad ha-Danfi and related events from Adam to 1900 CE. The Samaritan corpus included a variety of halakhic works, Pentaetuch commentaries, and grammatical studies.

In all cases, Samaritan literature was centred around the Pentateuch and the religious life of the community. The purpose of these works was to guide the community in understanding the meaning of Scripture, ensuring that the biblical precepts were fulfilled in the lives of the adherents. This religious orientation illustrates the traditionalism of the Samaritan sect despite its deviation from mainstream Judaism. Holding fast to the religious tenets of the faith, the Samaritans strictly adhered to the Jewish way of life as they understood it. In this respect they regarded themselves as following an authentic form of Judaism despite their divergence from the rabbis.

Throughout its history the Samaritan community was committed to observing the law and fulfilling its covenant duties as it understood them.

Below *A Samaritan priest with the ancient Pentateuch in the Samaritan synagogue in Nablus, West Bank.*

Sadducees

MEMBERS OF A 2ND-CENTURY BCE JEWISH SECT, POSSIBLY FORMED AS A POLITICAL PARTY, THE SADDUCEES BELIEVED THE TORAH WAS DIVINELY REVEALED AND BIBLICAL LAW MUST BE STRICTLY FOLLOWED.

According to tradition, the Sadducees were followers of the teachings of the High Priest Zadok. Scholars, however, have pointed out that this explanation is unlikely since the Sadducees made their debut in history as supporters of the Hasmonean high priests. Thus, the term 'Sadducees' may be a Hebraization of the Greek word *sundikoi*, or 'members of the council'. This would mark them out as councillors of the Hasmoneans even though they themselves came to associate their name with the Hebrew *zedek*, or 'righteous'. According to rabbinic sources, the Sadducees were not named after the High Priest Zadok, but rather

Below *A fanciful 19th-century lithograph showing the breastplate and supposed costume of the Jewish high priest.*

Right *Jewish historian Flavius Josephus, who described the Hasmonean revolt, is brought before Titus, Roman commander in Judea during the Jewish revolt 66CE.*

another Zadok who rebelled against the teachings of Antigonus of Soko, a government official of Judea in the 3rd century BCE who was a predecessor of the rabbis.

Despite these different interpretations, it is clear that the Sadducees were a priestly group, associated with the leadership of the Jerusalem Temple. Possibly, the Sadducees belonged to the aristocratic clan of the Hasmonean high priests who replaced the previous high priestly lineage that permitted the Syrian Emperor Antiochus IV Epiphanes to desecrate the Temple of Jerusalem with idolatrous sacrifices. The festival of Hanukkah celebrates the overthrowing of the Syrian forces, the rededication of the Temple, and the instalment of a new Hasmonean priestly line.

In the following years the Hasmoneans ruled as priest-kings; like other aristocracies across the Hellenistic world, they were increasingly influenced by Hellenistic ideas. Like the Epicureans, the Sadducees rejected the existence of an afterlife, thereby denying the Pharisaic doctrine of the resurrection of the dead. The Dead Sea Scrolls community – identified with the Essenes – were led by a high priestly caste who were believed to be the descendants of the legitimate high priestly lineage which the Hasmoneans removed. According to the Dead Sea Scrolls, the current high priests were interlopers since the Hasmoneans constituted a different priestly line.

THE INTERPRETATION OF SCRIPTURE

Most of what is known about the Sadducees is derived from the writings of the Jewish historian Josephus; other information is contained in the Talmud. According to these sources, the Sadducees rejected the Pharisaic belief in an oral Torah. Instead, they interpreted the Torah literally. In their personal lives this led to an excessively stringent lifestyle.

The fact that the Sadducees had a high opinion of the Five Books of Moses does not mean that they denied that the other books of the Bible – the prophets and historical writings – were divinely inspired. Yet they refused to accept the other biblical books as sources of law. When a Sadducee had to judge a case he would look in the written Torah and ignore the oral traditions that the Pharisees accepted as normative. One of the consequences of such an approach was that the Sadducees stressed the importance of the priests in the Temple cult, while the Pharisees insisted on the participation of all Jews.

In developing their approach to Scripture, the Sadducees had interpretative traditions of their own which were written down in a

Above *Ceremonies at the Temple in Jerusalem, from the Bible Mozarabe, a 10th-century Spanish manuscript.*

book of jurisprudence known as the Book of Decrees. The existence of this code is known from a rabbinical source, the *Megilla Ta'anit*, a calendar-like text, which states that the Book of Decrees was revoked on the 4th of Tammuz, although no year is given. The code that is described is very harsh. An example of the

Below *A section of the oldest surviving map of the Holy Land. This part of the 5th-century CE mosaic map from Madaba, Jordan, shows Jerusalem and the area around.*

Sadducean approach concerns the interpretation of the biblical law concerning 'an eye for an eye.' The Pharisees believed that the value of an eye was to be sought by the perpetrator of its loss rather than actually removing his eye in accordance with the law. The Sadducees, however, insisted that the law should be taken literally.

SADDUCEAN THEOLOGY

Regarding Sadducean belief, many sources stress that the Sadducees believed that souls die with their bodies. The rabbinical text known as *Avot de Rabbi Nathan* states that a discussion about this subject was the cause of the schism between the Sadducees and the Pharisees.

According to the *Avot de Rabbi Nathan*, the Pharisee teacher Antigonus of Soko had two disciples who used to study his words. They taught them to their disciples, and their disciples to their disciples. These proceeded to examine the words closely and demanded, 'Why did our ancestors see fit to say this thing? Is it possible that a labourer should do his work all day and not take his reward in the evening? If our ancestors, forsooth, had known that there is no other world and that there will be a resurrection of the dead, they would not have spoken in this manner.'

So they arose and withdrew from the study of the oral Torah, and split into two sects.

TEMPLE PRACTICES

With regard to Temple ritual, the Sadducees insisted that the daily burnt sacrifices were to be offered by the high priest at his own expense, whereas the Pharisees maintained that they were to be furnished as a national sacrifice at the cost of the Temple treasury. The Sadducees also held that the meal offering belonged to the priest's portion, whereas the Pharisees claimed it was for the altar.

Above *A 15th-century miniature showing that ritual animal slaughter is a part of the Jewish way of life.*

The Sadducees insisted on a high degree of purity in those who officiated at the preparation of the ashes of the Red Heifer. By contrast, the Pharisees opposed such strictness.

With regard to the kindling of the incense in the vessel with which the high priest entered the Holy of Holies on the Day of Atonement, the Sadducees claimed it should take place outside so that he might be wrapped in smoke while meeting the Shekhinah (divine presence) within; the Pharisees insisted that the incense be kindled inside.

In addition, the Sadducees opposed the popular festivity of the water libation and the procession that preceded it on each night of Sukkot, marking the end of the agricultural year. They also opposed the Pharisaic assertion that the scrolls of the Torah have the power to render ritually unclean the hands that touch them; the Pharisaic idea of the *eruv* (the merging of several private precincts into one so that food and vessels can be carried from place to place); and the formula introduced by the Pharisees in divorce documents.

Pharisees

ALONGSIDE THE SADDUCEES AND THE ESSENES, THE PHARISEES CONSTITUTED A MAJOR JEWISH PARTY IN THE HELLENISTIC PERIOD. AFTER THE FALL OF THE TEMPLE, THE PHARISEES DOMINATED JEWISH LIFE.

The Pharisees were a Jewish religious and political party who emerged shortly after the Hasmonean revolt in about 165–160BCE. In all likelihood they were the successors of the Hasideans who had promoted the observance of Jewish ritual and the study of the Torah. Regarding themselves as followers of Ezra, they maintained the validity of the Oral Torah as well as of the Written Torah.

THE EMERGENCE OF THE PHARISEES

The origin of their name is uncertain, though it is generally believed that the name Pharisees derives from the word *parash*, or 'to be separated' – thus Pharisees would mean the separated ones or the separatists. Determined to adapt biblical law to new conditions, they formulated a complex system of scriptural interpretation. Initially the Pharisees were small in number, but by the 1st century CE they had profoundly influenced the religious beliefs, practices and social attitudes of the majority of the nation.

The Pharisees' first bid for power took place in a period two centuries after the Babylonian exile, during the struggle to remove the Temple and religious control from the leadership of the Sadducees. The inception of synagogue worship was an attempt by the Pharisees to undermine the privileged authority of the Sadducees; in addition, ceremonies that were originally part of the Temple cult were carried over to the home, and scholars of non-priestly descent came to play an important role in national affairs. Unlike the Sadducees, the Pharisees believed that the Written Torah required expansion. As a consequence, Pharisaic sages developed an elaborate system of biblical interpretation.

PHARISAIC SCHOLARSHIP

According to rabbinic writings, Pharisaic sages first appeared as the men of the Great Assembly. Subsequently there were five generations of *zugot* (pairs) of outstanding Pharisees who served as leaders of the Pharisaic supreme court until the beginning of the 1st century CE. During the civil war of the reign of Alexander Janneus, the Pharisees were among the king's enemies. Later they were restored by Salome Alexandra. The Pharisees then exacted retribution on the Sadducees. The Jewish historian Josephus records there were

Above *The prophet Ezra reads the law, which was expanded by the Pharisees. A 2nd-century CE painting from Dura-Europos synagogue, Syria.*

Below *Jesus on trial before the Sanhedrin, the Jewish supreme court, which was dominated by the Sadducees. A 6th-century CE mosaic from Ravenna.*

about 6,000 Pharisees during King Herod's reign. By the second or third decades of the 1st century CE, the Pharisees had become divided into two schools of thought: the school of Hillel and the school of Shammai.

While scholars disagree on whether the Pharisees were the dominant group in Erez Israel before 70CE, there is no doubt that once the Temple in Jerusalem was destroyed by the Romans they became the leading party. As such, the Pharisees exerted a profound influence on Jewish life. The hereditary priestly caste was superseded by a new form of leadership that was based on learning, knowledge and wisdom. The most important relationship among the Pharisees was between a teacher and student. A sage's reputation was based on learning transmitted orally from him to his students. Pharisaic maxims from this period deal with such ethical issues as honesty in judging, ethical responsibility and serving God.

THE DEVELOPMENT OF PHARISAIC JUDAISM

Towards the end of the 1st century CE under Rabban Gamaliel II, the Sanhedrin (rabbinical assembly) at Yavneh strengthened a post-Temple form of Judaism. The term rabbi came into general use for a sage recognized as such by his peers. The sages at Yavneh summarized the teachings of the earlier schools of Hillel and

Above *Giacomo Giaquerio's shifty painting of a Pharisee from a 15th-century north Italian fresco about the life of Jesus, at the Castello della Manta.*

Shammai. In addition, they canonized the Scriptures, gave a more precise form to daily prayer, and transferred to the synagogue and the Sanhedrin various observances associated with the Temple. An ordination procedure for rabbis was instituted and the Sanhedrin exerted control over all aspects of Jewish life.

As far as the belief system of the Pharisees was concerned, Pharisaic theology was based on the conviction that God is an omnipotent, spiritual being who is all-wise, all-knowing and all-merciful. God, they believed, loves all his creatures and expects human beings to act justly and compassionately. Although God is omniscient and omnipotent, he endowed human beings with the power to choose between good and evil. Every person, the Pharisees stressed, has two impulses: the *yetzer tov* (good inclination) and the *yetzer ha-ra* (evil inclination). Yet despite

Left *This floor mosaic from an ancient synagogue in Jericho shows a menorah above the inscription 'Shalom al Israel' (Peace upon Israel').*

the belief in free will, the Pharisees held that everything in the world was ordained by God. Unlike the Sadducees, Pharisees believed in the resurrection of the dead. This concept of a future life made possible the belief in the divine justice in the face of calamity and suffering.

Pharisaic theological reflection is found in various collections of midrashim (commentaries on Scripture). Unlike the Mishnah, which consists of legislation presented without explicit reference to Scriptural sources, rabbinic aggadah (commentary on the Bible) focuses on the contemporary relevance of specific texts. Though the sages were not speculative philosophers, they expressed their religious views in these works and attempted to apply this teaching to daily life. These midrashic sources, along with the aggadic sections of the Talmud, serve as the basis for reconstructing the theology of early rabbinic Judaism.

Below *A 15th-century German Torah scroll. Unlike the Sadducees, the Pharisees believed the Written Torah needed expansion.*

Essenes

THE ESSENES WERE THE THIRD PRINCIPAL SECT IN THE HELLENISTIC PERIOD. CONGREGATED IN SEMI-MONASTIC COMMUNITIES, THEY SAW THE HELLENIZERS AND SADDUCEES AS VIOLATORS OF GOD'S LAW.

The dispute between the Pharisees and the Sadducees centred around the religious leadership of the Jewish people. However, there were other smaller groupings that withdrew from society into holy communities who rejected the priests who controlled the Temple. Preeminent among these groups were the Essenes, who, according to the Jewish historian Josephus (37/38–100CE), believed in fate and the immortality of the soul. They lived as a separatist association in the towns of Judea and also in rural communes, where members engaged in agricultural and artisan labour as well as the study of religious writings.

Admission to this order occurred only after several periods of probation and preparation. Those initiated into the faith had to swear obedience to the rules and leadership of the community and promise that they would keep secret its special doctrines. Discipline was enforced by the expulsion of lax members after a vote by the council. Among the inner circle, property was owned jointly. Food, clothing and other necessities were administered by overseers. Essene rituals included wearing white garments, taking frequent ritual baths and eating community meals accompanied by prayer and a reading from Scripture.

According to Josephus, the Essenes numbered about 4,000 in the 1st century CE. He asserted that Essene prophets were held in high regard by the masses and the kings for the accuracy of their predictions and medical knowledge.

THE DEAD SEA SECT

According to modern scholars, an Essene-like group lived between 150BCE and 68CE in the Judean desert near the Dead Sea. In 1947 Arab shepherds discovered a group of documents – the Dead Sea Scrolls – which were traced to 11 caves not far from Jerusalem where they were preserved by the desert climate. The Dead Sea Scrolls include communal rule books, hymns and biblical commentaries. Near this site was uncovered the remains of a community that flourished from about 130BCE to the time of the Roman–Jewish war. The ruins discovered on a cliff north of the Wadi Qumran include a tower, assembly chamber, kitchen, writing room and worship space. It appears that the members of this sect slept in tents, caves or upper rooms of this building.

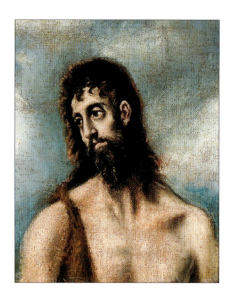

Above *El Greco's 16th-century painting of John the Baptist, cousin of Jesus, who may have had contact with the Essenes.*

An elaborate system of cisterns ensured an adequate supply of water for the members of this group. The community's cemetery contained a thousand burials. For nearly two centuries, Qumran was the headquarters of a well-organized settlement,

Below *This fragment of the Dead Sea Scrolls shows the Song of Degrees, one of the Psalms of King David.*

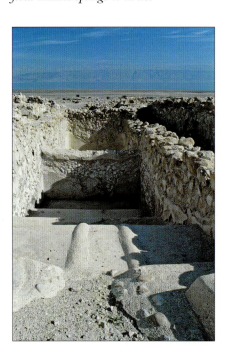

Below *A ritual bath or* mikveh *of the Essene sect at Qumran, 2nd century* BCE. *Water in* mikvehs *should come from natural springs or rivers.*

Right *The Qumran caves in the Judean desert, where the Dead Sea Scrolls were discovered 1946–56.*

which at its height numbered about 200. The Dead Sea Scrolls were most likely the remains of the Qumran library, which was hidden during the Roman–Jewish war when Qumran was destroyed by the Romans.

QUMRAN AND THE ESSENES

Assuming that Qumran was an Essene community and the Dead Sea Scrolls a collection of their writings, then the movement was both quietistic and philosophical. The scrolls depict a priest-dominated group who viewed the Temple as dominated by corrupt men who had usurped power.

From references in Qumran texts, the site seems to have been founded by a priestly 'Teacher of Righteousness', who was persecuted as a wicked priest. The community regarded the *Kittim* (possibly the Romans) with hostility and regarded itself as the true heir of the Mosaic covenant and of God's promises. Members of the order had been preserved from the domination of evil powers. The group had been saved from the domination of these forces in order to settle in the wilderness under the leadership of true priests, until they could return to a Temple that had been purified.

As members of the covenant, these individuals constituted the divine elect of God, who had predetermined whether they would join the holy community (Sons of Light) or remain outside with those hostile to God (Sons of Darkness). Eventually the Sons of Light would issue forth in ritual combat under the leadership of their divinely appointed leaders to reestablish the remnant of Israel in the Promised Land and to witness the victory of God over the entire earth.

INDIVIDUAL CHARISMATICS

In the Judean desert there were also individual charismatics who, though not formally affiliated with the Essenes, adopted similar attitudes and practices. John the Baptist, for example, was described in the New Testament as clothed with camel's hair, a leather girdle around his waist, and eating locusts and wild honey. According to Scripture, he preached a baptism of repentance for the forgiveness of sins. Another figure was John's mentor, Bannus. According to the Jewish historian Josephus, Bannus dwelt in the wilderness, wearing only such clothing as trees provided, feeding on such things as grew of themselves and using frequent ablutions of cold water, by day and night for purity's sake. In the 40s of the 1st century CE, Theudas declared himself a prophet and persuaded crowds to follow him to the River Jordan. A decade later an Egyptian prophet led his group to the Mount of Olives outside Jerusalem, proposing to force his way into the city, overpower the Roman garrison and set himself up as ruler of the people.

CHAPTER 2

RABBINIC JUDAISM

From the 1st century BCE to the 2nd century CE, rabbinic scholars engaged in the interpretation of Scripture. In their view, the Five Books of Moses were given by God to Moses on Mount Sinai. This belief implies that God is the direct source of all laws recorded in the Torah, and is also indirectly responsible for the authoritative legal judgements of the rabbis. Alongside their exegesis of biblical law, scholars also produced interpretations of Scripture in rabbinic commentaries and the Talmud. Within these texts is a wealth of theological, philosophical and mystical speculation.

The Karaites, a radical sect, later challenged rabbinic Judaism. Their guiding interpretative principle was: 'Search thoroughly in Scripture and do not rely on my opinion.' Further challenges were posed by the Shabbateans and Frankists. In the 17th century, a self-proclaimed messianic king, Shabbetai Tzvi, electrified the Jewish world with his claims. After his conversion to Islam, the majority of his followers were despondent, yet a number continued to believe in his messiahship. These Shabbateans and a later Shabbatean sect, the Frankists, remained convinced that the messianic era had begun.

Opposite *The title page of a Hebrew manuscript of the* Guide for the Perplexed *by the 12th-century Jewish philosopher and rabbinic scholar Moses Maimonides.*

Above *In 1999, Menachem Joskowicz, Chief Rabbi of Poland, asked John-Paul II to remove a large Christian cross from land bordering the concentration camp of Auschwitz.*

Introducing Rabbinic Judaism

THE RABBIS CONSTITUTED A SCHOLARLY CLASS DRAWN FROM THE PHARISEES. THEY PRODUCED A MASSIVE CORPUS OF LEGAL TEXTS, BIBLICAL EXEGESIS, THEOLOGICAL WORKS AND ETHICAL REFLECTIONS.

With the destruction of the Second Temple in 70CE, the Pharisees emerged as the dominant religious group. These sages were determined to forge a new form of Judaism based on scriptural precedent. In their view, both the written and the oral Torah were expressions of God's will.

During the Tannaitic period (1st century BCE–2nd century CE) and the Amoraic period (2nd–6th century CE) rabbinic scholars – referred to as the Tannaim and the Amoraim respectively – actively engaged in the interpretation of Scripture. According to the Pharisaic tradition, both the written Torah and its interpretation (oral Torah) were given by God to Moses on Mount Sinai. This belief, which implies that God is the direct source of all laws recorded in the Pentateuch and indirectly responsible for the authoritative legal judgements of the rabbis, served as the justification for the rabbinic exposition of scriptural ordinances.

INTERPRETING SCRIPTURE

Alongside the halakha, or the 'exegesis of Jewish law', scholars also produced aggadah, or 'interpretations of Scripture in which new meanings of the text were expounded' in midrashim or 'rabbinic commentaries', and in the Talmud. Within the aggadic texts is found a wealth of theological speculation about such topics as the nature of God, divine justice, the coming of the Messiah and the hereafter. In addition, ethical considerations were of considerable importance in the discussions of these teachers of the faith.

Early rabbinic Judaism thus covered a wide variety of areas that were all embraced by the holy word revealed on Mount Sinai, and this literature served as the foundation of later Judaism as it developed through the centuries.

Above Sage and pupil learning Hillel's golden rule –'What is hateful to you, do not do to another'. *From the Coburg Pentateuch by Samuel Halevi, 1395.*

RABBINIC EXEGESIS

The exegesis found in rabbinic literature of the Tannaitic and Amoraic periods is largely of two types: direct and explicit exegesis where the biblical text is commented on or accompanied by a remark, and indirect exegesis where a scriptural text is cited to support an assertion. In the case of direct exegesis, the rabbis frequently reinforced their exhortations by a biblical sentence which expressed their sentiments. It was also a usual custom in rabbinic circles to cite a text and then draw out its meaning. Further, the rabbis frequently stressed that a word should be understood in its strictest sense. Occasionally they also employed typological exegesis to explain the meaning of Scripture.

Turning to the method of indirect exegesis, it was a common practice in rabbinic literature to draw deductions from scriptural texts by means of a number of formal hermeneutical rules. Hillel the elder, who flourished about a century before the destruction of the Second Temple, is reported to have been the first to lay down these principles. In the 2nd century CE Ishmael ben Elisha expanded Hillel's seven rules

Below Moses ben Yekuthiel Hakohen *commissioned what is now known as* The Rothschild Miscellany *in 1479 to show customs of religious and secular life as expounded by rabbinic sages in a Jewish Renaissance household.*

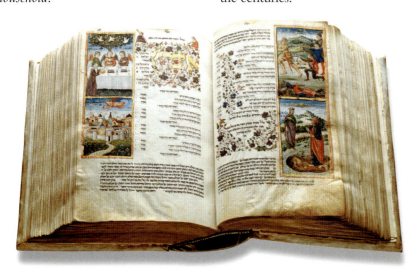

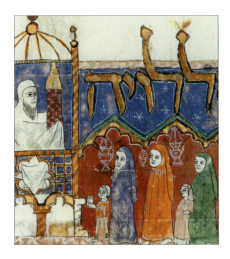

Above *A rabbi reads to his people from a* Sefer Torah, *the handwritten copy of the Pentateuch. From the 14th-century Barcelona Haggadah.*

into thirteen by sub-dividing them, omitting one, and adding a new one of his own.

These various methods of exegesis were based on the deeply held conviction that the Bible is sacred, that it is susceptible of interpretation and that, when properly understood, it will guide the life of the worthy. By means of this process of explanation of God's revelation, rabbinic authorities were able to infuse the tradition with new meaning and renewed relevance.

RABBINIC THEOLOGY

Unlike the Mishnah, which consists of legislation presented without explicit reference to a Scriptural source, rabbinic aggadah focuses on the contemporary relevance of specific biblical texts. The early halakhic midrashim consists of Tannaitic commentaries on the legal verses of the Bible. Narrative midrashim, on the other hand, derive from sermons given by the Amoraim in synagogues and academies. Within these texts the rabbis propounded their theological views by means of stories, legends, parables and maxims based on Scripture. Within aggadic sources, the rabbis expressed their profound reflections on human life and God's nature and activity in the world. Unlike the legal precepts of the Torah and the rabbinic expansion of these scriptural ordinances, these theological opinions were not binding on the Jewish community. They were formulated instead to educate, inspire and edify those to whom they were addressed. Study of the Torah was a labour of love that had no end, a task whose goal was to serve the will of God.

Above *A contemporary North African rabbi wearing Arab-style headgear and clothing and studying a Hebrew book.*

RABBINIC ETHICS

Supplementing these theological reflections, the rabbis in midrashic and talmudic sources also encouraged the Jewish people to put the teachings of the law into effect in their everyday lives. In their view the kingdom of God is inconsistent with injustice and social misery – the effort to bring about the perfection of the world so that God will reign in majesty is the responsibility of every Jew. Jewish ethics as enshrined in rabbinic literature were inextricably related to the coming of God's Kingdom. Throughout rabbinic sources, Jews were encouraged to strive for the highest conception of life, in which the rule of truth, righteousness and holiness will be established among humankind. Such a desire is the eternal hope of God's people – a longing for God's Kingdom. The coming of his rule requires a struggle for the reign of justice and righteousness on earth. This Kingdom is not an internalized, spiritualized, other-worldly concept, rather it involves human activity in a historical context.

Below *Rabbinic study group at Bircas Hatorah in Jerusalem, 1994, a yeshiva which is dedicated to Torah education.*

Early Mystical Judaism

ALONGSIDE OTHER MODES OF SCRIPTURAL INTERPRETATION, RABBINIC SCHOLARS ENGAGED IN MYSTICAL EXEGESIS. THEY FORMULATED COSMOLOGICAL THEORIES AS WELL AS METHODS OF HEAVENLY ASCENT.

Within aggadic sources, the rabbis also engaged in mystical speculation. These doctrines were often of a secret nature; in a midrash on Genesis it is reported that these mystical traditions were repeated in a whisper so that they would not be overheard by those for whom they were not intended. These secret doctrines served as the basis for the evolution of a mystical form of the Jewish tradition.

THE DIVINE CHARIOT

In the rabbis' mystical reflections, the first chapter of Ezekiel played an important role. In this biblical text the *merkavah*, or 'divine chariot', is described in detail, and this scriptural source served as the basis for rabbinic speculation about the nature of the deity. It was the aim of the mystic to be a 'merkavah rider'

Below *God creating the earth, planets and stars, from a 15th-century Armenian* Sefer Yezirah *or 'Book of Creation'.*

Right The Vision of Ezekiel *from a 15th-century Bible, showing the winged symbols of the four Christian evangelists – a man, a lion, an ox and an eagle.*

so that he would be able to penetrate the heavenly mysteries. Within this contemplative system, the rabbis believed that the pious could free themselves from the fetters of bodily existence and enter paradise. A further dimension of this theory is that certain pious individuals can temporarily ascend into the unseen realm and, having learnt the deepest secrets, may return to earth. These mystics were able to attain a state of ecstasy, to behold visions and hear voices. As students of the merkavah they were the ones to attain the highest degree of spiritual insight.

THE MYSTICS AND CREATION

Closely associated with this form of speculation were *Maaseh Bereshit*, or 'mystical theories about creation'. Within aggadic sources the rabbis discussed the hidden meanings of the Genesis narrative. The most important early treatise, possibly from the 2nd century CE, which describes the process of creation is *Sefer Yezirah*, or 'Book of Creation'. According to this cosmological text, God created the universe by 32 mysterious paths consisting of 22 letters of the Hebrew alphabet together with ten *sefirot*, or 'emanations'. Concerning these 22 letters, the *Sefer Yezirah* states: 'He hewed them, combined them, weighed them, interchanged them and through them produced the whole creation and everything that is destined to come into being.'

DIVINE EMANATION

These recondite doctrines were supplemented by a theory of divine emanation. The first of the sefirot is the spirit of the living God; the second is air and is derived from the first – on it are hewn the 22 letters. The third sefirah is the water that comes from the air; the fourth is the fire that comes from water through which God made the heavenly wheels, the seraphim and the ministering angels. The remaining six sefirot are the six dimensions of space – north, south, east, west, height and depth.

These ten sefirot are the moulds into which all created things were originally cast. They constitute form

HEAVENLY HALLS

A description of the experiences of these merkavah mystics is contained in *hekhalot*, or 'heavenly hall', literature from the later Gaonic period (from the 7th to the 11th century CE). In order to make their heavenly ascent, these mystics followed strict ascetic disciplines, including fasting, ablution and the invocation of God's name. After reaching a state of ecstasy, the mystic was able to enter the seven heavenly halls and attain a vision of the divine chariot.

EARLY MYSTICAL JUDAISM

rather than matter. The 22 letters are the prime cause of matter: everything that exists is due to the creative force of the Hebrew letters, but they receive their form from the sefirot. According to this, God transcends the universe; nothing exists outside him. The visible world is the result of the emanations of the divine. God is the cause of the form and matter of the cosmos. By combining emanation and creation, the *Sefer Yezirah* tries to harmonize the concept of divine imminence and transcendence. God is imminent in that the sefirot are an outpouring of his spirit. He is transcendent in that the matter, which was shaped into the forms, is the product of his creative action.

MEDIEVAL MYSTICISM

Drawing on these ideas, early medieval Jewish mystics elaborated a complex system of mystical thought. Referring to the traditions of early rabbinic mysticism, writers expanded and elaborated many of the doctrines found in midrashic and talmudic sources as well as in the *Sefer Yezirah*. In their writings these mystics saw themselves as the transmitters of a secret tradition which describes the supernal world to which all human beings are linked. One strand of this heritage focused on the nature of the spiritual world and its relationship with the terrestrial plane. The other more practical side attempted to use energies from the spiritual world to bring about miracle-working effects. According to these mystics, all of creation is in a struggle for redemption and liberation from evil, and their goal was to restore world harmony so that universal salvation would be attained through the coming of the Messiah and the establishment of the Kingdom of God.

Pre-eminent among these early medieval mystics were Jewish settlers in the Rhineland, the Hasidei Ashkenaz. Among the greatest figures of this period were the 12th-century Samuel ben Kalonymus of Speyer, his son Judah ben Samuel of Regensburg, and Eleazar ben Judah of Worms, who composed the treatise *The Secret of Secrets*. In their writings these mystics were preoccupied with the mystery of divine unity. God himself, they believed, cannot be known by human reason. The aim of the Hasidei Ashkenaz was to attain a vision of God's glory through the cultivation of the life of piety, which embraced devotion, saintliness and contemplation.

Below *A medieval Jewish hamsa, sometimes known as the hand of Miriam. Amulets like this were used to protect people from evil spirits.*

Above *This 19th-century Russian icon shows the prophet Elijah contemplating his ascent to heaven in a fiery chariot. Jewish mystics saw themselves as chariot riders on an ascent towards the Divine.*

295

KABBALISTIC JUDAISM

MEDIEVAL MYSTICS, KNOWN AS KABBALISTS, CONTINUED THE TRADITIONS OF EARLIER THINKERS. THE AIM OF THE KABBALISTS WAS TO ATTAIN THE HIGHEST LEVELS OF SPIRITUAL ILLUMINATION.

Parallel with the emergence of the Hasidei Ashkenaz, Jewish Kabbalists in southern France engaged in speculation about the nature of God, the existence of evil and the religious life. In 12th-century Provence the earliest Kabbalistic text, the *Bahir*, reinterpreted the concept of the sefirot as depicted in the *Sefer Yezirah*. According to the *Bahir*, the sefirot are conceived as vessels, crowns or words that constitute the structure of the divine realm.

Basing themselves on this work, various Provence Jews engaged in similar mystical reflection. Isaac the Blind conceived of the sefirot as emanations of a hidden dimension of the Godhead. Using neo-Platonic ideas, he argued that out of the *En Sof*, or 'infinite', emanated the first supernal essence (divine thought) from which came the remaining sefirot.

KABBALISTS IN GERONA

In Gerona, the traditions from Isaac the Blind were broadly disseminated. One of the most important was Azriel ben Menahem who replaced divine thought with the divine will as the first emanation of the En Sof. The most famous figure of this circle was Nahmanides (1194–1270CE) who helped this mystical school gain general acceptance. In his commentary on the Torah he frequently referred to Kabbalistic notions to explain the true meaning of the text. During the time these Geronese writers were propounding their Kabbalistic theories, other mystical schools of thought developed in Spain. Influenced by the Hasidei Ashkenaz and the Sufi traditions of Islam, Abraham ben Samuel Abulafia wrote meditative texts concerning the technique of combining the letters of the alphabet as a means of realizing human aspirations toward prophecy. They developed a complex system of mystical speculation coupled with mystical practice.

SPANISH KABBALISTS

Other Spanish Kabbalists were more attracted to Gnostic ideas. Isaac ha-Kohen elaborated the theory of a demonic emanation. The mingling of such Gnostic teaching with the Kabbalah of Gerona resulted in the major mystical work of Spanish Jewry, the Zohar, composed by Moses ben Shem Tov de Leon in Guadalajara. The author places the work in a 2nd-century CE setting, focusing on Simeon ben Yohai and his disciples, but the doctrines of the Zohar are of a much later origin. Written in Aramaic, the text is largely a midrash in which the Torah is given a mystical or ethical interpretation.

Above *A Kabbalist at festivities in Meron, Israel, to celebrate Simeon ben Yohai, commemorated in the Zohar.*

Below *A Hebrew book in the garden of the Nahmamid Institute, housed in a former synagogue in Gerona, Spain, once a centre of Jewish Kabbalah.*

THE EN SOF

According to these various Kabbalistic systems, God in himself lies beyond any speculative comprehension. To express the unknowable aspect of the Divine, the early Kabbalists of both Provence and Spain referred to the Divine Infinite as En Sof – the absolute perfection in which there is no distinction or plurality. The En Sof does not reveal itself; it is beyond all thought and at times is identified with the Aristotelian First Cause. In Kabbalistic teaching, creation is bound up with the manifestation of the hidden God and his outward movement.

DIVINE EMANATION

These sefirot emanate successively from above to below, each one revealing a stage in the process. The common order of the sefirot and the names most generally used are:

(1) supreme crown; (2) wisdom; (3) intelligence; (4) greatness; (5) power (or judgement); (6) beauty (or compassion); (7) endurance; (8) majesty; (9) foundation (or righteous one); (10) kingdom.

These ten sefirot are formally arranged in threes. The first triad consists of the first three sefirot and constitutes the intellectual realm of the inner structure of the Divine. The second triad is composed of the next three sefirot from the psychic or moral level of the Godhead. Finally, sefirot 7, 8 and 9 represent the archetypes of certain forces in nature. The remaining sefirah, kingdom, constitutes the channel between the higher and the lower worlds. The ten sefirot together demonstrate how an infinite undivided and unknowable God is the cause of all the modes of existence in the finite plane.

SPIRITUAL REALITY

In explaining this picture of Divine creation, Kabbalists adopted a neo-Platonic conception of a ladder of spiritual reality composed of four worlds in descending order. First is the domain of Atzilut, or 'emanation', consisting of the ten sefirot which form Adam Kadmon, or 'primordial man'. The second world, based on hekhalot, or 'heavenly hall', literature, is the realm of Beriyah, or 'creation', which is made up of the throne of glory and the seven heavenly palaces. In the third world, Yezirah, or 'formation', most of the angels dwell, presided over by the angel Metatron. This is the scene of the seven heavenly halls guarded by angels to which merkavah, or 'chariot', mystics attempt to gain admission. In the fourth world of Asiyah, or 'making', are the lowest order of angels – the ophanim, who combat evil and receive prayers. This is the spiritual archetype of the material cosmos, heaven and the earthly world.

Asiyah is both the last link in the Divine chain of being and the domain where the Sitra Ahra, or 'the realm of demonic powers', is manifest; in this sphere the forces of good struggle with the demons.

COSMIC REPAIR

For the mystic, deeds of *tikkun*, or 'cosmic repair', sustain the world, activate nature to praise God, and bring about the coupling of the tenth and the six sefirot. Such repair is accomplished by keeping the commandments which were conceived as vessels for establishing contact with the Godhead and for ensuring divine mercy. Such a religious life provided the Kabbalist with a means of integrating into the divine hierarchy of creation – the Kabbalah was able to guide the soul back to its Infinite source. The supreme rank attainable by the soul at the end of its sojourn is *devekut*, or 'mystical cleaving to God'. Devekut does not completely eliminate the distance between

Left *A Kabbalistic roll of 1604 by Jacob Hebron, showing the names of God, the 10 sefirot, the 32 paths, the mystery of the letters and vowels, and the Temple.*

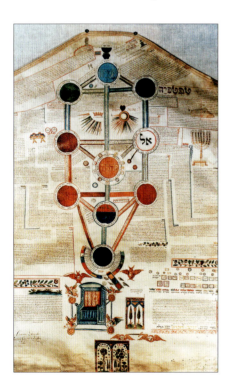

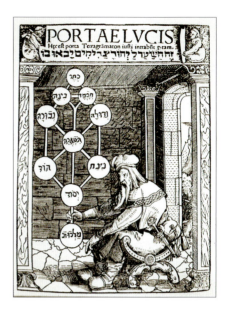

Above *German woodcut from 1516 showing a Jewish Kabbalist holding the Sefirot Tree of Life.*

God and human beings – it denotes instead a state of beatitude and intimate union between the soul and its source.

Below Tree of Life Showing the Ten Spheres *or sefirot, by Mark Penney Maddocks, 1976, illustrating the ten sefirot or divine emanations.*

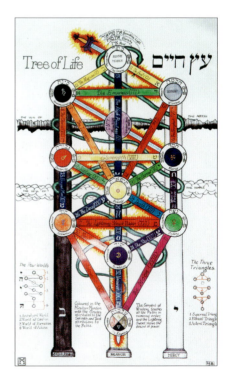

Philosophical Judaism

JEWISH THINKERS INTERPRETED THEIR TRADITION PHILOSOPHICALLY. THE INTERPRETATION OF THE NATURE OF GOD AND HIS ACTION CONSTITUTED AN ALTERNATIVE CONCEPTION OF THE JEWISH FAITH.

In the Hellenistic world the Jewish philosopher Philo tried to integrate Greek philosophy and Jewish teaching into a unified whole. By applying an allegorical method of interpretation to Scripture, he explained the God of Judaism in Greek philosophical categories and reshaped Jewish notions about God, human beings and the world. Philo was the precursor of medieval Jewish philosophy which also attempted to combine alternative philosophical systems with the received biblical tradition.

Below Islamic theology had a profound impact on Jewish medieval thought. This 1237 illustration of medieval Muslim scholars is from Maqamat *by poet and Seljuk empire government official al-Hariri of Basra (1054–1122).*

The beginnings of this philosophical development took place in 9th-century CE Babylonia during the height of the Abbasid caliphate, when rabbinic Judaism was challenged by Karaite scholars who criticized the anthropomorphic views of God in midrashic and talmudic sources.

Added to this internal threat was the Islamic contention that Mohammed's revelation in the Koran superseded the Jewish faith. In addition, Zoroastrians and Manicheans attacked monotheism as a viable religious system. Finally, some gentile philosophers argued that the Greek scientific and philosophical world view could account for the origin of the cosmos without reference to an external deity. In combating these challenges,

Above This statue of Spanish poet and philosopher Solomon Ibn Gabirol stands in Malaga, where he was born in 1022.

Jewish writers were influenced by the teachings of *kalam*, or 'Muslim schools' of the 8th to the 11th century CE; in particular the contributions of one school of Muslim thought – the Mutazilite kalam – had a profound effect on Jewish thought. These Islamic scholars maintained that rational argument was vital in matters of religious belief and that Greek philosophy could serve as the handmaiden of religious faith. In their attempt to defend Judaism from internal and external assault, rabbinic authorities frequently adapted the Mutazilite kalam as an important line of defence, and as time passed they also employed other aspects of Graeco-Arabic thought in their expositions of the Jewish faith.

SOLOMON IBN GABIROL

After the 11th century CE the Mutazilite kalam ceased to play a central role in Jewish philosophical thought. In Islam the Mutazilites were replaced by the more orthodox Asharyites, who attempted to provide a rational basis for unquestioning traditionalism. During this period the

PHILOSOPHICAL JUDAISM

Above *Hebrew manuscript of 1356 of Maimonides' classic* Guide for the Perplexed. *From Huesca, Spain.*

first Spanish Jewish philosopher to produce a work in the neo-Platonic tradition was Solomon Ibn Gabirol (1022–58). In his *Fountain of Life*, he argued that God and matter are not opposed as two ultimate principles – instead matter is identified with God. It emanates from the essence of the creator, forming the basis of all subsequent emanations.

MAIMONIDES

In the following century, Moses Maimonides (1135–1204), arguably the greatest philosopher of the Middle Ages, produced *The Guide for the Perplexed*, based on Aristotelianism. Like Saadia, he addressed the question of anthropomorphic terms in the Bible. In his view, a literal reading of these passages implies that God is a corporeal being. Yet, according to Maimonides, this is a mistake. No positive attributes should be predicated of God, he argued, since the Divine is an absolute unity. Thus when God is described positively in the Bible, such ascriptions must refer to his activity. The only true attributes are negative ones – they lead to a knowledge of God because in negation no plurality is involved.

MAIMONIDEANS AND ANTI-MAIMONIDEANS

By the 13th century, most of the important philosophical texts of medieval thinkers had been translated into Hebrew by Jews living in southern France. This led to bitter antagonism between Maimonideans and anti-Maimonideans who believed that Maimonides had corrupted the tradition. Yet, in later centuries other philosophers emerged who continued to produce treatises grounded in Greek thought. The most prominent Jewish philosopher after Maimonides who was attracted to Aristotelianism was Gersonides (1288–1344). In his *The Wars of the*

SAADIA GAON

The earliest philosopher of the medieval period was the 10th-century CE thinker, Saadia ben Joseph al-Fayyumi. As *Gaon*, or 'head', of one of the Babylonian academies, he wrote treatises on a wide range of subjects and produced the first major Jewish theological treatise of the Middle Ages, *The Book of Beliefs and Opinions*. In this study Saadia attempted to refute the religious claims of Christians, Muslims and Zoroastrians. Adapting the teaching of the Mutazilites, he argued that religious faith and reason are fully compatible. On this basis he sought to demonstrate that God exists since the universe must have had a starting point. The divine creator, he believed, is a single, incorporeal being who created the universe out of nothing. Anthropomorphic descriptions of God in the Bible, he argued, should therefore be understood figuratively rather than literally.

Above *Statue of Maimonides, the greatest medieval Jewish philosopher, in his birthplace, Cordoba in Spain.*

Lord, he wrestled with the question of divine omniscience. In his opinion, God only knows human events if they are determined by heavenly bodies; he does not know them in so far as they are dependent on individual choice. This limitation to divine knowledge, Gersonides believed, is entirely consonant with Scripture and is coherent with the concept of the freedom of the will.

Gersonides was followed by other Jewish philosophers such as the 14th-century Spanish thinker Hasdai Crescas (1340–1410), whose work *The Light of the Lord* offered an alternative account of the basic principles of the Jewish faith in opposition to Maimonides' 13 principles.

However, after Crescas the philosophical approach to religion lost its appeal for most thinkers in Spain. By the end of the 15th century, the impulse to rationalize the Jewish tradition in the light of Greek philosophy had come to an end, and succeeding generations of Jews turned to the mystical tradition as a basis for speculation about God's nature and his creation.

LURIANIC KABBALAH

IN THE 1500s ISAAC LURIA MADE MAJOR CONTRIBUTIONS TO JEWISH MYSTICISM. HIS INFLUENCE ON A CIRCLE OF DISCIPLES HAD HUGE CONSEQUENCES FOR THE DEVELOPMENT OF KABBALISTIC JUDAISM.

By the early modern period the centre of Kabbalistic activity had shifted to Israel. In this milieu Isaac Luria (1534–72), the greatest mystic of the period, reinterpreted Kabbalistic doctrine – his teaching propounded theories about divine contraction, the shattering of the vessels and cosmic repair. These reflections profoundly influenced the subsequent development of Jewish mysticism.

MOSES CORDOVERO
One of the greatest mystics of the town of Safed, Moses Cordovero (1522–70), collected, organized and interpreted the teachings of earlier mystical scholars. His work is a systematic summary of the Kabbalah up to his time, and in his most important treatise, *Pardes*, he outlined the Zoharic concepts of the Godhead, the sefirot, the celestial powers and the earthly processes.

In this study he described the sefirot as vessels in which the light of the En Sof is contained and through which it is reflected in different forms. For Cordovero, the Godhead is in this way manifest in every part of the finite world. In another important work, *The Palm Tree of Deborah*, he expressed the notion that in order to achieve the highest degree of the religious life, one should not only observe the commandments but also imitate divine processes and patterns.

ISAAC LURIA AND CREATION
Originally brought up in Egypt where he studied the Talmud and engaged in business, Isaac Luria withdrew to an island on the Nile where he meditated on the Zohar for seven years. In 1569 he arrived in Safed and died some two years later after having passed on his teaching to a small group of disciples. Of primary importance in the Lurianic system is the mystery of creation. In the literature of early Kabbalists creation was understood as a positive act. For Luria, however, creation was a negative event: the En Sof had to bring into being an empty space in which creation could occur since divine light was everywhere, leaving no room for creation to take place. This was accomplished by the process of *zimzum*, or 'the contraction of the Godhead into itself'.

After this act of withdrawal, a line of light flowed from the Godhead into *tehiru*, or 'empty space', and took on the shape of the sefirot in the form of Adam Kadmon. In this process divine lights created the vessels – the external shapes of the sefirot – which gave specific characteristics to each divine emanation. Yet these vessels were not strong enough to contain such pure light and they shattered. This *shevirat ha-kelim*, or 'breaking of the vessels', brought disaster and upheaval to the emerging emanations: the lower vessels broke down and fell; the three highest emanations were damaged; and the empty space was divided into two parts. The first part

Above *Torah shrine at Ha'ari synagogue in Safed, Israel, where Rabbi Isaac Luria lived and taught.*

Below *A view of Safed and Mount Meron, Israel. Simeon ben Yohai is buried on Mount Meron, and thousands camp out near the tomb on the anniversary of his death on Lag B'Omer, or the 'Scholars' Feast'.*

consisted of the broken vessels with many divine sparks clinging to them; the second part was the upper realm where the pure light of God escaped to preserve its purity.

THE COSMOS

Following the shattering of the vessels the cosmos was divided into two parts: the kingdom of evil in the lower part and the realm of divine light in the upper part. For Luria evil was seen as opposed to existence; therefore it was not able to exist by its own power. Instead it had to derive spiritual force from the divine light. This was accomplished by keeping captive the sparks of the divine light that fell with them when the vessels were broken and subsequently gave sustenance to the satanic domain. Divine attempts to bring unity to all existence now had to focus on the struggle to overcome the evil forces. This was achieved by a continuing process of divine emanation, which at first created the sefirot, the sky, the earth, the Garden of Eden and human beings.

Below *A Hasidic Jew studying in Safed, Israel. The blue colour on the door is thought to protect against the evil eye. Hasidic Judaism is deeply influenced by Kabbalistic thought.*

Humanity was intended to serve as the battleground for this conflict between good and evil. In this regard Adam reflected symbolically the dualism in the cosmos – he possessed a sacred soul while his body represented the evil forces. God's intention was that Adam defeat the evil within himself and bring about Satan's downfall. But when Adam failed, a catastrophe occurred parallel to the breaking of the vessels; instead of divine sparks being saved and uplifted, many new divine lights fell and evil became stronger.

THE JEWISH PEOPLE

Rather than relying on the action of one person, God then chose the people of Israel to vanquish evil and raise up the captive sparks. The Torah was given to symbolize the Jews' acceptance of this allotted task. When the ancient Israelites undertook to keep the law, redemption seemed imminent. Yet the people of Israel then created the golden calf, a sin parallel to Adam's disobedience. Again, divine sparks fell and the forces of evil were renewed. For Luria, history is a record of attempts by the powers of good to rescue these sparks and unite the divine and earthly spheres. Luria and his disciples believed that they were living in the

Above *Strictly Orthodox Jews pray for peace in the Lebanon at the grave of mystic Isaac Luria in Safed, Israel.*

final stages of this last attempt to overcome evil, in which the coming of the Messiah would signify the end of the struggle.

TIKKUN

Related to the contraction of God, the breaking of the vessels and the exiled sparks, was Luria's conception of tikkun. This concept refers to the mending of what was broken during the breaking of the vessels. After the catastrophe in the divine realm, the process of restoration began and every disaster was seen as a setback in this process. In this battle, keeping God's commandments was understood as contributing to repair – the divine sparks which fell down can be redeemed by ethical and religious deeds. According to Luria, a spark is attached to all prayers and moral acts; if the Jew keeps the ethical and religious law these sparks are redeemed and lifted up.

By the beginning of the 17th century Lurianic mysticism had had a major impact on Sephardic Jewry, and in succeeding centuries Luria's mystical theology became a central feature of Jewish life.

KARAITES

THE EMERGENCE OF THE KARAITE MOVEMENT IN THE 8TH CENTURY CE POSED A MAJOR CHALLENGE TO THE RABBINIC ESTABLISHMENT. IT CONTINUED TO EXERT A PROFOUND INFLUENCE ON JEWISH LIFE.

In the early medieval period the emergence of Karaism as an anti-rabbinic movement constituted a major threat to the tradition. Deriving its name from the Hebrew word *mikrah*, or 'Scripture', the Karaites believed that God had revealed his word exclusively in the Written Torah. In their view, the oral Torah as passed down by rabbinic sages was a human reflection on the divine commandments.

ORIGIN OF THE KARAITES

During the 8th century CE messianic movements appeared in the Persian Jewish community, leading to armed uprisings against Muslim authorities. Such revolts were quickly crushed, but an even more serious threat to traditional Jewish life was posed later in the century by the emergence of an anti-rabbinic sect, the Karaites. This movement was founded in Babylonia in the 760s by Anan ben David, who had earlier been passed over as exilarch (head of the Jewish community in Babylonia). The Karaites traced its origin to the time of King Jeroboam in the 8th century BCE. According to some scholars, Anan's movement absorbed elements of an extra-talmudic tradition and took over doctrines from Islam.

Right *An 18th-century silver* yad *or finger pointer used when reading from the Torah. For the Karaites the Torah was of pre-eminent importance.*

The guiding interpretative principle formulated by Anan, 'Search thoroughly in Scripture and do not rely on my opinion', was intended to point to the Bible as the sole source of law. Jewish observances, the Karaites insisted, must conform to biblical legislation rather than rabbinic ordinances. Anan, however, was not lenient concerning legal matters. For example, he did not recognize the minimum quantities of forbidden foods fixed by the rabbis; in addition, he introduced more complicated regulations for circumcision, added to the number of fast days, interpreted the prohibition of work on the Sabbath in stricter terms than the rabbis, and extended the prohibited degrees of marriage. In short, he made the yoke of the law more burdensome.

THE DEVELOPMENT OF THE KARAITE MOVEMENT

After the death of the founder, new parties within the Karaite movement soon emerged. The adherents of Anan

Left *A prophet of God denounces the idolatry of Jeroboam. Painting by William Hole (1846–1917). For the Karaites God's world was revealed exclusively in Scripture.*

Above *The Karaite synagogue is the oldest active synagogue in Jerusalem, founded in the 8th century CE. The synagogue is currently below street level, which has risen over the years.*

were referred to as the 'Ananites' and remained few in number. In the first half of the 9th century CE, the Ukarite sect was established by Ishmael of Ukbara (near Baghdad). Some years later another sect was formed in the same town by Mishawayh Al-Ukbari. Another group was formed by a contemporary of Mishawayh, Abu Imram Al-Tiflisi. In Israel, yet another sect was established by Malik Al-Ramli. By the end of the 9th century CE, Karaism had become a conglomerate of groups advocating different anti-rabbinic positions, but these sects were short-lived and in time the Karaites consolidated into a uniform movement.

The central representative of mainstream Karaism was Benjamin ben Moses Nahavendi (of Nahavendi in Persia), who advocated a policy of free and independent study of Scripture, which became the dominant ideology of later Karaism. By the 10th century CE, a number of Karaite communities were established in Israel, Iraq and Persia. These groups rejected rabbinic law and devised their own legislation, which led eventually to the foundation of a Karaite rabbinical academy in Jerusalem. There the Karaite community produced some of the most distinguished scholars of the period, who composed legal handbooks, wrote biblical commentaries, expounded on Hebrew philology and engaged in philosophical and theological reflection.

ANTI-KARAITES AND THE DEVELOPMENT OF KARAISM

The growth of Karaism provoked the rabbis to attack it as a heretical movement. The first prominent authority to engage in anti-Karaite debate was Saadia Gaon, who in the first half of the 9th century CE wrote a book attacking Anan. This polemic was followed by other anti-Karaite tracts by eminent rabbinic authorities.

By the 10th century CE, the Karaites had successfully established a network of synagogues in the Middle East. In addition, the movement produced some of the most distinguished literary figures of eastern Jewry. Karaite scholars composed handbooks of law, wrote commentaries on the Bible, contributed to theology and philosophy, and furthered the growth of Hebrew philology.

However, traditionalists continued to compose diatribes against what they perceived as a heretical sect. But as the social composition of the movement changed, Karaism became less severe, and members of the movement in Egypt and elsewhere became prosperous merchants. As a consequence, the ascetic features of Karaite ritual were modified, and the concept of a post-biblical tradition was gradually accepted.

After the Jerusalem community was destroyed during the First Crusade, the centre of Karaite literary activity shifted to the Byzantine empire. From there Karaites established communities in the Crimea and medieval Poland and Lithuania. In Egypt the Karaite community continued to maintain itself. Subsequently, relations between Karaites and Rabbanites (the rabbinical establishment) varied – at times ties were close whereas at other periods the differences between the Karaism and traditional Judaism were emphasized. Yet, after the 11th century Karaism lost its base of support, and it survived only as a small minority group.

Right *The Karaite synagogue in Yevpatoria, Ukraine. Yevpatoria became a residence of the Hakham, spiritual leader of the Karaites, when Russia annexed the Crimea in 1738.*

Shabbateans

THE ARRIVAL OF SHABBETAI TZVI ELECTRIFIED THE JEWISH WORLD. CONVINCED THAT THE LONG-AWAITED MESSIAH HAD COME, FOLLOWERS ANTICIPATED THAT MESSIANIC REDEMPTION WAS IMMINENT.

Through the centuries, Jews anticipated the coming of a messianic redeemer who would bring about the transformation of human history. In the middle of the 17th century, Jewry was electrified by the arrival of Shabbetai Tzvi who was proclaimed the long-awaited Messiah by his disciple Nathan of Gaza. Despite his subsequent apostasy and death in 1676, a circle of followers – the Shabbateans – continued to proclaim his messiahship.

THE ARRIVAL OF SHABBETAI TZVI

By the beginning of the 17th century, Lurianic mysticism had made a major impact on Sephardic Jewry, and messianic expectations had also become a central feature of Jewish life. In this milieu the arrival of a self-proclaimed messianic king, Shabbetai Tzvi, brought about a transformation of Jewish life and thought. Born in Smyrna into a wealthy family, Shabbetai had received a traditional Jewish education and later engaged in the study of the Zohar.

After leaving Smyrna in the 1650s Shabbetai spent ten years in various cities in Greece as well as in Constantinople (Istanbul) and Jerusalem. Eventually he became part of a Kabbalistic group in Cairo and travelled to Gaza where he encountered Nathan of Gaza who believed that Shabbetai was the Messiah. In 1665 Shabbetai's messiahship was announced, and Nathan sent letters to Jews in numerous communities asking them to repent and recognize Shabbetai Tzvi as their redeemer. Shabbetai, he announced, would take the Sultan's crown, bring back the lost tribes and inaugurate the period of messianic redemption.

After a brief sojourn in Jerusalem, Shabbetai went to Smyrna, where he encountered strong opposition on the part of some local rabbis. In response he denounced the disbelievers and declared that he was the Anointed of

Below *A view of 19th-century Smyrna, Turkey, where the false Messiah Shabbetai Tzvi was born in 1626.*

Above *Shabbetai Tzvi, who declared he was the Messiah or the Anointed of the God of Jacob, engraved in 1666.*

the God of Jacob. This action evoked a hysterical response – a number of Jews fell into trances and had visions of him on a royal throne crowned as king of Israel. He journeyed to Constantinople in 1666, but on the order of the grand vizier he was arrested and put into prison. Within a short time the prison quarters became a messianic court; pilgrims from all over the world made their way to Constantinople to join in messianic rituals and ascetic activities. In addition, hymns were written in his honour and new festivals were introduced. According to Nathan who remained in Gaza, the alteration in Shabbetai's moods from illumination to withdrawal symbolized his soul's struggle with demonic powers. At times he was imprisoned by the *kelippot*, or 'powers of evil', but at other moments he prevailed against them.

DEFENDING SHABBETAI'S MESSIAHSHIP

Shabbetai's act of apostasy scandalized most of his followers, but he defended himself by asserting he had become a Muslim in obeisance to God's commands. Many of his followers accepted this explanation and refused to give up their belief. Some thought it was not Shabbetai who had become a Muslim, but rather a phantom who had taken on his appearance; the Messiah himself had ascended to heaven.

Others cited biblical and rabbinic sources to justify Shabbetai's action. Nathan explained that the messianic task involved taking on the humiliation of being portrayed as a traitor to his people.

Furthermore, Nathan argued on the basis of Lurianic Kabbalah that there were two kinds of divine light – a creative light and another light opposed to the existence of anything other than the En Sof (Infinite). While creative light formed structures of creation in empty space, the other light became after *zimzum*, or 'divine contraction', the power of evil. According to Nathan, the soul of the Messiah had been struggling against the power of evil from the beginning; his purpose was to allow divine light to penetrate this domain and bring about *tikkun*, or 'cosmic repair'. In order to do this, the soul of the Messiah was not obligated to keep the law, but was free to descend into the abyss to liberate sparks and thereby conquer evil. In this light, Shabbetai's conversion to Islam was explicable.

THE SHABBATEAN MOVEMENT

After Shabbetai's act of apostasy, Nathan visited him in the Balkans and then travelled to Rome where he performed secret rites to bring about the end of the Papacy. Shabbetai remained in Adrianople and Constantinople where he lived as both Muslim and Jew. In 1672 he was deported to Albania where he disclosed his own Kabbalistic teaching to his supporters. After he died in 1676, Nathan declared that Shabbetai had ascended to the supernal world.

Eventually a number of groups continued in their belief that Shabbetai Tzvi was the Messiah, including a sect, the Doenmeh, or 'dissidents', which professed Islam publicly but nevertheless adhered to its own traditions. Marrying among themselves, they eventually evolved into antinomian sub-groups, which violated Jewish sexual laws and asserted the divinity of Shabbetai and their leader, Baruchiah Russo.

In Italy several Shabbatean groups also emerged and propagated their views. In the 18th century the most important Shabbatean sect was led by Jacob Frank, who was influenced by the Doenmeh in Turkey. Believing himself to be the incarnation of Shabbetai, Frank announced that he was the second person of the Trinity and gathered together a circle of disciples who indulged in licentious orgies.

Below *Interior of the house of Shabbetai Tzvi in Izmir, formerly Smyrna, in Turkey.*

Above *The anointing of Shabbetai Tzvi as King of the Jews by Nathan of Gaza, in a 17th-century engraving.*

Frankists

IN THE 18TH CENTURY, JACOB FRANK ESTABLISHED A SHABBATEAN MOVEMENT. ALARMED BY THE RADICAL NATURE OF THIS GROUP, THE RABBINIC ESTABLISHMENT DENOUNCED THE FRANKISTS AS HERETICS.

The 18th-century Jacob Frank (1726–91) established a new Shabbatean group, the Frankists, whose theology constituted a radical departure from the tradition. Not surprisingly, Frank and his followers were anathematized by the rabbinic establishment for their heretical views and practices.

ORIGIN OF THE FRANKISTS
Jacob Frank was born Jacob ben Judah Leib in Korolowka, a small town in Podolia. Educated in Czernowitz and Sniatyn, he lived for a number of years in Bucharest. Although he went to heder, or 'Jewish primary school', he had no knowledge of the Talmud. In Bucharest he began to earn his living as a dealer in cloth and precious stones.

Frank appears to have been associated with Shabbateans during his youth. He began to study the Zohar, making a name in Shabbatean circles as a person possessed of certain powers. In 1752 he married Hannah, the daughter of a respected merchant in Nikopol. Accompanied by Shabbateans, he visited Salonika in 1753 and became involved with the Doenmeh, a radical wing of this group. Eventually he became the leader of the Shabbateans in Poland where he was perceived by his followers as a reincarnation of the divine soul which had previously resided in Shabbetai.

Subsequently, Frank journeyed through the communities of Podolia, which contained Shabbatean groups. Although he was received enthusiastically by Shabbateans, Frank's appearance in Lanskroun caused considerable consternation when he was discovered conducting a Shabbatean ritual with his followers – his Jewish opponents claimed that a religious orgy was taking place. Although Frank's followers were imprisoned, he was released because the authorities thought he was a Turkish subject.

At the request of the local rabbis an enquiry was instituted that examined the practices of the Shabbateans.

FRANKIST THEOLOGY
In his teaching, Frank revealed himself as the embodiment of God's power who had come to complete Shabbetai's task. He was, he believed, the true Jacob, like Jacob in the Bible who had completed the work of his predecessors, Abraham and Isaac. In short statements and parables, Frank explained the nature of his mission. It was necessary, he argued, for those who belonged to his group to adopt Christianity outwardly in order to keep their true faith secret. In his view, all religions were only stages through which believers had to pass, like a person putting on different suits of clothes that could later be discarded.

Above *Jonathan Eybeschutz, rabbi of the 'Three Communities', was accused by Jacob Emden of being a secret Shabbatean. He was cleared in 1753.*

Below *Caricature of Archbishop Dembowski of Lemberg, who arranged a public burning of the Talmud and other Hebrew writings after the Shabbateans informed him they rejected the Talmud in the late 1750s.*

Above *Kamenietz: the capital of Podolia in Russian Poland, where the Frankist movement developed.*

In place of the Shabbatean trinity in which all were united in divinity, Frank argued that the true and good God is hidden and divested of any connection with the created order. It is he who conceals himself behind 'the King of Kings' whom Frank also refers to as 'the Great Brother', or 'He who stands before God'. He is the God of the true faith whom one must attempt to approach; in doing so, it is possible to break the domination of the three 'leaders of the world' who rule earth, imposing on it an inappropriate system of law.

FRANKISTS AND THE CHURCH

Frank prepared his followers to accept baptism as the step that would open before them this new way. Paralleling the pattern in the Gospels, he appointed 12 emissaries who were destined to become his chief disciples. At the same time he appointed 12 'sisters' who were to act as his concubines. Continuing the tradition of the Baruchiah sect, Frank also instituted licentious sexual practices.

As time passed, it became clear that Frank and his followers would need to be baptized, and they requested that Archbishop Lubienski in Lvov receive them into the Church. In making this application, they expressed the desire to be allowed to lead a separate existence. The Church, however, replied that no special privileges would be granted.

In July 1759 a disputation took place in Lvov, as a precondition of conversion, when the leading rabbis and members of the Frankist sect debated a variety of theological topics. In September 1759 Frank was baptized, and by the end of 1760 in Lvov alone more than 500 Frankists followed his example. Despite such widespread conversion, the Church became increasingly suspicious of the Frankists: it appeared that the real object of their devotion was Frank as the living incarnation of God.

In February 1760 Frank was arrested and an inquisition took place, resulting in Frank's imprisonment, though he was later released. In 1791 Frank died, mourned by hundreds of his followers.

Below *Street in the Jewish area of Lvov, in the Ukraine, where a Frankist disputation took place in 1759.*

THE NEW ROAD

According to Frank all great religious leaders from the patriarchs to Shabbetai Tzvi and Baruchiah, had endeavoured to find the way to God, but failed. In Frank's view, it is necessary to embark on a completely new road, untrodden by the people of Israel. This path is the road to consistent religious anarchy – in order to achieve this goal it is necessary to abolish and destroy Jewish laws, teachings and practices that constrict the power of life. Some believers had already passed through Judaism and Islam; now they had to complete their journey by taking on the Christian faith, using its beliefs and practices to conceal the real core of their belief in Frank as the true Messiah and the living God.

CHAPTER 3

MODERN JUDAISM

On the far right of the religious spectrum, Haredim (strictly Orthodox Jews and Hasidism) hold tenaciously to the belief system of the past, believing the Torah in its entirety was given by God to Moses on Mount Sinai; in addition, the rabbinic interpretation of the law is sacrosanct. However, recent times have seen the emergence of new forms of Judaism with radically different ideologies some of which do not accept the Torah as the basis of Jewish life.

In the early 19th century, Reform Jews were anxious to modernize the tradition. They felt it was no longer necessary for Jews to adhere to the minutiae of the law and set aside certain central tenets of traditional Judaism. Conservative Jews adopted a less radical view, yet also sought to make Judaism relevant in the modern world. More recently, Reconstructionist and Humanistic Jews argued that Judaism must divest itself from supernaturalism. A growing number of Jews sought to revitalize the faith through Jewish renewal. And, at the margin of Jewish life, Messianic Jews believed that a new era had dawned with the coming of the messianic age.

Opposite *A Hasidic Jew, arms outstretched with joy, celebrates the reunification of Jerusalem on the first Jerusalem Day in 1968. He is carried by a soldier at the Western Wall.*

Above *In 1954, US architect Frank Lloyd Wright designed his only synagogue, Beth Shalom at Elkins Park, Pennsylvania, a startling modernist version of an ancient temple.*

Orthodox Judaism

BOUND BY THE JEWISH LEGAL SYSTEM, ORTHODOX JEWS KEEP ALIVE THE TRADITIONS OF THEIR ANCESTORS. THE RITUALS OF ORTHODOX JUDAISM BRING THE CHAIN OF TRADITION INTO THE PRESENT AGE.

The origins of Orthodox Judaism stretch back 4,000 years to the birth of the Jewish nation. From the time of the patriarchs to rabbinic Judaism, Jews were bound by the covenant with Moses. Orthodox Jews today adhere to the tenets of the faith in an uncompromising fashion.

ORIGINS OF ORTHODOXY

Orthodox Judaism is the branch of Judaism that adheres most strictly to halakha, or 'Jewish law'. By the 18th century local Jewish communities had lost much of their authority. This led to the disintegration of the traditional religious establishment as well as the prestige of communal leaders. Coupled with the aspirations of Jewish emancipationists, new interpretations of the faith and an altered conception of the relationship between Jews and non-Jews, Orthodox Judaism was a response to these changes in Jewish life.

Below *Sephardic Mordechai Eliyahu and Ashkenazi Avraham Shapira were Orthodox chief rabbis of Israel, 1983–93.*

In the first half of the 19th century, traditionalist Jews in Hungary and Germany were profoundly critical of the efforts of Reform Jews to adapt halakha to modern society as well as modify the traditional synagogue service. These reformers argued that such alterations were a condition for Jewish emancipation as well as civil equality. Traditionalists viewed this attitude a violation of God's will.

At the end of the 19th century, Eastern European Orthodox leaders similarly championed Torah Judaism in the face of increased secularism.

ORTHODOX THEOLOGY

Until the growth of the Enlightenment in the 18th century, the Jewish people affirmed their belief in one God who created the universe. As a transcendent deity he brought all things into being, continues to sustain the cosmos, and guides humanity to its ultimate destiny. In the unfolding of this providential scheme, Israel has a central role – as God's chosen people, the nation is to serve as a light to all peoples.

Above *A strictly Orthodox family in Jerusalem. Note the girls' sober clothing and the boy's side curls and fringes.*

Scripture does not contain a dogmatic formulation of such beliefs, but the Orthodox prayer book contains the medieval philosopher Moses Maimonides' formulation of the '13 Principles of the Jewish Faith'.

As Maimonides explained, anyone who denies any of these tenets is to be regarded as a heretic: God's existence; God's unity; God's incorporeality; God's eternity; God alone is to be worshipped; prophecy; Moses is the greatest of the prophets; the divine origin of the Torah (Pentateuch); the Torah is immutable; God knows the thoughts and deeds of human beings; reward and punishment; the Messiah; resurrection of the dead. Maimonides' principles as well as parallel dogmatic formulations by other medieval thinkers served as the basis for theological speculation through the centuries.

MODERN TRADITIONALISTS

Today Orthodox Jews continue to subscribe to these fundamental doctrines, secure in the knowledge that they are fulfilling God's will. Such a commitment serves as the framework for traditional Orthodox practice. Wary of modernity, traditional Orthodox Jews are anxious to preserve the Jewish way of life through a process of intensive education – for these Jews there can

Right *Friday night in Jerusalem. Jewish tradition encourages everyone to dress finely for Shabbat.*

be no compromise with secularism. Such attitudes permeate all aspects of Jewish life from the earliest age. Among traditional Orthodox Jews, education for boys is rigorous, following the curriculum laid down in ancient times. Within strictly Orthodox circles, expectations for girls are of a different nature; Jewish young women are reared to become loyal and dedicated mothers and homemakers.

Strict adherence to Jewish law is demanded within the context of traditional orthodoxy. Committed to the doctrine of Torah Mi Sinai (the belief that God revealed the Torah to Moses on Mount Sinai), Orthodox Jews are obliged to keep all biblical and rabbinic ordinances. To accomplish this in a modern setting requires both determination and scrupulous care. Although the traditional Orthodox constitute only a minority of the Jewish community, there is a growing element anxious to draw other Jews to the traditional faith.

Below *Pupils crowd round the desk of a teacher at an Orthodox elementary school in Jerusalem.*

ORTHODOX JUDAISM TODAY
The dominant trend in Orthodoxy since World War II has been its increased emphasis of adherence to the traditional Jewish way of life. What is required is religious zealotry, observance of the mitzvot, or commandments, and a rejection of modern values and culture.

Throughout the Jewish world, Orthodox Jews have actively encouraged the establishment of schools, synagogues, political organizations, a press and summer camps. Both Orthodox rabbis and lay leaders have been anxious to counter the threats of secularism and modernity.

Today most Orthodox Jews reside in Israel or the United States. In Israel religiously observant Jews make up about 15–20 per cent of the Jewish population. These neo-traditionalists, who were once marginal to Israeli society, play an increasingly important role in communal and political life. Within their ranks the Edah Haredit (community of the pious) consist of thousands of families with numerous sympathizers. These are the most intransigent of the Orthodox. They relate to the state of Israel with various degrees of hostility. A more moderate neotraditionalism is found in Israeli Agudah circles.

Among Israeli Orthodox Jews, the heads of the yeshivot and a number of Hasidic rebbes are dominant. In the United States, neo-traditionalists have been supportive of their own institutions.

With the exception of pockets of neo-traditional extremists such as the Edah Haredit in Israel, American Orthodox Jews are generally familiar with modern culture, and most are willing to work with the non-Orthodox on behalf of general Jewish interests.

Below *An Orthodox Jew wearing the traditional prayer shawl and tefillin, boxes worn on the forehead and arm.*

Hasidism

SINCE THE 18TH CENTURY HASIDISM HAS BEEN A POWERFUL FORCE IN JEWISH LIFE. TODAY THE HASIDIC COMMUNITY IS DIVIDED INTO A NUMBER OF SUB-GROUPS, EACH WITH ITS OWN REBBE.

In the 18th century, Hasidism emerged as a challenge to the rabbinic establishment. Founded by the Ba'al Shem Tov (1700–60), the movement stressed the importance of eliminating selfhood and the ascent of the soul to divine light. Unlike the arid scholasticism of traditional Judaism, Hasidism offered to the Jewish masses a new outlet for religious fervour.

THE ORIGINS OF HASIDISM

During the second half of the 18th century, this new popular movement attracted thousands of followers. Pietistic in orientation, Hasidism was based on Kabbalistic ideas and reinterpreted the role of the rabbi as a spiritual guide. It first appeared in the villages of the Polish Ukraine, especially Podolia, where Shabbatean Frankists had been active. According to tradition, Israel ben Eliezer, known as the Ba'al Shem Tov or Besht, was born in Southern Poland and in his twenties journeyed with his wife to the Carpathian mountains. In the 1730s he travelled to Medzhybizh where he performed various miracles and instructed his disciples in Kabbalistic lore. By the 1740s he had attracted a considerable number of disciples who passed on his teaching. After his death in 1760, Dov Baer became the leader of this sect and Hasidism spread to southern Poland, the Ukraine and Lithuania.

CRITICISM

The growth of Hasidism engendered considerable hostility on the part of rabbinic authorities. In particular the rabbinic leadership of Vilna issued an edict of excommunication. The Hasidim were charged with permissiveness in their observance of the commandments, laxity in the study of the Torah, excess in prayer, and preference for the Lurianic rather than the Ashkenazic prayer book. In subsequent years the Hasidim and their opponents (Mitnaggedim) bitterly denounced one another. Relations deteriorated further when Jacob Joseph of Polonnoye published a book critical of the rabbinate; his work was burned, and in 1791 the Mitnaggedim ordered that all relations with the Hasidim cease.

By the end of the century, the Jewish religious establishment of Vilna denounced the Hasidim to the Russian government, an act resulting in the imprisonment of several leaders. Despite such condemnation, the movement was eventually recognized by the Russian and Austrian governments. In the ensuing years the movement divided into a number of separate groups under different leaders who passed on positions of authority to their descendants.

HASIDIC THEOLOGY

Hasidism initiated a profound change in Jewish religious pietism. In the medieval period, the Hasidei Ashkenaz attempted to achieve perfection through various mystical activities. This tradition was carried on by Lurianic Kabbalists who engaged in various forms of

Above *Hasidic women behind a mechitza screen that affords them a limited view of the service at Viznitz synagogue, Stamford Hill, London.*

Below *A Hasidic Jew holds the lulav and etrog in a sukkah built for Sukkot in Williamsburg, New York.*

Above *Dancing at a Chabad-Lubavitch bar mitzvah. Chabad-Lubavitch is now one of the largest Hasidic organizations in the world.*

self-mortification. In opposition to such ascetic practices, the Ba'al Shem Tov and his followers emphasized the omnipresence of God rather than the shattering of the vessels and the imprisonment of divine sparks by the powers of evil. For Hasidic Judaism there is no place where God is absent; the doctrine of *zimzum*, or 'divine contraction', was interpreted by Hasidic sages as only an apparent withdrawal of the divine light. Divine light, they believed, is everywhere. As the Ba'al Shem Tov explained, in every one of a person's troubles, physical and spiritual, even in that trouble God himself is there.

For some Hasidim, devekut, or 'cleaving to God in prayer', was understood as the annihilation of selfhood and the ascent of the soul to divine light. In this context joy, humility, gratitude and spontaneity were seen as essential features of Hasidic worship. The central obstacles to concentration in prayer are distracting thoughts; according to Hasidism, such sinful intentions contain a divine spark which can be released. In this regard, the trad-

Right *The Rebbe and his Hasidim during Hanukkah at the Premishlan congregation in Bnei Brak, Israel.*

itional Kabbalistic stress on theological speculation was replaced by a preoccupation with mystical psychology in which inner bliss was conceived as the highest aim rather than *tikkun*, or 'repair of the cosmos'.

For the Hasidim, it was also possible to achieve devekut in daily activities including eating, drinking, business affairs and sex. Such ordinary acts became religious if in performing them one cleaves to God, and devekut is thus attainable by all Jews rather than just by a scholarly elite. Unlike the earlier mystical tradition, Hasidism provided a means by which ordinary Jews could reach a state of spiritual ecstasy. Hasidic worship embraced singing, dancing and joyful devotion in anticipation of the period of messianic redemption.

THE ZADDIK

Another central feature of this new movement was the institution of the zaddik, which gave expression to a widespread disillusionment with rabbinic leadership. According to Hasidism, the zaddikim are spiritually superior individuals who have attained the highest level of devekut. The goal of the zaddik was to elevate the souls of his flock to the divine light. His tasks included

Above *Rabbi Menachem Schneerson giving funds to a follower as a blessing. He led the Chabad-Lubavitch movement in the late 20th century.*

pleading to God for his people, immersing himself in their everyday affairs, and counselling and strengthening them. As an authoritarian figure, the zaddik was seen by his followers as possessing the miraculous power to ascend to the divine realm. In this context, devekut to God involved cleaving to the zaddik. Given this emphasis on the role of the zaddik, Hasidic literature included summaries of the spiritual and Kabbalistic teachings of various famous zaddikim as well as stories about their miraculous deeds.

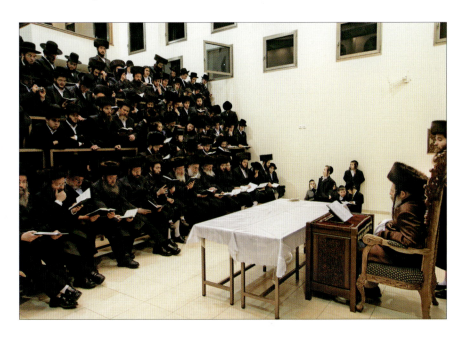

Conservative Judaism

CONSERVATIVE JUDAISM ADOPTS A MIDDLE POSITION BETWEEN ORTHODOX AND REFORM JUDAISM, ADVOCATING LOYALTY TO THE TRADITION COUPLED WITH AN ACCEPTANCE OF MODERN VALUES.

Above *Seder plate showing traditional foods eaten at Passover – an egg, lamb, green vegetables, haroset and bitter herbs. Conservative Judaism stresses the importance of ritual in Jewish life.*

In the wake of the Enlightenment of the 18th century, reformers sought to modernize the Jewish tradition. Initially, Reform Judaism constituted a radically new approach to the tradition. Yet more conservative reformers were alarmed by the radicalism of their co-religionists. Eventually, Conservative Judaism emerged as a more moderate form of Jewish modernism.

ZACHARIAS FRANKEL

The founder of what came to be known as Conservative Judaism was Zacharias Frankel (1801–75). An advocate of moderate reform, Frankel was committed to a historically evolving dynamic Judaism. The aim of such an approach (positive historical Judaism), he believed, would be to uncover the origins of the Jewish people's national spirit and the collective will. Both the past as enshrined in tradition and the present as embodied in the religious consciousness of the people, he argued, should determine the nature of Jewish life.

In 1845 Frankel left the Reform rabbinical conference in Frankfurt because a majority of the participants had voted that there was no need to use Hebrew in the Jewish worship service. Although he agreed with other reformers that Judaism needed to be revised, he disputed with them over the legitimate criteria for religious change. None the less, he broke with Orthodoxy in asserting that the Oral law was rabbinic in origin, that the halakha, or 'Jewish law', had evolved over time, and that the source of religious observance was not divine.

SOLOMON SCHECHTER

In the United States a similar approach to the tradition was adopted by a number of leading figures including the Jewish scholar Solomon Schechter (1847–1915) who argued that Conservative Judaism should combine elements of both traditional and non-traditional Judaism. Disdainfully Schechter rejected both Reform and Orthodoxy. Instead, he emphasized the importance of traditional rituals, customs, observances as well as belief, while simultaneously stressing the need for a historical perspective.

In February 1913 a union of 22 congregations was founded, committed to maintaining the Jewish tradition in its historical continuity. In the preamble to its constitution, the United Synagogue stated its intention to separate from Reform Judaism – it was committed to a heterogeneous, traditional mode of belief and practice through the observance of ritual in the home and synagogue. As Conservative Judaism expanded in the 1920s and 1930s a degree of uniformity developed in congregational worship. Services usually began late Friday evening and early Saturday morning; head coverings

Left *Prime Minister David Ben-Gurion of Israel and Louis Finkelstein, Chancellor of the Jewish Seminary for Conservative Judaism, New York, look at rare books at the seminary, 1960.*

were required; prayer shawls were usually worn on Sabbath morning; rabbis conducted the service and preached English sermons; prayer books other than the Union Prayer Book of the Reform movement were used; and many congregants participated in afternoon study with the rabbi. In addition, many synagogues had organs, mixed choirs, family pews, and *minyans*, or 'quorum for a religious service', that met three times a day for prayer.

CONSERVATIVE THEOLOGY

Conservative Jews viewed Judaism as an evolving organism that remained spiritually vibrant by adjusting to environmental and cultural conditions. In consequence, Conservative thinkers attempted to preserve those elements of the tradition that they believed to be spiritually meaningful while simultaneously setting aside those observances that actually hinder the continued growth of Judaism. Such obsolete practices were not abrogated, but simply ignored. In a similar spirit, Conservative Jews, in contrast with Orthodoxy, felt no compulsion to accept theological doctrines which they believed were outmoded – thus Conservative Judaism broke with Orthodoxy regarding the belief that the Torah was revealed in its entirety to Moses on Mount Sinai.

In its quest to modernize the faith, Conservative scholars sought to establish an authoritative body to adapt Judaism to contemporary circumstances. As early as 1918 there was a considerable desire to establish a body of men learned in the law who would be able to advise the movement concerning pressing contemporary issues. Thus, even though the Conservative movement refused to formulate a detailed platform or series of credal statements, these features of Conservative Judaism provided a coherent and imaginative approach to the tradition.

CONSERVATIVE BELIEFS

Regarding belief in God, Conservative thinkers have generally subscribed to the traditional understanding of the Deity as omnipotent, omniscient, and all-good. Yet, in contrast with Orthodoxy, there remains considerable ambiguity about the nature of divine communication. Unlike Orthodox thinkers who view revelation as verbal in nature and Reform theologians who conceive of the Torah as a largely human product, the Conservative movement has generally attempted to bridge these two extremes. Within Conservative Judaism revelation is understood as a divinely initiated process involving human composition. As to what constitutes the nature of such a divine human encounter, Conservative writers vary: some argue that human beings correctly recorded the divine will as revealed at Sinai; others that those who wrote the Scriptures were simply divinely inspired.

Regarding halakha, Conservative thinkers emphasized the importance of conserving the laws of traditional Judaism, including dietary observances, Sabbath, festival and liturgical prescriptions, and ethical precepts. Nevertheless,

Above *In 1963, Martin Luther King received the Solomon Schechter Award. Schechter (1847–1915) was a leading figure of the Conservative movement.*

Conservative scholars advocated change and renewal. On the whole they stressed the historical importance of the Jewish heritage. Guided by such an approach to law, the Conservative movement resorted to what Schechter called 'the conscience of catholic Israel' in reaching decisions about the status of biblical and rabbinic law.

Concerning Jewish peoplehood, the Conservative movement has consistently affirmed the pre-eminence of K'lal Yisrael, or 'the body of Israel'. Yet despite this insistence there has not been the same unanimity about the nation of God's chosen people. Although the Sabbath and High Holy Day prayer books have retained the traditional formula ('You have chosen us from all the nations'), there has been a wide diversity of interpretation of the concept of chosenness among Conservative thinkers. Yet, as a consequence of its dedication to the peoplehood of Israel, the Conservative movement has from its inception been dedicated to the founding of the State of Israel.

Reform Judaism

THE ENLIGHTENMENT HAD A DEEP IMPACT; NO LONGER WERE JEWS FORCED TO LIVE IN GHETTOS. REFORM JUDAISM EMERGED AS A REVOLUTIONARY MOVEMENT WHOSE AIM WAS TO MODERNIZE THE FAITH.

At the end of the 18th century, such advocates of Jewish enlightenment as Moses Mendelssohn encouraged fellow Jews to integrate into the mainstream of western European culture. Subsequently early reformers tried to reform Jewish education by widening the traditional curriculum of Jewish schools. Preeminent among these figures was Israel Jacobson, who founded a boarding school for boys in Westphalia and subsequently established other schools throughout the kingdom. In these new foundations, general subjects were taught by Christian teachers while a Jewish instructor gave lessons about Judaism.

Simultaneously a number of Reform temples were opened in Germany with innovations to the liturgy, including prayers and sermons in German as well as choral singing and organ music. The central aim of these early reformers was to adapt Jewish worship to contemporary aesthetic standards. For these innovators, the informality of the traditional service seemed foreign and undignified. They therefore insisted on greater decorum, more unison in prayer, a choir, hymns and music responses, as well as alterations in prayers and service length.

REFORMING JUDAISM

In response to such developments, Orthodoxy asserted that any change to the tradition was a violation of the Jewish heritage. For these traditionalists the Written and Oral Torah constitute an infallible chain of divinely revealed truth. Despite this reaction, some German rabbis began to re-evalute the Jewish tradition. In this undertaking the achievements of Jewish scholars who engaged in the scientific study of Judaism had a profound impact. In Frankfurt the Society of Friends of Reform was founded and published a proclamation stating that they recognized the possibility of unlimited progress in the Jewish faith and rejected the authority of the legal code as well as the belief in messianic redemption.

Above *US Reform rabbi Isaac Mayer Wise became President of the Hebrew Union College, the rabbinical seminary of the Reform movement in 1875.*

A similar group was founded in Berlin in 1844 and called for major changes in the Jewish tradition. That year the first Reform synod took place at Brunswick in which the participants formulated a programme of reform. This was followed by a series of synods. In England similar developments took place with the establishment of the West London Synagogue in the 1840s. In the USA, Reform congregations were established first in Charleston, South Carolina and later in New York City. Isaac Mayer Wise founded the Union of American Hebrew Congregations with lay and rabbinical representatives in 1873, and the Hebrew Union College, the first Reform rabbinical seminary in America in 1875.

PHILOSOPHY

In 1885 a gathering of Reform rabbis met in Pittsburgh, Pennsylvania, and adopted a programme of reform: the Pittsburgh Platform. This document insisted on a number of central principles of this new movement. According to these reformers,

Below *The West London Synagogue of British Jews, founded 1840. They chose this name to emphasize their patriotism.*

Above *Reform rabbi Sally Priesand was ordained in 1972. She is the first American female Reform rabbi.*

Judaism presents the highest conception of the God-idea as taught in holy Scripture and developed and spiritualized by Jewish teachers. They believed the Bible is the record of the consecration of the Jewish people to its divine mission, yet it should be subjected to scientific research. The Mosaic legislation, they declared, is a system of training the Jewish people, but today only the moral laws are binding; rabbinic legislation is apt to obstruct rather than further modern spiritual elevation. Further, the reformers rejected the belief in the Messiah as well as the doctrine of heaven and hell. It is the duty of modern Jewry, they asserted, to strive for justice in modern society.

Fifty years after the Pittsburgh meeting of 1885, the Jewish world had undergone major changes: America had become the centre of the Diaspora; Zionism had become a vital force in Jewish life; and Hitler was in power.

The Columbus Platform of the Reform movement adopted in 1937 reflected a new approach to liberal Judaism. In later years the Reform movement underwent further change. In the 1960s new liturgies were used, and in the 1970s a new Reform prayer book was published which changed the content as well as the format of worship. In 1972 the first woman rabbi was ordained, and by the early 1980s more than 75 women had entered the rabbinate. In 1976 the Reform movement produced the San Francisco Platform – the purpose of this statement was to provide a unifying document which would bring a sense of order to the movement.

Another platform was issued by the Central Conference of American Rabbis in 1991. At the onset of the 21st century, this rabbinic body set out a new statement of principles that affirmed the central tenets of Judaism – God, Torah and Israel – while acknowledging the diversity of Reform Jewish belief and practice. In this platform the movement affirmed the reality and oneness of God despite the differing theological interpretations. Further, it affirmed that the Jewish people are bound to God by an eternal covenant and that all human beings are created in the image of God. The Torah was conceived as the foundation of Jewish life; in this context the study of Hebrew, the language of Torah and the Jewish liturgy were extolled. The Jewish quest to bring Torah into the world was regarded as a central aspect of the faith. Finally, the movement stressed that the Reform movement is committed to strengthening the people of Israel and to furthering the interests of the Jewish State.

Below *A Reform Yom Kippur service held at the Reform Temple De Hirsch Sinai, Seattle, Washington.*

Reconstructionist Judaism

SEEKING TO MODERNIZE THE CENTRAL TENETS OF THE FAITH, RECONSTRUCTIONIST JUDAISM EMERGED IN THE EARLY 1900S AS A RADICAL ALTERNATIVE TO MAINSTREAM JEWISH MOVEMENTS.

The Reconstructionist movement emerged in the first half of the 20th century in the United States as a radical interpretation of the faith. Inspired by its founder, Mordecai Kaplan (1881–1983), the movement rejected the concept of a supernatural deity, and focused on the sociological dimensions of the tradition. Reconstructionists view Judaism as an evolving religious civilization in which spiritual symbols play a fundamental role.

ORIGINS

Unlike Reform and Conservative Judaism, Reconstructionist Judaism developed out of the thinking of an individual teacher. Born in Lithuania in 1881, Mordecai Kaplan served as professor of homiletics at the Jewish Theological Seminary in New York. During the 1910s and 1920s he engaged in wide-ranging congregational work; later he officiated as a rabbi at a synagogue-centre in New York. In 1922 Kaplan initiated a policy of reconstructing Judaism to meet the demands of modern life. After publishing *Judaism as a Civilization* in 1934, he launched the *Reconstructionist* magazine.

In *Judaism as a Civilization* Kaplan evaluated the main religious groupings of American society. In his view, Reform had correctly recognized the evolving character of Judaism, yet it ignored the social basis of Jewish identity as well as the organic character of Jewish peoplehood. Neo-Orthodoxy, on the other hand, acknowledged Judaism as a way of life and provided an intensive programme of Jewish education. None the less, it mistakenly regarded the Jewish religion as unchanging. In contrast, Conservative Judaism was committed to the scientific study of the history of the Jewish faith while recognizing the unity of the Jewish people. However it was too closely bound to the halakha, or 'Jewish law' to respond to new circumstances. All of these movements failed to adjust adequately to the modern age; what was needed, Kaplan argued, was a definition of Judaism as an evolving religious civilization.

A RECONSTRUCTED JUDAISM

In the light of this vision of a reconstructed Judaism, Kaplan called for the re-establishment of a network of organic Jewish communities that would ensure the self-perpetuation of the Jewish heritage. Membership of this new movement would be voluntary; leadership should be elected democratically; and private religious opinions would be respected. Kaplan proposed a worldwide Jewish assembly, which would adopt a covenant defining the Jews as a

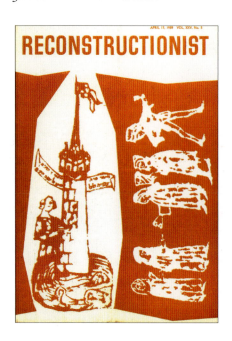

Below *The* Reconstructionist, *1959. Since 1935 the magazine has traced the growth of Reconstructionist Judaism in North America.*

Above *First page of the manuscript of Mordecai Kaplan's* Judaism as a Civilization, *dated New York, 1934, with handwritten notes by Kaplan.*

Below *Mordecai Kaplan, founder of Reconstructionist Judaism, at Camp Modin, Maine, 1958. Modin began in the summer of 1922 as 'The Camp with a Jewish Idea'.*

> **RECONSTRUCTIONIST LITURGY**
>
> Many of the ideas found in Kaplan's writings were reflected in the movement's religious literature. *The New Haggadah for Passover*, for example, applied Kaplan's theology to liturgical texts, subordinating miracles and plagues in the traditional Haggadah to the narrative of Israel's redemption from Egypt. *The Sabbath Prayer Book* was designed for those who were dissatisfied with synagogue worship – its aim was to arouse emotion by eliminating theologically untenable passages and adding inspirational material drawn from the tradition. This new prayer book deleted all references to the revelation of the Torah on Mount Sinai, the chosenness of Israel, and the doctrine of a personal Messiah.

Above Reconstructionist rabbi Sharon Kleinbaum dances the Hora, a popular Jewish circle dance, after officiating at a same-sex wedding in New York, 2010.

transnational people. In Kaplan's view, religion is the concretization of the collective self-consciousness of the group, which is manifest in spiritual symbols such as persons, places, events and writings. These symbols inspire feelings of reverence, commemorate what the group believes to be most valuable, provide historical continuity, and strengthen the collective consciousness of the people. In order for the Jewish community to survive, Kaplan believed it must eliminate its authoritarian dogmatic features.

SUPERNATURAL BELIEF

In particular, Judaism must divest itself of supernatural belief. The spiritual dimension of the faith must be reformed in humanistic and naturalistic terms. For Kaplan, God is not a supernatural being but the power that makes for salvation. God, he wrote, is the sum of all the animating organizing forces and relationships that are forever making a cosmos out of chaos. In Kaplan's view, the idea of God must be understood fundamentally in terms of its effect. In his view, God is a 'trans-national', 'super-factual' and 'super-experiential' transcendence, which does not infringe on the laws of nature. Such a notion was far-removed from the biblical and rabbinic concept of God as the creator and sustainer of the universe who chose the Jewish people and guides humanity to its final destiny.

THE MOVEMENT

In the 1940s and 1950s the leaders of Reconstructionist Judaism insisted they were not attempting to form a new branch of Judaism. Throughout this period, Reconstructionists hoped to be able to infuse the three major groups within North American Judaism (Orthodox, Conservative and Reform) with its ideas.

However, by the end of the 1960s the Reconstructionist movement had become a denomination – it had established a seminary to train Reconstructionist rabbis and had instituted a congregational structure. Regarding halakha or Jewish law, the Reconstructionist Rabbinical Association issued a statement at its 1980 convention that placed authority in the Jewish people (as opposed to the rabbis) and created a process whereby each congregation would be free to evolve its own *minhag*, or custom. Three years later, the Association produced guidelines on intermarriage, encouraging rabbis to welcome mixed couples (a Jew and a non-Jew), permit them to participate in Jewish synagogue life, and recognize their children as Jewish if raised as Jews. In addition, the Association decreed that rabbis could sanctify an intermarriage as long as it was accompanied by a civil, rather than a religious, ceremony.

Below Celebrating Sukkot at the Reconstructionist Rabbinical College in Wyncote, Pennsylvania, USA.

Humanistic Judaism

THIS RADICAL MOVEMENT HAS BECOME AN ALTERNATIVE FOR SOME JEWS. IT OFFERS JEWISH SECULAR HUMANISTS A NEW FORM OF JUDAISM DEVOID OF A BELIEF IN A SUPERNATURAL DEITY.

Like Reconstructionist Judaism, Jewish humanism offers a non-theistic interpretation of the Jewish faith. Originating in the 1960s in Detroit, Michigan under the leadership of Rabbi Sherwin Wine, Humanistic Judaism now numbers about 40,000 members in the United States, Israel, Europe and elsewhere. The movement originated in 1965, when the Birmingham Temple in a suburb outside Detroit began to publicize its philosophy of Judaism. In 1966 a special committee for Humanistic Judaism was organized at the Temple to share service and educational material with rabbis and laity. The following year a meeting of several leaders of the movement met, issuing a statement, which affirmed that Judaism should be governed by empirical reason and human needs. A new magazine, *Humanistic Judaism* was founded. Two years later, two new Humanistic congregations were established: Temple Beth Or in Deerfield, Illinois, and a Congregation for Humanistic Judaism in Fairfield County, Connecticut.

In 1969 the Society for Humanistic Judaism was established in Detroit to provide a basis for cooperation among Humanistic Jews, and in 1970 the first annual conference of the Society took place. During the next ten years new congregations were established in Boston, Toronto, Los Angeles, Washington, Miami, Long Beach and Huntington, New York. In subsequent years Secular Humanistic Judaism became an international movement with supporters on five continents. The National Federation currently comprises nine national organizations in the United States, Canada, Britain, France, Belgium, Israel, Australia, Argentina and Uruguay.

Above *Rabbi Sherwin Wine founded the Society for Humanistic Judaism in North America, in 1969.*

THE IDEOLOGY OF HUMANISTIC JUDAISM

In 1986 the Federation issued a proclamation stating its ideology and aims. According to this document, Humanistic Jews value human reason and the reality of the world which reason discloses. In their view, the natural universe stands on its own, requiring no supernatural intervention. In this light, Humanists believe in the value of human existence and in the power of human beings to solve their problems individually and collectively. Life, they maintain, should be directed to the satisfaction of human needs. In their view, Judaism, as the civilization of Jews, is a human creation: it embraces all manifestations of Jewish life, including Jewish languages, ethical traditions, historic memories, cultural heritage, and especially the emergence of the state of Israel in modern times.

The Jewish people, Humanists insist, is a world with a pluralistic culture and civilization all its own. Judaism, as the culture of the Jews, is thus more than theological content. It encompasses many languages, a vast body of literature, historical memories and ethical values. Yet, unlike other modern movements, Humanistic Judaism seeks to welcome all people who seek to

Below *Blowing the Shofar for Yom Kippur at a humanistic service at Morris County, NJ, USA. In a break with tradition, the service is about atonement – but not to God.*

identify with Jewish culture and destiny. Hence, Humanists have redefined the notion of Jewishness. A Jew, they state, is a person of Jewish descent or any person who declares himself or herself to be a Jew and who identifies with the history, ethical values, culture, civilization, and community of the Jewish nation.

JEWISH FESTIVALS

Dedicated to Jewish survival, Humanistic Judaism emphasizes the importance of Jewish festivals in fostering Jewish identity. Yet, for Humanistic Jews, they must be detached from their supernatural origins and reinterpreted in the light of modern circumstances. Such a reorientation provides a basis for extolling human potential.

So, too, does Humanistic Judaism's understanding of life-cycle events: the ceremonies connected with these events emphasize the importance of group survival. Beginning with birth, Humanistic Jews stress the connection of the child with the future of the family, the Jewish people and humanity. Likewise, Humanistic Judaism fosters a Humanistic maturity ceremony, which reflects the ethical commitments of Humanistic Jews.

As an important transitional event, the marriage ceremony should also embody Humanistic values. For Humanistic Jews, the wedding should embrace the conception of the bride and groom publicly declaring their commitment and support and loyalty to one another.

Rituals connected with death should similarly be expressive of Humanistic principles. Humanistic Judaism asserts that mortality is an unavoidable and final event. Accepting this truth, it is possible to live courageously and generously in the face of tragedy. A Humanistic Jewish memorial service serves as

Above *A young man at his bar mitzvah, held as a humanistic service, Detroit, Michigan, 2006.*

an opportunity to teach a philosophy of life. Both the meditations and the eulogies are designed to remind people that the value of personal life lies in its quality, not in its quantity.

A NEW APPROACH

Humanistic Judaism, then, offers an option for those who wish to identify with the Jewish community despite their rejection of the traditional understanding of God's nature and activity. Unlike Reconstructionist Judaism, with its emphasis on the observances of the past, Humanistic Judaism fosters a radically new approach. The Jewish heritage is relevant only in so far as it advances Humanistic ideals.

In addition, traditional definitions and principles are set aside in the quest to create a Judaism consonant with a scientific and pluralistic age. Secular in orientation, Humanistic Jews seek to create a world in which the Jewish people are dedicated to the betterment of all humankind.

Left *Altar at a humanistic wedding scattered with natural objects – flowers, stones, incense and a glass goblet.*

Jewish Renewal

FOSTERING A NON-TRADITIONAL COMMITMENT TO JEWISH HERITAGE, JEWISH RENEWAL IS A PRODUCT OF THE COUNTER-CULTURE MOVEMENTS, ORGANIZED AROUND EXPERIMENTAL FELLOWSHIPS.

The Jewish Renewal movement brings Kabbalistic and Hasidic theory and practice into a non-Orthodox, egalitarian framework. In this respect, Jewish Renewal is characterized by its Hasidic orientation. Renewal Jews often add ecstatic practices such as meditation, chant and dance to traditional worship. In addition, some Renewal Jews borrow from Buddhism, Sufism and other faiths to enhance their spiritual approach.

HISTORY

Jewish renewal has its origins in the North American counter-movements of the late 1960s and early 1970s. During this period, a number of young rabbis, academics and political activists founded experimental havurot, or 'fellowships', for prayer and study in a reaction to what they perceived as the overly organized institutional structures of mainstream Judaism. Initially the main inspiration was the pietistic fellowship of the Pharisees as well as other early sects. In addition, some of these groups attempted to function as fully fledged communes after the model of their secular counterparts. Others formed communities within urban and suburban contexts.

Founders of the havurot movement included the liberal political activist Arthur Waskow, Conservative rabbi Michael Strassfeld and perhaps Jewish Renewal's most prominent leader, Zalman Schachter-Shalomi. Even though the original leadership consisted of men, US Jewish feminists were later actively engaged in Jewish Renewal, including Rabbis Shefa Gold, Lynn Gottlieb and Waskow's partner Phyllis Berman. Initially the movement attracted little attention in the US Jewish community despite various articles in Jewish magazines. However, in 1973 Michael and Sharon Strassfeld published *The Jewish Catalogue: A Do-It-Yourself Kit*. This was patterned after the counter-culture *Whole Earth Catalogue* and served as a basic reference book dealing with a wide range of Jewish subjects, including traditional observances as well as crafts, recipes and meditational practices. In time the havurah movement increased in numbers and included self-governing havurot within Reform, Conservative and Reconstructionist congregations. By 1980 a number of havurot moved away from traditional patterns of Jewish worship as members added English readings, chants, poetry and other elements from various spiritual traditions.

Above *Liberal political activist Rabbi Arthur Waskow (right), co-founder of the havurot movement and a leading figure in Jewish Renewal, with Muslim imam Mahdi Bray.*

RENEWAL LEADERSHIP

Pre-eminent among leaders of this new movement was Zalman Schachter-Shalomi, a Hasidic-trained rabbi who was ordained in the Lubavitch movement. In the 1960s he broke with Orthodox Judaism and founded his own organization, the B'nai Or Religious Fellowship. The name 'B'nai Or' means 'sons'

Left *Rabbi Zalman Schachter-Shalomi, with the Dalai Lama in Dharamsala, India, 1990. The rabbi is holding a chart explaining the similarities between Jewish and Tibetan views.*

or 'children' of light, and was taken from the Dead Sea Scrolls where the sons of light battle with the sons of darkness.

Schachter-Shalomi viewed B'nai Or as a semi-monastic ashram community, based on various communal models of the 1960s and 70s. The community never materialized as he wished, yet it produced a number of important Renewal leaders. The *B'nai Or Newsletter* presented articles on Jewish mysticism, Hasidic stories and Schachter-Shalomi's philosophy, which was influenced by Buddhism and Sufism. Rabbi Zalman later held the Wisdom Chair at Naropa Institute, America's only Buddhist university.

After the first national Kallah conference in Radnor, Pennsylvania in 1985, the name B'nai Or was changed to P'nai Or (Faces of Light) to reflect the more egalitarian nature of Jewish Renewal. Together with Arthur Waskow, Schachter-Shalomi broadened the focus of the organization. In 1993 it merged with the Shalom Centre, founded by Rabbi Waskow to become ALEPH (Alliance for Jewish Renewal). This organization served as an overarching association for like-minded havurot.

However, some more Orthodox members of B'nai Or were not con-

Right *Wearing a prayer shawl and skullcap, a Jew practises yoga on the beach at Ashdod, Israel — an example of how Judaism is reinterpreted in contemporary life.*

tent with these changes and left the Renewal movement. This brought about significant leadership changes, with Waskow taking an increasingly important role. During this period his magazine *Menorah* merged with the *B'nai Or Newsletter* to become *New Menorah*. This new publication addressed such issues as Jewish feminism, the nuclear arms race, new forms of prayer, social justice, and gay rights.

B'nai Or/ALEPH and its magazine led to the spread of Jewish Renewal throughout the United States and other countries. This has brought about the institutionalization of the movement in the form of the administrative ALEPH, the rabbinical association OHaLaH, and formalized rabbinic ordination programme.

THE MOVEMENT
Statistical information about the number of Jews who affiliate with Jewish Renewal is not available. None the less, the movement has had a profound impact on various non-Orthodox streams of Judaism within the United States. Arguably the greatest impact has been on Reconstructionist Judaism. Initially based on the rationalistic philosophy of Mordecai Kaplan, under the influence of Jewish Renewal, Reconstructionism has come to embrace Jewish mystical beliefs and practices, particularly in the prayer books that were issued in the 1990s.

Jewish Renewal has also had an impact on other non-Orthodox movements in terms of the increased leadership roles of women, the acceptance of gays and lesbians, and liberal political activism.

In addition, it is not uncommon for synagogues not associated with Jewish Renewal to feature workshops on Jewish meditation and yoga. Various melodies and liturgical innovations have been introduced through the influence of Renewal.

Despite such an impact on Jewish life, critics of Jewish Renewal maintain that the movement puts too much emphasis on individual spiritual experience over communal norms. Dismissed as a 'New Age' phenomenon, they argue that the borrowing from non-Jewish traditions has had a deleterious effect on Jewish life.

Left *The Jewish Voice for LGBTI rights marching at the Gay Pride Parade, New York, USA.*

Messianic Judaism

AT THE CENTRE OF MESSIANIC JEWISH BELIEF AND PRACTICE IS THE CONVICTION THAT JESUS, WHO IS REFERRED TO AS YESHUA, IS THE LONG-AWAITED MESSIAH OR ANOINTED ONE.

Firmly rejected by the Jewish community as a whole, Messianic Judaism claims to be an authentic interpretation of the Jewish tradition. In the last few decades it has emerged as a controversial movement on the religious scene. Although followers see it as a legitimate interpretation of the tradition, this claim is firmly rejected by the Jewish community.

At the core of Messianic Jewish theology is the belief that Jesus (whom Messianic Jews refer to as Yeshua) is the long-awaited Messiah. Messianic believers contend that they are not Christians – rather they are determined to live Jewish lives in fulfilment of God's will. In this quest, Messianic Jews have reinterpreted the major Jewish festivals including Sabbath, Passover, Shavuot and Sukkot as well as festivals of joy and life-cycle events. At the centre of their practice and worship is the belief that the world has been redeemed and transformed.

Below *Rembrandt's* Head of Christ, *painted in 1748, shows the Christian Messiah as a Jewish man.*

BIRTH OF A MOVEMENT

In the early 1970s a considerable number of American Jewish converts to Christianity (known as Hebrew Christians) were committed to a church-based conception of Hebrew Christianity. At the same time emerged a growing segment of the Hebrew Christian community seeking a more Jewish lifestyle. Particularly among the youth, there was a strong urge to identify with their Jewish roots. In their view, the acceptance of Yeshua should be coupled with a commitment to the cultural and religious features of the faith.

Eventually a clear division emerged between those who wished to forge a new lifestyle and those who sought to pursue traditional Hebrew Christian goals. The advocates of change sought to persuade older members of the need to embrace Jewish values, yet they remained unconvinced. In time the name of the movement was changed to Messianic Judaism – this brought about a fundamental shift in orientation. Any return to Hebrew Christianity was ruled out, and a significant number of older members left the movement.

THEOLOGY

Messianic Judaism is grounded in the belief that Yeshua is the long-awaited Messiah. In this respect, Messianic Judaism and the earlier Hebrew Christian movement are based on the same belief system. None the less, Messianic Jews are anxious to point out there are important distinctions between their views and those of Hebrew Christians. Hebrew Christians see themselves as of Jewish origin and may desire to affirm their background, yet at the same time they view themselves as coming into the

Above *Messianic Jews do not celebrate Mass but they mark festivals, such as the blessing of bread and wine on the Sabbath.*

New Covenant. The Old Covenant has passed away. Hence, the direct practice of anything Jewish is contrary to their being part of the new people of God and the body of Christ. Messianic Jews, however, believe that the Jew is still called by God.

In the view of Messianic Jews, all of the prophecies in the *Tanakh* (Hebrew Bible) relating to messianic atonement were fulfilled in Yeshua. Repeatedly they affirm that the Messiah Yeshua came to the Jews, and his followers transmitted his message to the world. Although the Torah demands a blood sacrifice, the Messiah is able to offer himself as a means of atonement. Whereas traditional Judaism stresses the importance of the mitzvot, what is required instead is belief in God's word and acceptance of the Messiah's atonement for sin. Only in this way can the faithful receive God's forgiveness and the promise of salvation.

Messianic Judaism asserts the world will be changed during the Second Coming. Drawing on the Suffering Servant passages in the Book of Isaiah, Messianic Jews argue that Yeshua fulfilled this role on earth but he will come again to deliver the world, defeat Israel's enemies, and establish God's Kingdom on earth.

Above *Members of Sha'ar Adonai, a Messianic congregation, dancing in Central Park in New York.*

Right *A painting of Jesus, the Virgin and the Child by Jewish master Marc Chagall. The artist stresses the Jewishness of Jesus as the suffering Messiah.*

OBSERVANCE

Messianic Jews see themselves as the true heirs of the early disciples of the risen Lord. Anxious to identify with the Jewish nation, Messianic Jews have sought to observe the central biblical festivals. In their view, the Sabbath and the various festivals prescribed in Scripture are as valid today as they were in ancient times.

Customs regulating the life-cycle and lifestyle of Jews in biblical times are binding on members of the Messianic community. Believers are united in their loyalty to the Jewish heritage as enshrined in Scripture.

None the less, Messianic Jews are not legalistic in their approach to Judaism. Traditional observance is tempered with the desire to allow the holy spirit to permeate the Messianic community and animate believers in their quest to serve the Lord. For this reason, there is considerable freedom among Messianic Jews in the ways they incorporate the Jewish tradition into their daily lives.

Right *Minister Jacques Elbaz preaches to Messianic Jews in Tel Aviv, Israel.*

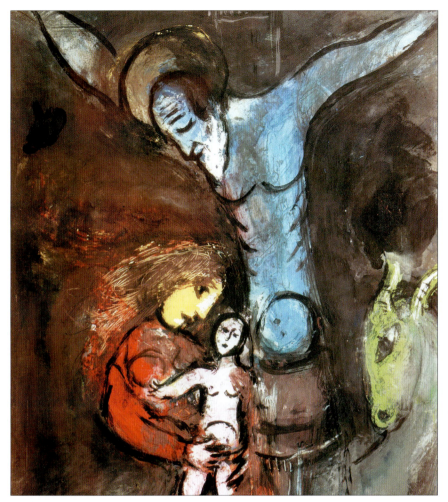

The nature of contemporary Messianic practice, means that congregations do not rigidly follow the patterns recommended in the various Messianic prayer books produced by the movement; instead, they modify their observance in accordance with their own spiritual needs. Visitors to Messianic congregations will thus be struck by the considerable variation that exists within the movement.

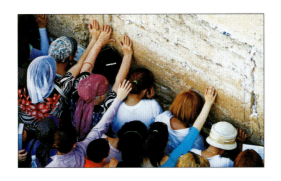

CHAPTER 4

UNTRADITIONAL JUDAISM

Over the last two centuries, new interpretations of Jewish life have emerged. In the 1900s, Zionist thinkers argued a Jewish commonwealth must be established in the Holy Land, with a few religious Zionists arguing that Jewry must actively bring about the creation of a Jewish presence in Palestine prior to the arrival of the Messiah. Secular Zionists maintained Jews would never be secure from anti-Semitism unless they had a nation state.

In recent years, other non-traditional movements have emerged in the Jewish community. Modern Kabbalists have tried to revitalize traditional Kabbalistic doctrines in the quest to live a more spiritual life. Jewish socialists have pressed for the restructuring of modern society. Jewish feminists have pressed for gender equality. Jewish Buddhists have reinterpeted Judaism. Jewish vegetarians espouse animal welfare. Other Jews advocate the acceptance of the pluralistic nature of modern Jewish life. Today Jews in Israel and the Diaspora follow a wide variety of different and conflicting paths in their quest to live an authentically Jewish existence.

Opposite *Tree of Life, part of the Ardon Windows by Mordecai Ardon, National Library of Israel, Jerusalem.*

Above *Jewish women reach out to touch the Western Wall in Jerusalem, 2010. In modern times, Jewish feminists have reevaluated the role of women in Jewish life.*

Religious Zionism

TRADITION IS THAT THE MESSIAH WILL LEAD THE JEWS BACK TO ZION. IN CONTRAST, RELIGIOUS ZIONISTS ADVOCATED THE RETURN OF JEWRY TO ISRAEL IN ANTICIPATION OF MESSIANIC DELIVERANCE.

For thousands of years Jews anticipated that the coming of the Messiah would bring about a final ingathering of the Jewish people to their ancient homeland. This was to be a divinely predetermined miraculous event, which will inaugurate the messianic age. However, in the early 19th century within religious Orthodox circles there emerged a new trend, the advocacy of an active approach to Jewish messianism.

THE STIRRINGS OF RELIGIOUS ZIONISM

At the beginning of the 19th century, a number of Jewish writers maintained that, rather than adopt a passive attitude towards the problem of redemption, the Jewish nation must engage in the creation of a homeland in anticipation of the advent of the Messiah. Preeminent among such religious Zionists was Yehuda hai Alkalai, born in 1798 in Sarajevo to Rabbi Sholomo Alkalai, the spiritual leader of the local Jewish community. During his youth, Yehuda lived in Palestine, where he was influenced by Kabbalistic thought. In 1825 he published a booklet entitled *Shema Yisrael* in which he advocated the establishment of Jewish colonies in Palestine, a view at variance with the traditional Jewish belief that the Messiah will come through an act of divine deliverance.

When in 1840 the Jews of Damascus were charged with the blood libel (killing a child and using its blood in an act of ritual), Alkalai became convinced that the Jewish people could be secure only in their own land. Henceforth he published a series of books and pamphlets explaining his plan of self-redemption. In *Minhat Yehuda* he argued on the basis of the Hebrew Scriptures that the Messiah will not miraculously materialize; rather, he will be preceded by various preparatory events. In this light the Holy Land needs to be populated by Jewry in preparation for messianic deliverance. For Alkalai, redemption is not simply a divine affair – it is also a human concern requiring labour and persistence.

Above *Abraham Isaac Kook, philosopher, mystic and defender of religious Zionism, who became the first Ashkenazi chief rabbi of Palestine before independence.*

THE GROWTH OF RELIGIOUS ZIONISM

Another early pioneer of religious Zionism was Zvi Hirsch Kalischer, the rabbi of Toun in the province of Posen, in Poland. An early defender of Orthodoxy against the advances made by Reform Judaism, he championed the commandments in prescribing faith in the Messiah and devotion to the Holy Land. In 1836 he expressed his commitment to Jewish settlement in Palestine in a letter to the head of the Berlin branch of the Rothschild family. The beginning of redemption, he maintained, will come through natural causes by human effort to gather the scattered of Israel into the Holy Land. Later he published *Derishat Zion*. In this work he argued that the redemption of Israel will not

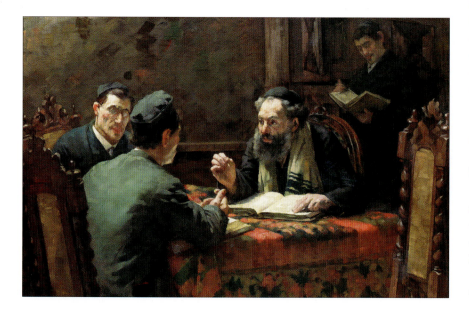

Below *A Theological Debate by Eduard Frankfort, 1888. By this date, the idea of a Jewish state was being fiercely debated among Orthodox Jews.*

take place miraculously. Instead, it will occur slowly through awakening support from philanthropists and gaining the consent of other nations to the gathering of the Jewish people into the Holy Land.

Following in the footsteps of Alkalai and Kalischer, Abraham Isaac Kook formulated a vision of messianic redemption integrating the creation of a Jewish state. Born in Latvia in 1865, Kook received a traditional Jewish education and in 1895 became rabbi of Bausk. In 1904 he emigrated to Palestine, eventually becoming the first Ashkenazi chief rabbi after the British Mandate. Unlike secularists who advocated practical efforts to secure a Jewish state, Kook embarked on the task of reinterpreting the Jewish religious tradition to transform religious messianic anticipation into the basis for collaboration with the aspirations of modern Zionism.

ORTHODOXY AND RELIGIOUS ZIONISM

Although some Orthodox Jewish figures endorsed the Zionist movement, Orthodoxy in Germany, Hungary and Eastern European countries protested against this new development in Jewish life.

To promote this policy, an ultra-Orthodox movement, Agudat Yisrael, was created to unite rabbis and laity against Zionism. Determined to counter Zionist ideology, Agudat denounced the policies of modern Zionists and refused to collaborate with religious Zionist parties such as the Mizrachi. In Palestine itself the extreme Orthodox movement joined with Agudat Israel in its struggle against Zionism.

Eventually, however, these critics of Zionist aspirations modified their position and began to take a more active role in Jewish settlement. This was owing to the immigration of members of Agudat Yisrael to Palestine, as well as the massacre of Orthodox Jews in Hebron, Safed and Jerusalem during the riots of 1929. None the less, the ultra-right refused to join the National Council of Palestinian Jewry, which had been established in the 1920s. In the next decades the rise of the Nazis and the events of the Holocaust brought about a split in the movement.

In 1934 Isaac Breuer, a leading Orthodox spokesman, cautioned

Left Hasidic Jew in Mea Shearim, home to ultra-Orthodox Jews in Jerusalem, 1985. Some Hasidic Jews oppose the idea of a Zionist state.

Above Entrance to a house in Mea Shearim, Jerusalem, a quarter outside the Old City walls, whose name means 'Hundred Gates'.

that it would be a mistake to leave Jewish history to the Zionists. If Agudat wished to gain the upper hand against the Zionists, it was obligated to prepare the Holy Land for the rule of God. In the unfolding of God's providential plan, he declared, the extreme Orthodox had a crucial role to play. Between the end of the war and the founding of the Jewish state, a zealous extreme group, the Neturei Karta in Jerusalem, accused the Agudat of succumbing to the Zionists. Yet, despite such criticism, the leaders of Agudat continued to support the creation of a Jewish homeland, and a year before its establishment they reached an understanding with Palestinian Zionists concerning such matters as Sabbath observance, dietary laws and regulations regarding education and marriage. Such a conciliatory policy paved the way for the creation of Orthodox religious parties in Israel, which continue to play a central role in the government of the Jewish state. Today, religious Zionists in Israel and the Diaspora regard the modern State of Israel as the fulfilment of God's promise to Abraham, Isaac and Jacob.

Secular Zionism

IN THE 1880S AND 90S SECULAR ZIONISTS PROMOTED THE CREATION OF A JEWISH HOMELAND IN PALESTINE. IN THEIR VIEW, ONLY THE CREATION OF A JEWISH STATE WOULD PROTECT JEWS FROM THEIR ENEMIES.

The Russian pogroms of 1881–2 forced many Jews to emigrate to the United States, but a sizeable number were drawn to Palestine. These earlier pioneers were the vanguard of the Zionist movement, which agitated for the creation of a Jewish commonwealth in the Holy Land. In their view, anti-Semitism was inevitable; hence, they argued, Jewry could only be secure in a country of their own. This ideology was fuelled by an intense commitment to Jewish survival in a hostile world.

ORIGINS

In the Russian Pale of Settlement, nationalist zealots organized Zionist groups (Lovers of Zion) which collected money and organized courses in Hebrew and Jewish history. In 1882 several thousand Jews left for Palestine, where they worked as shopkeepers and artisans; other Jewish immigrants known as Bilu (from the Hebrew 'House of Jacob, let us go') combined Marxist ideals with Jewish nationalist fervour and worked as farmers and labourers.

During this period, Leon Pinsker, an eminent Russian physician, published *Autoemancipation* in which he argued that the liberation of Jewry could only be secured by the establishment of a Jewish homeland. 'Nations', he wrote, 'live side by side in a state of relative peace, which is based chiefly on fundamental equality between them. But it is different with the people of Israel. This people is not counted among the nations, because when it was exiled from its land it lost the essential attributes of nationality.'

THE ZIONIST MOVEMENT

In the 1890s the idea of Jewish nationalism had spread to other countries in Europe. Foremost among its proponents was the Austrian journalist Theodor Herzl (1860–1904) who was profoundly influenced by the Dreyfus affair. In 1897, the first Zionist Congress took place in Basle, which called for a national home for Jews based on international law. At this congress Herzl stated that emancipation of the Jews had been an illusion. Jews were everywhere objects of contempt and hatred. The only solution to the Jewish problem, he argued, was the reestablishment of a Jewish homeland in Palestine.

In the same year the Zionist Organization was created with branches in Europe and America. After establishing these basic institutions of the Zionist movement, Herzl embarked on diplomatic negotiations. In 1898 he met with Kaiser Wilhelm II (ruled 1888–1918) who promised he would take up the matter with the Sultan. When nothing came of this, Herzl himself attempted to arrange an interview, and in 1901 a meeting with the Sultan took place. In return for a charter of Jewish settlement in Palestine, Herzl suggested that wealthy Jewish bankers might be willing to pay off the Turkish debt. In the following year the Sultan agreed to approve a plan of Jewish settlement throughout the Ottoman empire but not a corporate Jewish homeland in Palestine.

Unwilling to abandon a diplomatic approach, Herzl sought to cultivate contacts in England. In 1903 Joseph Chamberlain, the Secretary of State for Colonial Affairs, suggested the possibility of Uganda as a homeland for the Jews. At the next Zionist Congress in Basle this proposal was presented for ratification. When Chamberlain's scheme was explained, it was emphasized that Uganda was not meant to serve as a permanent solution but rather

Below *Theodor Herzl, founder of political Zionism, a movement which promoted Jewish immigration to Palestine.*

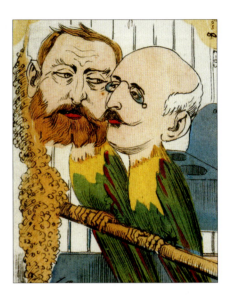

Above *French editor Jean Jaurès (left), one of the most energetic defenders of Alfred Dreyfus (right). The Dreyfus affair persuaded Theodor Herzl of the necessity of a Jewish state to protect Jews.*

SECULAR ZIONISM

Above *During an 1880s pogrom in Kiev, Russian Jews were assaulted while police did nothing. Such attacks convinced Zionists of the need for a Jewish state.*

as a temporary residence. When the resolution was passed by a small margin, delegates from eastern Europe walked out. Eventually the offer was withdrawn.

EVOLUTION
After Herzl's death in 1904, David Wolffsohn became President of the Zionist movement. Under his leadership Orthodox Jews joined the Zionist Organization as members of the Mizrahi Party; socialist Jews also became members through the Labour Zionist Party. In the 1907 congress a resolution was passed which pledged the movement to the quest for a charter, the physical settlement of Palestine and the revival of the Hebrew language. During the next decade the major developments in the Zionist movement took place in Israel and by the beginning of the 20th century a sizeable number of Jews had migrated to Palestine.

Most of these pioneers lived in cities, but a small minority worked on farm colonies under the control of the Palestine Jewish Colonization Association. By 1929 the Jewish community in Palestine (*yishuv*) numbered 160,000 with 110 agricultural settlements; in the next ten years the community increased to 500,000 with 233 agricultural communities. During this time, rival Jewish factions emerged within Palestine with different political orientations. The President of the World Zionist Congress, Chaim Weizmann (1874–1952), for example, was committed to co-operating with the British. Vladimir Jabotinsky (1880–1940), leader of the Union of Zionist Revisionists, stressed that the central aim of Zionism was the establishment of an independent state in the whole of

Above *Arabs ready to attack Jewish buses from Jerusalem, 1948. As the Jewish population in Palestine increased, Zionists were constantly threatened by Arabs.*

THE CREATION OF A JEWISH STATE

The Holocaust and the establishment of the State of Israel were organically related events: the death of millions of Jews in World War II profoundly affected Jewry throughout the world. During the war and afterwards, the British prevented illegal immigrants entering the Holy Land. In response, Jewish military forces joined together in resisting British policy. Eventually the British Government handed the problem of Palestine over to the United Nations. The UN discussed the Palestinian problem in May 1947. A special committee issued two reports; a minority recommended a federated bi-national state; the majority advocated a new plan of partition with a Jewish and Arab state as well as an international zone in Jerusalem.

This latter proposal was endorsed by the General Assembly of the United Nations on 29 November 1947.

Once the UN plan of partition was endorsed, the Arabs began to attack Jewish settlements. By March 1948 more than thousand Jews had been killed, but in the next month David Ben-Gurion (1886–1973) ordered the Haganah to link up all the Jewish enclaves and consolidate the territory given to Israel under the UN partition plan.

On 14 May 1948 Ben-Gurion read out the Scroll of Independence in which he reiterated the goal of the Zionist movement: 'The Land of Israel was the birthplace of the Jewish people ... In the year 1897 the First Zionist Congress, inspired by Theodor Herzl's vision of the Jewish State, proclaimed the right of the Jewish people to national renewal in their own country.'

Left *David Ben-Gurion, the first Prime Minister of modern Israel, appointed two days after independence.*

MODERN KABBALISM

DRAWING ON ANCIENT KABBALISTIC TEACHING, MODERN KABBALISTS STRESS THE IMPORTANCE OF JEWISH MYSTICAL BELIEF AND PRACTICE. IN RECENT YEARS, THE KABBALAH CENTRE HAS ATTRACTED MILLIONS.

In contemporary society the Kabbalistic tradition has served as a rich spiritual resource for many Jews. In their quest to attain enlightenment, these religious seekers have embraced the teachings of modern Kabbalists. Pre-eminent among contemporary mystics Rav Philip Berg has drawn millions of Jews to the Kabbalistic tradition through the creation of Kabbalah Centres throughout the Jewish world.

ORIGINS
The fundamentals of the medieval Kabbalistic system were expanded by such luminaries as Moses Cordovero, Isaac Luria, the Ba'al Shem Tov, Nachman of Bratslav, Levi Yitzhak of Berdichev, Kalonymus Kalman Epstein, Dov Baer of Mezhirich and Shneur Zalman. In the modern period, interest in Kabbalistic thought outside the Hasidic circle generally diminished with the exception of such figures as Yehuda Ashlag, the author of *Sulam*, or 'Ladder', who influenced the development of popular Kabbalah. In recent years through his disciple Rav Berg, the international Kabbalah Centre has today become the most influential proponent of Kabbalistic thought worldwide.

Born in Warsaw in 1885, Ashlag was a descendent of scholars connected to the Hasidic courts of Prosov and Belz. In 1921 he moved to Palestine and worked as a labourer; later he was appointed rabbi of Givat Shaul, Jerusalem. In the 1930s he gathered around him a group of disciples who studied Kabbalah and promoted the study of Kabbalistic doctrine even for those who had not mastered rabbinic texts. In his view, knowledge of Kabbalah can provide all persons with a taste of Godliness that will enable them to conquer their evil inclinations and advance spiritually.

During this period Ashlag published *The Talmud of the Ten Sephirot*, which was a reworking of the thought of Isaac Luria; in addition he wrote an extensive commentary on the Zohar. In this work Ashlag stressed the transformation of human consciousness from a state of desiring to receive, to desiring to give. Through the study of Kabbalah, he believed, the mind opens to God's light, and the desire to give to others is developed. Ashlag believed that the coming of the Messiah meant that humans would give up their selfishness and devote themselves to loving each other.

Above *American rabbi Philip Berg of the Kabbalah Centre, which has had a powerful effect on Jews seeking inspiration from the Kabbalistic tradition.*

THE KABBALAH CENTRE
Ashlag's main disciples included his sons Baruch Shalom and Shlomo Benyamin as well as Rabbi Yehuda Brandwein. Rabbi Baruch and Rabbi Brandwein influenced students who spread Ashlag's interpretation of Kabbalah. Brandwein's son-in-law Rabbi Avraham Sheinberger founded a commune in Israel, Or Ganuz, or 'The Hidden Light', which combines Ashlag's communal ideas with a devotion to Kabbalistic teaching.

In 1962 Rabbi Brandwein met Rav Philip Berg who had visited Israel from America. Trained in traditional yeshivot, Rav Berg was no longer a practising rabbi, but was deeply influenced by Rabbi Brandwein's teaching. In his autobiography, *Education of a Kabbalist*, Berg explained that he received the honour and responsibility of bringing the ancient wisdom of Kabbalah to the world.

As Brandwein's devoted student, Berg established the Kabbalah Research Centre, which today has 50 branches worldwide and has become the leading educational institution teaching the wisdom of the Kabbalah. Together with his sons Michael Berg and Yehuda Berg, Rav

Below *The Chamsah, an amulet used to ward off the evil eye, from Safed, Israel, where Kabbalah developed.*

Above *The Kabalah centre, Los Angeles, USA was opened in 1984.*

Berg has spread Kabbalistic teaching to millions of adherents. In a wide range of publications the Bergs have spread Ashlagian Kabbalism to disciples seeking spiritual knowledge and insight.

KABBALISTIC THEOLOGY
Of central importance in the Kabbalistic system propounded by Rabbi Ashlag as explained by Rabbi Brandwein is the Desire to Share. This, he argued, should replace the Desire to Receive. According to Brandwein, human beings have been the gift of the desire to receive; this can be understood as an unusually large spiritual vessel containing the divine light. Yet it is a mixed blessing. Although it allows them to be persons to be filled with light, it can block them from true goodness. If individuals cannot transform their Desire to Receive into a Desire to Share, this will have the most negative results. The Desire to Receive will grow larger and larger until it swallows everything around it. Human history, Brandwein observed, is simply a record of self-serving desire run rampant, fuelled by hatred, envy and distrust.

Developing Brandwein's views, Rav Berg explains how spiritual growth is possible. Our souls, he asserted, are created for one reason only – the Creator in whom all things are invested, had a Desire to Share. But, when the Creator existed alone, sharing could not occur. There were no vessels to hold the endless bounty pouring out of him. So, with nothing more than desire, he created those vessels which are our souls. Initially these created souls received the divine light with no motive other than to receive for themselves alone. But as they were filled, a new yearning evolved – one that put them on a collision course with the Creator. Suddenly, in emulation of the Creator, our souls developed a Desire to Receive for the purpose of sharing. But they were faced with the same dilemma as that which faced the Creator himself before he created the vessels. With every soul filled, there was no one and nothing with whom to share.

Thus what Berg referred to as the 'Bread of Shame' came into being. This was shame at receiving so much and giving nothing in return. Shame at being in a position in which the soul had no opportunity to say yes or no to the Creator and, by that exercise of will, prove itself worthy to receive and thus dispel the shame. The shame led to rebellion – a mass rejection of the Creator's beneficence. When that happened, the light was withdrawn, darkness and the unclean worlds were created and all became finite – or limited – and thus in need of receiving. With those worlds came the clay bodies – vessels desiring only to receive for themselves alone – in which our souls reside. Here they forever struggle against body energy, to share. For the modern Kabbalist, this quest to eliminate the 'Bread of Shame' by sharing with others is the fundamental spiritual goal.

Below *Kabbalistic Jews mark the end of the Sabbath with Havdalah, reciting blessings over wine, a candle and spices.*

333

THE JEWISH LEFT

IN THE LATE 19TH CENTURY SOCIALIST IDEALS INSPIRED A GROWING SEGMENT OF THE JEWISH COMMUNITY. CONTINUING THIS TRADITION, THE JEWISH LEFT PROMOTES SOCIAL ACTION IN MANY CONTEXTS.

The term Jewish Left refers to Jews who identify with or support left-wing causes either as individuals or through organizations. The Jewish Left is not a movement, yet those who support this political stance have been identified with various groups, including the US labour movement, the women's rights movement and anti-fascist organizations.

In contemporary society many well-known figures on the left have been Jews; these individuals were born into Jewish families and have in various ways been connected with the Jewish community, Jewish culture and the Jewish faith.

ORIGINS

In the age of industrialization in the 19th century, a Jewish working class emerged in Eastern and Central Europe. Before long, a Jewish labour movement had emerged. The Jewish Labour Bund (or federation) was formed in Vilna in Lithuania in 1897. In addition, Jewish anarchist and socialist organizations were formed and spread across the Jewish Pale of Settlement in the Russian Empire. As Zionism grew in numbers, socialist Zionist parties were established. There were also non-Zionist left-wing forms of Jewish nationalism, such as territorialism (which advocated the creation of a Jewish national home but not necessarily in Palestine), autonomism (which supported non-territorial national rights for Jews in multinational empires), and folkism (which celebrated Jewish culture).

As Eastern European Jews emigrated in the 1880s, these ideological positions took root in various Jewish communities, particularly in England, New York and Buenos Aires. In the United States, the Jewish socialist movement embraced various organs including the Yiddish-language daily, the *Forward*, trade unions such as the International Ladies Garment Workers' Union, and the Amalgamated Clothing Workers.

Above *Rose Pesotta, a Ukrainian Jew who came to the USA in 1917, became a feminist organizer and vice president of the International Ladies' Garment Workers' Union.*

In the late 19th and early 20th centuries, Jews played a major role in the Social Democratic parties in Germany, Russia, Austria–Hungary and Poland.

STALINISM AND FASCISM

Many Jews worldwide welcomed the Russian Revolution of 1917, celebrating the eclipse of a regime which had fostered anti-Semitism. In their view, the new order in Russia would bring about the amelioration of Jewish life. A number of Jews joined the Communist party in Great Britain and the United States. As a result, there were Jewish sections of various Communist parties such as the Yevsektsiya in the Soviet Union. In the USSR the Communist regime adopted an ambivalent attitude

Left *Many Jews welcomed the Russian Revolution. These members of the Jewish Society in St Petersburg are holding a banner in Yiddish that reads, 'Jewish Socialist Workers Party', 1918.*

Above *Political theorist Hannah Arendt, a German Jew, who reported for* the New Yorker *on the war crimes trial of the Nazi Adolf Eichmann.*

towards Jewry and Jewish civilization; at times it supported the development of a Jewish national culture, yet the party also carried out anti-Semitic purges. With the rise of fascism in Europe in the 1920s and 1930s, many Jews became involved in the left, particularly within Communist circles, which were fiercely opposed to fascism. During World War II the Jewish left played a major role in the resistance to Nazism.

THE LEFT IN CENTRAL AND WESTERN EUROPE

Alongside Jewish working-class movements, assimilated middle-class Jews in Central and Western Europe began to search for sources of radicalism in the Jewish tradition. Martin Buber, for example, was influenced by Hasidic texts in formulating his philosophy; Walter Benjamin was inspired by Marxism and Jewish messianism; Jacob Israel de Haan combined socialism with Orthodox Judaism; in Germany, Walther Rathenau was an important figure of the Jewish Left.

SOCIALIST ZIONISM

In the 20th century, socialist Zionism became an increasingly important factor in Palestine. Poale Zion, or 'Workers of Zion', the Histadrut labour union and the Mapai party were important in Israel and included within their ranks such politicians as Israel's first and fourth prime ministers David Ben-Gurion and Golda Meir. At the same time, the kibbutz movement was grounded in socialist ideals.

In the 1940s many on the left advocated a bi-national state in Israel/Palestine rather than an exclusively Jewish state. This position was supported by such figures as Hannah Arendt and Martin Buber. Since Israeli independence in 1948, the left has been represented by the Labour Party, Meretz and the Palestine Communist Party, Maki. There are two worldwide left-wing Zionist organizations: namely the World Labour Zionist Movement and the World Zionist Organization.

Left *This anti-Semitic cartoon of 1900 alleges Jews were plotting to destabilize Russia. Many Russian Zionists supported the creation of a Jewish homeland in Palestine.*

Above *Israel's first and fourth prime ministers Golda Meir and David Ben-Gurion at London Airport, 1961.*

THE CONTEMPORARY LEFT

The Jewish working class died out following World War II, but there are still some survivals of the Jewish working class left, including the Jewish Labour Committee and *Forward* newspaper in New York, the Bund in Melbourne, Australia, and the Labour Friends of Israel in the UK.

Throughout the 1960s and 1970s there was a renewal of interest in the West in working-class culture and in various radical positions of the past. This interest led to the development of a new form of radical Jewish organizations that were interested in Yiddish culture, Jewish spirituality and social justice, such as the New Jewish Agenda, the Jewish Socialists' Group in Britain, and the magazine *Tikkun*.

In addition, there has been a strong Jewish presence in the anti-Zionist movement, including such figures as Norman Finkelstein and Noam Chomsky. In Israel, left-wing political parties and blocs continue to play a significant role in the Jewish state.

Jewish Feminism

INSPIRED BY THE FEMINIST MOVEMENT, JEWISH FEMINISM PROMOTES THE RIGHTS OF JEWISH WOMEN. CRITICAL OF MALE DOMINANCE IN RELIGIOUS LIFE, THEY WORK FOR AN EQUAL ROLE IN ALL SPHERES.

The Jewish feminist movement seeks to improve the status of women within Judaism and to open up new opportunities for religious experience and leadership. An offshoot of the feminist movement, it originated in the early 1970s in the United States and has had a profound influence on contemporary Jewish life.

ORIGINS

Jewish feminism was spurred by a grassroots development that took place in the 1970s. In the previous decade, many Jewish women had participated in the second wave of American feminism. At this time most of these women did not link their feminism to their religious or their ethnic indentification. However, eventually some women whose Jewishness was central to their self-understanding applied feminist insights to their condition as American Jewish women. Faced with a male religious establishment, these women envisaged a new form of Jewish life, one that would embrace women's concerns.

At this stage two important articles appeared which pioneered the evolution of American Jewish feminism. In the latter half of 1970 Trude Weiss-Rosmarin criticized the liabilities of Jewish women in 'The Unfreedom of Jewish Women' which appeared in the *Jewish Spectator* which she edited. Several months later, Rachel Adler, an Orthodox Jew, published an indictment of the status of women in *Davka*, a counter-culture journal.

THE DEVELOPMENT OF JEWISH FEMINISM

Following these publications, Jewish feminism became a public phenomenon. A small group of feminists, calling themselves Ezrat Nashim (women's help), associated with the New York Havurah, a counter-cultural fellowship, and took the issue of equality of women to the 1972 convention of the Conservative Rabbinical Assembly. In meetings with rabbis and their wives, members of Ezrat Nashim called for a change in the status of Jewish women. In their view, women should have equal access with men in occupying public roles of status and honour in the Jewish community. The group focused on eliminating the subordination of women by equalizing their rights in marriage and divorce laws, the study of sacred texts, including women in the *minyan*, or 'quorum necessary for communal prayer', and

Above *Bertha Pappenheim, Austrian feminist and founder of the Jüdischer Frauenbund (League of Jewish Women) in 1904.*

Below *Jewish feminists, politician Bella Abzug and writer Gloria Steinem, with the Revd Jesse Jackson.*

Below *Elena Kagan has been an Associate Justice of the Supreme Court of the United States since 2010.*

providing opportunities for women to assume positions of leadership in the synagogue as rabbis and cantors. In the same year, the Reform movement took a fundamental step in this direction by ordaining Sally Priesand as the first female American Reform rabbi.

In the following year, secular and religious Jewish feminists under the auspices of the North American Jewish Students' Network convened a conference in New York City. The next year a short-lived Jewish feminist organization was founded at a similar Jewish feminist conference. As time passed, Jewish feminists brought their message to a wider audience through various publications. Activists from Ezrat Nashim and the North American Jewish Students' Network published an issue of *Responsa* magazine dedicated to Jewish feminist concerns. In 1976, an expanded version entitled *The Jewish Woman: New Perspectives* appeared. The same year a Jewish feminist magazine *Lilith* was published.

RITUALS AND RABBIS

Through their efforts, Jewish feminists gained increasing support. Innovations, such as baby-naming ceremonies, feminist Passover seders and ritual celebrations of the New Moon were introduced into communal settings in the home or synagogue. These ceremonies were aimed at the community rather than the individual; in this way, Jewish feminists aimed to enhance women's religious roles in Jewish life. The concept of egalitarianism evoked a positive response from many American Jews. In the Reform movement, the principle of equality between the sexes became a cardinal principle. Similarly, within the Reconstructionist movement women were granted equal status, and in 1974 Sandy Eisenberg Sasso was ordained as a rabbi. In time the Conservative movement also accepted the princi-

Above *Women of the Wall wear prayer shawls and tallit, ritual garments traditionally associated with men, at the Western Wall, Jerusalem.*

ple of equality: Amy Eilberg became the first female Conservative rabbi in 1985, and women were welcomed into the Conservative cantorate in 1987.

BLU GREENBERG AND JOFA

In support of feminist principles, Blu Greenberg founded the Jewish Orthodox Feminist Alliance (JOFA) in 1997 to advocate women's increased participation in modern Orthodoxy and to create a community for women and men dedicated to principles of equality. In its mission statement, JOFA declares: 'The mission of the Jewish Orthodox Feminist Alliance is to expand the spiritual, ritual, intellectual and political opportunities for women within the framework of halakha. We advocate meaningful participation and equality for women in family life, synagogues, houses of learning and Jewish communal organizations to the full extent possible within halakha.'

ORTHODOX FEMINISM

Even though the Conservative movement led the way for Jewish feminism in the 1970s and 1980s, Jewish feminism was interpreted in different ways in the Orthodox community. In 1981 Blu Greenberg made a case for Orthodox feminism in *On Being a Jewish Feminist*. Alongside this work, a small number of Orthodox feminists established women's *tefilah*, or 'prayer', groups that respected halakhic restraints on the role of women in Jewish life.

Even though the Orthodox leadership deny feminist claims of the secondary status of women within traditional Judaism, Jewish feminism has had an important impact on American Orthodoxy. Girls are provided with a more comprehensive education in Orthodox schools, and Orthodoxy has embraced such rituals as celebrations of the birth of a daughter and bat mitzvah rites.

GENDER ISSUES

WITHIN THE JEWISH WORLD THERE ARE A SUBSTANTIAL NUMBER OF GAY AND LESBIAN JEWS. YET THE VARIOUS MOVEMENTS WITHIN JUDAISM DIFFER IN THEIR VIEW OF HOMOSEXUALITY.

In the Western world, many countries now legalize civil partnerships between people of the same sex. Orthodox Jews may condemn such unions, but some non-Orthodox communities adopt a more liberal attitude.

TRADITIONAL JUDAISM AND HOMOSEXUALITY

In the Bible, homosexual conduct between men is more frequently mentioned and condemned than homosexual practices between women. There is no reference to a homosexual tendency, rather it is the act which is forbidden. Thus Leviticus 19:20 states: 'Thou shalt not lie with mankind, as with womankind, it is an abomination.' Again, Leviticus 20:13 declares: 'And if a man lie with mankind, as with womankind, both of them have committed abomination; they shall surely be put to death; their blood shall be upon them.'

In the 2nd century CE, a debate is recorded in the Mishnah in which Rabbi Judah forbids two unmarried men to sleep together in the same bed, while the sages permit it. According to the Talmud, the reason why the sages disagree with Rabbi Judah is that Jews are not suspected of engaging in homosexual practices. Although the code of Jewish law records the opinion of the sages, it states: 'But in these times, when there are many loose-livers about, a man should avoid being alone with another male.' According to the rabbis, Gentiles too are commanded by the Torah to abstain from male homosexual acts.

The sources, however, are less clear about lesbianism. The *Sifra* (midrash on Scripture) comments on Leviticus 18:3 ('After the doings of the land of Egypt wherein ye dwelt shall ye not do; and after

Right Chabad Lubavitch Hasidim protesting at the annual gay pride parade in Tel Aviv, Israel.

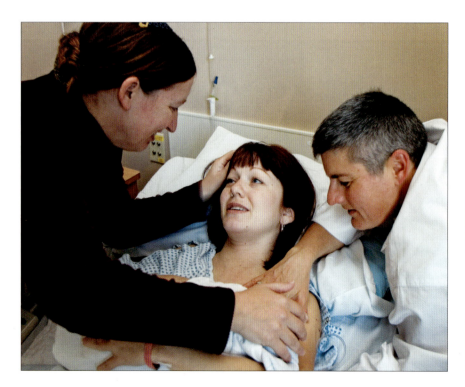

Below A mother and her lesbian partner with their newborn son and female rabbi, California, 2004, the first year that same-sex marriages were permitted in the US state.

WORLD CONGRESS

Today the movement for the acceptance of gay and lesbian Jews is a worldwide phenomenon. The World Congress of Gay, Lesbian, Bisexual and Transgender Jews, Keshet Ga'avah, consists of more than 25 member organizations. The Hebrew subtitle Keshet Ga'avah – Rainbow of Pride – emphasizes the importance of Hebrew and of Israel to the World Congress. Since its establishment in 1975, conferences have been held all over the world. Their vision is 'an environment where Lesbian, Gay, Bisexual and Transgender Jews worldwide can enjoy free and fulfilling lives.'

the doings of the land of Canaan, whither I bring you, shall ye not do; neither walk in their statutes.'), stating that what is being referred to are the sexual practices of the Egyptians and the Canaanites. The sin being referred to is marrying off a man to a man and a woman to a woman. The Talmud rules that women who perform sexual acts with one another should not be viewed as harlots, but as indulging in lewd practices.

According to the 12th-century Jewish philosopher and legalist Moses Maimonides, while lesbian practices are forbidden, a woman guilty of them should not be treated as an adulteress.

CONSERVATIVE JUDAISM AND HOMOSEXUALITY

Despite such teaching, the more liberal branches of Judaism have in recent years embraced both gays and lesbians. Conservative Judaism did not allow for the ordination of openly gay men and women for over one hundred years. In addition, Conservative rabbis who performed same-sex commitment ceremonies did so without the Law Committee's sanction. Yet on 6 December 2006 the Committee on Jewish Law and Standards of the Rabbinical Assembly decreed that Conservative rabbis, synagogues and institutions can perform or host same-sex commitment ceremonies and are free to hire openly gay rabbis and cantors if they so wish. The decisions of the CJLS are only advisory, yet this body does represent the movement as a whole.

Above *A same-sex couple participating in a Jewish wedding ceremony at Beverly Hills, California, in 2008.*

REFORM JUDAISM

More liberal in its outlook, the Reform movement actively supports the rights of gays and lesbians. Over the last two decades the Union of American Hebrew Congregations has admitted to membership several synagogues with an outreach to gay and lesbian Jews. Hundreds of men and women who previously felt alienated from Judaism have joined these synagogues and added their strength to the Jewish community.

In 1977 the Union of American Hebrew Congregations called for an end to discrimination against homosexuals, and in 1987 they expanded upon this by calling for inclusion of gay and lesbian Jews in all aspects of synagogue life. Subsequently the movement has embarked on a programme of heightened awareness and education to achieve the fuller acceptance of gay and lesbian Jews.

Left *Portrait of a gay Jewish couple marrying under the traditional* huppah *(a canopy with open sides) in Manhattan, New York.*

Jewish Buddhists

JUBUS OR BUJUS SEEK TO BLEND THEIR JEWISH BACKGROUND WITH PRACTICES DRAWN FROM THE BUDDHIST TRADITION. THIS SPIRITUAL PATH OFFERS BELIEVERS A MEANS OF ENTRY INTO JUDAISM.

The members of the Jewish Buddhist movement (known as Jubus or Bujus) seek to combine their Jewish background with practices drawn from the Buddhist tradition. The term Jubu was first brought into circulation with the publication of *The Jew in the Lotus* by Rodger Kamenetz. The majority of Jewish Buddhists maintain their religious convictions and practices in Judaism coupled with Buddhist beliefs and observances.

The first instance of an American being converted to Buddhism in the USA occurred at the 1893 exposition on world religions. The convert, Charles Strauss, stated that he was a Buddhist at a public lecture that followed the World Conference on Religions in the same year. Strauss later became an author and an expositor of Buddhism in the West. After World War II there was an increasing interest in Buddhism among Jews associated with the Beat generation. At that time Zen Buddhism was the most widely known form of the Buddhist tradition.

In the 1960s more Jews became interested in Buddhist teachings; prominent teachers included Joseph Goldstein, Jack Kornfield and Sharon Salzberg who founded the Insight Meditation Society and learned vipassana meditation primarily through Thai teachers.

THE ATTRACTION OF JUDAISM

Jewish Buddhists report that the encounter between Jews and Buddhism leads to a journey into a deeper spirituality by blending

Above *An iconic image of a stone Buddha embedded in tree roots at Wat Mahathat temple, Ayutthaya, Thailand.*

various elements of both traditions. For Jubus the Buddhist tradition provides a means of entry into the religious treasures of their own faith. As many individual followers are keen to point out, both Judaism and Buddhism contain a number of common practices: they both emphasize acting ethically. Each is based on a body of teachings passed on for thousands of years. Each teaches respect for spiritual teachers. Both stress that actions have consequences, but that errors can be atoned for and purified. Neither Jubus nor Bujus proselytize, though both accept newcomers. Jews and Buddhists alike treat their texts and holy objects with veneration. And significantly, some of their mystical teachings are similar.

BRIDGING TRADITIONS

On the surface it appears that the beliefs and rituals of Judaism and Buddhism could not be more different. Yet, Jubus argue that an immersion into Buddhism can serve to help Jews to discover their Jewish roots. The Jewish history of persecution and displacement, for example, is echoed by the treatment of Tibetan Buddhists at the hands of the Chinese; both Moses

---

THE JEW IN THE LOTUS

In October 1990, the Jewish poet Rodger Kamenetz journeyed to Dharamsala, India, with a small group of rabbis and other Jewish leaders. There they met the Dalai Lama, the leader of Tibetan Buddhism who had been exiled from Tibet by the Chinese regime.

The book that emerged from this expedition was *The Jew in the Lotus: A Poet's Rediscovery of Jewish Identity in Buddhist India* (1994). This volume explores Kamenetz's reflections on his own Jewishness and the attraction that Buddhism holds for a significant number of Jews whom he referred to as Jubus.

In this study, Kamenetz expounds an interpretation of Judaism that offers a new form of spirituality to Jews so they need not turn to Buddhism or anywhere else. Candidly he chronicles his own struggles with what it means to be Jewish. Without knowing why, he sensed it is not enough to be a secular Jew; rather, he insisted, life calls for a spirituality of some sort.

Above *Rodger Kamenetz's The Jew in the Lotus.*

JEWISH BUDDHISTS

Above *The Dalai Lama, the leader of Tibetan Buddhism, praying at the Western Wall in Jerusalem.*

Above *Rabbi David Saperstein, the Dalai Lama and Rodger Kamenetz at the Seder for Tibet, 1997, an example of Jewish–Buddhist dialogue.*

and the Buddha had life-changing experiences that caused them to flee the royal court: both wandered – Buddha as a yoga practitioner and Moses as a shepherd. There is also a similarity between the tree of knowledge in Genesis and the Bodhi tree under which the Buddha was first enlightened. Jubus further point out that both traditions encourage questioning and debate. Despite the icons and statues associated with Buddhism, both religions reject images and forms of the Ultimate, conceiving the Absolute to transcend all form and limitation. For some Jubus, the eight-fold path of Buddhism helps to focus their spiritual and moral life.

JUDAISM AND BUDDHISM

Critics of the Jewish–Buddhist movement are anxious to point out the differences between Judaism and Buddhism. The most conspicuous difference concerns belief in God. While Judaism is theistic, Buddhists do not espouse belief in a supernatural deity.

Right *Singer Leonard Cohen was ordained as a Buddhist monk but says 'I'm not looking for a new religion. I'm quite happy with the old one, with Judaism.'*

According to tradition, when the historical Buddha was asked whether or not God exists, he remained silent. This silence was interpreted in two ways: either he intended to demonstrate that God is beyond words, or that he considered theism as irrelevant to his doctrine. This latter approach has been widely accepted among Buddhists through the centuries.

The doctrine of no-self is also foreign to Jewish consciousness. According to Buddhist philosophy, the annihilation of the ego is conceived as seeing through the illusion of the historically conditioned self as a fixed entity. Even though Jewish mysticism extols the transcendence of the ego, this path is not an end in itself. The Jewish mystic is obliged to continue to keep the mitzvot and to remain an individual member of a Jewish community. Selfhood is fundamental to the Jewish notion of obedience to the divine will. Yet, despite such observations, Jubus insist that they are living an authentic Jewish existence enlightened by insights from a rich tradition of spiritual resources.

Jews and the Environment

ALONGSIDE CONCERNS ABOUT ANIMAL WELFARE, MANY JEWISH PEOPLE TODAY ALSO FOCUS ON THE SIGNIFICANCE OF NUMEROUS ENVIRONMENTAL THREATS.

Acid rain, the greenhouse effect, ozone layer depletion, erosion of topsoil, destruction of forests and other habitats, pollution of water and soil, and toxic waste pose fundamental problems in the modern world. Given that Judaism teaches that the earth is the Lord's and that we are to be partners and co-workers with God in protecting the environment, Jews have ecological responsibilities towards the planet. Across the religious spectrum, a growing number of Jews embrace ecological principles rooted in the tradition.

HUMAN RESPONSIBILITY FOR NATURE

In the 21st century, concern with the preservation of the planet has become of central importance. The proliferation of vast industries throughout the globe, the danger of overpopulation, the risk of global warming – these and a range of other issues have contributed to anxiety about the ecological state of the world. In the past, these problems were not central to Judaism. On the contrary, Scripture asserts that human beings are to master the environment: 'And replenish the earth, and subdue it; and have dominion over the fish of the sea, and over the fowl of the air, and over every living thing that creepeth upon the earth' (Genesis 1:28). This does not mean, however, that in the older Jewish sources there was no concern with conservation. On the contrary, human beings are to exercise care in dealing with nature. Human freedom to act should be in God's name and by his authority.

Right *A Haredi Jewish man showers after bathing in the Dead Sea, where Orthodox Jews have dedicated areas. Such rituals are linked to respect for the natural world.*

CREATION AND STEWARDSHIP

Genesis 1.31 declares that God found all of creation 'very good'. This implies that creation is sufficient, structured and harmonious. Scripture teaches that God has absolute ownership over creation. The environmental implications are that human beings are not to misuse nature. Everything belongs to God – as a consequence the use of the natural world must always be related to the larger good, and human concerns should not be elevated above everything else. Having been created in the image of God, humans are to have a special place and role. Of all of God's creatures, only they have the power to disrupt the natural world. This power comes from special characteristics that no other creature possesses. Humanity was placed on earth to act as God's agents and to actualize his presence as his stewards.

Left *Due to climate change, raging forest fires are becoming more and more frequent. Jewish environmentalists seek to take responsibility for protecting the planet from such devastation.*

LOVE AND AWE

As God's representatives on earth, humanity is connected to the rhythms of nature, the biogeochemical cycles, and the complex diversity of ecological systems. In Judaism, human responsibility growing out of such awareness is perceived as the fulfilment of the commandment to love and fear God. As the 12th-century Jewish philosopher Maimonides explained in the *Mishnah Torah*: 'When a person observes God's works and God's great and marvellous creatures, and they see from them God's wisdom that is without estimate or end, immediately they will love God, praise God and long with a great desire to know God's great name ... And when a person thinks about these things they draw back and are afraid and realizes that they are small lowly and obscure, endowed with slight and slender intelligence, standing in the presence of God who is perfect knowledge.'

THE BIBLE AND THE ENVIRONMENT

A central text in understanding the Jewish concern for the environment concerns the prohibition of cutting down trees in a time of war. Deuteronomy 20:19–20 teaches: 'When in your war against a city you have to besiege it a long time in order to capture it, you must not destroy the trees wielding the axe against them. You may eat of them, but you must not cut them down. Are trees of the field human to withdraw before you into the besieged city? Only trees that you know do not yield field food may be destroyed; you may cut them down for constructing siegeworks against the city that is waging war on you, until it has been reduced.'

In rabbinic sources this law was expanded to include the prohibition of the wanton destruction of household goods, clothes, buildings, springs, food and the wasteful consumption of anything. The underlying idea is the recognition that everything we own belongs to God. When we consume in a wasteful manner, we damage creation and violate the commandment to use creation only for legitimate ends. Restraint in consumption is hence a cardinal value within the tradition.

THE SABBATH

Sabbath observance is one way to engender this sense of love and humility before creation. For one day out of seven, observant Jews limit their use of resources. Traditionally they do not do any work; the day is set aside for contemplation of the meaning of life.

Through Sabbath prayer the Jewish community is able to recognize that everything comes from God. Hence when Jews recite a blessing, they create a sacred pause in the flow of time to contemplate their place in the universe. At this moment they can see the world as an object of divine concern and place themselves beyond selfish desire.

Above *Since Israel's founding in 1948, agriculture and ecology has played an important part there. Poster of an Israeli farmer harvesting grapes, 1949.*

Jewish Vegetarianism

IN THE MODERN WORLD, A GROWING NUMBER OF JEWS FROM ACROSS THE RELIGIOUS SPECTRUM HAVE EMBRACED VEGETARIANISM AS AN AUTHENTIC MODE OF JEWISH LIVING.

Many people see Jewish vegetarianism as both a philosophy and a life style based on Jewish theology.

THE BIBLICAL BACKGROUND

According to Rabbi Abraham Isaac Kook (1865–1935), the first chief rabbi of Israel, vegetarianism is the ideal, symbolizing the ultimate peace between human beings and the animal kingdom. In his view, in the Messianic Age as prophesied in the Book of Isaiah, everyone will adopt a vegetarian diet. The only sacrifices that will be offered in the Temple will be the minhah sacrifice, which is of vegetable origin. Even though there has been some debate regarding Kook's consistency in following a vegetarian diet, Rabbi She'ar Yashuv Cohen, the Chief Rabbi of Haifa, declared: 'I am a vegetarian, following in the footsteps of my late father, Rabbi David Cohen, and his teacher, the saintly first Chief Rabbi of Israel, Abraham Isaac Kook.'

According to Jewish vegetarians, in the ideal state of Gan Eden (the Garden of Eden) humans were described as vegetarian, and this state of affairs continued until after the Great Flood in the time of Noah. Other prominent figures who have followed a vegetarian lifestyle based on such biblical ideas include Rabbi David Rosen, former Chief Rabbi of Ireland, the late Rabbi Shlomo Goren, Chief Rabbi of Israel, and Avraham Burg, an elected Knesset Speaker.

Above *Abraham Isaac Kook, 20th-century philosopher, who promoted vegetarianism as a Jewish ideal.*

ETHICAL PRINCIPLES

Judaism forbids the infliction of unnecessary pain and suffering. The principle of *tsaar baalei hayyim*, or 'preventing the suffering of living creatures', is extolled in biblical and rabbinic sources. Although this principle is not explicitly formulated in Scripture, it is based on biblical teaching concerning the compassionate treatment of God's creatures. Such an attitude shows an early appreciation of the sentiency of other creatures, and according to the rabbis, Israel was unique among the nations in advocating this approach.

On this assumption, rabbinic codes of law enshrine the principle of tsaar baalei hayyim as an important feature of the faith. Specifically, the rabbis continued to legislate concerning Sabbaths and festivals. For example, rabbinic legislation stipulates that animals – like human beings – should be allowed to move about wearing bandages and splints for their wounds, and that cushions should be supplied if needed.

Further, one is allowed to put salve and oil on an animal's wound and seek assistance of a gentile if

Below *Jewish rug depicting Adam and Eve, made in Turkey, late 19th century. According to tradition, humans were vegetarian until the time of the Flood.*

milking is required. Again, it is allowed to put an animal in cold water so as to cool it off as a remedy for congestion, or raise it out of a body of water into which it has fallen. It is also permitted to relieve a burden from an animal if it is in pain. Given the centrality of this concept of tsaar baalei hayyim, Jewish vegetarians maintain that their lifestyle is the ideal ethical option, one that more clearly approximates to the original will of the creator.

HEALTH CONCERNS

Recently a number of medical scientists have stressed that a plant-based diet is more healthy than a diet which includes meat. The Jewish tradition emphasizes the importance of maintaining health. Hence Jews are commanded in Deuteronomy 4:15: 'You shall guard yourselves most diligently.' This implies that everything possible must be done to protect health and avoid unnecessary risks. Further, Jews are obliged to 'choose life above all'. (Deuteronomy 30:19). The Talmud states that a danger to health takes precedence over ritual obligations. The Torah also declares that prevention is the highest form of health. In this light, Jewish vegetarians maintain that they are following both biblical and rabbinic principles in adopting a vegetarian lifestyle.

In this regard, Jewish vegetarians point out that elevated blood cholesterol levels, high blood pressure and diabetes, all of which contribute to heart disease, can be alleviated by a high fibre, low-fat vegetarian diet coupled with a vigorous regime of exercise and stress reduction.

Similarly, the risk of lung cancer may be increased by animal-fat consumption. Meat consumption is a major risk factor for prostate cancer. Breast cancer may be linked with higher oestrogen levels and may reflect childhood dietary practices. Cancer of the colon is strongly linked to red and white meat consumption. Further, meat consumption is a risk factor for pancreatic cancer. Ovarian cancer has also been linked with dairy, egg and meat consumption.

Left *Jewish vegetarianism is varied and includes colourful dishes such as Hatzilim Pilpel, a fiery tomato and aubergine stew (shown here) that is typical of Israeli cooking.*

Above *The deforestation of the Amazon in recent years is an issue important to Jews concerned with the conservation of our planet.*

Further, lymphoma has been linked with beef and dairy consumption. Finally, the risk of bladder cancer in non-vegetarians is twice that of vegetarians.

ECOLOGICAL CONCERNS

As an extension of the concern with animal welfare, many Jewish vegetarians also focus on the significance of numerous environmental threats. Acid rain, the greenhouse effect, ozone layer depletion, erosion of topsoil, destruction of forests and other habitats, pollution of water and soil, and toxic waste pose fundamental problems in the modern world.

Given that Judaism teaches that the earth is the Lord's and that we are to be partners and co-workers with God in protecting the environment, Jews have ecological responsibilities towards the planet. Hence, it is vital that Jewish values be applied in the solution of these pressing problems.

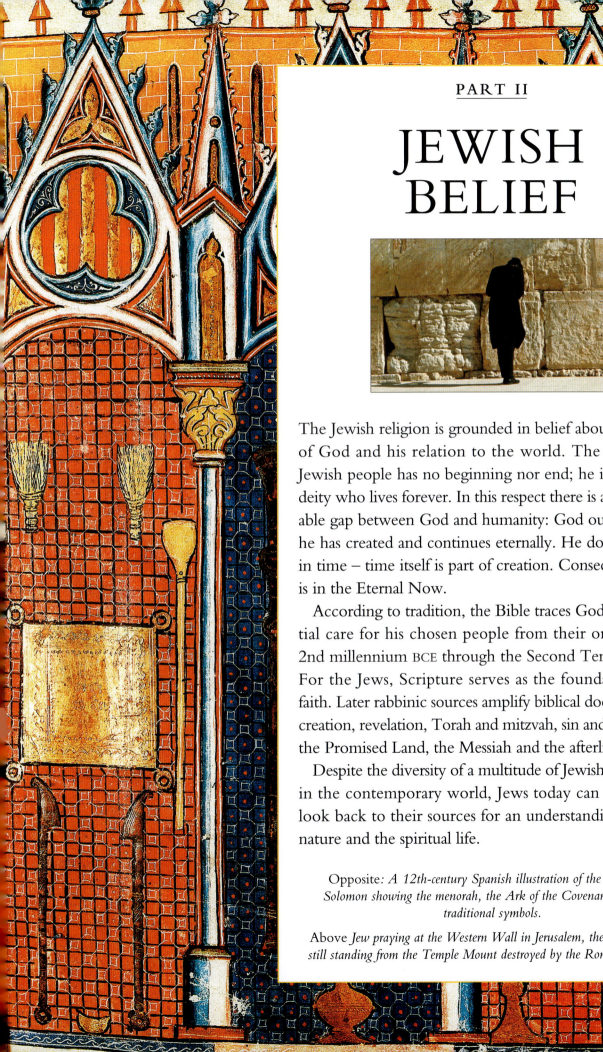

PART II

JEWISH BELIEF

The Jewish religion is grounded in belief about the nature of God and his relation to the world. The God of the Jewish people has no beginning nor end; he is the eternal deity who lives forever. In this respect there is an unbridgeable gap between God and humanity: God outlasts all that he has created and continues eternally. He does not dwell in time – time itself is part of creation. Consequently God is in the Eternal Now.

According to tradition, the Bible traces God's providential care for his chosen people from their origins in the 2nd millennium BCE through the Second Temple period. For the Jews, Scripture serves as the foundation of the faith. Later rabbinic sources amplify biblical doctrines about creation, revelation, Torah and mitzvah, sin and repentance, the Promised Land, the Messiah and the afterlife.

Despite the diversity of a multitude of Jewish movements in the contemporary world, Jews today can continue to look back to their sources for an understanding of God's nature and the spiritual life.

Opposite: A 12th-century Spanish illustration of the Temple of Solomon showing the menorah, the Ark of the Covenant and other traditional symbols.

Above Jew praying at the Western Wall in Jerusalem, the only structure still standing from the Temple Mount destroyed by the Romans in 70CE.

CHAPTER 5

GOD

According to the Bible, the struggle against Canaanite belief and practice was a constant concern. Later in the rabbinic period, scholars cautioned against worshipping two gods in heaven. Worship of one God was of paramount importance. With the rise of Christianity, Jews were admonished to remain faithful to monotheism, and Jewish theologians insisted on God's unity. For the Jewish people, God is both imminent and transcendent. He created the universe, yet is in no sense remote from his creation. In the rabbinic period, Jewish sages formulated the concept of the *Shekhinah* to denote God's abiding presence. It is the Shekhinah that serves as an intermediary between God and human beings.

For God there is no past, present, nor future. In rabbinic literature, the word *emet*, or truth, one of the names of God, is interpreted as having the first, middle and final letters of the Hebrew alphabet. According to Jewish thinkers, God is both omnipotent and omniscient. His power is unlimited as is his knowledge. Past, present and future lie unrolled before his eyes, and nothing is hidden from him. It is he who has created all things in his infinite goodness. From him benevolence and compassion flow as a mighty stream.

Opposite *Abraham smashing idols. From the Leipnik Haggadah (1740) by Joseph of Leipnik, the most influential scribe of the Hamburg-Altona school of Hebrew illuminated manuscripts.*

Above The Creation of Adam, *in the Sistine Chapel, Rome, is one of the most famous paintings by the 16th-century artist Michelangelo.*

THE GOD OF THE JEWS

THE STORY OF THE JEWISH PEOPLE BEGAN IN MESOPOTAMIA. IT WAS HERE THAT SUCCESSIVE EMPIRES ROSE AND FELL BEFORE THE JEWS EMERGED AS A SEPARATE PEOPLE, BELIEVING IN ONE INVISIBLE GOD.

According to the Bible, Abraham was the father of the Jewish nation. Living in Ur of the Chaldeans, a Sumerian city near the head of the Persian Gulf, he was called by God to go to Canaan. As Genesis 12:1–2 records, God proclaimed: 'Go from your country and your kindred and your father's house to the land I will show you. And I will make of you a great nation.'

ANCIENT MESOPOTAMIAN RELIGION

The rise of ancient Mesopotamian civilization occurred at the end of the 4th century BCE in southern Mesopotamia, where the Sumerians created city states, each with its local gods. During the 3rd millennium BCE, waves of Semitic peoples settled amid the Sumerians, adopting their writing and culture. These Semites identified some of their gods with the Sumerian ones. In their view, life was under the control of the gods. To obtain happiness, it was essential to keep them in a good humour through worship and sacrifice – yet the gods were unpredictable. It was here in the 2nd century BCE that God called the Jewish nation to be his chosen people.

Right *A vision of the prophet Jeremiah showing Greek fire, an incendiary weapon, being poured over Jerusalem. From the 12th-century Souvigny Bible.*

EARLY MONOTHEISM

According to some scholars, the origins of Israelite monotheism stemmed from Abraham's disillusionment with Mesopotamian religion. These scholars attribute this radical break to Abraham's discovery that the concept of universal justice must rest on the belief in one supreme God. Other scholars see Moses as the principal architect of Israelite monotheism. Such scholars point out that before Moses there was evidence of monotheistic belief in the religious reforms of the Egyptian Pharaoh Akhenaton in the 14th century BCE. In this light, Moses is seen as following the path of this Egyptian revolutionary figure.

MONOLATRY

There are other scholars, however, who contend that it is unlikely that monotheism can be attributed to Abraham or Moses. Such a view, they believe, conflicts with the biblical narratives of the tribal and monarchial periods that give evidence of a struggle on the part of some Israelites to remain faithful to God in the face of competing deities. For these writers, monotheism should be

Left *Daily life in Mesopotamia, showing weaving and farming, from a wall painting in the Museum of the Jewish Diaspora in Tel Aviv, Israel.*

Above *The Hospitality of Abraham. A Russian icon by Andrei Rublev, painted around 1410.*

> ### THE PSALMIST
>
> According to some scholars, Psalm 82 gives evidence of the transition from monolatry to monotheism: in it God rebukes the other gods for their injustice and deprives them of divine status and immortality:
>
> God has taken his place in the divine council;
> In the midst of the gods he holds judgement;
> How long will you judge unjustly, and show partiality to the wicked? Selah.
> Give justice to the weak and the fatherless;
> maintain the right of the afflicted and the destitute.
> Rescue the weak and the needy;
> deliver them from the hand of the wicked –
> They have neither knowledge, nor understanding,
> they walk about in darkness;
> all the foundations of the earth are shaken –
> I say, 'You are gods,
> sons of the Most High, all of you;
> nevertheless you shall die like men, and fall like any prince.'
> Arise, O God, judge the earth,
> for to thee belong all the nations!

understood as the result of a clash of cults and religious concepts over the centuries.

According to this latter view, ancient Israelite religion was not monotheism but monolatry: the worship of one God despite the admitted existence of other gods. Arguably, this may have been the meaning of Deuteronomy 6:4: 'Hear, O Israel: the Lord our God is one Lord.' With this view, the God of Israel was understood as the Divine Being who revealed his will to Israel, inspired its leaders, protected the Israelites in their wanderings, and led them to the Promised Land. The worship of any other deity was, according to Exodus 20:3, betrayal and blasphemy: 'You shall have no other gods before me.'

The God of Israel was not like any other gods of Mesopotamia, Egypt or Canaan, and it was forbidden to make an image of him. It was this God, not the Canaanite El, who was the creator of heaven and earth; he, not Baal, was the source of rain and agricultural fertility; it was through his action, rather than that of any of the gods of Mesopotamia, that the Assyrian and Babylonian conquest took place.

Monotheism is thus understood as a later development in the history of Israel; it took place when foreign gods were seen as simply the work of human hands. Possibly this was the view of Elijah in the 9th century BCE when, confronting the prophets of Baal, he declared: 'The Lord He is God; the Lord He is God' (1 Kings 18:39). But certainly by the time of Jeremiah (several decades before the Babylonian exile in the 6th century BCE), monotheism appears to have taken a firm hold on the Israelite community. In the words of Jeremiah: 'Their idols are like scarecrows, in a cucumber field, and they cannot speak; they have to be carried for they cannot walk. Be not afraid of them, for they cannot do evil, neither is it in them to do good' (Jeremiah 10:5).

Below *The Sacrifice of Isaac, a 6th-century floor mosaic from the Bet Alpha synagogue, Israel.*

Below *The Assyrian goddess of abundance, a stylised marble idol dating from around 1950–1700 BCE.*

UNITY OF GOD

THE MOST UNCOMPROMISING EXPRESSION OF GOD'S UNITY IS THE PRAYER IN DEUTERONOMY: 'HEAR, O ISRAEL, THE LORD OUR GOD IS ONE LORD.' THIS BELIEF HAS SERVED AS THE FOUNDATION OF THE FAITH.

THE REJECTION OF DUALISM

According to Scripture, the universe owes its existence to the one God, the creator of heaven and earth, and since all human beings are created in his image, all men and women are brothers and sisters. Thus the belief in one God implies that there is one humanity and one world.

At the heart of Jewish biblical teaching is an emphasis that God alone is to be worshipped. As the prophet Isaiah declared:

I am the Lord, and there is no other,
besides me there is no God; ...
I form light and create darkness,
I make weal and create woe,
I am the Lord,
  who do all these things.
    (Isaiah 45:5,7)

Within the Bible, the struggle against polytheism became a dominant motif, continuing into the rabbinic period. Combating the dualistic doctrine that there are two gods in heaven, the rabbis commented on Deuteronomy 32:39 ('See now that I, even I, am he, and there is no god beside me'): 'If anyone says that there are two powers in heaven, the retort is given to him: "There is no god with me".'

In a passage in the *Mekhilta* (midrash on Exodus), the dualistic doctrine is rejected since when God said, 'I am the Lord your God' (Exodus 20:2) no one protested. Again the Mishnah states that if a person says in his prayers, 'We acknowledge Thee, we acknowledge Thee', implying belief in two gods, he is to be silenced.

Above *William Blake's vision of God writing on the Tablets of the Covenant, the laws given to Moses on Mt Sinai. For Jews, God is transcendent, yet directly involved in their history.*

JUDAISM AND CHRISTIANITY

In the early rabbinic period Jewish sages were troubled by the Christian doctrine of the incarnation, which they viewed as dualistic in character. In 3rd-century CE Caesarea, for example, Abahu commented on the verse: 'God is not man, that he should lie, or a son of man, that he should repent. Has he said, and will he not do it? Or has he spoken, and will he not fulfil it?' (Numbers 23:19). According to Abahu, the last part of this verse refers to man rather than God. Thus he declared: 'If a man says to you, "I am a god", he is lying; "I am the Son of Man", he will not end by being sorry for it; "I am going up to heaven", he will not fulfil what he has said.'

In the Middle Ages the Christian doctrine of the Trinity was frequently attacked by Jewish scholars since it appeared to undermine pure monotheism. In contrast to Christian exegetes who interpreted the Shema with its three references to God as denoting the Trinity, Jewish scholars maintained that the Shema implies that there is only one God, rather

---

THE KABBALAH

In the Middle Ages. Kabbalistic belief in divine unity was also of major importance. The early Kabbalists of Provence and Spain referred to the Divine Infinite as En Sof – the absolute perfection in which there is no distinction or plurality. The En Sof does not reveal itself; it is beyond all thought. In Kabbalistic thought, creation is bound up with the manifestation of the hidden God and his outward movement. According to the Zohar, a mystical work of the time, the *sefirot*, or 'divine emanations', come successively from above to below, each one revealing a stage in the process. The ten sefirot together demonstrate how an infinite, undivided and unknowable God is the cause of all the modes of existence in the finite plane.

Left *A 17th-century Greek codex showing the Moon surrounded by Kabbalistic symbols.*

UNITY OF GOD

Above Torah scroll from the 16th-century Ha'ari synagogue in Safed, Israel, one of the homes of Kabbalah.

was awakened within the Godhead and this resulted in a long process of emanation. For Luria, however, creation was a negative event: the En Sof had to bring into being an empty space in which creation could occur since divine light was everywhere, leaving no room for creation to take place. This was accomplished by the process of *zimzum* – the contraction of the Godhead into itself.

After this act of withdrawal a line of light flowed from the Godhead into empty space and took on the shape of the sefirot in the form of Adam Kadmon (primeval man). In this process divine lights created the vessels – the external shapes of the sefirot – which gave specific characteristics to each emanation. Yet these vessels were not strong enough to contain such pure light and they shattered. This breaking of the vessels brought disaster and upheaval to the emerging emanations: the lower vessels broke down and fell, the three highest emanations were damaged and the empty space was divided into

Above In Kabbalah, the term Adam Kadmon means Primeval Man. Copy of an illustration from Kabbala Denudata (1684) by Knorr von Rosenroth.

two parts. Despite the complexity of this Kabbalistic theory of creation, Jewish mystics affirmed their belief in the unity of the Godhead. The sefirot were ten in number, yet God himself is one.

than Three Persons of the Godhead. For medieval Jewish theology, the belief in divine unity was a fundamental principle of Judaism. For a number of Jewish theologians the concept of God's unity implies that there can be no multiplicity in his being. Thus the 12th-century philosopher Moses Maimonides argued in *The Guide for the Perplexed* that no positive attributes can be predicated of God since the divine is an absolute unity. The only true attributes are negative ones; they lead to a knowledge of God because in negation no plurality is involved.

LURIANIC KABBALAH

The elaboration of early mystical ideas took place in the 16th century through the teachings of Isaac Luria. Of primary importance in the Lurianic system is the mystery of creation. In the literature of early Kabbalists, creation was understood as a positive act; the will to create

Right Prayer at the tomb in Meron, Israel, of Rabbi Simeon ben Yohai, traditionally the author of the Zohar, the most important medieval text of Kabbalistic Judaism.

Transcendence and Immanence

ACCORDING TO TRADITIONAL JUDAISM, GOD TRANSCENDS THE UNIVERSE YET IS MANIFEST IN HIS CREATION. THROUGHOUT SCRIPTURE GOD IS DEPICTED AS ACTIVE IN HUMAN HISTORY.

Transcendence is the concept of being entirely beyond the universe. For Jews, God is conceived as the transcendent creator of the universe. It is he who created the heavens and the earth; he reigns supreme over all creation. Yet, he does not remain remote from the cosmos. Repeatedly he is described as actively involved in the natural world and human affairs.

DIVINE TRANSCENDENCE

Throughout Scripture the theme of transcendence is repeatedly affirmed. Thus the prophet Isaiah proclaimed:

Have you not known?
Have you not heard?
Has it not been told you
    from the beginning?
Have you not understood from
    the foundations of the earth?
It is he who sits above the circle
    of the earth,
and its inhabitants are like
    grasshoppers;
who stretches out the heavens
    like a curtain
and spreads them like a tent
    to dwell in.
(Isaiah 40:21–22)

Later in the same book, Isaiah declared that God is beyond human understanding:

For my thoughts are not
    your thoughts
neither are your ways my ways, says
    the Lord.
For as the heavens are higher than
    the earth,
so are my ways higher than
    your ways
and my thoughts than
    your thoughts.
(Isaiah 55:8–9)

In the Book of Job the same idea is repeated – God's purposes transcend human understanding:

Can you find out the deep things of
    God?
Can you find out the limit of the
    Almighty?
It is higher than heaven – what can
    you do?
Deeper than Sheol – what can
    you know?
Its measure is longer than the earth,
and broader than the sea.
(Job 11:7–9)

Left *A 12th-century miniature of the prophet Job afflicted by boils. The book of Job considers the dual themes of God's justice and human suffering.*

Above *North and South America from space. For Jews, God is seen as the transcendent creator of the universe.*

IMMANENCE

Despite this view of God's remoteness from his creation, he is also viewed as actively involved in the created order. In the Bible his omnipresence is continually stressed.

Whither shall I go from thy Spirit?
Or whither shall I flee from thy
    presence?
If I ascend to heaven, thou art there!
If I take the wings of the morning
and dwell in the uttermost parts of the
    sea,
even there thy hand shall lead me.
(Psalm 139:7–12)

In the rabbinic period, Jewish scholars formulated the doctrine of the *Shekhinah*, or 'divine presence', to denote God's presence in the world. The Shekhinah is compared to light. Thus the midrash paraphrases Numbers 6:25 ('The Lord make his face to shine upon you, and be gracious to you'): 'May He give thee of the light of the Shekhinah'. In another midrash, the 'shining' of the Shekhinah in the Tent of Meeting is compared to a cave by the sea. When the sea rushes in to fill the cave, it suffers no diminution of its waters. Likewise, the divine presence filled the Tent of Meeting, but simultaneously filled the world.

In the Middle Ages, the doctrine of the Shekhinah was further elaborated by Jewish scholars. According to the Jewish philosopher Saadia Gaon (9th to 10th century), the Shekhinah is identical with the glory of God, which serves as an intermediary between God and man during the prophetic encounter. For Saadia the 'Glory of God' is a biblical term whereas the Shekhinah is a rabbinic concept that refers to the created splendour of light that acts as an intermediary between God and human beings. At times this manifestation takes on human form. Thus when Moses asked to see God's glory, he was shown the Shekhinah. Similarly when the prophets in their vision saw God in human form, what they actually perceived was the Shekhinah.

In his *Guide for the Perplexed*, the 12th-century philosopher Moses Maimonides embraced Saadia's belief that the Shekhinah is a created light, identified with glory. In addition, he associated the Shekhinah with prophecy. According to Maimonides, prophecy is an overflow from God, which passes through the mediation of the active intellect and then to the faculty of imagination. It requires perfection in theoretical wisdom, morality and development of the imagination. On the basis of this conception, Maimonides asserted that human beings can be divided into three classes according to the development of their reasoning capabilities. First there are those whose rational faculties are highly developed and receive influences from the active intellect, but whose imagination is defective – these are wise men and philosophers. The second group consists of those where the imagination alone is in good condition, but the intellect is defective – these are statesmen, lawgivers and politicians. Thirdly there are prophets – those whose imagination is consistently perfect and whose active intellect is fully developed.

In Kabbalistic teaching, the Shekhinah also played an important role. In early Kabbalistic thought it is identified as the feminine principle in the world of the *sefirot*, or 'divine emanations'. Later the Shekhinah was understood as the last in the hierarchy of the sefirot, representing the feminine principle. Like the moon, this sefirah has no light of her own, but instead receives the divine light from the other sefirot. As the divine power closest to the created world, she is the medium through which the divine light passes. Further, in Kabbalistic thought the Shekhinah is the divine principle of the Jewish people. Everything that happens to Israel is reflected upon the Shekhinah, which grows stronger or is weakened with every meritorious or sinful act of each Jew and of the people as a whole. Finally, the Shekhinah is viewed as the goal of the mystic who attempts to achieve communion with the divine powers.

Below *The tide turns, and the sea floods into the cave. God is seen as actively present in his creation.*

Above *A vision of glory. Moses before the Burning Bush by Dieric Bouts the Elder, c.1465–70. According to Scripture, God was present in the Burning Bush.*

ETERNITY

THROUGHOUT SCRIPTURE, GOD IS DESCRIBED AS HAVING NEITHER BEGINNING NOR END. UNLIKE THE REST OF CREATION, WHICH MAY SEE ETERNITY AS ENDLESS TIME, HE WAS, IS AND FOREVER WILL BE.

Above *Some Jewish theologians think that God is outside time in the way that sand dunes appear to stretch for ever.*

Many people have tried to define the concept of God and eternity. As the Psalmist declared:

Before the mountains were brought forth,
or ever thou hadst formed the earth and the world,
from everlasting to everlasting thou art God.
  (Psalm 90:2)

ETERNAL EXISTENCE

In the Bible the term *olam* is most frequently used to denote the concept of God's eternity. In Genesis 21:33 he is described as the Eternal God; he lives for ever (Deuteronomy 32:40), and reigns for ever (Exodus 15:18; Psalm 10:16). He is the living God and everlasting King (Jeremiah 10:10); his counsel endures for ever (Psalm 33:11), as does his mercy (Psalm 106:1). For the biblical writers, God's eternal existence is different from the rest of creation – he exists permanently without beginning or end.

THE RABBIS

This biblical teaching was elaborated by the rabbis. According to the Talmud, there is an unbridgeable gap between God and human beings. In midrashic literature God's eternal reign is similarly affirmed. Thus, according to a midrash, when Pharaoh was ordered by Moses and Aaron in the name of God to let the people go, Pharaoh declared that God's name is not found in his list of gods. In reply Moses and Aaron declared: 'O fool! The dead can be sought among the living but how can the living be sought among the dead. Our God lives, but those you mention are dead. Our God is "the living God, and everlasting King"' (Jeremiah 10:10). In response Pharaoh asked whether this God is young or old, how old he is, how many cities he has conquered, how many provinces he has subdued, and how long he has been king. In reply they proclaimed: 'The power and might of our God fill the world. He was before the world was created and he will be when all the world comes to an end and he has created thee and gave thee the spirit of life.'

THEOLOGICAL SPECULATION

Although the rabbis were convinced that God would endure for ever, they discouraged speculation about the nature of eternity. Such reluctance is reflected in the Mishnah's dictum: 'Whoever reflects on four things, it were better for him that he had not come into the world: What is above? What is beneath? What is before? What is after?'

In the Middle Ages, Jewish theologians debated this issue. In the *Guide for the Perplexed*, the 12th-century Jewish philosopher Moses Maimonides argued that time itself was part of creation. Therefore, when God is described as existing before the creation of the universe, the notion of time should not be understood in its normal sense.

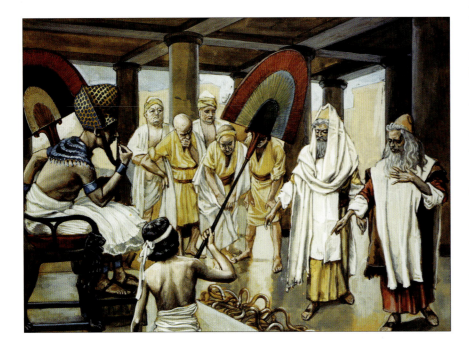

Below *Moses and Aaron show God's power before Pharaoh in a painting by James Tissot. For Jews, God is present in history, having neither beginning nor end.*

Above *Maimonides argued that time was part of creation in his* Guide for the Perplexed, *shown here in a 14th-century Italian illumination.*

This concept of time as part of creation was later developed by the 15th-century Jewish philosopher Joseph Albo. In his *Ikkarim* he maintained that the concepts of priority and perpetuity can only be applied to God in a negative sense. That is, when God is described as being 'before' or 'after' some period, this only means he was not non-existent before or after that time. However, these terms indicating a time span cannot be applied to God himself. Following Maimonides, Albo asserted that there are two types of time: measured time, which depends on motion, and time in the abstract. This second type of time has no origin – this is the infinite space of time before the universe was created.

ETERNAL NOW

According to other Jewish thinkers, God is outside time altogether – he is in the 'Eternal Now'. Thus the 13th-century theologian Bahya ibn Asher ibn Halawa, in his commentary on the Pentateuch, discussed the verse, 'The Lord will reign for ever and ever' (Exodus 15:18): 'All times, past and future, are in present so far as God is concerned, for he was before time and is not encompassed by it.' In the same way, the 16th-century scholar Moses Almosnino commented on the statement 'For now I know' (Genesis 22:12). According to Almosnino, God is in the 'Eternal Now', and he uses this notion to explain how God's foreknowledge is not incompatible with human free will.

According to these writers, God is outside time – he does not live in the present, have a past, or look forward to the future. On this view, God is experiencing every moment in the past and future history of the created world simultaneously and eternally. What for us are fleeting moments rushing by, bringing one experience after another, are for God a huge static tapestry, of which he sees every part continually. This conception of God's eternity – that he is outside time – and the alternative view that God exists in infinite duration before creation constitute the two central Jewish interpretations of the deity's relation to time. Yet for most Jews God's eternal existence is an impenetrable mystery.

None the less, the doctrine of God's eternity is a major feature of the Jewish faith. Through the centuries, Jews have been convinced that God was, is, and forever will be. Hence in Maimonides' formulation of the 13 central principles of the Jewish faith, the belief that God is eternal is the fourth tenet. In the Ani Maaimin prayer this principle is formulated as follows: 'I believe with perfect faith that the Creator, blessed be his name, is the first and the last.' And at the conclusion of synagogue services in all branches of Judaism, the faithful voice their commitment that God is eternal in time in the Adon Olam prayer:

He is the Lord of the universe,
Who reigned ere any creature yet
  was formed,
At the time when all things
  shall have had an end,
He alone, the dreaded one,
  shall reign:
Who was, who is, and who will
  be in glory.

Below *Rain over the Golan Heights in Israel. Jewish thought suggests God sees every part of time continually – the time before, after and during the rain.*

Omnipotence

AS LORD OF THE UNIVERSE, GOD IS CAPABLE OF ALL ACTIONS. IN GUIDING HIS CHOSEN PEOPLE, HE BROUGHT ABOUT THEIR DELIVERANCE AND REDEMPTION AND LEADS THEM TO THEIR ULTIMATE DESTINY.

From biblical times, the belief in God's omnipotence, that God is all powerful, has been a central doctrine.

GOD IN SCRIPTURE
According to the Book of Genesis, when Sarah expressed astonishment at the suggestion that she should have a child at the age of 90, she was criticized: 'The Lord said to Abraham, "Why did Sarah laugh, and say 'Shall I indeed bear a child now that I am old?' Is anything too hard for the Lord?"' Again, in the Book of Jeremiah, when the city was threatened by invaders, God declared: 'Behold I am the Lord the God of all flesh: is anything too hard for me?' (Jeremiah 32:27). Given such a view, there is nothing God cannot do. What appears impossible is within his power.

IMPOSSIBLE ACTIONS
Despite the conviction that God can do anything, in the Middle Ages Jewish theologians wrestled with the philosophical problems connected with this belief. Preeminent among their concerns was the question whether God could do absolutely everything. The 10th-century Jewish philosopher Saadia Gaon, for example, in his *Book of Beliefs and Opinions*, stated that the soul will not praise God for causing five to be more than ten without further addition, nor for being able to put the world through the hollow of a signet ring without making the world narrower and the ring wider, nor for bringing back the day that has passed in its original state. These, he argued, are absurd acts.

Later, the 15th-century Jewish philosopher Joseph Albo explored the same issue. In his opinion, there are two kinds of impossibility.

Some things are intrinsically impossible so that even God cannot make them possible. For example, we cannot imagine that God can make a part equal to the whole, a diagonal of a square equal to one of its sides, nor the angle of a triangle equal to more than two right angles. Further, it is impossible for God to make two contradictory propositions true at the same time, or the affirmative and negative true simultaneously. Likewise, it is impossible to believe that God could create another being like himself. In all these cases, the human intellect cannot conceive of such a state of affairs.

The other kind of impossibility is that which contradicts the law of nature, such as the resurrection of the dead. In such instances, it is possible to imagine such an occurrence. Thus Albo argued, God can bring about such events since they are not inherently impossible. Hence logical impossibilities are impossible for God, but not physical impossibilities.

LOGICAL IMPOSSIBILITIES
The 12th-century Jewish philosopher Maimonides argued along similar lines in his *Guide for the Perplexed*. There he explored the notion of God's omnipotence. In Maimonides' view, although God is all-powerful, there are certain actions that he cannot perform because they are logically impossible. That which is impossible, he wrote, has a perma-

Above *The prophet Elijah wrote that God's true spirit was not in the heart of the storm but in the still small voice. For Jews, God is the cause of all things.*

Left *The complex geometrical puzzles of 20th-century artist M.C. Escher reflect the complexity of the belief that God can do anything.*

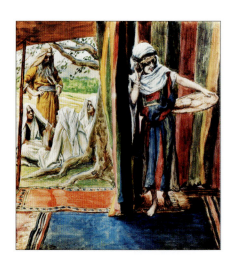

Below *Nothing is impossible with God. Sarah, Abraham's ageing wife, hears that she is to bear a son, and laughs. Painting by French artist James Tissot.*

Above *As the wave breaks on the shore and withdraws, so God allows humans space for the exercise of personal freedom.*

nent and constant property which is not the result of some agent. It cannot in any way change, and thus it is a mistake to ascribe to God the power of doing what is impossible. It is impossible, he went on, for God to produce a square with a diagonal equal to one of its sides, or a solid angle that includes four right angles. Thus Maimonides concluded: 'We have thus shown that according to each one of the different theories there are things which are impossible, whose existence cannot be admitted, and whose creation is excluded from the power of God.'

THE HOLOCAUST

In addressing the religious perplexities connected with the Holocaust, a number of modern writers have advanced the concept of a limited God. In the view of these writers, God intentionally limited himself when he bestowed free will on human beings. Thus, the Orthodox rabbi and Jewish theologian Eliezer Berkovits (1908–92) argued in *Faith After the Holocaust* that if God did not respect human freedom, morality would be abolished and men and women would cease to be fully human. God, he insisted, did not intervene to save the Jewish nation because he had bestowed human free will on humanity at the time of creation.

In *God and Evil*, the Orthodox scholar David Birnbaum similarly argued that human beings must accept that God is 'Holy Potential', allowing through the process of divine contraction space for the exercise of personal freedom. In Birnbaum's view, men and women are able to attain spiritual maturity in the exercise of liberty, and thereby attain their fullest possible potential. This view serves as the basis for reconciling the tragedy of the Holocaust with the traditional understanding of God's nature.

RADICAL THEOLOGY

A more radical approach was adopted by the Reform rabbi Steven Jacobs in *Rethinking Jewish Faith*. Here he argued that the concept of God in the Bible and rabbinic Judaism must be reformulated in the post-Holocaust world. What is now needed, he wrote, is a notion of a deity compatible with the reality of radical evil at work and at play in our world. To continue to affirm the historically traditional notions of faith in God as omnipotent is a theological error. Similarly the feminist Jewish theologian Melissa Raphael argued in *When God Beheld God* that the patriarchal model of God should be set aside. Drawing on the records of women's experiences during the Nazi period, she offered a post-Holocaust theology of relation that affirms the redemptive presence of God at Auschwitz.

Right *Jewish thought rules that God is all-powerful.* The Creation of Adam *by Michelangelo in the Sistine Chapel in Rome represents this idea.*

Above *Jewish quarter, Barcelona, Spain. Birthplace of Hasdai Crescas, author of* Or Adonai, The Light of the Lord, *in which he wrestles with a range of theological issues.*

OMNISCIENCE

ACCORDING TO THE JEWISH TRADITION, GOD KNOWS ALL. YET THIS CONCEPT GAVE RISE TO THEOLOGICAL SPECULATION ABOUT GOD'S KNOWLEDGE OF THE FUTURE.

According to the Jewish tradition, God knows everything: past, present and future. Nothing is hidden from his sight. As an all-knowing deity, he looks down from heaven on all his creation. This does not imply that human beings lack free will since God knows in advance what their actions will be. Rather, Judaism asserts that God knows all, yet men and women possess freedom of the will.

FOREKNOWLEDGE AND FREE WILL

In line with this biblical view, rabbinic Judaism asserted that God's knowledge is not limited by space and time. Instead, nothing is hidden from him. Moreover, the rabbis stated that God's knowledge of events does not deprive human beings of free will. Thus in the Mishnah, the 2nd-century CE sage Akiva declared: 'All is foreseen but freedom of choice is given.'

In the *Guide for the Perplexed* Maimonides argued that God knows all things before they occur. None the less, human beings are unable to understand the nature of God's knowledge because it is of a different order from that of human beings. On this account, it is not possible to comprehend how divine foreknowledge is compatible with human freedom. Other medieval writers, however, were unconvinced by such an explanation. In *The Wars of*

Above *The Middle East and the Red Sea from the air. God's knowledge is not limited by time or space.*

Below *15th-century painting of God as the divine architect. The act of creation is part of the tapestry of God's knowledge.*

> **THE BIBLICAL VIEW**
> According to the Hebrew Bible, God is aware of all human action. As the psalmist proclaimed:
>
> The Lord looks down from heaven,
> He sees all the sons of men...
> He who fashions the hearts of them all,
> and observes their deeds. (Psalm 33:13,15)
>
> Again, in Psalm 139:2–3, the psalmist declared:
>
> Thou knowest when I sit down and when I rise up;
> thou discernest my thoughts from afar.
> Thou searchest out my path and my lying down,
> and art acquainted with my ways.

the Lord, the 14th-century theologian Gersonides argued that only God knows things in general. Hence the world is constituted so that a range of possibilities is open to human beings. Since men and women are able to exercise free will, these are possibilities rather than certainties, which they would be if God knew them in advance.

Thus, although God knows all it is possible to know, his knowledge is not exhaustive. He does not know how individuals will respond to the possibilities open to them since they are only possibilities. For Gersonides, such a view does not undermine God's providential plan. Although God does not know all future events, he is aware of the outcome of the whole process. In the same century, however, the Jewish theologian Hasdai Crescas (1340–1410) held a different view in *The Light of the Lord*. According to Crescas, human beings only appear to be free, but in reality all their deeds are determined by virtue of God's foreknowledge. Therefore, rather than attempting to reconcile free will and omniscience, he asserted that God's knowledge is absolute and free will is an illusion.

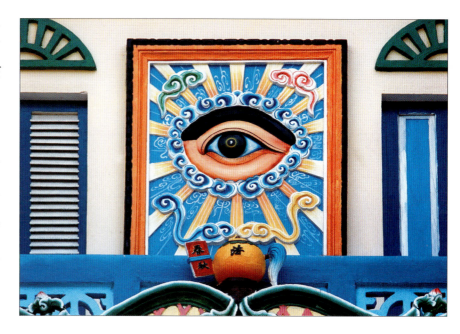

MODERN JUDAISM

In recent times the devout have been less concerned about such philosophical perplexities. Jewish scholar Michael Friedländer was best known for his English translation of Maimonides' *Guide for the Perplexed*. In 1890 he considered the subject of divine foreknowledge in *The Jewish Religion*: 'His knowledge is not limited, like the knowledge of mortal beings, by space and time. The entire past and future lies unrolled before his eyes, and nothing is hidden from him.

Above *An omniscient eye on the Cao Dai temple in the Mekong Delta, Vietnam, portrays the idea of God's all-encompassing knowledge.*

Although we may form a faint idea of the knowledge of God by considering that faculty of man that enables him within a limited space and time, to look backward and forward, and to unroll before him the past and the future, as if the events that have happened and those that will come to pass were going on in the present moment, yet the true nature of God's knowledge no man can conceive. ... It is the will of God that man should have free will and should be responsible for his actions; and his foresight does not necessarily include predetermination.'

In the modern period, there has been a universal reaffirmation of the traditional belief that God knows past, present and future and that men and women have freedom of choice.

Left *The Creation from the Sarajevo Haggadah, c.1350, one of the oldest Sephardic Haggadahs. Images include the separation of light from darkness, and the spirit of God hovering over the waters of chaos. According to Judaism, God knows and does all things.*

CREATION

THE DOCTRINE OF CREATION IS A CENTRAL ELEMENT OF THE JEWISH FAITH. YET AMONG JEWISH THEOLOGIANS THIS BELIEF GAVE RISE TO SPECULATION ABOUT THE CREATIVE PROCESS.

According to the Bible, God created the cosmos. This belief became a central feature of the synagogue liturgy. Repeatedly, Jews praise God for his creative works and extol his providential concern for all that he has formed. The doctrine of divine creation also became a central doctrine of Jewish philosophy and mysticism.

THE BIBLE
According to Genesis 1:1–4 God created the universe:

In the beginning God created
   the heaven and the earth.
The earth was without form
   and void,
and darkness was upon the face
   of the deep;
and the Spirit of God was moving
   over the face of the waters.
And God said,

Below This early 13th-century mosaic for Monreale Cathedral, Sicily, shows God creating Heaven and Earth.

Right According to the Bible God created the cosmos and everything in it. Animals in the Rothschild Miscellany, *a 15th-century Italian illumination.*

'Let there be light':
   and there was light.
And God saw that the light was good.
Based on the Psalms, synagogue liturgy depicts God as the creator of all:

Blessed be He who spake, and the
   world existed:
Blessed be He;
Blessed be He who was the Master
   of the world in the beginning.

In the Ani Maamin prayer, the first principle of the Jewish faith concerns creation:

I believe with perfect faith that
the creator, blessed be his name, is
the author and guide of everything
that has been created, and that He
   alone
has made, does make, and will
   make all things.

RABBINIC LITERATURE
In rabbinic sources, scholars speculated about the creative process. In Genesis Rabbah (midrash on Genesis), for example, the concept of the world as a pattern in the mind of God is expressed in relation to the belief that God looked into the Torah and then created the universe. Here the Torah is conceived as a primordial blueprint. Regarding the order of creation, the School of Shammai stated that

---

EXTRATERRESTRIAL CREATION

Regarding the question whether in the process of creating the cosmos, God also formed intelligent beings on other planets, the Bible provides no information. Even though rabbinic sources attest to the creation of other worlds, they similarly contain no reference to the existence of other sentient creatures. However, in the 19th century Phineas Elijah ben Meir Hurwitz of Vilna discussed this topic. On the basis of Isaiah 45:18 ('For thus says the Lord who created the heavens, who formed the earth and made it, he established it; he did not create it a chaos; he formed it to be inhabited: "I am the Lord; and there is no other."'), he stressed that there are creatures on other planets than the earth. He went on to say that creatures on other planets may have intelligence, yet he did not think that they would have free will since only human beings have this ability. Consequently, he wrote, there is only room for Torah and worship in this world, for neither Torah nor worship has any meaning where there is no free will.

CREATION

Left *Adam and Eve, the first created humans, in a scene from Genesis. From a 1438 manuscript of the Tur Even HaEzer, a compilation of Hebrew laws.*

the heavens were created first and then the earth. The School of Hillel, however, maintained that the heaven and the earth were created simultaneously. According to one rabbinic source, all things were formed at the same time on the first day of creation, but appeared on the other six days just as figs are gathered simultaneously in one basket but each selected individually.

Again, in the Genesis Rabbah midrash, scholars stressed that God created several worlds but destroyed them before creating this one. The goal of creation is summed up in the rabbinic claim that God created the world for his glory.

THE MEDIEVAL PERIOD

In the Middle Ages, a number of Jewish philosophers argued that God created the cosmos *ex nihilo*. The Kabbalists, however, interpreted the doctrine of *ex nihilo* in a special sense. In their view, God should be understood as the Divine Nothing because as he is in and of himself nothing can be predicated. This is because the divine is beyond human comprehension. Creation *ex nihilo* therefore refers to the creation of the universe out of God, the Divine Nothing. This took place, they stated, through a series of divine emanations.

For the Kabbalists the first verses of Genesis allude to the process within the Godhead prior to the creation of the universe. In Lurianic Kabbalah, the notion of God creating and destroying worlds before the creation of this world is viewed as referring to spiritual worlds. Thus *tohu*, or 'void', in Genesis denotes the stage of God's self-revelation known as world of the void that precedes the world of perfection. In later Kabbalistic thought, the 14th-century Kalonymus Kalman of Cracow in his *Maor Va-Shemsh* maintained that the void in Genesis is the primordial void remaining after God's withdrawal to make room for the universe. On this reading, God's decree 'Let there be light' (Genesis 1:3) means that God caused his light to be emanated into the void in order to provide sustaining power required for the worlds that were later to be formed.

Below *Map showing the Earth, planets and zodiac circling the Sun, by Nicolaus Copernicus, c.1543.*

363

Goodness

BIBLICAL AND RABBINIC SOURCES EXTOL GOD'S GOODNESS. TRADITION SAYS HE IS BENEVOLENT, MERCIFUL AND COMPASSIONATE. YET SUCH A BELIEF GAVE RISE TO SPECULATION ABOUT THE ORIGIN OF EVIL.

As the supreme ruler of the universe, God is depicted in biblical and rabbinic sources as all-good. He is the beneficent creator who watches over all he has formed and extends mercy to his chosen people. As the Psalmist declared, he is good and ready to forgive (Psalm 86:5).

THE RABBIS
According to rabbinic literature, God is the supremely beneficent deity who guides all things to their ultimate origin. In the unfolding of his plan, God has chosen Israel as his messenger to all peoples – as creator and redeemer, he is the father of all. Such affirmations about God's goodness have given rise to speculation about the existence of evil. In the Bible, the authors of Job and Ecclesiastes explore the question why the righteous suffer, and this quest extended into the rabbinic period. However, it was not until the Middle Ages that Jewish theologians began to explore the philosophical perplexities connected with the origin of evil.

THE SOURCE OF EVIL
In the 12th century, the Jewish philosopher Abraham Ibn Daud argued that both human reason and the Jewish tradition teach that God cannot be the cause of evil. Reason demonstrates that this is the case because God is all-good; it would be self-contradictory for him to be the source of evil. Since God does not have a composite nature, it is logically impossible for him to bring about both good and evil. Why then does evil exist? Poverty, he argued, is in fact the absence of wealth; darkness the absence of light; folly the absence of understanding. It is an error to believe that God creates any of these

Above *The Rabbi by Martin Archer-Shee, 1837, shows its subject as wise, knowing and benevolent.*

things just as it would be an error to assume that God made no elephants in Spain. Such a lack of elephants is not divinely willed. Likewise, evil is not created by God. It occurs when goodness is not present. The absence of good is not an inherent evil. Rather, imperfections in the world exist so that God can benefit a multitude of creatures in different forms.

THE KABBALISTS
According to Jewish Kabbalists, the existence of evil constitutes a central problem for the Jewish faith. One tradition asserts that evil has no objective reality. Men and women are unable to receive all of the influx from the *sefirot*, or 'divine emanations'; it is this inability that is the origin of evil. Created beings are estranged from the source of emanation and this results in the illusion that evil exists. Another view depicts the sefirah of power as an attribute whose name is evil. On the basis of such teaching, Isaac the Blind (*c.* 1160-1235) concluded that there must be a positive root of evil and death. During the process of differentiation of forces below the sefirot, evil became concretized. This inter-

Below *According to the Bible, Adam and Eve were expelled from the Garden of Eden because of their disobedience. 12th-century Spanish painting.*

pretation led to the doctrine that the source of evil is the supra-abundant growth of judgement – this was due to the separation and substitution of the attribute of judgement from its union with compassion. Pure judgement produced from within itself the Sitra Ahra, or 'the other side'. The Sitra Ahra consists of the domain of emanations and demonic powers. Though it originated from one of God's attributes, it is not part of the divine realm.

THE ZOHAR

According to the Zohar, the major Kabbalistic source of the Middle Ages, evil is like the bark of a tree of emanation – it is a husk or shell in which lower dimensions of existing things are encased. Evil is perceived as a waste product of an organic process. It is compared to bad blood, foul water, dross after gold has been refined and the dregs of wine. Yet despite this depiction, the Zohar asserts that there is holiness even in the Sitra Ahra, whether it is understood as a result of the emanation of the last sefirah or a consequence of human sin. The domains of good and evil are intermingled, and it is a person's duty to separate them.

MODERN JEWISH THOUGHT

In modern times philosophical theories about the existence of evil have ceased to attract attention within Judaism, and most Jews have ignored the mystical theories in early and medieval Jewish literature. Instead, writers have wrestled with the question whether it is possible to believe in God's goodness after the Holocaust.

Above *Peter Eisenman's Holocaust Memorial to the Murdered Jews of Europe, Berlin, 2005. For theologians, the Holocaust poses fundamental questions about human evil and God's omnipotence.*

In *The Face of God after Auschwitz* (1965) Reform Jewish theologian Ignaz Maybaum contended Jews died in the concentration camps for the sins of humanity as God's suffering servant. For Maybaum, Jews suffer in order to bring about the rule of God over the world and its peoples – their God-appointed role is to serve the course of historical progress and bring human beings into a new era.

An alternative approach to the Holocaust is to see in the death camps a manifestation of God's will that his chosen people survive. Such a view was expressed by the Reform Jewish philosopher Emil Fackenheim (1916–2003), who asserted that God revealed himself to the Jewish people out of the furnaces and through the ashes of the victims of the death camps. Through the Holocaust, he argued, God issued an additional 614th commandment to the 613 commandments found in Scripture: 'Jews are forbidden to hand Hitler posthumous victories.' In this way, God commanded his people to survive as Jews, lest the Jewish people perish.

Below *Evil can triumph when good men do nothing. The Holocaust Memorial at Mauthausen Concentration Camp is in the shape of a menorah.*

CHAPTER 6

GOD AND ISRAEL

According to traditional Judaism, God is understood as the providential Lord of all creation. In the Hebrew Bible, God is depicted as ever-present, directing the course of human affairs. In rabbinic sources, he is intimately involved with his people, continually leading them to their ultimate redemption. The revelation to Moses on Mount Sinai is the basis of the 613 commandments in the Torah, which were later interpreted by rabbinic scholars. According to tradition, God's eternal covenant with Israel means both the Written and the Oral Law are binding for all time.

As the all-good ruler of the universe, God chose the Jews as his special people. Israel was to be a messenger to all nations in the unfolding of God's divine plan for humanity. In acceptance of God's love, the Jewish people were to worship God and keep his commandments. In biblical times, worship and sacrifice were carried out in the Temple. Sacrifices were offered to God to obtain his favour and atone for sin. With the destruction of the Temple, the synagogue became the focus for divine worship. Prayers replaced sacrifices, which could no longer be offered. A new ritual, referred to as 'service of the heart', became a central focus of Jewish life.

Opposite *This magnificent illustration from the Golden Haggadah of 1320 shows, anti clockwise from top right, Pharaoh letting the people of Israel go, the strangling of the firstborn, the Egyptians pursuing the people of Israel, and the drowning of the Egyptians in the Red Sea.*

Above *This 6th-century Byzantine mosaic from Madaba, Jordan, is the oldest extant map of Palestine.*

Providence

FOR THE JEWISH PEOPLE, GOD IS THE TRANSCENDENT CREATOR OF THE UNIVERSE AND ACTIVELY INVOLVED IN HISTORY. PROVIDENTIALLY, HE INTERVENES IN EVERYDAY LIFE, SUSTAINING AND GUIDING HIS CREATURES.

In Scripture, God is continually presented as controlling and guiding his creation. The Hebrew term for such divine intervention is *hashgahah*, derived from Psalm 33:14: 'From where he sits enthroned he looks forth [*hisgiah*] on all the inhabitants of the earth.' This view implies that the dispensation of a wise and benevolent providence is manifest everywhere.

THE BIBLE
According to the Hebrew Bible, there are two types of providence: general providence (God's provision for the world in general) and special providence (God's care for each person). In the Bible, God's general providence was manifest in his freeing the ancient Israelites from bondage; special providence relates to God's care for each individual. In the words of Jeremiah:

Below *When God told Abraham to send Hagar and Ishmael into the desert, was this general or special providence? By Italian painter Veronese, 1580.*

'I know, O Lord, that the way of man is not in himself, that it is not in man who walks to direct his steps' (Jeremiah 10:23).

THE RABBINIC TRADITION
The doctrine of divine providence was developed in rabbinic sources. According to the Mishnah, 'everything is foreseen'. Developing this concept, the Talmud states: 'No man suffers so much as the injury of a finger when it has been decreed in heaven.' This belief became a major feature of the Rosh Hashanah, or New Year, liturgy where God, the judge of the world, provides for the destiny of individuals as well as nations on the basis of their actions.

THE MIDDLE AGES
Jewish medieval theologians were preoccupied with the problem of divine causality. In the *Guide for the Perplexed*, the 12th-century Jewish philosopher Moses Maimonides defended both general and special

Above *14th-century Spanish drawing of the ancient Hebrews as slaves in Egypt. For Jews, the Exodus from Egypt was an act of divine deliverance.*

providence. Special providence, he argued, extends only to human beings and is in proportion to a person's intellect and moral character. This view implies God is concerned about non-human species, but not with every individual. Only men and women come under divine care as they rise in intellectual and moral stature.

However, in the 15th century, the Jewish theologian Hasdai Crescas (1340–1410) maintained that God created human beings out of his love for them. Therefore, his providential care is not related to their personal characteristics. Instead, all persons enjoy God's special providence.

THE KABBALISTS
Jewish Kabbalists were also concerned about providence. In his *Shomer Emunim*, the 18th-century scholar Joseph Ergas explained there are various types of providence. 'Nothing', he wrote, 'occurs by accident, without intention and divine providence, as it is written: "Then will I also walk with you in chance." (Leviticus 21:24). You see that even the state of chance is attributed to God, for all proceeds

> ### HASIDIC TEACHERS
> Such a restriction of special providence was rejected by a number of Hasidic thinkers. Divine providence, they insisted, is exercised over all things. In the 18th century, for example, Phineas of Koretz (1726–91) wrote in his *Peer La-Yesharim* that 'a man should believe that even a piece of straw that lies on the ground does so at the decree of God.' Hayim of Sanz (1793–1876), the founder of the Sanz Hasidic dynasty, stated: 'It is impossible for any creature to enjoy existence without the creator of all worlds sustaining it and keeping it in being, and it is all through divine providence.'

from him by reason of special providence.' None the less, Ergas limited special providence to human beings. 'The guardian angel', he continued, 'has no power to provide for the special providence of non-human species. For example, whether this ox will live or die, whether this ant will be trodden on or saved, whether this spider will catch this fly ...There is no special providence for this kind of animals, to say nothing of plants and minerals.'

Below *Cosmographical Diagram from the Catalan Atlas by Abraham Cresques, 1375. For Jews, God is both transcendent and immanent in human history.*

MODERN JUDAISM
In the contemporary world, such theological issues have not been at the forefront of Jewish thought. Rather, the rise of science has challenged the traditional understanding of God's providential activity. In place of the religious interpretation of the universe as controlled by God, scientific investigation has revealed that nature is governed by complex natural laws. Thus it is no longer possible for most Jews to accept the biblical and rabbinic concept of divine providential activity. As a result, many Jews have simply abandoned the belief in providence.

Others envisage God as working through natural causes. As creator of all, he established the laws that regu-

Above *The destruction of the Temple of Jerusalem can be seen as providentially willed or as the result of human action. Painting by Francesco Hayez, 1867.*

late the natural order. Regarding special providence, many Jews would want to say that God is concerned with each individual, even though he does not miraculously intervene in the course of human affairs. Divine providential concern should thus be understood as a mode of interaction in which God affects the consciousness of individuals without curtailing their free will. Knowing the innermost secrets of the human heart, he introduces into the conscious awareness of individuals aims consonant with his will.

Revelation

TRADITION IS THAT GOD REVEALED HIMSELF TO THE JEWISH NATION. THIS BELIEF SERVES AS THE FOUNDATION OF THE LEGAL SYSTEM AND THE AUTHORITATIVE BASIS OF JEWISH THEOLOGY.

According to the Jewish tradition, God revealed the Torah to Moses on Mount Sinai and, therefore, 613 commandments in the Five Books of Moses are binding for all time. In addition, God's revelation on Mount Sinai serves as basis for the conviction that the descriptions of God's nature and activity found in Scripture are authoritative and unchanging.

THE RABBIS

In rabbinic sources a distinction is drawn between the revelation of the Torah and the prophetic writings. This is frequently expressed by saying that the Torah was given directly by God, whereas the prophetic books were given by means of prophecy. The other books of the Bible, however, were conveyed by means of the holy spirit. Yet despite these distinctions, all the writings in the Hebrew Bible constitute the canon of Scripture. The Hebrew term referring to the Bible as a whole is Tanakh. This word is made of the first letters of the three divisions of Scripture: Torah, Neviim (Prophets), and Ketuvim (Writings).

THE ORAL TORAH

For the rabbis, the expositions and elaborations of the Written Law were revealed on Mount Sinai and passed down from generation to generation. This process is referred to as the Oral Torah. Hence, traditional Judaism affirms that God's revelation is two-fold and binding. Committed to this belief, Jews pray in the synagogue liturgy that God will guide them to do his will.

THE MEDIEVAL PERIOD

In the Middle Ages, the traditional belief in the Written and Oral Torah was repeatedly affirmed. The Jewish writer Nahmanides (1194–1270) stated in his *Commentary to the Pentateuch* that Moses wrote the Five Books of Moses at God's dictation. It is likely, he observed, that Moses wrote Genesis and part of Exodus when he came down from Mount Sinai. After 40 years in the wilderness, he completed the rest of the Torah.

Nahmanides stated that this view follows the rabbinic tradition that the Torah was given scroll by scroll. For Nahmanides, Moses was like a scribe who copied an older work. Underlying this conception is the mystical idea of a primordial Torah, which contains the words describing events long before they occurred. This entire record was in heaven before the creation of the world. Further, Nahmanides maintained that the secrets of the Torah were revealed to Moses and are referred to in the Torah by the use of special letters, and by the adornment of Hebrew characters.

KABBALAH

Parallelling Nahmanides' mystical interpretation of the Torah, the medieval mystical work the Zohar

Above *Revelation at Sinai as Moses receives the Ten Commandments. From the mid 9th-century Moutier-Grandval Hebrew Bible.*

Left *The first Great Sanhedrin of French Jews in Paris, 1807. The Jewish legal system is based on God's revelation of Mount Sinai, as interpreted by rabbinic sages through the centuries.*

asserts that the Torah contains mysteries beyond human comprehension. As Rabbi Simeon ben Yohai, traditionally thought to be the author of the Zohar, explained, 'Alas for the man who regards the Torah as a book of mere tales and everyday matters! If that were so, even we could compose a Torah dealing with everyday affairs, and of even greater excellence. Nay, even the princes of the world possess books of greater worth which we could use as a model for composing such Torah. The Torah, however, contains in all its words supernal truths and sublime mysteries.'

BIBLICAL SCHOLARSHIP

In the modern period it has become increasingly difficult to sustain the concept of divine revelation in the light of scholarly investigation and discovery. According to biblical scholars, the Torah is composed of various sources from different periods in the history of ancient Israel.

Below *Tradition teaches that God revealed the Torah to Moses. This new Torah scroll is being completed before it is paraded in procession to an Ashkenazi synagogue in Stamford Hill, London.*

Some scholars stress that these sources themselves contain early material; thus it is a mistake to think they originated in their entirety at particular periods. Other scholars reject the theory of separate written sources; instead, they argue that oral traditions were modified throughout the history of ancient Israel and only eventually were compiled into a single narrative. Yet, despite these rival claims, there is a general recognition that the Torah was not written by Moses; rather, it is seen as a collection of traditions originating at different times.

Above *1350 Passover Haggadah. In following such liturgy, Jews pray God will guide them to do his will.*

MODERN JUDAISM

Orthodox Jews remain committed to the view that the Written and the Oral Torah were imparted by God to Moses on Mount Sinai. This is the basis of the legal system and doctrinal beliefs about God. Non-Orthodox Jews have a general acceptance of the findings of biblical scholarship. The Five Books of Moses are perceived as divinely inspired, but at the same time the product of human reflection.

THE TORAH

According to the Jewish tradition, the Torah was given by God to the Jewish nation. Moses Maimonides explained: 'The Torah was revealed from heaven. This implies our belief that the whole of the Torah found in our hands this day is the Torah that was handed down by Moses, and that it is all of divine origin. By this I mean that the whole of the Torah came unto him from before God in a manner which is metaphorically called "speaking". But the real nature of that communication is unknown to everybody except Moses.'

GOD AND ISRAEL

Torah and Commandments

JEWISH OBSERVANCE IS BASED ON THE BELIEF THAT GOD REVEALED 613 COMMANDMENTS TO MOSES ON MOUNT SINAI – THESE ARE RECORDED IN THE TORAH AND SERVE AS THE BASIS OF JEWISH LAW.

Traditional Judaism affirms that Moses received the Oral Torah in addition to the Written Law. These commandments were passed down from generation to generation and were the subject of rabbinic discussion and debate.

THE RABBINIC TRADITION

The first authoritative compilation of the Oral Law was the Mishnah, composed by Yehuda Ha-Nasi in the 2nd century CE. This work is the most important book of law after the Bible – its aim was to supply teachers and judges with a guide to the Jewish legal tradition.

In later centuries, sages continued to discuss the nature of Jewish law. Their deliberations and conclusions are recorded in the Palestinian and Babylonian Talmuds. Both Talmuds incorporate the Mishnah and later rabbinic debate known as the Gemara. The Gemara text preserves the proceedings of scholarly academies in both Palestine and Babylonia. The central purpose of these works was to elucidate the Mishnah text.

CODES OF LAW

After the compilation of the Talmuds in the 6th century CE, outstanding scholars continued the development of halakha, or 'Jewish law', by issuing answers to specific questions. These responsa, or 'responses', touched on all aspects of the Jewish tradition and insured a standardization of practice. In time, various scholars felt the need to produce codes of Jewish law so that all members of the community would have access to the legal tradition. Isaac Alfasi (1013–1103) produced a work in the 11th century that became the standard code for Sephardic Jewry. Two centuries later, Asher ben Jehiel (c.1250–1327) wrote a code for Ashkenazi Jews. In the 12th century Moses Maimonides wrote the Mishneh Torah, which had a wide influence, as did the code by Jacob ben Asher in the 14th century. In the 16th century, Joseph Caro (1488–1575) published the *Shulkhan Arukh*, which together with the glosses by Moses Isserles (c.1525–72) has served as the standard code of Jewish law for Orthodox Jews.

THE KABBALAH

In Kabbalistic sources the observance of the *mitzvot*, or 'commandments', takes on cosmic significance. For the Jewish mystic, deeds of *tikkun*, or 'cosmic repair', sustain the world, activate nature to praise God, and bring about the coupling of the 6th and 10th sefirot, or 'divine emanations'. Such repair is brought about

Above *Brass hanging lamp in the shape of a Jewish 'Sabbath lamp', lit on the eve of Sabbath and festivals. Jews are commanded to rest and worship on the Sabbath.*

Below *Dutch artist Rembrandt's painting of* Moses with the Ten Commandments, *1659*.

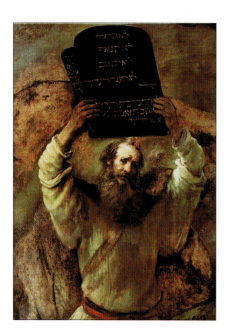

Below *The rabbi in his pulpit reading a Torah scroll to his congregation, from the Barcelona Haggadah, c.1350.*

TORAH AND COMMANDMENTS

> ### LURIANIC KABBALAH
> According to the 16th-century Kabbalist Isaac Luria (1534–72), when the vessels were shattered the cosmos was divided into two parts: the kingdom of evil in the lower part and the realm of divine light in the upper part. God, he believed, chose Israel to vanquish evil and raise up the captive sparks. The Torah was given to symbolize the Jews' acceptance of this task. Luria and his disciples believed they were living in the final stages of the last attempt to overcome evil, in which the coming of the Messiah would signify the end of the struggle. For Lurianic mystics, the concept of tikkun refers to the mending of what was broken during the shattering of the vessels. By keeping God's commandments it is possible for the righteous to redeem the world.

by keeping the commandments, which were conceived as vessels for establishing contact with the Godhead and for enduring divine mercy. Such a religious life provided the Jewish mystic with a means of integrating into the divine hierarchy of creation.

MYSTICAL CLEAVING

The highest rank attainable by the soul at the end of its sojourn on earth is mystical cleaving to God. Early Kabbalists of Provence defined such cleaving as the ultimate goal.

According to the 13th-century mystic Isaac the Blind, the principal task of the mystics and of those who contemplate the divine name is to cleave to God. This, he argued, is a central principle of the Torah and of prayer. The aim should be to harmonize one's thoughts above, to conjoin God in his letters and to link the ten sefirot to him. For the 13th-century writer Nahmanides, such cleaving is a state of mind in which one constantly remembers God and his love.

MODERN JUDAISM

In the modern world, such traditional mystical ideas have lost their force except among the Hasidim. Today the majority of those who profess allegiance to Orthodox Judaism do not live by the code of Jewish law. Instead, each individual Jew feels free to write his or her own *Shulkhan Arukh*. This is also the case within the other branches of Judaism. For most Jews the legal tradition has simply lost its hold on Jewish consciousness. This means that there is a vast gulf fixed between the requirements of legal observance and the actual lifestyle of the majority of Jews, both in Israel and the Diaspora.

Above *Jews kissing the Torah scrolls, Nevatim, Israel. Tradition states that God revealed the words of the Torah to Moses.*

Below *Hasidic life is regulated by Jewish law. A Hasidic couple walk through the Mea Shearim, one of the oldest Jewish neighbourhoods in Jerusalem.*

Left *Cover page of Leviticus, dated 1350, which covers laws about sacrifice, the sanctuary, impurity and holiness.*

373

CHOSEN PEOPLE

ACCORDING TO TRADITION, GOD CHOSE THE JEWS FROM AMONG ALL PEOPLES. THEY ARE TO BE HIS SERVANTS AND DO HIS WILL. THIS BELIEF HAS ANIMATED JEWISH CONSCIOUSNESS THROUGH THE AGES.

According to Scripture, God chose the Jewish nation as his special people. As the Book of Deuteronomy proclaims: 'For you are a people holy to the Lord your God: The Lord your God has chosen you to be a people for his own possession out of all the peoples that are on the face of the earth' (Deuteronomy 7:6).

DIVINE LOVE
According to the Hebrew Bible, God's selection of Israel was motivated by divine love. The Book of Deuteronomy states: 'It was not because you were more in number than any other people that the Lord set his love but it is because the Lord loves you' (Deuteronomy 7:7–8). Such affection was later echoed in the synagogue liturgy, particularly in the prayer for holy days: 'Thou has chosen us from all peoples; thou has

Below *The Book of Genesis from a 1472 Pentateuch, showing Adam, Eve and a unicorn, which in Jewish tradition stands for the final redemption of Israel.*

loved us and found pleasure in us and hast exalted us above all tongues; thou hast sanctified us by thy commandments and brought us near unto thy service, O king, and hast called us by thy great and holy name.'

AN HISTORIC MISSION
By its election, Israel was given an historic mission to bear truth to all humanity. Hence, before God proclaimed the Ten Commandments on Mount Sinai, he admonished the people to carry out this role: 'You have seen what I did to the Egyptians, and how I bore you on eagles' wings, and brought you to myself. Now, therefore, if you will obey my voice, and keep my covenant, you shall be my own possession among all peoples; for all the earth is mine, and you shall be to me a kingdom of priests and a holy nation' (Exodus 19:4-6).

OBLIGATION AND RESPONSIBILITIES
Such a choice of Israel carries with it numerous responsibilities: 'For I have chosen him, that he may charge his children and his household after him to keep the way of the Lord by doing righteousness and justice' (Genesis 18:19). Divine choice therefore brings about reciprocal response: Israel is obliged to keep God's law. In doing so, the nation will be able to persuade other nations that there is only one universal God. Israel is to be a prophet to the nations in that it will bring them to salvation. However, despite such an obligation, the Bible asserts that God will not abandon his chosen people even if they go astray. The wayward will be punished, but God will not reject them: 'Yet for all that,

Above *The Ark of the Law, 6th-century CE mosaic at Beth Alpha synagogue, Israel. Tradition says God chose the Jews from all nations to be his special people and observe his commandments.*

when they are in the land of their enemies, I will not spurn them, neither will I abhor them so as to destroy them utterly and break my covenant with them: for I am the Lord their God' (Leviticus 26:44).

THE RABBINIC VIEW
In rabbinic literature the concept of the chosen people is a constant theme. While maintaining that God chose the Jews from all peoples, the rabbis argued their election was due to an acceptance of the Torah. This belief was based on Scripture: 'If you will hearken to my voice, indeed, and keep my covenant, then you shall be my own treasure from among all the peoples' (Exodus 19:5). For the rabbis, the Torah was offered first to other nations of the world, but they all rejected it because its precepts conflicted with their way of life. Only Israel was willing to keep his covenant.

THE MEDIEVAL PERIOD
In the Middle Ages, the Jewish claim to be God's chosen people was disputed by Church authorities

who regarded the Church as the true Israel. In response, such Jewish philosophers as the 12th-century Spanish Jew Judah Halevi stressed that the entire Jewish people were endowed with a special religious sense. According to Halevi, this faculty was first bestowed on Adam, and then it was passed on through a line of Jewish representatives. As a result, the Jewish nation was able to enter into communion with God. Moreover, because of this divine influence, the election of Israel implies dependence on special providence, which sustains the people while the remainder of the human race is subject to the general workings of the laws of nature and general providence.

Below *The Spanish philosopher Judah Halevi held that Jewish people had a special religious sense. Thus Moses could talk to God on Mount Sinai. A 14th-century Italian fresco by Bartolo di Fredi.*

KABBALAH

The concept of Jewish chosenness is a central theme of medieval Kabbalistic thought. According to medieval Kabbalah, the Jewish people on earth has its counterpart in the Shekhinah, or 'divine presence', in the sefirotic realm – the sefirah, or 'divine emanation', *Malkhut* is known as 'the community

Above *Israel and the Mediterranean from the Catalan Atlas by Jewish cartographer Abraham Cresques, 1375. According to tradition, Israel was chosen to be a light to all nations.*

of Israel' which serves as the archetype of the Israelite people on earth. For the Kabbalists, Israel's exile mirrors the cosmic disharmony in which the Shekhinah is cast into exile from the Godhead. The dynamic of Israel's exile and its restoration reflects the dynamic of the upper worlds.

MODERN JUDAISM

In the contemporary Jewish world, the notion of Israel's chosenness remains an important doctrine. Yet within Reform Judaism the concept of Jewish mission was developed, stressing the special message of God that is to be passed on to all peoples. Within the various non-Orthodox branches of the faith a number of writers have expressed unease about the claim that the Jews constitute a divinely chosen people. The rejection of this traditional doctrine derives from universalistic and humanistic tendencies. Although the Jewish community has a unique history, the people of Israel are not perceived as divinely chosen. Instead, the God of Israel is also the Lord of history who loves all peoples and guides their destiny.

LOVE OF GOD

OF CENTRAL IMPORTANCE IN JUDAISM IS THE LOVE OF GOD. THE OBLIGATION TO LOVE GOD INVOLVES BEING FAITHFUL, EVEN IF THIS REQUIRES THE LOSS OF ONE'S WEALTH OR ONE'S LIFE.

At the heart of Judaism lies the love of God. According to Scripture: 'You shall love the Lord your God with all your heart and with all your soul and with all your might' (Deuteronomy 6:5). The Mishnah teaches that this biblical verse implies that human beings must love God not only for the good that befalls them, but for their sufferings as well. This explanation is based on an interpretation of three expressions in this verse: 'with all your heart' means with both the good and evil inclinations; 'with all your soul' means even if God takes away your soul through martyrdom; 'with all your might' means with all your wealth.

MIDRASHIC TEACHING

Alongside the Mishnah, the midrash also comments on this biblical verse. Concerning the phrase 'You shall love the Lord your God', the *Sifra* (midrash on Exodus) declares: 'Do it out of love. Scripture distinguishes between one who does it out of love and one who does it out of fear. Out of love, his reward is doubled and gain doubled. Scripture says: "You shall fear the Lord your God: you shall serve him and cleave to him" (Deuteronomy 10:20). A man who fears his neighbour will leave him when his demands become too troublesome, but you do it out of love. For love and fear are never found together except in relation to God.'

THE MIDDLE AGES

Among medieval Jewish writers, stress was placed on mystical love. Thus the Jewish philosopher Saadia Gaon (882–942CE) in *Beliefs and Opinions* asked how it is possible to have knowledge of God, much less love him, since we have not perceived him with

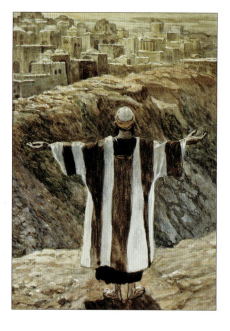

Above I Will Worship toward Thy Temple. *A 19th-century painting of Jerusalem by the French artist James Tissot shows the obligation to love God.*

our senses. In response he asserted that certain statements are believed to be true even though they cannot be proved. For Saadia, it is possible to acquire knowledge of God through rational speculation and the miracles afforded by Scripture. Hence, truth about God is able to mingle with the human spirit. For this reason the prophet Isaiah stated: 'My soul yearns

Below *This carving of 1420 from Roskilde, Denmark, depicts Job, a righteous man who is put to the test with illness and the loss of his wealth and family, but remains faithful to God.*

BAHYA IBN PAKUDAH

In the 11th century the Jewish philosopher Bahya Ibn Pakudah viewed the love of God as the final goal – this is the aim of all virtues. According to Bahya, the love of God is the soul's longing for the creator. When human beings contemplate God's power and greatness, they bow before his majesty until God stills whatever fear they might have. Individuals who love God in this fashion have no other interest than serving him. With complete faith they accept all their sufferings.

Above *Paradise by Lucas Cranach the Elder, 1530. Scripture says, Adam and Eve were driven out of Paradise for failing to observe God's commandments.*

for thee in the night, my spirit within me earnestly seeks thee' (Isaiah 26:9). As a consequence, the soul is filled with love.

MOSES MAIMONIDES

In the Mishneh Torah, the 12th-century thinker Moses Maimonides discussed the love of God in relation to the nature of the universe. 'It is a religious obligation to love and fear this glorious and tremendous God,' he wrote. 'And it is said: "You shall love the Lord your God" (Deuteronomy 6:5). And it is said: "You shall fear the Lord your God" (Deuteronomy 6:13). How does a man come to love and fear God? No sooner does man reflect on his deeds and on his great and marvellous creatures, seeing in them his incomparable and limitless wisdom, than he is moved to love and to praise and to glorify and he has an intense desire to know the great Name.'

Right *Jews praying before the Western Wall in Jerusalem. Such prayer should be based on love of God.*

According to Maimonides, one who truly loves God serves him disinterestedly rather than out of an ulterior motive. When a person loves God, he automatically carries out the divine commandments. This state is like being lovesick, unable to get the person he loves out of his mind, pining constantly when he stands, sits, eats or drinks. Yet Maimonides maintained that not everyone is able to attain such a state of pure love. God, he maintained, can only be loved in proportion to the knowledge one has of him.

KABBALAH

In Kabbalistic literature the love of God is highly important. Concerning the verse, 'You shall love the Lord your God', the Zohar states that human beings are here commanded to cleave unto God with selfless devotion: 'It is necessary for man to be attached to God with a most elevated love, that all man's worship of the Holy One, blessed be he, should be with love; for no form of worship can be compared to the love of the Holy One, blessed be he.'

LATER KABBALISTS

In the writings of later Kabbalists the theme of the love of God was further elaborated. According to the 16th-century writer Elijah de Vidas in his *Reshite Hokhmah*, it is impossible for human beings to love a disembodied spirit. Here the love of God must refer to something that is embodied. Since God as En Sof has no body, human love of the divine must be understood as love of the Shekhinah (God's presence). For de Vidas, the Shekhinah is in no way apart from God; rather God manifests himself through the Shekhinah in order to provide human beings with something tangible they are able to grasp so as to rise above worldly desires.

FEAR OF GOD

THE FEAR OF GOD IS TO BE COUPLED WITH THE LOVE OF GOD. ACCORDING TO MEDIEVAL JEWISH THINKERS, SUCH FEAR SHOULD BE UNDERSTOOD AS AWE BEFORE GOD'S GREATNESS.

Above *Molten lava flowing from an active volcano. Accepting the power of the natural world may be seen as a way of interpreting the fear of God.*

In the Jewish tradition, there are numerous references to the fear of God. In the Book of Job, for example, Job is described as 'blameless and upright, one who feared God and turned away from evil' (Job 1:1). In rabbinic sources the Hebrew terminology for such awesome reverence is *yirat shamayim*, or 'the fear of heaven'. In the medieval period a distinction was drawn between fear of punishment and fear in the presence of the exalted majesty of God.

MEDIEVAL THEOLOGIANS

In the 12th century, the Jewish philosopher Abraham Ibn Daud (1040–1105) discussed the concept of the fear of God in *Emunah Ramah*. Referring to Deuteronomy 10:20 ('You shall fear the Lord your God'), he argued that the reference is to the fear produced by God's greatness, not to the fear of harm. There is a fundamental difference between these two types of fear, he stated. A person may be afraid of an honourable prophet who would certainly not harm him, or he might be afraid of a hyena or a snake. The first type is fear at the greatness of the one feared and shame in his presence. Fear of God, he asserted should be of this kind, not of the kind of fear we have for kings whom we are afraid will do harm to us.

In *Duties of the Heart*, the 11th-century theologian Bahya Ibn Pakudah drew a similar distinction. Only fear in the presence of the exalted majesty of God can lead to pure love. A person who attains this degree of reverence will neither fear nor love anything other than the creator. In this regard Bahya referred to a saint who found a God-fearing man sleeping in the desert. He asked if he were afraid of lions sleeping in such a place. In reply, the God-fearer said: 'I am ashamed that God should see that I am afraid of anything apart from him.'

LATER PHILOSOPHERS

In the 15th century, Jewish philosopher Joseph Albo defined fear as the receding of the soul and the gathering of all her powers into herself, when she imagines some fear-inspiring thing. Yet there is another type of fear in which the soul is awestruck not because of any fear of harm, but because of her unworthiness in the face of majesty. For Albo this higher fear is elevating. Fearing God in this way, a person will stand in awe before him and be ashamed to transgress his commandments.

In the following century, Elijah de Vidas maintained in *Reshite Hokhmah* that the fear of God is the gate through which every servant of the Lord must pass. It is a necessary condition for loving God and doing his will. Basing his views on Kabbalah, de Vidas stated that, since human beings are created after the pattern of the upper world, all acts have a cosmic effect. Good deeds cause the divine grace to flow through all worlds, whereas evil actions arrest this flow. The fear of sin thus has cosmic significance.

Below *The reading of the Torah in a synagogue is interrupted by a crowd led by a Christian priest, 1868. Out of love and fear of God, Jews have revered the Torah and God's commandments.*

Right *The fear of the Lord. Elijah curses the boys who have mocked his baldness, and they are eaten by bears. Painting by James Tissot (1836–1902).*

HASIDIM

Among the Hasidim, the fear of God was also an important issue. In the 19th century, Zevi Elimelech Spira in *Bene Yisakhar* argued that effort is required to reach this state. He wrote: 'The disciples of the Ba'al Shem Tov wrote in the name of their master that human effort is only required in order to attain to the state of worship out of fear, whereas God himself sends man the love of him since the male pursues the female; and you know that fear is the category of the female and love that of the male.' In the 18th century Levi Isaac of Berdichev argued in *Kedushat Levi* that a distinction should be drawn between the lower fear of sin and the higher fear whereby one is overawed by God's majesty. In this state a person has no self-awareness. Yet, this higher fear can only be attained as a product of the lower fear.

THE ZOHAR

According to the medieval mystical work the Zohar, there are three types of fear. Two of these have no proper foundation, but the third is the main source of fear. A person may fear God in order that his sons may live and not die, or because he is afraid of some punishment. Because of this he is in constant fear. Or there is a person who fears God because he is terrified of punishment in the next world. Both these types of fear do not belong to the main foundation of fear. The fear that does have a proper foundation is when a person fears his master because he is the great and mighty ruler. This is the highest type of fear.

MUSAR

This was a movement for ethical education in the spirit of the halakha or Jewish law. It emerged in the 19th century in Lithuania, where fear of punishment was viewed as essential for those struggling to reach perfection. According to Isaac Blazer (1837–1907), the highest fear is the ultimate aim, but it is impossible to attain it without serious reflection on the fear of punishment. Only serious contemplation of severe punishment can penetrate the human heart so that this deeper understanding can be gained.

Below *Living with fear. An anti-Semitic riot outside a synagogue in 1750, by Daniel Chodowiecki.*

Promised Land

TRADITIONAL JUDAISM MAINTAINS THAT THE HOLY LAND WAS PROMISED BY GOD TO ISRAEL. THROUGH THE CENTURIES, JEWS HAVE LONGED TO RETURN TO THEIR ANCESTRAL HOME.

According to Scripture, God told Abraham to travel to Canaan: 'Go from your country and your kindred and your father's house to the land that I will show you. And I will make of you a great nation' (Genesis 12:1–2). This divine promise became the basis of the Jewish claim to the Holy Land, a conviction that animated Jewish aspirations in the Diaspora to return to the land of their ancestors.

ANCIENT ISRAEL

God's promise to Abraham was repeated to his grandson Jacob who was renamed Israel (meaning 'he who struggles with God'). After Jacob's son Joseph became a vizier in Egypt, the Israelite clan settled in Egypt for several hundred years.

Eventually they were freed from Egyptian bondage by Moses, who led them into the desert. Under Joshua's leadership, the Jewish nation conquered the Canaanites and settled in the land, establishing a monarchy. A sacred Temple was built in Jerusalem by King Solomon which became the central cult for the nation. This was followed by a rebellion by the Northern tribes and the establishment of two kingdoms: Israel in the north and Judah in the south. In 722BCE the Northern Kingdom was devastated by Assyrian invaders, and two centuries later the Southern Kingdom was conquered by the Babylonians. Although Jews were allowed to return to Judah by Cyrus of Persia in 538BCE, the Romans destroyed the Temple in 70CE.

Above *The sack of Antioch, 1098. Some Jews saw Jewish deaths in this crusade as a sign that the Messiah was on his way.*

MESSIANIC REDEMPTION

Following these events, the Jews were bereft of a homeland. In their despair the Jewish people longed for a messianic deliverer who would lead them back to Zion. Basing their beliefs on biblical prophecy, they foresaw a period of redemption in which earthly life would be transformed and all nations would bow down to the one true God. This vision animated rabbinic reflection about God's plan for his people.

According to rabbinic sources, the process of divine deliverance involved the coming of a messianic

Below *The fall of the Temple in 70CE marked the loss of the Jews' homeland for nearly 2,000 years. From the Hours of Neville of Hornby, c. 1340.*

Below *Palestine and the Promised Land; a map of 1603 after Flemish Abraham Ortelius, generally recognized as the creator of the first modern atlas.*

Above *View of Jerusalem Seen From the Mount of Olives by the Russian artist N.G. Chernezov, 1863.*

figure, Messiah ben Joseph, who would serve as the forerunner of the second Messiah, Messiah ben David. This second messiah would bring back all the exiles to Zion and usher in the messianic age. At the end of this period all human beings would be judged: the righteous would enter into heaven whereas the wicked would be condemned to eternal punishment. This vision served as a means of overcoming the nation's trauma at suffering the loss of the Holy Land.

FALSE MESSIAHS

In the early rabbinic period some Jews believed that Jesus was the long-awaited redeemer of Israel. Although mainstream Judaism rejected such claims, the Jewish community continued to long for deliverance. In 132 CE the Palestinian military leader Simeon bar Kochba was acclaimed by many Jews as the Davidic Messiah. When his rebellion against Rome resulted in failure, Jews put forward the year of redemption until the 5th century CE, when another messianic pretender, Moses from Crete, declared he would lead Jewish inhabitants from the island back to their homeland. After this plan failed, Jews continued to hope for a future return and their aspirations are recorded in various midrashic sources.

This longing continued into the early Middle Ages. The traveller Eldad Ha-Dani brought news from Africa of the ten lost tribes, which stimulated messianic longing. Many Jews viewed the year of the First Crusade (1096) as a year of deliverance: when Jews were slaughtered, their suffering was viewed as the birth pangs of the Messiah. In later years the same yearning for a return to Zion was expressed by Jews who continued to be persecuted by the Christian population. The early modern period witnessed this same aspiration for redemption. In 1665 the arrival of Shabbetai Tzvi electrified the Jewish world. Claiming to be the Messiah, he attracted a large circle of followers; however, his conversion to Islam evoked widespread despair.

THE ZIONIST MOVEMENT

With the apostasy of Shabbetai Tzvi, the Jewish preoccupation with messianic deliverance diminished. Many Jews became disillusioned with messianic anticipation. Yet despite this shift in orientation, a number of Jews continued to pray for the coming of the Messiah, and linked this yearning to an advocacy of Zionism. Paralleling these religious aspirations to establish a Jewish settlement in the Holy Land prior to the coming of the Messiah, modern secular Zionists encouraged such a development in order to solve the problem of anti-Semitism.

As time passed, the Zionist cause gained increasing acceptance in the Jewish world. The first steps towards creating a Jewish homeland were taken at the end of the 19th century with the first Zionist Congress. Subsequently, Zionists attempted to persuade the British government to permit the creation of a Jewish home in Palestine. Although Britain eventually approved of such a plan, the British government insisted that the rights of the Arab population be protected. After World War II, the creation of a Jewish state was approved by the United Nations. Yet despite such an official endorsement, this plan was rejected by the Arabs. In subsequent years, Arabs and Jews have engaged in a series of conflicts, and this antagonism has continued until the present day.

Below *The Zionist dream. This Israeli poster shows a Hebrew soldier removing a yellow Star of David armband from an old man, c.1950.*

Prayer

THROUGHOUT THE AGES, JEWS HAVE TURNED TO GOD IN PRAYER. THROUGH PRAYERS OF PRAISE, THANKSGIVING AND PETITION, THEY HAVE EXPRESSED THEIR LONGINGS AND ASPIRATIONS.

Within the Jewish faith, worship is of fundamental importance. From the biblical period to the present, Jews have turned to God in times of distress. In the synagogue, prayers are addressed to God during daily and Sabbath services and during festivals. In the belief that God listens to the voices of those who turn to him, Jews have expressed their deepest longings and hopes in words of prayer.

THE BIBLE

The Hebrew Scriptures list more than 80 examples of formalized and impromptu worship. Initially no special prayers were required for regular prayer. It was only later that worship services became institutionalized through sacrifices and offerings. Sacrifices to God were made to obtain his favour or atone for sinful acts. Unlike the Canaanites, who sacrificed human beings, the ancient Israelites slaughtered only animals. In biblical times there were three types of sacrifice offered in the Temple: animal sacrifice, made as a burnt offering for sin; meal offerings; and libations. The rituals and practices governing these acts were set down in Leviticus 2, 23 and Numbers 28, 29.

FIXED WORSHIP

According to the Mishnah, priests serving in the Temple participated in a short liturgy comprising the Shema (Deuteronomy 6:4), the Ten Commandments (Exodus 20:3–17), and the priestly blessing (Numbers 6:24–6). During this period the entire congregation began to pray at fixed times; later, an order of service was established by the men of the Great Assembly. Regular services were held four times daily by the delegations of representatives from the 24 districts of the country. These services consisted of *shacharit*, or 'morning', *musaf*, or 'additional', and *neilat shearim*, or 'evening'.

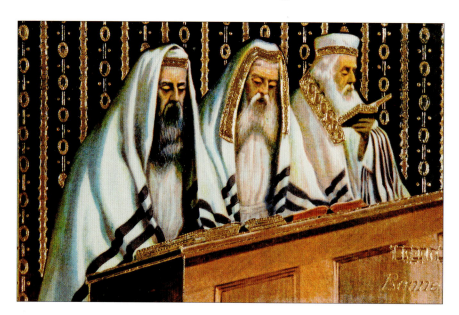

Below *A French postcard for Jewish New Year showing worshippers in prayer shawls, c.1920.*

Above *A 5th-century Roman mosaic of Daniel in the lions' den, from Bordj El Loudi, Tunisia. According to Scripture, God protected Daniel from harm.*

RABBINIC TIMES

Several orders of prayers coexisted until Gamaliel II produced a regularized standard after the Temple was destroyed in 70 CE. Prayers officially replaced the sacrificial system since they could no longer be offered in the Temple. This new ritual – the service of the heart – was conducted in the synagogue. The core of the liturgy included the prayer formula 'Blessed are You, O God', the Shema, and the Amidah (known also as the tefillah), consisting of 19 benedictions. On special occasions, an additional Amidah was included.

Prayers were recited by a *minyan*, or 'quorum of ten men': if such a number could not be found, certain prayers had to be omitted (including the Kaddish, Kedushah and the reading of the Law). The Alenu prayer, originating from the New Year liturgy, and the Kaddish were the two concluding prayers of all services.

HEBREW BIBLE READINGS

During the worship service, portions of the Torah (Five Books of Moses) and the Prophets were recited, and this became a normal practice by the time of the Mishnah in the 2nd

Above *Prayer ceremony from an illustrated Hebrew prayer book, Germany, 1471.*

century CE. By the end of the talmudic period (6th century CE), the prayer service was supplemented by piyyutim, or 'liturgical hymns'. These compositions were produced in Palestine as well as Babylonia from geonic times until the 12th century.

The Palestine rite was distinguished by a triennial cycle of reading from the Torah, a recension of the benedictions of the Amidah, and an introductory blessing before the recitation of the Shema.

The Babylonian rite was first recorded by Amram Gaon in the 9th century CE. This work served as the official ordering of prayers with their legal requirements. This act of setting down liturgical arrangements led to the dissolution of the ban against committing prayers to writing. In the 10th century CE the first authoritative prayer book (*siddur*) was edited by Saadiah Gaon (882–942CE).

JEWISH MYSTICISM

For Jewish mystics, *devekut*, or 'cleaving to God in prayer', was of fundamental importance. For the early Kabbalists of Provence devekut was the goal of the mystic way. According to the 13th-century Jewish philosopher Nahmanides, devekut is a state of mind in which one constantly remembers God and his love to the point that when a person speaks with someone else, his heart is not with them at all but is still before God. In Nahmanides' view, the true Hasid, or 'pious individual', is able to attain such a spiritual state – devekut does not completely eliminate the distance between God and human beings. Rather, it denotes a state of beatitude and intimate union between the soul and its source.

MYSTIC PRAYER

In ascending to the higher worlds, the path of prayer paralleled the observance of the commandments. Yet, unlike the *mitzvot*, or 'commandments', prayer is independent of action and can become a process of mediation. Mystical prayer, which is accompanied by meditative *kavvanot*, or 'intention', focusing on each prayer's Kabbalistic content, became a feature of various stems of Kabbalah. For the Kabbalist, prayer was understood as the ascent of human beings into the higher realm where the soul can integrate with the higher spheres. By using the traditional liturgy in symbolic fashion, prayer repeats the hidden processes of the cosmos.

HASIDISM

In the 19th century, Hasidim incorporated Kabbalistic ideas into their understanding of prayer. According to Hasidic thought, the Kabbalistic type of kavvanot brings about an emotional involvement and attachment to God. In Hasidism, prayer is seen as a mystical encounter with the divine in which the human heart is elevated towards its ultimate source. Frequently the act of prayer was seen as the most important religious activity.

MODERN JUDAISM

In modern times the emergence of various Jewish movements led to the reinterpretation of the liturgical tradition. Reform Jews modified the worship service through eliminating various prayers, and introducing the organ and communal singing as well as addresses in the vernacular. The aim of Reform Judaism was to adapt Jewish worship to contemporary needs. Within the Conservative and Reconstructionist movements, prayer books adhered more closely to the traditional *siddur*, or 'prayer book'. Yet, despite such a diversity of approaches, prayer continues to serve as a focal point of the faith.

Below *In the Synagogue, c.1900, the focus of divine worship and service.*

CHAPTER 7

THE SPIRITUAL PATH

The Bible serves as a guide to Jewish spirituality. Later Jewish sources – including the midrash and the Talmud – similarly provide a basis for the spiritual path. In this context, ethical values are of primary importance. Through their election, the Jewish people are to serve as God's servants, proclaiming God's truth and righteousness. Jews are called to action, to turn humanity away from wickedness and sin. In this quest, the Jewish nation is to become holy, just as God is holy. Through moral living, Jews are to reflect God's compassion, mercy and justice.

In the Jewish tradition, compassion is perceived as a cardinal virtue. Those who suffer are to be consoled. God's mission for his people is for them to act as comforters of the oppressed. This message is highlighted during the Passover *seder*, or 'religious meal'. The Jewish people are to remember that they were once enslaved; their responsibility is to free those who are in bondage. Yet such compassionate care is to be tempered by the quest for justice. By choosing such a moral life, the Jew is to complete God's work of creation.

Opposite Synagogue Service Imploring Divine Favour and Grace. *A devout Jew pictured by 19th-century Russian painter Nikolai Bogdanoff-Bjelski.*

Above *Simchat Torah is the holy day on which the completion of the annual reading of the Torah is celebrated. This particular festival procession took place at Livorno synagogue, Italy, in 1850.*

BIBLE

THE BIBLE SERVES AS THE BEDROCK OF THE JEWISH FAITH. IN THE HEBREW SCRIPTURES, KNOWN AS THE TANAKH, THE ANCIENT ISRAELITES RECORDED THEIR HISTORY AND RELIGIOUS BELIEFS.

For the Jewish people, the Hebrew Scriptures serve as the basis of belief and practice. Through the ages the nation has looked to the Bible for inspiration and sustenance. In times of tribulation as well as joy, Jews have turned to this sacred literature as a source of comfort and hope.

THE HEBREW SCRIPTURES

The Jewish faith is a revealed religion. Its basis is the Bible. The Hebrew name for the canon of Scripture is *Tanakh*: the Hebrew term is an abbreviation of the principal letters of the words standing for its divisions: *Torah*, or 'teaching'; *Neviim*, or 'prophets'; *Ketuvim*, or 'writings'. The Torah consists of Genesis, Exodus, Leviticus, Numbers and Deuteronomy. According to

Below *Samuel, prophet and judge in the Bible, beheads Agad, king of the Amalekites. From the North French Hebrew Miscellany, compiled in 1278 at a time of upheaval for European Jews.*

tradition, these five books were revealed by God to Moses on Mount Sinai. The second division of the Hebrew Bible – the Prophets – is divided into two parts. The first – Former Prophets – contains the books of Joshua, Judges, 1 and 2 Samuel and 1 and 2 Kings. The second part – Latter Prophets – is composed of the major prophets (Isaiah, Jeremiah and Ezekiel) and the minor prophets (Hosea, Joel, Amos, Obadiah, Jonah, Micah, Nahum, Habakkuk, Zephaniah, Haggai, Zechariah and Malachi). The third division consists of a variety of divinely inspired books: Psalms, Proverbs, Job, Song of Songs, Ruth, Lamentations, Ecclesiastes, Esther, Daniel, Ezra, Nehemiah and 1 and 2 Chronicles.

NON-CANONICAL LITERATURE

During the Second Temple period and afterwards, a large number of other books were written by Jews in Hebrew, Aramaic and Greek that were not included in the biblical canon. None the less, these texts did gain canonical status in the Roman Catholic and Eastern Orthodox churches. Known as the Apocrypha, they had an important impact on Christian thought. The most substantial is the Wisdom of Jesus Son of Sirah (also known as Ben Sira or Ecclesiasticus). Other works include: the Wisdom of Solomon, 1 and 2 Maccabees, Tobit and Judith. Additional literary sources of the Second Temple period are known as the Pseudepigrapha – these non-canonical books consist of such works as the Testament of the Twelve Patriarchs, 1 and 2 Enoch and Jubilees.

Above *Samson, an Israelite judge and man of great strength, defeats a lion in a German illustration from 1360.*

RABBINIC JUDAISM

In rabbinic literature a distinction is drawn between the revelation of the Pentateuch (Torah in the narrow sense) and the prophetic writings. This is frequently expressed by saying that the Torah was given directly by God, whereas the prophetic books were given by means of prophecy. The remaining books of the Bible were conveyed by means of the holy spirit rather than through prophecy. Nevertheless, all these writings constitute the canon of Scripture.

According to the rabbis, the expositions and elaborations of the *Torah She-Bi-Ketav*, or 'Written

Below The Judgement of Solomon, *greatest of the judges, by Valentin de Boulogne, 1625.*

Law', were also revealed by God to Moses on Mount Sinai. Subsequently they were passed from generation to generation, and through this process additional legislation was incorporated. This process is referred to as the *Torah She-Be-Al-Peh*, or 'Oral Torah'. Thus traditional Judaism affirms that God's revelation is twofold and binding for all time. Committed to this belief, Orthodox Jews pray in the synagogue that God will guide them to do his will as recorded in their sacred literature.

THE MEDIEVAL PERIOD

In the Middle Ages this traditional belief was affirmed. Thus the 12th-century Jewish philosopher Moses Maimonides (1135–1204) declared that the belief in *Torah*

Below *The coming of the prophet Elijah, from the Washington Haggadah, created in Italy by Joel ben Simeon, 1478.*

Left *The text of every Sefer Torah, kept in the synagogue, is identical because it is copied from an original by a* sofer *(scribe).*

MiSinai, or 'Torah from Sinai', is a fundamental principle of the faith: 'The Torah was revealed from heaven. This implies our belief that the whole of the Torah found in our hands this day is the Torah that was handed down by Moses, and that it is all of divine origin. By this I mean that the whole of the Torah came unto him from before God in a manner which is metaphorically called "speaking"; but the real nature of that communication is unknown to everybody except to Moses to whom it came.'

THE ZOHAR

The medieval mystical work the Zohar asserts that the Torah contains mysteries beyond human comprehension. According to Simeon ben Yohai, traditionally identified as the author of the Zohar: 'Alas for the man who regards the Torah as a book of mere tales and everyday matters! If that were so, even we could compose a Torah dealing with everyday affairs, and of even greater excellence. Nay, even the princes of the world possess books of greater worth which we could use as a model for composing such Torah. The Torah, however, contains in all its words supernal truths and sublime mysteries.'

MODERN JUDAISM

Orthodox Judaism remains committed to the view that the Written as well as the Oral Torah were imparted by God to Moses on Mount Sinai. This act of revelation serves as the basis for the entire legal system as well as doctrinal beliefs about God. Yet despite such an adherence to tradition, many modern Orthodox Jews pay only lip service to such a conviction. The gap between traditional belief and contemporary views of the Torah is even greater in the non-Orthodox

Above *The Book of Exodus recounts that the Israelites built cities for Pharaoh. From a Hebrew Haggadah, 1740.*

branches of Judaism. Here there is a general acceptance of biblical scholarship. Such a non-fundamentalist approach rules out the traditional belief in the infallibility of Scripture and thereby provides a rationale for changing the law and reinterpreting the theology of the Hebrew Scriptures.

> ### THE PENTATEUCH
> Like Maimonides, the 13th-century philosopher Nahmanides (1194–1270) in his *Commentary to the Pentateuch* argued that Moses wrote the Five Books of Moses at God's dictation. It is likely, he observed, that Moses wrote Genesis and part of Exodus when he descended from Mount Sinai. At the end of 40 years in the wilderness he completed the rest of the Pentateuch. Nahmanides observed that this view follows the rabbinic tradition that the Torah was given scroll by scroll. For Nahmanides, Moses was like a scribe who copied an older work.

MISHNAH, MIDRASH AND TALMUD

IN THE 2ND CENTURY CE, THE MISHNAH WAS COMPILED BY YEHUDA HA-NASI AS THE FIRST COLLECTION OF RABBINIC LAW. IN LATER CENTURIES, THE PALESTINIAN AND BABYLONIAN TALMUDS WERE PRODUCED.

With the rise of rabbinic Judaism, scholars engaged in the exposition of the biblical text and the interpretation of Jewish law. In academies in Erez Israel and Babylonia, sages devoted themselves to interpreting God's will and edifying the Jewish people. Initially their teachings were passed on orally, but in time they were written down in the Mishnah, Talmud and midrashic sources.

EARLY RABBINIC JUDAISM

During the early rabbinic period – between the 1st century BCE and the 6th century CE – rabbinic scholars referred to as Tannaim (70–200 CE) and Amoraim (200–500 CE) engaged in the interpretation of the biblical text. According to tradition, both the Written and the Oral Torah were given by God to Moses on Mount Sinai. This belief implies that God is the direct source of the *mitzvot*, or 'commandments', recorded in the Five Books of Moses and is also indirectly responsible for the legal judgements of the rabbis. Such a conviction serves as the justification for the rabbinic exposition of scriptural ordinances.

Alongside this halakha, or 'exegesis of Jewish law', Jewish sages also produced interpretations of Scripture in which aggadah, or 'new meanings of the text', were expounded in midrashim, or 'rabbinic commentaries', and in the Talmud. Within aggadic sources is found a wealth of theological speculation about topics such as the nature of God, divine justice, the coming of the Messiah and the afterlife. In addition, ethical considerations were of considerable importance in the discussions of these teachers of the faith.

MISHNAH

During the age of the Tannaim, Jewish scholars produced teachings dealing with Jewish law which were codified in the Mishnah by Yehuda Ha-Nasi (135–220CE) in about 200 CE. This work is a compilation of oral traditions (Oral Law); it is divided into six orders (which are subdivided into 63 tractates). The first order, Zeraim, or 'seeds', deals largely with agricultural law, although it begins with a section about prayer. The second order, Moed, or 'season', deals with the sacred calendar. In the third order, Nashim, or 'women', matrimonial law is discussed in extensive detail. The fourth order, Nezikim, or 'damages', contains both civil and criminal law and also contains a tractate of Avot, or 'moral maxims'. The fifth order, Kodashim, or 'holy things', gives a detailed account of the rules for sacrifice. Finally, the sixth order, Tohorot, or 'purity', is concerned with ritual purity.

Above Menorah, *or seven-branched candlestick, and sarcophagus at Beit She'arim, where the great Mishnah scholar Yehuda Ha-Nasi lived.*

Below The Talmud *is a compilation of Jewish laws. This page, from a German Talmud of the early 1300s, shows when God created his world.*

MIDRASH

Parallel with the legal tradition, Jewish sages also expounded the narrative parts of Scripture. In the Tannaitic period such midrashim dealt with the Five Books of Moses. Some of these traditions allegedly derive from the School of Akiva; others are attributed to the School of Ishmael. These midrashic sources are: the *Mekilta* on the book of Exodus; the *Sifra* on Leviticus; and the *Sifrei* on Numbers and Deuteronomy. Other midrashic sources deal with material from the Amoraic period.

Like the tannaitic midrashim, some are in the form of running commentaries known as exegetical midrashim. Others are collections of sermons arranged according to the sabbaths or festivals for which they

Above *Studying the Scriptures with rabbinic commentary is an integral part of Jewish life. Photo taken in the Great Synagogue in Moscow.*

were written. These are known as homiletical midrashim. The largest collection of midrashim is *Midrash Rabbah*, consisting of works that were separate commentaries on the Torah plus the Five Scrolls (the Song of Songs, Ruth, Lamentations, Ecclesiastes, Esther). Homiletical midrashim are exemplified by *Pesikta de-Rav Kahana*, *Pesikta Rabbati* and *Midrash Tanhuma* (known also as *Yelammedenu*).

TALMUD

In the centuries following the composition of the Mishnah and the early midrashim, Jewish sages in Palestine and Babylonia continued to expand Jewish law. By the 4th century CE scholars in Erez Israel had collected together the teachings of generations of sages in the academies of Tiberius, Caesarea and Sepphoris. The extended discussions of the Mishnah became the Palestinian Talmud. The text of this multi-volume work covers four sections of the Mishnah (seeds, set feasts, women and damages), but here and there various tractates are missing. No doubt the discussions in these academies included matters on these missing tractates, but it is not known how far the recording, editing and transmission of these sections had progressed before they were lost.

The views of these sages had an important influence on scholars in Babylonia, though their work never attained the same prominence as that of the Babylonian Talmud. In Babylonia, sages completed the redaction of the Babylonian Talmud by the 6th century CE – an editorial task begun by Ashi in the 5th century CE. This massive work is largely a summary of the discussions that took place in the Babylonian academies. Although the Babylonian Talmud deals with slightly fewer Mishnaic tractates, it is nearly four times larger than the Palestinian Talmud and came to be regarded as more authoritative.

The texts of these Talmuds consists largely of summaries of rabbinic discussion: a phrase of Mishnah is interpreted, discrepancies are resolved and redundancies are explained. In this compilation, conflicting opinions of the earlier sages are contrasted, unusual words are explained and anonymous opinions are identified. Frequently, individual teachers cite specific cases to support their views, and hypothetical eventualities are examined to reach a solution on the discussion. Debates between outstanding scholars in one generation are often cited, as are differences of opinion between members of an academy or a teacher and his students. The range of talmudic explorations is much broader than that of the Mishnah, and includes a wide range of teachings about such subjects as theology, philosophy and ethics.

Below *A painting of a* Jewish Wedding *by Italian Pietro Longhi (1701/2–85). A section of the Mishnah concerns women, marriage, divorce and vows.*

ETHICS

ETHICAL CONCERNS ARE OF PARAMOUNT IMPORTANCE IN THE JEWISH TRADITION. ALONGSIDE THE ETHICAL TEACHING IN SCRIPTURE, A WIDE RANGE OF MITZVOT DEAL WITH THE MORAL LIFE.

In the Jewish faith, ethical values are of primary importance. For Jews, moral action is fundamental – since it is through the rule of the moral law that God's kingdom on earth can be realized. This is the goal of the history of the world in which God's chosen people have a central role. It is their destiny to be a light to the nations.

THE MORAL LIFE

Through the centuries Judaism did not separate religion from life. Rather, the Jewish people were called to action. It was their duty to turn men and women away from violence, wickedness and falsehood. In this quest it was not the hope of bliss in a future life that was the primary goal – rather, the aim was to establish a kingdom of justice and peace on earth. Ethical action is thus at the heart of the tradition. Each Jew was to be like the creator, mirroring the divine qualities revealed to Moses: 'The Lord, the Lord, a God merciful and gracious, slow to anger, and abounding in steadfast love and faithfulness, keeping steadfast love for thousands, forgiving iniquity and transgression and sin' (Exodus 34:6–7).

Right *When God destroyed humanity with a flood because of its great wickedness, Noah's family were saved in an ark, shown here under a rainbow, in a mosaic from Kykko, Cyprus.*

THE TORAH

In the Hebrew Scriptures, deeds and events involving ethical issues are found in abundance: the punishment of Cain for murdering his brother; the violence of the generation that brought about the flood; the early prohibition against murder; the hospitality of Abraham and his plea for the peoples of Sodom; the praise of Abraham for his ethical character; the condemnation of Joseph's brothers; Joseph's restraint in Egypt in the house of Potiphar; Moses' plea for the exploited.

Yet it is in the legal codes of the Torah that we encounter moral guidelines formulated in specific laws. The Ten Commandments in particular illustrate the centrality of Jewish ethics. The first commandments are theological in nature, but the last six deal with relationships between human beings. These *mitzvot*, or 'commandments', provide a means of expressing love of others. The Decalogue thus makes it clear that moral standards are fundamental to the Jewish faith.

Left *Moses receives the Ten Commandments, a central part of Jewish ethics. From a 1305* Bible Historiale, *the predominant medieval translation of the Bible into French.*

THE PROPHETS

Ethical principles are at the core of prophetic teaching. The books of the prophets are rooted in the Torah of Moses. The prophets saw themselves as messengers of the divine word – their task was to denounce the nation for its transgressions and call it to repentance. In all this they pointed to concrete ethical action as the only means of sustaining their covenantal relationship with God. In their view, God demands righteousness and justice above all else.

Emphasis on the moral life was reflected in the prophetic condemnation of cultic practices that were devoid of ethical concern. These passages illustrate that ritual laws are of instrumental value – morality is intrinsic and absolute. The primacy of ethics was also reflected in the prophetic warning that righteous action is the determining factor in the destiny of the Jewish nation. Moral transgressions referred to in such contexts concern exploitation, oppression and the perversion of justice. These transgressions have the potential to bring about the destruction of the nation.

Below *Chabad volunteers sort food for poor Jewish families in Sderot, Israel.*

Above *An old man blessing a child. Such ritual is a feature of Jewish ethical teaching on the relationship between children and adults.*

PROVERBS

The Book of Proverbs reinforces the teaching of the Torah and the prophets. Here wisdom is conceived as a capacity to act morally. It is a skill that can be learned. Throughout the book of Proverbs dispositional traits are catalogued: positive moral types include the righteous person, the wise individual and the upright; negative ones include the evil person, the fool, the mocker and the simpleton. Thus, here as in the rest of Scripture, the moral life is seen as the basis of the faith. Theology is defined in relation to action – it is through the moral life that humanity encounters the divine.

RABBINIC LITERATURE

Rabbinic sages continued this emphasis on the moral life. Convinced that they were the authentic expositors of the Bible, the rabbis amplified scriptural law. In their expansion of the mitzvot, rabbinic exegetes differentiated between the laws governing human relationships to God and those that concern relationships to others. By choosing the moral life, the Jew is able to complete God's work of creation. To accomplish this task the sages formulated an elaborate system of traditions that were written down in the Mishnah, subsequently expanded in the Talmud and eventually codified in the Code of Jewish law. According to rabbinic Judaism, this expansion of biblical law is part of God's revelation. Both the Written and Oral Torah are binding on Jews for all time. Such a conviction implies that the entire corpus of moral law is an expression of the divine will and must be obeyed.

THE CODE OF JEWISH LAW

For Jews the moral law is absolute and binding. In all cases it was made precise and specific – it is God's word made concrete in the life of the nation. The commandment to love one's neighbour embraces all humanity. In the code of Jewish law the virtues of justice, honesty and humane concern are regarded as central to community life. Hatred, vengeance, deceit, cruelty and anger are condemned. The Jew is to exercise loving kindness to all: to clothe the naked, feed the hungry, care for the sick and comfort the mourner. By fulfilling these ethical demands, the Jewish nation can help bring about God's kingdom on earth in which exploitation, oppression and injustice are eliminated.

SIN AND REPENTANCE

IN THE JEWISH TRADITION, REPENTANCE IS REGARDED AS A VIRTUE. SINNERS ARE TO RECOGNIZE THEIR WICKEDNESS, REPENT OF THEIR ACTIONS, AND RESOLVE TO CHANGE THEIR EVIL WAYS.

According to the Jewish tradition, sin is understood in terms of the rejection of God's will. Human beings are thought of as being pulled in two directions: the *yetzer ha-tov*, or 'good inclination', draws individuals towards the good, whereas the *yetzer ha-ra*, or 'evil inclination', binds them in sin. Sin occurs when the evil inclination is overpowering in this struggle.

THE LEGAL SYSTEM

According to Jewish law, there are two types of sin: sins of commission and sins of omission. The former are more serious, but in some cases a positive commandment pushes aside a negative one if this is the only way that it can be carried out. Sins involving the transgression of negative precepts are of two types: offences against God and offences against one's neighbour. Yom Kippur, the Day of Atonement brings about forgiveness for those sins committed against God. But for offences against other human beings, the wrong done to the victim must be put right.

THE EVIL INCLINATION

The yetzer ha-ra is often identified with sexual lust, but the term also applies to physical appetites in general and aggressive desires. It is perceived as the force in human beings that drives them to gratify their instincts. Although it is referred to as 'evil' because it can lead to wrong-doing, it is essential to life. As the midrash remarks: 'Were it not for the yetzer ha-ra, no man would build a house or marry or have children or engage in commerce.' This is the reason why Scripture states: 'And God saw everything that he had made and behold, it was very good' (Genesis 1:31). In a similar vein, there is a legend that the Men of the Great Synagogue wished to kill the yetzer ha-ra. But the yetzer ha-ra warned them that if they were successful, then the world would be destroyed.

Above *The shofar is blown at the end of Yom Kippur, to remind Jews of their sins during the previous year. From a 1400s German manuscript.*

REPENTANCE

Given the ever-present danger of sin, how are human beings to repent of their sinfulness? This is the constant theme of prophetic literature, and it continued into the rabbinic period. According to the 12th-century Jewish philosopher Moses Maimonides (1135–1204), if a person wittingly or unwittingly transgresses any commandment, he is required to repent and turn away from his wickedness and confess his sins to God. How should one confess one's sins? Maimonides wrote: 'He says, "O God! I have sinned, I have committed iniquity. I have transgressed before you by doing such and such. Behold now I am sorry for what I have done and am ashamed and

Below *The serpent tempts Adam and Eve leading to their expulsion from the Garden of Eden. French manuscript of Ovid's* Metamorphoses, *1494.*

I shall never do it again."' True repentance takes place if the sinner has the opportunity of committing once again the sinful act, but he refrains from doing so. The sinner must strive to relinquish his sin, remove it from his thoughts and resolve never to repeat it.

LITERARY WORKS

In addition to the numerous references to repentance in rabbinic sources, there exist medieval works devoted to this theme. One of the most important, *Shaare Teshuvah* (Gates of Repentance) by Jonah ben Abraham Gerondi (1200–64), lists 20 essential features of sincere repentance: remorse; relinquishing the sin; pain for the sin; affliction of the body in fasting and weeping; fear of the consequences of the sin and of repeating it; shame for the sin; submission to God in humility and contrition; gentleness in future conduct; breaking the physical lusts by asceticism; the use by the sinner of that organ with which he sinned to do good; constant self-scrutiny; reflection by the sinner on the pun-

Right *The Kapparot ceremony, in which a chicken is slaughtered and given to the poor, is performed before Yom Kippur, the annual Day of Atonement for sin.*

ishment he deserves; the treatment of minor sins as major; confession; prayer; putting right the sin; almsgiving; the sinner should be conscious of his sin to refrain from repeating the sinful act when the opportunity presents itself; leading others away from sin.

PHYSICAL MORTIFICATION

For the rabbis, repentance is effected by such sincere resolve. There is no need for physical mortification in order to win pardon. The need for such mortification came into Jewish thought in the Middle Ages. The self-tortures required for true repentance are detailed in the ethical work *Rokeah* by Eleazer of Worms (1160–1238). No doubt Christian monasticism of the period influenced such practices. It is recorded that sages used to roll naked in the snow in the depths of winter, smear their bodies with honey and allow themselves to be stung by bees and fast for days on end. However, such extreme practices were only carried out by a relatively few pietists, and in later centuries mortification of the flesh was condemned by the teachers of the Hasidic movement.

Below *Penitence in a German synagogue, 1723. Flagellation was a practice influenced by Christian monks.*

> ### THE HUMAN STRUGGLE
> According to rabbinic Judaism, human beings are engaged in a constant struggle against the evil that exists within themselves. The means whereby they can overcome this destructive force is provided by the Torah and its precepts. In the Talmud we read that when a person submits to the discipline provided by the Torah and studies it, then he will become free of morbid guilt. His life is then unclouded by the fear that the evil within will drag him down and bring his ruin. God has wounded human beings by creating the evil inclination – but the Torah serves as a plaster on the wound.

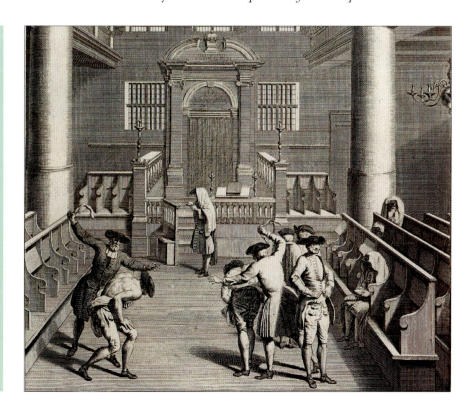

Compassion

JUST AS GOD IS COMPASSIONATE, JEWS ARE TO TREAT OTHERS WITH COMPASSION. ALONGSIDE BENEVOLENCE AND MODESTY, IT IS REGARDED AS AN IDENTIFYING CHARACTERISTIC OF THE JEWISH NATION.

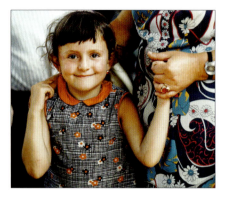

Within the Jewish faith, compassion is regarded a central virtue. Empathy for the suffering of others and the desire to remove their pain are extolled as moral imperatives.

THE TRADITION OF COMPASSION

In Hebrew the word for compassion is *rahmanut*; this has the same root as the word *rehem*, or 'womb'. It denotes the tenderness and pity a mother should have for her child. According to the rabbis, compassion is one of the three distinguishing marks of Jews (the others being benevolence and modesty). This does not imply that non-Jews are less compassionate; rather compassion is understood as part of human nature. When compassion is ascribed to Jews, this simply means that the Jewish people should be true to this basic element of human nature.

The Torah trains Jewry in the ways of compassion; the rabbis maintain that the ancestors of a person lacking in compassion did not stand at the foot of Mount Sinai. Just as God is described in the Bible as compassionate, so too should Jews strive to resemble the creator and be God-like in their sympathy for others.

THE CONCEPT

Rahmanut, or compassion, is understood as the tear which is shed for the sick and the poor; the hand that is outstretched in friendship; concern for the handicapped; commiseration with failure; and prayer for humanity overwhelmed with suffering. Even though rahmanut should result in action, it is in itself desirable. When a person is described as kind and sympathetic, this is compassion. Its opposite is indifference.

DIVINE COMPASSION

A common phrase used in the Talmud for 'God states' is 'The Compassionate says'. The second benediction of the Amidah prayer declares God's compassion for his creatures: 'Thou sustainest the living with loving kindness, revivest the dead with great compassion. Thou supportest the falling, healest the sick, loosest the bound, and keepest thy faith to them that sleep in the dust.'

One of God's names in the Jewish liturgy is *Av ha-Rahamin*, or 'Father of compassion'. The Grace after Meals speaks of God as feeding the world with goodness, with grace, with loving kindness, and with compassion. The end of the Amidah prayer refers twice to God's compassion.

UNIVERSAL RESPONSIBILITY

In Judaism, compassion is regarded as a virtue for all peoples. The prophets criticized non-Israelites for their lack of compassion to one another. Thus Jeremiah described people of the north country who 'lay hold on bow and spear, they are cruel and have no compassion' (Jeremiah 6:23). Amos pronounced God's verdict of doom on those nations who com-

Right *Compassion for the displaced. Fleeing anti-Semitism in the USSR in 1979, a Soviet Jewish child refugee and her mother arrive at Vienna.*

Below *Giving charity at the entrance to the grave of the Moroccan rabbi and Kabbalist Baba Saki in Netivot, Israel.*

mitted atrocities against one another, among them Edom, who 'pursued his brother with the sword, and cast off all pity' (Amos 1:11).

COMPASSION FOR ANIMALS

According to the Jewish tradition, compassion must be extended to all of God's creatures. The principle of compassion toward animals is expressed by the Hebrew concept *tza'ar baalei hayyim*, or 'causing pain to living creatures'.

In the rabbinic tradition, this notion is developed in detail. Hence, according to the dietary laws, the purpose of *shehitah*, or 'ritual slaughter', is to adopt as painless a form of killing as possible. It is the principle of tza'ar baalei hayyim which underlies biblical prohibitions to avoid: muzzling the ox while ploughing (Deuteronomy 25:4), yoking an ox with an ass (22:10), taking the young before sending away the mother bird (22:76-7), and killing an animal and its young on the same day (Leviticus 22:28).

THOSE IN NEED OF COMPASSION

Judaism teaches that those whom fate has treated harshly should become objects of compassion. This applies particularly to the stranger, the widow and the orphan. According to rabbinic Judaism, it is wrong to suggest to those who mourn or suffer in other ways that this is the result of sin.

Although it is important to be self-critical, the temptation to be hard on others should be resisted. It is important in showing compassion that others should not be put to shame. Steps should always be taken not to cause distress. The Talmud, for example, asserts that in the presence of a family of a criminal who has been hanged for murder, one should refrain from referring to anything that is hanging from the ceiling. Even when it is necessary to rebuke someone for his or her action, this should be done with tact.

THE LIMIT OF COMPASSION

Despite the importance of compassion, Judaism rules that there are limits. If a judge comes to the conclusion that a person is in the right and another in the wrong, it would be a perversion of justice if in feeling compassion for the guilty, there should be a miscarriage of justice. Thus the Talmud rules there must be no compassion in a law suit. The law must be decided objectively. What the judge must never do is to bend the law through a miscalculation based on sympathy for the accused.

Compassion is also misapplied when it is expressed to individuals who are deliberately cruel. There is a rabbinic dictum which states that whoever has compassion on the cruel will in the end be cruel to the compassionate.

Right *A 15th-century miniature showing* sheitah, *the ritual slaughter of animals, which is carried out as painlessly as possible. According to Jewish law, animals are to be treated humanely.*

BENEVOLENCE

LIKE THE ATTITUDE OF COMPASSION, THE PRACTICE OF BENEVOLENCE IS OF KEY IMPORTANCE IN THE JEWISH FAITH. COMPASSION SHOULD LEAD TO BENEVOLENCE – THE JEWISH IDEAL IS TO PRACTISE BOTH.

Above *A man begs for alms in Israel. Giving to the needy is a means of exercising benevolence.*

There are two related concepts of benevolence in Judaism. The first is *gemilut hasadim*, or 'bestowing loving kindness', and *tzedakah*, 'charity'. In the Bible, *tzedakah* means righteousness, and is synonymous with *mishpat*, or 'justice'. Yet, by rabbinic times, the word had assumed the meaning of charity. The Talmud states that there are three main differences between gemilut hasadim and tzedakah. Tzedakah is for the benefit of the poor, whereas gemilut hasadim is for everyone. It is not possible to contribute charity to the rich, but gemilut hasadim can be extended to all including the rich. Further, tzedakah refers to a contribution of money. The poor need financial assistance, but gemilut hasadim implies the giving of oneself.

Finally, tzedakah is given to the living. One cannot give charity to the dead. But gemilut hasadim can be extended to those who have died by burying them and attending their funerals.

RABBINIC SOURCES

There are numerous examples of gemilut hasadim in rabbinic literature. Prominent among acts of benevolence is visiting the sick. An entire section of the Shulkhan Arukh, or 'Code of Jewish Law', is devoted to the rules for visiting the sick. The rabbis declared that the Shekhinah, or 'divine presence', is with the sick because God shares in that person's suffering. Comforting mourners is another example of gemilut hasadim. In talmudic times it was a custom to take gifts of food to those who had suffered loss. To attend a funeral is an act of benevolence. Other examples include lending money to help a person with a financial difficulty, speaking words of encouragement, greeting others warmly, helping the aged, and providing hospitality.

RELIEF FOR THE POOR

In giving charity, there should always be an element of benevolence. The poor should be spoken of kindly, and whatever is given should come from the heart without being patronizing. In ancient times there was a complex system of tzedakah: charity overseers made separate collections. One was for a weekly distribution; the other was for those who were passing through a town. Jewish communities provided a number of societies, each with its own charitable purposes.

Below *Comforting mourners at a funeral is an example of* gemilut hasadim. *Italian painting, 1750.*

DEGREES OF CHARITY

According to the medieval philosopher Moses Maimonides, there are eight degrees of charity:

1 A man gives, but is glum when he gives. This is the lowest degree of all.
2 A man gives with a cheerful countenance, but gives less than he should.
3 A man gives, but only when asked by the poor.
4 A man gives without having to be asked, but gives directly to the poor who know therefore to whom they are indebted, and he, too, knows whom he has benefited.
5 A man places his donation in a certain place and then turns his back so that he does not know which of the poor he has benefited, but the poor man knows to whom he is indebted.
6 A man throws his money into the house of a poor man. The poor man does not know to whom he is indebted but the donor knows whom he has benefited.
7 A man contributes anonymously to the charity fund, which is then distributed to the poor. Here the poor man does not know to whom he is indebted, neither does the donor know whom he has benefited.
8 Highest of all is when a man gives money to prevent another person from becoming poor, as by providing him with a job or by lending him money to tide him over during a difficult period. There is no charity greater than this because it prevents poverty in the first instance.

Above *Charitable giving is a sign of benevolence. Donation box in Elijah's Cave synagogue, Haifa, Israel.*

The education of poor children and other religious needs of the poor were also provided.

WHO ARE 'THE POOR'?

In determining who qualifies as a poor person, the Jewish tradition specifies that someone who has 200 zuz (an ancient silver coin) in ready cash or 50 zuz invested in business can no longer be considered poor and entitled to public assistance. A person who has a smaller amount does qualify since he meets the terms of the law. The official rabbinic view concerning the amount to be given is that a person should give a tenth of his income. However, the rabbis discourage giving more than a fifth of their income in case they might become poor themselves. Regarding the question who should come first in terms of preference, the rabbis state that when it is a question of food, a man should come before a woman because he has a family to support. If it is a question of clothing, a woman should take precedence because she suffers greater deprivation if she does not have proper clothes to wear. A person should help his poor relatives before he helps others; similarly, the poor of one's own town should be helped first.

Below *Benevolence includes being with the sick. An Orthodox woman with a baby at the neonatal ICU in Shaarei Tzedek hospital, Jerusalem, Israel.*

Below *Russian Jewish refugees in the Poor Jews Temporary Shelter, Leman Street, east London, 1891.*

THE SPIRITUAL PATH

JUSTICE

THE CONCEPT OF JUSTICE IS FUNDAMENTAL TO THE JEWISH TRADITION. WITHIN RABBINIC SOURCES, JUSTICE IS UNDERSTOOD IN TERMS OF LAW. THE PRACTICE OF GIVING A JUST RULING IS OF CENTRAL IMPORTANCE.

In legal cases, justice comes into operation when two parties are in conflict. For example, two individuals (A and B) might claim ownership of land: one (A) inherited the property from his father, while the other (B) claims he bought it from A and produces evidence to support this assertion. (A), however, denies ever having sold the land and rejects the evidence. In many instances, the available evidence does not provide a basis for reaching a just solution. Yet even here there is a possibility of solving the problem. Jewish law gives the benefit of the doubt to the person who is in possession of the disputed property. The general rule in such a dispute is that, in the absence of factual evidence, the court would not be justified in removing the property from where it is for this would be deciding, without sufficient cause, in favour of one of the parties. Where evidence is insufficient, the court has no right to decide in favour of either party. The only fair procedure is to leave the property where it is until further evidence is available.

CRIME AND PUNISHMENT

In cases of crime, justice involves weighing the claims of society against the criminal. In a just society, the right of the criminal to prey on others should be rejected in favour of the right of society to protect itself. However, justice is involved when society has to determine how far to punish the offender. As far as the punishment affords such protection, it is just. But if it exceeds the degree of protection required, it is unjust to the criminal.

COURTS

Proper courts are necessary for the administration of justice. According to rabbinic sages, this is one of the demands of the Torah made even to non-Jews – it is one of the seven commandments of the sons of Noah to have a legal system. The Hebrew term for a court is *bet din*, or 'house of justice'. For civil cases, a bet din is composed of three Jewish scholars.

Above *The* bet din *shown here is the court of justice of the Sephardic Orthodox community in Israel.*

Here the decision of the majority is followed. Judges must be unbiased, and no one should serve as a judge if one of the parties is a friend or enemy. The laws regarding judges is contained in Deuteronomy 16:18–19: 'Judges and officers shalt thou make thee in all thy gates, which the Lord thy God giveth thee, tribe by tribe; and they shall judge the people with righteous judgement. Thou shalt not wrest judgement; thou shalt not show partiality; neither shalt take a bribe, for a bribe doth blind the eyes of the wise, and pervert the words of the righteous.' Scripture rules that judges must never take bribes, but the rabbis extend this ruling to include any form of gift even from the party he thinks is in the

Below *The Bible records that after God had judged the world and sent the Great Flood, Noah emerged from the Ark. 13th-century mosaic, St Mark's, Venice.*

COMPROMISE

According to rabbinic Judaism, if both parties to a dispute are willing to compromise, this is a form of justice. It is especially desirable in a complicated case, where it is unlikely right is solely on one side, for the parties to compromise with one another. In marital disputes, both parties may be right in some respects and wrong in others. In such cases, the path of compromise is often the best solution.

JUSTICE

Above *Arbitration at a* bet din *(Jewish court that deals with religious questions) in a Czech Jewish community, 1925.*

Above *The tombs of Zechariah and Jehoshaphat in the Kidron Valley, Israel. The prophet Zechariah stressed the importance of justice.*

right. Witnesses in a law suit must be respectable individuals who can be relied on to tell the truth. Anyone who has a bad reputation in money matters is disqualified. No relative is permitted to serve as a witness.

THE VIRTUE OF JUSTICE

In the Mishnah, the first chapter of the Ethics of the Fathers concludes with a statement from Simeon ben Gamaliel: 'On three things the world rests: on justice, truth and peace.' Here the words of the prophet Zechariah are quoted: 'These are the things that ye shall do: Speak ye every man the truth with his neighbour; execute the judgment of truth and in your gates' (Zechariah 8:16). Commentators on this passage remark that where there is truth, there is justice; and where there is justice, there is peace. A peace based on injustice is no peace and will not endure.

JUSTICE IN PRACTICE

It is not only in courts that justice should be found – Judaism demands that Jews must be just in their dealings with one another. The relationship between employer and employee must be based on fairness. Shopkeepers should charge fair prices and not take advantage of customers – they should have just weights and measures. A principle of everyday justice is the demand that no one should take advantage of another's helplessness. The Bible declares: 'Thou shalt not curse the deaf, nor put a stumbling block before the blind, but thou shalt fear thy God: I am the Lord' (Leviticus 19:14). This principle is extended in rabbinic sources to cover every instance of causing harm to another by allowing someone to err through weakness. Thus, the rabbis forbid giving advice one knows to be bad.

Right *A horrifying vision of Hell by Renaissance painter Hieronymus Bosch. Belief in punishment in the Hereafter is a feature of rabbinic theology.*

HOLINESS

WITHIN THE JEWISH FAITH, THE TERM HOLINESS REFERS TO WHAT IS ELEVATED ABOVE THE MATERIAL PLANE. THE CONCEPT RELATES TO A WIDE RANGE OF TOPICS INCLUDING GOD HIMSELF.

According to the Bible, holiness is a characteristic of God. He is apart from the universe and beyond its limitations. In the Book of Isaiah, the Serafim declare: 'Holy, holy, holy is the Lord of Hosts: the whole earth is full of his glory' (Isaiah 6:3). Here Scripture asserts that God is apart from the world he created, yet there are intimations of his holiness everywhere. Anything that is dedicated to God is called holy, such as the Temple or the synagogue. The implication is that to be near God it is necessary to be holy – such an idea is expressed in Leviticus 19:12: 'Speak unto all the congregation of the children of Israel, and say to them: Ye shall be holy; for I the Lord your God am holy.'

Below *A 19th-century drawing of the Western Wall in Jerusalem by Alexandre Bida. Popularly known as the Wailing Wall, Jews regard it as a central holy site of pilgrimage.*

THE JEWISH PEOPLE

According to the Jewish tradition, Jewish communities are referred to as holy: a community is called *kehillah kedoshah*, implying that where Jews are gathered together for sacred purposes, holiness is present. Holiness is not reserved for select individuals, but for persons living normal lives. Jews become holy through their involvement with spiritual affairs: this involves the willingness to give up worldly things as well as a separation from physical pleasures.

SELF-CONTROL

While it is true that Judaism does not encourage asceticism, self-denial is regarded as a virtue. Thus the rabbis stated: 'Sanctify yourself by denying yourself even something of that which is otherwise permitted.' This dictum implies that self-control must be exhibited even when doing what the Torah permits. Whatever the Torah forbids is

Above *Seraphim with wings (Isaiah 6) decorated with an all-seeing eye motif, from a 1537 Romanian fresco.*

forbidden; but this does not mean that one should indulge oneself. Each person must exercise restraint. It is ultimately left to each individual to determine how much self-control should be exercised so that worldly pleasure does not become a barrier to spiritual growth.

THE QUEST FOR HOLINESS

For ordinary people, Judaism prescribes various aids to holiness. Prominent among these are the 'holy days', which include the Sabbath and festivals when secular concerns are set aside and there is time for spiritual refreshment. Yom Kippur (the Day of Atonement) in particular is referred to as Yom ha-Kodesh (the Holy Day); this is a time when the needs of normal physical life are transcended and Jews are called to be near to God. Classical Jewish sources are called 'holy' – by studying these it is possible for the individual to achieve a degree of spirituality. Further, there are various symbols of the Jewish religion including *tefillin*, or 'phylacteries', the *Sefer Torah*, or 'Torah scroll', and the *mezuzah*, or

Right Among the Hasidim, the Rebbe is revered as a holy leader. The Tish (Yiddish: 'table') is a meal taken by the Rebbe with his followers. Seen here in the Betz Yeshiva in Mea Shearim, Jerusalem, 2005.

'rolled parchments with scriptural references', which are connected with holiness. Conversely, there is the need to avoid the opposite of what is holy.

SELF-DENIAL

According to the Talmud, there are two views of self-denial. One is that those who deny themselves are sinners, presumably because they reject legitimate gifts of food and drink which God has given to them. The second is that on the contrary those who pursue self-denial are holy. A number of thinkers hold that it all depends on one's motives. If a person is sincere in the quest for God and appreciates how necessary it is to forego many of life's pleasures to attain a spiritual state, then he is holy.

Below Blowing the shofar to signal the end of the Yom Kippur fast, London, 1929. The High Holy Days begin with Rosh Hashanah and end with Yom Kippur.

But if his reasons are a hatred of life or a wish to demonstrate religious superiority, he is a sinner.

PRAISE OF HOLINESS

Rabbinic sources extol the state of holiness. Hence, the rabbis ruled that before carrying out a *mitzvah*, or 'commandment', it is essential to recite the benediction: 'Blessed art thou, O Lord our God, King of the universe, who has sanctified us with his commandments.' Through observing God's laws we become holy. In rabbinic sources the usual name for God is *Ha-Kadosh Barukh Hu*, or 'The Holy One, blessed be he'. There are degrees of holiness and one should make an attempt to ascend to a higher level. The Zohar states nothing is more holy than the Torah, and both students of the Torah and those who help them to study are to be called holy.

> ### THE GIFT OF HOLINESS
> According to the tradition, the attainment of holiness is not possible through one's own efforts. Rather, it is a gift from God. According to the Talmud, a person who makes a little effort to be holy is given much holiness from on high. In this quest, there are stages of development. As the 2nd-century CE teacher Phinehas ben Yair explained: 'The knowledge of the Torah leads to watchfulness, watchfulness to zeal, zeal to cleanliness, cleanliness to abstinence, abstinence to purity, purity to saintliness, saintliness to humility, humility to the fear of sin, and the fear of sin to holiness. Holiness leads to the holy spirit and the holy spirit leads to the resurrection of the dead.'

CHAPTER 8

MESSIAH AND THE HEREAFTER

For thousands of years the Jewish people have longed for messianic deliverance; sustained by this belief the community has endured persecution and suffering, confident that they will ultimately be rescued from earthly travail. In the Hebrew Bible, God declared to Abraham, Isaac and Jacob that their descendants will inherit a land of their own. In biblical times, such deliverance was understood as pertaining to human history. Yet, with the emergence of rabbinic Judaism, the concept of the Messiah was transformed. In rabbinic sources, sages maintained that prior to the coming of the Messiah, the world would be subject to a series of tribulations defined as the 'birth pangs of the Messiah'. The Messiah would then usher in a period of deliverance, and all Jewish exiles would be returned to Zion. This messianic age would usher in the concept of perfect peace in the end of days. At the end of this messianic period, all human beings would undergo judgement and either be rewarded with heavenly bliss or punished everlastingly.

Opposite The Resurrection of the Dead, *an important expectation of the messianic tradition. From the* Très belles heures *of Notre Dame, 1410, commissioned by the Duc de Berry.*

Above *Section of* The Last Judgment *showing the deceased in Paradise. A painting c.1465 by Giovanni di Paolo, one of the most important painters of the Sienese School.*

Biblical Messiah

IN SCRIPTURE THE MESSIAH IS CONCEIVED OF AS THE REDEEMER OF ISRAEL. AS GOD'S ANOINTED, HE WILL USHER IN A PERIOD OF PEACE IN WHICH ALL PROPHECIES WILL BE FULFILLED.

Biblical history foretells of a future redemption, which will be brought about through an appointed agent of the Lord. According to the early prophets, such a kingly figure will be a descendant of David. Eventually there arose the view that the house of David would rule over Israel as well as neighbouring peoples. Later prophets predicted the destruction of the nation because of its iniquity, yet they were convinced that God would eventually deliver the Israelites and usher in a new redemption of the nation.

THE CONCEPT OF THE MESSIAH

The term 'Messiah' is an adaptation of the Hebrew *Ha-Mashiah*, or 'the anointed'. In time it came to refer to the redeemer at the End of Days.

Below *Ethiopian icon from the 18th–19th century, showing the Messiah celebrating Passover with his disciples.*

Although there are no explicit references to such a figure in the Torah, the notion of the redemption of the Jewish nation is alluded to in the promises made to the patriarchs. Such references form the background to the development of the doctrine of deliverance.

It was in the Book of Samuel that the notion of redemption through a divinely appointed agent was explicitly expressed; here Scripture asserts that the Lord had chosen David and his descendants to rule over Israel to the end of time.

This early biblical doctrine assumed that David's position would endure throughout his lifetime and would be inherited by a series of successors who would carry out God's providential plan. With the fall of the Davidic empire after the death of King Solomon in the 10th century BCE, there arose the view that the house of David would eventually rule over the two divided

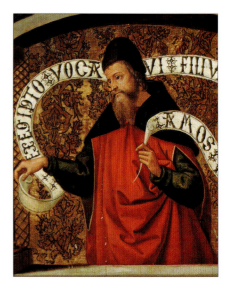

Above *The Prophet Amos, who foretold the coming of the Day of the Lord, by Juan de Borgoña, 1535.*

kingdoms as well as neighbouring peoples. Yet despite such a hopeful vision of Israel's future, the pre-exilic prophets were convinced that the nation would be punished for its iniquity. Warning the people of this impending disaster, the Northern 8th-century BCE prophet Amos spoke of the Day of the Lord when God would unleash his fury against those who had rebelled against him. None the less, the prophets predicted that those who had been led away into captivity would eventually return to their own land.

Below *Prophet Jonah rests under a gourd vine in Nineveh; a 4th-century CE mosaic pavement from the basilica in Aquileia, northern Italy.*

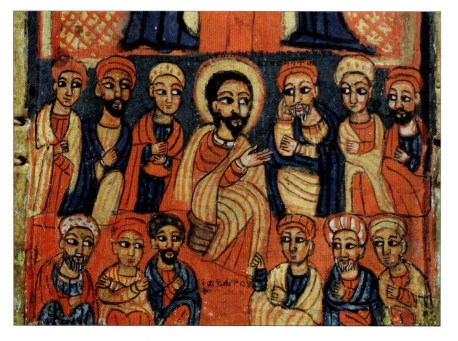

404

Above *The Earthly Paradise, 1607, Jan Brueghel the Elder. According to tradition, the Messiah will bring about God's kingdom on earth.*

REDEMPTION AND REBIRTH

In the Southern Kingdom the 8th-century BCE prophet Isaiah predicted that the inhabitants of Judah would be destroyed because of their iniquity. None the less, he predicted the eventual triumph of God's kingdom on earth. In his view, only a faithful remnant will remain, from which a redeemer will issue forth to bring about a new epoch in the nation's history. A contemporary of Isaiah, the prophet Micah, also predicted that the nation would not be cut off. God, he stated, had a purpose for them in the future. Confident of the restoration of the people, he looked forward to an age of fulfilment and prosperity. Like Isaiah, he predicted a time of messianic redemption. All nations will go to the mountain of the Lord and dwell together in peace. In those days swords will be turned into ploughshares and each man will sit under his vine and fig tree.

POST-EXILIC PROPHECY

Dwelling in Babylon in the 6th-century BCE, the prophet Ezekiel castigated Israel for their iniquity – because they had turned away from God further punishment would be inflicted on them. Yet, despite the departure of God's glory from the Temple, the prophet reassured the nation that it will not be abandoned. In his view, God takes no delight in the death of sinners; what he requires instead is a contrite heart. Using the image of a shepherd and his flock, Ezekiel reassuringly declared that God will gather his people from exile and return them to the Promised Land. In a vision of dry bones, Ezekiel predicts that, although the nation had been devastated, it will be renewed in a future deliverance: a future king will rule over his people and under his dominion Jerusalem will be restored. In a similar vein Second Isaiah offers words of consolation to those who had experienced the destruction of Judah. In place of oracles of denunciation, the prophet offered the promise of hope and restoration.

The Bible thus presents a picture of destruction that is followed by redemption. According to the prophets, the Lord will have compassion upon his chosen people and return them to their former glory. Reassured by these words of comfort, the ancient Israelites were secure in the knowledge that they had not been forsaken. The Messiah will usher in an era of peace and tranquillity. God will be reunited with his people and Zion will undergo future glory. These words of comfort provided the framework for the evolution of the concept of messianic deliverance, which was expanded by Jewish writers during the Second Temple period.

Below *The prophet Samuel anoints David. From a wall painting in the Dura-Europos synagogue, Syria, c. 2nd century CE.*

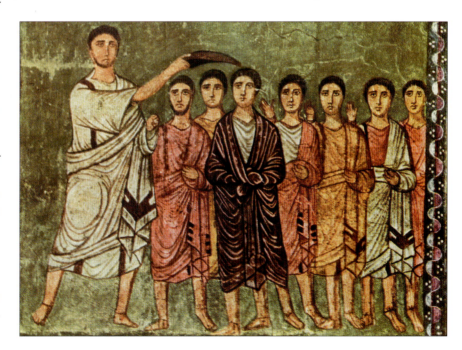

POST-BIBLICAL MESSIAH

DRAWING ON BIBLICAL THEMES, POST-BIBLICAL JEWISH LITERATURE DEVELOPED THE CONCEPT OF THE MESSIAH. IN THESE WRITINGS THE STAGES OF MESSIANIC DELIVERANCE ARE DESCRIBED IN DETAIL.

In post-biblical Jewish literature, which is known as the Apocrypha and Pseudepigrapha, the concept of a future redemption was not forgotten, and there are frequent references to the ingathering of the exiles. Although the messianic predictions in these writings vary considerably, they bear witness to the deep longing for divine deliverance and redemption.

MESSIANIC ANTICIPATION

Throughout the book of Ben Sira composed in the 2nd century BCE, the love of Israel is manifest. In this work the author outlines the various stages of messianic anticipation – the destruction of Israel's enemies, the sanctification of God's name by elevating the Jewish nation, the performance of miracles, the ingathering of the exiles, the glorification of Jerusalem and the Temple, reward for the righteous and punishment for the wicked, and the fulfilment of prophetic expectations. Although Ben Sira does not specify that redemption will come through Davidic rule or an individual Messiah, the author does specify that the house of David will be preserved.

RETURN OF THE EXILES

In the Apocryphal Baruch, which was also written in the 2nd century BCE, there is a reference to the idea that God will bring about the return of the exiles to the land of their fathers once they have turned from their evil ways. Later in the book the author describes Jerusalem, which is to be renewed. The book continues with a description of the return of the exiles: 'Arise, O Jerusalem, and stand upon the height; And look about thee toward the east; And behold thy children gathered from the going down of the sun unto the rising thereof.' Alluding to Second Isaiah's vision of the ingathering of the exiles, the author depicts the re-establishment of Zion in glowing terms.

Above *Head of the Messiah, 1648*, by Rembrandt, who lived in the Jodenbreestraat in Amsterdam, in what was then becoming the Jewish quarter.

THE MESSIANIC AGE

Composed after the destruction of the Temple, the author of the Apocryphal Baruch presented a variety of reflections about the messianic age beginning with the Day of Judgement. During this period the Day of the Lord was identified with the 'birth pangs of the Messiah' – this did not refer to any suffering of the Messiah himself, but to the tribulations of the messianic age. In his view the Holy Lord will come from his dwelling, appear from the highest of

---

THE WORLD TO COME

Unlike other post-biblical work, the Wisdom of Solomon is preoccupied with the world to come, eternal life, and divine retribution. In chapter 3 the author describes the reward for the righteous: 'But the souls of the righteous are in the hand of God; and no torment shall touch them. In the eyes of fools they seemed to die; and their departure was accounted to be their hurt; and their going from us to be their ruin: but they are in peace.' Turning to the destruction of the wicked, he described the future Day of the Lord: 'He shall sharpen stern wrath for a sword: and the world shall go forth with him to fight against his insensate foes; shafts of lightning shall fly with true aim; and from the clouds, as from a drawn bow, shall they leap to the mark.'

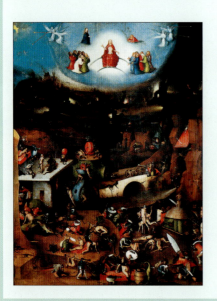

Left *The Last Judgement* by Hieronymus Bosch, 1500.

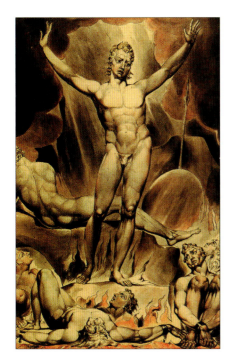

Above *Satan Arousing the Rebel Angels, 1808. An illustration by English visionary William Blake for John Milton's poem* Paradise Lost.

their spirits will grow strong when they see the Messiah, and heaven and earth will be transformed. The elect will then dwell in a new and blessed earth upon which sinners and evildoers will not set foot. The Messiah will be a staff to the righteous and holy and a light to the gentiles. All who dwell on earth will worship and bless him and praise the God of Spirits.

REDEMPTION
Another work of this period, *The Testaments of the Twelve Patriarchs*, consists of stories about the tribal patriarchs. In the Testament of Judah, there are vivid descriptions of messianic redemption. The star of heavens and tread on Mount Sinai. Not only will the wicked be chastised, so too will Satan and the angels who have corrupted the earth be brought to judgement. At the end of days the righteous will be delivered, beget a thousand children, and complete all their days in peace. The whole earth will be filled with righteousness and the fields prosper. The Lord will open the storehouses of heavenly blessing, which he will pour out upon the faithful.

THE MESSIAH
The Ethiopic Book of Enoch, another apocryphal work, continues with a description of the Messiah himself. According to the author, the Messiah existed before the creation of the world, and his dwelling place is under the wings of the God of Spirits where the elect shall pass before him. On that day the Elect One will sit on the throne of glory and choose the occupations of men and their dwelling places; peace will arise and walk in meekness among men. The heavens will be opened and pour out their blessings. The spirit of truth will come upon the children of Judah. A shoot will come forth from the stock of Judah and the rod of righteousness will be in his hand to judge and save all those who call upon him. All the tribes will become one people and have one language. Those who died in grief will arise and awake to everlasting life.

Below *German engraving of the Tribes of Israel around the Ark of the Covenant, c.1630. Tradition says the Messiah will transport the scattered people of Israel back to Zion.*

Rabbinic Messiah

During the rabbinic period, Jewish sages developed the concept of the Messiah: messianic redemption would be divided into a series of stages leading to the World to Come.

Once the Temple had been destroyed and the Jewish people driven out of their homeland, the nation was bereft. In their despair the rabbis longed for a kingly figure who would deliver them from exile and rebuild their holy city. Drawing on messianic ideas that are found in Scripture, the Apocrypha and Pseudepigrapha, they foresaw the coming of a future deliverance when all peoples would be converted to the worship of the one true God.

THE COMING OF THE MESSIAH

In rabbinic sources, sages elaborated the themes found in Scripture as well as in Jewish literature of the Second Temple period. In midrashic collections and the Talmud they formulated a complex eschatological scheme divided into a series of stages. In their view, this chain of events

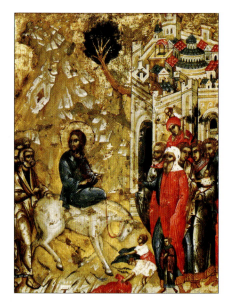

Right *This 1400s Russian icon shows the Messiah's entry into Jerusalem.*

will begin with devastation. As in the Pseudepigrapha, such sufferings are referred to as the 'birth pangs of the Messiah'. As the Talmud states: 'With the footprints of the Messiah, insolence will increase and death reach its height; the vine will yield its fruit but the wine will be costly. There will be none to offer reproof, and the whole empire will be converted to heresy.'

Not only will natural disasters come upon the land, the word of the Lord will also be forgotten during the time of messianic travail. As the Talmud states: 'When our teachers entered the vineyard (school) at Yabneh, they said: "The Torah is destined to be forgotten in Israel, as it is written (Amos 8:11): 'Behold the days come, saith the Lord God, that I will send a famine in the land, not a famine of bread, nor a thirst for water, but of hearing the words of the Lord.'

THE PROPHET ELIJAH

Despite these dire predictions, the rabbis maintained that the prophet Elijah will return prior to the coming of the Messiah to solve all earthly problems. In addition, his role in the messianic era will be to certify the ritual uncleanliness of families that suffered from mixed marriages or forbidden unions, and also to grant permission to hitherto excluded peoples from marrying Jews. Moreover, Elijah's task will be to bring back to the Jewish people those who had been wrongfully excluded from the community. All this is to be done in anticipation of the coming of the Messiah. As a forerunner of messianic redemption, Elijah will announce from the top of Mount Carmel that the Messiah is coming who will initiate the end of history and the advent of God's kingdom on earth.

Left *Gog and Magog. A woodcut for the Martin Luther Bible of 1534, from the workshop of Lucas Cranach the Elder. According to tradition, the Messiah will engage in battle with Gog and Magog.*

MESSIAH BEN JOSEPH

Drawing on earlier conceptions, the rabbis formulated the doctrine of a second Messiah – the son of Joseph – who will precede the King-Messiah, the Messiah ben David. According to legend, this Messiah will engage in battle with God and Magog, the traditional enemies of Israel, and be slain. Only after his defeat will the Messiah ben David arrive in glory. As a hero, the Messiah ben Joseph will be mourned by the Jewish people. As the Talmud states, quoting Scripture: 'And the land shall mourn, every family apart; the family of the house of David apart, and their wives apart' (Zechariah 12:12).

In this final struggle against the nation's enemies, God will act on behalf of Israel. Thus in the midrash, the rabbis maintain that: 'There are four shinings forth: the first was in Egypt, as it is written (Psalm 80:1), "Give ear, O Shepherd of Israel, thou that leadest Joseph like a flock, thou that art enthroned upon the cherubim shine forth"; the second was at the time of the giving of the Law, as it is written (Deuteronomy 33:2), "He shone forth from Mount Paran"; the third will take place in the days of Gog and Magog, as it is written

Below *The Return to Jerusalem, after Raphael. Tradition is that the Messiah will bring about the return of all Jews to the Holy Land.*

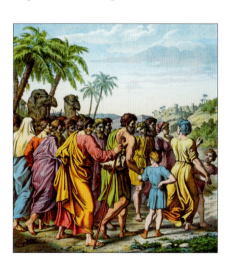

(Psalm 94:1), "Thou God to whom vengeance belongeth shine forth"; the fourth will be in the days of the Messiah (ben David) as it is written (Psalm 50:2), "Out of Zion, the perfection of beauty, shall God shine forth."

Regarding this struggle, the rabbis speculated that God had already revealed the defeat of Gog and Magog to Moses. Hence Rabbi Nehemiah stated that in Numbers 11:26 Eldad and Medad prophesied concerning this battle: 'As it is written (Ezekiel 38:17), "Thus saith the Lord God: Art thou he of whom I spoke in old time by my servants the prophets of Israel, that prophesied in those days [from many] years that I would bring thee against them?"' and so on. According to Simeon ben Yohai (2nd century CE), the war with Gog and Magog was one of the most terrible evils to befall humanity. Yet after Israel is delivered from this struggle, the King-Messiah will come to bring about the messianic age.

MESSIAH BEN DAVID

During the early rabbinic period, numerous legends emerged about the names and personality of this glorious figure. His moral character and spiritual integrity were frequently exalted and with his coming the dispersion

Above *The beloved city. View of Jerusalem, Russian painting, 1821, by Maxim N. Vorobyev.*

would cease. Thus Simeon ben Yohai proclaimed: 'Come and see how beloved is Israel before the Holy One, blessed is he; for wherever they went into exile the Shekinah [God's presence] was with them, as it is written (I Samuel 2:27), "Did I indeed reveal myself unto the house of thy father when they were in Egypt." They went into exile in Babylonia, and the Shekinah was with them, as it is written (Isaiah 43:14), "For your sake I was sent to Babylonia." Likewise, when they shall be redeemed in the future, the Shekinah will be with them, as it is written (Deuteronomy 30:3), "Then the Lord thy God will return with thy captivity." It does not say "will bring back thy captivity" but "will return with thy captivity" – teaching that the Holy one, blessed is he, returns with them from the places of exile.'

Here God is described as accompanying his chosen people in exile, sharing their sufferings. Yet with messianic redemption, the exiles will return to Zion in triumph with God at their head. Clouds of glory shall be spread over them, and they will come singing with joy on their lips.

The Messianic Age and Heaven

AT THE CULMINATION OF THE MESSIANIC AGE, ALL WILL BE JUDGED. THE RIGHTEOUS WILL ENTER HEAVEN. THIS IS DIVIDED INTO A SERIES OF CHAMBERS FOR VARIOUS CLASSES OF INDIVIDUALS.

Rabbinic literature contains frequent speculation about the Days of the Messiah (also referred to as 'The World to Come'). At the end of this messianic period, all human beings will undergo judgement and either be rewarded with heavenly bliss or punished everlastingly. This vision of a future hope was animated by the Jewish conviction that God will not abandon his people.

THE MESSIANIC AGE

In their depictions of the messianic age, Jewish sages stressed that the Days of the Messiah will be totally different from the present world. Concerning the fruitfulness of the harvest, for example, they stressed his era 'is not

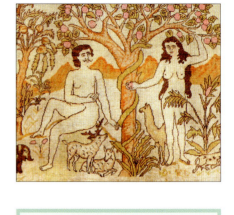

Right *Detail of a Turkish Jewish rug showing Adam and Eve, late 19th century. The Garden of Eden symbolizes heavenly bliss.*

of this world. In this world, there is the trouble of harvesting and treading [grapes]; but in the world to come a man will bring one grape on a wagon or in a ship, put it in the corner of his house, and use its contents as if it had been a large wine cask...There will be no grape that will not contain 30 kegs of wine.'

Speculating on the length of this period, the early rabbinic sages differed as to its duration. Eliezer, for instance, stated: 'The Days of the Messiah will be 40 years; for it is written in one place (Deuteronomy 8:3), "And he afflicted thee, and suffered thee to hunger and fed thee with manna", and in another place it is written (Psalm 90:15), "Make us glad

Below *Adam and Eve driven from the Garden of Eden by James Tissot. In the tradition, Heaven is referred to as* Gan Eden *(Garden of Eden).*

HEAVEN

The principal qualification for divine reward is obedience to God's law; those who are judged righteous will enter into Heaven (Gan Eden). One of the earliest descriptions is in a compilation called Midrash Konen:

There are five chambers for various classes of the righteous. The first is built of cedar with a ceiling of transparent crystal. This is the habitation of non-Jews who become true and devoted converts to Judaism. The second is built of cedar, with a ceiling of fine silver. This is the habitation of the penitents, headed by Manasseh, king of Israel, who teaches them the Law. The third chamber is built of silver and gold, ornamented with pearls ... [here] rest Abraham, Isaac, and Jacob, the tribes, those of the Egyptian exodus, and those who died in the wilderness, headed by Moses and Aaron ... The fourth chamber is made of olive-wood and is inhabited by those who have suffered for the sake of their religion... The fifth chamber is built of precious stones, gold and silver, surrounded by myrrh and aloes. ... This chamber is inhabited by the Messiah ben David, Elijah and the Messiah ben Joseph.

THE MESSIANIC AGE AND HEAVEN

Above *Vine of the Promised Land. 12th-century Romanesque enamel from the Rhenish School.*

according to the days wherein thou hast afflicted us according to the years wherein we have seen evil."' Dosa said: 'Four hundred years; for it is written in one place (Genesis 15:13), "And they shall serve them, and they shall afflict them 400 years"; and in another place it is written (Psalm 90:15), "Make us glad according to the days wherein thou has afflicted us."' Jose the Galilean said: 'Three hundred and sixty-five years, according to the number of days in the solar year, as it is written (Isaiah 63:4), "For the day of vengeance was in my heart, and my year of redemption has come."'

According to another Baraitha: 'It was taught in the school of Elijah: The world will endure 6,000 years; 2,000 in chaos, 2,000 under the Law and 2,000 during the messianic age; but because of our many iniquities time has been lost from the last period (that is, 4,000 years have already passed, yet the Messiah has not yet arrived).' Other traditions, however, stress that such reckoning is fruitless. Hence the Talmud records: 'Seven things are hidden from men. These are the day of death, the day of consolation, the depth of judgement, no man knows what is in the minds of his friend; no man knows which of his business ventures will be profitable, or when the kingdom of the house of David will be restored or when the sinful kingdom will fall.'

WORLD TRANSFORMATION
Despite such disagreement about the length of this period, there was a general acceptance among the sages that at the end of the Days of the Messiah all will be changed. At the close of this era, a final judgement will come upon all humankind. Yet for such judging to take place, all those who have died will need to be resurrected. Given that there is no explicit belief in eternal salvation in the Bible, the rabbis of the post-biblical period were faced with the difficulty of proving that the doctrine of resurrection of the dead is contained in Scripture that they regarded as authoritative. To do this, they employed a number of principles of exegesis based on the assumption that each word of the Torah was transmitted by God to Moses.

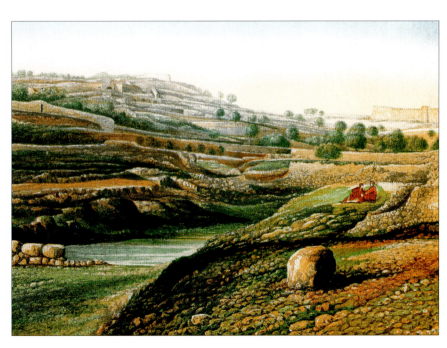

Right *The Valley and Lower Pool of Gihon, Jerusalem, c.1870, by W. Dickens. According to tradition, the exiles will return to Jerusalem at the time of Messianic redemption.*

HELL

ACCORDING TO JEWISH SAGES, THOSE WHO SIN WILL BE CONDEMNED TO ETERNAL TORMENT. RABBINIC LITERATURE DEPICTS THEIR SUFFERING IN GRAPHIC DETAIL.

As with heaven, we find extensive and detailed descriptions of hell in Jewish literature. In the Babylonian Talmud, Joshua ben Levi deduces the division of hell from biblical quotations. This talmudic concept of the sevenfold structure of hell was greatly elaborated in rabbinic sources.

DIVISIONS OF HELL

According to one midrashic source, it requires 300 years to traverse the height or width or the depth of each division, and it would take 6,300 years to go over a tract of land equal in extent to the seven divisions. Each of these seven divisions of hell is in turn divided into seven subdivisions, and in each compartment there are seven rivers of fire, and seven of hail. The width of each is 100 ells (measurement equivalent to about 45 ins/114cm), its depth 1,000, and its length 300. They flow from each other and are supervised by the Angels of Destruction. Besides, in each compartment there are 700 caves, and in each cave there are 7,000 crevices. In each crevice there are 7,000 scorpions. Every scorpion has 300 rings, and in every ring 7,000 pouches of venom from which flow seven rivers of deadly poison. If a man handles it, he immediately bursts, every limb is torn from his body, his bowels are cleft, and he falls upon his face.

PUNISHMENT

Confinement to hell is the result of disobeying God's Torah as is illustrated by a midrash concerning the evening visit of the soul to hell before it is implanted in an individual. There it sees the Angels of Destruction smiting with fiery scourges; the sinners all the while crying out, but no mercy is shown to them. The angel guides the soul and then asks: 'Do you know who these are?' Unable to respond the soul listens as the angel continues: 'Those who are consumed with fire were created like you. When they were put into the world, they did not observe God's Torah and his commandments. Therefore they have come to this disgrace, which you see them suffer. Know, your destiny is also to depart from the world. Be just, therefore, and not wicked, that you may gain the future world.'

VISIT TO HELL

According to this midrash, the soul was not alone in being able to see hell; a number of biblical personages entered into its midst. Moses, for example, was guided through hell by an angel, and his journey there gives us the most complete picture of its torments: 'When Moses and the Angel of Hell entered hell together, they saw men being tortured by the Angels of Destruction. Some sinners were suspended by their eyelids, some by their ears, some by their hands, and some by their tongues. In addition, women were suspended by their hair and their breasts by chains of fire. Such punishments were inflicted on the basis of sins that were

Above *The Ungodly Shall Not Stand* by the 19th-century French artist James Tissot.

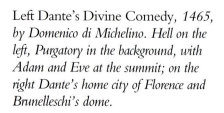

Left Dante's Divine Comedy, *1465, by Domenico di Michelino. Hell on the left, Purgatory in the background, with Adam and Eve at the summit; on the right Dante's home city of Florence and Brunelleschi's dome.*

Right *Fire, the devil and separation in a 19th-century Japanese painting of Hell.*

committed: those who hung by their eyes had looked lustfully upon their neighbours' wives and possessions; those who hung by their ears had listened to empty and vain speech and did not listen to the Torah; those who hung by their tongues had spoken slanderously; those who hung by their hands had robbed and murdered their neighbours. The women who hung by their hair and breasts had uncovered them in the presence of young men in order to seduce them.

In another place, called Alukah, Moses saw sinners suspended by their feet with their heads downwards and their bodies covered with long black worms. These sinners were punished in this way because they swore falsely, profaned the Sabbath and the Holy Days, despised the sages, called their neighbours by unseemly nicknames, wronged the orphan and the widow, and bore false witness. In another section, Moses saw sinners prone on their faces with 2,000 scorpions lashing, stinging and tormenting them. Each of these scorpions had 70,000 heads, each had 70,000 mouths, each mouth 70,000 stings, and each sting 70,000 pouches of poison and venom. So great was the pain they inflicted that the eyes of the sinners melted in their sockets. These sinners were punished in this way because they had robbed other Jews, were arrogant in the community, put their neighbours to shame in public, delivered their fellow Jews into the hands of the gentiles, denied the Torah, and maintained that God is not the creator of the world.

Below *The Angel of Death and Destruction visits Rome during a plague. Painting by Jules-Elie Delaunay, 1869.*

THE NATURE OF HELL

This eschatological scheme, which was formulated over the centuries by innumerable Jewish scholars, should not be seen as a flight of fancy. It was a serious attempt to explain God's ways. Israel was God's chosen people and had received his promise of reward for keeping his law. Since this did not happen on earth in this life, the rabbis believed it must occur in the World to Come. Never did the rabbis relinquish the belief that God would justify Israel by destroying the power of the oppressing nations. This would come about in the messianic age. The individual who had died without seeing the justification of God would be resurrected to see the ultimate victory of the Jewish people. And just as the nations would be judged in the period of messianic redemption, so would each individual. Those deemed wicked would be punished everlastingly. In this way, the vindication of the righteous was assured in the hereafter.

Jewish Messiahs

OVER THE YEARS VARIOUS PSEUDO-MESSIAHS APPEARED, EACH CLAIMING THEY HAD COME TO USHER IN THE MESSIANIC AGE. THEY ALL FAILED TO FULFIL THE EXPECTATIONS OF DELIVERANCE AND REDEMPTION.

JESUS THE MESSIAH

From the Gospels it appears that a Jewish sect of Christians emerged in the 1st century BCE. In consonance with messianic expectations of this period, these believers expected their Messiah to bring about the fulfilment of human history. According to the New Testament, Jesus of Nazareth spent most of his life in Galilee where he preached the coming of the Kingdom of God. After a brief association with John the Baptist, he attracted disciples from among the most marginalized sectors of society to whom he proclaimed his message.

Despite his popularity among the masses, he soon aroused suspicion and hostility from both Jewish and Roman officials and was put to death during the reign of Pontius Pilate in about 30CE. Afterwards his followers believed he had risen from the dead, appeared to them and promised to return to usher in the period of messianic rule. The Jewish community, however, rejected these claims; in their view, Jesus did not fulfil the messianic role as outlined in Scripture and portrayed in rabbinic sources. Despite the growth of the Christian community in the years after Jesus' death, Jews continued to wait for the advent of a Messiah-King who would return the exiles to Zion, resurrect the dead and usher in a period of messianic redemption.

EARLY MESSIAHS

The destruction of Jerusalem and the Temple in 70CE profoundly affected Jewish life and led to intensified longing for messianic deliverance. With the loss of both the Northern and Southern Kingdoms, Jews looked to the advent of the messianic age when the nation would be restored to its ancient homeland. Although mainstream Jewry rejected Jesus as the long-awaited Messiah, the Jewish community continued to long for divine deliverance.

In 132CE a messianic revolt against Rome was led by the warrior Simeon bar Kochba. This rebellion was inspired by the conviction that God sought to overthrow Roman oppression. When this uprising was crushed, Jews put forward the year of messianic deliverance until the 5th century CE. In fulfilment of this prediction, a figure named Moses appeared in Crete, declaring that he would be able to lead Jews across the seas to Judaea. However, after this plan failed, Jews continued to engage in messianic speculation, believing that they could determine the date of their deliverance on the basis of scriptural texts.

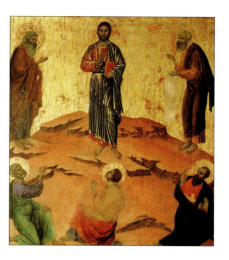

Above *Jesus talking to Moses and Elijah with his disciples Peter, John and James below, c.1278, by Duccio di Buoninsegna.*

Left *Herodium, the ancient palace-fortress built by Herod the Great on a Judean hilltop, who lived at the time of Jesus, the Christian Messiah.*

MEDIEVAL MESSIAHS

During the early medieval period a series of messianic pretenders appeared such as Abu Isa al-Isphani, Serene and Yugdhan, and the traveller Eldad Ha-Dani brought reports of the ten lost tribes, an event which stimulated the Jewish desire to return to Zion. At the end of the 11th and throughout the 12th century a number of pseudo-Messiahs appeared in the Jewish world. In 1096 the arrival of the Crusaders gave rise to widespread excitement among Jews living in the Byzantine empire. As a consequence, the French Jewish community sent a representative to Constantinople to obtain information about the advent of the Messiah. In Khazaria 17 communities marched to the desert to meet the ten lost tribes. In Salonika the arrival of the prophet Elijah was announced. During this period a proselyte, Obadiah, journeyed to northern Palestine, where he encountered the Karaite Solomon

Below *Shabbetai Tzvi, a Jewish rabbi and Kabbalist who claimed to be the long-awaited Jewish Messiah, 1670s.*

Above *Bishop John of Speyer (r. 1090–1104) protecting Jews from Crusaders, from* A Popular History of Germany, *1878. Messianic expectations increased during the Crusades.*

ha-Kohen who declared he was the Messiah and would soon redeem the Jewish nation. In Mesopotamia another messianic figure, ben Chadd, appeared but was subsequently arrested by the caliph of Baghdad.

In the next century a messianic forerunner in Yemen was described by the 12th-century Jewish philosopher Moses Maimonides. But the most important pseudo-Messiah of this period was David Alroy who appeared in 1147 at the time of the Second Crusade. Born in Amadiya, his real name was Menahem ben Solomon, but he called himself David owing to his claim to be king of the Jews. The movement to recognize his messiahship probably began among mountain Jews of the north-east Caucasus before 1121 and gathered momentum in the ferment accompanying the struggles between Christianity and Islam following the First Crusade and during the wars preceding the Second Crusade.

EARLY MODERN MESSIAHS

In the following centuries other messianic pretenders appeared, including Solomon Molko, a 16th-century Kabbalist and mystic. When Rome was sacked in 1527 he believed he saw the signs of impending redemption. In 1529 he preached about the coming of the Messiah. To fulfil the talmudic legend about the suffering of the Messiah, he dressed as a beggar and sat for 30 days, fasting among the sick on a bridge over the Tiber. Eventually he was burned at the stake for refusing to embrace Christianity. After his death, many of his disciples refused to accept that he had died and remained loyal to the belief that he was the long-awaited Messiah.

THE MYSTICAL MESSIAH

At the beginning of the 17th century, Lurianic mysticism had made a major impact on Sephardi Jewry, and messianic expectations had become a central feature of Jewish life. In this milieu, the arrival of Shabbetai Tzvi brought about a transformation of Jewish life and thought. In 1665 his messiahship was proclaimed by Nathan of Gaza. Eventually Shabbetai was brought to court and given the choice between conversion and death. In the face of this alternative, he converted to Islam. Despite this act of apostasy, a number of his followers remained loyal, justifying his action on the basis of Kabbalistic ideas. In subsequent years such belief was continued by various branches of the Shabbatean movement.

ANTI-MESSIANISM

DESPITE THE CENTRALITY OF BELIEF IN THE MESSIAH IN THE JEWISH TRADITION, IN RECENT TIMES THE WORLD HAS WITNESSED THE EROSION OF SUCH CONVICTION.

With the conversion of Shabbetai Tzvi in the 17th century, the Jewish preoccupation with messianic calculation diminished. As time passed, many Jews found it increasingly difficult to believe in a miraculous divine intervention that will change the course of human history.

DISILLUSIONMENT

Not surprisingly the failure of the Messiah to appear through thousands of years of history coupled with the repeated appearance of false messiahs throughout the centuries led to wide-spread disillusionment with the Jewish eschatological hope. As a consequence, the longing for the Messiah who will bring about the end of history appeared to many Jews as a misguided aspiration. Instead, 18th- and early 19th-century Jewry hailed the breaking down of the ghetto walls and the elimination of social barriers between Jews and Christians. In this milieu the belief in the Kingdom of God inaugurated by the Messiah-King receded in importance; in its place the clarion call for liberty, equality and fraternity signified the dawning of a golden age for the Jewish people.

REFORM JUDAISM

Within Reform Judaism in particular, the doctrine of messianic redemption was radically modified in the light of these developments. In the 19th century, Reform Jews interpreted the new liberation in the Western world as the first step towards the realization of the messianic dream. For these reformers messianic redemption was understood in this-worldly terms. No longer, according to this view, is it necessary for Jews to pray for a restoration in Erez Israel. Rather, Jews should view their own countries as Zion, and their political leaders as bringing about the messianic age.

Such a conviction was enshrined in the Pittsburgh Platform of the Reform movement, which was formulated in 1885. As a central principle of the Platform, the belief in a personal Messiah was replaced by the concept of a messianic age, which will come about through social causes: 'We recognize in the modern era of universal culture of heart and intellect the approach of the realization of Israel's great messianic hope for the establishment of the kingdom of truth, justice and peace among all men. We consider ourselves no longer a nation but a religious community, and therefore expect neither a return to Palestine, nor a sacrificial worship under the administration of the sons of Aaron, nor a restoration of any of the laws concerning the Jewish state.'

Above *Moses Hess (1812–75), German socialist who argued for the creation of a Jewish homeland.*

Below *A Rabbinical Disputation by Jacob Toorenvliet (1640–1719). As messianic expectations faded, Jews debated whether a Jewish homeland should be established in Palestine.*

Right *Jewish ghetto in Rovigo, Italy, 1867, by Giovanni Biasin. At the end of the 19th century, Zionists pressed for the creation of a Jewish state to solve the problem of discrimination against Jews in Europe and elsewhere.*

ZIONISM

These sentiments were shared by secular Zionists who similarly rejected the traditional belief in the coming of the Messiah and the in-gathering of the exiles. The early Zionists were determined to create a Jewish homeland, even though the Messiah had not yet arrived.

Rejecting the religious categories of the Jewish past, such figures as Moses Hess (1812–75), Leon Pinsker (1821–91) and Theodor Herzl (1860–1904) pressed for a political solution to the problem of anti-Semitism. In their view there is no point in waiting for a supernatural intervention to remedy Jewish existence.

As Pinsker explained: 'Nowadays, when in a small part of the earth our brethren have caught their breath and can feel more deeply for the sufferings of their brothers; nowadays, when a number of other dependent and oppressed nationalities have been allowed to regain their independence, we, too, must not sit even one moment longer with folded hands; we must not admit that we are doomed to play on in the future the hopeless role of the "wandering Jew" ... it is our bounded duty to devote all our remaining moral force to re-establish ourselves as a living nation, so that we may finally assume a more fitting and dignified role.'

BEYOND MESSIANISM

Such attitudes are representative of a major transformation in Jewish thought. In the past, Jews longed for the advent of a personal Messiah who would bring about the messianic age, deliver the Jewish people to their homeland, and inaugurate the fulfilment of human history. Although this doctrine continues to be upheld by a large number of devout Orthodox Jews, it has been largely eclipsed by a more secular outlook. Most contemporary Jews prefer to interpret the messianic hope in naturalistic terms, abandoning the belief in the coming of the Messiah, the restoration of the sacrificial system, and the idea of direct divine intervention. On this view, it is argued that Jews should free themselves from the absolutes of the past. Jewish views about the Messiah should be seen as growing out of the life of the people. In the modern world, these ancient doctrines can be superseded by a new vision of Jewish life, which is human-centred in orientation. Rather than await the coming of a divinely appointed deliverer who will bring about peace and harmony on earth, Jews should themselves strive to create a better world for all peoples.

Right *This Israeli poster of Theodor Herzl celebrates the 50th anniversary of the meeting of the first Zionist Congress in Basle, Switzerland, in 1897, which later became the World Zionist Organization.*

Death of the Afterlife

IN THE PAST JEWS BELIEVED EARTHLY LIFE WAS NOT THE END. AFTER DEATH THE RIGHTEOUS WOULD BE REWARDED AND THE WICKED PUNISHED. SUCH A CONVICTION HAS LOST ITS HOLD ON MODERN JEWISH CONSCIOUSNESS.

On the basis of the scheme of salvation and damnation – which is at the heart of rabbinic theology throughout the centuries – it might be expected that modern Jewish theologians of all shades of religious observance and opinion would attempt to explain contemporary Jewish history in the context of traditional eschatology. This, however, has not happened: instead many Jewish thinkers have set aside doctrines concerning messianic redemption, resurrection, final judgement and reward for the righteous and punishment for the wicked.

JEWISH THEOLOGY

This shift in emphasis is in part due to the fact that the views expressed in the narrative sections of the midrashim and Talmud are not binding. All Jews are obliged to accept the divine origin of the law, but this is not so with regard to theological concepts and theories expounded by the rabbis. Thus it is possible for a Jew to be religiously pious without accepting all the central beliefs of mainstream Judaism. Indeed, throughout Jewish history there has been widespread confusion as to what these beliefs are. In the 1st century BCE, for example, the sage Hillel stated that the quintessence of Judaism could be formulated in a single principle: 'That which is hateful to you, do not do to your neighbour. This is the whole of the Law; all the rest is commentary.' Similarly, in the 2nd century CE, the Council of Lydda ruled that under certain circumstances the laws of the Torah may be transgressed in order to save one's life, with the exception of idolatry, murder and unchastity.

PRINCIPLES OF JEWISH FAITH

In both the above cases, the centre of gravity was in the ethical rather than the religious sphere. However, in the medieval period Moses Maimonides (1135–1204) formulated what he considered to be the 13 principles of the Jewish faith. Other thinkers, though, challenged this formulation. Hasdai Crescas (1340–1410), Simon ben Zemah Duran (1361–1444),

Above *Joseph Hertz (1872–1946) was born in Hungary, became chief rabbi of Great Britain, and wrote on the theme of resurrection.*

Below *A 19th-century photograph of the city of Lydda, where the Council of Lydda ruled c. 135 CE that in certain circumstances the laws of the Torah could be transgressed in order to save life.*

DEATH OF THE AFTERLIFE

Above *Sigmund Freud (1865–1939), Austrian Jewish psychologist, was critical of traditional Jewish theology.*

Joseph Albo (c.1380–c.1444) and Isaac Arami elaborated different creeds, and some thinkers argued that it is impossible to isolate from the whole Torah essential principles of the Jewish faith. As David ben Solomon Ibn Abi Zimra (c.1479–1573) stated: 'I do not agree that it is right to make any of the perfect Torah into a "principle" since the whole Torah is a "principle" from the mouth of the Almighty.' Thus when formulations of the central theological tenets of Judaism were propounded, they were not universally accepted since they were simply the opinions of individual teachers. Without a central authority whose opinion in theological matters was binding on all Jews, it has been impossible to determine the correct theological beliefs in Judaism.

REINTERPRETING MESSIANIC REDEMPTION

Given that there is no authoritative bedrock of Jewish theology, many modern Jewish thinkers have felt fully justified in abandoning the various elements of traditional rabbinic eschatology, which they regard as untenable. The doctrine of messianic redemption, for example, has been radically modified. In the 20th century, Reform Jews interpreted the new liberation in the Western world as the first step towards the realization of the messianic dream. But messianic redemption was understood in this-worldly terms. No longer, according to this view, was it necessary for Jews to pray for a restoration in Erez Israel; rather they should view their own countries as Zion and their political leaders as bringing about the messianic age. Secular Zionists, on the other hand, saw the return to Israel as the legitimate conclusion to be drawn from the realities of Jewish life in Western countries, thereby viewing the State of Israel as a substitute for the Messiah himself.

THE JEWISH HOPE

Traditional rabbinic eschatology has thus lost its force for a large number of Jews in the modern world, and in consequence there has been a gradual this-worldly emphasis in Jewish thought. Significantly this has been accompanied by a powerful attachment to the Jewish state. For many Jews, the founding of Israel is the central focus of their religious and cultural identity. Jews throughout the world have deep admiration for the astonishing achievements of Israelis in reclaiming the desert and building a viable society. As a result, it is not uncommon for Jews to equate Jewishness with Zionism, and to see Judaism as fundamentally nationalistic in character – this is a far cry from the rabbinic view of history that placed the doctrine of the hereafter at the centre of Jewish life and thought.

Left *Partying in a Tel Aviv nightclub. For many young Jews, enjoying this life is more important than the afterlife.*

> ### RESURRECTION
> The earlier doctrine of the resurrection of the dead has in more recent times been largely replaced by the belief in the immortality of the soul.
>
> The original belief in resurrection was an eschatological hope bound up with the rebirth of the nation in the Days of the Messiah, but as this messianic concept faded into the background, so did this doctrine. For most Jews, physical resurrection is simply inconceivable in the light of a scientific understanding of the world. As the former Chief Rabbi of Great Britain, Joseph Herman Hertz (1872–1946) wrote: 'Many and various are the folk beliefs and poetical fancies in the rabbinical writings concerning Heaven, Gan Eden, and Hell, Gehinnom. Our most authoritative religious guides, however, proclaim that no eye hath seen, nor can mortal fathom, what awaiteth us in the Hereafter; but that even the tarnished soul will not forever be denied spiritual bliss.'

PART III

JEWISH PRACTICE

According to the Jewish heritage, God revealed the Five Books of Moses to Moses on Mount Sinai. Traditional Judaism maintains that in addition Moses received the Oral Tradition. This was passed down from generation to generation and was the subject of rabbinic debate. This first authoritative compilation of the Oral Law was the Mishnah, composed by Yehuda Ha-Nasi in the 2nd century CE. In subsequent centuries sages continued to discuss the content of Jewish law; their deliberations are recorded in the Palestinian and Babylonian Talmuds.

In time, Jewish scholars felt the need to produce codes of Jewish law so that all members of the community would have access to the legal tradition. The most important code, the *Shulkhan Arukh*, was composed in the 16th century by Joseph Caro, together with glosses by Moses Isserles. This has served as the standard Code of Jewish Law for Orthodox Jewry until the present day. Alongside the Orthodox community, the various non-Orthodox branches of Judaism draw on this sacred tradition in their reinterpretation of Jewish observance for the modern world.

Opposite Members of a Hasidic community dancing on Simchat Torah as the scrolls of the Torah are carried round a synagogue at Bnei Brak, Israel.

Above A 17th-century illustration from the Barcelona Haggadah of the Passover Seder meal, celebrated in Jewish homes each year.

CHAPTER 9

WORSHIP

Throughout the history of the nation, Jews have turned to God for comfort and support. In ancient times the Tabernacle and the Temple served as the focus of religious life; subsequently the synagogue became the place for public worship.

The Jewish year consists of 12 months based on the lunar cycle, and is 354 days long. Throughout the year, believers gathered together to recite the traditional liturgy. According to Scripture, God rested on the Sabbath day; as a consequence, the Jewish people are to rest from all forms of labour on *Shabbat*, or 'the Sabbath'. During the rabbinic era, Jewish sages formulated 39 categories of work that were later interpreted by scholars as forbidding a wide range of activities. For Orthodox Jews these regulations are authoritative and binding. Alongside the Sabbath, the pilgrim festivals (Passover, Sukkot and Shavuot) occupy a central place in the Jewish calendar. In ancient times pilgrims went to offer sacrifices in the Temple in Jerusalem. Later special prayers were recited in the synagogue, and each festival has its own special liturgical characteristics, ceremonies and customs.

Opposite Morning service in a synagogue in Teaneck, New Jersey, USA. Young boys gather round the Scrolls of the Law.

Above Jews praying in the Portuguese Sephardic Synagogue in Amsterdam, the Netherlands, built in 1671 by Jews who escaped from the Inquisition in Iberia.

Jewish Calendar

Running from Nisan to Adar, a variety of festivals are celebrated throughout the Jewish year, many of which commemorate historical events in the life of the nation.

According to tradition, the first work of chronology is the *Seder Olam* attributed to Yose ben Halafta (2nd century CE). In this work, calculation is based on biblical genealogical tables, the length of lives recorded in the Hebrew Bible, and the creation of the world in six days. On this basis the year of creation was 3761BCE. The Jewish calendar is lunar, not solar, consisting of a lunar year of 12 months of 29 or 30 days. The year is thus 354 days. The shortage of 11 days between lunar and solar years is made up by adding a 13th month (Adar 2) in certain years. In 356CE the sage Hillel II introduced a permanent calendar based on mathematical and astrological calculations.

CALENDAR REFORM

In modern times there have been several attempts at calendar reform so as to arrange a calendar with the same number of days in each month. This would result in a uniform pattern so that the same date would fall on the same day of the week each year. The year would be divisible into two equal halves and four quarters. The main objection to such an alteration is that it would disturb the regularity of a fixed Sabbath after every six working days. If the reform were carried out, it would fall on a different day each year.

THE MONTHS

There are 12 months in the Jewish calendar. New Year (Rosh Hashanah) takes place in the seventh month in autumn and begins the spiritual year.

1 NISAN

Shabbat ha-Gadol This Sabbath takes place before Passover.
14 The Fast of the First-Born A fast is observed by every male first-born in gratitude for God's deliverance during the Exodus.
15–22 Passover Passover lasts for eight days and commemorates God's deliverance of the Israelites from Egypt. It is also referred to as the festival of unleavened bread. This term refers to the unleavened bread which the Israelites baked when they fled from the Egyptians.
16 The Counting of the Omer The Israelites were commanded to count 49 days from the second day of Passover when the omer was brought to the Temple. The 50th day was celebrated as a wheat harvest.
17–20 Hol Hamoed Intermediate days of Passover and Sukkot which are observed as semi-holy days.

Left *Rabbis drinking with pilgrims at Lag B'Omer at the El Ghriba synagogue, Djerba, Tunisia.*

Above *Passover lamb being taken into a synagogue. Copper plate from the Verdun Altar, Klosterneuburg, of 1181 made by Nicholas of Verdun.*

23 Isru Hag Day after the festival of Passover.
28 Yom Yerushalaim Jerusalem Reunification Day.

2 IYYAR

5 Yom ha-Atsmaut Celebration of the day of the State of Israel's independence.
Second, fifth and seventh days of the week During the month of Iyyar and Marheshvan these days are kept as fast days to atone for any sins committed during the preceding Passover or Sukkot.
14 Second Passover The Paschal lamb was to be sacrificed only on 14 Nisan. Those who were unable to make this sacrifice because they were in a state of ritual impurity or a long way from home could make this offering on 14 Iyyar.
18 Lag B'Omer The period between Passover and Shavuot was a time of tragedy. During the days of Akiva a plague occurred among his disciples and only stopped on 18 Iyyar. This day became known as the Scholars' Feast. The day itself is a time of joy when pilgrims go to Meron where Simeon ben Yohai (2nd century CE) is buried.

3 SIVAN

3–5 Three Days of Bordering This day commemorates the time when the Israelites prepared themselves for the revelation on Mount Sinai.

6–7 Shavuot This festival is celebrated seven weeks after the bringing of the omer on the second day of Passover. It commemorates the giving of the law on Mount Sinai.

8 Isru Hag Day after Shavuot.

4 TAMMUZ

17 The Fast of the 17 of Tammuz This fast commemorates the day when the walls of Jerusalem were breached by the Romans as well as other disasters.

5 AV

Sabbath of the 'Vision' The Sabbath before Tishah B'Av.

9 Tishah B'Av This fast commemorates the day when the Temple was destroyed by Nebuchadnezzar (604–561BCE), and the Second Temple by Titus (ruled 79–81CE).

Sabbath of 'Comfort Ye' The Sabbath after Tishah B'Av.

15 The 15 of Av A joyous day in ancient times when the people participated in a wood offering.

6 ELLUL

7 TISHRI

1–10 Ten Days of Penitence The period begins with Rosh Hashanah and concludes with Yom Kippur. It is a time for spiritual cleansing.

1–2 Rosh Hashanah The New Year festival.

3 Fast of Gedaliah This fast commemorates the assassination of Gedaliah, the Governor of the Jews appointed by Nebuchadnezzar.

10 Yom Kippur Day of Atonement.

15–21 Sukkot This festival commemorates God's protection of the Israelites in the wilderness. Sukkot, or 'booths', are built during this festival to symbolize the temporary shelter used by the Israelites.

17–21 Hoi Hamoed Atzeret Intermediate days of the festival, observed as semi-holy days.

21 Hoshanah Rabbah Name given to the seventh day of Sukkot since seven circuits are made around the Torah while Hoshanah prayers are recited.

22–3 Shemini Atzeret This two-day festival is observed at the end of Sukkot. A special prayer for rain is recited during the Musaf or additional service.

23 Simchat Torah On this festival the annual cycle of Torah readings is completed and begun again.

24 Isru Hag The day after the Sukkot festival.

8 MARHESHVAN

Second, fifth and seventh During Iyyar and Marheshvan these days are kept by some as fast days to atone for sins committed during Sukkot.

9 KISLEV

25–2/3 of Tevet Hanukkah This festival is celebrated for eight days. It commemorates the re-dedication of the Temple by the Maccabees after the Seleucids were defeated in 165BCE.

10 TEVET

10 The Fast of 10 Tevet This day commemorates the siege of Jerusalem by Nebuchadnezzar.

11 SHEVAT

15 New Year for Trees Joyous festival celebrated in Israel by the planting of trees.

Sabbath relating to the shekels Sabbath that takes place before or on 1 Adar.

12 ADAR

Sabbath of 'Remember' Sabbath before Purim.

13 Fast of Esther This fast commemorates Queen Esther's fast before she asked Ahasuerus (486–465BCE) to revoke his decree against the Jews.

14 Purim This festival commemorates the defeat of Haman's plot against the Jews.

15 Shushan Purim This festival commemorates the victory of the Jews of Shushan.

Sabbath of the Red Heifer Sabbath that occurs on the first or second Sabbath after Purim.

Sabbath of the Month Sabbath that occurs before or on 1 Nisan.

NAMES OF THE MONTHS

The names of the months in the Jewish year are of Babylonian origin. In the pre-exilic books they are identified by their numerical order. Concerning the days themselves, they begin at sunset and end at nightfall on the next day. As a result, the Sabbath begins at sunset on Friday and ends the next night when three stars appear. This same pattern apples to all holy days. The Hebrew date is normally given by indicating the name of the month first; this is followed by the date and then the year. When the year is written in Hebrew, it is usual to omit the thousands.

Above *Calendar page from a Spanish Bible manuscript of 1301.*

Places of Worship

AT FIRST, JEWISH WORSHIP TOOK PLACE IN THE SANCTUARY. LATER THE TEMPLE BECAME THE CENTRAL PLACE OF PRAYER. AFTER ITS DESTRUCTION IN 70CE, IT WAS REPLACED BY THE SYNAGOGUE.

Above *An imaginary view of the Temple of Solomon. Copper engraving by Pierre Mariette, 1670.*

Throughout their history Jews have gathered together for worship. In the desert the ancient Israelites transported a portable shrine; this was subsequently superseded by the Temple built in Jerusalem by King Solomon (10th century BCE). In later centuries the synagogue served as a meeting place for prayer and study.

SANCTUARY
Scripture relates that Moses made a portable shrine (sanctuary) following God's instructions in the Book of Exodus. This structure travelled with the Israelites in the desert and was placed in the centre of the camp in an open courtyard. The fence surrounding it consisted of wooden pillars from which a cloth curtain was suspended. Located in the eastern half of the courtyard, the Sanctuary measured 50 cubits by 10 cubits (about 75 x 15 ft/23 x 4.5m; at its end stood the Holy of Holies, which was separated by a veil hanging on five wooden pillars on which were woven images of the cherubim. Inside the Holy of Holies was the Ark of the Covenant, the table on which the shewbread was placed, the incense altar, and the *menorah*, or 'candelabrum'. In the courtyard there was also an outer altar on which sacrifices were offered, as well as a brass laver for priests.

TEMPLE
In time this structure was superseded by the Temple, which was built by King Solomon in Jerusalem in the 10th century BCE. From the time of Solomon's reign, the Temple served as the site for prayer and the offering or sacrifices to God. In addition to the communal sacrifices made daily, there were additional communal sacrifices offered on the Sabbath, festivals, and the New Moon. The Temple was also the site to which the *omer*, or the first barley measure harvested on the second day of Passover, and the first fruits were brought on Shavuot. On Passover all families were required to come to Jerusalem to offer the paschal sacrifice.

ORIGINS OF THE SYNAGOGUE
In the 6th century BCE the Temple was destroyed by the Assyrians when they invaded the country. After the exile during the same century, Jews in Babylonia established a new institution for public worship: the synagogue (meaning 'assembly' in Greek). There they came together to study and pray. On their return to Jerusalem in the latter part of the 6th century BCE, the Jewish populace continued to gather in synagogues as well as offer sacrifice in the Temple. Thus the synagogue developed alongside the Second Temple.

THE SYNAGOGUE
In the synagogue itself, there are a number of elements, which parallel the Sanctuary and the Temple. Firstly, there is the Holy Ark – this is symbolic of the Holy of Holies, the most important part of the Sanctuary and the Temple. The Ark itself is located on the eastern wall so that Jews are able to pray in the direction of the Temple in Jerusalem. Secondly, the eternal light hangs before the Ark. This represents the lamp that burned continually in the Sanctuary.

The third major element in the synagogue is the Torah scroll, which is placed in the Ark. The Torah is written in Hebrew by a scribe who uses a special ink on parchment. A breastplate covers the Torah, and over it hangs a pointer, which is used for the chanting or recitation of the Torah. There are two rollers on which the Torah scroll is wrapped; in addition, various ornaments, usually in silver, adorn the Scroll. These are symbolic of the ornaments of the High Priest in Temple times.

A fourth feature of the synagogue is the *bimah*, or 'platform', which was in previous times used only for the reading of the Law and the Prophets,

Below *A modern synagogue in Teaneck, New Jersey, USA, with a beautiful stained-glass window.*

PLACES OF WORSHIP

Above *Siege of Jerusalem by Assyrians under Nebuchadnezzar, 587*BCE. *From Merian's Illustrated Bible, c.1627.*

Above *Eternal light or* Ner Tamid *burns before the Ark in a synagogue in Westchester County, New York.*

ter. Men attended services three times a day, and the local rabbinic court frequently convened there. Classes took place in the sanctuary or in an annexe, and oaths as well as bans of excommunication were pronounced in its environs. In addition, communal offices, the ritual bath, a library, a hospice for travellers and a social hall were located in synagogue rooms or adjacent buildings.

THE MODERN PERIOD

In the early modern period, synagogues were constructed in Western European ghettos; Poland's wooden synagogues influenced synagogue architecture all over Eastern Europe. From the 19th century, reformers influenced major innovations. Reform synagogues (temples) were large, imposing buildings with organs. The section for women was abolished, and decorum during the service was emphasized. Head coverings for men were abandoned, and the reader's platform was shifted from the centre to the area in front of the Ark.

Yet, despite such changes, Reform temples, together with Orthodox synagogues occupy a major role in Jewish life.

as well as for rabbinical sermons. Finally, men and women sit separately; the women are usually seated in a balcony during the service.

SYNAGOGUE HISTORY

According to tradition, there were about 400 synagogues in Jerusalem when the Second Temple fell. Although this figure may be exaggerated, there is considerable evidence of synagogue building in the Jewish world during the Second Temple period. By the 5th century BCE it was widely attested that wherever Jews lived they built structures which became the focus of Jewish life and thought. Unlike the Temple, where ritual was carried out exclusively by priests, the only requirement for synagogue worship was the presence of a *minyan*, or 'quorum of ten men'. Any service could be led by a lay person. This shift away from Temple hierarchy marked a fundamental democratization of Jewish life.

THE MIDDLE AGES

The medieval synagogue dominated Jewish life; in most communities it was at the heart of the Jewish quar-

Right *Moses receives the Tablets of the Law, builds the Ark of the Covenant and makes offerings. From the medieval Bible by Guiars de Moulins.*

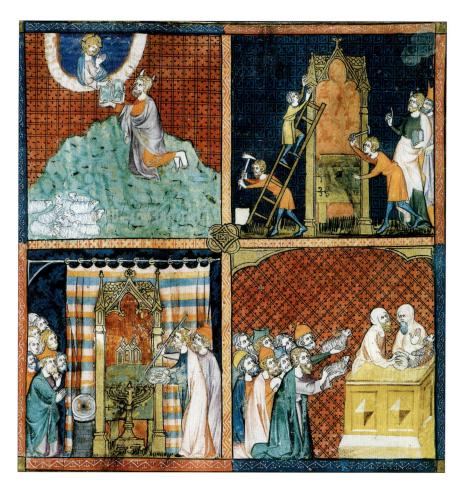

WORSHIP

ACTS OF WORSHIP MAY BE PERFORMED INDIVIDUALLY OR IN A GROUP WITH OR WITHOUT A LEADER. THROUGH IT JEWS EXPRESS THEIR JOYS, SORROWS AND HOPES, ESPECIALLY IN TIMES OF CRISIS AND CALAMITY.

In the Hebrew Bible, the patriarchs often addressed God through personal prayer. Abraham, for example, begged God to spare Sodom since by destroying the whole population the righteous as well as the wicked would be destroyed. At Beth-El Jacob vowed: 'If God will be with me, and will keep me in this way that I go, and will give me bread to eat, and raiment to put on ... then shall the Lord be my God (Genesis 28:20–1). After Israel made a golden calf to worship, Moses begged God to forgive them for this sin (Exodus 32:31–2).

THE TEMPLE

In ancient times the Temple in Jerusalem served as the central focus for worship. Twice daily – in the morning and afternoon – the priests offered sacrifices while the Levites chanted psalms. Additional services were added on Sabbaths and festivals. As time passed it became customary to include other prayers with the recitation of the Ten Commandments and the Shema (Deuteronomy 6:4–9, 11, 13–21; Numbers 15:37–41). When the Temple was destroyed in 70 CE, sacrificial offers were replaced by the prayer service in the synagogue. To enhance uniformity, the sages introduced fixed periods for daily prayer, which corresponded with the times sacrifices had been offered in the Temple. By the completion of the Talmud in the 6th century CE, the major elements of the synagogue service were established. In the 8th century CE the first prayer book was composed by Rav Amram, Gaon of Sura.

THE ORDER OF SERVICE

Jews are commanded to recite the Shema during the morning and evening services in accordance with the commandment, 'You shall talk of them when you lie down and when you rise' (Deuteronomy 6:7), The first section (6:4–9) opens with 'Shema Yisrael' ('Hear, O Israel: the Lord our God is one Lord'). This teaches the unity of God, and emphasizes the duty to love God, meditate on his commandments and impress them on one's children. In addition, it contains laws about the tefillin

Above *An engraving by Bernard Picart showing the Simchat Torah ceremony at an Amsterdam synagogue, Holland.*

Below *A watercolour by Richard Moser of the elaborately decorated interior of a synagogue in Vienna, 1920.*

Above *Amsterdam Jews at Yom Kippur, 1723, in the Second Synagogue built when the Great Synagogue proved too small.*

and the mezuzah. Tefillin consists of two black leather boxes containing scriptural verses, which are bound by black leather straps on the arm and forehead in accordance with the commandment 'you shall bind them as a sign upon your hand, and they shall be frontlets between your eyes' (Deuteronomy 6:8). They are worn by men during morning prayer except on the Sabbath and festivals. The mezuzah consists of a piece of parchment containing two paragraphs of the Shema, which is placed into a case and fixed to the right-hand side of an entrance. Male Jews wear

Below *Stained-glass window featuring the menorah at the Great Synagogue in Jerusalem, Israel.*

an undergarment with fringes (the smaller tallit) and a larger tallit, or 'prayer shawl', for morning services. The silk or wool shawl has black or blue stripes with tzizit, or 'fringes', at each of the four corners.

A central feature of the synagogue service is the *Shemoneh Esreh*, or '18 Benedictions' or the Amidah. Composed over a long period of time, the prayers received their full form in the 2nd century CE. They consist of 18 separate prayers plus an additional benediction dealing with heretics. The first and last three benedictions are recited at every service; the 13 other prayers are recited only on weekdays. On Sabbaths and festivals they are replaced by one prayer dealing with the Holy Day. Other prayers are added on special occasions.

THE SYNAGOGUE SERVICE

From earliest times, the Torah was read in public gatherings; later regular readings of the Torah on Sabbaths and festivals were instituted. The entire Torah is divided into 54 sections, each of which is known as a *sidrah*. Each of these sections is subdivided into parashot, or 'portions'. Before the reading of the Torah in the synagogue, the Ark is opened and the Torah Scroll is removed.

The number of men called up to the reading on the Sabbath is seven; on other occasions the number varies. In former times those who were called up to the Torah read a section of the weekly sidrah; later an expert in Torah reading was appointed to recite the entire sidrah, and those called up recited blessings instead. After the reading of the Torah, a section from the *Haftarah*, or 'prophetic books', is recited. Once the Torah scroll is replaced in the Ark, a sermon is usually delivered based on the sidrah of the week. Another central feature of the synagogue service is the kaddish prayer. Written in Aramaic, it takes several forms in the prayer book and expresses the hope for universal peace under the kingdom of God – this prayer is recited by mourners at the end of the service.

THE MODERN PERIOD

The traditional liturgy was essentially the same until the Enlightenment. Reformers in Central Europe then altered the worship service and introduced new prayers into the liturgy. They decreed that the service should be shortened and conducted in the vernacular as well as in Hebrew. In addition, they introduced melodies accompanied by a choir and organ and replaced the chanting of the Torah with the recitation of the sidrah. Prayers viewed as anachronistic were abandoned, and prayers of a particularistic character were amended so they became more universalistic in scope.

In recent years, all groups across the Jewish spectrum have produced new liturgies. Moreover, a wide range of occasional liturgies exist for camps, youth groups and *havurot*, or 'informal prayer groups'. Among non-Orthodox denominations there is a growing emphasis on more egalitarian liturgies with gender-free language and an increasing democratic sense of responsibility.

Below *Rabbi carries the Torah scrolls during a Yom Kippur service in the Great Synagogue, Budapest, Hungary.*

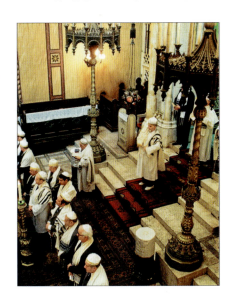

SABBATH

WITHIN THE JEWISH FAITH, SABBATH DAY OBSERVANCE IS OF PARAMOUNT IMPORTANCE. JEWS GATHERED TOGETHER TO COMMEMORATE THE CREATION OF THE UNIVERSE AND GOD'S SPECIAL DAY OF REST.

According to Genesis, God finished the work he had made on the seventh day. He blessed the seventh day and hallowed it and ceased his labour. Genesis 2:1–3 is the basis of the decree no work is to be done on the Sabbath.

During their time in the wilderness, the Israelites were commanded to observe the Sabbath. They were told to work on five days and collect a single portion of manna. On the sixth day they were told to collect a double portion for the following day; it was to be 'a day of solemn rest, a holy sabbath of the Lord' (Exodus 16:23). On the seventh day when several people looked for manna, the Lord said: 'How long do you refuse to keep my commandments and my laws? See! The Lord has given you the sabbath, therefore on the sixth day He gives you bread for two days; ... let no man go out of his place on the seventh day' (Exodus 16:23–9).

Below *Table set for the Sabbath meal with candles, wine and a challah loaf.*

Several weeks later God revealed the Ten Commandments, including regulations concerning the Sabbath day: 'Remember the sabbath day, to keep it holy. Six days you shall labour, and do all your work, but the seventh day is a sabbath to the Lord your God; in it you shall not do any work, you, or your son, or your daughter, your manservant, or your maidservant, or your cattle, or the sojourner who is within your gates; for in six days the Lord made heaven and earth, the sea, and all that is in them, and rested the seventh day; therefore the Lord blessed the sabbath day and hallowed it' (Exodus 20.8–11).

RABBINIC JUDAISM

By the time of the Sanhedrin, Sabbath observance was regulated by Jewish law. Following Exodus 20:10, the primary aim was to refrain from work. In the Torah only a few provisions are delineated. Such regulations were expanded by the rabbis who listed 39 categories of work.

According to the Mishnah, the 39 categories of work are: sowing; ploughing; reaping; binding sheaves; threshing; winnowing; sorting; grinding; sifting; kneading; baking; shearing sheep; washing wool; beating wool; dyeing wool; spinning; sieving; making two loops; weaving two threads; separating two threads; tying; loosening; sewing two stitches; tearing in order to sew two stitches; hunting a deer; slaughtering; flaying; salting; curing a skin; scraping the hide; cutting; writing two letters; erasing in order to write two letters; building; pulling down a structure; extinguishing a fire; lighting a fire; striking with a hammer; and, finally, moving something.

Above *A Jewish woman lighting Sabbath candles. A 17th-century Dutch woodcut.*

In the Talmud these 39 categories were discussed and expanded to include within each category a range of activities. In order to ensure that individuals did not transgress these prescriptions, the rabbis enacted further legislation, which serves as a fence around the law.

SABBATH OBSERVANCE

The Sabbath begins on Friday at sunset. Candles are lit by the woman of the house about 20 minutes before sunset, as she recites the blessing: 'Blessed are you, O Lord our God, King of the universe, who has hallowed us by your commandments and commanded us to kindle the Sabbath light.' In the synagogue service preceding Friday *maariv*, or 'who brings on twilight', takes place at twilight. Known as Kabbalat Shabbat, it is a late addition dating to the 16th century when Kabbalists in Safed went to the fields on Friday afternoon to greet the Sabbath queen.

Traditionally, when the father returns home from the synagogue he blesses his children. With both hands placed on the head of a boy, he says: 'May God make you like Ephraim and Manasseh'; for a girl: 'May God make you like Sarah, Rebekah, Rachel and Leah.' In addition, he recites the priestly blessing. Those assembled then sing Shalom Aleikhem, which welcomes the Sabbath angels. At the Sabbath table the father recites the Kiddush prayer over a cup of wine. This is followed by the washing of the hands and the blessing of the bread. The meal ends with the singing of *zemirot*, or 'table hymns', and concludes with the *Birkhat ha-Mazon*, or 'grace after meals'.

SYNAGOGUE SERVICE
On Sabbath morning the liturgy consists of a morning service, a reading of the Torah and the *Haftarah*, or 'selective readings from the prophets', and the additional service. In the service itself, introductory prayers prior to the Shema differ from those of weekdays, and the Amidah is also different. Seven individuals are called to the reading of the law, and an eighth for the reading from the prophets. In the Reform movement the worship is abridged and has no additional service. On returning home, the morning Kiddush and the blessing over bread are recited, followed by the Sabbath meal and then the grace after meals. In the afternoon service, the Torah is read

Below *A woman praying before the Shabbat candles.*

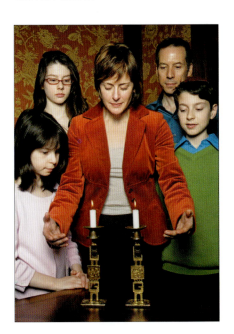

prior to the Amidah; three persons are called to the Torah, and the first portion of the reading of the law for the following week is recited. Customarily three meals are to be eaten on the Sabbath day; the third meal is known as the Seudah Shelishit. It should take place just in time for the evening service. At the end of the Sabbath, the evening service takes place and is followed by the Havdalah service.

HAVDALAH
The Havdalah ceremony marks the conclusion of the Sabbath period; it is divided and consists of four blessings. Three are recited over wine, spices and lights, and the service concludes with the Havdalah blessing. The final blessing opens with the phrase, 'Blessed are you, O Lord our God, King of the universe, who distinguishes'; it is followed by a series of comparisons: between the holy and the profane, light and darkness, Israel and the nations, between the seventh day and the six days of the week. The hymn Ha-Mavdil follows the Havdalah ceremony and asks for forgiveness of sins and for the granting of a large number of children. A number of customs, including filling a cup and

Above *Abraham sees Sodom in Flames by James Tissot, shows the importance of keeping God's law.*

extinguishing the Havdalah candle in wine poured from it, are associated with the Havdalah ceremony. Within Reform Judaism an alternative Havdalah service incorporates additional readings with traditional blessings.

Below *An Orthodox Jew at daily prayer at the Western Wall in Jerusalem.*

SPECIAL SABBATHS

IN THE JEWISH CALENDAR, A NUMBER OF SABBATHS ARE OF SPECIAL IMPORTANCE AND CELEBRATED IN TRADITIONAL SYNAGOGUES. ON THESE OCCASIONS, THE WORSHIP SERVICE ALTERS IN VARIOUS WAYS.

Throughout the Jewish year, special sabbaths are held to mark the coming or ending of a festival.

THE SABBATH OF BLESSING
On this Sabbath before a New Moon, worshippers using the Ashkenazi liturgy recite a formula based on sage Rav's prayer that 'it will be God's will to renew the coming month for good service' and with four expressions of hope it will be God's intention to re-establish the Temple, rescue his people from all afflictions, maintain Israel's sages and grant a month of good tidings. The service continues with the prayer 'He who performs miracles', an announcement of the date of the New Moon, and a benediction.

SHABBAT MAHAR HODESH
This Sabbath, which falls on the eve of the New Moon, has a biblical origin (1 Samuel 20:18). The Torah reading is that for the week. The Haftarah (1 Samuel 20:18-42) depicts the covenant between Jonathan and David on the eve of the New Moon.

SABBATH OF THE NEW MOON
In the Sabbath service which falls on the New Moon the Hallel is recited after the morning service. The Torah reading is that for the week and the additional reading is Numbers 28:9–15. The Haftarah is Isaiah 66:1–24.

SABBATH OF RETURN
The origin of the name of this Sabbath is derived from the opening words of the Haftarah: 'Return [*shuvah*], O Israel, to the Lord your God.' Since this Sabbath occurs during the Days of Penitence, it is also known as the Sabbath of Repentance.

SABBATH DURING SUKKOT
In the service for this Sabbath, which occurs during the intermediate days of Sukkot, the Hallel and the Book of Ecclesiastes are read after morning service. In some traditional congregations, religious poems are recited.

SABBATH OF GENESIS
The origin of the name of this Sabbath is derived from the opening words of the Book of Genesis which are included in the reading of the law for this Sabbath (which follows the Simchat Torah festival): 'In the beginning God created ...' On this Sabbath the annual reading cycle of the Torah commences with Genesis 1:1–6,8, and the Haftarah is that for the week.

Left *Silver goblet used for kiddush, a prayer recited before the meal on the eve of Shabbat and Jewish holidays.*

Above *David's Farewell from Jonathan by Rembrandt, commemorated on Shabbat Mahar Hodesh.*

Included among those who are called to the Torah is the person chosen as 'bridegroom of Genesis' on Simchat Torah. He normally provides a festival meal to which all are invited after the Sabbath morning service.

SABBATH OF HANUKKAH
This Sabbath takes place during the Hanukkah festival. After the morning service, the Hallel is recited. The Torah reading is that for the week. The additional reading is Numbers 7:1–7. If the Sabbath also falls on the eighth day of Hanukkah the weekly portion is Genesis 41:1–44.17 and the additional reading is Numbers 7:54–8.4. If this Sabbath coincides with the New Moon, Numbers 28:9–15 is recited from a second scroll before the additional reading.

SABBATH OF THE SONG
The origin of the name of this Sabbath is the song Moses and the Israelites sang at the Red Sea (Exodus 15:1–18), which is included in the Torah reading. In some congregations special religious poems are also recited. The Torah reading is the weekly portion (Exodus 13:17–17:16).

Above *The Parting of the Red Sea, an 18th-century lithograph by Becquet for a French catechism, forms a part of the Exodus story. The Hallel and Song of Songs are recited on the Sabbath during Passover.*

SABBATH OF THE SHEKEL TAX
The origin of the name of this Sabbath, which precedes or coincides with the New Moon, Rosh Hodesh Adar, is derived from the Mishnah that states that 'on the first day of Adar they gave warning of the shekel dues.' The additional reading concerns the half-shekel levy, which was used to support the Sanctuary. In some congregations the rabbi urges that contributions be made to religious institutions in Israel.

SABBATH OF REMEMBRANCE
On the Sabbath before Purim, the additional reading emphasizes the obligation to 'remember what Amalek did to you' (since traditionally Haman was regarded as a descendant of Amalek).

SABBATH OF THE RED HEIFER
This Sabbath precedes the Sabbath of the New Moon. The additional reading deals with the red heifer whose ashes were used for ritual purification by the ancient Israelites.

SABBATH OF THE MONTH
The origin of the name for this Sabbath is derived from the opening words of the additional reading: 'This month [*ha-Hodesh*] shall mark for you the beginning of the months.'

THE GREAT SABBATH
The origin of the name of this Sabbath is uncertain but it may derive from the last verse of the Haftarah: 'Lo, I will send the prophet Elijah to you before the coming of the awesome [*gadol*], fearful day of the Lord'(Malachi 4:5).

SABBATH DURING PASSOVER
This Sabbath takes place during the intermediate days of Passover. In the service the Hallel and Song of Songs are recited after the morning service.

SABBATH OF PROPHECY
The Sabbath precedes the ninth day of Av. Its name is derived from the Haftarah, which refers to Isaiah's vision [*hazon*] about the punishments that will be inflicted on Israel.

SABBATH OF COMFORT
The origin of this name is derived from the opening words of the Haftarah: 'Comfort [*nahamu*], O comfort my people.' The Torah reading is Deuteronomy 3:23–7:11 which includes the Ten Commandments and the first paragraph of the Shema.

Below *Jewish high priests, a 14th-century fresco from Ohrid, Macedonia. The high priesthood ended with the fall of the Temple, and synagogue services took the place of Temple worship.*

WORSHIP

Passover

THE FESTIVAL OF PASSOVER COMMEMORATES THE EXODUS FROM EGYPT. THE SEDER MEAL TAKES PLACE ON THE FIRST NIGHT. DURING THE PASSOVER CELEBRATIONS, JEWS ARE COMMANDED TO EAT MATZAH.

Through the centuries the Jewish people celebrated the festival of Passover, which commemorates the exodus from Egypt. The term 'passover' is derived from the account of the tenth plague in Egypt when firstborn Egyptians were killed, whereas God passed over the houses of the Israelites (whose door-posts and lintels were sprinkled with the blood of the paschal lamb).

THE FESTIVAL OF UNLEAVENED BREAD
Passover is also known as the festival of unleavened bread. Once the Egyptian Pharaoh gave permission for the Israelites to go, they were in such a hurry to leave that they did not wait for their bread to rise. Subsequently God commanded that no leaven was to be eaten at future Passover celebrations, nor should any leaven be found in the house. As a consequence, it became the custom just before the festival to conduct a thorough spring-clean. All leavened foods were removed, and special Passover cutlery and crockery were brought out. This was accompanied by a final ritual search for leaven.

FESTIVAL CELEBRATIONS
Passover is also described as the festival of spring – this refers back to its traditional agricultural connections. Primarily the festival is perceived as a celebration of liberation. Traditionally it is kept for eight days and its main focus is the Passover Seder (meal), which takes place on the first night. Even the most secular Jews often attend a Passover Seder: it is an opportunity for the extended family to meet one another in an atmosphere of fellowship and joy.

PREPARATION
In preparation for Passover, Jewish law stipulates that all leaven must be removed from the house. On the 14th of Nisan a formal search

Below *Passover Seder, from a 15th-century missal; manuscript attributed to the school of Van Eyck.*

Below *Father distributing loaves of unleavened bread and haroset, from the Spanish Golden Haggadah, c.1320.*

Above *Three matzahs. The unleavened bread plays an important part in the Seder meal.*

is made for any remains of leaven. This is then put aside and burned on the following morning. The first night of Passover is celebrated in the home; the ceremony is referred to as the Seder. This is done to fulfil the biblical commandment to relate the story of the Exodus to one's son: 'And you shall tell thy son on the day, saying: "It is because of what the Lord did

---

ORDER OF THE SEDER

At the Seder, the Haggadah, or 'Passover prayer book', details the order of service. It is as follows:

The kiddush is recited.
The celebrant washes his hands.
Parsley is dipped in salt water.
Celebrant divides the middle matzah and sets the afikoman aside.
Celebrant recites the Haggadah narration.
Participants wash their hands.
Blessing over bread is recited.
Blessing over matzah is recited.
Bitter herbs are eaten.
The matzah and *maror*, or 'bitter herbs', are combined.
The meal is eaten.
The afikoman is eaten
Grace after meals is recited.
The Hallel is recited.
The service is concluded.
Hymns and songs are sung.

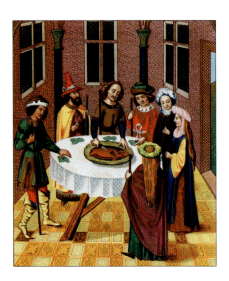

434

Right *Passover in the London Hasidic Jewish community. Hasidim dip their cutlery and crockery in a ritual bath of fresh rainwater to purify them.*

for me when I came out of Egypt'" (Exodus 13:8). The order of the service dates back to Temple times. During the ceremony celebrants traditionally lean on their left sides – this was the custom of freemen in ancient times.

MATZAH

Three *matzot*, or 'unleavened bread', are placed on top of one another, usually in a special cover. The upper and lower matzot symbolize the double portion of manna that provided for the Israelites in the wilderness. The middle matzah (which is broken in two at the beginning of the Seder) represents the 'bread of affliction'.

The smaller part of the matzah is eaten to comply with the ancient commandment to eat matzah. The larger part is set aside for the *afikoman*, which recalls Temple times when the meal was completed with the eating of the paschal lamb. These three matzot also symbolize the three divisions of the Jewish people: Cohen, Levi and Yisrael.

FOUR CUPS OF WINE

According to tradition, each Jew must drink four cups of wine at the Seder. The first is linked to the recital of Kiddush; the second with the account of the Exodus and the Blessing for Redemption; the third with the grace after meals; and the fourth with the *Hallel*, or 'psalms', and prayers for thanksgiving. These cups also symbolize four expressions of redemption in Exodus 6:6–7. Today the cups are usually small.

CUP OF ELIJAH

This cup symbolizes the hospitality awaiting the passer-by and wayfarer. According to tradition, the Messiah will reveal himself at the Passover, and Malachi declared that he will be preceded by Elijah. The cup of Elijah was also introduced because of the doubt as to whether five cups of wine should be drunk rather than four.

Below *Clockwise from top left: Plague of the first born, the Israelites leave Egypt, the passage of the Red Sea and the pursuit by the Egyptians. From the Golden Haggadah, c.1320.*

THE SEDER PLATE

The Seder plate displays a number of other symbols for Passover in addition to the matzah. Bitter herbs symbolize the bitterness of Egyptian slavery. Parsley is dipped in salt water and eaten after the Kiddush, or 'prayer over wine'. It is associated with spring. Haroset is a mixture of apples, nuts, cinnamon and wine. It is a reminder of the bricks and mortars that Jews were forced to use in Egypt. A roasted shankbone symbolizes the paschal offering. A roasted egg commemorates the festival sacrifice in the Temple. Salt water recalls the salt that was offered with all sacrifices. It also symbolizes the salt water of the tears of all ancient Israelites.

Above *Table set for Seder meal with foods associated with Passover.*

Shavuot

THE FESTIVAL OF SHAVUOT COMMEMORATES THE GIVING OF THE LAW ON MOUNT SINAI. IT CULMINATES THE PROCESS OF LIBERATION OF THE JEWISH NATION WHICH BEGAN WITH THE EXODUS AT PASSOVER.

The festival of Shavuot, or 'Festival of Weeks', is based on Leviticus 23:15: 'and from the day you bring the *omer*, or 'sheaf offering', of 'wave offering', you shall count off seven weeks [Shavuot].' Through the centuries, this festival has been observed as a celebration of the giving of the law.

ORIGINS

On the second day of Passover a meal offering was brought to the Temple, consisting of a sheaf of barley that was waved by the priest. This accounts for the fact that it is referred to as a 'wave offering'. Strictly speaking, the word *omer* is the name of a 'measure'. A sheaf that had this measure was brought as an offering in thanks for the barley harvest. Seven weeks were counted from the second day of Passover. At the end of seven weeks (on the 50th day), Shavuot was celebrated.

Below *A mid-19th-century image of a festival procession at a synagogue at Livorno, Italy.*

Initially, Shavuot was a harvest festival. However, the revelation on Mount Sinai took place during the month of Sivan according to Exodus 19: the date of Shavuot (on the sixth of Sivan) and Sinaitic revelation thus occurs at the same time. For this reason Shavuot came to be seen as a celebration of revelation, rather than a harvest festival. During the prayers for the day, Shavuot is referred to as 'the season of the giving of the Torah'.

SHAVUOT RITUALS

There are no special rituals for Shavuot as there are for Passover and Sukkot. Originally, Shavuot appears to have been an adjunct of Passover. But an adjunct festival does not require its own rituals. Further, even when Shavuot became the festival celebrating the giving of the law, new rituals expressing this theme were not created. Yet, during the Middle Ages, Shavuot customs began to develop. It is the practice, for example, to decorate the synagogue with flowers and plants. This symbolizes what occurred on Mount Sinai when the Torah was given. When God gave the law, it was covered with luxuriant plants and fragrant flowers.

Above *Children celebrate Shavuot in a kindergarten in Jerusalem.*

Another custom is to eat dairy dishes. One of the reasons given is that the Torah is like milk, which soon turns sour if it is left in vessels of gold or silver. Students of the Torah who have golden opinions of themselves and lack humility are not true representations of Jewish scholarship. They turn sour the nourishing milk of the Torah.

Below *Ruth harvesting, from the 1520s Latin Bible of St Amand Abbey, France. The Book of Ruth is read on Shavuot.*

SHAVUOT

Above *A boy learning how to fire an arrow from a bow. Archery plays a part in the celebration of Lag B'Omer.*

CELEBRATION

Shavuot is celebrated for two days on the 6th and 7th of Sivan. Seven weeks are counted from the bringing of the omer on the second day of Passover. The festival is also referred to as Pentecost, a Greek word meaning 50, since it was celebrated on the 50th day. Symbolically, the day commemorates the culmination of the process of emancipation, which began with the Exodus at Passover. It is concluded with the proclamation of the Law on Mount Sinai.

During the Temple period, farmers set out for Jerusalem to offer a selection of the first ripe fruits as a thanks-offering. In post-Temple times, the festival focuses on the giving of the law on Mount Sinai. In some communities it is a practice to remain awake during Shavuot night. In the 16th century, Solomon Alkabets and other Kabbalists began the custom of *tikkun*, in which an anthology of biblical and rabbinic material was recited. Today in the communities where this custom is observed, this lectionary has been replaced by a passage of the Talmud or other rabbinic literature.

Some congregations in the Diaspora read a book of psalms on the second night. Synagogues are decorated with flowers or plants. Jews should count the days until the Law was given on Sinai. This is like a slave counting the days to his freedom, or lovers counting the days until reunion. In the Middle Ages, the omer period was one of mourning. One reason given for this is that the disciples of Akiva died during this period. It is the custom not to have a haircut during this time, except on certain days. In addition, weddings are not to be celebrated except at specific times.

LAG B'OMER

The word 'lag' has the numerical equivalent of 33. This day, which is the 33rd day of the omer, is a minor festival because Simeon ben Yohai, traditionally viewed as the author of the Zohar, died on this day. The ascent of his soul to Heaven is described as his wedding, the reunion of the soul with God. Weddings are permitted on this day, even though it takes place during the omer. Lag B'Omer became a scholars' festival, celebrated as a day of joy. In some communities, teachers and students go out into the woods to shoot bows and arrows.

Right *Poem for the first day of Shavuot from* Laudian Mahzor, *a German book of Jewish liturgy for festivals, c.1275.*

SUKKOT

THE FESTIVAL OF SUKKOT COMMEMORATES THE WANDERING OF THE ISRAELITES IN THE DESERT. DURING THIS FESTIVAL JEWS ARE COMMANDED TO CONSTRUCT SUKKOT (BOOTHS) AND DWELL IN THEM.

Sukkot is a pilgrim festival prescribed in the Bible: 'On the 15th of the month and for seven days is the feast of tabernacles to the Lord' (Leviticus 23:34). Beginning on the 15th of Tishri, it commemorates God's protection of the Israelites during their sojourn in the desert. Leviticus demands that Jews are to construct booths during this period as a reminder that the people of Israel dwelt in booths when they fled from Egypt (Leviticus 23:42–3).

BIBLICAL LAW

The Book of Leviticus goes on to explain how the festival of Sukkot is to be celebrated: 'You shall take on the first day the fruit of goodly trees, branches of palm trees and boughs of leafy trees and willows of the brook; and you shall rejoice before the Lord your God for seven days ... You shall dwell in booths for seven days ... that your generation may know that I made the people of Israel dwell in booths when I brought them up out of the land of Egypt' (Leviticus 23:40, 42–3).

THE SUKKAH

The feast of tabernacles was thus ordained to remind Jews of their wandering in the wilderness before they reached the Promised Land. This was a time when they were particularly close to God. Today Jews are expected to build their own *sukkah*, or 'tabernacle', and the sages of the Talmud explained how this is to be done. The sukkah has to be at least four square cubits in size (a cubit is about 18ins/45 cm). It must have at least three walls and it should have a covering of things that were once growing. However, this does not imply that it should have a complete roof. When pious Jews stand in the sukkah, they should be able to see the stars through the branches of the covering. Meals should be eaten in the sukkah for the duration of the festival, although in cold climates there is no obligation to sleep in it or even to remain in it if it rains.

LULAV

In addition to constructing a sukkah, Jews are to perform a ceremony involving the fruit and the branches. This is done by holding an *etrog*, a citron, which is a large citrus fruit, in one hand and branches of palm, willow and myrtle (which are collectively known as the *lulav*) in the other. During the synagogue service, the lulav is waved in six directions: north, south, east, west, up and down. In all likelihood this symbolizes God's control of all the points of the compass and space.

Various explanations have been given regarding the composition of the lulav: possibly the most attractive is that it symbolizes the different types of Jews that make up the community, that all are necessary and should work in harmony while keeping their individuality. In any case, the lulav is waved while the Hallel (Psalms 113–118) is recited, and it is taken in a circuit around the synagogue while a prayer is recited for a good harvest.

Above *Serving food at a Sukkot celebration in the Grand Choral Synagogue, St Petersburg, Russia.*

Below *An Orthodox Jew and a secular youth blessing the four species during the Feast of Tabernacles in Jerusalem.*

Above *Hollow eggs with sacred texts were used to decorate European sukkahs for the holiday of Sukkot. This 19th-century Polish egg is decorated with text from the Song of Solomon.*

THE GREAT HOSHANAH

On the seventh day of the festival known as the Great Hoshanah (God saves), seven circuits are made in the synagogue. This is often viewed as the culmination of the whole season of repentance (the New Year, the Ten Days of Penitence and the Day of Atonement). Since Sukkot is celebrated during the course of the Tabernacles festival, it is a mixture of joy and solemnity. The next day, the day of the holy convocation, is Shemini Atzerert (the eighth day of the solemn assembly) and Simchat Torah (the rejoicing of the law). Shemini Atzeret and Simchat Torah are traditionally commemorated on the same day, but it has become customary for Shemini Atzeret to be observed on the eighth day and Simchat Torah on the ninth.

Below *Jews eating in a public sukkah during Sukkot. Some congregations build community sukkahs.*

Above *Hasidim celebrate Simchat Torah at the Premishian congregation's synagogue, Bnei Brak, Israel.*

SIMCHAT TORAH

Simchat Torah is a time of joy. It is a holy day on which the annual reading of the Torah is finished and the whole cycle begins again with the first portion from the Book of Genesis. It is considered to be an honour to be called up to read the last section of the Book of Deuteronomy, and the person chosen is called 'Bridegroom of the Torah'. The next person who is called up to read the first section of the Book of Genesis is known as the 'Bridegroom of Genesis'.

During the service, the Torah scrolls are taken from the Ark and carried in procession around the synagogue. In Hasidic communities, the enthusiasm is overwhelming and the procession spills out into the street amid singing and dancing. Children are called up and given sweets and fruits. In some communities it is the custom for the two 'bridegrooms' to give a party for the whole community.

CHAPTER 10

FESTIVALS

Celebrating Jewish high days and holidays is a vital part of being a Jew. Communities come together to mark not just the happiest festivals but also those that commemorate sad and serious times such as Holocaust Remembrance Day and Yom Kippur. The Jewish New Year begins in the autumn of the first day of Tishri and marks the start of the Ten Days of Penitence, which end on the Day of Atonement. In the Bible, Rosh Hashanah is referred to as falling on the first day of the seventh month (Leviticus 23:24). During the rabbinic period, it came to be regarded as a day of judgement for the entire world, on which each person's fate is inscribed in the Book of Life. Today the High Holy Days can continue to serve as the focus for reflection and introspection. Throughout the Jewish year, the community also celebrates a numbers of days of joy, including Hanukkah, Purim, Rosh Hodesh, the New Year for Trees, the Fifteenth of Av and Israel Independence Day. During these celebrations, Jews remember joyous historical events and times of tragedy in the history of their nation as well as seasons of the year when thanks are due to God for his blessings.

Opposite Blowing the shofar, a ceremonial wind instrument originally made from a ram's horn, on Rosh Hashanah to mark the beginning of the Jewish New Year.

Above A late 18th-century engraving showing Jews in a synagogue in Amsterdam, Holland, celebrating Purim. At Purim, Esther delivered the Jews from Haman's plot to destroy them.

ROSH HASHANAH

ROSH HASHANAH (NEW YEAR) MARKS THE COMMENCEMENT OF THE SPIRITUAL YEAR. AT THIS TIME JEWS ARE COMMANDED TO REPENT OF THEIR SINS AND RESOLVE TO IMPROVE DURING THE NEXT 12 MONTHS.

The New Year is commemorated for two days on the 1st and 2nd of Tishri. It marks the beginning of the Ten Days of Penitence, which ends on Yom Kippur, or 'the Day of Atonement'. From ancient times to now, Rosh Hashanah has been seen as the start of the spiritual year. It is a time for reflection and self-examination.

BIBLICAL JUDAISM
In ancient times, the Jewish New Year took place on one day; in subsequent centuries it became a two-day festival. The term Rosh Hashanah occurs only once in Scripture – in Ezekiel 40:1. Nevertheless, this festival had three other biblical designations: (1) Shabbaton – a day of solemn rest to be observed on the first day of the seventh month; (2) Zikhron Teruah – a memorial proclaimed with the blast of the horn (Leviticus 23:24); and (3) Yom Teruah – a day of blowing the horn (Numbers 29:1).

Below Sounding the shofar on Rosh Hashanah. 1723 engraving by Bernard Picart from his series on Judaism.

Later it was referred to by the sages as Yom ha-Din (the Day of Judgement) and Yom ha-Zikkaron (the Day of Remembrance).

DIVINE JUDGEMENT
The Mishnah declares that all human beings will appear before God on the New Year. The Talmud expands this idea by stressing the need for self-examination. In rabbinic sources each individual stands before the throne of God, and judgement on each person is entered on the New Year and sealed on the Day of Atonement.

According to the Talmud, there are three ledgers opened in heaven: one is for the completely righteous, who are immediately inscribed and sealed in the Book of Life. Another is for the thoroughly wicked, who are recorded in the Book of Death. A third is for the intermediate, ordinary type of individual, whose fate hangs in the balance and is suspended until the Day of Atonement. In this light, Rosh Hashanah and Yom Kippur are called Yamim Noraim, or 'Days of Awe'.

Above At Rosh Hashanah it is customary to eat apples dipped in honey for 'a good and sweet year'.

SYNAGOGUE OBSERVANCE
On New Year Day, the Ark curtain, reading desk and Torah scroll mantles are decked in white, and the rabbi, cantor and person who blows the *shofar*, or 'ram's horn', all wear a white *kittel*, or 'robe'. In the synagogue service the Amidah or the Musaf service contains three sections relating to God's sovereignty, providence and revelation: Malkhuyyot deals with God's rule; Zikhronot portrays God's remembrance of the ancestors of the Jewish people when he judges each generation; Shofarot contains verses relating to the shofar, and deals with the revelation on Mount Sinai and the messianic age. Each introductory section is followed by three verses from the Torah, three from the Writings; three from the Prophets, and a final verse from the Torah.

The Torah readings at Rosh

Below A poem for Rosh Hashanah, has a drawing of the sacrifice of Isaac by Abraham. From a 14th-century German Jewish book of prayers for festivals.

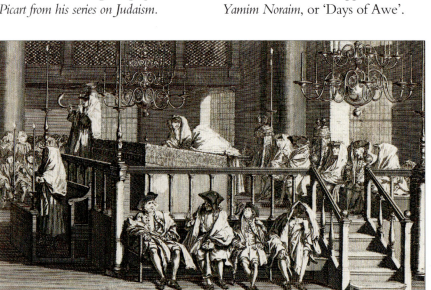

ROSH HASHANAH

Above *A Central European postcard from 1900 showing the blowing of the shofar, or horn, for Rosh Hashanah.*

> ### AVINU MALKENU
>
> *Avinu Malkenu* is said from Rosh Hashanah to Yom Kippur. The phrase means 'Our father, our king'.
>
> Avinu Malkenu, we have no king but you.
> Avinu Malkenu, help us for your own sake.
> Avinu Malkenu, grant us a blessed New Year.
>
> Avinu Malkenu, annul all evil decrees against us.
> Avinu Malkenu, annul the plots of our enemies.
> Avinu Malkenu, frustrate the designs of our foes.
> Avinu Malkenu, rid us of tyrants.
> Avinu Malkenu, rid us of pestilence, sword, famine, captivity, sin and destruction.
>
> Avinu Malkenu, forgive and pardon all our sins.
> Avinu Malkenu, ignore the record of our transgressions.
> Avinu Malkenu, help us return to you fully repentant.
> Avinu Malkenu, send complete healing to the sick.
> Avinu Malkenu, remember us with favour.
>
> Avinu Malkenu, inscribe us in the book of happiness.
> Avinu Malkenu, inscribe us in the book of deliverance.
> Avinu Malkenu, inscribe us in the book of prosperity.
> Avinu Malkenu, inscribe us in the book of merit.
> Avinu Malkenu, inscribe us in the book of forgiveness.

Hashanah concern the birth (Genesis 12:1–34) and the binding of Isaac (Genesis 22:1–24). On both days the shofar is blown at three points during the service: 30 times after the reading of the Law; 30 times during Musaf; and 10 before Alenu. In the liturgy there are three variants of the blowing of the shofar: *tekiah*, or 'a long note'; *shevarim*, or 'three tremulous notes'; and *teruah*, 'nine short notes'. According to the 12th-century Jewish philosopher Moses Maimonides, the shofar is blown to call sinners to repent.

TASHLICH

Traditionally, it was the custom to go to the seaside or the banks of a river on the afternoon of the first day. The ceremony of Tashlich symbolizes the casting of one's sins into a body of water. The prayers for Tashlich and the three verses from the Book of Micah (Micah 7:18–20) express confidence in divine forgiveness. In the home, a piece of bread is dipped in honey followed by a piece of apple, and a prayer is recited that the year ahead may be good and sweet.

A SOLEMN DAY

The Ten Days of Penitence begin with the New Year and last until the Day of Atonement. This is regarded as the most solemn time of the year when all are judged and their fate determined for the coming year. During the Ten Days various additions are made to the liturgy, especially in the morning service. Selihot Penitential prayers are recited during the morning service, and various additions are made to the Amidah and the reader's repetition of the Amidah. The reader's repetition is followed by the Avinu Malkenu prayer.

Right *A Rosh Hashanah service at the Moscow Choral Synagogue, Russia.*

YOM KIPPUR

YOM KIPPUR CONCLUDES THE TEN DAYS OF PENITENCE, WHICH BEGINS WITH ROSH HASHANAH. DURING YOM KIPPUR, JEWS ARE COMMANDED TO REPENT OF THEIR SINS AND SEEK FORGIVENESS.

Yom Kippur is the holiest day of the Jewish year. Observed on the 10th of Tishri, it is prescribed in Scripture: 'On the tenth day of the seventh month is the Day of Atonement; and you shall afflict yourselves. It shall be to you a sabbath of solemn rest, and you shall afflict yourselves; on the ninth day of the month, beginning at evening, from evening to evening' (Leviticus 23: 27, 32).

The rabbis stress that the Day of Atonement enables human beings to atone for sins committed against God. However, regarding transgressions committed against others, pardon cannot be obtained unless forgiveness has been sought from the persons injured. As a result, it is customary for Jews to seek reconciliation with anyone they might have offended during the year.

Below *The Day of Atonement as observed by Ashkenazi Jews in the 18th century, by Bernard Picart.*

KAPPAROT

The kapparot ritual takes place before Yom Kippur among Sephardi and Eastern communities as well as among some Ashkenazim. During this ceremony a fowl is slaughtered and either eaten before the fast or sold for money, which is given to charity. Its death symbolizes the transfer of guilt from the person to the bird that has been killed. In some congregations, Jews substitute coins for the fowl, and charity boxes are available at the morning and afternoon services before Yom Kippur.

Previously *malkot*, or 'lashes', were administered in the synagogue to impart a feeling of repentance, but this custom has largely disappeared.

YOM KIPPUR RITUAL

Customarily, Jews were able to absolve vows on the eve of Yom Kippur. In addition, afternoon prayers are recited earlier than normal, and the Amidah is extended by two for-

Above *Emperor Hadrian expelled the Jews from Jerusalem. His persecution is referred to in the Yom Kippur liturgy.*

A DAY OF FASTING

According to the sages, afflicting one's soul involves abstaining from food and drink. Thus every male over the age of 13 and every female over 12 is obliged to fast from sunset until nightfall the next day. Sick people may take medicine, and small amounts of food and drink. Those with chronic illnesses like insulin-dependent diabetes may be forbidden to fast. During the day normal Sabbath prohibitions apply, but worshippers are to abstain from food and drink, marital relations, wearing leather shoes, using cosmetics and lotions and washing the body, except for fingers and eyes.

Below *Leather shoes are not worn on the day of Yom Kippur.*

Right *The Kol Nidre, the first of the Yom Kippur services, in the Great Synagogue, Budapest, Hungary.*

mulae of confession. Some pious Jews immerse themselves in a *mikveh*, or 'ritual bath', in order to undergo purification before the fast. In the home, a final meal is eaten, and, before lighting the festival candles, a memorial candle is lit to burn through-out the day. Leather shoes are replaced by non-leather shoes. The *tallit*, or 'prayer shawl', is worn throughout all the services, and a white curtain adorns the Ark and Torah scrolls. The reader's desk and other furnishings are covered in white. Among Ashkenazim, rabbis, cantors and other officials also wear a white kittel (gown).

CONFESSION

On Yom Kippur five services take place. The first, Kol Nidre, takes place on Yom Kippur eve. Among the Orthodox, it was a custom to spend the night in the synagogue reciting the entire Book of Psalms as well as other readings. Among Sephardim and Reform Jews the memorial prayer is recited on Kol Nidre. In addition to selihot and other hymns, the morning service includes a Torah reading describing the Day of Atonement ritual in the Sanctuary. Before the Musaf service, a special prayer – Hineni He-Ani Mi-Maas – is recited. A number of liturgical hymns are included in the reader's repetition of the Amidah, including the 11th-century U-Netanneh Tokef passage, which states that prayer and charity avert judgement.

MARTYROLOGY

Interpolated among the selihot and confessions towards the end of Musaf is the Elleh Ezkerah martyrology. Based on a medieval midrash, this describes the plight of the Ten Martyrs persecuted for defying Hadrian's ban on studying of the Torah. In some rites this part of the service is expanded to include Holocaust readings. In the afternoon service, Leviticus 18 is read, dealing with prohibited marriages and sexual offences. The second reading is the Book of Jonah.

CONCLUDING SERVICE

Before the neilah, or 'concluding service', the hymn El Nora Alilah is chanted among the Sephardim. This part of the liturgy is recited as twilight approaches. In some congregations, the Ark remains open and worshippers stand throughout the service. They ask God to inscribe each person for a good life and to seal them for a favourable fate. At the end of the service, the shofar is blown, and the congregations recite *La-Shanah ha-Baah Bi-Yerushalayim*, or 'next year in Jerusalem'. After the service concludes, it is customary to begin the construction of the sukkah, or 'booth'.

Below *Jews in preparation for Yom Kippur perform the kapparot ritual, in which a chicken is sacrificed.*

Fasts

THROUGHOUT THE JEWISH YEAR, THE COMMUNITY COMMEMORATES A VARIETY OF EVENTS WITH FASTING. ALONGSIDE YOM KIPPUR, THERE IS A RANGE OF FAST DAYS WHICH HIGHLIGHT TRAGIC PAST EVENTS.

Fasting or abstinence from food plays its part in Jewish religion. Individuals may fast as a sign of repentance or mourning, or to make atonement.

THE FIRST TEMPLE
In the ritual of the First Temple, fasting was a permanent feature: the death of a national leader such as King Saul could initiate a day-long fast or even a weekly fast. The purpose of such fasting was manifold: its most important function was to avert or terminate calamities. In addition, fasting served as a means of obtaining divine forgiveness.

THE BIBLE
In Scripture, there is no record of specific fast days in the annual calendar except for the Day of Atonement. Fixed fast days were first mentioned in the post-exilic period by the prophet Zechariah. According to tradition, these fasts commemorate events which resulted in the destruction of the Temple: the 10th of Tevet – the beginning of the siege of Jerusalem; the 17th of Tammuz – the breaching of the walls; the 9th of Av – the destruction of the Temple; the 3rd of Tishri – the assassination of Gedaliah, the Babylonian-appointed governor of Judah. As a result, the practice of fasting, which was initially spontaneous, later entered the calendar as a recurring event in the commemoration of historical tragedies.

OBSERVANCE
Jewish texts lay down a series of prescriptions to regularize the process of fasting. During the First Temple period, the devout offered sacrifice, confessed sins and uttered prayers. From the Second Temple period onwards, public fasts were accompanied by a reading from Scripture. On solemn fasts, four prayers were recited as well as Maariv. The Amidah of the fast day consisted of 24 benedictions (the normal 18 and six others), and the liturgy was elaborated with passages of *selihot*, or 'supplication', and prayers for mercy. During the service the shofar, or 'ram's horn', was sounded, accompanied by other horns.

In the Temple, the blowing of shofarot and trumpets was performed differently from other localities. Prayers were normally uttered in the open, and all the people tore their clothes, wore sackcloth and put ashes or earth on their heads. Holy objects were also humiliated. It was common for the altar to be covered with sackcloth and the Ark, containing the Torah scrolls, was frequently taken into the street and covered with ashes. During the mass assembly, one of the elders rebuked the people for their failings, and the affairs of the community were scrutinized. It was normal for young children and animals to fast as well. The sages, however, exempted young children and animals, the sick, those obliged to preserve their strength and pregnant and nursing women.

ORDINARY AND IMPORTANT FAST DAYS
Ordinary fast days lasted during the daylight hours; important fasts were 24 hours in length. Fasts were held either for one day, or, on some occasions, for a series of three or seven days. In some cases they took place daily for a continued period.

In unusual cases, fasts were held on Sabbaths and festivals, but it was normally forbidden to fast on these days. So as not to mar the celebration of joyful events in Jewish history, Hananiah ben Hezekiah ben Garon (1st century CE) formulated a Scroll of Fasting which lists 35 dates on which a public fast should not be proclaimed. Eventually, however, this list was abrogated. It was customary to hold fast days on Mondays and Thursdays. After the destruction of the Second Temple, individuals took upon themselves to fast every Monday and Thursday.

Above *The Suicide of Saul*, 1562, by Pieter Brueghel the Elder. *Saul's death initiated fasting and mourning.*

Below *On the 9th of Av, Jews wearing jute bags gather to pray at the Western Wall in Jerusalem, to mark the fall of the First and Second Temples.*

Left *This 13th-century fresco from Anagni, Italy describes the events in 1 Samuel 6 when the Philistines returned the Ark of the Covenant. During fasts, the Ark was taken into the streets covered with ashes.*

5 7th of Adar is a traditional date of the death of Moses.
6 Yom Kippur Katan is a fast day which takes place on the last day of each month.
7 The Fast of the First-Born takes place on 14th Nisan to commemorate the sanctification of the first-born who were saved during the time of the last plague of Egypt.
8 Days commemorating various calamitous events in the history of the Jewish nation.

Jewish law specifies that in such cases these persons should fast during the afternoon of the preceding day. It was also possible to fast for a certain number of hours. On some occasions, the fast was only partial, with those fasting refraining only from meat and wine.

BIBLICAL FASTS

1 The Day of Atonement (Yom Kippur) is to be a fast day.
2 The Ninth of Av (Tishah B'Av) was the day when Nebuchadnezzar (fl. 7th–6th centuries BCE) destroyed the Temple in 586BCE and Titus later devastated the Second Temple in 70CE.
3 The Seventeenth of Tammuz commemorates the breaching of the walls of Jerusalem, which occurred on 9th of Tammuz in the First Temple period.
4 The Tenth of Tevet is a fast that commemorates the commencement of the siege of Jerusalem by Nebuchadnezzar.
5 The Fast of Gedaliah takes place on 3rd of Tishri to commemorate the fate of Gedaliah, the governor of Judah who was assassinated on this day.
6 The Fast of Esther takes place on the 13th of Adar, the day before Purim.

RABBINIC FASTS

1 The especially pious are encouraged to fast during the Ten Days of Penitence and for as many days as possible during the month of Elul.
2 The first Monday and Thursday and the following Monday after Passover and Sukkot are observed as fast days.
3 Shoavim Tat is observed during the Three Weeks of Mourning.
4 A fast is observed during the Three Weeks of Mourning between 17th of Tammuz and 9th of Av.

PRIVATE FASTS

1 The anniversary of the death of a parent.
2 Grooms and brides fast on the day before their wedding.
3 Fasting occurs to prevent the consequences of nightmares taking place.
4 Fasting takes place if a Torah scroll is dropped.

Below *German Jews from Nuremberg, 1734, commemorate Tishah B'Av in memory of the destruction of the Temple in Jerusalem.*

HANUKKAH

HANUKKAH IS A JOYOUS FESTIVAL COMMEMORATING THE TRIUMPH OF THE JEWS OVER THEIR ENEMIES IN ANCIENT TIMES. FOR EIGHT DAYS A HANUKKAH MENORAH IS LIT AND TRADITIONAL PRAYERS RECITED.

The festival of Hanukkah, or 'dedication', is celebrated for eight days beginning on the 25th of Kislev – it commemorates the victory of the Maccabees over the Seleucids in the 2nd century BCE. Originally a Jewish rebel army the Maccabees took control of Judea, which had been a client state of the Seleucid empire, and founded the Hasmonean dynasty, which ruled from 164BCE to 63BCE, reasserting the Jewish religion and expanding Israel's borders.

At this time the Maccabees were engaged in military conflict with the Seleucids who had desecrated the Temple. After a three-year struggle (165–163BCE), the Maccabees under Judah Maccabee (*d.* 160/161 BCE) conquered Jerusalem and rebuilt the altar. According to the Talmud, one day's worth of oil miraculously kept the menorah burning in the Temple for eight days.

I MACCABEES

The First Book of Maccabees 4:36–59 states that Judah Maccabee, after defeating Lysias, entered Jerusalem and purified the Temple. The altar, which had been defiled, was destroyed and a new one was constructed.

Judah then made new holy vessels including a candelabrum, an altar for incense and a table, and established the 25th of Kislev as the date for the rededication of the Temple. This day coincided with the third anniversary of the proclamation of the edicts of Antiochus Epiphanes (*c*.215–164BCE) in which he decreed idolatrous sacrifices should be offered in the Temple. The altar was to be consecrated with the renewal of the daily sacrificial service; this was to be accompanied by song, the playing of musical instruments, the chanting of the Hallel, and the offering of sacrifice.

Above *In this scene from 1 Maccabees, Mattathias kills a Jew who comes to make a sacrifice at an altar. By Gabriel Bodenehr the Elder (1673–1765).*

These festivities lasted for eight days, and Judah decreed they should be designated as a time for rejoicing.

II MACCABEES

The Second Book of Maccabees 1:8; 10:1–5 parallels 1 Maccabees. It adds that the eight-day celebration was performed on an analogy with Solomon's consecration of the Temple. The eight days were celebrated with gladness like the Feast of Tabernacles, which recalled how the ancient Israelites had been wandering like wild beasts in the mountains and caves. Thus, bearing wands wreathed with leaves, boughs and palms, they offered hymns of praise.

Hanukkah is therefore called Tabernacles or Tabernacles and Fire. Fire had descended from heaven at the dedication of the altar during the time of Moses and at the sanctification of the Temple of Solomon. At the consecration of the altar in the time of the prophet Nehemiah there was also a miracle of fire, and similarly in the days of Judah Maccabee.

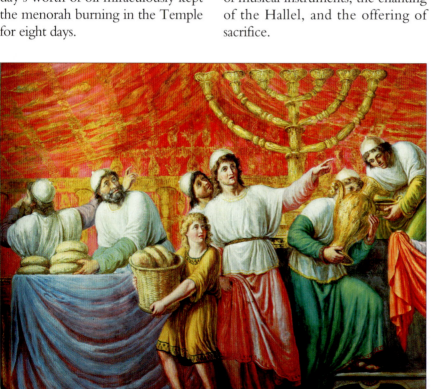

Left *A menorah dominates this fresco of preparations for a Jewish festival by Luigi Ademollo. In the 2nd century BCE, the Maccabees under Judah Maccabee drove out the Seleucid oppressors, rebuilt the Temple and rekindled the menorah.*

Right *Children playing with dreidels at Hanukkah. This traditional Jewish toy bears the initial letters of the Hebrew words 'A great miracle happened there.'*

THE KINDLING OF LIGHTS

None of these early sources mention the kindling of lights on Hanukkah. This is referred to first in a *baraita*, or 'religious law outside teaching': 'The precept of light on Hanukkah requires that one light be kindled in each house; the zealous require one light for each person; the extremely zealous add a light for each person each night. According to Bet Shammai: "On the first day, eight lights should be kindled, thereafter they should be progressively reduced" while Bet Hillel held that: "On the first night one light should be kindled, thereafter they should be progressively increased."'

HANUKKAH OBSERVANCE

The main observance of this festival is the kindling of the festive lamp on each of the eight nights. This practice gave this holiday the additional

Below *Hanukkah recalls when a day's oil kept the Temple menorah burning for eight days. In this 1299 Hebrew Bible from Spain, oil is poured into a menorah.*

name of *Hag ha-Urim*, or 'festival of lights'. In ancient times this lamp was placed in the doorway or in the street outside; subsequently the lamp was placed inside the house. The lighting occurs after dark (except on Friday night, when it must be done before the kindling of the Sabbath lights). The procedure for lighting the Hanukkah candles is to light one candle (or an oil lamp) on the first night, and an additional candle each night until the last night when all eight candles are lit. The kindling should go from left to right. An alternative tradition prescribes that the eight candles are lit on the first night, seven on the second night and so forth. These candles are lit by an additional candle called the *shammash*, or 'serving light'. In addition to this home ceremony, candles are lit in the synagogue.

THE SYNAGOGUE LITURGY

In the synagogue this festival is commemorated by the recitation of the Al ha-Nissim prayer in the Amidah, and Grace after Meals. In the morning service the Hallel is recited, and a special reading from the law takes place on each day. In both the home and the synagogue the hymn Maoz Tsur is sung in Ashkenazi communities; the Sephardim read Psalm 30 instead. During Hanukkah it is customary to hold parties, which include games and singing. The most well-known game involves a *dreidel*, or 'spinning top'. The dreidel is inscribed with four Hebrew letters (*nun, gimmel, he, shin*) on its side – this is an acrostic for the phrase *nes gadol hayah sham*', or 'a great miracle happened there'. During Hanukkah, *latkes*, or potato pancakes, and *sufganiyyot*, or doughnuts, are eaten. In modern Israel the festival is associated with national heroism and a torch is carried from the traditional burial site of the Maccabees at Modiin to various parts of the country.

Below *Children lighting a menorah for the eight-day holiday of Hanukkah, commemorating the rededication of the Holy Temple in Jerusalem.*

PURIM

THE FESTIVAL OF PURIM CELEBRATES THE DELIVERANCE OF THE JEWISH PEOPLE FROM THEIR OPPRESSORS. THE BOOK OF ESTHER IS READ DURING THE FESTIVAL.

According to Scripture, this feast was instituted by Mordecai to celebrate the deliverance of the Jews from the plot by Haman, chief minister of King Ahasuerus (486–465BCE), to kill them. The term 'purim' refers to the lots cast by Haman in order to determine the month when this massacre was to take place. Purim is celebrated on the 14th of Adar, and is a time of joy and thanksgiving.

OBSERVANCE
The central feature of this festival is the reading of the Book of Esther, from the *megillah*, or 'scroll', with special cantillation (ritual chanting or intoning). Megillot scrolls are often decorated, sometimes with scenes from the narrative. It is customary to fold the megillah over and spread it out before the reading. The four verses of redemption (Esther 2:5; 8:15–16 and 10:3) are read in a louder voice than other verses. It is the custom of children to make a loud noise with rattles whenever the name of Haman is read. It is the practice for the reader to recite the names of the ten sons of Haman (Esther 9:7–9) in one breath to demonstrate that they were executed simultaneously. According to one interpretation, this is done so that a person will not gloat over the downfall of one's enemies.

GIFTS
The Book of Esther (9:22) describes the practice of sending portions to friends on Purim and giving gifts to the poor. The rule is to send at least two portions of eatables, confectionery and so forth to a friend and to give a present of money to at least two poor men. A special festival meal is often consumed on Purim afternoon: among Purim foods are boiled beans and peas, which are viewed as a reminder of the cereals Daniel ate in the king's palace in order to avoid infringing dietary laws. Three-cornered pies, known as *hamantashen*, or 'Haman's hats', are also eaten. According to the Babylonian sage Rava (270–350CE), a person is obliged to drink so much wine on Purim that he becomes incapable of knowing whether he is cursing Haman or bless-

Above *Children in Old Jerusalem dress in colourful costumes as angels, clowns and police officers for Purim.*

Below *Mordecai and Haman. A 2nd-century fresco from Dura-Europos Synagogue, Syria.*

> ### SACRED LITERATURE
> Parodies of sacred literature produced for Purim include *Massekeht Purim*, a parody of the Talmud with its theme of the obligation to drink wine and abstain from water. The institution of the Purim rabbi as a merry fool became a norm in many communities. This can be seen as an annual attempt to find psychological relief from an overwhelming burden of loyalty to the Torah. Under influence from the Italian carnival, people dressed up on Purim in fancy dress. Men were even allowed to dress as women, and vice versa.

Above Jews celebrating Purim in a synagogue in Amsterdam, Holland. A late 18th-century engraving.

ing Mordecai. The laws concerning this festival are found in the Code of Jewish Law.

KABBALAH

In Kabbalistic and Hasidic literature much is made of Purim as a day of joy and friendship. Unlike Passover, which celebrates God's intervention in human life, God is not mentioned in the Book of Esther. The lots of Purim are compared with the 'lots' cast on the Day of Atonement when human beings call fate and luck into being. Kabbalists esteemed Purim so highly that they reported in the name of Isaac Luria that the Day of Atonement is like Purim. Although a few Reform congregations abolished Purim, the majority continue to regard the day as one of encouragement and hope.

PURIM KATAN

Following the talmudic injunction that one must recite a special thanksgiving benediction on returning to the place where one was once miraculously saved from danger, the custom arose of celebrating the anniversary of the Jews escape from destruction by reciting special prayers with a ritual similar to that of Purim. These communal Purims are referred to as 'Purim Katan' or 'Moed Katan' or 'Purim', followed with the name of the community. In some cases special Purims were preceded by a fast comparable to the Fast of Esther.

In addition, on the Purim Katan itself the story of personal or communal salvation is recited from a scroll in the course of the synagogue service in which special prayers are recited. Sometimes the Al ha-Nissim prayer and the Hallel are inserted into the ritual. The traditional Purim observance of enjoying a festival meal and giving charity to the poor were also added to these Purims.

PURIM-SHPIL

The term *Purim-shpil*, or 'Purim play', refers to the group performances or monologues given at the traditional family meal held on the festival of Purim. There is evidence that the use of the term 'Purim-shpil' was widespread among Ashkenazi communities as early as the mid-16th century. At the beginning of the 18th century, the biblical Purim-shpil reflected various trends of the contemporary European theatre in its literary style, choice of subject and design.

As time passed, the Purim-shpil became a complex drama with a large cast, comprising thousands of rhymed lines performed to musical accompaniment. The play invariably maintained a strong connection with Purim.

Below Kurdish Jews celebrating the festival of Purim wearing traditional dress and reading from a scroll of the Book of Esther.

FESTIVALS OF JOY

DURING THE YEAR JEWS CELEBRATE A NUMBER OF JOYOUS FESTIVALS. IN MODERN TIMES, ISRAEL INDEPENDENCE DAY HAS GAINED CONSIDERABLE SIGNIFICANCE IN THE JEWISH CALENDAR.

In addition to the festivals of Hanukkah and Purim, Jews celebrate several other festivals of joy. The first, Rosh Hodesh, celebrates the New Moon; the second, Tu b'Shevat, is related to tree planting; the third, 15th of Av, is a folk festival; and the fourth, Israel Independence Day, commemorates the creation of the State of Israel.

NEW MOON

Originally Rosh Hodesh, or 'new moon', was not fixed by astronomical calculations; instead it was proclaimed after witnesses had observed the reappearance of the crescent of the moon. On the 30th of every month, members of the High Court assembled in a courtyard in Jerusalem; there they waited

Above *A young boy pats down the soil around a sapling he has planted for Tu b'Shevat in Herzlia, Israel.*

to receive information from reliable witnesses. They then sanctioned the New Moon. If the moon's crescent was not seen on the 30th day, the New Moon was celebrated on the next day. To inform the population of the beginning of the month, beacons were lit on the Mount of Olives and from there throughout the country as well as in the Diaspora.

Later the Samaritans began to light beacons, and the High Court sent out messengers to far-removed communities. Those Jews who lived far from Jerusalem always celebrated the 30th day of the month as Rosh Hodesh. On these occasions, when they were informed of its postponement to the next day, they also observed a second day as Rosh Hodesh. By the middle of the 4th century CE, however, the sages established a permanent calendar and the public proclamation of the New Moon ceased. A relic of this original practice is retained in the synagogue custom of announcing the New Moon on the Sabbath preceding its celebration.

Although the biblical commandment of joy is not prescribed in relation to Rosh Hodesh, the rabbis

Left *A lighted beacon in a window at the Great Synagogue, Jerusalem, for the New Moon or Rosh Hodesh.*

ISRAEL INDEPENDENCE DAY

Israel's national day is Israel Independence Day, which commemorates the proclamation of its independence on the 5th of Iyyar 1948. The Chief Rabbinate of Israel declared it a religious holiday and established a special order of service for the evening and morning worship. This service includes the Hallel, and a reading from the Book of Isaiah. The rabbinate also suspended any fast that takes place on the day and various other restrictions. In Israel, the preceding day is set aside as a day of remembrance for soldiers who died in battle. Memorial prayers are recited, and next-of-kin visit the military cemeteries. At home, memorial candles are lit, and Psalm 9 is recited in many synagogues.

Right *Celebrating Independence Day at the Western Wall, Jerusalem.*

inferred its relevance from the fact that the Bible equated the New Moon with the festivals as well as from the duty to recite the following on Rosh Hodesh: 'This is the day which the Lord hath made. We will rejoice and be glad in it' (Psalm 118:24). Hence it is forbidden to fast on the New Moon, and any funeral service is abbreviated. On the New Moon it is customary to partake of a festive meal.

During the period of the First Temple, Rosh Hodesh was observed with the offering of special sacrifices, the blowing of shofars, feasting and a rest from work. By the end of the 6th century BCE, Rosh Hodesh became a semi-holiday. Eventually this status disappeared, and Rosh Hodesh became a normal working day except for various liturgical changes. In the morning service the Hallel psalms of praise are recited. The Bible reading is from Numbers and describes the Temple service for the New Moon. An additional service is also included, corresponding to the additional sacrifice which was offered on the New Moon.

NEW YEAR FOR TREES

A further joyous festival is Tu b'Shevat (New Year for Trees), which occurs on the 15th of Shevat. Even though this festival is not referred to in the Bible, it appeared in the Second Temple period as a fixed cut-off date for determining the tithe levied on the produce of fruit trees. Once the Temple was destroyed, the laws of tithing were no longer applicable. As a consequence, this festival took on a new character. Wherever Jews resided, it reminded them of their connection with the Holy Land.

During the 15th century, a number of new ceremonies and rituals were instituted by the mystics of Safed. Owing to the influence of Isaac Luria (1534–72), it became customary to celebrate the festival with gatherings where special fruits were eaten and hymns and readings from the Bible were included. Among the fruits eaten on Tu b'Shevat were those of the Holy Land. In modern Israel new trees are planted during this festival.

15TH OF AV

Another joyous occasion is the 15th of Av, which was a folk festival during the Second Temple period. At this time bachelors selected their wives from unmarried maidens. According to the Mishnah, on both this day and the Day of Atonement, young girls in Jerusalem dressed in white garments and danced in the vineyards where young men selected their brides. In modern times this festival is marked only by a ban on eulogies or fasting.

FESTIVALS

HOLOCAUST REMEMBRANCE DAY

THE HOLOCAUST HAS CAST A SHADOW OVER THE MODERN JEWISH COMMUNITY. HOLOCAUST MEMORIAL DAY COMMEMORATES THOSE WHO LOST THEIR LIVES AT THE HANDS OF THE NAZIS.

It is now well over half a century since the Holocaust took place. For survivors, the Holocaust is an ever-present memory, but for others it is an event of the past. To ensure that this tragedy is not forgotten, *Yom ha-Shoah*, or 'Holocaust Remembrance Day', is now commemorated throughout the Jewish world. Inaugurated in 1959, Holocaust Remembrance Day was signed into law by the Prime Minister of Israel, David Ben-Gurion (1886–1973), and the President of Israel, Yitzhak Ben-Zvi (1884–1963).

The original proposal was to hold Holocaust Remembrance Day on the anniversary of the Warsaw ghetto uprising on 19 April 1943, but this was problematic since the 14th of Nisan is the day before Passover. The date was therefore moved to the 27th of Nisan, eight days before Israel Independence Day. Most Jewish communities hold a ceremony on this day but there is no institutional ritual. Generally Jews light a memorial candle and recite the Kaddish prayer for the dead.

ORTHODOX JUDAISM
After the war, the Chief Rabbinate of Israel decided that the 10th of Tevet should be a national remembrance day for victims of the Holocaust. It recommended traditional forms of remembering the dead, such as the study of the Mishnah section about ritual baths, saying psalms, lighting a yahrzeit candle and saying Kaddish. On other occasions, the Chief Rabbinate recommended Tisha b'Av as the appropriate day for remembrance. In April 1951, the Knesset decreed that 27th Nisan should become Yom ha-Shoah, ignoring the Rabbinate's decision. In turn, the Chief Rabbinate decided to ignore the Knesset's chosen date.

Above *Holocaust memorial in Miami Beach, Florida, USA, designed by Kenneth Treister.*

Below *The women's compound at Bergen-Belsen concentration camp, where Margot and Anne Frank died in March 1945. Painting by Leslie Cole.*

COMMEMORATION
On the eve of Holocaust Remembrance Day, there is a state ceremony at Yad Vashem, the Holocaust Martyrs' and Heroes' Remembrance Authority. At 10 a.m. on Yom ha-Shoah, air-raid sirens are sounded throughout Israel for two minutes, During this time, people stop working and stand at attention. On the eve of Yom ha-Shoah and the day itself, places of public entertainment are closed by law. Documentaries about the Holocaust are screened on television and songs are played on the radio. Flags on public buildings are flown at half mast.

Above Dr Laszlo Tauber, Holocaust survivor, lights a menorah in memory of victims and survivors of the Holocaust at a service in Washington DC, 1985.

Although there are Orthodox Jews who commemorate the Holocaust on Yom ha-Shoah, others in the Orthodox world – especially the Hasidim – remember the victims of the Holocaust on traditional days of mourning which were in place before World War II, such as Tishah B'Av. In Israel most Orthodox Zionists stand still for two minutes during the siren. Others, especially in Haredi areas, do not pay attention to this event: most stores remain open, schools continue, and most people carry on with their activities when the siren sounds. The non-participation of the Haredim has caused friction with the rest of the Israeli population.

NORTH AMERICA

Jews in North America observe Yom ha-Shoah within the synagogue as well as in the broader American community. Commemorations range widely from synagogue services to communal vigils and educational programmes. Some congregations find it more practical to have a commemorative ceremony on the closest Sunday to Yom ha-Shoah. It is usual to have a talk by a Holocaust survivor, recitation of songs and reading, and viewing of a film dealing with the Holocaust. Some communities stress the loss that Jews experienced during the Holocaust by reading out the names of Holocaust victims.

HOLOCAUST RITUALS

Rituals associated with Yom ha-Shoah are continually being created and vary widely. Attempts have also been made to observe this day of mourning and remembrance in the home. A common practice is to light a yahrzeit candle.

There have also been attempts to compose a Holocaust liturgy such as the 'Six Days of Destruction' produced by the Reform movement. It was intended to serve as a modern addition to the five scrolls that are read on special holidays.

It has also been suggested that a programme of observance for Yom ha-Shoah should include fasting, and a Holocaust Haggadah has been written in which the story of the Holocaust is told.

Despite the variations in practice, the overriding theme of Yom ha-Shoah or Holocaust Remembrance Day is the importance of remembering this tragedy and ensuring that it never occurs again.

Below Memorial in Berlin for the murdered Jews of Europe, designed by Peter Eisenman; comprising a field of thousands of concrete steles.

Tishah B'Av

THE FESTIVAL OF TISHAH B'AV RECALLS THE DESTRUCTION OF THE TEMPLE BY THE BABYLONIANS IN THE 6TH CENTURY BCE, AND LATER THE ROMAN CONQUEST OF JERUSALEM IN THE 1ST CENTURY CE.

This day of mourning commemorates the destruction of the Temple in Jerusalem by the Babylonians and later by the Romans. In synagogues throughout the Jewish world Jews gather together to mourn this tragic event as well as other calamities in Jewish history which occurred at about the same time. Tishah B'Av serves to remind Jewry of its vulnerability throughout the ages.

HISTORICAL BACKGROUND
In 586BCE the Temple (First Temple) was destroyed by King Nebuchadnezzar of Babylonia

Below *A dramatic depiction of* The Destruction of Jerusalem *by David Roberts (1796–1864).*

(7th–6th century BCE) on the 10th of Av. The rebuilt Temple (Second Temple) was destroyed by the Romans in 70CE on the same day. In time the 9th of Av became the anniversary of both destructions. The Talmud justifies this date because a series of calamities occurred on this day throughout Jewish history in addition to the destruction of the Temple on the 10th of Av.

MOURNING RITES
It is uncertain whether the 9th of Av was observed as a day of mourning before 70CE, in memory of the destruction of the First Temple. The Talmud recounts that Eliezer ben Zadok, who lived before and after the destruction of the Second Temple, did not fast on the 9th of

Above *An aerial view of Temple Mount, a hill in the old city of Jerusalem. This holy site has been venerated for thousands of years by Judaism, Christianity and Islam alike.*

Av, which was deferred because of the Sabbath to the following day since it was his family's traditional holiday of wood offerings for the altar. This indicates that fasting on the 9th of Av was observed during the period of the Second Temple. In any event, fasting on the 9th of Av was observed during the mish-

Above *Rebuilding the Temple in Jerusalem, manuscript illumination from a 13th-century Bible.*

naic period. Some rabbis advocated permanent abstention from wine and meat in memory of the destruction of the Temple, but this was regarded as excessive.

The general rule in the Talmud for the mourning rites of Tishah B'Av is that a person is obliged to observe on it all mourning rites that apply in the case of the death of a next of kin. These rites have to be followed from sunset to sunset. Some mourning rites are already observed during the weeks prior to Tishah B'Av from the fast of the 17th of Tammuz. On the 1st of Av, the mourning rites are intensified. On the eve of Tishah B'Av, at the final meal before the fast, one should not partake of two cooked dishes nor eat meat nor drink wine. It is customary to eat a boiled egg at this meal, and to sprinkle ashes on it. Grace after this meal is said silently by each individual.

RULES FOR TISHAH B'AV

These rules are observed on the fast of Tishah B'Av:

1 There should be complete abstention from food and drink.
2 Bathing is forbidden. Washing of the hands and the face, however, are permissible for cleansing.
3 The use of oils for anointing or the application of perfumes is forbidden.
4 Sexual intercourse is forbidden.
5 Footwear made of leather is not to be worn.
6 One should sit on the ground or on a low stool.
7 It is customary to abstain from work.
8 The study of Torah is forbidden, except for the reading of the Book of Lamentations and its midrash, the Book of Job, the curses in the Book of Leviticus (Leviticus 26:14–42), several chapters in the Book of Jeremiah, and aggadic tales in the Talmud describing the destruction of Jerusalem.

NIGHT OF TISHAH B'AV

On the night of Tishah B'Av pious individuals used to sleep on the floor with a stone as a pillow. It was customary to fast until noon of the 10th of Av. Meat and wine should not be consumed until the afternoon of the 10th, although some of the mourning rites are lessened from Tishah B'Av afternoon onwards based on the belief that Tishah B'Av will again be a holiday since the Messiah will be born then. At the end of the 17th century, strict observance of Tishah B'Av also became a mark of adherence to traditional Judaism after Shabbetai Tzvi abolished the fast of Tishah B'Av and turned the day into a time of joyous celebration.

SYNAGOGUE OBSERVANCE

In the synagogue the following practices are observed:

1 The lights are dimmed and only a few candles lit. This is a symbol of the darkness which befell Israel.
2 The curtain of the Ark is removed in memory of the curtain in the Holy of Holies in the Temple. According to talmudic legend, it was stabbed and desecrated by Roman emperor Titus (39–81BCE).
3 Congregants sit on low benches or on the floor.
4 The cantor recites the prayers in a monotonous and melancholy fashion.
5 Some people change their customary seats.
6 In some congregations the Torah Scroll is placed on the floor and ashes are sprinkled on it.
7 The prayer service is the regular weekday service with a number of changes.
8 In some congregations it is customary not to wear prayer shawls and *tefillin*, or 'phylacteries', during the morning service. Instead they are worn during the afternoon service.
9 It is customary to sprinkle ashes on the head as a symbol of mourning. In Jerusalem, it is customary to visit the Western Wall where the Book of Lamentations is recited.

Below *Prayer with Torah scroll at the Western Wall, Jerusalem, on the 9th of Av, the anniversary of the destruction of both the First and Second Temples.*

CHAPTER 11

HOME CEREMONIES

In Judaism religious observance in the home is of central importance. According to the sages, the home is a *mikdash me-at*, or 'minor sanctuary'. Like the synagogue, home continues various traditions of the ancient Temple. The Sabbath candles, for example, recall the Temple menorah and the dining table symbolizes the altar. *Kashrut* or dietary laws and the discipline of keeping a kosher kitchen, together with ritual immersion, are seen as a part of a person's freewill choices about aligning one's life with God. In this context, honouring and respecting parents is regarded as an ideal. Most significantly, in the home family life is sanctified.

This chapter also considers personal piety and duties of the heart in Jewish religious practice. A good person shows humility, compassion, mercy and justice. Alongside the home, communal life is of fundamental importance. Within the context of community and synagogue, Jews express their loyalty to the traditions of their ancestors and their dedication to God.

Opposite A father putting the Passover basket on his son's head in the ritual meal held annually to mark the Exodus from Egypt. From the Barcelona Haggadah c.1340.

Above A family in Seattle, Washington DC, USA, holding a Passover seder, to commemorate the Jews' escape from slavery in Egypt.

HOME

ACCORDING TO THE TRADITION, THE HOME IS REGARDED AS A MINOR SANCTUARY. THROUGHOUT THE YEAR VARIOUS RELIGIOUS CEREMONIES TAKE PLACE IN A FAMILY SETTING.

The Jewish home is a *mikdash me'at* or minor sanctuary. Religious observance is of fundamental importance.

THE HOME AND THE TEMPLE

Like the synagogue, the home continues various traditions of the ancient Temple. The dining table symbolizes the altar and the Sabbath candles recall the Temple menorah.

Most significantly, within the home, family life is sanctified. As head of the family, the father is to exercise authority over his wife and children. He is obligated to circumcise his son, redeem him from Temple service in a special ceremony if he is the first-born, teach him the Torah, marry him off and teach him a craft. Moreover, the father of the family is required to serve as a role model for the transmission of Jewish ideals to his offspring.

Below *A Jewish woman hiding leavened bread for her husband to find, 1723. At the beginning of Passover, leavened bread must be removed from the house.*

WIFE AND MOTHER

The prevailing sentiment is that the wife's role is to bear children and exercise responsibility for family life.

According to Jewish law, womanhood is a separate status with its own sets of rules. In terms of religious observance, women were classed as slaves and children, disqualified as witnesses, excluded from the study of the Torah and segregated from men. Moreover, they were viewed as ritually impure for extended periods of time. In general, they were exempted from time-bound commandments. As a consequence, they were not obliged to fulfil those commandments that must be observed at a particular time. The purpose of these restrictions was to ensure that their attention and energy be directed towards completing their domestic duties.

In the modern world, however, a growing number of women have agitated for equal treatment and the role of women has undergone a major transformation.

Above *An Orthodox Jewish father from Tiberias, Israel, holding his son. Family life is central to Judaism.*

CHILDREN

Young people are to carry out the commandment to honour and respect their parents. For the rabbis, the concept means providing parents with food, drink, clothing and transportation. Respect requires children do not sit in a parent's seat, interrupt them, or express an opinion in a dispute involving a parent. The Talmud extols this: 'There are three partners in man, the Holy One, blessed be He, the father and the mother. When a man honours his [parents], the Holy One, blessed be He, says, "I will ascribe [merit] to them as though I had dwelt among them and they had honoured me."'

DOMESTIC HARMONY

The ideal of home life is domestic harmony. The Talmud specifies the guidelines for attaining this goal: 'A man should spend less than his means on food, up to his means on clothes, and more than his means in honouring wife and children because they are dependent on him.' Such harmony is attained through give and take, as well as the observance of Jewish ritual. When the family follows God's commandments, the home is permeated with sanctity.

Left *Hebrew postcard from the 1920s showing a Hungarian Jewish family gathered around the dinner table.*

SYMBOLS AND OBSERVANCE

Mezuzahs on each doorpost characterize the Jewish home. In Scripture it is written that 'these words' shall be written on the mezuzot, or 'doorposts', of the house (Deuteronomy 6:4–9; 11:13–21). This is understood literally; these two passages are copied by hand on to parchment, put into a case and fixed to the doorpost of every room in the house.

Sabbath candles are important home ritual objects. At least two candles should be used in honour of the dual commandment to remember and observe the Sabbath day. This ceremony is performed before sunset on Sabbath eve as well as at festivals symbolizing light and joy. Lighting the candles is normally the wife's task.

The cycle of the year provides various opportunities for home observances. On Passover normal dishes are replaced. Traditional law excludes the use of all domestic utensils, crockery and cutlery. As a result sets are kept especially for this holiday. The seder, or 'religious meal', itself is observed on the first night of Passover. On Sukkot it is customary to dwell in a *sukkah*, or 'booth', built for the festival in a yard, garden or balcony. It is covered by foliage through which the stars can be seen at night. During Hanukkah a festival lamp is kindled at home on each day of the festival in memory of the victory of the Maccabees over the Seleucids. Life-cycle events also provide an occasion for special observances in the home.

MODERN JUDAISM

In contemporary society Orthodox Judaism continues to carry out these home activities. However, within the various branches of non-Orthodox Judaism modifications have been made to those traditions and a number of home festivities have been eliminated because they are no longer viewed as spiritually significant. None the less, there is a universal recognition among Jewry that the home is central to Jewish existence and survival.

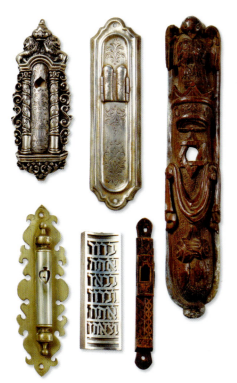

Left *Mezuzah cases. Such cases contained Bible scrolls and were fixed to doorposts to protect the household.*

Below *A family reads the Haggadah during the Passover celebration.*

COMMUNITY LIFE

IN THE JEWISH WORLD, COMMUNAL LIFE IS OF FUNDAMENTAL SIGNIFICANCE. IT IS WITHIN THE COMMUNITY THAT JEWS ARE ABLE TO CARRY OUT THEIR RITUAL AND MORAL RESPONSIBILITIES.

Through the centuries, community life had been of central importance in the Jewish faith. Alongside the home, Jews have encouraged active participation within the community. Community centres, synagogues and other venues help unite the Jewish people into a collective whole.

THE ANCIENT WORLD

In ancient Israel, Jews constituted a Hebrew clan. Later, as they changed from a nomadic to an agricultural existence, they lived in towns. As a result, their leadership became urbanized. Leaders were responsible for administering justice and towns were organized into territorial units. During the Babylonian exile, Jewish institutions established a pattern for later communal development. As early as the 2nd century BCE, Jews in Alexandria formed their own corporation with a council that regulated its affairs in accordance with Jewish law. It also constructed synagogues and sent taxes which were collected for the Temple in Jerusalem. In the Roman Empire, Jews were judged by their own courts: this system established the basis for legal autonomy which became a standard for Jewish life throughout the world.

THE DIASPORA

When the Temple was destroyed in 70CE, Jewish life underwent a transformation. In Israel the patriarchate together with the Sanhedrin served as the central authority. In Babylonia, on the other hand, the exilarch was the leader of the community along with the heads of the rabbinical academies. Jews were bound together by the law, and synagogues, law courts, schools, philanthropic institutions and ritual baths constituted the framework of communal life. In North Africa and Spain, the *nagid* ('prince') was the head of the community. Later in the medieval period in the Franco-German region, rabbinical authorities exercised communal leadership. As in Babylonia, a wide range of institutions regulated daily life, and taxes were raised to provide for the needy. In this milieu the synagogue served as the centre for Jewish worship and study.

Above *A kosher butcher weighing beef in his shop at the Orthodox Jewish community headquarters in Budapest. Kosher (Kashrut) meat is required as part of Jewish dietary law.*

COMMUNAL STATUTES

In order to regulate communal affairs, *takkanot ha-kahal*, or 'statutes', were established; these were amplified by special ordinances and enactments. To ensure their enforcement, a *bet din*, or 'court', was presided over by a panel of *dayyanim*, or 'judges'. These courts excommunicated offenders. The parnas, or 'community's head', was recognized by the secular or church authorities. He and the local rabbi were often designated as Master of the Jews or Bishop of the Jews. From the 14th century, Polish Jewry gained dominance in Eastern Europe and communal autonomy was often invested in the Jewish community of a central town which had responsibilities for smaller communities in the region. In Poland – Lithuania,

Below *Conversation in the street. Polish Jews in the ghetto at Vienna, Austro-Hungary, c.1873.*

the Council of the Four Lands functioned as a Jewish parliament. By contrast, in the Ottoman empire a chief rabbi was recognized as the Jewish community's representative. Each province of the empire had its own chief rabbi.

THE ENLIGHTENMENT

With the advent of the Enlightenment in the 18th century, the traditional pattern of Jewish life was fundamentally altered. Previously, Jews were unable to opt out of the community. However, with full citizenship rights, Jews assimilated into the wider community. In modern times, Jews have adjusted communal life to contemporary demands. In contrast with previous centres where Jewish life was uniform in character, the Jewish community has fragmented into a number of different religious groupings.

MODERN JUDAISM

On the far right of the Jewish spectrum, Orthodoxy has sought to preserve the beliefs and practices of the past. From the late 18th century, Orthodox Jews opposed changes to Jewish existence brought about by the Enlightenment. Moving to the centre of the religious spectrum, Conservative Judaism advocates a moderate stance in which traditional law is observed, but modified according to contemporary needs. As an offshoot of the Conservative movement, Reconstructionist Judaism rejects supernaturalism while adopting a moderately traditional approach to Jewish life. Reform Judaism has adopted a more liberal stance, intent on modernizing Judaism for the contemporary world. Humanistic Judaism espouses a more radical position; like Reconstructionist Judaism it rejects any form of supernaturalism and focuses on humanistic values. Alongside these movements, there are a variety of alterna1tive approaches to Jewish existence that espouse a range of differing ideologies.

Above *The circular city of Nahalal, Israel. An aerial view of the first moshav, a co-operative settlement consisting of small separate farms, founded in the Jezreel Valley.*

THE COMMUNAL IDEAL

Throughout Jewish history, communal life has undergone enormous change. Yet despite the variations in form, the Jewish people have been united in their determination to preserve and transmit their religious traditions. Despite their varied forms of organization, Jews remain loyal to the concept of *K'lal Yisrael*, or 'the community of Israel', and are intent on ensuring the survival of Judaism and the Jewish people. It is within the context of community that Jewry continues to gain spiritual sustenance and strength.

Below *A bet din (Jewish court dealing especially with religious questions) in London's East End, 1930s.*

PRAYERS AND BLESSINGS

PRAYER IS AT THE HEART OF THE JEWISH TRADITION. THE TALMUD DESCRIBES IT AS BELONGING TO THE HIGHEST THINGS OF THE WORLD. IT LETS JEWS ESTABLISH A DIRECT CONTACT WITH THE CREATOR.

Jewish prayer is usually recited in Hebrew; this is the language of the Bible, the prophets and the sages of Israel. It is customary for prayers to be chanted, since this endows the words with a more profound meaning. The Ashkenazim and the Sephardim use different traditions of chant, and there are also different chants in the traditions of German, French, Italian, Lithuanian and Polish Jews. These forms of chanting vary depending on the context: the weekday mode of chanting differs from that of the festivals. On Rosh Hashanah and Yom Kippur the chanting is more solemn.

Below *An illuminated heading from a German prayer book, c.1320, for the Day of Atonement, which is observed by praying and fasting.*

Right The Rabbi, *1892, by Jan Styka. The leather box and straps are the tefillin and contains four Torah texts.*

GESTURES

Traditionally a number of movements and gestures are made during various parts of the liturgy. Bowing and prostrating the body are frequently described in the Bible. The Talmud limits bowing to four stages in the Amidah prayer, which is recited while standing. These four bows take place at the beginning and end of the first benediction and at the beginning and end of the thanksgiving benediction near the end of the Amidah. The correct procedure for bowing is to bend the head and the body from the waist while reciting *Barukh Atah*, or 'Blessed art Thou'. Then one should straighten the head and after it the body so that head and body are upright when saying *Adonai*, or 'O Lord'.

During the biblical period it was customary for total prostration of the body to take place with the face to the ground and arms and legs outstretched. Today this only takes place during the Alenu prayer on Rosh Hashanah and Yom Kippur and while reciting the account of the Temple service on Yom Kippur. Some Jews also cover the eyes with the right hand while reciting the first verse of

SWAYING

It is customary for traditional Jews to sway while reciting prayer. In Yiddish this is known as *shocklen*. In the past some sages were opposed to swaying since they believed it lacked decorum. Other scholars permitted a gentle form of swaying of the head as an aid to concentration. Others, such as the Hasidim, however, advocated the use of violent movements and gestures. Advocates of such a practice cite Psalm 35: 10 to emphasize the necessity of swaying: 'All my bones shall say, Lord who is like unto Thee' – in their view, this verse suggests that the entire body should move in praise of God.

Above *Tashlich prayer by the Yarkon River, Israel. On the first day of Rosh Hashanah, prayers are recited near water.*

the Shema: 'Hear, O Israel, the Lord our God, the Lord is One.' This is done so that one is not distracted during the recitation of this prayer.

TEMPLE AND SYNAGOGUE

Since the destruction of the Temple in Jerusalem in the 1st century CE, the synagogue has become the central place of prayer. No longer are sacrifices offered as they were in ancient times, and the use of incense, which was associated with the Temple cult, has been abandoned. It is also incorrect to have a seven-branched menorah in the synagogue like the one used in the Temple. However, since the 19th century, Reform Jews have referred to their place of worship as a 'temple', but such a designation is regarded by traditional Jews as a misnomer.

COVERING THE HEAD

During the talmudic period, it was a mark of piety to cover the head. This is because heaven is described as above in both spatial and spiritual terms. For this reason it has become customary for Jewish men to cover their head; by doing so they create a barrier between themselves and the heavenly domain. Both Orthodox and non-Orthodox men cover their head during worship services, and recently this practice has been adopted by some women in non-Orthodox synagogues. It is also common for Orthodox men (as well as some traditionalists) to wear head coverings at all times.

SYNAGOGUE DECORUM

According to tradition, the synagogue should be a place where Jews worship in a spirit of holiness. One should not eat or drink in the synagogue; conversation during prayers should be avoided unless necessary for the conduct of the service; and a synagogue should not be used as a short-cut from one place to another. Yet, despite such a spirit of decorum, traditionally the synagogue should be regarded as a familiar place where Jews gather together for religious purposes.

BLESSINGS

There are four types of blessings in Judaism. The first are blessings to be recited when enjoying God's bounty. For each type of enjoyment (such as eating bread or fruit) a specific blessing was introduced. Another group of blessings is recited before the performance of a *mitzvah* or commandment: 'Blessed art thou ... Who has sanctified us with his commandments and has commanded us to ...'. A third type of blessing consists of those said on beholding the wonders of nature. Finally, there are blessings of general

Above *Rabbi's Blessing, 1871, by Moritz Daniel Oppenheim, one of the leading German Jewish artists.*

praise such as the blessing of the kiddush on the Sabbath and festivals, or the blessings at a wedding.

PRAYERS OF THE DAY

There are three daily prayers: *shaharit* or morning prayer, *minhah* (afternoon) and *ma'ariv* (evening). Morning prayer should be recited just after sunrise; afternoon prayer can be recited from 20 minutes after midday until nightfall; evening prayer can be recited at any time during the night until dawn, but it is customary for minhah and ma'ariv to be recited one after the other. The central feature of all three prayers is the Amidah, which consists of 18 benedictions. There are three opening benedictions, a series of intermediate benedictions, and three closing benedictions. These benedictions were written at various times between 100BCE and 100CE and were gathered together in their final form by Rabban Gamaliele II. Before the Amidah in the morning and evening service, the Shema is recited together with a number of blessings.

Parents and Children

ACCORDING TO SCRIPTURE, IT IS THE DUTY OF CHILDREN TO HONOUR AND REVERE PARENTS. IN RABBINIC LITERATURE, SUCH DUTIES ARE ELABORATED IN DETAIL.

In the Jewish faith respect for parents is a cardinal virtue. Scripture uses two different expressions to describe such an attitude. In Exodus 20:12 Jews are instructed to 'honour thy father and thy mother'; Leviticus 19:3 states: 'Each one of you shall revere his mother and his father'.

RABBINIC JUDAISM

On the basis of these two passages, rabbinic sages taught that there is a double obligation to honour parents and revere them. They point out that in the verse from Exodus the father is mentioned first, whereas in the verse from Leviticus the mother is referred to first. The reason given is that children are more ready to honour their mother than their father, but are more ready to revere their father than their mother. As a result, the parent who might be neglected is mentioned first. This is as if to say, you may not need reminders to honour your father and to revere your mother. But do not forget to honour both and to revere both.

Above *Father, son and great grandfather at a circumcision ceremony in Tel Aviv, Israel.*

PARENTAL DUTIES

According to rabbinic Judaism, the duty to honour parents is defined as the obligation to provide them with food and drink, clothe them and escort them. The duty to revere parents is defined as the obligation not to stand or sit in their place, contradict them or take sides in a dispute involving them. The duty to honour parents is conceived as positive – to do what they require. But the duty to revere them is a negative requirement: not to do that which causes them distress.

OBLIGATIONS OF CHILDREN

These requirements require clarification. For example, to give parents food and drink and clothe them can mean either it is the responsibility of children to support their parents financially or, alternatively, it could mean simply that children should be courteous to their mother and father, serving them with their meals, and helping them on with their clothes – in such cases food and clothing would have been purchased by the parents themselves. This issue was debated by later scholars. The final ruling is that children have no obligation to support their parents financially. Yet, if

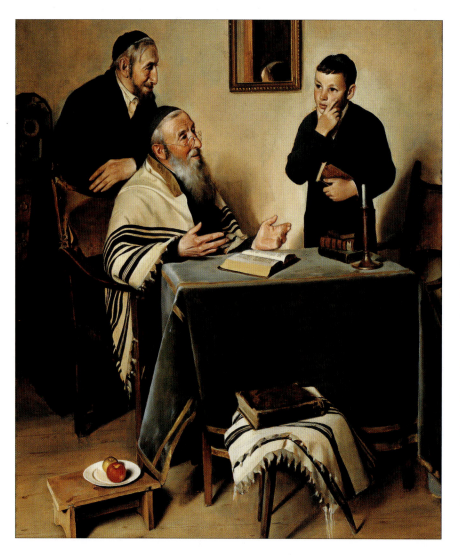

Left The Lesson. *A boy studies the Talmud in this Austrian painting of 1930 by F.X. Wolf.*

Left *Across the generations. Grandparents and grandchildren lighting candles for Hanukkah.*

their parents are too poor to provide for their own needs, then their children must support them financially. Regarding the obligation not to contradict parents or patronize them, this does not imply that children are not permitted to disagree with their mother and father. It means instead that children should not give the impression of judging their parents' opinions in a patronizing fashion. Children do not have to forfeit their own opinions; on the contrary, they have a right to their own views. The obligation not to stand or sit in a parent's place is understood both literally and figuratively. If a father has a special place at home, a child should not occupy it unless a parent has no objection. Further, the injunction means that if a parent has a special position in the community, children should not take the same role. However, it is permitted for parents to forgo their rights in these matters.

LIMITATIONS

Despite such obligations to parents, there are limits to what a mother and father can demand. The commandment to honour parents does not give parents the right to act in a dictatorial fashion. Children have rights, and the wishes of parents should be set aside if children are expected to commit a crime or disobey the *mitzvot*, or 'commandments'. According to a number of authorities, there is not an obligation for children to obey their parents other than in the cases specified by Jewish law. Thus, if a parent objects to the person their son or daughter chooses to marry, the parents' wishes do not have to be respected. When parents divorce, children can be tempted to take sides, but this should be resisted. Children should avoid playing one parent against another. When there are contradictory demands to the father and mother, the children must do their best to be impartial.

HONOUR

The obligation to honour and revere parents is extended by rabbinic sages in various ways. Honour is to be paid to parents who are no longer alive. The institutions of *kaddish*, or 'reciting a prayer for the dead', and *yahrzeit*, or 'lighting a memorial candle', were introduced for this purpose. There are also other categories of individuals to whom respect is due – this is a further extension of this commandment. These include grandparents, parents-in-law, step-parents, older siblings, and teachers. Yet, duties to parents must always come first.

Below *Grandfather, father, son. Three generations of Jews reading from the Torah for the son's bar mitzvah.*

Dietary Laws

SCRIPTURE DIFFERENTIATES BETWEEN FOOD WHICH IS KOSHER AND FOOD WHICH IS FORBIDDEN. THESE REGULATIONS WERE EXPANDED IN RABBINIC SOURCES.

According to Scripture, food must be *kosher*, or 'ritually fit', if it is to be consumed. Through the centuries, Jews have observed these biblical regulations as well as rabbinic prescriptions. The laws of *kashrut* are of seminal importance in the tradition.

BIBLICAL LAW

The Bible declares that laws of kashrut were given by God to Moses on Mount Sinai. As a result, Jews are obligated to follow this legislation due to its divine origin. Nevertheless, various reasons have been adduced for such observance. Allegedly, forbidden foods are unhealthy; that is why they are forbidden. Another explanation is that those who refrain from eating particular kinds of food serve God even while eating. Thereby they are able to attain an elevated spiritual state. Some of these laws, such as refraining from eating pork, have gained such significance that Jews were prepared to sacrifice their lives rather than violate God's law.

ANIMALS, BIRDS AND FISH

The laws concerning which animals, birds and fish may be eaten are contained in Leviticus 11 and Deuteronomy 14:3–21. The Bible states that only those animals that chew the cud and have split hooves may be eaten. Such animals include cows and sheep. However, no similar formula is stated concerning which birds may be consumed; instead a list is given of forbidden birds. Although no reasons are given to explain these choices, it has been suggested that forbidden birds are in fact birds of prey. By not eating them, human beings are able to express their abhorrence of cruelty as well as the exploitation of the weak over the strong. Regarding fish, the law states that only fish that have both fins and scales are allowed. Again, no reason is given to support this explanation. Yet various explanations have been proposed, such as the argument that fish that do not have fins and scales frequently live in the depths of the sea, which was regarded as the abode of the gods of chaos.

Above *A rabbi wearing a prayer shawl supervises production of kosher wines at a winery in Tuscany, Italy.*

SLAUGHTER

A further category of kashrut deals with *shehitah*, or 'the method of killing animals for food'. Even though the Torah does not specify the details of this procedure, the Talmud states this method has divine authority since it was explained by God to Moses on Mount Sinai. According to tradition, the act of slaughter must be done with a sharpened knife without a single notch, because that might tear the animal's food pipe or windpipe.

Numerous other laws govern this procedure. A person must be trained in the law if he is to act as a *shohet*, or 'slaughterer'. According to rabbinic scholars, the central idea underlying the laws of ritual slaughter is to give the animal as painless a death as is possible. Judaism does not require that the devout become vegetarians, but when animals are killed for food this must be done

Below *A Jewish bakery in the le Marais district of Paris.*

so as to cause the least amount of suffering possible.

Another aspect of ritual slaughter is the concern that no animal is eaten if it has a defect. In such cases it is referred to as *terefah*, or 'torn'. The prohibition against terefah is based on Exodus 22:31. This law is elaborated in the Mishnah where the sages decree that terefah refers not only to the meat of an animal torn by wild beasts but to any serious defect in an animal's or a bird's organs. On the basis of this law, the shohet is obliged to examine the lungs of an animal after it has been slaughtered to ensure that no defect is found. If any irregularity is found in an animal that has been slaughtered it should be taken to a rabbi to determine if it is kosher. In the preparation of meat, it is imperative that adequate salting takes place. This prescription is based on the biblical prohibition against consuming blood.

MILK AND MEAT

Another restriction concerning ritual food is the prohibition against eating milk and meat together. This stipulation is based on Exodus 23:19: 'Thou shalt not boil a kid in its mother's milk'. According to rabbinic Judaism, this rule does not

Below *A German Jewish slaughtering yard in the 1700s. Animals are killed according to Jewish dietary laws by cutting the animal's throat and allowing the blood to drain out.*

refer only to the act of boiling a kid in its mother's milk. Tradition stipulates that it is forbidden to cook meat and milk together. Later, this law was expanded to eating milk and meat products at the same time. Eventually the law was introduced that dairy dishes should not be eaten after a meal until a stipulated period of time had passed. Meat, on the other hand, may be eaten after dairy produce; none the less, it is usual to wash the mouth out beforehand. Not only should milk and meat products not be consumed at the same time, dairy food should not be cooked in meat utensils, and vice versa.

MODERN JUDAISM

Although the Bible does not attempt to explain the origin of these various dietary laws, it does associate them with holiness. The rabbis of the Talmud and midrash explored the rationale of the system of kashrut. Generally they believed that observance of such laws aids the development of self-discipline and moral conduct.

Today, kosher food is obtainable in kosher food stores and some supermarkets. Observant Jews eat in kosher restaurants, which have been inspected by supervisors.

Above *Purifying dishes for Passover, an important part of the preparations, in Mea Shearim neighbourhood, Jerusalem.*

Up until modern times the rules of kashrut were universally practised by Jewry. Yet, in the 19th century, the Reform movement broke with tradition. For this reason, most Reform Jews have largely ignored the prescriptions of the dietary system. Conservative Judaism, however, adheres to the laws of kashrut, although allowance is made for personal selectivity. Orthodox Judaism, on the other hand, strictly follows the tradition.

Below *Seal of approval. Packaged kosher food is sealed with a label, often called a hechsher.*

Conversion

ACCORDING TO TRADITION, A PERSON IS JEWISH IF HIS OR HER MOTHER IS JEWISH. HOWEVER, CONVERSION HAS ALWAYS BEEN A ROUTE OF ENTRY INTO THE JEWISH COMMUNITY.

Although there is no formal term for the process of conversion in the Hebrew Bible, there are several biblical terms that are suggestive of such an act. Such terms illustrate that conversion was practised during the biblical period in order to assimilate conquered peoples as well as those who came to live within the Israelite community. During the tannaitic and amoraic periods (100BCE–600CE), conversion was frequently extolled by various authorities. According to the early rabbinic sage Elazar, for example, conversion was viewed as part of God's salvationist scheme. According to Hoshiah, another early rabbinic authority, God acted righteously towards Israel when he scattered them among the nations. In another passage in the Talmud it is asserted that the proselyte is dearer to God than the Israelite since he has come of his own accord.

As a result of such openness to converts, a number of gentiles converted to Judaism during the early rabbinic period. However, the rise of Christianity led to the cessation of Jewish missionizing. None the less, during the talmudic and post-talmudic period occasional conversions did take place in accordance with rabbinic law. Eventually the regulations governing conversion were drawn together and edited by Joseph Caro (1488–1575), the compiler of the *Shulkhan Arukh*, which since its publication in 1565 has served as the authoritative Code of Jewish Law.

CANDIDATE CONVERSION

In the *Shulkhan Arukh* the requirements for conversion as laid down in the Talmud and other codes are detailed. When a man or woman

Above *Ethiopian immigrants to Israel demonstrate against a ruling by the rabbinate that they must undergo conversion to be considered Jews, 1996.*

appears as a candidate, the person is asked: 'What motivates you? Do you know that, in these days, Jews are subject to persecution and discrimination, that they are hounded and troubled?' If the individual replies: 'I know this and yet I regard myself as unworthy of being joined to them,' the convert is accepted immediately. The root principles of the faith, namely the unity of God and the prohibition of idol worship, are expounded to the candidate at considerable length. The proselyte is taught, too, some of the simpler and some of the more difficult commandments, and is informed of the punishment involved in violating the commandments.

Similarly, the convert is told of the rewards of observing them, particularly that by virtue of keeping the commandments he or she will merit the life of the world to come. He or she is told that no one is considered wholly righteous except those who understand and fulfil the commandments. Further, the convert is told that the world to come is intended only for the righteous. If the male convert finds these doctrines acceptable, he is circumcised immediately. After his circumcision has completely healed, he undergoes ritual immersion. Three learned Jews stand by

Below *Passover Haggadah showing Savants at the Table of Maimonides. From left: Joseph Caro, Isaac Alfasi, Maimonides, Jacob ben Asher and Rashi. Laws regulating conversion are contained in compendiums of Jewish law compiled by such rabbinic scholars.*

Above *Jews washing in a small spring mikveh (ritual bath) outside the Tomb of the Prophet Samuel, north of Jerusalem. Traditionally, converts undergo ritual immersion in a mikveh.*

Above *American entertainers Frank Sinatra and Sammy Davis Jr were members of the Rat Pack. Both championed Jewish civil rights and causes in the USA, and Davis became a Jew.*

while he is in the water and instruct him in some of the easy and some of the difficult commandments.

In the case of the female proselyte, Jewish women accompany her and supervise her immersion. The three learned male Jews remain outside the *mikveh*, or 'pool', and give the convert instruction while she is in the water.

THE CANDIDATE'S MOTIVES

The *Shulkhan Arukh* states: 'When the would-be proselyte presents himself, the convert should be examined lest the person be motivated to enter the congregation of Israel by hope of financial gain or social advantage or by fear. A man is examined lest his motive be to marry a Jewish woman, and a woman is questioned lest she have similar desires towards some Jewish man.' If no unacceptable motive is found, the candidate is told of the heaviness of the yoke of the Torah and how difficult it is for the average person to live up to the commandments of the Torah. This is done to give the candidate a chance to withdraw if he so desires. Once a man is circumcised and a man or woman is ritually immersed, the convert is no longer a non-Jew. The central feature of these regulations governing the traditional conversion procedure is the emphasis on joining the Jewish community and accepting the law.

MODERN JUDAISM

Up until the present day, the procedure outlined in the *Shulkhan Arukh* has been rigorously followed. Within modern Orthodox Judaism, the emphasis is on living a Jewish way of life within the community. For this reason, converts are given extensive religious instruction. Conservative Judaism generally follows these legal requirements, but Reform Judaism has departed from the traditional practice in a variety of ways. Emphasizing the universalistic mission of Judaism, Reform Jews very early in their history abrogated the necessity of ritual immersion for converts. On the question of circumcision, opinion was at first divided. Eventually, however, it was generally accepted that the only requirements were that the person freely seek membership, that the candidate be of good character and be sufficiently acquainted with the faith and practices of Judaism. Unlike Orthodoxy, Reform Judaism accepts conversion for the sake of marriage.

Right *Harvest scene from the Book of Ruth, 1320. According to Scripture, Ruth was a Moabite woman who joined the Jewish people.*

HOME CEREMONIES

DUTIES OF THE HEART

NOT ONLY ARE JEWS OBLIGATED TO FULFIL RITUAL AND MORAL DUTIES, THEY ARE ALSO COMMANDED TO DIRECT THEIR SPIRITUAL LIFE IN ACCORDANCE WITH GOD'S WILL.

In *c.* 1080 the 11th-century Jewish philosopher Bahya Ibn Pakudah wrote an important treatise *Duties of the Heart*. In this he described Jewish obligations as comprising duties which he calls practices of the limbs: these are acts a Jew is obliged to perform. In addition, he listed a second category – duties of the heart – which relate to the inner life.

SPIRITUALITY

In the past, Jewish writers promoted inwardness. What is clear is that the norm for these sages was different from the attitude of modern Jews. For example, Bahya discussed the concept of equanimity. In his view, it is essential for a person to adopt such an attitude if God is to be truly worshipped. In other words, a spiritual person must be indifferent to the praise and blame of others. Such an individual should so love God that he does not care what others think. His mind and heart should be directly focused on the Divine. Yet, for most Jews today such an attitude of disinterestedness is not based on the love of God, but on a disdain of the opinions of others. Moreover, such an attitude can result in indolence. If a person does good only to satisfy others, his motivation is not adequate. On the other hand, one who aspires to do good only for the sake of heaven is leaving it up to himself to decide if and when God is satisfied. Indeed, he may in fact trying to deflect criticism by believing that his motives are for God alone. This can result in complacency and self-satisfaction.

Right *Prayer at Home, c.1470. A facsimile of a Hebrew book of sacred texts painted by the Italian Renaissance master Leonardo Bellini.*

CHARACTER

According to Judaism, one who has a good character should possess the traits of humility, compassion, love of mercy and a sense of justice. Conversely, he or she should avoid such attitudes as pride, vanity, cruelty, falsehood and bad temper. To be humble does not mean that a person should be unaware of his talents. Rather, such an individual should regard all his positive qualities as a gift

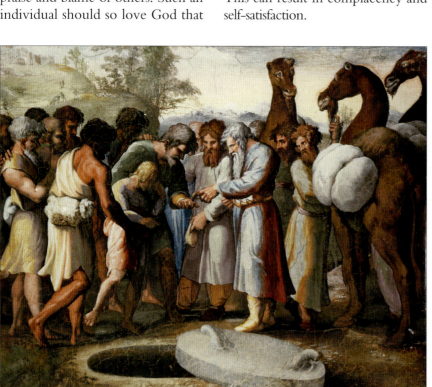

Left *When Joseph's brothers sold him into slavery they betrayed their brotherly duty. From a painting by Raphael.*

> ### THE ASCETIC LIFE
> Bahya and others' views on the ascetic life should be viewed with caution by those with no saintly pretensions. Judaism demands correct action. But there is no requirement to be a saint. Ascetics in previous centuries have denied themselves food and drink and rarely slept in a comfortable bed. At times they flogged themselves and performed other acts of self-torture. Such actions are not required; indeed, such can even lead to morbid self-hatred.

Right *A cantor reads the Haggadah to illiterate members of a Spanish synagogue so that all can take part. 14th-century Sephardi manuscript.*

from God for which he can claim no credit. In this regard, there is a religious dimension of a good character. The pursuit of truth, for example, is connected with the God of truth. Falsehood is a distortion of reality, an affront to God.

PEACE

Rabbinic sages stated that it is permitted to tell harmless lies for the sake of peace. An example of this is Joseph's statement to his brothers that their father, Jacob, had ordered him to forgive them for their wrongdoing. This was not true, but Joseph was telling a lie to preserve family peace. The rabbis also say that a lie is in order if a person is asked indelicate questions about his married life. In such a case, he has no obligation to tell the truth. Again, it is permissible to lie about how much Torah learning one has in order to avoid appearing as a braggart.

Below *A woman prays at the Tomb of the Righteous Rabbi Ovadia in the Upper Galilee, Israel.*

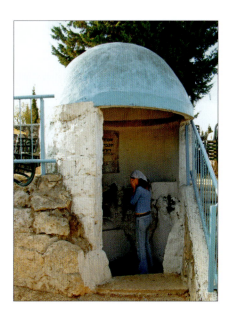

BAD TEMPER

Within the Jewish tradition, a bad temper is severely criticized. A person who breaks things in a fit of temper is compared to an idolator because the loss of self-control is due to an inadequate awareness of God's presence. Even when a parent or teacher is obliged to show disapproval, they should retain control, making only the outward signs of displeasure. As the Ethics of the Fathers states in the Mishnah: 'The man who is quick to become angry but is easily appeased, his virtue outweighs his fault. The person who rarely flies into a rage but when he does so is hard to appease – his fault outweighs his virtue. The man who is quick to be angry and hard to appease is wicked. The man who rarely loses his temper and on the occasions when he does so is easily appeased – that person is a saint.'

THE LOVE AND FEAR OF GOD

Love and fear of God are duties of the heart that have received a range of interpretations. In the Bible, they are usually synonymous with righteous action. It is not only that justice and righteousness lead to love and fear of God, but in a sense they are the love and fear of God. In rabbinic literature the love of God generally means love of God's law; the fear of God refers to the avoidance of sin. Among medieval mystics, the love and fear of God is viewed as a yearning of the human soul for the nearness of the Creator and its dread and awe at his majesty.

Ritual Immersion

A MIKVEH, OR 'COLLECTION OF WATER', REFERS TO ANY POOL OR BATH OF CLEAR WATER WHICH IS USED FOR RITUAL IMMERSION. SUCH IMMERSION RENDERS A PERSON RITUALLY CLEAN.

From ancient times to the present, the mikveh has played a central role in Jewish life. By immersing in a mikveh a person who has become ritually unclean through contact with the dead or any other defiling object, or through an unclean flux from the body, can become ritually clean. The mikveh is also used for vessels that have become unclean.

In the modern world, the chief use of the mikveh is for a woman who has just menstruated. According to Jewish law, the contracting of marital relations with a wife who is in an unclean state is a serious offence.

The mikveh is also commonly used for the immersion of proselytes, or converts to Judaism, as part of the ceremony of conversion.

In addition, immersion in the mikveh is practised by various groups as an aid to spirituality, particularly on the Sabbath and festivals, especially the Day of Atonement.

SPIRITUALITY

The purpose of immersion is not physical, but spiritual. According to the 12th-century philosopher Moses Maimonides, the laws about immersion as a means of freeing oneself from uncleanness are decrees laid down by Scripture. They are not matters that human beings can rationally comprehend. Uncleanliness thus should not be viewed as mud or filth which water can remove, but rather of a spiritual nature and depending on the intention of the heart. For this reason the sages stated: 'If a man immerses himself, but without special intention, it is as though he has not immersed himself at all.'

THE MORAL RATIONALE

There is a moral basis for immersion. Just as one who sets his heart on becoming clean becomes clean as soon as he has immersed himself (although nothing new has occurred to his body), so, too, one who sets his heart on turning away from evil becomes clean as soon as he resolves to change his ways. For this reason, Scripture states: 'And I will sprinkle clean water upon you and you shall be clean, from all your uncleanliness and from all your idols will I cleanse you' (Ezekiel 36:25).

THE WATER

All natural spring water, provided it is clean and has not been discoloured by any admixtures, is valid for a mikveh. With regard to rainwater, melted snow or ice, care must be taken to ensure the water flows freely. The water must

Above *Mikveh (ritual bath) at Masada, Israel. The water in a mikveh should come from a natural spring or river.*

Left *Jewish women in the mikveh or ritual bath. An engraving from 1726 by Johann Georg Puschner.*

Below *A non-traditional Jewish group in Pennsylvania, USA, have a mikveh in a swimming pool.*

RITUAL IMMERSION

Left *A Kosher mikveh, still used to this day in the old city of Jerusalem.*

the correct amount of valid water, it does not become invalid even though someone adds drawn water to it.

TYPES OF MIKVEH

When there is a plentiful supply of valid water which can replenish the mikveh, the only condition to be fulfilled is to ensure the water does not become invalidated by the construction of the mikveh, which renders it a vessel, or by going through metal pipes, which are not sunk into the ground. Since most mikvaot are constructed in urban areas where such supplies are not freely available, the technological and halakhic solution of a valid mikveh depends essentially upon constructing a mikveh with valid water and replenishing it with invalid water, taking advantage of the fact the addition of this water to an originally valid one does not invalidate it.

Below *A Hungarian Orthodox Jew prays in the yard of the mikveh after making his dishes kosher.*

BIBLICAL LAW

According to biblical law, any collection of water, drawn or otherwise, is suitable for a mikveh as long as it contains enough for a person to immerse himself. The rabbis, however, enacted that only water which has not been drawn in a vessel or receptacle may be used. The rabbis further established that the minimum quantity for immersion is 250–1,000 litres/55–220 gallons. A mikveh containing less than this amount becomes invalid should a specified amount of drawn water be added to it. If the mikveh contains more than this amount, it can never become invalid no matter how much water is added. A mikveh may be be hewn out of rock or built in or put on the ground, and any material is suitable. It must be watertight, otherwise it becomes invalid. Finally, the height must be 47 inches (119.3 cm) to enable a person standing in it to be completely immersed even though he has to bend the knees.

not reach the mikveh through vessels made of metal or other materials. This is avoided by attaching the pipes and other accessories to the ground, which means they cease to have the status of vessels. The mikveh should be emptied from above by hand, by vacuum or by electric or automatic pumps. There is one regulation that eases the problems of constructing a valid mikveh. Once the mikveh has

CHAPTER 12

LIFE CYCLE EVENTS

The Jewish life cycle is marked by a series of religious events which celebrate various stages of development. Beginning at birth, a number of ceremonies mark the acceptance of the child into the Jewish community. For male infants, the act of circumcision symbolizes the child's identification as a Jew. The Redemption of the First-Born recalls the ancient practice of redeeming the child from Temple service. Bar and bat mitzvah constitute steps towards Jewish adulthood. Finally, the Jewish marriage service binds the bride and groom in the presence of God.

At the end of life, the utmost regard and consideration is shown to the dying. Jewish law stipulates that the body must be buried as soon as possible after death. The general pattern for funerals involves the ritual rending of garments, the funeral procession, the eulogy, either in a funeral chapel or beside the grave, and memorial prayers. Once the funeral is over, it is customary for the family to return home to begin a period of mourning.

Opposite A Jewish marriage contract from the Netherlands, 1648. The purpose of Jewish marriage is to create a Jewish home and a family and thus continue the Jewish community.

Above A Jewish Wedding, 1903, by the Dutch artist Jozef Israëls, is a portrait that explores marital tenderness.

LIFE CYCLE EVENTS

BIRTH

IN THE BIBLE THE FIRST COMMANDMENT IS TO BE FRUITFUL AND MULTIPLY. IT IS THEREFORE AN OBLIGATION FOR JEWISH PARENTS TO HAVE CHILDREN WHO WILL CONTINUE THE TRADITION.

From ancient times there have been various ceremonies connected with childbirth.

THE BIBLE

In biblical times childbirth took place in a kneeling position or sitting on a special birthstool. Scriptural law imposes various laws on ritual purity and impurity of the mother. If she gives birth to a boy, she is considered ritually impure for seven days. For the next 33 days she is not allowed to enter the Temple precincts or handle sacred objects. For the mother of a girl, the number of days are respectively 14 and 66. According to Jewish law, if a woman in childbirth is in mortal danger, her life takes precedence over that of an unborn child. Only when more than half of the child's body has emerged from the womb is it considered to be fully human so that both lives are of equal worth.

THE BIRTH OF A CHILD

In ancient times the birth of a child was accompanied by numerous superstitious practices, including the use of amulets to ward off the evil eye. After the birth, family and friends gathered nightly to recite prayers to ward off evil spirits such as Lilith, the female demon who allegedly attempts to kill off all newly born children. Among German Jews it was frequently the practice for parents of a son to cut off a strip of swaddling in which the child was wrapped during his circumcision; this is known as the wimple, and it is kept until his bar mitzvah, when it is used for tying the scroll of the law. From the medieval period Ashkenazi mothers visited the synagogue after the birth of a child to recite a blessing that expresses gratitude to God as well as other prayers. It was also customary for the congregation to recite a prayer for the welfare of the mother and the child.

BABY NAMING

The naming of a child takes place either when a baby boy is named at the circumcision ceremony or when a baby girl is named in the synagogue on the first time the Torah is read after her birth. The Hebrew form of a person's name consists of the individual's name followed by *ben*, or 'son', or *bat*, or 'daughter', of the father. This form is used in all Hebrew documents as well as for the call to the reading of the Torah. In contemporary society it is still the practice to give a child a Jewish name in addition to their ordinary name. Ashkenazi Jews frequently name a child after a deceased relative; Sephardi Jews after a person who is still alive. Alternatively, a Hebrew name is selected that is related to the ordinary name either in meaning or sound, or the secular name may be transliterated in Hebrew characters.

Above *Painting by English Jewish painter Abraham Solomon of his brother Simeon as a baby, 1841.*

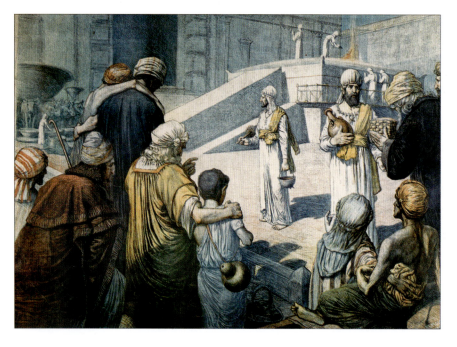

Below *In this 1900 lithograph, people are giving offerings for sacrifice to the priests at the Temple in Jerusalem. First-born boys were dedicated to God.*

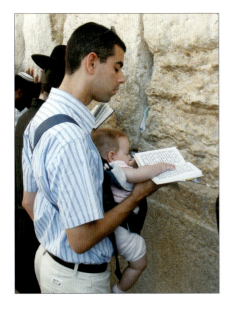

Above A father prays with his baby at the Western Wall in Jerusalem. Prayer is an important part of family life.

Traditionally it was customary to change the name of a person at the time of a serious illness. According to rabbinic Judaism, changing the name is a way of misdirecting the angel of death. On this basis, it became a custom to add a further name to the ill person's. From that point the individual was known by their original name, together with the new one.

Above The redemption of the first-born son ritual requires payment of gold to a Cohen, a member of a priestly clan that traces its paternal lineage back to Aaron, the first priest in the Jewish religion.

REDEEMING THE FIRST-BORN

The custom of redeeming first-born male children (*Pidyon ha-Ben*) is based on the scriptural prescription that first-born sons should be consecrated to the Temple. Just as first fruits and first-born animals had to be handed over to the priests, so first-born boys were dedicated to God. The obligation to redeem first-born sons from this service is referred to in Numbers 3:44–51. Here redemption is to take place by a payment of five shekels to the priest. Detailed laws are outlined in the Mishnah tractate Bekhorot and further expanded in the talmudic commentary on this passage.

According to Jewish law, the sons of priests and Levites are exempt from redemption. Similarly, first-born sons whose mother is the daughter of either a priest or Levite are exempt. During the geonic period, a ceremony was instituted in which the father of the child declares to the priest on the 31st day after its birth that the child is the first-born son of his mother and the father, and that as a father, he is obliged to redeem him. The priest then asks the father if he prefers to give his son to the priest or redeem his son, and the father hands the priest the required amount. The father then recites a blessing concerning the fulfilment of the precept of redeeming the child, and another expressing gratitude to God. This procedure has served as the basis for the ceremony since the Middle Ages.

Left A young girl wearing a tichel, the traditional headscarf worn by Jewish women all over the world.

RITES OF PASSAGE

ACCORDING TO SCRIPTURE, ABRAHAM WAS COMMANDED BY GOD TO CIRCUMCISE HIS SON ISAAC. THE PRACTICE OF CIRCUMCISION HAS CONTINUED THROUGH THE AGES.

From ancient times, Jewish male children were circumcised; this practice was based on biblical law and was perceived as a sign of the covenant. At the age of 13, Jewish boys reach the age of adulthood, which is celebrated by a bar mitzvah ceremony. In modern times, a bat mitzvah ceremony has been introduced for Jewish girls.

CIRCUMCISION

According to Jewish law, all male children are to undergo circumcision in accordance with God's command to Abraham in the Book of Genesis. Jewish ritual involves the removal of the entire foreskin of the penis. This act is to be performed on the eighth day after the birth of the child by a person who is qualified (*mohel*). Jewish law specifies that this ceremony can be performed even on the Sabbath, festivals and the Day of Atonement. However, postponement is permitted if there is a danger to the child's health.

Laws concerning the ceremony are derived from both biblical and rabbinic sources. Traditionally circumcision is to take place in the presence of a *minyan*, or 'quorum of ten adult Jewish men'. On the morning of the eighth day, the child is taken from the mother by the godmother who hands him to the *sandak*, or 'godfather'. The sandak then carries the child in to the room where circumcision is to take place. He then hands him to the individual who places the child on a chair called the Chair of Elijah. Another person then takes him and passes him to the child's father who puts him on the lap of the godfather who holds the boy during the ceremony. The circumcision is performed by a mohel or specially trained person who performs circumcision. Formerly, blood was drawn orally but today an instrument is used. The infant is then handed to the person who will hold him during the ceremony of naming, and circumcision ends with a special blessing over a cup of wine, followed by the naming of the child.

BAR MITZVAH

At the age of 13, a boy attains the age of Jewish adulthood. From this point he is considered as part of a minyan. According to Jewish law, the 13th year is when a boy should observe the commandments. The essentials of the bar mitzvah ceremony involve prayer with *tefillin*, or 'phylacteries', for the first time, and reading from the Torah. It is now a universally accepted practice that the bar mitzvah boy is called to the reading at Sabbath morning services where he recites the Torah blessings, chants a maftir, or 'portion of the Law', and reads from the Prophets.

Above *A 17th-century circumcision set from Prague, elaborately ornamented and engraved, in gold and steel.*

Below *Circumcision, from* The Rothschild Miscellany, *the most lavish Hebrew manuscript of the 15th century, which details almost every custom of religious and secular Jewish life.*

Above *A bar mitzvah is held at the Western Wall in Jerusalem, a remnant of the ancient Temple.*

In both Ashkenazi and Sephardi communities the bar mitzvah ceremony included a discourse by the bar mitzvah boy, which demonstrates his knowledge of rabbinic sources. In time other practices became associated with the ceremony. Some boys chanted the entire weekly reading; others were trained as prayer leaders; some conducted the Sabbath eve service on Friday night as well as the Sabbath morning. In some communities the bar mitzvah boy reads a special prayer standing before the Ark. In modern times it is usual for the rabbi to address the bar mitzvah boy after the reading of the law.

BAT MITZVAH

Unlike the bar mitzvah, there is no legal requirement for a girl to take part in a religious ceremony to mark her religious majority. None the less, a ceremonial equivalent of bar mitzvah has been designed for girls. In Orthodoxy this was an innovation in the 19th century and subsequently became widespread. In the early 20th century the Conservative scholar Mordecai Kaplan (1881–1983) pioneered the bat mitzvah ceremony in the USA as part of the synagogue service, and since then this has become widely accepted by many American communities. In non-Orthodox congregations, a 12-year-old girl celebrates her coming of age on a Friday night or during the Sabbath morning service where she conducts the prayers, chants the Haftarah or reading from the Prophets, and in some cases also reads from the Torah and delivers an address. In Orthodox synagogues, however, the bat mitzvah's participation in services is more limited. At a woman's minyan or quorum for prayer, she is called to the reading of the Torah and may even chant one of the portions, together with the Haftarah.

Outside the USA the bat mitzvah ceremony takes various forms. In Reform congregations the ceremony is in line with the American pattern. Orthodox girls, however, do not participate in the synagogue service. Rather, a bat mitzvah's father is called to the Torah on the appropriate Sabbath morning. His daughter then recites a prayer, and the rabbi addresses her in the synagogue or at a Kiddush reception afterwards. Alternatively, the ceremony takes place at home or in the synagogue hall on a weekday.

In Britain and South Africa the procedure is different; bat mitzvah girls must pass a special examination enabling them to participate in a collective ceremony.

Below *Surrounded by friends, a Jewish girl lights candles at her bat mitzvah celebration in Manhattan, New York.*

EDUCATION

IN JUDAISM EDUCATION IS OF CENTRAL IMPORTANCE. IT IS A PARENTAL DUTY TO ENSURE THEIR CHILDREN RECEIVE EDUCATION AND ARE FAMILIAR WITH THE VARIOUS ASPECTS OF THEIR RELIGIOUS HERITAGE.

Above *Orthodox Jewish boys studying the Torah at the Yeshiva Kol Yaakov in Monsey, New York, USA.*

Judaism stipulates that it is the responsibility of parents to educate children. The Book of Deuteronomy declares: 'And you shall teach them diligently to your children, and shall talk of them when you sit in your house, and when you walk by the way, and when you lie down and when you rise' (6:7). For this reason, Jewish education has been of paramount importance through the ages.

PARENTAL DUTY

The Hebrew Bible repeatedly refers to a father's obligation to teach his children about their religious past. The Book of Exodus states: 'You may tell in the hearing of your son and of your son's son how I have made sport of the Egyptians and what signs I have done among them' (Exodus 10:2). Exodus 13:8 says: 'And you shall tell your son on that day, "It is because of what the Lord did for me when I came out of Egypt."' The Book of Deuteronomy stipulates that 'When your son asks you in the time to come, "What is the meaning of the statutes and the ordinances which the Lord our God has commanded you?" then you shall say to your son, "We were Pharaoh's slaves in Egypt; and the Lord brought us out of Egypt with a mighty hand"' (Deuteronomy 6:20–21). In addition to such parental duties, it was the responsibility of the Levites to teach the people: 'They shall teach Jacob thy ordinances, and Israel the law' (Deuteronomy 33:10).

THE BIBLE

From the earliest times the study of the tradition was of central importance in the life of the nation. For this reason, the Hebrew Bible contains numerous references to the process of learning. The Book of Joshua, for example, states: 'This book of the law shall not depart out of your mouth, but you shall meditate on it day and night, that you may be careful to do according to all that is written in it' (Joshua 1:8). Again, the Book of Proverbs contains a number of references to the process of education: 'He who spares the rod hates his son' (Proverbs 13:24); 'Train up a child in the way he should go, and when he is old he will not depart from it' (Proverbs 22:6).

When the Israelites returned from Babylonian exile, Scripture records that Ezra gathered the people and taught them the law. When they heard his words, they vowed to observe the religious practices and festivals of their ancestors. According to the rabbis, it was Ezra who instituted the Torah reading on Monday and Thursday when people attended local markets.

Below *Morning prayer in this Jewish girls' school in Jerusalem takes place in the classroom.*

Below *A rabbi teaching boys Hebrew in a synagogue after school hours, 1891, from the* London Illustrated News.

RABBINIC JUDAISM

According to the tradition, parents are obliged to begin a child's education as soon as possible. When the child begins to speak, he should be taught the verse: 'Moses commanded us a law, as a possession for the assembly of Jacob' (Deuteronomy 33:4). During this period the 1st century BCE sage Simeon ben Shetah (120–40BCE) established schools. However, it was his contemporary Joshua ben Gamla who is credited with the establishment of a formal system of education. He decreed that teachers had to be engaged in each locality at the community's expense and all children were to be given an education. Later the Talmud stipulated the size of classes. One teacher was permitted to handle up to 25 students. If students exceeded this number, an assistant was to be hired. More than 40 students required two teachers.

THE PALESTINIAN ACADEMY

Instruction in the law was to be carried out in the Palestinian academy. The first such institution was founded in Javneh after the destruction of the Temple in 70CE. According to tradition, Johanan ben Zakkai (fl. 1st century CE) arranged to have himself smuggled out of the city in a

Above *Schoolchildren on a historical visit, Jerusalem, Israel.*

Below *A young girl writes 'Shalom' in Hebrew at her local school.*

coffin. He was then brought before the Roman commander, Vespasian (9–79CE) and requested permission to found a centre of learning. This institution took over from the great Sanhedrin. Later other academies flourished under Johanan ben Zakkai's disciples.

BABYLONIAN ACADEMIES

In Babylon, schools of higher learning were also established in the 1st century CE. In the next century, under the leadership of Rav Shila and Abba bar Abba, the academy of Nehardea became the Babylonian spiritual centre, maintaining contact with the Palestinian Jewish community. When Rav returned to Babylonia from Palestine, he founded another academy at Sura in 200CE. In 259CE the Nehardea academy was destroyed; under Judah ben Ezekiel it was transferred to Pumbedita where it remained for the next 500 years. From then it functioned in Baghdad until the 13th century.

THE POST-TALMUDIC AND MODERN PERIOD

During the period between the completion of the Talmud in the 6th century CE and the Enlightenment the majority of male Jews received some sort of education. This was generally limited to the study of sacred texts. However, in some periods secular subjects were also included. Prior to Jewish emancipation, the typical pattern of Jewish study involved a teacher with several students who studied religious texts. In the 19th century, organized *yeshivot*, or 'rabbinical seminaries', emerged in eastern Europe. In these institutions students progressed from one level to another – throughout the subject matter was Talmud and halakha, or 'Jewish law'. With the emancipation of Jewry, Jews began to study in secular schools and this has been the pattern up until the present. Jewish religion schools operating alongside secular schooling as well as Jewish day schools now serve as the primary means of Jewish education.

Higher Education and Courtship

AMONG THE ORTHODOX, JEWISH LEARNING CONTINUES AT A HIGH LEVEL. TRADITIONALLY, YOUNG MEN CONTINUED THEIR EDUCATION IN YESHIVOT OR ACADEMIES DEDICATED TO STUDYING SACRED TEXTS.

For the strictly Orthodox, in the modern world religious education does not end with bar or bat mitzvah. Four years of Jewish high school follow which combine secular and Jewish studies. Then young men go off to a *yeshiva* for several years.

ANCIENT ACADEMIES

A yeshiva (pl. yeshivot) is an academy dedicated to the study of the Talmud and other sacred texts. Academies of higher learning were created in Palestine and Babylonia in the 1st century CE. These institutions kept in contact with one another and attracted students from other lands. In Palestine the most famous was the academy founded by Johanan ben Zakkai (fl. 1st century CE) in Javneh after the destruction of Jerusalem in 70CE. In Babylonia the academies of Sura and Pumbedita, founded in the 3rd century CE, exerted an enormous influence on Jewish learning.

NON-ORTHODOX YOUTH

Most young people in the Diaspora do not pursue such a rigorous course of study. They go to secular schools and attend Jewish religious schools at the weekend. In non-Orthodox congregations, boys and girls attend confirmation classes, culminating in a confirmation ceremony. Alongside such study, summer camp offers opportunities for Jewish youth to learn about the tradition. Many Jewish children go on a trip to the Holy Land, where they are given a chance to experience Jewish life in Israel.

ORTHODOX COURTSHIP

According to the tradition, marriage is a sacred institution. Jews are expected to marry. Early marriage is the norm for the strictly Orthodox. Boys and girls are taught separately,

Above *An engaged couple at a meal, facsimile of Schecken Bible of 1470, painted by Leonardo Bellini of Venice.*

Below *An example of Yeshiva education: male students in the study hall building of Kerem B'Yavneh Yeshiva.*

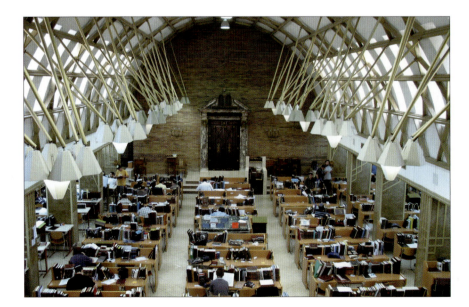

> ### THE YESHIVA WORLD
> In the 19th century, yeshivot were organized throughout Eastern Europe, however they were destroyed in the Holocaust. After World War II, new yeshivot were set up in the United States, Israel and Europe. Today most yeshivot are organized along the traditional Lithuanian lines. Students generally study in pairs in a large hall; together they argue the meaning of ancient sources. The debate is often conducted in Yiddish as they pore over the Aramaic text. Twice a week, the head of the yeshiva will give a lecture on the portion of the Talmud that is being studied. There is also a moral tutor who gives regular talks on *musar*, or 'ethics'. Such study does not necessarily lead to a career in the practical rabbinate. The majority of graduates earn their living in secular occupations. However, almost every yeshiva has a kolel, an advanced section in which married men and their families are supported as they continue their studies.

Above *A couple under a huppah (bridal canopy), 1438, from Jacob ben Asher's* Even ha'Ezer, *on marriage and divorce.*

and they are largely kept apart during adolescence. During a young man's final years at a yeshiva, he is expected to get married and families, friends and teachers are co-opted to find a suitable bride. In the past, in Eastern Europe villages, an official matchmaker organized the brokering between families. Today, this process is more informal. Marriages are not exactly arranged, but parents keep a close eye on the proceedings.

THE NON-ORTHODOX

Most Jewish children go to secular, co-educational schools. They then attend secular universities, often far from home. As a result, parents are able to exert far less control. According to Jewish law, certain marriages have no validity – in particular those that are incestuous, those that are adulterous, and those between a Jew and a gentile. In contemporary society intermarriage poses a major threat to Jewish life. In the past, when Jews were isolated in their own communities or when there was rampant anti-Semitism, the danger of intermarriage was small. Today in the State of Israel, Jews are likely to marry Jews. But in the Diaspora, the rate of intermarriage is very high.

INTERMARRIAGE

The religious establishment is anxious to combat this trend. Part of the drive behind the creation of non-Orthodox Jewish day schools is to help children grow up in a more Jewish milieu. Children are sent to Jewish summer camps where they meet other Jews. There are university Jewish societies, and Jewish single events take place in major cities around the globe.

Parents also exert considerable pressure. In the past, if a child married a gentile, then he or she was cut off from the Jewish community. Today this state of affairs is usually inconceivable, and most families are touched by intermarriage.

SINGLE JEWS

Despite the importance of marriage in the Jewish tradition, a significant number of Jewish men and women remain unmarried. In some cases this is because they are homosexual. Others are happier to live by themselves. Some have had a bad early experience, or simply leave it too long. Non-marriage combined with intermarriage poses a danger to the survival of the Jewish way of life. It has been calculated that if present trends continue, the Jewish community will significantly diminish in size.

Below *A group of young Jews at a Jewish summer camp in Saratoga, California.*

LIFE CYCLE EVENTS

OUTWARD SIGNS

IN LIVING A JEWISH LIFE, JEWISH ADULTS ARE OBLIGED TO FOLLOW A RANGE OF LAWS RELATING TO OUTWARD SIGNS. SOME OF THESE REGULATIONS MUST BE OBSERVED BY MEN, OTHERS BY WOMEN.

All outward signs express determination to fulfil God's will as revealed to Moses on Mount Sinai and interpreted by rabbinic sages.

PHYLACTERIES

Once a Jewish boy has reached the age of maturity, he is required to wear *tefillin*, or 'phylacteries', for prayer. These consist of special boxes containing biblical verses written by hand on parchment. The verses are: (1) Exodus 13:1–10, concerning the laws relating to the dedication of the first born to God's service; (2) Exodus 13:11–16, repeating the laws of the first-born and the commandment to teach children about the miraculous deliverance from slavery in Egypt; (3) Deuteronomy 6:4–9, the first paragraph of the Shema prayer stressing the oneness of God; and (4) Deuteronomy 11:13–21, containing the second paragraph of the Shema prayer on reward and punishment. These boxes are attached to straps. One is placed over the head so that the box sits squarely upon the forehead and between the eyes. The other is wound round the left arm so that the box faces the heart. The strap is placed in a special way so that it forms

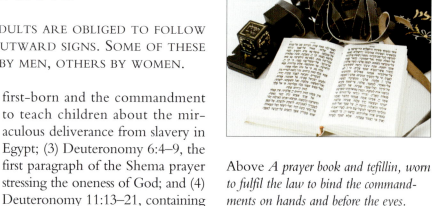

Above *A prayer book and tefillin, worn to fulfil the law to bind the commandments on hands and before the eyes.*

the Hebrew letter *shin*, the first letter of God's name Shaddai – God Almighty.

LAYING TEFILLIN

The action of putting on the boxes is known as laying tefillin. It is an ancient practice and should be observed by all male Jews of bar mitzvah age and above. It is performed every weekday at home or in the synagogue. Phylacteries are not worn on the Sabbath or festivals. The tradition among Ashkenazim is to wind the straps round the arm anti-clockwise whereas the Sephardim wind them clockwise. The Talmud emphasizes the importance of fulfilling this commandment, and it states that even God lays tefillin. Among the Hasidim it is said that if only every male Jew were to perform this duty then the Messiah would come.

THE BEARD

According to Leviticus, it is forbidden to cut the corners of the beard. In the medieval period, it was customary for Jewish men to have beards, and the Talmud describes the beard as the 'ornament of the face'. Later, this biblical verse was interpreted to mean Jews should not shave, but it was permissible to clip facial hair. Today

Left *Jew in Black and White, 1923, by Marc Chagall, showing the characteristic prayer shawl and tefillin.*

OUTWARD SIGNS

HEAD COVERING

The skull-cap (*yarmulke* in Yiddish; *kippah* in Hebrew) is one of the most recognizable signs of male Orthodox dress. The practice goes back to the 12th century and may have been introduced to distinguish Jewish from Christian prayer. Today Orthodox men keep their heads covered at all times. Conservative and Reform Jews generally wear a head-covering in the synagogue, but go bare-headed elsewhere.

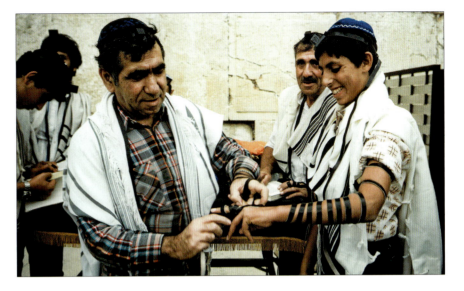

many Jewish men are clean-shaven – they use an electric razor or a chemical depilatory. Among the Hasidim and the strictly Orthodox, the passage from Leviticus is also understood to mean that men should let their *peot*, or side-locks grow.

FRINGES

An element of Orthodox appearance is *tziztzit*, or 'fringes'. According to the Book of Numbers, God told the Israelites to make tassels on the corners of their garments. Orthodox men wear an undergarment with fringes on the four corners; these are tied in a particular way to symbolize the numerical value of the name of God. Known as a *tallit katan*, it is largely hidden, though the fringes are brought out above the trouser waistband and are discreetly tucked into a pocket. Similar fringes are put on the four corners of the *tallit gadol*, or 'prayer shawl', which is worn in the synagogue during the morning service. A special blessing is said when both the prayer shawl and the undergarment are put on each day.

MODESTY

Women's dress is characterized by modesty. Traditionally, married women cover their heads, and the Orthodox continue this practice by wearing a wig or by swathing the head in a scarf. Skirts cover the knee and sleeves the elbow. The Book of Deuteronomy teaches that a woman shall not wear anything that pertains to a man, nor shall a man put on a woman's garment. Thus among the strictly Orthodox any unisex garment is perceived as an abomination. However, non-Orthodox women ignore these customs.

Above *A Jewish father wraps his son's arm in phylacteries at his bar mitzvah at the Western Wall, Jerusalem.*

FORBIDDEN CLOTH

The Book of Deuteronomy states it is forbidden to wear a *shatnes*, or mingled stuff, such as wool or linen mixed together. This regulation is one of many laws against mixing. Today modern technology can be employed to determine the precise composition of fabrics, and certify the legality of a particular material. The commandment is understood as forbidding the mingling of linen and wool. Any other combination is permissible. Again, this law is ignored by the non-Orthodox.

Below *A woman prays besides the Wailing Wall, Jerusalem, her head covered with the traditional tichel.*

Right *A customer trying on a wig. Many Strictly Orthodox Jewish women cover their heads once they marry to obey religious modesty edicts.*

Marriage

ACCORDING TO TRADITION, MARRIAGE IS GOD'S PLAN FOR HUMANITY. IN THE JEWISH FAITH IT IS VIEWED AS A SACRED BOND AS WELL AS A MEANS TO PERSONAL FULFILMENT.

In Judaism the purpose of marriage is to create a Jewish home, have a Jewish family and thereby perpetuate the Jewish community. Marriage is an institution with cosmic significance, legitimized through divine authority. Initially Jews were permitted to have more than one wife, but this practice was banned in Ashkenazi countries by Rabbenu Gershom (c.960–1028CE) in 1000. In modern society all Jewish communities follow this ruling.

ANCIENT JUDAISM

In the Bible, marriages were arranged by fathers. Abraham, for example, sent his servant to find a wife for Isaac, and Judah arranged the marriage of his first-born son. When the proposal of marriage was accepted by the girl's father, the nature and amount of the *mohar*, or 'payment by the groom', was agreed. By Second Temple times, there was a degree of choice in the selection of a bride: on 15th of Av and the Day of Atonement, young men could select their brides from among the girls dancing in the vineyards.

According to tradition, a period of engagement preceded marriage itself. The ceremony was a seven-day occasion for celebration during which love songs were sung in praise of the bride.

In the talmudic period, a major development occurred concerning the mohar. Since it could be used by the father of the bride, a wife could become penniless if her husband divorced or predeceased her. As a consequence, the mohar evolved into the *ketubah*, or 'marriage document', which gave protection to the bride. In addition, the act of marriage changed from being a personal civil procedure to a public religious ceremony, which required the presence of a *minyan*, or 'quorum', and the recitation of prayers.

Below *A classic image of the relationship of husband and wife in this Dutch painting of* A Jewish Wedding *by Jozef Israëls, 1903.*

Above *A Jewish couple share in a Passover Seder meal. From a 15th-century illuminated manuscript.*

MARRIAGE PROCEDURES

In biblical and rabbinic times marriage was divided into two stages – betrothal and marriage.

Betrothal involved the commitment of a couple to marry and the terms of financial obligations, and also a ceremony establishing a nuptial relationship independent of the wedding ceremony. In the Bible, the betrothal or nuptial ceremony takes place prior to the wedding and is referred to as *erusin*; in the rabbinic period the sages called it *kiddushin* to indicate the bride was forbidden to all men except her husband. According to the Mishnah, the bride could be acquired in marriage in three ways: by money, deed or intercourse. Traditionally, the method involved placing a ring on the bride's finger. At this stage the groom declared: 'Behold, you are consecrated unto me with this ring according to the law of Moses and Israel.' Then the blessing over wine was recited.

After this ceremony the bride remained in her father's house until the *nissuin*, or 'marriage ceremony'. During the second stage of this procedure the *sheva berakhot*, or 'seven blessings', are recited.

THE WEDDING

From the Middle Ages it became customary for Jewish communities to postpone the betrothal ceremony until just before the nissuin wedding ceremony. Prior to the wedding itself, the bride immerses herself in a mikveh, or 'ritual bath', usually on the evening before the ceremony. To facilitate this the wedding date is determined so that it does not occur during her time of menstruation, or the following week. In some Ashkenazi circles the bride when reaching the *huppah*, or 'marriage canopy', is led around the groom seven times. The wedding ceremony can be held anywhere, but from the Middle Ages, the synagogue or synagogue courtyard was commonly used. In modern times, the Orthodox wedding ceremony normally follows a uniform pattern based on traditional law.

Normally the groom signs the ketubah. He is then led to the bride and covers her face with her veil; the couple are next led to the marriage canopy with their parents walking with the groom and the bride. According to custom, those leading the couple carry lighted candles.

Below Marc Chagall painted The Wedding *in 1918, three years after his marriage. The fiddler and house symbolize their wedded state and a baby is drawn on the cheek of the bride.*

When the participants are under the canopy, the rabbi recites the blessing over wine. Then the bride and groom drink from the cup. The groom then recites the traditional formula: 'Behold you are consecrated unto me according to the law of Moses and of Israel.' He then puts the ring on the bride's right index finger. To demonstrate that the act of marriage consists of two ceremonies, the ketubah is read prior to the nissuin ceremony. The seven blessings are then recited

Above Indian–Jewish wedding in Mumbai. Tradition says the Bene Israel were shipwrecked while fleeing persecution in Galilee and reached India some 2,100 years ago.

over a second cup of wine. The ceremony concludes with the groom stepping on a glass and breaking it. Within Conservative and Reform Judaism the wedding service follows the traditional pattern with varying alterations.

THE SHEVA BERAKHOT OR SEVEN BLESSINGS

Blessed are you, O Lord Our God, King of the Universe, who creates the fruit of the vine,
- Who has created all things to your glory.
- Creator of man.
- Who has made man in your image, after your likeness ...
- Made she who was barren (Zion) be glad and exult when her children are gathered within her in joy. Blessed are you, O Lord, who makes Zion joyful through her children.
- O make these loved companions greatly to rejoice, even as of old you did gladden your creatures in the Garden of Eden. Blessed are you, O Lord, who makes bridegroom and bride to rejoice.
- Who has created joy and gladness, bridegroom and bride, mirth and exultation, pleasure and delight, love, brotherhood, peace and fellowship. Soon may there be heard in the cities of Judah and in the streets of Jerusalem, the voice of joy and gladness, the voice of the bridegroom and the voice of the bride, the happy sound of bridegrooms from their canopies, and of youths from their feasts of song.
- Blessed are you, O Lord, who makes the bridegroom to rejoice with the bride.

Divorce

Marriage is regarded as an ideal in Judaism, but relationships between men and women do break down. Jews recognize this, and the Bible specifies a procedure for divorce.

'When a man takes a wife and marries her, if then she finds no favour in his eyes because he has found some indecency in her, he writes her a bill of divorce and puts it in her hand and sends her out of his house' (Deuteronomy 24:1).

BIBLICAL AND RABBINIC LAW

This verse in Deuteronomy stipulates that the power of divorce rests with the husband, and the act of divorce must be in the form of a legal document. Among early rabbinic sages there was disagreement as to the meaning of the term 'indecency'. The School of Shammai interpreted it as referring to unchastity, whereas the School of Hillel understood the term more widely. It was not permitted for divorce to take place in two instances: if a man claimed that his wife was not a virgin and his charge was disproved; or if he raped a virgin whom he later married. Conversely, a person was not allowed to remarry his divorced wife if she had married someone else and had not been divorced or widowed. Nor could a priest marry a divorced woman.

THE TALMUDIC PERIOD

During the talmudic period, the law of divorce underwent considerable change, including the elaboration of various situations under which a court could compel a husband to divorce his wife. This applied if she remained barren over a period of ten years, if the husband contracted a loathsome disease, if he refused to support her or was not in a position to do so, if he denied his wife her conjugal rights, or if he beat her despite the court's warnings. In these cases the Talmud states that the husband is coerced by the court only to the extent that he would in fact want to divorce his wife.

Above *A 1906 edition of the Gittin tractate of the Talmud, which deals with the concepts of divorce.*

DIVORCE PROCEDURE

The procedure for a divorce is based on the Code of Jewish Law. The officiating rabbi asks the husband if he gives the get or bill of divorce of his own free will. After receiving the writing materials from a scribe, he instructs

> ### THE BILL OF DIVORCE
> A get, or 'bill of divorce', is to be drawn up by a scribe following a formula based on mishnaic law. This document is to be written almost entirely in Aramaic on parchment. Once it has been given to the wife, it is retained by the rabbi, who cuts it in a criss-cross fashion so that it cannot be used a second time. The husband then gives the wife a document that affirms that he has been divorced, and may remarry. The wife is permitted to remarry only after 90 days, so as to determine whether she was pregnant at the stage of divorce. This document must be witnessed by two males over the age of 13 who are not related to each other or to the divorcing husband and wife.

Below *The Bet Din grants a divorce. From* Jüdisches Ceremoniell *(1717) published by Paul Christian Kirchner, following his conversion to Judaism.*

Above *The Get c. 1930 by Moshie Rynecki. The Get is a document that seals a divorce.*

Left *A bet din (rabbinical court) in Jerusalem granting a divorce for a woman whose husband has left her.*

the scribe to write a get. The get is written, and the witnesses should be present during this process. They then make a distinguishing mark on the get. When it is completed, the witnesses read the get. Eventually the rabbi asks the husband if the get was freely given. The wife is then asked if she freely accepts the get.

The rabbi then tells the wife to remove all jewellery from her hands and holds her hands together with open palms upward to receive the bill of divorce. The scribe holds the get and gives it to the rabbi. The rabbi then gives the get to her husband; he holds it in both hands and drops it into the palms of the wife. When the wife receives the bill of divorce, she walks with it a short distance and returns. She gives the get to the rabbi who reads it again. The four corners of the get are cut, and it is placed in the rabbi's files. The husband and wife then receive written statements certifying that their marriage has been dissolved in accordance with Jewish law.

DIVORCE PROCEEDINGS

It is customary for the husband and wife to be present during the divorce proceedings. If this is not possible, Jewish law stipulates an agent can take the place of either party. The husband may appoint an agent to deliver the get to his wife. If this agent is unable to complete this task, he has the right to appoint another one, and the second agent yet another. The wife can also appoint an agent to receive the get. Thus it is possible for the entire procedure to take place without the husband or wife seeing one another.

NON-ORTHODOX JUDAISM

Since it is the husband who must give the bill of divorce to his wife, if he cannot be located, this presents an insurmountable obstacle. Similarly, in the Diaspora rabbinic scholars have discussed the status of a woman who is an *agunah*, or 'chained person', who is not able to remarry according to traditional Jewish law. To vitiate this the Conservative movement has called for the insertion of a clause in the marriage contract whereby both groom and bride in grave circumstances agree to abide by the decision of the *bet din*, or 'religious court'. Within Reform Judaism the traditional practice of granting a bill of divorce has been largely abandoned. Instead civil divorce is regarded as valid.

Below *At these divorce proceedings in Amsterdam, Netherlands, the Ashkenazi Jew passes a writ of divorce into the hands of a surrogate for his wife.*

Death and Mourning

THE JEWISH RELIGION SPECIFIES A DETAILED PROCEDURE FOR DEALING WITH THE DEAD. BURIAL SHOULD TAKE PLACE AS SOON AS POSSIBLE AFTER THE MEMBERS OF THE BURIAL SOCIETY HAVE TAKEN CARE OF THE BODY.

According to Scripture, human beings will return to the dust of the earth (Genesis 3:19). The Bible teaches that burial – especially in the family tomb – was the normal procedure for dealing with the deceased. Such a practice has been superseded by burial in the earth, preceded by a number of procedures. This is followed by a period of mourning for the dead.

THE ONSET OF DEATH

The rabbis of the Talmud decreed that death takes place when respiration has ceased. However, with the development of modern medical technology, this concept has been changed. It is now possible to resuscitate those who previously would have been viewed as dead. For this reason the Orthodox scholar Moshe Sofer (1762–1839) stated that death is considered to have occurred when there has been respiratory and cardiac arrest. Mosheh Feinstein (1895–1986) ruled that a person is considered to have died with the death of his brain stem. Despite such disagreements, it is generally accepted that a critically ill person who hovers between life and death is alive. It is forbidden to hasten the death of such a person by any positive action. However, it is permitted to remove an external obstacle, which may be preventing death.

DEALING WITH THE DEAD

Once death has been determined, the eyes and mouth of the person are to be closed, and if necessary the mouth is tied shut. The body is then put on the floor, covered with a sheet, and a lighted candle is placed close to the head. Mirrors are covered in the home of the deceased, and any standing water is poured out. A dead body is not to be left unattended, and it is considered a good deed to sit with the person who has died and recite psalms.

Above *At a Jewish cemetery in Budapest, Hungary. The rabbi chants prayers as family members use a shovel to put dirt on the casket in the open grave.*

BURIAL

The burial of the body should occur as soon as possible. No burial is allowed to take place on the Sabbath or on Yom Kippur, the Day of Atonement, and in contemporary practice it is considered unacceptable for it to take place on the first and last days of a pilgrim festival.

After the members of the burial society have taken care of the body, they prepare it for burial. It is washed and dressed in a white linen shroud. The corpse is then placed in a coffin. Traditional Jews only permit the use of plain wooden coffins. The deceased is then borne to the grave face upwards. Adult males are buried wearing their prayer shawl. A marker should be placed on a newly filled grave, and a tombstone should be erected and unveiled as soon as possible.

Among Reform Jews, burial practice differs from that of the Orthodox. Embalming and cremation are usually permitted and Reform rabbis often officiate at crematoria. Burial may be delayed for several days, and the person who has died is usually buried in normal clothing. No special places are reserved for priests, nor is any separate arrangement made for someone who has committed suicide or married out of the faith.

Below *The Acafoth, or seven turns around the coffin. A 1723 French engraving by Bernard Picart.*

Right *An Orthodox Jew gestures while praying as he stands in a Jewish cemetery on the Mount of Olives in Jerusalem.*

BURIAL SERVICE

Despite the differences between Ashkenazi and Sephardi Jews, there are a number of common features of the burial service. In both rites, mourners rend their garments and liturgical verses are chanted by the rabbi as he leads the funeral procession to the cemetery. Often a eulogy is given either in the funeral chapel or as the mourners help to fill the earth. Memorial prayers and a special mourners' kaddish are recited. Mourners present words of comfort to the bereaved, and all wash their hands before leaving the cemetery.

SHIVAH

The mourning period is known as *shivah*, 'seven', and lasts for seven days beginning with the day of burial. During this time mourners sit on the floor or on low cushions or benches and are forbidden to shave, bathe, go to work, study the Torah, engage in sexual relations, wear leather shoes, greet others, cut their hair or wear laundered clothing. Through these seven days, it is customary to visit mourners. Those comforting mourners are not to greet them but rather offer words of consolation.

SHELOSHIM

Shivah concludes on the morning of the seventh day and is followed by mourning of a lesser intensity for 30 days known as *sheloshim*, or 'thirty'. At this time mourners are not permitted to cut their hair, shave, wear new clothes or attend festivities. Those who mourn are not permitted to attend public celebrations or parties. Mourners are to recite kaddish daily throughout the period of mourning. In the case of those whose mourning continues for a year, it is at times customary to recite kaddish till one month or a week before the first anniversary of death.

Below *A mother mourns at the grave of her son in the military section of Mount Herzl cemetery, Jerusalem.*

Below *Four sons saying Kaddish over the coffin of their father in the Gaza Strip settlement of Ganei Tal, Israel.*

Glossary

ADAM KADMON primordial man, in Kabbalah the spiritual prototype of man created by God
ADAR twelfth month of the Jewish year. In leap years, Adar is followed by a month called Adar 2
ADON OLAM poem that begins, 'Lord of eternity'
AFIKOMAN part of the middle matzah
AKEDAH the binding of Isaac
ALENU prayer at the end of a service
AMIDAH major prayer originally consisting of 18 benedictions
AMORAIM Palestine sages (200-500CE)
ANTI-SEMITISM hostility towards Jews
ARK OF THE COVENANT chest in which the two ancient Tablets of the Law were placed
ASHKENAZIM one of the two main divisions of Jews. Initially applied to a biblical people, but now Jews originating in Eastern Europe
ASIYAH Kabbalistic realm ('making')
ATZILUT Kabbalistic term ('emanation')
AV fifth month of the Jewish year

BARAITA teachings not included in the Mishnah
BAR MITZVAH male adolescent ceremony ('son of the commandment') when a Jewish youth comes under the obligation to fulfill the commandments
BAT MITZVAH female adolescent ceremony ('daughter of the commandment')
BERIYAH Kabbalistic realm ('creation')
BET DIN rabbinic court
BIBLE the Hebrew Bible is divided into three sections: the Torah (Pentateuch), Nevim (Prophets) and Ketuvim (writings)
BIMAH platform
BINAH God's wisdom

CANTOR chanter
CHALLAH braided bread eaten on the Sabbath and holidays
CHOSEN PEOPLE the belief that God chose the Jews based on the covenant between Abraham and God
COHEN priest
COMMANDMENTS see Halakha, Mitzvah and Ten Commandments
CONSERVATIVE JUDAISM religious movement, which emerged in the mid-19th century as a mid-way between Orthodoxy and Reform
COVENANT binding agreement between person's nations or parties

DEVEKUT mystical cleaving to God
DIASPORA outside Israel
DREIDEL a spinning top used in a game at Hanukkah

ELUL sixth month of the Jewish year
ELOHIM one of the names of God.
EN SOF Infinite
EREZ ISRAEL land of Israel
ESSENES monastic Jewish sect, one of three main Jewish sects before the destruction of the Temple in 70CE
EXILE exclusion from the Promised Land, especially to Babylonia in the 6th century BCE

FRANKISTS Heretical movement founded by Jacob Frank

GAN EDEN Garden of Eden (or heaven)
GAON head of a Babylonian academy
GEHINNOM Hell
GEMARA rabbinic discussions on the Mishnah
GET bill of divorce

HABAD Hasidic movement whose name is based on the initials of the words *hokhmah* (wisdom), *binah* (understanding), and *daat* (knowledge)
HAFTARAH prophetic reading
HAGGADAH Passover prayer book
HALAKHA Jewish law
HALLEL Psalms 113-118
HANUKKAH festival of lights (dedication), lasting eight days
HAREDIM Strictly Orthodox Jews
HAROSET paste of fruit, spices, wine and matzah eaten at the Passover seder
HASID pious person
HASIDISM mystical Jewish movement founded in the 18th century
HASKALAH Jewish enlightenment
HAVDALAH service at the end of the Sabbath and festivals
HEDER school for children
HESHVAN eighth month of the Jewish year
HOKHMAH God's wisdom
HOLOCAUST destruction of the European Jewish community during the Second World War. Six million Jews are estimated to have died during the Holocaust.
HUMANISTIC JUDAISM non-supernaturalistic and humanistically oriented movement
HUPPAH marriage canopy

IYAR second month of the Jewish year

JEWISH RENEWAL Judaism inspired by counter-culture
JUBUS Jewish Buddhists

KABBALAH mystical teachings
KADDISH Aramaic prayer praising God
KARAITES Jewish sect, which rejected the rabbinic tradition

Below *A dreidel used at Hanukkah.*

GLOSSARY

Above Matzot, eaten at Passover.

KASHRUT dietary laws
KETUVIM Writings (third section of the Hebrew Scriptures)
KIBBUTZ collective village in Israel
KIDDUSH prayer recited over wine to consecrate the Sabbath or a festival
KIPPAH skullcap
KISLEV ninth month of the Jewish year
KITTEL robe
KNESSET Parliament of Israel
KOLLEL advanced institute for Talmud study
KOL NIDRE evening service, which starts the Day of Atonement ('all vows')
KOSHER ritually fit food

LADINO Judeo-Spanish dialect
LAG BA-OMER scholars' feast
LEKHAH DODI Sabbath hymn ('come, my beloved')
LEVITE priest
LULAV palm branch (used on Sukkot)
LURIANIC KABBALAH mysticism based on the teachings of Isaac ben Luria

MAARIV evening service
MAFTIR reader of the *Haftarah*
MAMZER offspring of any sexual relationship forbidden in Jewish law (that is, incest, or sexual intercourse between a married woman and a man who is not her husband)
MAROR bitter herbs
MARRANOS Jews who converted to Christianity (in Spain and Portugal)
MASKILIM followers of the Jewish Enlightenment
MATRIARCHS the wives of the three Patriarchs: Sarah, Rebecca, Leah and Rachel
MATZAH unleavened bread for Passover
MEGILLAH scroll

MENORAH a seven-branched candle-stick. A menorah with eight branches is used at Hanukkah.
MERKAVAH divine chariot
MESSIAH the anointed one
MESSIANIC JUDAISM a movement with a belief in Jesus (Yeshua)
MEZUZAH scroll in a box fixed to the doorpost of a Jewish home
MIDRASH rabbinic commentary on Scripture
MIKDASH ME-AT minor sanctuary
MIKVEH ritual bath. Used for immersion and ritual cleansing of both individuals and vessels
MINHAH meal offering (or afternoon service)
MINYAN quorum of ten men
MISHNAH compendium of the Oral Torah
MITNAGGEDIM rabbinic opponents of the Hasidim
MITZVAH commandment
MOHEL person who performs a circumcision
MOURNERS' KADDISH prayer said at the end of service
MUSAF additional service
MUSAR movement of return to traditional ethics founded in the modern period

NAGID head of a Spanish or North African community
NEILAH concluding service, originally recited daily one hour before sunset and the closing of the Temple
NEVIIM Prophets (second section of the Hebrew Scriptures)

Below A Hanukkah menorah.

Above A ritual Seder plate.

NISAN first month of the Jewish year
NISSUIN second stage of the marriage procedure

OLAM HA-BA the hereafter. Olam ha-Ba will begin with the resurrection of the dead and a final judgement. The righteous will be rewarded and the wicked punished.
OMER barley offering
ORTHODOXY Torah-observant Judaism

PARASHAH Torah portion
PARNAS head of the community
PASSOVER festival commemorating the Exodus from Egypt
PATRIARCHS the biblical ancestors of the Jewish people: Abraham, Isaac and Jacob
PENTATEUCH the Five Books of Moses (Genesis, Exodus, Leviticus, Numbers and Deuteronomy)
PESACH Passover festival
PHARISEES one of three main Jewish sects before the destruction of the Temple in 70CE
PIYYUTIM hymns
PURIM feast of Esther, marking the deliverance of the Jews from Haman

RABBI teacher
REBBE Hasidic leader
RECONSTRUCTIONIST JUDAISM modernizing movement founded by Mordecai Kaplan
REFORM JUDAISM progressive modernizing movement
RESPONSA answers to specific legal questions
ROSH HASHANAH New Year. The Jewish New Year begins on the 1st day of Tishri, the 7th month of the Jewish year

GLOSSARY

ROSH HODESH 1st of the month, celebrating the appearance of the new moon

SABBATH day of rest. Observed every week from before sunset on Friday until nightfall on Saturday
SADDUCEES priestly class, one of three main Jewish sects before the destruction of the Temple in 70CE
SAMARITANS people descended from the tribes of Ephraim and Manasseh
SANDAK godfather
SANHEDRIN central rabbinic court in ancient times
SEDER Passover ceremony at home
SEFER YETZIRAH Early Babylonian or Palestinian mystical tract
SEFIROT divine emanations
SELIHOT penitential prayers
SEPHARDIM Jews originating in Spain or North Africa
SEUDAH SELISHIT third meal
SHABBAT first tractate of the Mishnah and Talmud. It discusses Sabbath law and outlines the thirty-nine categories of work, forbidden on the Sabbath
SHABBATEANS followers of Shabbetai Tzvi
SHAHARIT morning service
SHAVUOT Festival of Weeks, commemorating the giving of the law on Mount Sinai
SHEHITAH ritual slaughter
SHEKHINAH divine presence
SHELOSHIM 30 days of mourning
SHEMA prayer ('Hear, O Israel')
SHEMINI ATZERET final day of the festival of Sukkot
SHEMONEH ESREH Amidah
SHEVAT eleventh month of the Jewish year
SHEWBREAD bread laid out in the Temple on the golden table
SHIVAH seven days of mourning
SHOFAR ram's horn
SHOHET slaughterer
SHTETL small town in eastern Europe with Jewish population
SHULKHAN ARUKH Jewish law code
SIDDUR traditional prayer book
SIDRAH section of the Torah reading
SIMHAT TORAH Festival of the Rejoicing of the Law
SITRA AHRA demonic realm
SIVAN third month of the Jewish year
SUKKAH booth built at Sukkot
SUKKOT Feast of Tabernacles, marking the end of the agricultural year
SYNAGOGUE place of worship

TABLETS OF THE LAW the Ten Commandments given by God to Moses on Mount Sinai
TALLIT (larger) prayer shawl
TALLIT (smaller) fringed undergarment
TALMUD compilation of the legal discussions based on the Mishnah
TAMUZ fourth month of the Jewish year
TANAKH Hebrew Bible
TANNAIM Jewish sages (70–200CE)
TASHLIKH casting away sin
TEFILLAH prayer (also the Amidah)
TEMPLE principal place of worship of the Jews in Jerusalem until 70CE
TEN COMMANDMENTS laws given by God to Moses on Mount Sinai
TENAIM betrothal document
TEVET tenth month of the Jewish year
TIK the wooden or metal case in which the Scroll of the Law is stored
TIKKUN cosmic repair
TISHA B'AV ninth of Av, commemorating the destruction of the Temples and other Jewish tragedies
TISHRI seventh month of the Jewish year

Below *Sabbath challah and wine.*

Above *Masks are worn at Purim.*

TORAH Law (or Pentateuch)
TOSEFTA additions to the Mishnah
TWELVE TRIBES according to the Bible Israel is divided into 12 tribes descended from the sons of Jacob: Reuben, Simeon (Levi), Judah, Issachar, Zebulun, Benjamin, Dan, Naphtali, Gad, Asher, Ephraim and Manasseh
TU B'SHEVAT New Year for Trees
TZIZTZIT fringes

YAD pointer used in the synagogue when reading the Torah
YAHRZEIT lighting a memorial candle
YAHWEH God's sacred name, which is never pronounced
YARMULKE skullcap
YARTZEIT anniversary of a death
YESHIVAH (pl. yeshivot) Jewish rabbinical college
YETSIRAH Kabbalistic realm
YETZER HA-RA evil inclination
YETZER HA-TOV good inclination
YHWH it is forbidden to pronounce the Hebrew name of God (YHWH), so substitutions were used
YIDDISH language of Ashkenazi Jews
YIZKOR memorial prayers
YOM ATZMAUT Israel Independence Day
YOM KIPPUR Day of Atonement

ZADDIK righteous person
ZEMIROT hymns
ZIMZUM contraction of the Godhead into itself
ZIONISM movement for a Jewish homeland
ZOHAR medieval mystical work

Further Reading

GENERAL INTRODUCTIONS

Baron, S. W., *A Social and Religious History of the Jews* (Columbia University Press, 1952–76)
Beck, L., *The Essence of Judaism* (Schocken, 1948)
Cohn-Sherbok, D., *Introduction to Zionism and Israel* (Continuum, 2012)
—, *Judaism Today* (Continuum, 2011)
—, *Judaism: History, Belief and Practice* (Taylor & Francis, 2003)
De Lange, N., *Judaism* (Oxford University Press, 1986)
Epstein, I., *Judaism* (Penguin, 1975)
Jacobs, L., *The Book of Jewish Practice* (Behrman House, 1987)
—, *The Book of Jewish Belief* (Behrman House, 1984)
—, *A Jewish Theology* (Darton, Longman and Todd, 1973)
—, *Principles of the Jewish Faith* (Jason Aaronson, 1988)
Joffe, L., *An Illustrated History of the Jewish People* (Lorenz Books, 2012)
Katz, S. T., *Jewish Ideas and Concepts* (Schocken Books, 1972)
Margolis, M. L. and Marx, A., *A History of the Jewish People* (Harper and Row, 1965)
Neusner, J., *The Way of Torah: An Introduction to Judaism* (Dickenson, 1974)
Pilkington, C.M., *Judaism* (Hodder and Stoughton, 1991)
Rosten, L., *The Joys of Yiddish* (W.H. Allen, 1968)
Roth, C., *A History of the Jews* (Schocken, 1973)
Scheindlin, R.P., *A Short History of the Jewish People* (Oxford University Press, 2000)
Trepp, L., *A History of the Jewish Experience* (Behrman House, 1973)
Waskow, A.I., *Seasons of Our Joy: Modern Guide to the Jewish Holidays* (Bantam, 1982)
Werbolowsky, R.J. and Wigoder, G. (eds), *Encyclopedia of the Jewish Religion* (Holt, Reinhardt and Winston, 1966)

Above *A Passover haggadah.*

DICTIONARIES AND ENCYCLOPEDIAS

Abrahamson, G. (ed.), *The Blackwell Companion to Jewish Culture* (Blackwell, 1989)
Brisman, S. (ed.), *A History and Guide to Judaic Bibliography* (Hebrew Union College Press and Ktav, 1977)
Cohn-Sherbok, D., *A Concise Encyclopedia of Judaism* (Oneworld, 1992)
—, *Dictionary of Kabbalah and Kabbalists* (Impress Books, 2009)
—, *Dictionary of Jewish Biography* (Oxford University Press, 2005)
De Lange, N., *Penguin Dictionary of Judaism* (Penguin, 2008)
Encyclopedia Judaica (Keter, 1972), second edition (Macmillan, 2007)
The Jewish Encyclopedia (Funk and Wagnalls 1901–6)
Kantor, M., *The Jewish Time Line Encyclopedia* (Jason Aaronson, 1989)
Shamir, I. and Shavit, S., *Encyclopedia of Jewish History* (Massada, 1986)
Shunami, S., *Bibliography of Jewish Bibliographies* (Magness Press, 1965; supplement, 1975)
Solomon, N., *Historical Dictionary of Judaism* (Scarecrow Press, 2006)
Waxman, M., *A History of Jewish Literature* (Thomas Yoseloff, 1960)
Wigoder, G., *Dictionary of Jewish Bibliography* (Jerusalem Publishing House, 1991)
Wigoder, G., *The Encyclopedia of Judaism* (Macmillan, 1989)

ATLASES

Barnavi, Eli (ed.), *A Historical Atlas of the Jewish People* (Hutchinson, 1992)
Cohn-Sherbok, D. *Atlas of Jewish History* (Routledge, 1994)
De Lange, N., *Atlas of the Jewish World* (Phaidon, 1984)
Friesel, E., *Atlas of Modern Jewish History* (Oxford University Press, 1994)
Gilbert, M., *Jewish History Atlas* (Weidenfeld & Nicolson, 1988)

ELECTRONIC TEXTS

Bar-Ilan's Judaic Library (Torah Education Software, 1990)
Dead Sea Scrolls Database (Brill, 1999)
Encyclopedia Judaica (TES, 1997)
Judaic Classic Library (Davka Corporation, 1991–5)

INTERNET

Useful web addresses at the time of publication include (please note that addresses may change):
www.jewishencyclopedia.com (the 1901–6 edition)
http://www.jewfaq.org
http://www.torah.org/

Below *The Torah is at the heart of Judaism.*

INDEX

Aaron 66, 277, 356, 410
Abahu 352
Abbas, Mahmoud 15
Abbasids 109, 112, 215
Abbaye 88
Abi Zimra, David ben Solomon Ibn 419
Abraham 18, 10, 31, 32–3, 35, 39, 102, 107, 262, 273, 274, 280, 348, 350–1, 358, 368, 380, 390, 403, 410, 428, 488
Abraham ben Samuel Abulafia 296
Abraham Ibn Daud 364, 378
Absalom 46
Absentee Property Law 226–7
Abu al-Fath 283
Abu Imram Al-Tiflisi 303
Abu Isa al-Isphani 415
Abulafia, Abraham 120
Abulafia, Haim 13
Abzug, Bella 336
Adam Kadmon 297, 300–1, 353, 375, 377
Adler, Rachel 336
Adon Olam 357
afterlife 403, 418–19
aggadah 88, 246, 287, 292–3, 294, 388
Agudat Yisrael 26
agunah 491
Ahab 49, 52
Ahaz 279
Ahijah 48
Akiva 360, 388, 424, 437

Below *Fall of the Second Temple, 70CE.*

Akiva, Rabbi 81, 86
al-Aqsa Intifada 15
al-Hariri of Basra 298
Al-Tolidah 283
Albo, Joseph 357, 358, 378, 419
Alenu 382, 465
ALEPH 323
Alexander the Great 10, 62–3
Alfasi, Isaac 372
Alfassi, Yitzhak 11, 127
Algeria 12, 102
Alhambra Decree 12
aliyot 13, 14, 188, 192, 210–11
Alkabets, Solomon 437
Alkalai, Yehuda hai 328
Almosnino, Moses 357
American Revolution 13, 166–7
Amidah 61, 382–3, 394, 429, 431, 442, 464–5
Amora'im 11, 88
Amos 50, 51, 263, 278, 386, 394–5, 404, 405
Amram Gaon 383, 428
Anan ben David 110, 265, 302–3
Ananites 303
Anatolia 147
angels 297, 407, 431
Ani Maaimin 357, 362
anti-Semitism 19, 11, 14, 100, 122, 132–3, 136–7, 142, 143, 170, 177, 179, 180–1, 189, 197, 198, 204–5, 223, 266, 267, 268, 330, 334–5, 381
Antigonus of Soko 284, 285
antinomian sects 305
Antioch 99
Apocrypha 386, 406–7
apostates 266
Arab nationalism 161, 214–5
Arab Revolt 213
Arab-Israeli War 14, 214–5, 220–1
Arabic 109, 110, 118
Arabs 11, 33, 102–3, 105, 108–9, 112, 134, 148, 161
Arafat, Yasser 19, 228–9
Aramaic 82, 110, 151
Arami, Isaac 419
Arba'ah Turim 12
architecture 256–7
Arendt, Hannah 335
Aristobulus 280

Aristotelianism 296, 299
Ark of the Covenant 10, 42, 44, 46, 276–7, 346, 426–7, 429
Armageddon 10, 47, 57
Armenia 168
artists 186, 244–5
Asa 48–9
Asatir 283
Asharyites 298–9
Asher, tribe of 41
Asher ben Jehiel 372
Ashi, Rav 88, 389
Ashkenazi, Solomon 149, 267, 295, 312–13, 372
Ashkenazim 19, 11, 13, 67, 100, 105, 114–5, 119, 123, 130, 131, 140, 144, 147, 149, 150–1, 161, 171, 178–9, 182
Ashlag, Yehuda 332–3
Asia Minor 85, 98, 99, 146
Asiyah 297
Assyria 18, 10, 31, 52–3, 55, 56–9
Assyrians 263, 278–9, 350–1, 380
Atzilut 297
Auschwitz 14, 104, 202, 203
Australia 13, 184, 237
Austria 123, 133, 144, 164–5, 171, 176–7, 182, 186, 200, 203, 235
auto-da-fé 136, 137, 141
Avinu Malkenu 443
Avot de Rabbi Nathan 285
Azriel ben Menahem 296

Baal 49, 52
Ba'al Shem Tov (Besht) 13, 158–9, 267, 312–13, 332, 379
Baasha 48–9
Babi Yar massacre 205, 206
Babylon 18, 10, 11, 35, 52, 83, 85, 93, 94–5, 109, 114, 262, 263, 265, 279, 282, 299, 302, 380, 456
Babylonian captivity 56, 57–60, 188
Babylonian rite 383
Babylonian Talmud 372, 388–9, 412
badges *see* clothing and badges
Badinter, Elisabeth 336
Baghdad 11, 215
Bahir 296
Bahya ibn Asher ibn Halawa 357
Bahya ibn Pakudah 376, 378, 472

Balfour Declaration 14, 173, 192–3, 210–11, 216
Balkans 147, 148, 177, 203
banking and money-lending 53, 100, 103, 128–9, 132, 133, 140, 145, 148–9, 152–3, 179
Bannus 289
bar Giora, Simon 79, 80
Bar Hiyya, Abraham 133
Bar Kochba revolt 10, 80–1, 84, 85, 90, 93
bar mitzvahs 27, 28, 240, 261, 313, 321, 477, 480–1
bar Zakkai, Simeon 121
Baraitha 411
Barak, Ehud 15, 229
Baruchiah Russo 305, 307
Basel Conference 189
Bassevi, Jacob 145
bat mitzvah 27, 28, 240, 337, 477, 481
beard 486–7
Begin, Menachem 15, 217, 221, 228
ben Asher, Jacob 12, 119
ben Chadd 415
Ben-Gurion, David 209, 211, 212–13, 220–1, 268–9, 314, 331, 335, 454
ben Hanokh, Moses 113
ben Napaha, Johanan 88, 95
Ben Sira 280, 406
ben Solomon, Isaac Israeli 133
ben Ya'ir, Eleazar 80
Ben-Yehuda, Eliezer 13, 218
ben Zakkai, Yohanan 80
benevolence 396–7
Benjamin, tribe of 41, 44, 48, 56, 278
Benjamin ben Moses Nahavendi 303
Benjamin of Tudela 126, 135
Benjamin, Walter 335
Benyamin, Shlomo 332
Berber Jews 127, 162
Berg, Philip 332–3
Beriyah 297
Berkovits, Eliezer 359
Bernadotte, Count Folke 221
Bernstein, Leonard 15
Besht see Ba'al Shem Tov
bet din 398, 462, 490–1
Bible 18, 31, 60, 63, 77, 92–3, 246, 370, 374, 382, 385, 386–7
  Books of Moses (Pentateuch) see Torah
  Gospels 72, 73, 74
  Old Testament see Tanakh
Bilu 13, 188, 330
bimah 426–7
Birkhat ha-Mazon 431
Birnbaum, David 359
Birnbaum, Nathan 14
Birobidzhan 195
Black Death 133
Blazer, Isaac 379
blood libel 12, 129, 132–3, 136, 328
B'nai Brit 183
B'nai Or 322–3
Bnei Akiva 210
Bnei Menashe 15
Bnei Yisrae 33
Bomberg, Daniel 142
Book of Decrees 285
Borochov, Ber 189
Brakhot 87
Brandwein, Yehuda 332–3
Breuer, Isaac 329
brit milah 28
Britain 12, 13, 128–9, 132, 139, 153, 164, 171, 172–3, 176, 177, 180–1, 182, 186, 200, 224, 232–3, 240
Bruriah 89
Buber, Martin 269, 335
Bund 179, 194
Burg, Avraham 344
Burning Bush 272, 355
Byron, Lord 180
Byzantine empire 11, 83, 91, 93, 96–7, 135

Cain 390
Caleb 39, 40, 42
calendar 11, 20, 26, 388, 423, 424–5, 432–3

Above *A ruined synagogue at Sardis.*

caliphates 107, 108–9
Canaan 10, 31, 32–5, 37, 39–41, 262, 25, 26, 102, 132–3
Canaanites 14, 273, 349, 380
Canada 177, 231
cantillation 450
Carmel, Mount 408
Caro, Joseph 12, 13, 147, 149, 150, 266, 267, 372, 421, 470
Carvajal, Antonio 153
Castro, Abraham 162
Caucasus 127
Central Conference of American Rabbis 317
Chabad 158
Chabad-Lubavitch 313, 338
Challah 26–7
charity 396–7
Charlemagne 101
Chasidism see Hasidism
children 459–60, 466–7, 478–83, 485
China 126–7
Chmielnicki, Bogdan 267
Chmielnicki massacres 13, 156, 158, 165
Chomsky, Noam 335
chosen people 32, 275, 301, 310, 315, 319, 365, 367, 374–5
Christianity 10, 11, 12, 19, 31, 32, 47, 71–5, 77, 83, 84–5, 91–3, 96–11, 225, 264–7, 349, 352–3, 414
Chronicles 46, 61, 277, 386
cinema 207, 250–1
circumcision 28, 33, 75, 274, 279, 281, 460, 470, 477, 478, 480
clothing and badges 136, 147, 150,

INDEX

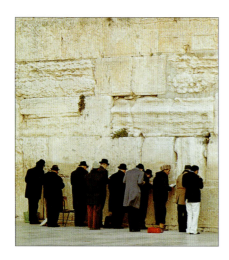

Above *The Western Wall, Jerusalem.*

159, 164, 169, 171, 202, 238, 311, 427, 442, 446, 465, 486–7
Cohen 53, 67, 84, 435, 479
Cohen, Leonard 341
Columbus Platform 317
commandments 262, 265, 275, 277, 283, 367, 370, 372–3, 374, 382, 388, 390–1, 430
community life 462–3
compassion 394–5
concentration camps 191, 199, 200–7, 217
Conservative Judaism 13, 14, 171, 183, 240, 268, 309, 314–5, 336, 338–9, 383, 463
Constantine the Great 11, 91, 92, 96, 264
conversion 470–1, 474
conversos 12, 137
Cordovero, Moses 13, 160, 266, 300, 332
Costa, Uriel da 143
Council of the Four Lands 13, 151, 158, 463
Council of Lydda 418
counter-culture 322, 336, 341
Counter-Reformation 267
court Jews 145, 151, 154–5, 172
covenant 33, 39, 262, 274, 275, 277, 289, 310, 352, 367, 374–5
Creation 294–5, 297, 300–1, 310, 353, 362–3, 368, 424
Crémieux, Adolphe 181, 187
Crémieux Decree 201
Crescas, Abraham 137, 152

Crescas, Hasdai 299, 359, 361, 368, 418–19
Crete 146, 147
Crimea 111, 168, 303
Crusades 12, 14, 97, 115, 117, 122, 129, 130–3, 134, 135, 303, 381, 415
Cuba 141, 236
cup of Elijah 435
Czechoslovakia 122, 123, 130, 139, 144, 145, 150–1, 156, 235

Dan, tribe of 41, 53, 126
dance 313, 3319, 325
Daniel 57, 58–9, 386
dati leumi 239
David 10, 31, 44, 45–7, 66, 72, 93, 126, 263, 404, 406, 432
David Alroy 415
Dayan, Moshe 226
de Haan, Jacob Israel 335
de Vidas, Elijah 377, 378
Dead Sea Scrolls 14, 73, 284, 288–9
death and funerals 477, 492–3
Deborah 42, 240
Defter 283
Deir Yassin massacre 220
Deluge 156
Deuteronomy 38, 39, 57, 61, 86, 351, 352, 374, 386, 388
devekut 297, 313, 383
Diaspora 10, 18, 19, 58, 63, 69, 77, 78, 80, 81, 83–5, 86, 98–103, 110, 126–7, 158, 184, 222, 262–13, 265, 280–1, 462
dietary laws 275, 302, 314, 344–5, 395, 434–5, 442, 449, 450, 459, 461, 462, 468–9
Diocletian 260
displaced persons camps 204, 205, 216, 217
Disputation of Barcelona 12
Disraeli, Benjamin 13, 153, 181, 187, 255
divine emanation 294–5
divorce 488, 490–1
'Doctors' Plot' 204–5
Doenmeh 305, 306
Dona Gracia 148–9, 240
Dosa 411
Dov Baer 267, 312, 332
Dov Ber 158
dreidels 22, 23, 449

Dreyfus, Alfred 14, 180–1, 189
Dreyfus affair 330
Duran, Simon ben Zemah 418–9

Eastern Europe 14–15, 19, 121–3, 130, 149–51, 164–5, 178–9, 204–5, 234–5
Ebionites 75
Ecclesiastes 364, 386, 389
Edah Haredit 311
Edom 395
Edomites 33, 65, 202–3
education 311, 316, 337, 482–3, 485
Egypt 10, 19, 32–3, 85, 108, 124–5, 146, 148, 161, 219–20, 262, 263, 274, 275, 280, 350, 380
 Jewish enslavement 10, 31–39
Einsatzgruppen 269
Einstein, Albert 14, 192, 199, 221, 232, 243
Eisner, Kurt 196
Elbaz, Jacques 325
Eldad Ha-Dani 381, 415
Eleazar ben Judah 295
Eleazar of Worms 393
Elephantine 77
Eli 44
Elijah 10, 50–1, 66, 263, 295, 351, 379, 387, 408, 410
Eliot, George 180–1
Elisha 51, 52, 263
emancipation 13, 14, 175, 176–7, 261, 268, 310
En Sof 296, 300, 305, 352, 353, 377
England *see* Britain

Below *Jewish quarter, Barcelona, Spain.*

500

INDEX

Enlightenment 164, 165, 170, 180, 240, 261, 268, 310, 314, 316, 463
Enlightenment movement *see* Haskalah
environmental issues 342–3, 345
Ephraim, tribe of 40, 41, 48, 278
Epicurianism 281, 284
Epstein, Kalonymus Kalman 332
Erasmus, Desiderius 142
Erez Israel 287, 416
Ergas, Joseph 368–9
eruv 285
Essenes 43, 71, 73, 84, 110, 271, 273, 281, 284, 288–9
Esther 23, 61, 240, 386, 389, 425, 447, 450–1
eternal light 426, 427
eternity 356–7, 403, 418–9
ethics 293, 344–5, 385, 390–1, 484
Ethiopia 15, 53, 126, 127, 226
Ethiopic Book of Enoch 407
etrog 312, 438–9
Eupolemus 290
Europe 265–7, 269–70
Evian Conference 200
evil 287, 297, 301, 305, 359, 364–5, 392
excommunication 462
exegesis 292–3, 294
exilarch 265
Exile 273, 274
Exodus 26, 36, 38–9, 61, 88, 126, 262, 275, 276, 283, 352, 368, 370, 386–7, 388, 424, 426, 434
Exodus affair 217
Ezekiel 18, 50, 61, 66, 120, 294, 386, 405
Ezra 10, 54, 59, 60–1, 66, 286, 387, 482
Ezra, Abraham Ibn 119
Ezrat Nashim 336–7

Fackenheim, Emil 365
Falasha 53, 126
false messiahs 13, 157, 158
family life 459–61, 466–7, 482, 488–9
fascism 197, 232
Fast of the First-Born 424, 447
fasting 444, 446–7, 457
fear of God 378–9, 473
feminism 322, 327, 334, 336–7
festivals 20–5, 87, 277, 283, 400, 423–5, 434–57

Finkelstein, Norman 335
Fircovitch, Abraham 111
food 21–6, 75, 88, 231 *also see* dietary laws
France 12–13, 14, 98, 100–1, 105, 114–5, 122, 128–9, 132–3, 136, 142–3, 144, 151, 176–7, 180, 181, 201, 203, 105, 224, 233
  French Revolution 13, 164, 166–7, 176, 210
Frank, Anne 206
Frank, Jacob 13, 158, 267, 305, 306–7
Frankel, Zacharias 268, 314
Frankists 260, 271, 291, 306–7, 312
free will 360–1
Freud, Sigmund 77, 187, 199, 232, 254
Friedländer, Michael 361

Gabirol, Solomon Ibn 119
Gad, tribe of 41
gaon 109, 110, 294
Ga'onim 11, 89
Garden of Eden 410–11
Gaza 15, 34, 134, 221, 227, 228, 269
Gedaliah 425, 446, 447
Ge'ez 126
Geiger, Abraham 171
Gemara 88
Genesis 26, 32–3, 61, 240, 273, 274–5, 276, 294, 350, 362–3, 370, 386–7, 430
Geonim 109
Gerizim, Mount 282, 283
Germany 13–15, 100–1, 123, 130, 133, 139, 140, 142, 144–5, 151, 164–5, 170–1, 176–7, 182, 192–3, 196–7, 198–203, 222–3, 234–5

Gerona 296
Gerondi, Jonah ben Abraham 393
Gershom, Rabbenu 11, 114, 130
Gershon, Abraham 13
Gersonides 12, 133, 137, 152, 99, 361
gestures 464
get 490–1
ghettos 12, 19, 123, 139, 140, 167, 176, 201, 267, 316, 417, 427
Gideon 43
Glückel of Hameln 151, 246
Gnosticism 59, 120, 296
Gog and Magog 408, 409
Golan 14, 15, 84, 220, 227
Gold, Shefa 322
Golden Calf 275, 301, 302, 428
Goldstein, Joseph 341
Golem 150
Goliath 43
Gomer 278
goodness 364–5, 392
Gordon, Aaron David 189
Goren, Shlomo 344
Gospels 414
Gottlieb, Phyllis 322
Grana 162–3
Great Assembly 10, 60, 66, 76
Great Hoshanah 439
Great Sanhedrin 149, 155
Greece 98–9, 146, 177, 185, 203
Greek civilization 280–1
Greenberg, Blu 337
Gush Emunim 15, 227, 239

Below *A 19th-century print of the ancient city of Jerusalem.*

INDEX

Above *A fifth-century mosaic of the City of Jerico and the River Jordan.*

Ha-Am, Ahad 188, 189
ha-Danfi, Av-Sakhva ben Asad 283
Ha-Mavdil 431
Habakkuk 50, 51, 386
Hadassah 13
Haftarah 61, 429, 431, 433
Haganah 14, 212, 213, 216–17, 331
Hagar 33, 102, 368
Haggadah 24, 88, 319, 371, 372, 434
Haggai 50, 60, 386
Haile Selassie 126
Haim of Volozhin 159
hakhamim 73
Halakha 88, 114, 222
Halevi, Yehuda 12, 110, 119
Hamas 15, 229
hamsa 295
HaNagid, Samuel 118
Hannah 44
Hanseatic League 144
Hanukkah 20, 22, 23, 65, 284, 425, 432, 448–9, 461
haredim 159, 238, 240
Harran 262, 274
Harun, Jacob ben 283
hashgahah 368–9
Hasideans 280, 286
Hasidei Ashkenaz 12, 295, 296
Hasidism 12, 29, 64, 67, 155, 158–9, 178, 238, 240, 267, 301, 308, 309, 311, 312–2, 329, 332, 338, 369, 372–3, 379, 383, 393, 420–1, 439, 451, 464
Hassidim Haskalah 13, 155, 170–1, 176, 177, 187, 210, 238, 268

Hasmoneans 10, 65, 67–70, 281, 284
Havdalah 27, 431
Havurah 231, 239
havurot movement 322–3
Hayim of Sanz 369
He-Halutz 213
Heaven 410–11, 418
Hebrew 13, 14, 34–5, 59, 63, 88, 97, 118, 142, 150, 151, 166, 170, 209, 212–3, 218, 247, 314, 317, 329, 426, 429, 464
Hebrews 18, 32–41
Hebron 15, 32, 160, 262
Heine, Heinrich 177, 246
hekhalot 294, 297
Helen of Adiabene 94, 95
Hell 412–13, 418
Hellenism 62–3, 273, 280–1, 288, 298
Herod the Great 10, 69–71, 72, 263, 414
Hertz, Joseph 418, 419
Herzl, Theodor 14, 188–9, 210, 211, 218, 226, 268, 330, 331, 417
Hesiod 280
Hess, Moses 13, 188, 416, 417
Hezekiah 10, 56–7
Hezekiah's Tunnel 56
Hilberg, Raul 207
Hillel 10, 76–7, 280, 287, 292–3, 363, 418
Hiram 47
Hirsch, Samson Raphael 171, 177
Hirsch, Samuel 171, 183
Histadrut 212
Hitler, Adolf 14, 191, 198–203, 207
Hizbollah 15, 228
Holdheim, Samuel 171

holiness 400–1
Holocaust 19, 14, 121, 191, 199, 200–207, 234, 269, 291, 329, 331, 359, 365, 454–5
Holy land 93, 115, 148–9
Holy of Holies 276, 277, 285, 426
Holy Roman Empire 144–5, 151, 164–5
Homer 280
homosexuality 319, 323, 338–39
Horowitz, Isaiah 150–1, 161
Hosea 50, 263, 278, 279, 386
Hovevei Tzion 188
Humanistic Judaism 239, 309, 320–1, 463
Humash 61
Hungary 13, 130, 149, 159, 164, 171, 177, 179, 186, 196–7, 203
huppah 29, 339, 485, 489
Hurwitz, Phineas Elijah ben Meir 362
Hyksos 36–7

idolatry 33, 35, 39, 48, 49, 52, 56
immanence, divine 354–5
India 15, 53, 126, 127, 237
Inquisition 12, 136–7, 141, 146, 266
intermarriage 319, 485
intifada 15, 229, 269
Iran *see* Persia
Iraq 58, 102, 108, 214–15, 219, 220
Irgun 14, 213, 216–17, 220
Isaac 18, 31, 32–3, 102, 262, 273, 274, 351, 403, 405, 410, 443
Isaac the Blind 296, 364–65, 373
Isaac ha-Kohen 296
Isaiah 10, 450–1, 60–1, 66–7, 72, 126, 263, 279, 352, 354, 386, 433
Ish-Boshet 45
Ishmael 33, 102, 368
Ishmael, School of 388
Ishmael ben Elisha 292–3
Ishmael of Ukbara 303
Ishmaelites 102
Islam 11, 19, 31, 32, 47, 102–3, 105–9, 113–15, 118–19, 134, 265, 298
Israel 380
Israel Independence Day 424, 452–3
Israel (kingdom) 10, 18, 31, 45–9, 52–3, 263, 278–9, 380, 404–5
Israel, Land of 18, 19, 32, 110, 161, 188–9
Israel (modern state) 14–15, 19, 56,

INDEX

205, 209, 220–1, 222, 224, 226–9, 239, 311, 315, 331, 381
  independence 268, 269, 331
  Occupied Territories 269
  secular Judaism 320
  Six Day War 269
  War of Independence 269
  Yom Kippur War 269
Israeli Agudah 311, 329
Israelite tribes 10, 18, 31, 40–3, 48, 52–3, 55, 56
Israelites 32–42
Issachar, tribe of 41
Isserles, Moses 12, 123, 372, 421
Italkim 69
Italy 12, 14, 69, 100, 132, 139–44, 147, 167, 176–7, 197, 203

Jabneh 263
Jabotinsky, Vladimir 213, 268–9, 331
Jacob 18, 33, 37, 39, 40, 262, 273–5, 278, 306, 380, 403, 410, 428
Jacobs, Steven 359
Jacobson, Israel 171, 316
Jason 280
Jeremiah 50, 57, 58–9, 61, 75, 276, 279, 350, 351, 368, 386, 394
Jericho 40, 41
Jeroboam 10, 32, 48, 49, 302
Jerusalem 10, 11, 14, 45, 48, 56, 64, 107, 108–9, 134, 169, 161
  Al Aqsa Mosque 103, 128
  as capital 10, 45
  Crusades 16, 97, 115, 117, 130–1, 134
  Dome of the Rock 11, 105, 109, 134
  First Temple 10, 19, 46–7, 58
  Holy Sepulchre 91, 96, 134
  Islamic rulers 134, 148–9
  Persians 102–3
  Second Temple 19, 55, 60, 64, 67, 70–2, 74, 78–9, 93, 92
  state of Israel 220, 227
  Yad Vashem 205
  Zionism 189
Jesse 45, 72
Jesus 10, 47, 51, 72–3, 77, 87, 93, 239, 286, 324–5, 381, 414
Jewish Agency 14, 196, 214, 217
Jewish Brigade 163, 216
Jewish Buddhist movement 327, 340–1

Jewish Enlightenment 261, 268, 316
Jewish Renewal 231, 322–3
Jews for Jesus 239
Jews in the Woods 239
Jezebel 49
Joab 46
Job 50, 61, 54, 364, 378, 386
Joel 50, 386
Joffe, Adolph 194–5
John of Giscala 79
John the Baptist 288, 289, 414
Jonah 50, 61, 386, 404
Jonathan 45, 432
Jordan 19
Jose the Galilean 411
Joselewicz, Berek 161
Joseph 10, 37, 40, 262, 275, 278, 390, 473
Joseph, Jacob 312
Josephus Flavius 79, 84–5, 94, 98, 281, 284, 287, 288, 289
Joshua 10, 39, 40–1, 50, 262, 273, 283, 380, 386
Joshua ben Hananiah 281
Joshua ben Levi 412
Josiah 10, 57
Josippon 15, 114
Joskowicz, Menachem 291
Judah, tribe of 40, 41, 45, 56 278, 488
Judah (kingdom) 10, 18, 31, 48–9, 52–3, 263, 278–9, 380, 404–5
Judah ben Samuel 295
Judah Halevi 375
Judea 55, 56–7
Judean revolt 78–9, 92
Judeo-Tat 127
Judezmo 113, 149
Judgement 10, 40, 41, 42–3, 44, 403, 406–7, 418, 442
judges 262–3, 278, 386
Judith 280
Juhuro 127
Justinian 11

Kabbalat Shabbat 430
Kabbalistic Judaism 12, 13, 120–1, 143, 152, 155, 157–60, 239, 266, 267, 296–7, 304–5, 327, 328, 352–3, 355, 383, 415, 437
  chosen people 375
  divine providence 368–9
  ex nihilo creation 363
  goodness and evil 364–5
  Hasidism 312–13, 332
  love of God 377
  Lurianic 300–1, 353, 363, 373, 415
  mitzvot 372–3
  modern 332–3
  Purim 451
  Zohar 296, 300, 304, 332, 352, 353, 365, 370–1, 377, 379, 387, 401
Kaddish 382, 429, 467
kakhya 148
kalam 298
Kalischer, Zvi Hirsch 328–9
Kallir, Eleazar 135
Kalonymous Kalman 363
Kamenev, Lev 194–5, 234
Kamenetz, Rodger 341
Kant, Emmanuel 170
Kaplan, Mordecai 239, 240, 255, 318–19, 323, 481
Kapparot 393, 444–5
Kapsali, Moses 147

Below *Reading the scriptures*.

INDEX

Above The Flight of the Prisoners *by James Tissot*.

Karaim 111
Karaites 11, 89, 105, 109, 110–11, 135, 148, 169, 260, 265, 271, 291, 298, 302–3
Kedushah 382
kehillah 147, 151
Kehset Ga'avah 339
ketubah 140, 245, 488–9
Khazars 11, 105, 110–11, 168
kibbutz movement 14, 211–13, 238, 241, 335
kiddush 21, 26, 27, 431, 432, 434, 435
Kindertransport 200
King David Hotel bombing 217
King-Crane Commission 211
Kingdom of God 295
Kings 10, 43–49, 52–3, 277, 386
Kishinev Pogrom 14
Kislev 425
kitl 22
Kitos Wars 10, 81
kittel 442
K'lal Yisrael 315, 463
klezmer 179, 252
Knaanic 151
Knights Hospitaller 148
Kodashim 87
Kol Nidre 22
kolel 484
Koliyivshchyna rebellion 158
Komfield, Jack 341
Konen 410
Kook, Abraham Isaac 328, 329, 344
Koran 107

Kosciusko Uprising 165
kosher 88
Kristallnacht 100, 269
Ku Klux Klan 197
kvutzot 192

La-Shanah ha-Baah Bi-Yerushalayim 445
Laaz 151
Ladino 113, 149, 150, 185, 222
Lag B'Omer 25, 300, 424, 437
Lamentations 61, 279, 386, 389
landsleitsverreine 182
law code 10–12, 22, 39, 75, 86, 89, 261, 285, 292–3, 370–1, 392, 398–9
  aggadah 287, 292–3, 294, 388
  commandments 367, 370, 372–3, 374, 388, 390–1, 430
  communal laws 462–3
  Conservative Judaism 314, 315
  education 482–3, 484
  ethical code 390–1
  homosexuality 338–9
  Kabbalistic Judaism 372–3
  Karaites 302
  Mishnah 293, 388, 391
  mitzvot 311, 372–3, 388, 390–1
  Mosaic 310, 311, 316–17, 427
  Musar 379
  Oral 286–7, 292, 302, 316, 367, 372, 387, 388, 391, 421
  Orthodox Judaism 310, 311, 314, 372, 373, 387, 421, 423
  outward signs 486–7
  rabbinic 291, 292, 302, 317, 344, 388–9, 391, 421, 423
  Reconstructionist Judaism 318

  revelation 370–1
  Shulkhan Arukh 267, 421, 470–1
  Talmuds 372, 388–9
  transgression 418
  Written 302–3, 316, 367, 372, 386–7, 391
Law of Return 221, 226
Leah 33, 40, 240
Lebanese civil war 15, 228
Lehi 14, 217, 220–1
Lemba 53
Lenin, Vladimir 194
Lessing, Gotthold 170
Levi 435
Levi, Primo 207
Levi, Nathan Benjamin 266
Lévi-Strauss, Claude 254, 255
Levi Strauss 173, 183
Levi Yitzhak of Berdichev 332, 379
Levites 41, 49, 56, 60, 61, 67, 84, 277, 428
Leviticus 38, 61, 86, 338, 376, 386, 388
Libya 98
Likud 15, 228, 229
literature 151, 179, 246–9
Lithuania 12, 14, 110, 111, 140, 150, 156, 159, 165, 168–9, 197, 201, 205, 235
Loew ben Betzalel, Rabbi Judah 12, 150, 156
Lopez, Rodrigo 153
Lot 274
love of God 376–7, 473
Lubavich Hassidim 159, 238–9
lulav 312, 438–9
Luria, Isaac 13, 120, 157–8, 160, 266–7, 300–1, 332, 353, 373, 453
Lurianic Kabbalah 304–5, 312–13, 353, 363, 373, 415
Lurianic prayer book 312
Luther, Martin 12, 142, 144–5, 266, 267
Luxemburg, Rosa 196
Luzzatto, David 170

Maaseh Bereshit 294
Maccabee, Judah ha- 281, 448
Maccabees 10, 23, 64–7, 73, 76, 98
Madrid Peace Conference 15
Maimon, Solomon 170
Maimonides, Moses 12, 66, 87, 124–5, 143, 152, 162, 242, 251, 299, 338,

504

INDEX

Above Tree of Life, part of the Ardon Windows by Mordecai Ardon.

343, 387, 392–3, 397, 415, 443, 474
  Guide for the Perplexed 290, 299, 353, 355–61, 368, 371
  Mishneh Torah 372, 377
  Principles of the Jewish Faith 310, 418
Mainz 265
Malachi 50, 60, 386
Malik Al-Ramli 303
Malkhut 375
malkot 444
Malta 137, 141
Manasseh, tribe of 40, 41, 48, 53, 278, 410
Manicheans 298
Maranos 141, 148–9, 152–3, 167, 214, 266, 267
Margolioth, Meir ben Tzvi Hirsch 152
marriage 28–9, 87–8, 222, 240, 388, 476–8, 484–5, 488–9
martyrology 445
Marx, Karl 13, 77, 177, 254
Masada 70, 71, 79, 80
maskilim 170, 178, 268
Masoretes 11
matrilineal descent 60, 222
matzah 434–5
May Laws 178–9, 161
Maybaum, Ignaz 365
mechitza 312
medicine 133, 148, 153, 242
medieval Judaism 264–5
Megiddo *see* Armageddon
Megilla Ta'anit 285

megillah 450
Meir 281
Meir, Golda 15, 220, 227, 241, 335
Meir, Rabbi 89
Meisel, Marcus 151
Mekhilta 352, 388
Mendelssohn, Moses 13, 170, 247, 268, 316, 346
Menelaus 280, 281
Menelik 126
menorah 23, 65, 76, 270, 276, 426, 448–9, 465
merkavah 120, 294, 295, 297
Meron, Mount 300
Mesopotamia 262, 263, 274, 281, 350
Messiah 266, 282, 291, 295, 301, 302, 304–5, 310, 319, 380–1, 403–17
  messianism 66, 67, 72, 74, 157, 160–1
  anti-Messianism 416–7
  modern interpretations 418–9
  rabbinic Judaism 403, 408–9
  Zionism 327, 328–9
Messiah ben David 381, 404, 409, 410
Messiah ben Joseph 381, 409, 410
Messianic Age 344, 381, 403, 404–7, 410–11, 414, 416
Messianic Judaism 239, 309, 324–5
Metatron 297
mezuzah 245, 401, 428–9, 461
Micah 50, 51, 263, 279, 386, 404, 443
Michal 45
Middle East 18, 148, 162–3, 214, 223
midrash 11, 73, 88, 246, 287, 293, 295, 338, 352, 356, 362–3, 376, 385, 388–9, 408, 410
mikrah 302, 445
mikveh 128, 288, 427, 435, 462, 471, 474–5, 489
mincha 61
minhag 114
minim 75
minyan 28, 29, 77, 240, 315, 336, 382, 427, 480, 488
Miriam 38, 240
Mishawayh Al-Ukbari 303
Mishnah 10, 11, 22, 25, 76, 86–8, 93, 97, 120, 124, 264, 287, 293, 356, 360, 372, 382, 388, 391, 421, 430
Mitnaggedim 312
mitzvot 39, 86, 311, 372–3, 388, 390–1, 401

Mizrachi Zionism 210
Mizrachi, Mizrahim 159, 182, 214–15, 219
Mizrah scroll 20, 162
Mizrahi 329
Modena, Leone 143
Mo'ed 87
Mohammed 11, 105, 106–7
mohel 28, 480
Molko, Solomon 415
monarchy 263, 273, 380
monolatry 350–1
monotheism 18, 32, 273, 310, 317, 341, 349–53
Montagu, Edwin Samuel 210–11
Montefiore, Moses 163, 181, 189
Morocco 11, 98, 119, 124, 127, 149, 203, 214–15, 219
Moses 10, 21, 24, 31, 36, 37, 38–9, 50, 67, 107, 126, 262, 264, 265, 272, 273, 275, 276, 280, 282, 310, 311, 315, 350, 355, 356, 367, 370–1, 372, 380, 386, 387, 388, 390, 410, 412, 421, 426, 427, 428, 432
  Books of 291–3, 309, 370–3, 386, 421
Moses ben Shem Tov 296
Moses de Leon 12, 121
Moses from Crete 381
moshavot 14, 210
Motzkin, Leo 196
Mount Sinai 21, 38, 39
Mountain Jews 127
Muna, Rav 88
Munich Olympics 19
Munk, Salomon 170
Musar movement 13, 379

Below *Caves in the Judean desert.*

Above *The Western Wall, Jerusalem. A 19th-century German painting by Gustav Bauernfeind.*

music and musicians 179, 186–7, 250–3, 313, 315, 316, 429, 431
Mutazilites 298, 299
mystical Judaism 120–1, 147, 155, 157, 160, 260, 266–7, 294–7, 300–1, 304–5, 312–3, 323, 341, 383
see also Kabbalistic Judaism

Nachman of Bratslav 332
Nahmanides 12, 119, 134, 296, 370, 373, 383, 387
Nahum 50 386
names 478
Naphtali, tribe of 41
Napoleon Bonaparte 167, 176
Nashim 87
Nasi, Don Joseph 148–9
Nasser, Gamal Abdel 269
Nathan of Gaza 157, 304–5, 415
Nazirites 43, 75
Nazism 14, 19, 185, 191, 196–207, 210–11, 234, 245, 250
Nebuchadnezzar II 57–9
Nehemiah 8, 60–1, 386
neilat shearim 382
Neo-Orthodox Judaism 171, 177
Neologs 171, 179
Netherlands 13, 139–40, 143–4, 145, 152, 156, 177, 203, 232, 267
Neturei Karta 329
New Sanhedrin 155, 167
Nezikin 87
Noah 36, 202, 390, 398

Nordau, Max 189
North Africa 140, 146, 148, 152–3, 214
Norway 13
Numbers 38, 40, 61, 81, 386, 388
Nuremberg Laws 199
Nuremberg Trials 204

Obadiah 50, 51, 386
OHaLaH 323
olam 356
Old Testament 10, 18, 28, 60
Olmert, Ehud 19
omer 25, 283, 424, 426, 436–7
omnipotence, God's 358–9
omniscience, God's 360–1
ophanim 297
Oppenheim, Moritz Daniel 260
Or Ganuz 332
oral law 10, 11, 39, 67, 76, 86
Orit 126
Orthodox Judaism 13, 67, 87, 159, 171, 183, 210, 238–41, 309–11, 329, 331, 337, 338, 370–1, 387, 463, 465, 486–7
  law code 310–11, 315, 372–3, 387, 421, 423
Oslo Accords 15, 228–9
Ostjuden 178–9
Othniel 42
Ottomans 12, 13, 14, 97, 134–5, 139, 140, 146–9, 156, 160–2, 175, 177, 185, 193, 215
outward signs 486–7

Pact of Omar 108–9
Pale of Settlement 13, 14, 155, 168–9, 176, 182, 191, 192, 194, 234
Palestine 18, 34, 268–9, 280, 329, 330–1
  Balfour Declaration 14, 173, 192–3, 210–2, 216
  British Mandate 14, 189, 210, 212–3, 216–17
  Islamic rulers 134, 148–9, 160–1, 193
  Jewish migration to 13, 14, 139, 160–1, 173, 175, 181, 188–9, 199–200, 204, 211–19
  Roman rule 90–1
Palestine Liberation Organization (PLO) 15, 227–9
Palestine rite 383
Palestinian Arabs 14–15, 161, 209, 211–5, 217, 220–1, 222, 226–9
Palestinian people 269, 381
Palestinian Talmud 372, 388–9
Palmach 216
Pappenheim, Bertha 336
pardes 88–9
Paris Disputation 16
paschal lamb 282, 283, 424, 426, 434–5
Passover 275, 277, 314, 421, 423, 424, 434–5, 461
patriarchs 10, 18, 32–3, 35, 50, 76, 273, 274–5, 276
patrilineal descent 19, 222
Paul, Saint 74–5, 84, 99
paytanim 97
Pentateuch see Torah
peot 159, 169, 487
Peres, Shimon 15, 228–9
Persia 58, 102–3, 108, 140, 141, 148, 163, 168
Perushim 161
Pesach 20–1, 24–5, 87, 88, 277
peshut 115
Pesotta, Rose 334
Pfefferkorn, Johannes 144
Pharisees 66–7, 68, 70, 73, 76, 84, 263, 264, 271, 273, 284, 286–7, 292, 322
Philippson, Ludwig 171
Philistines 10, 41, 43–7
Philo of Alexandria 77, 93, 143, 280–1, 298
philosophical Judaism 254–5, 260, 298–9
Phineas of Koretz 369
Phinehas ben Yair 401

phylacteries 28
Pidyon ha Ben/Bat 28
pietism 312–3
pilgrim festivals 277, 283, 423, 438–9
pilpul 50, 159
Pinsker, Leon 188, 330, 417
Pirkei Avot 76, 77
Pittsburgh Platform 316–7, 416
piyyutim 383
Platonism/Neo-Platonism 281, 296–7, 299
P'nai Or 323
pogroms 11, 14, 151, 155–6, 179–80, 183–4, 188, 200, 204, 265, 266, 267, 268, 330, 331
Polak, Jacob 150
Poland 12, 13, 14, 26, 122–3, 130, 133, 139, 140, 144, 150–1, 156, 159, 179, 182, 196–7, 200–1, 202, 204, 235
   partitions 13, 155, 158, 164–5, 168–9
Polanski, Roman 207
polygamy 11, 114, 150, 240
polytheism 274
Portugal 12, 137, 140–1, 148
Positive-Historical Judaism 13
Prague trials 14
prayer 312, 315, 319, 323, 382–3, 388, 428–9, 464–5, 479, 486–7
prayer shawl (tallit) 208, 260, 311, 314–5, 382, 429, 431, 445, 468, 486, 487
Principles of the Jewish Faith 310, 418
printing 12, 13, 139, 142–3, 146–7, 150, 152, 160–1, 185
Promised Land 18, 31, 32–3, 262, 350, 380–1, 403, 404–7, 410
Prophets 18, 44, 50–1, 61, 76, 273, 278–9, 310, 355, 370, 382–3, 386, 391
Protestant Reformation 12, 139, 142, 144–5
'Protocols of the Elders of Zion' 181, 197
Proverbs 47, 61, 386, 391
providence, divine 368–9
Prussia 164–5, 177, 180
Psalms 47, 58, 61, 171, 277, 351, 354, 356, 360, 362, 364, 368, 386, 428, 445
Pseudepigrapha 406
Ptolemies 10, 63, 85
Purim 20, 23, 61, 87, 425, 450–1
Purim-shpil 451

Pythagoreanism 280, 281

Qumran 288–9

Rabbah 362–3, 389
Rabban Gamaliel II 287
Rabbenu Tam 115
rabbinic Judaism 11, 260, 264, 266, 287, 291–307, 309, 356, 362–3, 386–7, 423
   aggadah 292–3, 294, 388
   Amoraim 292, 293, 388
   anti-rabbinic sects 300, 302–3
   chosen people 374–5
   divine providence 368
   exegesis 292–3, 294
   goodness and evil 364–5
   halakha 292–3
   and Hellenism 281
   law code 265, 291, 292, 317, 344, 388, 391, 421
   Messiah 403, 408–9
   midrash 388–9
   Mishnah 388, 391
   mystical 294–7
   Sabbath 430
   Tannaim 292, 293, 388
   Torah 291, 292–3, 367
Rabbanites 110, 135
rabbis 59, 76–7, 83, 84, 178, 261, 287, 312–3
   women as 317, 319, 322, 323, 337
Rabin, Yitzhak 19, 226, 227, 228–9, 239
Rachel 33, 40, 240
Radhanites 101, 103, 168
Rambam see Maimonides
Ramban see Nahmanides
Raphael, Melissa 359

Rathenau, Walther 335
Rashi 11, 114–15
rebbe see rabbis
Rebecca 33, 240
Reconstructionist Judaism 14, 171, 239, 240, 255, 309, 318–19, 323, 337, 383, 463
Redemption of the First-Born 477, 479
Reform Judaism 13, 14, 15, 19, 89, 155, 159, 170–1, 183, 210, 222, 238, 240, 268, 309, 310, 314, 316–7, 318, 337, 339, 375, 383, 416, 419, 427, 429, 431, 463, 465
refuseniks 19
Rehoboam 10, 47, 48, 49, 263
Reines, Yizhak 189
Renaissance 142
repentence 392–3
resurrection 282, 310, 402, 418–19
returnees to faith 159, 238–9
Reuben, tribe of 41, 275
Reuchlin, Johannes 142
revelation 370–1, 371
Revisionists 213, 216–17
Rhodes 148
Rif 9, 127
Rishonim 12
ritual bath see mikveh
ritual purity 388
Romania 13, 147, 159, 186, 196, 203
Romaniotes 98, 147, 148
Romans 10, 11, 55, 64–5, 67–71, 73, 74, 78–81, 83, 84–5, 90–1, 263, 264, 288–9, 380–1, 414, 456
Rosen, David 344
Rosh Hashanah 20, 21, 87, 368, 425,

Below *Modern-day Tel Aviv, Israel.*

INDEX

Above *Lighting the candles in the El-Ghriba synagogue, Djerba.*

441, 442–3, 464, 465
Rosh Hodesh 277, 432, 433, 452–3
Rossi, Azaria di 143
Rothschild family 13, 172–3, 176, 188, 193
Russia 11, 13–15, 135, 151, 155, 156, 159, 164–5, 168–9, 176–184, 186, 188, 192, 200–1, 203, 204–5, 234–5
   revolutions 14, 178–9, 181, 191, 192–5, 196
Ruth 45, 386, 389

Saadia Gaon 11, 109, 111, 299, 303, 355, 358, 376–7
Sabbath 277, 282, 311, 343, 382, 400, 423, 430–3, 461
Sabbath lamp 372
Sabra and Chatilla massacre 19
sacrifice 263, 274, 276–7, 282, 283, 285, 351, 367, 382, 388, 423, 426, 428, 448
   paschal lamb 282, 283, 424, 426, 434–5
Sadat, Anwar 15, 228
Sadducees 66–7, 68, 70, 73, 74, 84, 110, 271, 273, 284–5, 286
Safed 160–1, 266, 267
Saison 217
Saladin 12, 131, 134
Salanter, Israel 13, 255
Saliège, Archbishop 203
Salonika 185
Salzberg, Sharon 341
Samaritans 59, 65, 93, 271, 273, 282–3

Samson 43, 280, 386
Samuel 10, 43, 44, 45, 50, 263, 386, 404
Samuel ben Kalonymus 295
Samuel, Rabbi 89, 94, 95
San Francisco Platform 317
sanctuary 276
Sanhedrin 10, 70, 73, 76–7, 80–1, 84, 86, 90, 264, 286, 287, 370
Sarah 32, 33, 240, 274, 358
Satan 301, 407
Satmar Hassidim 159, 238
Saul 31, 44–5, 263, 280
savora'im 11, 89
Schachter-Shalomi, Zalman 322–3
Schechter, Solomon 183, 314–5
Schindler, Oskar 203, 207
scientists 133, 137, 186, 242–3
secularism 261, 310, 311, 320–1, 327, 330–1, 419
Seder 24
Seder Olam 424
Sefer ha-Bahir 121
Sefer Torah 400–1
Sefer Yezirah 121, 294–5, 296
Sefirah 25
sefirot 121, 294–7, 300, 352, 355, 372–3, 375
segregation 267
Seleucids 10, 63–4, 68, 95, 280, 281
self-denial 401
self-mortification 313, 393
Semites 36, 102, 274
Sens 265
Sephardic Jewry 301, 304, 372
Sephardim 12, 19, 67, 112–3, 114, 117–26, 136–7, 139, 140, 146–7,

149, 150, 152, 159, 162–3, 182, 183, 185, 214–5, 219
Septuagint 10, 63
Serene 415
service of the heart 367
services 382, 426–9
settler movement 15, 209, 228, 229, 239, 241
Seudah Shelishit 431
Shabazi, Shalom 163
Shabbat 26–7, 87, 171
Shabbateans 260, 266–7, 271, 291, 304–5, 312, 415
Shabbetai Tzvi 13, 155, 156, 157, 158, 161, 266–7, 291, 304–5, 307, 381, 415, 416, 457
shacharit 361, 82
Shakespeare, William 19, 153, 248
shaloch manot 23
Shalom Aleikhem 431
Shalom, Baruch 332
shamash 23
Shamir, Yitzhak 15
Shammai 10, 76–7, 287, 363
Shaprut, Hisdai Ibn 113
Sharett, Moshe 212
Sharon, Ariel 15, 229
Shas *see* Mishna
Shavuot 21, 25, 277, 283, 423, 425, 426, 436–7
Shealtiel 148
She'arit Israel 141, 166
Shechem 32, 35, 40, 41, 47, 48, 262
Sheinberger, Avraham 332
Shekhinah 285, 349, 354–5, 375, 377
Shem 36, 102
Shema 352–3, 382–3, 428–9, 431, 465
Shemini Atzeret 425
Shemoneh Esreh *see* Amidah
shepherd crusaders 133
Sheva Berakhot 489
shevirat ha-kelim 300–1
shewbread 276, 426
Shiloh 10, 42, 44
Shimlung 53
Shiva 29
shiviti 98
Shoavim Tat 447
shocklen 464
shofar 21, 252, 320, 392, 401, 441–3, 445, 446
shtetl 150, 169, 234

508

shtieblach 29, 171
Shulkhan Arukh 12, 147, 150, 267, 421, 470–1
Sicarites 71
Sicily 12, 141
siddur 11
Sifra 338, 376, 388
Sifrei 388
Simchat Torah 20, 385, 420–1, 425, 436
Simeon, tribe of 41, 56
Simeon Bar Kochba 263, 381, 414
Simeon ben Gamaliel 399
Simeon ben Yohai 296, 300, 353, 371, 387, 498, 424, 437
sin 392–3
Sinai 275, 282, 283, 291, 292, 367, 386, 421
Singapore 14
Sitra Ahra 292, 365
Six Day War 15, 227, 228, 269
Slansky, Rudolf 205, 235
slaughter, ritual 395, 468–9
social Darwinism 180
socialism 327, 330, 334–5
Socrates 280
Sokolow, Nahum 193
Solomon 10, 31, 46–8, 126, 263, 276–7, 280, 380, 386, 426
Solomon ben Isaac *see* Rashi
Solomon ha-Kohen 415
Solomon Ibn Gabirol 298–9
Song of Songs 47, 61, 246, 386, 389, 433
South Africa 14, 184, 237
South America 14, 141, 184, 236
Soviet Union *see* Russia
Spain 11, 12, 19, 98, 100–1, 105, 110–13, 117–20, 120, 177
  Inquisition 12, 136–7, 141, 146
  Jews expelled 19, 134, 136–7, 139, 140, 146
Spartacist League 196
Spinoza, Baruch 13, 77, 139, 152
Spira, Zevi Elimelech 379
spiritual path 385–401, 472–3
Stalin, Joseph 195, 205, 234
Stalinism 334–5
Star of David 45, 122
Steinem, Gloria 336
Stern Gang *see* Lehi
Stoicism 281
Strassfeld, Michael 322

Sufism 296
sukkah 312, 319, 438–9, 445, 461
Sukkot 20, 22, 87, 277, 285, 312, 423, 425, 432, 438–9, 461
synagogue 29, 58, 59, 61, 67, 77, 147, 256–7, 312, 367, 382, 422–3, 426–9, 431, 465
Switzerland 133, 144
synagogues 29, 58, 59, 61, 67, 77, 147, 256–7
Syria 10, 11, 14, 15, 98, 114, 134, 148, 161, 162, 220
Szold, Henrietta 13

Tabernacle 423
Taharot 87, 88
tallit *see* prayer shawl
tallit katan 487
Talmud 10, 11, 19, 83, 85–9, 110, 115, 120, 142–3, 150, 171, 242, 246, 265, 266, 267, 284, 291, 293, 356, 372, 385, 388–9, 408, 412, 483
  Babylonian 86, 88–9, 95, 147
  Jerusalem (Palestinian) 11, 86, 88, 147
Tanakh 50, 60, 61, 370, 386–7
Tanna'im 10, 88
Tashlich 121, 443, 464
tefillin 208, 260, 311, 400–1, 428–9, 183, 486
tehiru 300
Tel Aviv 14, 212, 213
Temple Judaism 271, 273, 276–7, 284–5, 367, 380, 382, 423, 426, 428, 446, 465
Temple Mount 276–7
Temple, Second 263, 281, 282, 426, 427, 456
Temple of Solomon 263, 273, 276–7, 380, 426, 456
Ten Commandments 10, 26, 39
Ten Days of Penitence 442–4, 447
ten emanations 121
Terah 35, 274
Testament of Joseph 280
Testaments of the Twelve Patriarchs 407
theatre 17, 151, 179, 187, 246
Theudas 289
Thirty Years War 145
Three Weeks of Mourning 447
Tibbon, Yehuda Ibn 114, 125
Tiberias 160, 161, 265

tikkun 297, 301, 305, 313, 372–3, 437
Timbuktu 163
Tishah B'Av 21, 61, 90, 425, 447, 456–7
Tobiads 280
Tobit 280
Toland, John 164
Torah 10, 11, 12, 18, 26, 32, 38–9, 57, 61, 76–7, 84, 86, 110, 120, 150, 161, 171, 245, 260, 268, 282–3, 284, 309, 370–1, 382–3, 385, 386, 401, 421, 426, 429
  biblical scholarship 371, 387
  commandments 262, 265, 275, 277, 283, 367, 370, 372–3, 374, 388, 390–1, 430
  the Creation 362–3
  divine origin 310, 311, 315, 319
  Oral 286–7, 292, 302, 316, 367, 370, 372, 387, 388, 391, 421
  rabbinic Judaism 292, 292–3, 367
  Sefer 293
  Torah Mi Sinai 310, 311, 315, 367, 370, 386, 387, 388
  Written 302–3, 316, 367, 372, 386–7, 391
  yad 302
Tosafists 115, 265
tosafot 12
Touro, Isaac 166
trade and commerce 47, 52–3, 100, 122, 140, 140, 152, 162, 168, 169, 172–3, 177
Transcendence 354–5

Below *The Jewish Quarter, Girona, Spain.*

Above *The Dome of the Rock, Jerusalem.*

Transjordan 14
Tree of Life 297
tribes of Israel 262–3, 276, 278–9, 381, 407, 415
Trotsky, Leon 194–5, 234
Troyes 265
tsaar baalei hayyim 344–5
Tu b'Shevat 20, 25, 425, 452–3
Tunisia 98, 162–3
Tur *see* Arba'ah Turim
Turkey 98, 137, 140, 146–7, 177, 185
tzadikim 178
tzizit 19, 429, 487

Ukarites 303
Ukraine 13, 14, 111, 151, 155, 156, 158, 165, 179, 205
Umayyads 114–13
United Kingdom *see* Britain
United Nations 269, 331, 381
United States 13, 14, 19, 141, 166–7, 171, 175, 178–9, 181, 182–3, 188, 189, 192, 197, 200, 204, 230–1
universities 13, 150, 186–7, 242
Ur of the Chaldeans 262, 274, 350

Vatican II 15, 235
vegetarianism 327, 344–5
Venice 12, 140
Verga, Solomon Ibn 143
Vilna Gaon 13, 159, 161, 169
Vital, Haim 157, 160

Wallenberg, Raoul 203
War of Attrition 15
Warsaw Ghetto 19, 201, 202
Waskow, Arthur 322, 323
Weiss-Rosmarin, Trude 336
Weizmann, Chaim 193, 195, 210, 211, 212, 221, 268, 331
Wertheimer, Samson 164–5
West Bank 15, 220, 221, 227
Western Wall 268, 347, 377, 400, 446, 479
Wiesel, Eli 206
Wine, Sherwin 320
Wise, Isaac Mayer 183, 268, 316
Wolffsohn, David 331
women 128, 159, 171, 183, 240–1, 460, 474, 481
   agunah 491
   feminism 322, 327, 334, 336–7
   Jewish Renewal 322, 323
   marriage 488–91
   Mishnah 388
   Orthodox Judaism 311, 337
   rabbis 271, 317, 319, 322, 337
   synagogue worship 312, 427
wonder rabbis 158–9
World Jewish Congress 14, 196
World War I 192–4, 210
World War II 191, 198–207, 216–17, 232, 234, 245
worship 382, 423–39
written law 86

Yacoub, Ibrahim ibn 122
Yahweh 36
Yavneh 287
Yehuda Ha-Nasi 10, 76, 77, 86, 88, 95, 264, 281, 372, 388, 421
Yehuda He-Hasid 13
Yemen 11, 14, 53, 102–3, 163, 219
yeshivas 87, 89, 94, 110, 158, 239
yeshivot 311, 483, 484
Yeshua *see* Jesus
Yevanic 98
Yevsektsiya 195, 234
yetzer ha-ra 287
yetzer tov 287
Yezirah 297
Yiddish 12, 13, 123, 129, 139, 150, 151, 178–9, 183, 218, 221, 246–8, 250, 484
Yiddishkeit 178
yishuv 331
Yizkor 21, 25
Yodfat 79
Yom Ha Shoah 21
Yom Hatsma'ut 21
Yom Kippur 20–2, 50, 61, 87, 392, 400, 425, 442, 444–5, 447, 464, 465, 474
Yom Kippur Katan 447
Yom Kippur War 19, 227, 269
Yose ben Halafta 424
Yossi, Rav 88
Yugdhan 415

zaddik 313
Zadok 66, 284
Zalman, Shneur 332
Zangwill, Israel 14, 211
Zealots 43, 71, 73, 78–9, 80, 94
Zebulon, tribe of 41
Zechariah 350, 86, 399, 446
zemirot 431
Zephaniah 50, 386
Zerubbabel 10, 282
zimzum 300, 305, 313, 353
Zinoviev, Grigory 194–5, 234
Zion 404–6, 415, 416
Zionism 13, 14, 15, 19, 173, 175, 179, 180–1, 188–9, 192, 194, 195, 197, 209–23, 238, 239, 268–9, 327, 328–31, 334–5, 381, 417, 419
Zohar 12, 121, 160, 246, 296, 300, 304, 332, 352, 353, 365, 370–1, 377, 379, 387, 401
Zoroastrianism 298
zugot 10, 76–17, 286
Zunz, Leopold 170

Picture Acknowledgements

THE HISTORY OF THE JEWS

akg-images: 4bl, 33b, 36t, 41t, 42t, 46b, 48b, 54, 84t, 86b, 100b, 101b, 107, 110b, 123t, 134t, 136b, 137b, 145t, 149b, 149t, 153t, 165t, 167b, 168b, 170b, 170t, 172b, 172t, 176t, 177t, 196t, 200t, 201t, 203b, 246t; /Bible Land Pictures 57t; Bible Land Pictures/Photo 91t, 98b, 121tr; Bible Land Pictures/www.Bi 158b; Bible Land Pictures/Z. Rad 4bl, 41b, 73br, 118b, 119b; Bildarchiv Pisarek 151b, 171t, 187b, 199b, 254t; British Library 20t, 43tr, 117, 121tl, 131t, 133t, 134br; Cameraphoto 71t; Electa 62b, 74b, 75t; Erich Lessing 10, 34b, 42b, 52t, 61t, 63tl, 75b, 79t, 90b, 137tr, 152t, 162t, 188t, 193bl, 197t; Gerard Degeorge 116; Heiner Heine 144b; /Hervé Champollion 81b, 125tr; IAM/WorldHistory Archive 157b; Israel Images 70b, 86t, 97b, 147t, 162b, 212b, 220t; Nimatallah 36b; Philippe Maillard 43tl; /Pirozzi 73t; Rabatti – Domingie 39t; Suzanne Heid 161b; ullstein bild 191, 202t; VISIOARS 115t. **Alamy:** © 19th era 157t; © AF archive 247b; © Arcaid Images 5tr, 257bl; © Arclight 129b; © Art Directors & TRIP 153b, 181b; © Art of Travel 146b; © Bernie Epstein 244b; © Carmen Sedano 12; © David Hoffman 232b; © dbimages 108t; © Eddie Gerald 56t, 239b, 256t; © Hanan Isachar 60b, 95t, 213t; © Idealink Photography 165b; © Interfoto 210t; © Israel Images 87t, 89b, 218b, 220bl, 221; © Israel Imagesi 238b, 257t; © Ivan Vdovin 158t; © Janice Hazeldine 231b; © John Norman 111t; © Laura S Goodman 184b; © Lebrecht Music and Arts Photo Library 185t; © Maria Adelaide Silva 110t; © Mary Evans Picture Library 77b, 126t; © Matthias Wassermann 114t; © Maurice Joseph 127b; © Mohammed Khaluf 94b; © Nathan Benn 112t, 1124b, 169t, 215t; © North Wind Picture Archives 175, 176b; © Paris Marais 233b; © Peter Horree 98t; © Peter Titmuss 184t; © PhotoStock-Israel 78t, 89t, 127t, 212t; © Pictorial Press Ltd 251t; © Robert Estall photo agency 53t; © Robert Fried 236t; © Russell Kord 84b; © Sally and Richard Greenhill 241bl; © Shaun Higson colour 156b; © Steve Allen Travel Photography 208; © The Art Gallery Collection 99b; © vario images GmbH & Co. KG 169b; © White House Photo 222b; © www.BibleLandPictures.com 53b; © Yurij Brykaylo 156t; ©Ken Welsh 119t; Art Directors & TRIP 233t; Dan Cohen 56b; Israel Images 226t; The Art Archive 34t. **The Art Archive:** 76t, 201b, 252b; Archaeological Museum Aleppo Syria/Collection Dagli Orti 57b; Archaeological Museum Baghdad /Gianni Dagli Orti 94t; Archaeological Museum Tehran/Gianni Dagli Orti 64b; Archaeological Museum Venice/ Collection Dagli Orti 68t; Bardo Museum Tunis/Gianni Dagli Orti 58t; Basilica San Marco Venice/Collection Dagli Orti 96t; Biblioteca Capitolare Padua/Gianni Dagli Orti 130t; Biblioteca Nazionale Marciana Venice/Gianni Dagli Orti 101t, 132b; Bibliothèque Municipale Arras/Gianni Dagli Orti 64t; /Bibliothèque Municipale Valenciennes/Collection Dagli Orti 60t; Bibliothèque Municipale Verdun/Kharbine-Tapabor /Coll. Jean Vigne 133b; Bodleian Library Oxford 44t, 47t, 55, 61b, 88t, 115b, 120b, 125tl; British Library 1, 36t, 59tr, 63b, 63tr, 76b, 112b, 136t; British Museum/Collection Dagli Orti 59tl; Church of Saint Francis Tecamachalco/ Gianni Dagli Orti 66t; Collection Dagli Orti 92t, 91t; Culver Pictures 194b, 242b; Domenica del Corriere/Collection Dagli Orti 178t; Egyptian Museum Cairo/Alfredo Dagli Orti 37b; Fondation Thiers Paris/Gianni Dagli Orti 155; Galleria d'Arte Moderna Venice/Collection Dagli Orti 67b, 256b; Galleria degli Uffizi Florence/Collection Dagli Orti 50t, 131b; Gianni Dagli Orti 18b, 105, 125b, 180b; Harper Collins Publishers 106t; Hazem Palace Damascus/Gianni Dagli Orti 109tl; Humor Monastery Moldavia/Collection Dagli Orti 92b; Israel Museum Jerusalem/ Gianni Dagli Orti 20b, 76t; Karl Marx Museum Trier/Alfredo Dagli Orti 254br; Kharbine-Tapabor 134t; Library of Congress 51t; Manuel Cohen 118t; Moldovita Monaastery Romania 135t; Musée Archéologique Naples/Collection Dagli Orti 62t; Musée Condé Chantilly/Gianni Dagli Orti 79b; Musée d'Art et d'Histoire Metz/Gianni Dagli Orti 130b; Musée Départemental des Vosges Epinal/Gianni Dagli Orti 145br; Musée des 2 Guerres Mondiales Paris/Gianni Dagli Orti 195b; Musée des Beaux Arts Orléans/Collection Dagli Orti 44b; Musée du Louvre Paris/ Collection Dagli Orti 163t; Museo Capitolino Rome/Collection Dagli Orti 90t; Museo Civico Bolzano/Gianni Dagli Orti 74t; Museo de Bellas Artes Zaragoza/Granger Collection 137tl; Museum of London 193t; National Archives Washington DC 176b, 204b; National Library Cairo/Gianni Dagli Orti 102b; National Museum Bucharest/Collection Dagli Orti 85; National Palace Mexico City/Gianni Dagli Orti 143t; Nationalmuseet Copenhagen Denmark/Collection Dagli Orti 144t; Navy Historical Service Vincennes France/Gianni Dagli Orti 148b; Nicholas J. Saunders 193br; Palatine Library Parma/Gianni Dagli Orti 88b; Palazzo Barberini Rome/ Collection Dagli Orti 45t; Palazzo Pitti Florence/Collection Dagli Orti 141t; Private Collection/ Marc Charmet 161t, 194t, 206b; Private Collection/Gianni Dagli Orti 126b; Rijksmuseum Amsterdam/Superstock 152b; Russian Historical Museum Moscow/Collection Dagli Orti 164t; Stephanie Colasanti 139, 140b, 237b; Szapiro Collection Paris/Gianni Dagli Orti 140t; Tate Gallery London 40t; Tate Gallery London/Eileen Tweedy 160t, 128bl; Topkapi Museum Istanbul/Gianni Dagli Orti 146t, 148t; Turkish and Islamic Art Museum Istanbul/Harper Collins Publishers 106b; Turkish and Islamic Art Museum Istanbul/Collection Dagli Orti 59b, 104; Turkish and Islamic Art Museum Istanbul/Gianni Dagli Orti 50b; University Library Istanbul/ Gianni Dagli Orti 154; Vezzolano, Italy 100t; Victoria and Albert Museum London/Sally Chappell 38t. **Bridgeman Images:** 7t, 9, 17b, 24, 40t, 45b, 52b, 59tl, 59tr, 60b, 66t, 87b, 136b, 137bl, 144b, 167b, 174t, 201b, 216t, 223b, 231t, 239t, 249t; Gift of James A. de Rothschild, London 22t; The Stieglitz Collection and donated with contribution from Erica & Ludwig Jesselson 18b; © Edifice 167t; © Look and Learn 114t; © SZ Photo 137br, 194b; © Zev Radovan 27t, 32b, 39b, 65b, 74t, 75t, 234t; Alinari 6t; Ancient Art and Architecture Collection Ltd 26t, 29t; Archives Charmet 25, 96t, 108b, 144t, 175t; extended loan from Michael and Judy Steinhardt, New York 37b; Gift of James A. de Rothschild, London 240b; Giraudon 43t, 59b, 61t, 64t, 81b, 89b, 132, 161t; Ken Welsh 118t; Peter Willi 69b, 180b; Photo © Christie's Images 168; Photo © Philip Mould Ltd, London 181t; Seth G. Sweetser Fund 160t; The Stapleton Collection 22b, 116b; The Steiglitz Collection and donated with contribition from Erica & Ludwig Jesselson 158b. **Cody Images:** 19b, 198b, 204b, 205b, 216b. **Corbis:** 178b, 216t, 241tl, 241tr, 243t; © Adrian Andrusier/Lebrecht Music & Arts 179; © Andy Aitchison/In Pictures 228b; © Ann Johansson 234b; © Araldo de Luca 69t; © Atlantide Phototravel 238t; © Bettmann 183t, 183b, 188b, 195t, 196b, 197b, 205t, 211b, 213b, 217t, 219b, 226b, 228t, 230t, 242t, 247t, 248t, 248bl, 254bl; © Bojan Brecelj 252t; © Cezaro de Luca/ epa 236b; © Charles and Josette Lenars 80bl; © Chris Hellier 99t; © Christel Gerstenberg 142t; © Claude Medale/Kipa 4bm; © Colin McPherson 249tr; © Daniel Deme/epa 128t; © Dave

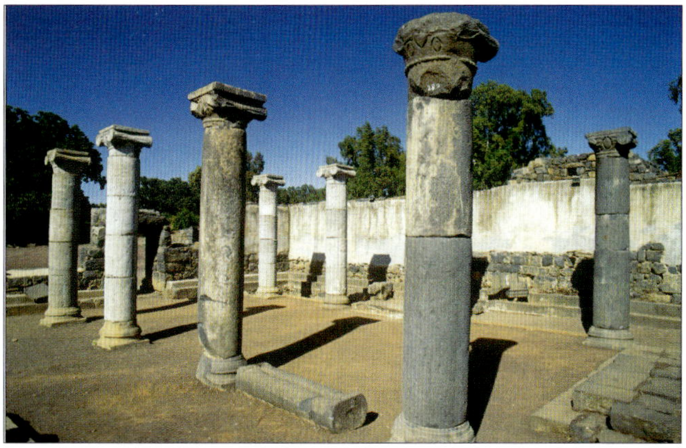

Above *The remains of a 5th–6th century* CE *synagogue in the Golan Heights.*

Bartruff 26b; © Dave G. Houser 14; © David Clapp/Arcaid 122t; © David James/Sygma 251b; © David Rubinger 219t; © David Sutherland 5tl, 204t; © DK Limited 113t; © Douglas Pearson 93t; © Ed Kashi 214t; © epa 203t; © Gianni Giansanti/Sygma 207t; © Hanan Isachar 73bl, 159t; © Hanan Isachar/JAI 257br; © Hulton-Deutsch Collection 177b, 198t, 214b, 217b, 218t, 227, 245b; © Ira Wyman/Sygma 249b; © Jon Arnold/ JAI 109tr; © Katarina Stoltz/Reuters 190; © Kevin Fleming 231t; © Lebrecht Arts & Music 234t, 253tl; © Lebrecht Authors/Lebrecht Music & Arts 129t; © Lee Snider/Photo Images 13, 166b; © Leland Bobbé 27b; © Li Erben 253tr; © Marc Garanger 235b; © Marcus Fhrer/epa 199t; © Melvyn Longhurst 185b; © Michael Freeman 215b; © Michael Nicholson 192t; © Michel Selboun/Sygma 162b, 163b; © Nathan Benn 123b; © Nathan Benn 5tm, 239t; © Nathan Benn/Ottochrome 3, 103b, 235t; © Nicolas Sapieha 69b; © Ocean 39b; © Pascal Parrot/Sygma 241br; © Patrick Ward 128br; © Peter M. Wilson 171b; © Pimentel Jean/Corbis KIPA 15; © Reuters 230b; © Richard T. Nowitz 74br, 159b; © Robert Holmes 141b; © Ronen Zvulin/Reuters 121b; © Sophie Bassouls/Sygma 248br; © Stapleton Collection 189; © Swim Ink, LLC 210b; © Ted Spiegel 4br, 225; © Walter Mcbride 249tl; ©Le-Dung Ly/Science Faction 256b. **Rex Features:** 29, 253b; Alinari 186t, 224; Assaf Shillo 229t; Chameleons Eye 223; Courtesy Everett Collection 232t; Everett Collection 250b, 250t; Israel Sun 209; Marco Marianella 243b; Roman Koszowski 206t; SIPA PRESS 211t, 244t, 255b.

JUDAISM

AKG-Images: 2, 16–17, 258–9, 260br, 262b, 265b, 266t, 267bl, 268b, 274br, 275b, 281b, 284b, 298b, 304t, 305t, 306b, 324b, 330t, 331b, 335b, 357t, 362b, 371t, 381t, 386t, 390b, 402, 406t, 408t, 409t, 425, 426t, 444bl, 465tl, 474bl, 478t&b; British Library 1, 367t, 373bl, 380bl, 386bl, 387tr, 392b, 408b; © Sotheby's 3664t, 466b; Bible Land Pictures, 283bl&br, 299tr, 439b, 451b; Bildarchiv Pisarek 328t, 344t, 399tl, 463b; Cameraphoto 369t; Electa 279b; Erich Lessing 263bl, 274bl, 280bl, 288bk, 302t, 305b, 348, 351bl, 368b, 374t, 383b, 386br, 396b, 405t, 424t, 433b; Horizons 342b, 468b; IAM 487bl; Israel Images 267br, 283b, 283t, 288br, 289, 296t, 300b, 310t, 311bl, 347, 373br, 391t, 394b, 398t, 401t, 417b, 429bl, 438b, 440, 457b, 466t, 467t, 469t&br, 473b, 439tl, 486t, 489t, 493bl; János Kalmár 291; Joseph Martin 404t; Jürgen Raible 455b; Laurent Lecat 401b; North Wind Picture Archives 266b; Rabatti – Domingie 403; RIA Nowosti 443b; Suzanne Held 300t, 329t, 329b, 353tl; ullstein – Archiv Gerstenberg 379b; ullstein bild, 365t, 418b, 429t, 447b; World History Archive/IAM 378b. **Alamy:** 477, 488b; © john norman 303b; © 19th era 2, 307t, 469bl; © Arcaid 309; © Art Directors & TRIP 316b; © ASAP 430b; © david sanger photography 341tl; © Eddie Gerald 323t, 397br; © Eden Akavia 490t; © Eitan Simanor 325b, 446b; © Hanan Isachar 303t; © INTERFOTO 336t; © Israel images 393t, 452b; © J. Wolanczyk 307b; © Jean Dominique Dallet 296b; © Jeff Morgan 260, 321b; © Jim West 321t; © Lebrecht Music and Arts Photo Library 275t, 293tr, 302b, 415b, 490b; © Moris Kushelevitch 353b; © Nathan Benn 345b, 423t, 429br, 445t, 491b; © Ohad Reinhartz 388t; © PhotoStock-Israel 338t; © Richard Levine 325tl; © Stefano Paterna 359tr; © The Art Gallery Collection 280t; © The Print Collector 411b; © www.BibleLandPictures.com 289, 267t, 277b, 278t, 280br, 295b, 311t. **The Art Archive:** 415t, 427tl, 457t, 498; American Colony Photographers/ NGS Image Collection, 282t; Anagni Cathedral Italy/Collection Dagli Orti 447t; Basilica Aquileia Italy/Collection Dagli Orti 404br; Biblioteca Nacional Lisbon/ Gianni Dagli Orti 449bl; Biblioteca Nazionale Marciana Venice/Gianni Dagli Orti 352b; Bibliothèque de l'Arsenal Paris 434bl; Bibliothèque Mazarine Paris/CCI, 276bl, 360b; Bibliothèque Municipale Amiens/Kharbine-Tapabor /Coll. J. Vigne 457t; Bibliothèque Municipale Moulins/Gianni Dagli Orti 350; Bibliothèque Municipale Valenciennes/Gianni Dagli Orti 276br, 436br; Bibliothèque Nationale Paris 380t; Bibliothèque Universitaire de Mèdecine, Montpellier/Gianni Dagli Orti 294t, 427b; Bodleian Library Oxford, 290, 363t, /Arch Selden A 5 folio2v, 388b, /Canon Or 62 folio 1r, 374b, /Canon or 79 folio 2v, 485t, /Laud Or 321 folio127v, 437b, /Mich 619 folio 464b, /MS. Reggio 1 fol. 407v, 442br, /Opp 776 folio 20v, 383t; British Library, 6r, 292t, 293tl, 363b, 366, 372br, 421, 434bm, 435bl, 458, 471b, 473t; Castello della Manta Piemonte/Collection Dagli Orti 287t; CCI 382b, 443t, 461t; Collection Antonovich/Gianni Dagli Orti 404bl; Collection Dagli Orti 376b; Culver Pictures 304b; DeA Picture Library/G. Nimatallah 406b; Eileen Tweedy 297br;

ACKNOWLEDGEMENTS

Fondation Thiers Paris/Gianni Dagli Orti 370b, 393b, 428t, 442bl, 460b, 492b; Gemaldegalerie Dresden 377t; Gianni Dagli Orti 367, 377b, Art Archive, Hermitage Museum Saint Petersburg/ Superstock, 432t; Horniman Museum/Eileen Tweedy 413t; Hunt Add E (R)/Bodleian Library Oxford 297bl; Imperial War Museum 454b; Israel Museum Jerusalem /Gianni Dagli Orti 389b; Jewish Museum, New York / Superstock 356b, 376t, 379t, 410b, 412t, 431t; Kunsthistorisches Museum Vienna/ Superstock 446t; Laud. Or.234 fol. 83V/Bodleian Library Oxford 299tl; Library of Congress 387b; Minneapolis Institute of Fine Art/Superstock 413b; Moldovita Monastery Romania /Collection Dagli Orti 400t; Museo del Bargello Florence/ Gianni Dagli Orti 411t; Museo del Prado Madrid 475t; Museum der Stadt Wien/ Collection Dagli Orti 428b; Museum of Anatolian Civilisations Ankara/Gianni Dagli Orti 351br; Museum of London 372t, 397bl, 482br; Art Archive, National Gallery London/Eileen Tweedy 414t; National Museum of Bosnia Herzegovina, Sarajevo 262t; Palatine Library Parma/Gianni Dagli Orti 276t; Palazzo Comunale Rovigo Italy/Collection Dagli Orti 417t; Palazzo Leoni-Montanari Vicenza/Gianni Dagli Orti 295t; Palazzo Pitti Florence/Collection Dagli Orti 448b; Private Collection/Gianni Dagli Orti 432b, 433t, 441, 451t; Private Collection Istanbul/Gianni Dagli Orti 472t; San Apollinare Nuovo Ravenna/Collection Dagli Orti 286b; Sistine Chapel Vatican/ Superstock 349; St. Peter's Basilica, The Vatican/Superstock 472b; Steve Raymer/ NGS Image Collection, 373t; Superstock, 261t, 384; University Library Istanbul/ Gianni Dagli Ort 277t, 294b, 370t, 385, 436bl, 484t; Victoria and Albert Museum London/V&A Images 407t. **The Bridgeman Art Library:** 6m, 8b, 9t, 285b, 285b, 288t, 297t, 306t,330b, 344b, 350b, 372bl, 375t, 380br, 382t, 399b, 410t, 412b, 416t, 439tl, 476; Gift of James A. de Rothschild, London 362t; Photo © Bonhams, London, UK 5l, 328b; © British Library Board. All Rights Reserved 281t; © National Gallery of Scotland, Edinburgh, Scotland 352t; Alinari 375b; Archives Charmet 392t, 407b, 409b, 470b; Bibliotheque Nationale, Paris, France 265t; DaTo Images 343, 381b; Gift of James A. de Rothschild, London 292b, 480b; Giraudon 263t, 285tl; Museo Diocesano de Solsona, Lleida, Spain 364b; Photo © AISA 346–7; Photo © Bonhams, London, UK 328b; Photo © Christie's Images 464t; Photo © Zev Radovan 7m, 272, 274t, 286t, 287br, 361b, 387tl, 405b, 449br, 450b; The Stieglitz Collection and donated with contribution from Erica & Ludwig Jesselson 480t. **Corbis:** 273, 313tl, 320b; © Mark Weiss 444br RF; © Abir Sultan/epa 471tl; © Alfredo Dagli Orti/The Art Archive 398b, 488t; © Andrew Aitchison/In Pictures, 371b; © Andrew Aitchison/In Pictures/ 312; © Andrew Holbrooke 482t; © Aristide Economopoulos/ Star Ledger 319t; © Austrian Archives 401b; © Bettmann 269tl, 310b, 314b, 315, 335tr, 336bl, 419t, 430t, 455t, 462b; © Bojan Brecelj 293b; © Catherine Karnow 339b; © Catherine Ledner 332t; © Chris Hellier 444t; © Christie's Images 260bl, 416b; © Courtesy of Museum of Maritimo (Barcelona), Ramon Manent 369b; © Daniele La Monaca/X01660/Reuters 468t; © Dave Bartruff 450t; © David H. Wells 474br, 485b; © David Rubinger 470t; © Ed Kashi 338b; © Eldad Rafaeli 396t; © Eliana Aponte/Reuters 487br; © Envision 464t; © Eyal Ofer 439b; © Frans Lanting 378t; © Gene & Karen Rhoden/Visuals Unlimited 358t; © Gianni Dagli Orti 278bl; © Gideon Mendel 435t; © Godong/Robert Harding World Imagery 397t; © Hanan Isachar 452t, 463t, 465tr, 474t; © Hanan Isachar/JAI 313b; © Herbert Spichtinger 355b; © Heritage Images 284t; © Historical Picture Archive 448t, 457b; © Hulton-Deutsch Collection 269tr, 418t; © Jacques Loew/Kipa 336br; © Jason Horowitz 311br; © Jim Hollander/epa 327; © Jim Zuckerman 359b; © John Bryson/Sygma 471tr; © John Stanmeyer/VII 345t; © Jonathan Ernst/Reuters 322t; © Karen Kasmauski 479tr; © Lebrecht Music & Arts 336b; © Leland Bobbé 314t, 431bl, 449t, 467b, © Les Stone/Sygma 333b; © Luca Tettoni 361t; © Lucy Nicholson/Reuters 339t; © Mark Peterson 7r, 313tr, 481b; © Michael Nicholson 279t; © Michael St. Maur Sheil 365b; © Miriam Alster/epa 337; © NASA 360t; © Nathan Benn 261b; © Nathan Benn/Ottochrome 312b, 394t, 462t, 487t, 492t; © Neal Preston 341b; © Nik Wheeler 424b; © Nir Alon/Demotix 445b; © Nir Elias/Reuters 493br; © Oscar White 335tl; © P Deliss/Godong 482bl; © Pauline St. Denis 437t RF; © Peter Turnley 389t; © Philadelphia Museum of Art 355t; © Philippe Lissac/Godong 460t; © Richard T. Nowitz 301b, 332b, 414b, 422, 426b, 431br, 436t, © Robert Mulder/ Godong 481t; © Roger Hutchings/In Pictures 357b; © Ron Dahlquist 359tl; © Roy Morsch 461br; © Scott Speakes 442t; © Shai Ginott 270–1, 287bl, 399tr; © Silvia Morara 271; © Sonntag/beyond 491tr RF; © Steve Raymer 190t; © STR/Reuters 53t; © Sung-Il Kim 356t; © Ted Spiegel 308, 317b, 427tr, 459; © Tetra Images/Tetra Images 435br; © The Gallery Collection 351t; © Tony Savino/Sygma 454t; © William Whitehurst 358bl; © Yannis Behrakis/Reuters 342t; Image © Bettmann 316t; 317t, 331tl, 331tr; IMAGE © Hanan Isachar 420–1, 439tr. **Photo12:** 268t, 285tr, 354b, 395; Ann Ronan Picture Library 263br, 264t; Eye Ubiquitous 390t; Oronoz 260t, 298t. **Rex Features:** Alinari 325tr, 486b, 489b; Europress Photo Agency 475b; Everett Collection 334t; Sipa Press 493t. **Rodger Kamenetz:** © Rodger Kamenetz 322b, 340b; John Bigelow Taylor/courtesy of the International Campaign for Tibet 341tr. **Eisenstein Reconstructionist Archives, Reconstructionist Rabbinical College,** Wyncote, PA: 318t, bl&r, 319b. **Society for Humanistic Judaism** (www.shj.org; www.hujews.org): 320t. **Superstock** 82, 323b, 342b, 354t, 356t, 358b, 378t, 391b, 419b, 461b, 479b, 483t, 483b, 484b, 487bl. **Wiki Commons** 83, 326b 333t 456t 474t, 491t.

This edition is published by Lorenz Books
an imprint of Anness Publishing Ltd
info@anness.com; wwww.annesspublishing.com

© Anness Publishing Ltd 2022

All rights reserved. No part of this publication may be reproduced, stored in a retrieval system, or transmitted in any way or by any means, electronic, mechanical, photocopying, recording or otherwise, without the prior written permission of the copyright holder.

Publisher: Joanna Lorenz
Editorial Director: Helen Sudell
Editor: Joy Wotton
Maps: Anthony Duke
Designer: Nigel Partridge
Production Controller: Ben Worley

Previously published as two volumes, *A History of the Jewish People* and *The Illustrated Guide to Judaism*.

PUBLISHER'S NOTE
Although the information in this book is believed to be accurate at the time of going to press, neither the authors nor the publisher can accept any legal responsibility or liability for any errors or omissions that may have been made.

Page 1: *Aaron the first high priest pours oil into the sacred seven-branched candelabrum, the menorah; from northern French manuscript c.1280.*
Page 2: Rabbi's Blessing, *1871, by Moritz Daniel Oppenheim.*
Page 3: *A Sephardi Jewish boy carries a Torah casket while celebrating his bar mitzvah by the Western Wall in Jerusalem.* Page 16: *Arch of the Titus, Rome.*
Page 258: A Theological Debate, *1888, by Eduard Frankfort.*
Above. The destruction of the Temple in Jerusalem, 70CE, *1867, by Francesco Hayez.*

In memory of Joy Wotton, who worked on this book.

For Lavinia LJ

Thanks to my parents Hyam and Vivienne, my sister Tamara and her husband David, and my nephew and niece, Daniel and Hannah DCS